The Resourceful Reader

Readings to Accompany the Harbrace and Hodges' Handbooks

FOURTH EDITION

✳

Suzanne Strobeck Webb
Texas Woman's University

with

Kimberly Jo Allison
Texas Woman's University

HARCOURT BRACE

HARCOURT BRACE COLLEGE PUBLISHERS
Fort Worth Philadelphia San Diego New York Orlando Austin San Antonio
Toronto Montreal London Sydney Tokyo

Publisher: Christopher P. Klein
Executive Editor: Michael Rosenberg
Acquisitions Editor: John Meyers
Developmental Editor: Kimberly J. Allison/Michell Phifer
Project Editor: Laura Miley
Art Director: Brian Salisbury
Production Manager: Kathleen Ferguson

ISBN: 0-15-505603-4
Library of Congress Catalog Card Number: 97-071102

Copyright © 1998, 1994, 1990, 1987 by Harcourt Brace & Company

Address for orders:
Harcourt Brace College Publishers
6277 Sea Harbor Drive
Orlando, FL 32887-6777
1-800-782-4479

Address for editorial correspondence:
Harcourt Brace & Company
301 Commerce Street, Suite 3700
Fort Worth, Texas 76102

Web site address:
http://www.hbcollege.com

Harcourt Brace & Company will provide complimentary supplements or supplement
packages to those adopters qulified under our adoption policy. Please contact your
sales representative to learn how you quality. If as an adopter or potential user you
receive supplements you do not need, please return them to your sales representative
or send them to: Attn: Returns Department, Troy Warehouse, 465 South Lincoln
Drive, Troy, MO 63379.

Printed in the United States of America

7 8 9 0 1 2 3 4 5 6   039   9 8 7 6 5 4 3 2 1

＊

To
T. V. B.
AND IN MEMORY OF
M. E. W.
SINE QUIBUS NON

＊

Preface

The Resourceful Reader, fourth edition, is designed expressly to accompany the *Harbrace College Handbook,* thirteenth edition, the *Harbrace College Handbook Brief,* thirteenth edition, and the thirteenth edition of the *Hodges' Harbrace Handbook.* This unique design provides a harmonious interaction between handbook and reader and, as a result, offers the instructor unprecedented efficiency in teaching. The sixty-four readings are arranged rhetorically in chapters according to the developmental strategies—namely, example, narration, description, process, cause and effect, comparison and contrast, classification and division, definition, and argument—outlined in sections 27d and 28e of both the thirteenth and Brief thirteenth editions of the *Harbrace College Handbook* and in sections 31d and 32e of the *Hodges' Harbrace Handbook,* thirteenth edition. In four additional chapters, *The Resourceful Reader* presents the arguments of a debate, the essay examination, the research paper, and a collection of classic essays. The readings balance classroom favorites with pieces seldom or never reprinted and amply represent a diversity of sources. Student essays, fifteen in all, appear throughout the book.

The Resourceful Reader offers a number of features that are lacking in the leading anthologies heretofore available for the teaching of writing:

- The pedagogical apparatus accompanying each reading focuses not only on meaning, purpose, audience, and rhetorical strategy in the whole essay but also on effective paragraphs, grammar, punctuation and mechanics, diction, effective sentences and vocabulary building—all with references to pertinent discussions in the full-length and brief versions of the thirteenth edition of the *Harbrace College Handbook* and *Hodges' Harbrace Handbook.*

- "Argument" (chapter 9) is followed by a mini-casebook (chapter 10) entitled "A Life-And-Death Issue Debated: The Environment," six short essays that show a variety of arguments, rhetorical strategies, and personal styles brought to bear on a single important issue.

- "The Essay Examination: A Student Writer across the Disciplines" (chapter 11) allows students to follow one undergraduate, Anne Nishijima, as she responds to the special demands of the essay test in the social sciences, the humanities, and science.

- Four documented papers supplement those in the *Harbrace College Handbook* (full length and brief editions) and the *Hodges' Harbrace Handbook.* Two are by students (in chapter 12, "Writing from Research") and follow the Modern Language Association's (MLA) and American Psychological Association's (APA) styles of documentation. Two in other sections are by professionals—one with MLA documentation in the text and one in an older documentation style that uses *Ibid.* and footnotes.

• A new feature in *The Resourceful Reader,* "Building Vocabulary," offers a new set of questions that encourage students to discover the origin and meanings of words. Drawing from the vocabulary used in the professionally written readings, these questions not only ask students to define words but to isolate and combine prefixes, suffixes, and roots, to identify and define synonyms and antonyms, and to use new words in their own sentences.

The general introduction stresses the interaction between reading and writing, focusing first on how active, critical reading informs writing—"Reading To Write"—and then on the writing process—"Writing To Be Read." It concludes with "About This Book," some suggestions to the student for making the most of the various features of *The Resourceful Reader.*

Chapter introductions explain the rhetorical strategies exemplified by the readings. Within both the general introduction and the chapter introductions, as well as the questions after individual readings, references connect *The Resourceful Reader* with both versions of the thirteenth edition of the *Harbrace College Handbook* and the *Hodges' Harbrace Handbook,* thirteenth edition. Each chapter introduction concludes with an annotated student essay that illustrates the principles discussed in the introduction. Noteworthy features of the student essay are identified in the margin, and a subsequent commentary discusses the writer's strategies and choices. Though possible further improvements to student essays are sometimes noted, the emphasis in the commentaries is always positive, stressing the student's *achievement.* Each professionally written piece is introduced by a note that puts the essay into a context, sometimes social, cultural, or biographical.

Throughout, *The Resourceful Reader* aims to demonstrate for students that "the rules"—necessarily presented concisely in a handbook—are not arbitrary but are simply principles that good writers apply in writing purposeful compositions. Each reading is followed by a strong pedagogical apparatus that includes two sets of questions keyed to the thirteenth and brief thirteenth editions of the *Harbrace College Handbook* (indicated by the reference to *Harbrace*) and to the thirteenth edition of the *Hodges' Harbrace Handbook* (indicated by the reference to *Hodges'*). Questions under "Responding to the Whole Essay" ask students to consider audience, purpose, and other concerns of the "Larger Elements" section of *Harbrace* (chapters 27–35) and *Hodges'* (chapters 31–39). References to *Harbrace* and *Hodges'* in the questions help students apply the handbook principles to the readings. Questions under "Analyzing the Elements" explore the concerns of *Harbrace* chapters 1–26 and *Hodges'* chapters 1–30. Students are asked to consider grammatical issues (*Harbrace* and *Hodges'* chapters 1–7) in relation to *meaning,* not merely "the rules." "Punctuation and Mechanics" questions explore the concerns of *Harbrace* chapters 17–26 and *Hodges'* chapters 8–17; "Diction" questions explore those of *Harbrace* 13–16 and *Hodges'* 18–22. "Effective

Sentences" questions (referring to *Harbrace* 8–12 and *Hodges'* 23–30) often ask students to experiment with alternative structures of their own devising or to comment on the difference, in effect, between the writer's version and an alternative supplied in the question. Questions under "Building Vocabulary" provide students an opportunity to discover the origins and meanings of words and to practice using these words in their own sentences. Throughout the questions in *The Resourceful Reader,* the emphasis is on *choice:* students are continually asked to put themselves in the writer's place and evaluate the writer's options. Finally, "Suggestions for Writing" are provided for each reading. These writing assignments are always related to the reading but are designed to afford students considerable freedom of choice.

A further advantage of *The Resourceful Reader* is that each reading observes as well as illustrates the principles in the *Harbrace College Handbook* and *Hodges' Harbrace Handbook:* no dangling modifiers, inexplicable fragments, or improper verb and case forms will crop up that the instructor has to excuse to the observant student. For example, where writers deliberately use fragments or where closely related independent clauses are connected by commas without a conjunction, the student is asked to analyze why and in each instance is also referred to the appropriate section of *Harbrace* or *Hodges'*. Not even the best of writers, of course, are exempt from occasional infelicity, a pronoun reference that could be clearer, a modifier that squints a little. Where these rare lapses do appear, they are *addressed*—turned to pedagogical advantage in the questions—rather than left unnoted to perplex the alert student and mislead the unwary.

The alternate list of contents by subject is intended to enhance the book's flexibility and to suggest combinations of essays that can spark classroom discussion or further writing assignments. An author-title index makes selections easy to find. As a further aid for the busy instructor, an Instructor's Manual is available.

Acknowledgments.   As with most books, a number of people have rendered invaluable help and advice in the preparation of *The Resourceful Reader.* Dr. Hilary Broadbent, formerly a student at Barnard College, provided help with student essays, as did Leslie Bivens, formerly a student at Texas Woman's University. Roy J. Fowler, Lisa Garrett, and Jackie Nye, students in my Fall 1996 freshman composition class, wrote the student essays I selected to refresh the chapters on example, narration, and description.

My continuing thanks go also to those who were particularly helpful and supportive on earlier editions: Tom Broadbent, Marilyn Keef, Bob Miller, and Larry Mapp. Debts of other kinds are owed to James Galloway, Texas Woman's University Library, who rendered valuable assistance locating material in local libraries, and John Hepner, also of the TWU library, who proved repeatedly his uncanny ability to ferret out hard-to-locate facts.

At Harcourt Brace College Publishers, my thanks go to Michael Rosenberg, who gave the book its new name and who has been a constant source of sanity and support, to developmental editor Michell Phifer, project editors Matt Ball and Laura Miley, production manager Kathy Ferguson, designer Brian Salisbury, and sales managers Ellen Wynn and Tom Hall, all of whom have made valuable suggestions and given other kinds of useful help.

Special thanks go to Kim Allison, without whose assistance I would still be looking for new essays, still be writing new exercises, still be trying to whip a manuscript into final shape, and still struggling with permissions. Her diligence and skill are apparent in every chapter, but she had major responsibility for revising the first four. And of course, no set of acknowledgments would be complete without expressing my thanks to my family—to my husband, Dick, who takes care of everything else when I am in the midst of working on a book, and to Aaron and Karl, my grown sons of whom I am inordinately proud, who generously agreed to be guinea pigs for exercises, and who gave good advice about revising them.

Contents

Introduction: Reading to Write, Writing to be Read   3

1 Example   13

Banesh Hoffman, "My Friend, Albert Einstein"   17
"He was one of the greatest scientists the world has ever known, yet if I had to convey the essence of Albert Einstein in a single word, I would choose simplicity.*"*

Noel Perrin, "Country Codes"   24
"So, next time you're in a country store and you get a sense that the locals are avoiding you, . . . you can be pretty sure of the reason. You've probably just said some dreadful thing in code."

Brent Staples, "Just Walk on By: A Black Man Ponders His Power to Alter Public Space"   30
"My first victim was a woman . . . more than a decade ago. . . . It was in the echo of that terrified woman's footfalls that I first began to know the unwieldy inheritance I'd come into—the ability to alter public space in ugly ways."

Dave Barry, "The Myth of College"   36
"College is basically a bunch of rooms where you sit for roughly two thousand hours and try to memorize things. The two thousand hours are spread out over four years; you spend the rest of the time sleeping and trying to get dates."

Paula Gunn Allen, "Where I Come from Is Like This"   40
"An American Indian woman is primarily defined by her tribal identity. . . . But in no tribal definitions is she perceived in the same way as are women in western industrial and postindustrial cultures."

2 Narration   49

water like an apocryphal hippo. . . . They have a penguin's alertness, combined with a build like a Brontosaurus when they rise up on tiptoe."

"June is the cruelest month in Tucson, especially when it lasts till the end of July. This is the season when every living thing in the desert swoons south toward some faint salt dream of the Gulf of Mexico: tasting the horizon, waiting for the summer storms. This year they are late."

"We hung our heads far back to watch migrating Canada geese and black brant pass over. . . . We drew nearer the border, wondering aloud how we would know it."

"Wherever things shake, the shaking will consist of all these waves. Half a minute will pass before the light towers move at Candlestick Park. Meanwhile, dogs are barking in Trout Creek Gulch. Car alarms and house alarms are screaming. If, somehow, you could hear all such alarms coming on throughout the region, you could hear the spread of the earthquake."

"You can't pick up a phone and call the future and tell them about our times. You have to pick up a piece of paper."

"Old pharaohs never died—they just took long vacations. . . . These days, dead pharaohs are admittedly a bit hard to come by. If you decide to practice mummification on a friend or relative, please make sure that the loved one in question is fully deceased before you begin."

"Who needs those restaurant guides telling you what's good or not? If you can tell the difference between pamplemousse and charlotte russe, samosas and mimosas, . . . well, you're on your way. No doctorate in Restaurant Critiquing required (or available)."

"When professional writers complete a first draft, they usually feel that they are at the start of the writing process. When a draft is completed, the job of writing can begin."

"When the grave is finished, the wasp returns to the tarantula to complete her ghastly enterprise. First she feels it all over once more with her antennae. Then her behavior becomes more aggressive."

visualized when he was The Man With No Name. But this late divestiture of the mystery he took to the bank for so long . . . has been earned by four decades of accumulating assurance and self-knowledge as director, star, and man."

Contents Arranged by Subject

Contemporary Issues

Cultural Values and Manners

Death

Education

Environment

Families

Growing Up

History

Humor and Irony

Law

Minorities and Poverty

Nature

People

Philosophy and Belief

Places and Local Color

Politics

Psychology and Behavior

Science and Technology

Society and Morality

Tradition

War and Weapons

Women

Work and Business

Writing, Thinking, and Language

The Resourceful Reader

*Readings to Accompany the
Harbrace and Hodges' Handbooks*

FOURTH EDITION

*

Introduction

Reading to Write, Writing to Be Read

Imagine you are digging on an archaeological site and one day you unearth a pot, intricately patterned, variously colored, miraculously whole after centuries of burial. As you hold the pot in your hand, your mind moves from admiration of the object to speculation about how, and by whom, it was created—an awareness that the pot is an artifact, something made by human hands and human intellect. Chances are, however, that it was not made on the first try. Not only did the potter probably have to make hundreds of pots to acquire the skill to produce those graceful lines, but also he or she undoubtedly shaped and reshaped the clay to get that very pot just right. Yet all you have is the pot. The earlier versions are gone, absorbed long ago into the final lovely thing you hold in your hand, and no record of the potter's labor to create it survives.

The essays in this book, too, are artifacts, things created by human intellect. The writers, like the potter, began with nothing more than their own hands and minds and experience. As readers, we see their finished creations, complete and as nearly perfect as the writers could make them—scarcely a seam anywhere, scarcely a lump or lopsidedness. Faced with a finished essay, readers seldom think much about the process (slow, seldom straightforward, often downright messy) that produced it—seldom are aware of how the writer may have labored to discover what was worth saying, then struggled to get the right words into phrases, clauses, sentences, paragraphs—that would enable the reader to re-create, from black marks on a page, the ideas that were in the writer's mind. Like anything made with skill and effort, the essay looks easy and natural—just as the writer wanted it to look.

But as you read the essays, you can reconstruct (though not perfectly) the process the writer went through, and in doing so learn much about writing well. This kind of reading requires the investment of time, effort, and attention, but it is an investment that will return a large profit because reading and writing go together: reading improves your writing, and writing makes you a better reader. When you tackle an essay as an active, involved reader, you go through much of the same process that you go through to write an essay, only in reverse. Beginning with the finished product, you take it apart

3

to see how another writer met challenges similar to those you face when you write. As you analyze the many kinds of choices the writer made, you increase your understanding of the options available to you. Reading can be a rehearsal for writing. *The Resourceful Reader,* designed to be used along with the thirteenth and brief thirteenth editions of the *Harbrace College Handbook* (hereafter referred to simply as *Harbrace*) and the *Hodges' Harbrace Handbook* (hereafter referred to as *Hodges'*), provides the materials for that rehearsal. You, of course, must supply the effort.

Reading to Write.   To get the most from any essay, you should read it at least twice, the first time for a general idea of what the writer is saying, the second time—and perhaps more times—to see how the writer has gone about saying it, to examine all the means the writer used to make the essay work.

As you reread the essay, do so actively, pencil in hand to jot down notes in the margin or mark important ideas. Certain kinds of information you can look for will help you understand many of the decisions the writer made while writing. Perhaps the most basic consideration is *purpose*—what the writer intends to accomplish in the essay. Is the author's aim to inform the reader, focusing on the topic as objectively as possible, as John McPhee does in "Loma Prieta" (chapter 3)? Or is the purpose to persuade, to sway the reader to take some action or adopt some point of view the writer considers desirable? For instance, "The Gift of Wilderness" (chapter 9) is one of many pieces in which Wallace Stegner has argued eloquently that we must act now to preserve what wilderness we have left. And sometimes writers are not so much concerned to inform or persuade a reader as to express themselves—that is, explore and share their own personal feelings and responses, as Barbara Kingsolver does in her delightful "Creation Stories" (chapter 3). But the question of purpose is not a simple one. As you read, bear in mind that in any effective piece of writing one purpose or another is likely to be dominant, but other purposes are sure to be present to some degree. Although Kingsolver's primary aim is expressive—a kind of celebration, a sharing of her own responses—her essay certainly conveys information, and unquestionably it aims to persuade us of something, too. And Stegner's "The Gift of Wilderness," though chiefly persuasive, is both informative and wonderfully expressive. (See *Harbrace* 28a or *Hodges'* 32a for further discussion of purpose.)

Whatever the writer's purpose, to be successful in achieving it the writer must have a clear sense of *audience*—indeed, purpose and audience can scarcely be separated, since all writing is presumably meant to be read by someone (if only the writer, as with a diary or a grocery list). You can learn a great deal about writing effectively for your own audiences from considering how other writers have written for theirs. Occasionally you will find that the writer explicitly names the intended audience, but more often you will have to infer from clues what kind of audience the writer had in mind. (One possible clue is external: if what you are reading has been published in, for example, a magazine—as some of the reprinted essays in this book originally were—what kind of audience is that magazine aimed at?) Consider the tone of the essay, for tone reflects the writer's attitude toward the audience as well as toward the subject (see *Harbrace* 28a; *Hodges'* 32a). Does the writer seem to assume that the audience will be sympathetic? Interested? Indifferent? Hostile? Consider, too, the writer's assumptions about the reader's knowledge. Does the writer either take pains to define specialized words or confine the vocabulary to words most general readers would be likely to understand? A piece written for specialists will assume considerable knowledge on the part of the reader and is likely to use a specialized vocabulary. (Although none of the essays in this book were written for highly specialized audiences, you can see a sample of such writing in *Harbrace* 28a; *Hodges'* 32a.

With the writer's purpose and intended audience clearly in mind, you will be ready to focus more specifically on other elements of the essay. Look for the *thesis*—the central or controlling idea, the main point the writer is making. Being able to pick out and evaluate the thesis of a piece of writing is the very essence of active reading. Often the thesis is stated, but if it is not, it will be implicit in what the writer has to say about the subject. Even in a piece of writing that is mainly descriptive, there will be some focus or reason for describing, some dominant impression the writer means to create in the reader's mind; the details will not be randomly chosen. Similarly, in a narrative some attitude toward the events will be suggested—if not explicitly, then implicitly through the writer's choice of events and details and of language appropriate to the writer's view. (For more discussion of thesis, see *Harbrace* 28d; *Hodges'* 32d.)

One of the most practical things you can do as a reader trying to become a better writer is to pay attention to how other writers use the various *methods of development* (around which the first nine chapters of this book are organized): example, narration, description, process, cause and effect, comparison and contrast, classification and division, definition, and argument. These are not hollow forms into which writers pour sentences to make essays; they are fundamental *thinking* strategies, basic ways human beings make sense of the world and communicate that sense to one another. Terms such as *narration* and *classification* may sound forbidding and technical, but if you run through the list of strategies again and consider the kinds of common questions each strategy answers, you will see how natural these methods are:

What are some instances?—example

What happened (or is happening)?—narration

How does it look (feel, taste, smell, sound)?—description

How does this work, or how is this done?—process

Why did this happen? What will be the result?—cause and effect

What is it like? How is it different?—comparison and contrast

What kinds are there?—classification and division

What is it? What does it mean?—definition

What should be done? What should we believe?—argument

Understanding and practicing these strategies will do more than teach you how to organize essays. You will use them every day, not only in all of your college courses but also in virtually every part of your life beyond the campus. (See also *Harbrace* 27d and 28d[1]; *Hodges'* 31d and 32d[1].)

Consider an essay's introduction, conclusion, and title. Does the introduction arouse your interest and get you oriented in the essay by suggesting what it is about? Would you have introduced the essay differently? Why? Does the conclusion bring the essay to a satisfying close? Is the title appropriate? How does it serve (and reveal) the writer's purposes? Does it help to establish the tone of the essay? (See also *Harbrace* 28f[1–3]; *Hodges'* 32f[1–3].)

Analyze the essay for logic and for unity and coherence. Has the writer avoided logical fallacies? (See also *Harbrace* 31; *Hodges'* 35.) Are there digressions, irrelevancies? What kinds of signposts does the writer provide to help readers follow the thought from paragraph to paragraph and sentence to sentence? Are the ideas presented in the most effective order? Is each idea adequately developed? Try to see how the writer's concern about these issues has contributed to making the essay effective. If you find weaknesses (no writer is perfect), ask yourself how the writer might have done better. (See also *Harbrace* 27 and 28c[1]; *Hodges'* 31 and 32c[1].)

Consider the essay at the level of the sentence and the word, with an eye to what you can learn for your own use as a writer. How are sentences constructed to avoid monotony, to achieve the exact emphasis desired, to convey the relationships among ideas precisely? Is anything unclear—for instance, the reference of a pronoun or the relation of a modifier to what it modifies? Are there awkward constructions or inappropriate choices of words or of figurative language to distract or confuse the reader? Can you think of better choices the writer could have made? Conversely, where the writer has said something more effectively than you think you would have said it yourself, see if you can explain the difference. (As you think about such matters, you will find *Harbrace* a useful reference, especially *Harbrace* 1–7 and 8–16; *Hodges'* 1–7 and 19–30.)

The writer's choices regarding punctuation and mechanics are also worth studying. Even though punctuation and mechanics are governed to a considerable extent by convention, there are more choices to be made than you realize—including, of course, the choice to be "correct," to avoid violating the conventions in ways that would distract the reader and undermine your credibility, thereby interfering with communication. Ask questions as you read: Why has the writer chosen to set off a particular parenthetical expression with dashes instead of parentheses or commas, when either of these alternatives would also be acceptable? Why has the writer put that word in italics when regular type would also have been correct? Why did the writer choose a semicolon between these two clauses instead of a period, or instead of a comma and a coordinating conjunction? Why is a colon better here than a semicolon? Why is this hyphen necessary? (Such decisions and many others are considered in *Harbrace* 17–25; *Hodges'* 9–17.)

As you consider all the choices, large and small, that other writers have made, you are continually reconstructing the processes they went through and, in a very real sense, rehearsing for your own writing. Let's now focus on what happens when you write for other readers.

Writing to Be Read.   Writing is never done in a vacuum. When you write, you are always in a specific situation that involves an *audience* (that is, a known or perhaps hypothetical reader, whose background and interests you must consider); a *purpose* for writing, something you mean to accomplish; and a *subject,* something you will write about. Often your writing situation will clearly dictate your subject; for instance, essay examinations in college courses often specify a topic, and letters and reports written on the job usually deal with subjects that are either assigned or obvious. When the subject is given, your purpose may seem obvious, too, but you will usually find it worthwhile to consider your purpose a little more carefully: it may not be as simple as you think. Consider the essay examination again. If the question is "Explain the difference between the budget deficit and the national debt," your purpose seems clear enough: *to explain.* And explain you must, of course, if you want to receive credit. But consider: your instructor *knows* the difference between the budget deficit and the national debt; so your main purpose is to *convince* the instructor, by your explanation, that you have mastered certain basic concepts. Similarly, much business writing is devoted primarily to giving information, but if the writers were not just as much concerned with persuasive aims—giving a favorable impression and winning customers—as with conveying information, business letters might read like this: "Dear Client: The widgets cost $5.00. Yours truly."

In a college writing course, you may sometimes be entirely free to choose your own subject. If you are, you can write an interesting paper on almost any subject you care about. Think about your personal knowledge, interest, and beliefs. What have you read lately? Do you know an interesting character? Has some particular place made a special impression on you? What do you do when you're not in school? Do you work? Do you have some special interest such as photography or playing in a band? What ambitions do you have for yourself? What are your convictions? What makes you angry? You can find subjects in any of these questions for papers that will interest other people.

More often, however, your freedom to choose will be limited in some way. Outside a composition classroom, rarely will you be free to choose a subject drawn from your own experience. For instance, your geology professor may give you complete freedom to write on any aspect of geology that interests you, but you are expected to write a paper demonstrating your mastery of some part of the subject matter of the course. Geologists are interested in mountains, but a paper about the elation you experienced when you successfully completed a difficult ascent of Mount St. Helens, despite the fact that the mountain is an active volcano, will not do. In such a situation, instead of relying on personal experience, look for an interesting subject in your text-book, in your lecture notes, in the subject catalog in the library; talk to other students or to your professor.

Whatever your subject, your writing task will be easier and your finished composition more effective if you take some time to explore your subject and get it sharply in focus before your begin drafting. You can use a number of different methods to generate ideas about your subject: listing, questioning, applying different perspectives, and surveying possible development strategies. (See *Harbrace* 28c[1]; *Hodges'* 32c[1].) Limiting and focusing a subject mean putting boundaries around it—perhaps reducing its scope—to make it man-ageable and, as with the subject of a photograph, deciding on the particular angle from which you will view it, what you will highlight and what you will eliminate as extraneous. (See *Harbrace* 28c[2]; *Hodges'* 32c[2].) Constructing a clear, specific thesis statement can help you decide whether you have lim-ited and focused your subject sufficiently and will also help you stay on the track as you draft the essay. (See *Harbrace* 28d; *Hodges'* 32d.)

If you have carefully considered your subject and purpose, chances are that the appropriate method of development will follow naturally. For in-stance, if exploring possible subjects for a history term paper led you to fo-cus on striking similarities between two battles that occurred in different wars, the development strategy of comparison and contrast would suggest itself to you. If, however, your main interest was in discovering what events and con-ditions had led to these confrontations, you would quite naturally find your-self using the strategy of cause and effect. As we've noted, these development strategies are ways in which our minds naturally work. Your problem is rarely to choose appropriate development strategies but rather to employ them ef-fectively. Reading and, above all, practice—writing—are the ways to learn.

Often—especially for a long paper—you may find it helpful to write down some kind of plan, an informal or even formal outline of your main ideas in what seems the most effective order, to guide you as you write (*Harbrace* 28e; *Hodges'* 32e). Remember, however, that such a plan is not written in stone; you can change it if you need to, and you probably will. When you begin drafting your essay, try writing quickly, without much con-cern for matters such as spelling, punctuation, and usage, which you can revise later. Most writers find that this approach is the most productive. The point is to get your ideas to flow as freely as you can, while keeping your purpose and audience in mind. Incidentally, no law says that you must begin at the beginning and slog straight through to the end in spite of any difficulties you may encounter on the way. Some writers find that writing chunks or blocks of an essay without worrying about the order makes their ideas flow more freely; then they put the chunks together, reshaping and connecting them as necessary. If you run out of steam in one part of your essay, try moving to another part you feel more comfortable with. Also, some writers find that when they're stuck it may help to turn back to what they've already written and look for ways to improve it, correcting errors, finding more exact words, restructuring sentences, or making paragraphs more coherent. (This is revision, but you don't have to wait until you have a complete draft to engage in it. You are, in fact, revising all the time, even as you are planning.) The value of this procedure is that it keeps you engaged with the essay while your unconscious mind has a chance to work on the problem that stopped you. However, you may find that sometimes the best remedy is simply to take a break and think about something entirely different for a while—perhaps take a walk or cook dinner—to give your mental batteries an opportunity to recharge, and then come back fresh to the draft. Researchers on creativity have found that breakthroughs commonly occur when the individual has first struggled hard to solve a problem and then temporarily turned away from it to think of something else. Experiment and find a method that works for you. You aren't exactly like anyone else; your writing process won't be exactly like anyone else's, either. (See *Harbrace* 28f; *Hodges'* 32f.)

When you have a complete draft, set it aside for a time (if possible a few days, but at least overnight). When you come back to it, try to see it as though someone else had written it. Reading it aloud may help—or having someone else read it to you. Go over your draft several times, looking first at the larger elements—unity and coherence, the arrangement and development of ideas, logic, and so on. What, if anything, is irrelevant? If you find material that is unrelated to your central idea, be ruthless in cutting it out. Where could your reader have difficulty seeing how an idea is related to the ones before it? Supply a transitional expression. Where do you need to provide more details to make yourself clear, and where are you guilty of overkill? (See *Harbrace* 29b; *Hodges'* 33b.)

Once you are reasonably satisfied with the overall shape of the essay, turn to the smaller elements. (The reason for looking at large things first is that it is more efficient: solving large problems often eliminates many smaller problems, too.) Read your sentences over. What kinds of changes will make them more effective? Can any words be replaced with more appropriate or exact ones? Look for problems with grammar, punctuation, mechanics, and spelling, and make whatever changes are needed. (You may wish to read Donald M. Murray's "The Maker's Eye: Revising Your Own Manuscripts" in chapter 4 of this text.)

When you have done your best, or the time comes when you must stop, put your essay into acceptable manuscript form. (See *Harbrace* 26; *Hodges'* 8.) Except in special circumstances, such as when writing an in-class essay or taking an examination (see *Harbrace* 30; *Hodges'* 34), make a clean copy, following your instructor's guidelines or those in *Harbrace* 10 and 29; *Hodges'* 26 and 33. Even if you are writing in class, reserve time to make sure that your insertions and deletions are clear and that your paper is as neat as you can make it. A little forethought will go a long way here to avoid problems.

About This Book.   Each of the first nine chapters of *The Resourceful Reader* focuses on one of the basic development strategies (or methods) that you will use in your college writing—and in all the writing you do. (These methods of development are also discussed in *Harbrace* 27d and *Hodges'* 31d in connection with paragraphs and in *Harbrace* 28c and *Hodges'* 32c as a tool for generating ideas about a subject.) The introduction to each chapter defines and explains the method, offers advice about using it, and concludes with an annotated student essay, illustrating it. Several essays from diverse sources follow. The authors of the selections have strikingly different personalities and voices, and they write on different subjects, with various purposes and for various audiences—but all use the particular development strategy being studied. A brief note that puts the essay into a social, cultural, or biographical context precedes each essay.

At the end of each selection, you will find several sets of questions. The first set, "Responding to the Whole Essay," directs your attention to overall considerations such as purpose, intended audience, and tone; thesis or central idea; method of development; coherence and unity; and so forth. This set of questions focuses on concerns treated in sections 27–35 of the *Harbrace College Handbook* and sections 31–39 of the *Hodges' Harbrace Handbook*. The second set of questions, "Analyzing the Elements," is divided into four parts, corresponding to sections of the *Harbrace* and *Hodges'* as follows: grammar (*Harbrace* 1–7; *Hodges'* 1–7), effective sentences (*Harbrace* 8–12; *Hodges'* 23–30), punctuation and mechanics (*Harbrace* 17–26; *Hodges'* 8–17), diction (*Harbrace* 13–16; *Hodges'* 18–22). Most of the individual questions contain references to specific discussions in *Harbrace* and *Hodges'*, which you can turn to if you need background information or simply want to read further. Answering these questions will start you thinking about the kinds of choices writers make—choices that are sometimes conscious ones, but often are unconscious. A conscious awareness on your part of the decisions other writers made will help you when you are faced with similar choices. A new set of questions, "Building Vocabulary," will help you understand where words come from and what they mean.

Following the questions you will find "Suggestions for Writing"—suggested writing projects (usually two) related in some way to the reading selection and designed to give you practice at meeting some of the challenges the author of the selection confronted.

Chapter 10, "A Life and Death Issue," is a special feature: a group of six essays all centering on a single controversial issue, the environment. The questions for this chapter are somewhat different in focus from those for chapters 1–9.

Finally, chapters 11–13 are entirely different from the chapters that precede them—and from each other. You may find chapter 11 one of the most interesting and immediately useful in the book. Here we see one student, Anne Nishijima, coping successfully with essay examination in three different college courses: humanities, social science, and natural science. This chapter, together with *Harbrace* 30 and *Hodges'* 34 on writing under pressure, can be of immediate practical help to you in your various college courses, and you may want to look at it even before it is assigned.

Chapter 12 illustrates the documented research paper—of which you will probably have to write a considerable number in the course of your college work—with two student papers to supplement those in *Harbrace* 34 and 35 and *Hodges'* 38 and 39. As you use this chapter, bear in mind that two of the essays in chapters 1–9 are also documented papers, giving you a total—between *Harbrace* (or *Hodges'*) and *The Resourceful Reader*—of nine* model research papers you can consult for help with your own papers. (All nine are mentioned in the introduction to chapter 12.)

Finally, no college writing anthology would be complete without some of the great pieces gathered in chapter 13, "For Further Reading: Some Classic Essays." Your instructor may not be able to work all seven of these essays into the course, but try to read them on your own. These are great voices, some from the distant past, some more recent, that speak powerfully to us.

If the subject of a particular essay happens to interest you and you would like to find other pieces dealing with the same or a closely related subject, you may wish to consult the listings in "Contents Arranged by Subject," which follows the regular table of contents. You can get a further glimpse of the content of various essays by looking at the brief annotations after their titles in the table of contents. Incidentally, very interesting papers can often be written comparing essays that approach the same subject with different rhetorical strategies. If you find yourself looking for a writing topic, you might consider this possibility, especially later on in the course when you have read essays in several different sections of *The Resourceful Reader*.

However you use *The Resourceful Reader* in your particular writing course, its editor hopes that you will enjoy it and learn much from it—as she did in preparing it. Here's wishing you good reading and writing!

---

*Note that between The Resourceful Reader, Fourth Edition and the Harbrace College Handbook, Brief Thirteenth Edition, six model research papers are available.

✳

Chapter 1

Example

One of the simplest but most effective ways for a writer to get an idea across clearly and forcefully is to provide a striking example or series of examples. In fact, a whole essay can be built with examples, as the readings in this chapter demonstrate.

An example may be as short as a word or two—for instance, a brief reference to a well-known figure (called an allusion):

> As Robin Hood and Baby Face Nelson show us, you don't always get what you pay for. Sometimes you get what others paid for. When a whole society begins to operate on that principle, that society is in trouble.
>
> —T. Breitfeld

Or a single example might extend to several pages. For instance (note that this phrase means "for *example*"), an essay aiming to persuade readers to support a program for the poor might rely on an account of one day in a family's struggle to live with dignity below the poverty line.

How will you know if you have used enough examples? There is no easy rule; perhaps the best advice is to put yourself in your reader's shoes and then ask yourself whether, from the reader's point of view, your points are as clear as they need to be. An essay discussing the horrors of college registration might benefit from two or three well-chosen examples but become tedious with more. On the other hand, an essay defining terrorism might require many examples to convey the complexity of that subject. The decision depends on your subject and purpose and, as always, the needs of your audience. In this chapter, Dave Barry's subject, the college experience, requires numerous brief examples. Paula Gunn Allen combines short examples and extended ones in her essay.

A single striking example often makes an effective beginning for an essay, quickly capturing the reader's interest while it prepares the way for the writer's main idea, or thesis. Banesh Hoffmann begins "My Friend, Albert Einstein" with a memorable anecdote that establishes his main point: Einstein's astonishing simplicity. Once that idea has been stated, Hoffmann presents a number of other examples to develop it.

p. 314 - 314

Sometimes you will want to give each example a paragraph of its own; at other times you may find that it works well to group several related examples in a single paragraph [*Harbrace* 27c(2); *Hodges'* 31c(2)]. And of course an extended example may require several or even many paragraphs.

A danger in using examples is that they may be so engrossing that you lose sight of the point you are trying to make. Keep your purpose and your point in mind. Another danger is that just as too few examples can make an essay weak, too many can overload it. Be selective (even ruthless) in choosing which examples you will use. Keep only the best.

Choosing examples is only part of the battle; you must also arrange them effectively. Any of several organizing principles might be appropriate: time, space, complexity, or importance. For a fuller discussion, see [*Harbrace* 27b(1); *Hodges'* 31b(1)].

In the following essay, Jackie Nye uses both brief and extended examples to explain how the reader might use relaxation techniques to reduce stress.

Stressed to the Max?

Generalization —thesis	Major report due on Monday? Research project moving too slowly? Family making demands? Grade-point in jeopardy? In a hurry-up world where deadlines crowd the pages of our day planners and where the push to produce seems paramount, finding ways to relax becomes increasingly important. Whether we need to recover from a busy day at the office or unwind from a semester of non-stop study, relaxation techniques invariably offer effective therapy.
Two brief examples	For instance, at day's end a long, leisurely soak in a warm eucalyptus-scented bath can loosen stiff, aching muscles, and a cup of good herbal tea can soothe the soul. A particularly stressful day may call for a deeper form of relaxation therapy, such as seeking a quiet place undisturbed by outside interruptions and influences and, once there, meditating to clear the
Third brief example	mind. For many, meditation coupled with a few minutes of yoga exercises results in a refreshed mind and body.
Transition	No time to get away for that quiet cup of tea? Too overwhelmed for solitary meditation? Deep breathing exercises offer an impromptu way to relax any time. Inhale and exhale slowly. While inhaling, imagine breathing in all good, nurturing forces; while exhaling, picture the stream of exhaled air carrying away all the negative, unhappy, unproductive thoughts. Ten deep breaths are usually enough to produce renewed vigor and well-being.
Extended example illustrating one method	

Example   15

Time and finances permitting, try a professional massage for an effortless way to relax. Feel the cares of the world melt away in the skilled hands of a massage therapist as warm oil is rubbed into the skin and muscles are gently kneaded. With such lavish attention, every muscle from the scalp to the toes tingles with increased circulation. In fact, massage can produce such a state of euphoria that some people report feeling as though they are floating on air. And experiencing the benefits of massage does not require the time and money to linger at a spa. This treatment can be enjoyed regularly by making a standing appointment with a local massage therapist or by learning massage basics with a friend or significant other.

Topic, restriction, series of illustrations

For those with the time and the money, a residential spa may be the answer. Planned exercise, managed diet, massage, and cosmetic pampering can make the cares of the world disappear for a few days. For those who feel the need for an extended period to rest and relax, an ocean cruise is hard to beat. Experienced, efficient ship's crew members attend to mundane matters and the gentle rocking of the ship enhances nightly sleep. No ringing phones jangle the nerves, no business crises require immediate attention--just seabreezes, good food and entertainment, exotic ports of call, and best of all, isolation from everyday cares. A week of this kind of pampering is a sure way to relax and restore the body and mind for returning to the real world.

Transition

Brief example leading in to an extended example illustrating a closely related point

Everyone needs to relax at various times, but choosing an effective means depends on time, money, and physical ability. And it also depends upon the kind and degree of stress to be overcome. A few simple neck rolls may be enough to relieve the tense shoulder muscles that come from long hours at a desk. Life-threatening high stress from a major change in lifestyle or work environment can cause high blood pressure or other kinds of heart disease and calls for more drastic measures. A daily regimen of exercise and meditation combined with a good diet may be enough to keep stress-induced high blood pressure from rising beyond an acceptable level. A healthy body is a relaxed body.

Extended transition to a new point

New point

Brief example

Health concerns give the art of relaxation new importance, so in the search for that perfectly relaxed state of balanced mind and muscle, it is worth remembering the wisdom of the Greek Stoic philosopher Epictetus. He taught that what affects us in life is

Example using allusion

not so much what happens to us as it is how we react
to what happens to us.

Conclusion
summarizes and
points to future
   While stress is inevitable, how to reduce or
eliminate it to maintain health or simply avoid inter-
ference with daily living is a matter of individual
choice. So choose well and choose often the way you
wish to relax, and then the stress of hurrying to produce with deadlines to meet can work for you instead
of against you.

Commentary. Jackie Nye gets the reader's attention with a catchy opening
sentence and keeps it by including interesting examples. Her introduction suggests that the stressful environment we all live in is reason enough to be interested in knowing more about managing stress.

  Nye's organization is more complex than it may seem at first. She begins
with simple, inexpensive remedies and then takes up the more expensive ones.
And the simple remedies are, incidentally, those we can do for ourselves,
whereas the expensive remedies require outside sources for fulfillment. In addition, Nye begins with remedies for relatively low levels of stress. As the essay moves along, the remedies address increasingly higher levels of stress. The
climax of the essay is the paragraph in which she talks about the dangers to
health that can result from unrelieved stress. Nye here points out that a change
of lifestyle may be the necessary therapy for stress-induced hypertension.

  Nye also uses a mix of brief and extended examples. In the second paragraph, she explains three ways to relax. The third paragraph focuses on a single technique, deep breathing. She signals that she is about to conclude when
she refers to Epictetus, and then she sums up and challenges her readers to
find suitable relaxation techniques.

My Friend, Albert Einstein
Banesh Hoffmann

Banesh Hoffmann (1906–1986) was born in England, the son of Polish immigrants, and educated at Oxford University and Princeton University. A distinguished mathematician and physicist, he taught briefly at the University of Rochester and then for forty years at Queens College of the City University of New York. He was also a member of Princeton's Institute for Advanced Study, and it was there, in 1935, that he came to know Albert Einstein, with whom he worked on a paper, "Gravitational Equations and the Problem of Motion." Author of numerous books during his long career, among them *The Strange Story of the Quantum* (1947) and *The Tyranny of Testing* (1962), Hoffmann wrote three books about Einstein: *Albert Einstein: Creator and Rebel* (1972) and *Albert Einstein: The Human Side* (1979), both with Einstein's personal secretary, Helen Dukas; and *Albert Einstein* (1975).

He was one of the greatest scientists the world has ever known, yet if I   1
had to convey the essence of Albert Einstein in a single word, I would choose
simplicity. Perhaps an anecdote will help. Once, caught in a downpour, he
took off his hat and held it under his coat. Asked why, he explained, with admirable logic, that the rain would damage the hat, but his hair would be none
the worse for its wetting. This knack for going instinctively to the heart of a
matter was the secret of his major scientific discoveries—this and his extraordinary feeling for beauty.

I first met Albert Einstein in 1935, at the famous Institute for Advanced   2
Study in Princeton, N.J. He had been among the first to be invited to the Institute, and was offered *carte blanche* as to salary. To the director's dismay,
Einstein asked for an impossible sum: it was far too *small*. The director had
to plead with him to accept a larger salary.

I was in awe of Einstein, and hesitated before approaching him about   3
some ideas I had been working on. When I finally knocked on his door, a gentle voice said, "Come"—with a rising inflection that made the single word
both a welcome and a question. I entered his office and found him seated at
a table, calculating and smoking his pipe. Dressed in ill-fitting clothes, his hair
characteristically awry, he smiled a warm welcome. His utter naturalness at
once set me at ease.

As I began to explain my ideas, he asked me to write the equations   4
on the blackboard so he could see how they developed. Then came the

staggering—and altogether endearing—request: "Please go slowly. I do not understand things quickly." This from Einstein! He said it gently, and I laughed. From then on, all vestiges of fear were gone.

Einstein was born in 1879 in the German city of Ulm. He had been no   5
infant prodigy; indeed, he was so late in learning to speak that his parents feared he was a dullard. In school, though his teachers saw no special talent in him, the signs were already there. He taught himself calculus, for example, and his teachers seemed a little afraid of him because he asked questions they could not answer. At the age of 16, he asked himself whether a light wave would seem stationary if one ran abreast of it. From that innocent question would arise, ten years later, his theory of relativity.

Einstein failed his entrance examinations at the Swiss Federal Polytechnic   6
School, in Zurich, but was admitted a year later. There he went beyond his regular work to study the masterworks of physics on his own. Rejected when he applied for academic positions, he ultimately found work, in 1902, as a patent examiner in Berne, and there in 1905 his genius burst into fabulous flower.

Among the extraordinary things he produced in that memorable year were   7
his theory of relativity, with its famous offshoot, $E = mc^2$ (energy equals mass times the speed of light squared), and his quantum theory of light. These two theories were not only revolutionary, but seemingly contradictory: the former was intimately linked to the theory that light consists of waves, while the latter said it consists somehow of particles. Yet this unknown young man boldly proposed both at once—and he was right in both cases, though how he could have been is far too complex a story to tell here.

Collaborating with Einstein was an unforgettable experience. In 1937, the   8
Polish physicist Leopold Infeld and I asked if we could work with him. He was pleased with the proposal, since he had an idea about gravitation waiting to be worked out in detail. Thus we got to know not merely the man and the friend, but also the professional.

The intensity and depth of his concentration were fantastic. When bat-   9
tling a recalcitrant problem, he worried it as an animal worries its prey. Often, when we found ourselves up against a seemingly insuperable difficulty, he would stand up, put his pipe on the table, and say in his quaint English, "I will a little tink" (he could not pronounce "th"). Then he would pace up and down, twirling a lock of his long, graying hair around his forefinger.

A dreamy, faraway and yet inward look would come over his face. There   10
was no appearance of concentration, no furrowing of the brow—only a placid inner communion. The minutes would pass, and then suddenly Einstein would stop pacing as his face relaxed into a gentle smile. He had found the solution to the problem. Sometimes it was so simple that Infeld and I could have kicked ourselves for not having thought of it. But the magic had been performed invisibly in the depths of Einstein's mind, by a process we could not fathom.

When his wife died he was deeply shaken, but insisted that now more than   11
ever was the time to be working hard. I remember going to his home to work

with him during that sad time. His face was haggard and grief-lined, but he put forth a great effort to concentrate. To help him, I steered the discussion away from routine matters into more difficult theoretical problems, and Einstein gradually became absorbed in the discussion. We kept at it for some two hours, and at the end his eyes were no longer sad. As I left, he thanked me with moving sincerity. "It was fun," he said. He had had a moment of surcease from grief, and those groping words expressed a deep emotion.

Although Einstein felt no need for religious ritual and belonged to no for- 12 mal religious group, he was the most deeply religious man I have known. He once said to me, "Ideas come from God," and one could hear the capital "G" in the reverence with which he pronounced the word. On the marble fireplace in the mathematics building at Princeton University is carved, in the original German, what one might call his scientific credo: "God is subtle, but he is not malicious." By this Einstein meant that scientists could expect to find their task difficult, but not hopeless: the Universe was a Universe of law, and God was not confusing us with deliberate paradoxes and contradictions.

Einstein was an accomplished amateur musician. We used to play duets, 13 he on the violin, I at the piano. One day he surprised me by saying Mozart was the greatest composer of all. Beethoven "created" his music, but the music of Mozart was of such purity and beauty one felt he had merely "found" it—that it had always existed as part of the inner beauty of the Universe, waiting to be revealed.

It was this very Mozartean simplicity that most characterized Einstein's 14 methods. His 1905 theory of relativity, for example, was built on just two simple assumptions. One is the so-called principle of relativity, which means, roughly speaking, that we cannot tell whether we are at rest or moving smoothly. The other assumption is that the speed of light is the same no matter what the speed of the object that produces it. You can see how reasonable this is if you think of agitating a stick in a lake to create waves. Whether you wiggle the stick from a stationary pier, or from a rushing speedboat, the waves, once generated, are on their own, and their speed has nothing to do with that of the stick.

Each of these assumptions, by itself, was so plausible as to seem primi- 15 tively obvious. But together they were in such violent conflict that a lesser man would have dropped one or the other and fled in panic. Einstein daringly kept both—and by so doing he revolutionized physics. For he demonstrated they could, after all, exist peacefully side by side, provided we gave up cherished beliefs about the nature of time.

Science is like a house of cards, with concepts like time and space at the 16 lowest level. Tampering with time brought most of the house tumbling down, and it was this that made Einstein's work so important—and controversial. At a conference in Princeton in honor of his 70th birthday, one of the speakers, a Nobel Prize winner, tried to convey the magical quality of Einstein's achievement. Words failed him, and with a shrug of helplessness he pointed to his wristwatch, and said in tones of awed amazement, "It all came from this." His very ineloquence made this the most eloquent tribute I have heard to Einstein's genius.

Although fame had little effect on Einstein as a person, he could not escape it; he was, of course, instantly recognizable. One autumn Saturday, I was walking with him in Princeton discussing some technical matters. Parents and alumni were streaming excitedly toward the stadium, their minds on the coming football game. As they approached us, they paused in sudden recognition, and a momentary air of solemnity came over them as if they had been reminded of a different world. Yet Einstein seemed totally unaware of this effect and went on with the discussion as though they were not there.   17

We think of Einstein as one concerned only with the deepest aspects of science. But he saw scientific principles in everyday things to which most of us would give barely a second thought. He once asked me if I had ever wondered why a man's feet will sink into either dry or completely submerged sand, while sand that is merely damp provides a firm surface. When I could not answer, he offered a simple explanation.   18

It depends, he pointed out, on *surface tension,* the elastic-skin effect of a liquid surface. This is what holds a drop together, or causes two small raindrops on a windowpane to pull into one big drop the moment their surfaces touch.   19

When sand is damp, Einstein explained, there are tiny amounts of water between grains. The surface tensions of these tiny amounts of water pull all the grains together, and friction then makes them hard to budge. When the sand is dry, there is obviously no water between grains. If the sand is fully immersed, there is water between grains, but no water *surface* to pull them together.   20

This is not as important as relativity; yet there is no telling what seeming trifle will lead an Einstein to a major discovery. And the puzzle of the sand does give us an inkling of the power and elegance of his mind.   21

Einstein's work, performed quietly with pencil and paper, seemed remote from the turmoil of everyday life: But his ideas were so revolutionary they caused violent controversy and irrational anger. Indeed, in order to be able to award him a belated Nobel Prize, the selection committee had to avoid mentioning relativity, and pretend the prize was awarded primarily for his work on the quantum theory.   22

Political events upset the serenity of his life even more. When the Nazis came to power in Germany, his theories were officially declared false because they had been formulated by a Jew. His property was confiscated, and it is said a price was put on his head.   23

When scientists in the United States, fearful that the Nazis might develop an atomic bomb, sought to alert American authorities to the danger, they were scarcely heeded. In desperation, they drafted a letter which Einstein signed and sent directly to President Roosevelt. It was this act that led to the fateful decision to go all-out on the production of an atomic bomb—an endeavor in   24 which Einstein took no active part. When he heard of the agony and destruction that his $E = mc^2$ had wrought, he was dismayed beyond measure, and from then on there was a look of ineffable sadness in his eyes.

There was something elusively whimsical about Einstein. It is illustrated by my favorite anecdote about him. In his first year in Princeton, on Christmas Eve, so the story goes, some children sang carols outside his house. Having finished, they knocked on his door and explained they were collecting money to buy Christmas presents. Einstein listened, then said, "Wait a moment." He put on his scarf and overcoat, and took his violin from its case. Then, joining the children as they went from door to door, he accompanied their singing of "Silent Night" on his violin.   25

How shall I sum up what it meant to have known Einstein and his works? Like the Nobel Prize winner who pointed helplessly at his watch, I can find no adequate words. It was akin to the revelation of great art that lets one see what was formerly hidden. And when, for example, I walk on the sand of a lonely beach, I am reminded of his ceaseless search for cosmic simplicity— and the scene takes on a deeper, sadder beauty.   26

✳

RESPONDING TO THE WHOLE ESSAY

1. This essay first appeared in *Reader's Digest*, a mass-circulation magazine with millions of readers. What features in the essay appeal to such an audience? How do you think the essay might have changed if Hoffmann had written it for *Scientific American*? [*Harbrace* 28a; *Hodges'* 32a]

2. What purpose can you discern in Hoffmann's reminiscences about Einstein? Is Hoffmann's aim primarily to entertain? to persuade the reader to a particular point of view? Explain. [*Harbrace* 28a; *Hodges'* 32a]

3. How does Hoffmann's selection of details contribute to the development of his thesis? How do paragraphs 5–7 and 14–15 fit in? [*Harbrace* 28d; *Hodges'* 32d]

4. What is interesting or arresting in Hoffmann's opening anecdote? Explain why this example entices the reader to keep reading. [*Harbrace* 28f(1); *Hodges'* 32f(1)]

5. What other examples in the essay do you find most memorable? What does each contribute?

6. In paragraph 10, Hoffmann writes of Einstein in the process of solving a problem: "There was no appearance of concentration, no furrowing of the brow—only a placid inner communion." In the very next paragraph, which discusses Einstein's grief following his wife's death, Hoffmann writes, "His face was haggard and grief-lined, but he put forth a great effort to concentrate." What do these opposing statements reveal?

7. What makes Hoffmann's final paragraph an effective conclusion? [*Harbrace* 28f(2); *Hodges'* 32f(2)]

ANALYZING THE ELEMENTS

Grammar

1. In the second sentence of paragraph 2, what time relationship does the past perfect tense of the first verb establish with the other verb? [*Harbrace* 7c; *Hodges'* 7c]
2. In the next-to-last sentence of paragraph 3, Hoffmann writes, "Dressed in ill-fitting clothes, his hair characteristically awry. . . ." What word in the main clause do these phrases modify? What advantages does this phrasal construction have over separate sentences conveying the same information? [*Harbrace* 1d(2); *Hodges'* 1d(2)]
3. The first sentence of paragraph 8 uses a gerund subject. Try rewriting the sentence to say the same thing without the gerund. Is the new version more or less successful than Hoffmann's? Why? [*Harbrace* 1d(1); *Hodges'* 1d(1)]
4. In the last sentence of paragraph 12, Hoffmann explains what Einstein meant when he said "God is subtle, but he is not malicious." Why does Hoffmann use the past tense for the part of the sentence following the colon? Would the meaning be different if he had used the present tense? [*Harbrace* 7c; *Hodges'* 7c]

Effective Sentences

1. The final sentence of paragraph 3 contains the modifier "at once." Some writers might place that phrase at the end of the sentence. What would be the effect of such a move? Which way do you think the sentence works better? Why? [*Harbrace* 11a; *Hodges'* 29a]
2. Paragraph 4 contains an inverted sentence—verb before subject. What is the inverted sentence, and what is the effect of that inversion? Explain the effect of inversion in the last sentence of paragraph 5. [*Harbrace* 11f; *Hodges'* 29f]
3. Although needless shifts in the person and number of pronouns are to be avoided, in the second sentence of paragraph 12 Hoffmann deliberately chooses the impersonal pronoun *one*. Why is *one* better here than if Hoffmann had said, "*I* could hear the capital G"? [*Harbrace* 8e(3); *Hodges'* 27b]

Punctuation and Mechanics

1. Explain why Hoffmann italicizes *simplicity* in the first sentence of the essay. (*Harbrace* 24f; *Hodges'* 10f]
2. The fourth sentence of paragraph 1 contains an indirect quotation. Rewrite the sentence as it might have been if Hoffmann had used a direct quotation. [*Harbrace* 20a; *Hodges'* 16a]
3. Explain the use of quotation marks in the last sentence of paragraph 25. [*Harbrace* 20b; *Hodges'* 16b]

Diction

1. What is the meaning of *dullard* in the second sentence of paragraph 5? What other word could Hoffmann have used? Are there any advantages to using *dullard*? If so, what? [*Harbrace* 14a; *Hodges'* 20a]

2. The first sentence of paragraph 9 contains the word *fantastic*. Write down what you think the word means and then look it up in your dictionary. What meaning do you think Hoffmann intended? [*Harbrace* 14a; *Hodges'* 20a]
3. Hoffmann creates a new word to describe the kind of simplicity Einstein possessed—*Mozartean*. Explain what connotations Hoffmann probably intended to evoke by using this word. [*Harbrace* 14a; *Hodges'* 20a]

BUILDING VOCABULARY

1. Define *recalcitrant*. From what Latin roots is *recalcitrant* borrowed? What do they mean? How did these roots change in Late Latin? Explain.
2. List and define two antonyms for *recalcitrant*. Write a sentence using each word you have listed.

SUGGESTIONS FOR WRITING

1. Write a character sketch of someone you know well, perhaps someone who has had an important influence on your life. As Hoffmann does, select examples that focus your essay on no more than one or two traits that have impressed you.
2. All of us—not only great geniuses—make our own discoveries of the natural world and experience a sense of wonder at its workings. Write a brief essay giving examples of your own discoveries and experiences.

Country Codes
Noel Perrin

Born in New York City, Noel Perrin (1927–   ) has lived in rural New England for more than a quarter-century and has made his adopted environment the subject of much of his writing. In addition to writing, Perrin teaches English at Dartmouth College and "scours a living from the flinty New England soil." His articles and essays appear regularly in *Country Journal,* the *New Yorker,* and the *New York Times Book Review.* "Country Codes" comes from his book *Second Person Rural: More Essays of a Sometime Farmer.* Much of what Perrin advises in this essay is reflected in his own writing: he observes the Power Code by keeping advice to the reader low-keyed, and he observes the Non-Reciprocity Code by never taking his audience for granted.

Robert Frost once wrote a poem about a "town-bred" farmer who was   1
getting his hay in with the help of two hired men, both locals. As they're working, the sky clouds over, and it begins to look like rain. The farmer instructs the two hired men to start making the haycocks especially carefully, so that they'll shed water. About half an hour later (it still isn't raining), one of them abruptly shoves his pitchfork in the ground and walks off. He has quit.

The farmer is utterly baffled. The hired man who stays explains to him   2
that what he said was a major insult.

> *"He thought you meant to find fault with his work.*
> *That's what the average farmer would have meant."*

This hired man goes on to say that he would have quit, too—if the order had been issued by a regular farmer. But seeing as it was a city fellow, he made allowances.

> *"I know you don't understand our ways.*
> *You were just talking what was in your mind.*
> *What was in all our minds, and you weren't hinting."*

Frost called that poem "The Code." He published it in 1914.

Sixty-four years later, the country code is still going strong, and it is still   3
making trouble for town-bred people who live in rural areas. Only I think the code is even more complicated than Frost had room to describe in his poem.

24

In fact, there isn't just one country code, there are at least three. What they all have in common is that instead of saying things out plainly, the way you do in the city, you approach them indirectly. You hint.

I am going to call these three the Power Code, the Non-Reciprocity Code, and the Stoic's Code. These are not their recognized names; they don't *have* recognized names. Part of the code is that you never speak of the code, and I am showing my own town-bredness in writing this exposition. (As Frost showed his in writing the poem. He was a city kid in San Francisco before he was a farmer in New Hampshire.) 4

In Frost's poem, it was the Power Code that the townie violated. Under the rules of the Power Code, you *never* give peremptory orders, and you ordinarily don't even make demands. You make requests. What the code says is that everybody is to be treated as an equal, even when financially or educationally, or whatever, they're not. Treat them as either inferiors or superiors, and you can expect trouble. 5

Just recently, for example, a young city doctor moved to our town, and began violating the Power Code right and left. Take the way he treated the boss of the town road crew. The house the doctor was renting has a gravel driveway that tends to wash out after storms. It washed out maybe a month after he had moved in. He is said to have called the road commissioner and given him a brisk order. "I want a culvert installed, and I want it done by this weekend." 6

Now in the city that would be a quite sensible approach. You're calling some faceless bureaucrat, and you use standard negotiating technique. You make an outrageous demand; you throw your weight around, if you have any; and you figure on getting part of what you ask for. You're not surprised when the bureaucrat screams, "*This week!* Listen, we got a hunnert and sixty-two jobs aheada you right now. If you're lucky, we'll get to you in October." You scream back and threaten to call the mayor's office. Then you finally compromise on August. 7

But it doesn't work that way in the country. The code doesn't encourage throwing your weight around. Our road commissioner had been given an order, and he instantly rejected it. " 'Tain't the town's job to look after folks' driveways. If you want a culvert, you can buy one down to White River Junction." 8

I happened to hear what the road commissioner told some friends later. The doctor had actually called at a good time. The town had several used culverts lying around—road culverts they had replaced, which were still good enough to go at the end of a driveway. "If he'd asked decent, we'd have been glad to put one in for him, some day when work was slack." If he'd used the code, that is. 9

That's nothing, though, compared with the way the young doctor handled one of our retired farmers. When the doctor decided to live in our town— it meant a fifteen-mile drive to the hospital where he worked—it was because he had gotten interested in country things. He wanted to have a garden, burn wood, learn how to scythe a patch of grass, all those things. During his first spring and summer in town, he probably asked the old farmer a hundred 10 questions. He got free lessons in scything. He consulted on fencing problems. Learned how thick to plant peas.

Then one day the farmer asked *him* a question. "I understand you know suthin' about arthritis," the farmer said. "Well, my wife's is actin' up." And he want on to ask a question about medication.   11

The young doctor's answer was quick and smooth. "I'll be glad to see her in office hours," he said.   12

Again, normal city practice. You've got to protect yourself against all the people at cocktail parties who want free medical advice. Furthermore, you probably really should examine a patient before you do any prescribing. All the same, what he was saying loud and clear in the country code was, "My time is worth more than yours; I am more important than you are. So I can ask you free questions, but you must pay for any you ask me." Not very polite. What he should have done was put down the scythe and say, "Let's go have a look at her."   13

Actually, if he had done that, he probably would have muffed it anyway. Because then he would have come up against the Non-Reciprocity Code, and he didn't understand that, either. The Non-Reciprocity Code says that you never take any favors for granted (or call in your debts, as city politicians say). Instead, you always pretend that each favor done you is a brand-new one. In the case of a young doctor, suppose he *had* stopped his free scythe lesson and gone to examine the farmer's wife. When he was ready to leave, the farmer would have said to him, "What do I owe you?" And then one of two things would have happened. Old habits would have asserted themselves, and he would have said smoothly, "That will be twenty-five dollars, please." Or else, a little cross with the farmer for not recognizing his generous motive (does the old fool think I make *house calls?*), he would have said that it was free, in a sort of huffy, look-what-a-favor-I'm-doing-you voice.   14

Both answers would have been wrong. The correct response would be to act as if the farmer was doing *you* a favor in letting you not charge. Something like, "Come on, if you can teach me to scythe, and how to plant peas, I guess there's no harm in my taking a look at your wife."   15

One of the funniest instances in which you see the Non-Reciprocity Code operating is after people get their trucks stuck, which during mud season in Vermont is constantly. You're driving along in your pickup, and there's your neighbor with two wheels in the ditch, unable to budge. You stop, get out your logging chain, hook on, and pull him out. "How much will that be?" he asks, as if his cousin Donald hadn't just pulled you out the week before. In a way it's a ritual question. He would be surprised out of his mind if you thought a minute and said, "Oh, I guess five dollars would be about right."   16

But it's not entirely ritual. He would be surprised. But he would hand over the five dollars. The point of the question is to establish that you don't *have* to pull him out just because he's a friend and will someday pull you out. It's treated as an act of free will, a part of New England independence.   17

The third code, the Stoic's Code, is sometimes confused with machismo, 18 but really has no connection with it. Country people of both sexes practice it with equal fervency. Basically, it consists of seeing who can go without complaining longest.

I first became aware of the Stoic's Code when I was helping two people 19 put hay bales into a barn loft about fifteen years ago. It was a hot day in late June, with the humidity running at least ninety percent. I function badly in hot weather. Within ten minutes I was pouring sweat—as were my coworkers. The difference was that I kept bitching about it. Finally, after three-quarters of an hour, I flopped down and announced I'd have to cool off before I touched another bale.

To me this just seemed common sense. We had no special deadline to meet 20 in loading that hay. What I really thought was that all three of us should go take a dip in the river.

But the Stoic's Code doesn't stress common sense. It stresses endurance. 21 Maybe that's because to survive at all as a farmer in New England you need endurance. In any case, the other two flicked me one quick scornful look and kept on working. One of them has never really respected me again to this day. The other, like the second hired man in Frost's poem, made allowances for my background and forgave me. We have since become fast friends. I have never dared to ask, but I think he thinks I have made real progress in learning to shut my mouth and keep working.

I could never be a stoic on the true native level, though. Consider the 22 story of Hayden Clark and Rodney Palmer, as Rodney tells it. A good many years ago, before there were any paved roads in town, Hayden ran a garage. (Rodney runs it now.) He also sold cordwood.

One day when there wasn't much doing at the garage, Hayden was saw- 23 ing cordwood just across the road, where he could keep an eye on the gas pumps. If you saw with a circular saw, and do it right, it takes three men. One person lifts up the logs, one does the actual cutting, and one throws the cut pieces into a pile. The three jobs are called putting on, sawing, and taking off. In all three you are doing dangerous work at very high speed.

On this day a man named Charlie Raynes was putting on, Hayden was 24 sawing, and young Rodney was taking off. Hayden kept the wood coming so fast that Rodney was always a beat behind. He never paused a second to let Rodney catch up, and this torture went on for nearly an hour. No one spoke. (Not that you could hear over a buzz saw, anyway.)

Then finally a customer pulled in for gas. Hayden left the other two saw- 25 ing, and went over to pump it. Charlie continued to put on, and Rodney sawed in Hayden's place.

Rather than interrupt their rhythm when he came back, Harden began to 26 take off. Rodney and Charlie exchanged a quick glance, and began putting the wood to Hayden so fast that *he* was off balance the whole time, and not infrequently in some danger of getting an arm cut off. At this speed and in this way they finished the entire pile. It was Rodney's revenge, and as he told me about it, his eyes gleamed.

It was only a year or two ago that Rodney told me the story. In the very act of telling it, he included me as one who knew the code. But I instantly betrayed it. My city background is too strong. I'm too verbal, too used to crowing over triumphs.   27

"After you were done sawing, Hayden never said anything about it?" I asked.   28

"Oh, *no*," Rodney answered, looking really shocked. "Any more than I'd have said anything to him."   29

So, next time you're in a country store and you get a sense that the locals are avoiding you as if you had the worst case of B.O. in the country, you can be pretty sure of the reason. You've probably just said some dreadful thing in code.

✴

RESPONDING TO THE WHOLE ESSAY

1. Would you say Perrin is more interested in expressing his own feelings about country codes or in informing the reader about how to talk with New Englanders? [*Harbrace* 28a; *Hodges'* 32a]
2. From evidence in the essay, what can you say about the audience for whom Perrin was writing? In particular, consider the references to *you* beginning with paragraph 7. [*Harbrace* 28a; *Hodges'* 32a]
3. "Country Codes" is developed with several extended examples. Explain why these examples are pertinent and then examine the rest of the essay to see what other methods of development may be present. [*Harbrace* 27c; *Hodges'* 31c]
4. Perrin uses a straightforward structure for organizing his essay. What is the function of his reference to Frost's poem? How does Perrin let the reader know what he will discuss in the essay? [*Harbrace* 28e; *Hodges'* 32e]
5. Explain how Perrin links paragraphs 5 through 10. [*Harbrace* 27d, *Hodges'* 31d]
6. Comment on Perrin's conclusion: Is it a good conclusion? If so, why? If not, what would make it better? [*Harbrace* 28f; *Hodges'* 32f]

ANALYZING THE ELEMENTS

Grammar

1. In paragraph 3, sentence 3, why it is necessary to use a comma between the clauses? [*Harbrace* 3a; *Hodges'* 3a]
2. Consider the fourth sentence of paragraph 3. In it, examine the relationship between the clauses. Comment on how each clause functions in the sentence. [*Harbrace* 1d; *Hodges'* 1d]
3. Does the relationship between the third and fourth sentences of paragraph 9 justify leaving out the main clause? Explain. [*Harbrace* 2; *Hodges'* 2]

Effective Sentences

1. What does Perrin's shift from the past tense to the present tense in the first paragraph of the essay accomplish? [*Harbrace* 8e(2); *Hodges'* 27a]
2. Identify the main way in which Perrin achieves sentence variety. [*Harbrace* 12; *Hodges'* 30]

Punctuation and Mechanics

1. In the first sentence of paragraph 6, how would you justify Perrin's using a comma between the two elements of a compound predicate. [*Harbrace* 17a; *Hodges'* 12a]
2. Consider Perrin's use of the semicolon in the third sentence of paragraph 7. Explain why he does not simply use commas instead. [*Harbrace* 18b; *Hodges'* 14b]
3. Justify omitting a comma between *quick* and *scornful* in the fourth sentence of paragraph 21. [*Harbrace* 17e; *Hodges'* 13d]

Diction

1. Rewrite the first sentence of paragraph 5 to make it less wordy. Why do you think Perrin wrote the sentence as he did? [*Harbrace* 15; *Hodges'* 21 and 15e]
2. Perrin used dialect in several places, among them the fifth sentence of paragraph 7 and the fourth sentence of paragraph 8. What effect does this use of regional language have? [*Harbrace* 13b; *Hodges'* 19d]

BUILDING VOCABULARY

1. From what language is *bureaucracy* derived? Identify and define the word, or words, from which bureaucracy is taken.
2. Define and write a sentence using *bureaucracy*.

SUGGESTIONS FOR WRITING

1. Perrin's New England farmers may seem unusual, perhaps even exotic, but the activities of the most ordinary folk can be made interesting with vivid examples and details. Select a day, or imaginatively construct a representative day, in the life of your community or of a closely knit group to which you belong and write a brief essay using carefully chosen examples to convey their way of handling strangers.
2. Pick an occupation that is strange or exotic to you (cowboy, pearl diver, treasure hunter) or one from times gone by (for example, fence viewer, trapper, wagon boss). Do a little research and in a short essay use examples to explain that occupation to a reader unfamiliar with it.

Just Walk on By: A Black Man Ponders His Power to Alter Public Space

Brent Staples

Born in 1951 in Chester, Pennsylvania, Brent Staples holds a bachelor's degree from Widener University and a Ph.D. in psychology from the University of Chicago. Currently a member of the editorial board of *The New York Times*, Staples began his work for the *Times* as the first assistant metropolitan editor in 1985. "Just Walk on By" first appeared in *Ms.* magazine in 1986.

My first victim was a woman—white, well dressed, probably in her early 1 twenties. I came upon her late one evening on a deserted street in Hyde park, a relatively affluent neighborhood in an otherwise mean, impoverished section of Chicago. As I swung onto the avenue behind her, there seemed be a discreet, uninflammatory distance between us. Not so. She cast back a worried glance. To her, the youngish black man—a broad six feet two inches with a beard and billowing hair, both hands shoved into the pockets of a bulky military jacket—seemed menacingly close. After a few more quick glimpses, she picked up her pace and was soon running in earnest. Within seconds she disappeared into a cross street.

That was more than a decade ago. I was twenty-two years old, a gradu- 2 ate student newly arrived at the University of Chicago. It was in the echo of that terrified woman's footfalls that I first began to know the unwieldy inheritance I'd come into—the ability to alter public space in ugly ways. It was clear that she thought herself the quarry of a mugger, a rapist, or worse. Suffering a bout of insomnia, however, I was stalking sleep, not defenseless wayfarers. As a softy who is scarcely able to take a knife to a raw chicken—let alone hold it to a person's throat—I was surprised, embarrassed, and dismayed all at once. Her flight made me feel like an accomplice in tyranny. It also make it clear that I was indistinguishable from the muggers who occasionally seeped into the area from the surrounding ghetto. That first encounter, and those that followed, signified that a vast, unnerving gulf lay between nighttime pedestrians—particularly women—and me. And I soon gathered that being perceived as dangerous is a hazard in itself. I only needed to turn a corner into a dicey situation, or crowd some frightened, armed person in a foyer somewhere, or make an errant move after being pulled over by a policeman. Where fear and weapons meet—and they often do in urban America—there is always the possibility of death.

In that first year, my first away from my hometown, I was to become thoroughly familiar with the language of fear. At dark, shadowy intersections in Chicago, I could cross in front of a car stopped at a traffic light and elicit the *thunk, thunk, thunk, thunk* of the driver—black, white, male, or female— hammering down the door locks. On less traveled streets after dark, I grew accustomed to but never comfortable with people who crossed to the other side of the street rather than pass me. Then there were the standard unpleas- antries with police, doormen, bouncers, cab drivers, and others whose busi- ness it is to screen out troublesome individuals *before* there is any nastiness.

I moved to New York nearly two years ago and I have remained an avid night walker. In central Manhattan, the near-constant crowd cover minimizes tense one-on-one street encounters. Elsewhere—visiting friends in SoHo,[1] where sidewalks are narrow and tightly spaced buildings shut out the sky— things can get very taut indeed.

Black men have a firm place in New York mugging literature. Norman Podhoretz[2] in his famed (or infamous) 1963 essay, "My Negro Problem—And Ours," recalls growing up in terror of black males; they "were tougher than we were, more ruthless," he writes—and as an adult on the Upper West Side of Manhattan, he continues, he cannot constrain his nervousness when he meets black men on certain streets. Similarly, a decade later, the essayist and novelist Edward Hoagland extols a New York where once "Negro bitterness bore down mainly on other Negroes." Where some see mere panhandlers, Hoagland sees "a mugger who is clearly screwing up his nerve to do more than just *ask* for money." But Hoagland has "the New Yorker's quick-hunch posture for broken-field maneuvering," and the bad guy swerves away.

I often witness that "hunch posture," from women after dark on the war- renlike streets of Brooklyn where I live. They seem to set their faces on neu- tral and, with their purse straps strung across their chests bandolier style, they forge ahead as though bracing themselves against being tackled. I understand, of course, that the danger they perceive is not a hallucination. Women are particularly vulnerable to street violence, and young black males are drasti- cally overrepresented among the perpetrators of that violence. Yet these truths are no solace against the kind of alienation that comes of being ever the sus- pect, against being set apart, a fearsome entity with whom pedestrians avoid making eye contact.

It is not altogether clear to me how I reached the ripe old age of twenty- two without being conscious of the lethality nighttime pedestrians attributed to me. Perhaps it was because in Chester, Pennsylvania, the small, angry in- dustrial town where I came of age in the 1960s, I was scarcely noticeable

---

[1]A district of lower Manhattan known for its art galleries.
[2]A well-known literary critic and editor of *Commentary* magazine.

against a backdrop of gang warfare, street knifings, and murders. I grew up one of the good boys, had perhaps a half-dozen fist fights. In retrospect, my shyness of combat has clear sources.

Many things go into the making of a young thug. One of those things is   8 the consummation of the male romance with the power to intimidate. An infant discovers that random flailings send the baby bottle flying out of the crib and crashing to the floor. Delighted, the joyful babe repeats those motions again and again, seeking to duplicate the feat. Just so, I recall the points at which some of my boyhood friends were finally seduced by the perception of themselves as tough guys. When a mark cowered and surrendered his money without resistance, myth and reality merged—and paid off. It is, after all, only manly to embrace the power to frighten and intimidate. We, as men, are not supposed to give an inch of our lane on the highway; we are to seize the fighter's edge in work and in play and even in love; we are to be valiant in the face of hostile forces.

Unfortunately, poor and powerless young men seem to take all this non-   9 sense literally. As a boy, I saw countless tough guys locked away; I have since buried several, too. They were babies, really—a teenage cousin, a brother of twenty-two, a childhood friend in his mid-twenties—all gone down in episodes of bravado played out in the streets. I came to doubt the virtues of intimidation early on. I chose, perhaps even unconsciously, to remain a shadow—timid, but a survivor.

The fearsomeness mistakenly attributed to me in public places often has   10 a perilous flavor. The most frightening of these confusions occurred in the late 1970s and early 1980s when I worked as a journalist in Chicago. One day, rushing into the office of a magazine I was writing for with a deadline story in hand, I was mistaken for a burglar. The office manager called security and, with an ad hoc posse, pursued me through the labyrinthine halls, nearly to my editor's door. I had no way of proving who I was. I could only move briskly toward the company of someone who knew me.

Another time I was on assignment for a local paper and killing time be-   11 fore an interview. I entered a jewelry store on the city's affluent Near North Side. The proprietor excused herself and returned with an enormous red Doberman pinscher straining at the end of a leash. She stood, the dog extended toward me, silent to my questions, her eyes bulging nearly out of her head. I took a cursory look around, nodded, and bade her good night. Relatively speaking, however, I never fared as badly as another black male journalist. He went to nearby Waukegan, Illinois, a couple of summers ago to work on a story about a murderer who was born there. Mistaking the reporter for the killer, police hauled him from his car at gunpoint and but for his press credentials would probably have tried to book him. Such episodes are not uncommon. Black men trade tales like this all the time.

In "My Negro Problem—And Ours," Podhoretz writes that the hatred he   12 feels for blacks makes itself known to him through a variety of avenues—one being his discomfort with that "special brand of paranoid touchiness" to which he says blacks are prone. No doubt he is speaking here of black men. In time, I learned to smother the rage I felt at so often being taken for a criminal. Not to be so would surely have led to madness—via that special "paranoid touchiness" that so annoyed Podhoretz at the time he wrote the essay.

I began to take precautions to make myself less threatening. I move about   13
with care, particularly late in the evening. I give a wide berth to nervous people on subway platforms during the wee hours, particularly when I have exchanged business clothes for jeans. If I happen to be entering a building behind some people who appear skittish, I may walk by, letting them clear the lobby before I return, so as not to seem to be following them. I have been calm and extremely congenial on those rare occasions when I've been pulled over by the police.

And on late-evening constitutionals along streets less traveled by, I employ what has proved to be an excellent tension-reducing measure: I whistle   14
melodies from Beethoven and Vivaldi and the more popular classical composers. Even steely New Yorkers hunching toward nighttime destinations seem to relax, and occasionally they even join in the tune. Virtually everybody seems to sense that a mugger wouldn't be warbling bright, sunny selections from Vivaldi's *Four Seasons*. It is my equivalent of the cowbell that hikers wear when they known they are in bear country.

✸

RESPONDING TO THE WHOLE ESSAY

1. What advantage does Staples gain by introducing his essay with an example of how one woman saw him as a threat? How does this example help Staples establish his main idea? [*Harbrace* 28d; *Hodges'* 32d]
2. Where is the main idea of paragraph 2 found? How do the examples that begin the paragraph prepare the reader for the main idea? [*Harbrace* 27a and 27c(2); *Hodges'* 31a and 31c]
3. How does Staples achieve coherence in paragraph 13? Mark and label all the devices he uses.
4. What clues do the vocabulary and the details of "Just Walk on By" provide about Staples's intended audience? Describe the audience. [*Harbrace* 28a; *Hodges'* 32a]
5. Does Staples ever state his purpose for writing "Just Walk on By"? If so, where? If not, what do you think his purpose is? [*Harbrace* 28a; *Hodges'* 33a]
6. Comment on the tone of Staples's essay. What evidence do you find for your assessment of the tone Staples takes? [*Harbrace* 29a; *Hodges'* 33a]

ANALYZING THE ELEMENTS

Grammar

1. In the first sentence of paragraph 14, Staples uses the clause "what has proved to be an excellent tension-reducing measure: I whistle melodies from Beethoven and Vivaldi and the more popular classical composers." How does this clause

function? As exactly as you can explain how this clause advances Staples's main idea. [*Harbrace* 1e; *Hodges'* 1e]
2. In the first sentence of paragraph 6, what advantage does Staples gain from using *warrenlike* to modify *streets*? [*Harbrace* 4; *Hodges'* 4]
3. In the final clause of the third sentence in paragraph 10 Staples uses the passive voice. Would the active voice be better? Explain your answer. [*Harbrace* 7c; *Hodges'* 7c]

Effective Sentences

1. Paragraph 2 begins with the word *that*. What is the antecedent of this pronoun, and what advantage does Staples gain from beginning the paragraph this way? [*Harbrace* 6b; *Hodges'* 28]
2. Explain why rewriting the fourth sentence of paragraph 11 as follows has a different effect: She stood with the dog extended toward me. She was silent to my questions. Her eyes bulged nearly out of her head. [*Harbrace* 9; *Hodges'* 24]
3. As fully as possible, explain what makes the fourth sentence of paragraph 13 effective.

Punctuation and Mechanics

1. Explain the reason for quotation marks around *hunch posture* in the first sentence of paragraph 6. Why is *before* italicized in the last sentence of paragraph 3? [*Harbrace* 20c and 24f; *Hodges'* 16c and 10f]
2. Comment on the reason for each comma and each semicolon in the final sentence of paragraph 8. [*Harbrace* 17d and 18a; *Hodges'* 12d and 14a]
3. Justify the capitalization of *Upper West Side* in the second sentence of paragraph 5. [*Harbrace* 23a; *Hodges'* 9a]

Diction

1. How does Staples use the word *victim* in the first paragraph? Explain why he refers to the woman as a *victim*. [*Harbrace* 14c; *Hodges'* 20c]
2. Look up the following words in your dictionary: *affluent* (paragraph 1), *quarry* and *dicey* (paragraph 2), *bandolier* (paragraph 6), *perilous* and *posse* (paragraph 10), *skittish* (paragraph 13), *warbling* (paragraph 14). What synonyms could Staples have used? In each case, which is better, the synonym or the word Staples uses? Why? [*Harbrace* 13a and 14a; *Hodges'* 19a, 20a, and 23e(2)]
3. Staples's use of the phrase "less traveled" (paragraphs 3 and 14) seems to echo the language of Robert Frost's line, "I took the one less traveled by," from the poem, "The Road Not Taken." Comment on how that possible *allusion* contributes to Staples's main point. (You may find it helpful to look up the poem.) [*Harbrace* 14c; *Hodges'* 20c]

BUILDING VOCABULARY

1. What are the Greek roots from which *paranoid* is borrowed? What do they mean? Write a sentence using a word derived from one of these Greek roots.

2. What is the meaning of the Latin suffix *-able*? List and define three words ending in this suffix. What is their grammatical function?

SUGGESTIONS FOR WRITING

1. Write an essay in which you use examples to describe how someone judged you unfairly and how you responded to the judgment.
2. Write an essay using examples to illustrate how you once had to alter your public behavior for reasons beyond your control. For instance, people often modify their public behavior because of the expectations of their families, because of peer group pressures, or because of standards imposed by an institution such as a school or the military.

The Myth of College
Dave Barry

Dave Barry is a Pulitzer Prize–winning journalist and syndicated humor columnist whose essays are published in nationwide and international newspapers and magazines. Additionally, Barry has gained recognition as an author, publishing a number of books, including his most recent titles, *Dave Barry's Guide to Guys*, *Dave Barry Is Not Making This Up*, and *Dave Barry in Cyberspace*. Many of his earlier books have become the subjects for the syndicated television show *Dave's World*. Barry currently works for the *Miami Herald's Tropic Magazine*, but in his spare time, he plays lead guitar in the rock band Rock Bottom Remainders, which is made up of distinguished writers, including Stephen King, Barbara Kingsolver, Amy Tan, and Robert Fulghum. In 1993, the band toured the United States, donating its profits to literacy and First Amendment causes. In "The Myth of College," Barry offers prospective students some humorous but insightful advice about choosing a major, using examples from his own experience and observations.

Many of you young persons out there are seriously thinking about going to college. (That is, of course, a lie. The only things you young persons think seriously about are loud music and sex. Trust me: these are closely related to college.) College is basically a bunch of rooms where you sit for roughly two thousand hours and try to memorize things. The two thousand hours are spread out over four years; you spend the rest of the time sleeping and trying to get dates. 1

Basically, you learn two kinds of things in college: 2

- *Things you need to know later in life (2 hours).* These include how to make collect telephone calls and get beer and crepe-paper stains out of your pajamas.
- Things you will not need to know in later life (1,998 hours). These are the things you learn in classes whose names end in "-ology", "-osophy", "-isty", "-ies", and so on. The idea is you memorize these things, then write them down in little exam books, then forget them. If you fail to forget them, you become a professor and have to stay in college for the rest of your life.

It's very difficult to forget everything. For example, when I was in college, I had to memorize—don't ask me why—the names of the metaphysical poets other than John Donne. I have managed to forget one of them, but I still remember that the other two were named Vaughan and Crashaw. 3

Sometimes, when I'm trying to remember something important, like 4 whether my wife told me to get tuna packed in oil or tuna packed in water, Vaughan and Crashaw just pop up in my mind, right there in the supermarket. It's a terrible waste of brain cells.

After you've been in college for a year or so, you're supposed to choose 5 a major, which is the subject you intend to memorize and forget the most things about. Here is a very important piece of advice: *be sure to choose a major that does not involve Known Facts and Right Answers.*

This means that you must not major in mathematics, physics, biology, or 6 chemistry, because these subjects involve actual facts. If, for example, you major in mathematics, you're going to wander into class one day and the professor will say: "Define the cosine integer of the quadrant of the rhomboid binary axis, and extrapolate your result to five significant vertices." If you don't come up with exactly the answer the professor has in mind, you fail. The same is true of chemistry: if you write in your exam book that carbon and hydrogen combine to form oak, your professor will flunk you. He wants you to come up with the same answer he and all the other chemists have agreed on. Scientists are extremely snotty about this.

So you should major in subjects like English, philosophy, psychology, and 7 sociology—subjects in which nobody really understands what anybody else is talking about, and which involve virtually no facts. I attended classes in all these subjects, so I'll give you a quick overview of each:

English. This involves writing papers about long books you have read little 8 snippets of just before class. Here is a tip on how to get good grades on your English papers: never say anything about a book that anybody with any common sense would say. For example, suppose you are studying *Moby Dick*. Anybody with any common sense would say that Moby Dick is a big white whale, since the characters in the book refer to it as a big white whale roughly eleven thousand times. So, in **your** paper, **you** say Moby Dick is actually the Republic of Ireland. Your professor, who is sick to death of reading papers and never liked *Moby Dick* anyway, will think you are enormously creative. If you can regularly come up with lunatic interpretations of simple stories, you should major in English.

Philosophy. Basically, this involves sitting in a room and deciding there is no 9 such thing as reality and then going to lunch. You should major in philosophy if you plan to take a lot of drugs.

Psychology. This involves talking about rats and dreams. Psychologists are obsessed with rats and dreams. I once spent an entire semester training a rat to punch little buttons in a certain sequence, then training my roommate to do the same thing. The rat learned much faster. My roommate is now a doctor. If you like rats or dreams, and above all if you dream about rats, you should major in psychology.

Sociology. For sheer lack of intelligibility, sociology is far and away the num-   11
ber one subject. I sat through hours of sociology courses, and read gobs of
sociology writing, and I never once heard or read a coherent statement. This
is because sociologists want to be considered scientists, so they spend most of
their time translating simple, obvious observations into scientific-sounding
code. If you plan to major in sociology, you'll have to learn to do the same
thing. For example, suppose you have observed that children cry when they
fall down. You should write: "Methodological observation of the sociometrical behavior tendencies to prematurated isolates indicates that a causal relationship exists between groundward tropism and lachrimatory, or 'crying' behavior forms." If you can keep this up for fifty or sixty pages, you will get a
large government grant.

✳

RESPONDING TO THE WHOLE ESSAY

1. Which would you say predominates in this essay: the writer's interest in his own
    feelings, an interest in exploring the possibilities offered by an unusual topic, or
    a wish to persuade readers to think differently about their own lives? Do you
    discern other purposes? Point to evidence in this essay to support your answers.
    [*Harbrace* 28a; *Hodges'* 32a]
2. From the evidence in the essay, what can you infer about the audience for whom
    "The Myth of College" was written? [*Harbrace* 28a; *Hodges'* 32a]
3. Which paragraphs are built on a single example? Which contain clusters of ex-
    amples? Explain. [*Harbrace* 27c(2); *Hodges'* 31c(2)]
4. How would you identify the tone of the essay? Be as specific as you can.
    [*Harbrace* 29a; *Hodges'* 33a]

ANALYZING THE ELEMENTS

Grammar

1. Explain whether *this* in the third sentence of the last paragraph is a broad or ex-
    plicit reference. Identify similar references for *this* in the essay. Are these refer-
    ences clear? Why or why not? [*Harbrace* 6b; *Hodges'* 28]
2. The first sentence of paragraph 4 contains a verb with a particle: *pop up*. Explain
    why the particle belongs with the verb rather than serving as a preposition. Find
    at least one other verb with particle in the essay. [*Harbrace* 1a; *Hodges'* 1a]

Effective Sentences

1. In most sentences, the verb directly follows the subject. However, the subject and
    verb in the next-to-last sentence in paragraph 8 are separated by the clause *"who
    is sick to death of reading papers and never liked* Moby Dick *anyway"*. Could

this clause be moved to a different part of the sentence? Explain. [*Harbrace* 1e and 9a(4); *Hodges'* 1e and 24a(4)]
2. Comment upon the parallel structure of the clause following the colon in the first sentence of paragraph 2 and the fourth sentence of paragraph 2. What is the rhetorical effect of this parallelism? [*Harbrace* 10 and 11g; *Hodges'* 26 and 29g]

Punctuation and Mechanics

1. Explain the use of dashes in the second sentence of paragraph 3. Could the author have used parentheses in place of the dashes, and if so, would the sentence have the same effect? Explain. [*Harbrace* 21e and 21f; *Hodges'* 17e and 17f]
2. Following the colon in the sixth sentence of the last paragraph, Barry uses a combination of single and double quotation marks. Explain why both types of quotation marks are necessary. Be as specific as you can. [*Harbrace* 20; *Hodges'* 16]
3. Notice that each of the last four paragraphs (8–11) begin with a word followed by a period. Because a colon has been used to begin this list, punctuating each of the listed items with a colon would be chancy. Usage is divided concerning this problem, so Barry has chosen the period as an alternative. What do you think of Barry's choice of punctuation? Do you find it effective or confusing? Explain.

Diction

1. In the second sentence of paragraph 6 and the sixth sentence of paragraph 11, Barry introduces technical jargon into the essay. What effect does Barry achieve by doing this? Explain. [*Harbrace* 13c(1); *Hodges'* 19g]
2. Look up each of the words in the following sentence from "The Myth of College" and rewrite the sentence without using technical jargon: "Methodological observation of the sociometrical behavior tendencies of prematurated isolates indicates that a causal relationship exists between groundward tropism and lachrimatory, or 'crying' behavior forms." Which sentence is easier to understand: the original or your revision? Explain. [*Harbrace* 13c(1); *Hodges'* 19g]

BUILDING VOCABULARY

1. Look up the meanings of the following words: rhomboid, binary, vertices, cosine, integer.
2. Create at least two words ending in each of the following suffixes: *-ology*, *-istry*, and *-ic*. Write sentences using each of the words that you have listed.

SUGGESTIONS FOR WRITING

1. Write an essay using examples to explain how most college students live.
2. Write an essay using examples to illustrate (and explain and justify) the myth of single or married life, or the myth of adulthood.

Where I Come from Is Like This
Paula Gunn Allen

Of Laguna-Sioux/Lebanese-Jewish ancestry, Paula Gunn Allen was born in Cubero, New Mexico, in 1939. She has taught at Fort Lewis College, the University of Albuquerque, the University of New Mexico, San Francisco State University, and the University of California at Berkeley. A member of the MLA commission on the Literature and Language of America and a former editor of *Sail* magazine, Allen has published numerous articles; one novel, *The Woman Who Owned the Shadows* (1983); five books of poetry, *The Blind Lion* (1975), *Cannon Between My Knees* (1978), *Coyote's Daylight Trip* (1978), *Shadow Country* (1982), and *Skin and Bones* (1988); and two cultural studies, *Sipapu, A Cultural Perspective* (1975) and *The Sacred Hoop: Recovering the Feminine in American Indian Traditions* (1986). In addition, she has served as editor of *From the Center: A Folio of Native American Art and Poetry* (1981) and *The Spider Woman's Granddaughters: Traditional Tales and Contemporary Writing by Native American Women* (1990). She was also awarded a grant for creative writing from the National Endowment for the Arts and a fellowship for Native American Studies from the University of California, Los Angeles. The essay which follows is taken from *The Sacred Hoop*.

I

Modern American Indian women, like their non-Indian sisters, are deeply 1 engaged in the struggle to redefine themselves. In their struggle they must reconcile traditional tribal definitions of women with industrial and postindustrial non-Indian definitions. Yet while these definitions seem to be more or less mutually exclusive, Indian women must somehow harmonize and integrate both in their own lives.

An American Indian woman is primarily defined by her tribal identity. In 2 her eyes, her destiny is necessarily that of her people, and her sense of herself as a woman is first and foremost prescribed by her tribe. The definitions of woman's roles are as diverse as tribal cultures in the Americas. In some she is devalued, in others she wields considerable power. In some she is a familial/clan adjunct, in some she is as close to autonomous as her economic circumstances and psychological traits permit. But in no tribal definitions is she perceived in the same way as are women in western industrial and postindustrial cultures.

40

In the west, few images of women form part of the cultural mythos, and these are largely sexually charged. Among Christians, the madonna is the female prototype, and she is portrayed as essentially passive: her contribution is simply that of birthing. Little else is attributed to her and she certainly possesses few of the characteristics that are attributed to mythic figures among Indian tribes. This image is countered (rather than balanced) by the witch-goddess/whore characteristics designed to reinforce cultural beliefs about women, as well as western adversarial and dualistic perceptions of reality.

The tribes see women variously, but they do not question the power of femininity. Sometimes they see women as fearful, sometimes peaceful, sometimes omnipotent and omniscient, but they never portray women as mindless, helpless, simple, or oppressed. And while the women in a given tribe, clan, or band may be all these things, the individual woman is provided with a variety of images of women from the interconnected supernatural, natural, and social worlds she lives in.

As a half-breed American Indian woman, I cast about in my mind for negative images of Indian women, and I find none that are directed to Indian women alone. The negative images I do have are of Indians in general and in fact are more often of males than of females. All these images come to me from non-Indian sources, and they are always balanced by a positive image. My ideas of womanhood, passed on largely by my mother and grandmothers, Laguna Pueblo women, are about practicality, strength, reasonableness, intelligence, wit, and competence. I also remember vividly the women who came to my father's store, the women who held me and sang to me, the women at Feast Day, at Grab Days, the women in the kitchen of my Cubero home, the women I grew up with; none of them appeared weak or helpless, none of them presented herself tentatively. I remember a certain reserve on those lovely brown faces; I remember the direct gaze of eyes framed by bright-colored shawls draped over their heads and cascading down their backs. I remember the clean cotton dresses and carefully pressed hand-embroidered aprons they always wore; I remember laughter and good food, especially the sweet bread and the oven bread they gave us. Nowhere in my mind is there a foolish woman, a dumb woman, a vain woman, or a plastic woman, though the Indian women I have known have shown a wide range of personal style and demeanor.

My memory includes the Navajo woman who was badly beaten by her Sioux husband; but I also remember that my grandmother abandoned her Sioux husband long ago. I recall the stories about the Laguna woman beaten regularly by her husband in the presence of her children so that the children would not believe in the strength and power of femininity. And I remember the women who drank, who got into fights with other women and with the men, and who often won those battles. I have memories of tired women, partying women, stubborn women, sullen women, amicable women, selfish women, shy women, and aggressive women. Most of all I remember the women who laugh and scold and sit uncomplaining in the long sun on feast days and who cook wonderful food on wood stoves, in beehive mud ovens, and over open fires outdoors.

Among the images of women that come to me from various tribes as well   7
as my own are White Buffalo Woman, who came to the Lakota long ago and brought them the religion of the Sacred Pipe which they still practice; Tinotzin, the goddess who came to Juan Diego to remind him that she still walked the hills of her people and sent him with her message, her demand and her proof to the Catholic bishop in the city nearby. And from Laguna I take the images of Yellow Woman, Coyote Woman, Grandmother Spider (Spider Old Woman), who brought the light, who gave us weaving and medicine, who gave us life. Among the Keres she is known as Thought Woman who created us all and who keeps us in creation even now. I remember Iyatiku, Earth Woman, Corn Woman, who guides and counsels the people to peace and who welcomes us home when we cast off this coil of flesh as huskers cast off the leaves that wrap the corn. I remember Iyatiku's sister, Sun Woman, who held metals and cattle, pigs and sheep, highways and engines and so many things in her bundle, who went away to the east saying that one day she would return.

II

Since the coming of the Anglo-Europeans beginning in the fifteenth cen-   8
tury, the fragile web of identity that long held tribal people secure has gradually been weakened and torn. But the oral tradition has prevented the complete destruction of the web, the ultimate disruption of tribal ways. The oral tradition is vital; it heals itself and the tribal web by adapting to the flow of the present while never relinquishing its connection to the past. Its adaptability has always been required, as many generations have experienced. Certainly the modern American Indian woman bears slight resemblance to her forebears—at least on superficial examination—but she is still a tribal women in her deepest being. Her tribal sense of relationship to all that is continues to flourish. And though she is at times beset by her knowledge of the enormous gap between the life she lives and the life she was raised to live, and while she adapts her mind and being to the circumstances of her present life, she does so in tribal ways, mending the tears in the web of being from which she takes her existence as she goes.

My mother told me stories all the time, though I often did not recog-   9
nize them as that. My mother told me stories about cooking and childbearing; she told me stories about menstruation and pregnancy; she told me stories about gods and heroes, about fairies and elves, about goddesses and spirits; she told me stories about the land and the sky, about cats and dogs, about snakes and spiders; she told me stories about climbing trees and exploring the mesas; she told me stories about going to dances and getting married; she told me stories about dressing and undressing, about sleeping and waking; she told me stories about herself, about her mother, about her

grandmother. She told me stories about grieving and laughing, about thinking and doing; she told me stories about school and about people; about darning and mending; she told me stories about turquoise and about gold; she told me European stories and Laguna stories; she told me Catholic stories and Presbyterian stories; she told me city stories and country stories; she told me political stories and religious stories. She told me stories about living and stories about dying. And in all of those stories she told me who I was, who I was supposed to be, who I came from, and who would follow me. In this way she taught me the meaning of the words she said, that all life is a circle and everything has a place within it. That's what she said and what she showed me in the things she did and the way she lives.

Of course, through my formal, white, Christian education, I discovered   10 that other people had stories of their own—about women, about Indians, about fact, about reality—and I was amazed by a number of startling suppositions that others made about tribal customs and beliefs. According to the un-Indian, non-Indian view, for instance, Indians barred menstruating women from ceremonies and indeed segregated them from the rest of the people, consigning them to some space specially designed for them. This showed that Indians considered menstruating women unclean and not fit to enjoy the company of decent (nonmenstruating) people, that is, men. I was surprised and confused to hear this because my mother had taught me that white people had strange attitudes toward menstruation: they thought something was bad about it, that it meant you were sick, cursed, sinful, and weak and that you had to be very careful during that time. She taught me that menstruation was a normal occurrence, that I could go swimming or hiking or whatever else I wanted to do during my period. She actively scorned women who took to their beds, who were incapacitated by cramps, who "got the blues."

As I struggled to reconcile these very contradictory interpretations of   11 American Indians' traditional beliefs concerning menstruation, I realized that the menstrual taboos were about power, not about sin or filth. My conclusion was later borne out by some tribes' own explanation, which, as you may well imagine, came as quite a relief to me.

The truth of the matter as many Indians see it is that women who are   12 at the peak of their fecundity are believed to possess power that throws male power totally out of kilter. They emit such force that, in their presence, any male-owned or -dominated ritual or sacred object cannot do its usual task. For instance, the Lakota say that a menstruating woman anywhere near a yuwipi man, who is a special sort of psychic, spirit-empowered healer, for a day or so before he is to do his ceremony will effectively disempower him. Conversely, among many if not most tribes, important ceremonies cannot be held without the presence of women. Sometimes the ritual woman who empowers the ceremony must be unmarried and virginal so that the power she channels is unalloyed, unweakened by sexual arousal and penetration by a male. Other ceremonies require tumescent women, others the presence of mature women who have borne children, and still others depend for empowerment on postmenopausal women. Women may be segregated from the company of the whole band or village on certain occasions, but on certain occasions men are also segregated. In short, each ritual depends on a certain balance of power, and the positions of women within the phases of womanhood are used by tribal people to empower certain rites. This does not derive from a male-dominant view; it is not a ritual observance imposed on women by men. It derives from a tribal view of reality that distinguishes tribal people from feudal and industrial people.

Among the tribes, the occult power of women, inextricably bound to our   13
hormonal life, is thought to be very great; many hold that we possess innately the blood-given power to kill—with a glance, with a step, or with a judicious mixing of menstrual blood into somebody's soup. Medicine women among the Pomo of California cannot practice until they are sufficiently mature; when they are immature, their power is diffuse and is likely to interfere with their practice until time and experience have it under control. So women of the tribes are not especially inclined to see themselves as poor helpless victims of male domination. Even in those tribes where something akin to male domination was present, women are perceived as powerful, socially, physically, and metaphysically. In times past, as in times present, women carried enormous burdens with aplomb. We were far indeed from the "weaker sex," the designation that white aristocratic sisters unhappily earned for us all.

I remember my mother moving furniture all over the house when she   14
wanted it changed. She didn't wait for my father to come home and help— she just went ahead and moved the piano, a huge upright from the old days, the couch, the refrigerator. Nobody had told her she was too weak to do such things. In imitation of her, I would delight in loading trucks at my father's store with cases of pop or fifty-pound sacks of flour. Even when I was quite small I could do it, and it gave me a belief in my own physical strength that advancing middle age can't quite erase. My mother used to tell me about the Acoma Pueblo women she had seen as a child carrying huge ollas (water pots) on their heads as they wound their way up the tortuous stairwell carved into the face of the "Sky City" mesa, a feat I tried to imitate with books and tin buckets. ("Sky City" is the term used by the Chamber of Commerce for the mother village of Acoma, which is situated atop a high sandstone table mountain.) I was never very successful, but even the attempt reminded me that I was supposed to be strong and balanced to be a proper girl.

Of course, my mother's Laguna people are Keres Indian, reputed to be   15
the last extreme mother-right people on earth. So it is no wonder that I got notably nonwhite notions about the natural strength and prowess of women. Indeed, it is only when I am trying to get non-Indian approval, recognition, or acknowledgment that my "weak sister" emotional and intellectual ploys get the better of my tribal woman's good sense. At such times I forget that I just moved the piano or just wrote a competent paper or just completed a financial transaction satisfactorily or have supported myself and my children for most of my adult life.

Nor is my contradictory behavior atypical. Most Indian women I know 16
are in the same bicultural bind: we vacillate between being dependent and
strong, self-reliant and powerless, strongly motivated and hopelessly insecure.
We resolve the dilemma in various ways: some of us party all the time; some
of us drink to excess; some of us travel and move around a lot; some of us
land good jobs and then quit them; some of us engage in violent exchanges;
some of us blow our brains out. We act in these destructive ways because we
suffer from the societal conflicts caused by having to identify with two hopelessly opposed cultural definitions of women. Through this destructive disso-
nance we are unhappy prey to the self-disparagement common to, indeed de-
manded of, Indians living in the United States today. Our situation is caused
by the exigencies of a history of invasion, conquest, and colonization whose
searing marks are probably ineradicable. A popular bumper sticker on many
Indian cars proclaims: "If You're Indian You're In," to which I always find
myself adding under my breath, "Trouble."

III

No Indian can grow to any age without being informed that her people 17
were "savages" who interfered with the march of progress pursued by respectable, loving, civilized white people. We are the villains of the scenario
when we are mentioned at all. We are absent from much of white history except when we are calmly, rationally, succinctly, and systematically dehuman-
ized. On the few occasions we are noticed in any way other than as howling,
bloodthirsty beings, we are acclaimed for our noble quaintness. In this definition, we are exotic curios. Our ancient arts and customs are used to draw
tourist money to state coffers, into the pocketbooks and bank accounts of
scholars, and into support of the American-in-Disneyland promoters' dream.

As a Roman Catholic child I was treated to bloody tales of how the sav- 18
age Indians martyred the hapless priests and missionaries who went among
them in an attempt to lead them to the one true path. By the time I was
through high school I had the idea that Indians were people who had benefited mightily from the advanced knowledge and superior morality of the
Anglo-Europeans. At least I had, perforce, that idea to lay beside the other
one that derived from my daily experience of Indian life, an idea less de-
humanizing and more accurate because it came from my mother and the
other Indian people who raised me. That idea was that Indians are a people who don't tell lies, who care for their children and their old people. You
never see an Indian orphan, they said. You always know when you're old
that someone will take care of you—one of your children will. Then they'd
list the old folks who were being taken care of by this child or that. No
child is ever considered illegitimate among the Indians, they said. If a girl
gets pregnant, the baby is still part of the family, and the mother is too.
That's what they said and they showed me real people who lived according
to those principles.

Of course the ravages of colonization have taken their toll; there are or-   19
phans in Indian country now, and abandoned, brutalized old folks; there are
even illegitimate children, though the very concept still strikes me as absurd.
There are battered children and neglected children, and there are battered
wives and women who have been raped by Indian men. Proximity to the "civ-
ilizing" effects of white Christians has not improved the moral quality of life
in Indian country, though each group, Indian and white, explains the situation differently. Nor is there much yet in the oral tradition that can enable us
to adapt to these inhuman changes. But a force is growing in that direction,
and it is helping Indian women reclaim their lives. Their power, their sense of
direction and of self will soon be visible. It is the force of the women who
speak and work and write, and it is formidable.

Through all the centuries of war and death and cultural and psychic de-   20
struction have endured the women who raise the children and tend the fires,
who pass along the tales and the traditions, who weep and bury the dead,
who are the dead, and who never forget. There are always the women, who
make pots and weave baskets, who fashion clothes and cheer their children
on at powwow, who make fry bread and piki bread, and corn soup and chili
stew, who dance and sing and remember and hold within their hearts the
dream of their ancient peoples—that one day the woman who thinks will
speak to us again, and everywhere there will be peace. Meanwhile we tell the
stories and write the books and trade tales of anger and woe and stories of
fun and scandal and laugh over all manner of things that happen every day.
We watch and we wait.

My great-grandmother told my mother: Never forget you are Indian. And   21
my mother told me the same thing. This, then, is how I have gone about remembering, so that my children will remember too.

✳

RESPONDING TO THE WHOLE ESSAY

1. What is Allen's main purpose: to express how she feels, to let the reader know
    more about American Indian women's roles, or to move the reader to some ac-
    tion? How can you tell? [*Harbrace* 28a; *Hodges'* 32a]
2. How would you describe the tone of Allen's essay? Point to some specific details
    in the essay that contribute to the tone. [*Harbrace* 29a; *Hodges'* 33a]
3. As nearly as you can, describe the audience you think Allen is writing for. [*Har-
    brace* 28a; *Hodges'* 32a]
4. How does Allen's introduction capture the interest of the kind of reader you have
    described? What does the first sentence contribute? [*Harbrace* 28f; *Hodges'* 32f]
5. How does Allen achieve coherence in paragraph 6? Mark and label all the devices
    she uses. [*Harbrace* 27c; *Hodges'* 31c]

ANALYZING THE ELEMENTS

Grammar

1. Allen frequently uses a series of *who*-clauses to emphasize the points she is making. Find at least three instances of this technique and comment upon its effectiveness in each case. [*Harbrace* 1e; *Hodges'* 1e]
2. Each sentence in paragraph 17 contains a passive verb. Rewrite at least two of them as active verbs. What problems do you encounter? What advantage does the passive construction offer? [*Harbrace* 7; *Hodges'* 7]
3. Identify all of the clauses in the fifth sentence of paragraph 5. What kind of sentence is it? Comment upon the rhetorical effect Allen gains by constructing the sentence this way. [*Harbrace* 1f; *Hodges'* 1f]

Effective Sentences

1. Explain why some people would suggest rewriting the beginning of the sixth sentence of paragraph 14 as follows: "My mother used to tell me that as a child she saw Acoma Pueblo women carrying huge ollas (water pots) on their heads. . . ." Justify leaving the sentence as it stands. [*Harbrace* 5; *Hodges'* 25]
2. What is the rhetorical effect of repeating *woman* in the final sentence of paragraph 5? [*Harbrace* 11e; *Hodges'* 29e]
3. Comment upon the rhetorical effect gained by inverting the structure of the first sentence of paragraph 20. [*Harbrace* 11f; *Hodges'* 29f]

Punctuation and Mechanics

1. The period in the second from the last sentence in paragraph 14 appears inside the parentheses. Explain. [*Harbrace* 21f; *Hodges'* 17f]
2. Explain the use of commas and semicolons in the first sentence of paragraph 19. [*Harbrace* 17 and 18; *Hodges'* 12 and 14]
3. Explain the use of colons and semicolons in the third sentence of paragraph 16. [*Harbrace* 18 and 21d; *Hodges'* 14 and 17d]

Diction

1. Allen uses a rich and varied vocabulary in this essay. Look up the following words in your dictionary: *mythos* (paragraph 3), *demeanor* (paragraph 5), *amicable* (paragraph 6), *consigning* (paragraph 10), *fecundity* (paragraph 12), *aplomb* (paragraph 13), and *vacillate* and *exigencies* (paragraph 16). Explain how the connotations and denotations of these words are appropriate. [*Harbrace* 14a; *Hodges'* 20a and 23e(2)]
2. Explain why Allen uses *effect* rather than *affect* in the third sentence of paragraph 19. [*Harbrace* Usage Glossary; *Hodges'* Usage Glossary]

BUILDING VOCABULARY

1. What are the Greek roots from which *autonomous* is borrowed? What do they mean? Write a sentence using a word derived from one of these Greek roots.
2. List and define three synonyms for *autonomous*. Write a sentence using one of these synonyms.

SUGGESTIONS FOR WRITING

1. Write an essay using examples to explain how your culture defines women's/men's roles.
2. Using stories and examples, explain some of your own family traditions.

Chapter 2

Narration

Narration is storytelling; that is, the writer of a narrative unfolds for the reader a sequence of events, either true or fictional. Although narratives usually proceed in chronological order, they may also begin in the middle or at the end of the story and provide "flashbacks" to earlier events. And occasionally a narrative recounts events in the order of their importance rather than in the time sequence in which they occurred.

Narratives come in all sizes and flavors: they may be short—jokes are often narratives—or long, as are Victorian novels. They may be humorous, as is Rogers' "Dead Air" in this chapter, or serious, as is Turner's "The Harlem Renaissance."

Narratives often contain conflict and suspense. For instance, in this chapter all the writers—Angelou, Alburty, Rogers, Dillard, and Turner—present a conflict as the core of their tales. The conflict may be with oneself, as it is for Dillard and Rogers, or with society, as in the essay by Angelou; or it may be with an idea, as it is in the essays by Alburty and Turner.

Narratives have a point of view: they may be told in the first person ("I") or third person. First-person narratives are often deeply subjective (although they need not be), emphasizing the writer's reactions to events, as Angelou's, Rogers', and Dillard's do. Third-person narratives, on the other hand—although they may display the writer's feelings—are usually more objective. Examples are Turner's "The Harlem Renaissance" and Alburty's "E-mail."

Narratives (excluding fictional narratives, which are beyond the scope of this book) may have an expressive, informative, or persuasive purpose or a combination of these. (For a full discussion of purpose, see [*Harbrace* 28a; *Hodges'* 32a.]) When a narrative is primarily expressive, it focuses on the writer's feelings about events; when primarily informative, it focuses on the events themselves; when primarily persuasive, it uses the events to influence the reader's opinion or to move the reader to some course of action. Evidence of all three purposes can be found in the readings in this section.

As you write narratives, always keep your purpose and your audience clearly in mind. Doing so will enable you to decide which events are significant and how they can best be arranged to achieve the effect you want, as

p. 351 ~ def. Thesis

49

well as help you choose the kinds of specific details that will make the events real for your reader.

Five questions that are sure to be in your reader's mind can help you plan your narrative strategy. In addition to learning *what* happens (action), your reader will want to know *who* is involved in the events (actors), and *when* (time) and *where* (place) the events occur (often referred to as the setting). Especially, the reader will be interested in *why* (cause).

Notice how Roy Fowler, a nontraditional student, provides answers to these questions as he recounts a frustrating experience.

Road Blocks

Introduction
Context

Point

Setting—where and when

Minor conflict

Precipitating event

Background and details
Event

Event

Last week I arrived ten minutes late for a major anatomy exam. It wasn't my fault. I left my part-time job with plenty of time for driving to campus, parking, and getting to my seat in the classroom, but two trucks—a semi and a dump truck—collided on the interstate and stopped traffic for thirty minutes. It never fails. Why is it, whenever I really need to be somewhere, someone or something is always in my way, just like when I was on that Air Force training exercise in southern Germany.

It was a very cold morning back in January, 1990. The snow crunched beneath my feet, and the cold breeze stung my face as I quickly walked back from the breakfast tent to my sleeping tent where I removed my coat, gloves, scarf, and sweater and lay down on my cot trying to get warm. I only had an hour, and I wanted to soak up as much heat as possible before I had to go outside for the rest of the day. As I drifted between sleep and wakefulness, someone roughly shook me back to consciousness. Had time passed that quickly? Surely my hour wasn't up. The captain was shaking me awake to congratulate me on becoming the father of a little girl. I became fully alert as I realized he was also holding something back: There were complications; my newborn daughter was in the intensive care unit in San Antonio, Texas; she might not live.

The military has a system for everything, even getting people home for emergencies. I quickly packed my bags, changed into civilian clothing, and hurried towards the administration tent to sign out of the unit before leaving for Frankfurt International Airport. But I had to wait nearly an hour until someone was available to drive me to the division support unit (DSU) that handled all the Red Cross notifications for emergency leave. There, I completed leave forms and picked up plane tickets—paperwork required for me to leave Germany. But then, there I was, stuck sitting in another tent, waiting for another ride. Finally, after lunch, I got into an old army-green VW bus, top speed 80 kph—about 50 mph. Three hours dragged by as that old bus lumbered down the autobahn toward Frankfurt. I mentally cheered as we arrived at the U. S. Air Force side of the airport. I was ready to fly across the ocean to my gravely ill baby girl. I wasn't ready for the surprise that waited for me at the personnel office, though.

The last flight back to the states had left at two o'clock. I was so close, but I was not going home that day. The chaplain, there to give me support, said, "We'll get you out of here tomorrow morning." There was nothing to do but call the hospital in Texas to check on my family. My wife was fine, but my little girl was scheduled for surgery the next morning, surgery she had only a fifty-percent chance of surviving. I spent that evening sitting in the Air Force club, I soon realized that, though drinking myself to sleep might make the night seem to pass more quickly, it wouldn't bring me any closer to my wife and little girl in Texas. After all, there were no flights until the next day.

Early the next day one of the chaplain's drivers gave me a ride to the other side of the airport for my 10:00 flight. Ticket in hand, I checked in at the gate and boarded the plane. After everyone settled into their seats, I watched the flight attendant close the cabin door, felt the bump of the tug as it hooked to the plane, and rejoiced as it pushed us away from the gate. We taxied away from the terminal and traveled down the taxiway, feeling every crack in the asphalt, and lined up for takeoff. Waiting for the plane to take off, I drifted so deeply into thoughts of home and my baby daughter that I never felt the plane roar down the runway and leap into the air. I was startled when, ten minutes after the plane was in the air, the pilot announced, "We are having trouble with the landing gear. We can't make it retract, we do not have enough fuel to fly to the United States with the gear down, and we are too heavy to land back at Frankfurt. We are going to fly out over the ocean, and if we still

Marginal notes:

Event

Event

Note expressive aim

Events

Note effect of details

First set of complicating events

Expressive aim

Event details

Second set of
complicating
events

Details

Details here
parallel details in
paragraph 5

Resolution of
travel conflict

Resolution of
conflict about
family

cannot get the gear to retract, we will have to dump some fuel and return to Frankfurt." One moment my stomach turned with anticipation, and the next it churned with frustration. Four hours later I was back at the Frankfurt terminal and no closer to home.

But I wasn't licked yet, and Delta was not the only American carrier in Frankfurt. I ran to the TWA ticket counter and exchanged my ticket for the 7:00 p.m. flight to London with an early-morning flight from there to the USA. The clock in the airport lounge where I waited slowly ticked away four hours before I stood in front of the departure gate ready to board another plane. The gate attendant announced a delay. There was a problem with the fuel lines. I waited until 10:00 p.m. when it was announced that the repair could not be made and the flight was canceled. There were no flights to the States until the following day. The airline put us up at a small hotel an hour away from the airport.

Day three, six in the morning; I waited for a taxi to the airport to change my ticket yet again. And then I was back at the Delta departure gate waiting to board for the third time. I entered the plane, located my seat, sat down, watched the flight attendant close the door, felt the tug connect to the plane, felt our movement away from the terminal. I was back on the runway waiting for takeoff, just as I had been the day before, but this day, this time, this plane was going to take me home even if I had to fly it myself. Once in the air and dreading an announcement that might cancel my flight home, I settled into my seat with a sigh of relief when I felt the landing gear thump into place and I began to compute my arrival time in Dallas.

Seven hours later the plane landed at DFW airport. At least I was in the United States; I could manage any roadblocks here. Once in the terminal, I called my home unit at Fort Hood to make arrangements to get to San Antonio. As the plane they booked me on taxied toward the Killeen terminal, I saw the turning rotor blades of the waiting army helicopter. I left the plane, ran across the ramp, boarded the helicopter, and ninety minutes later, landed on the grass in front of the army hospital in San Antonio. My father and father-in-law greeted me and took me to see my wife. And then I went to ICU where my pretty baby girl fought for life. (Six years old now, with wheels, she gives perpetual motion a new definition.)

Conclusion—
summarizes major
conflict, puts it in
perspective and
ties it to initial
minor conflict

In this supersonic age it had taken me three days to fly from Germany to the USA. Roadblocks: bureaucracy, scheduling problems, technical difficulties all conspired to delay me in a time of serious family crisis. Traffic jams, dead batteries, traffic lights— they're still hidden behind every corner and occasionally slow me down, but they can never hold me back. I took my family home intact and I aced my anatomy exam.

Commentary.   Fowler's introduction establishes the context for the essay; he begins by recounting a recent event, being late for an exam. His analysis of the source of his frustration provides a rationale for the essay. Then he moves backward in time to a specific event in 1990.

From this point on, Fowler's essay is organized in straightforward chronological order, moving from the background events in Germany through the events which followed. Within this chronological frame he establishes why the events occurred at the same time that he makes the setting (the military and other bureaucracies) concrete by offering details about how he continually had to hurry up and wait. These details, as well as those he includes to tell us about how worried he was about his newborn daughter, contribute to his expressive aim.

Fowler's frustration about not getting to class on time is a conflict that frames the primary conflict between Fowler and the roadblocks that delay him on his journey home from Germany—bureaucracy, scheduling inadequacies, and technical failures. Although how he misses his exam is not fully developed, this incident lends force to the main conflict by emphasizing his feelings of urgency and irritation as he discovers each successive delay.

Fowler makes skillful use of parallelism when he reports the sequence of his actions as he boards each plane. In the first instance, the actions emphasize his worried anticipation; in the second they function almost as a scale upon which he measures his frustration.

Note, too, how Fowler's reference to roadblocks in his conclusion echoes his introduction. The essay ends snappily, tightly drawing together the two events in a single sentence: "I took my family home intact and I aced my anatomy exam."

E-mail: Families Gather 'Round a Digital Hearth

Stevan Alburty

Internet issues and online services are the subjects Stevan Alburty explores in his columns and feature articles. Alburty has published articles about online technology in such national publications as *Connect Time, The Net,* and *The New York Times,* but his writing career is focused around his position as columnist and feature writer for *Fast Company* magazine. Writing is only one facet of Alburty's involvement with technology. Before taking up writing, Alburty worked for seventeen years as the Director of Information Services for Chiat/Day Advertising, and he continues to act as a consultant to companies wanting to establish themselves in the electronic marketplace, offering them strategies for designing and marketing themselves online. In "E-mail: Families Gather 'Round the Digital Hearth," Alburty uses anecdotes to extol the virtues of electronic mail.

1   It's 8 p.m., and all 16 emus have finally settled down for the night.

2   Barbara Wands Pierce strolls in from the barn on her farm in Benton City, Wash., where she and her husband, Jeff, are raising a flock of the large, flightless birds. She pulls off her boots and sits down for a long Sunday night chat with her sisters. She will not talk to them on a telephone, even though her three siblings live a total of 8,500 miles away.

3   Three hours to the north, sister Kathy Meredith looks at her watch, sets aside the lesson plan for her fifth-grade music class and walks to her desk in the den to join Barbara in conversation.

4   Sister number three, Susan Wands, sits in her New York apartment, rehearsing her lead role in a one-act play that will open at a small Greenwich Village theater the following week. She lays her script down and seats herself at a small worktable in the kitchen to chat with Kathy and Barb.

5   In Los Angeles, Cynthia Wands, the fourth and final sister to join the conversation, is running late. She is typing final revisions into her computer on a script she'll present to a producer over lunch tomorrow. She makes one last change, closes the file and double-clicks on the icon for America Online.

6   Her modem crackles and whines as it links up her computer with the nationwide online service, and soon Cynthia has navigated her way into an electronic gathering spot, the location of which is a well-kept secret among the sisters. "Hey there . . ." she types, and almost instantaneously her screen comes alive with electronic greetings from the other three women.

"What's been keeping you?" Susan wants to know. Kathy interrupts with   7
her critique of McDonald's new Arch Deluxe, while Barb complains about
having to get up at 5:30 a.m. to do farm chores.

Although all four women are in their 30s, the chatter is as random and   8
rowdy as if they were children again, giggling under a blanket with a flashlight.

This evening, and every Sunday evening, they are all in the same elec-   9
tronic "room." Barbara, Kathy, Cynthia and Susan, all members of the America Online computer network, have created their own "chat room," a little
private corner of cyberspace that lets each of them type messages that are simultaneously displayed like a rolling transcript on all four of the women's
computer screens.

The "conversation" is mildly disjointed; the speed at which questions get   10
answered depends on the respondent's typing abilities.

Susan: Barb, what did you do for your birthday?

Kathy: We had 5 minutes of hail this morning that pummeled my iris beds

Cynthia: Did you still get up at 5:30 to do chores even tho' it was your
birthday?

Barb: Was a party pooper. Made everyone stay home and watch the Lilac
Parade on TV

Tonight, their "talk" is abundant with the minor news and humble triv-
ialities of which lives are woven—a pet's latest antic, a trip taken, a bargain
obtained—but usually the conversation revolves around a more somber subject, the one that inspired these electronic meetings in the first place: their
mother.

Margaret Wands, 63, is engaged in her third battle with cancer. And so   11
this evening the conversation turns to blood counts and moods.

These Sunday night "chats" have become a way for the four daughters   12
to stick together during their mother's debilitating illness. Kathy and Barbara
both live within driving distance of their mother's home in Spokane, Wash.
This proximity brings with it all the responsibilities and pressures of being on
a front line.

"It's really been tough on Barbara and Kathy, since they're so hands-on   13
with the situation," Susan says, "so this chat room gives them a real chance
to get some emotional support from Cynthia and me."

The Wands daughters are a dramatic demonstration of how many Amer-   14
ican families, after years of using their personal computers to organize everything from finances to recipes, are now using them to keep track of one other
important element of their lives: each other.

Linking millions of personal computers to an online network with global   15
reach enables new forms of communication, which help make the often geographically diverse American family seem just a little less extended.

None of the four Wands women considers herself exceptionally adept   16
at using a computer. Yet each has become comfortable enough with the

technology that their Sunday night conversations feel perfectly normal, virtually no different from gabbing on a party line.

Since each of them is dialing into the nationwide computer network 17
through a local number, there are no long-distance charges.

When it comes to the battle of the budget, e-mail trounces the telephone 18
and licks a first-class stamp. An electronic message can be composed in leisure
while disconnected and then sent in seconds through one of the commercial
online services such as America Online, CompuServe or Prodigy. The Electronic
Messaging Association estimates the cost per message of e-mail sent from the
home to be a little more than a penny a piece, or $0.013, to be exact.

That price was right for Merritt Walters. She found the value of e-mail 19
after she moved from Austin, Texas, to New York City. Tortured by homesickness, she called her mother almost daily. Her phone bills could have funded
a small New York apartment.

She and her mother still talk once a week on the telephone but use e-mail 20
to fill in the gaps with "the little things," says Walters, 27, who also fires off
requests for recipes to her mother on a regular basis.

E-mail can save time, too, something else American families enjoy con- 21
serving almost as much as money. Paper mail (or "snail mail" as it's mockingly referred to by the wired generation) can take up to five days to travel
coast to coast, while an e-mail can zip around the globe in a matter of milliseconds.

The ease and convenience of e-mail is apparently catching on. In a recent 22
U.S. survey by the communications company MCI, 60 percent of the 1,000
polled said e-mail allows them to keep in touch with more people.

Active personal lifestyles, combined with the hectic pace and geographic 23
range of modern business, have cut into the serendipitous communications the
phone was meant to enable. People have become so frustratingly mobile that
"phone tag" has practically become a contact sport.

"There's no such thing as 'e-mail tag'," says Jim Smith of Hartford, 24
Conn., who works in the finance department of an insurance company. Smith
uses e-mail as the only logical means of keeping in touch with relatives who
trot the globe for their jobs.

The Software Publishers Association estimates that of the 34 million 25
owners of home personal computers in America, 23 million have modems.
And they're apparently a chatty lot. According to the Electronic Messaging
Association, home e-mail users will send more than 80 billion—yes billion—
messages to each other in 1996.

Yet despite its rising popularity, there are still pockets of resistance. Don't 26
try to send e-mail, for example, to William Gibson, the author who coined
the word "cyberspace." "I do not use e-mail," he recently confessed in an essay in *The New York Times Magazine.* "I have avoided it because I am lazy
and because unanswered mail, 'e-' or otherwise, is a source of discomfort."

Those who shun e-mail often criticize it for its sanitizing effect on human 27
communications, preferring instead to use the telephone.

Electronic mail is often left to handle the simple housekeeping chores, like   28
current events and relaxed chatter, while the phone is saved for more intimate
contact. Some families have even adopted almost formal codes of electronic
conduct. Kaye Folsom, a retired English teacher from Chicago, uses e-mail to
keep in touch with several of her seven children. "But we have a strict rule:
No bad news through e-mail," she says.

Frank Bouley of Teaneck, N.J., insists that e-mail has virtually cured what   29
he himself labels his "dysfunctional" family. At 68, he is the eldest and has
made an effort to reach out electronically to his kin, a gumbo of stepsiblings
and demirelatives scattered throughout the United States and Canada.

"We used to only keep in contact at Christmastime with cards. I hardly   30
knew they were alive," Bouley says. "But with e-mail, we trade letters at least
once a week."

Living next door to your family in cyberspace is not without its dark side.   31
Years ago, if you didn't like your relatives, you moved to another state, safe
in the knowledge that they were too far away to visit and too cheap to call.
Now you never know when one of them is going to pop up unannounced on
your computer screen.

Charlene Kurhani confesses to having had "a minimal amount of com-   32
munication" in the past with her sister, who recently retired to Florida, bought
a computer and now shows up on Kurhani's electronic doorstep almost daily.
"Suddenly, I'm having to become 'e-mail chatty' with a sister with whom I
have very little in common," Kurhani says.

The planet shrinks, the family extends. Our lives are constantly being tem-   33
pered by the climate of a society in perpetual adaptation. Even the digerati,
the pundits who are paid to think great thoughts about technology, are sometimes left slack-jawed by the pervasiveness of the digital revolution.

Nicholas Negroponte is the founder of MIT's Media Lab and author of   34
the best-selling "Being Digital." He has two electronic mail addresses. One he
publishes in his articles and books. The other he divulges to a select group
and uses for his personal correspondence.

One day he received an e-mail in his private mailbox with a return ad-   35
dress he did not recognize. After worrying about how his security had been
broken, he realized that the unfamiliar address belonged to someone who had
just joined an online service and was sending him her first e-mail.

It was from his mother.   36

* * *

RESPONDING TO THE WHOLE ESSAY

1. Alburty's purpose in "E-mail: Families Gather 'Round a Digital Hearth" is predominantly informative, but the essay also includes expressive elements. Alburty
   opens the essay with a narrative account of the Wands sisters' experience with

e-mail and commentary upon this story. What effect do you think Alburty intends to achieve by this opening anecdote? Is it effective? Why or why not? Do you find other expressive elements in the informative section that makes up the second half of the essay? How do these elements contribute to the overall effectiveness of the essay? [*Harbrace* 28a; *Hodges'* 32a]

2. Does Alburty ever state his thesis directly? If so, where? What is the thesis? [*Harbrace* 28d; *Hodges'* 32d]

3. Alburty discusses several benefits to be gained by using e-mail. What are they? Does Alburty make any concessions to people who disagree with his positive view of e-mail? If so, what negative consequences of using e-mail does he mention?

4. Identify the topic, the restriction, and the illustration in paragraph 9. [*Harbrace* 27c(2); *Hodges'* 31c(2)]

5. Explain the function of paragraph 14. [*Harbrace* 27b(4); *Hodges'* 31b(4)]

ANALYZING THE ELEMENTS

Grammar

1. Alburty uses the progressive form of the present tense verb *engage* in the first sentence of paragraph 11. What does this usage suggest about Margaret Wands's battle with cancer? [*Harbrace* 7c(1); *Hodges'* 7c(1)]

2. What is the grammatical function of the verbal phrase *Living next door to your family in cyberspace* in paragraph 31? [*Harbrace* 1d(3); *Hodges'* 1d(3)]

3. Justify the use of the fragment *Was a party pooper* in paragraph 10. [*Harbrace* 2; *Hodges'* 2]

Effective Sentences

1. In the last sentence of paragraph 33, the appositive *the pundits who are paid to think great thoughts about technology* separates the main subject and main verb (*digerati are*). What is the purpose of this appositive? Would the sentence be more or less effective if the phrase were removed? [*Harbrace* 1d(3) and 14a(2); *Hodges'* 1d(3) and 23e(2)]

2. Explain why the first sentence of paragraph 33 is or is not effective. [*Harbrace* 11g; *Hodges'* 29g]

Punctuation and Mechanics

1. Comment upon the use of commas in the first sentence of paragraph 2. [*Harbrace* 17c and 17d(5); *Hodges'* 12c and 12d]

2. Explain the use of double quotation marks in the first sentence of paragraphs 9 and 10, the first sentence of paragraph 12, and the second sentence of paragraph 26. [*Harbrace* 20; *Hodges'* 16]

3. Alburty spells out *Texas* in paragraph 19 but abbreviates the names of states in the first sentence of paragraph 2, 24, and 29. Why do you think Alburty chooses to abbreviate these state names? [*Harbrace* 25; *Hodges'* 11]

4. Explain the use of italics in the third sentence of paragraph 26. [*Harbrace* 24a; *Hodges'* 10a]

Diction

1. In paragraph 10, *though* is deliberately misspelled as *tho'*. Explain why, in this case, this nonstandard spelling is acceptable. [*Harbrace* 13b(4); *Hodges'* 19e]
2. In the last sentence of paragraph 34, Alburty uses *divulges* instead of *makes known*. Why is *divulge* the more exact verb in this sentence? [*Harbrace* 14a; *Hodges'* 20a and 23e(2)]

BUILDING VOCABULARY

1. Alburty creates the word *demirelatives* by adding to *relatives* the Latin prefix *demi-*. Look up the meaning of *demi-* and explain what it suggests about these relatives. Create two more words using the prefix *demi-* and explain what each word means.
2. Alburty uses several words that begin with the prefix *re-*. Explain the origin and meaning of *re-*. Make a list of five words that begin with the prefix *re-*. Define each of these five words and then write sentences using at least two of them.

SUGGESTIONS FOR WRITING

1. Write a narrative essay informing a high school student about the benefits of studying writing.
2. Write a short narrative essay informing your readers about the benefits of using a telephone, a computer, or another form of technology.

Dead Air
Tim Rogers

Tim Rogers (1970–), a graduate of the University of Notre Dame, is the major general editor for *The Met,* the weekly journal of culture and entertainment for Dallas/Fort Worth. Along with his duties as editor, Rogers writes a weekly column for *The Met,* enlightening his readers about the humorous and absurd sides of life. He has also written for *The Dallas Morning News,* the *Klinefelter's Syndrome Newsletter,* and the inflight magazine for American Airlines entitled *American Way,* at which Rogers worked as the assistant editor.

1   It happened suddenly. One day she was with us, bringing joy and love to me and Roommate Joe. Then she was gone. I found her in the living room, sitting motionless next to the stereo. Our television was dead.

2   First there was denial. Roommate Joe suggested the remote might be broken. We tried to turn her on the old-fashioned way, but of course that didn't work. We tried plugging her into a different outlet: nothing. We tried the Fonzarelli maneuver, wherein you stand behind the television and deliver quick, upward thrusts to the screen (little known fact: Dr. Heimlich stole his maneuver from Fonz's jukebox version of this move).

3   It quickly got ugly, Roommate Joe banging his fists on her screen, tearing out his hair, begging her through tears not to leave us so soon.

4   Eventually, we brought her to a wise man who divined the cause of death, as far as we could tell, by reading the intestines of a chicken. According to him, our television had a faulty warp coil . . . or a bad dilithium crystal . . . or something like that. To fix it, he wanted $130.

5   After careful deliberation, Roommate Joe and I concluded $130 is a lot of money. And even though our VCR and Sega would now be useless, we decided to act like men, to do the courageous thing. We resolved to try life without television.

6   We thought we would become more productive without her. Unburdened by "American Gladiators" and "Rescue 911," we would have time to do those things we'd been putting off, like volunteering at the homeless shelter or writing long-overdue letters to distant loved ones.

7   But, for the most part, we wound up sitting on the couch with our hands in our pants, staring at the empty space next to the stereo, where our

television had once sat. Roommate Joe and I were like soldiers who lose arms in battle, but who swear they can still feel their fingers. We were having trouble coming to terms with our loss.

By week's end, we had succumbed to a paralyzing depression. We called 8 in sick to work. We didn't bathe. I'm ashamed to admit that one Thursday evening we ate a whole tube of Häagen-Dazs Triple Fudge Brownie Overload and drank a fifth of bourbon. We were emotionally wrecked. We were missing a lot of "must-see TV."

In a pathetic attempt to fill the void, Roommate Joe and I several times 9 went to friends' houses to watch their televisions. With their sets, though, we felt naughty. We always returned home from our interludes regretting our infidelity, promising ourselves to never let it happen again.

Going without "Star Trek: The Next Generation" hurt most of all. To 10 call us "fans" would be like calling gang violence "a nuisance." (Roommate Joe has an honorary degree from Star Fleet Academy and has decorated his bathroom to resemble a holodeck.) We became so starved for "Star Trek" that we resorted to playacting our favorite characters. Joe, invariably, was Captain Picard; I was Riker. He barked all manner of commands at me:

ME: "Captain, we desperately need to buy toilet paper."

ROOMMATE JOE: "Form an away team, Number One. Make it so." 11

After two weeks, we thought the healing process had at last begun. We stopped comparing everyday occurrences to "Star Trek" plots and avoided all mention of our dearly departed television. We resumed our daily routine, leading our empty lives. 12

Then, one day, Roommate Joe and I found ourselves at Best Buy, surrounded by shiny new televisions. We had come ostensibly to shop for extension cords, but I think we both knew the real reason we were there. We knew it was time to move on, to live as she would have wanted us to. 13

We flirted with one television in particular, a sassy number with stereo speakers, 181 channels and on-screen programming. She said, "What are your names? Because in my dreams, I just call you two 'Honey' and 'Muffin.'" It was an old line, but we fell for it. I'll never forget Roommate Joe's eloquent and heartfelt words when I asked if he thought we were ready to take home another television: "We're here. Might as well." 14

So now we have a new set in our lives. Oh, there are still a lot of unresolved issues we haven't dealt with yet. We feel guilty for replacing her after such a short period of mourning. Sometimes it feels like we're cheating on her. But then the *Enterprise* goes hurtling across our new screen at Warp 9, her engines roaring through our living room in Dolby stereo, boldly going where no one has gone before; and it seems that it might be true, time does heal all wounds.

Of course, the bourbon helps. 15

✳

RESPONDING TO THE WHOLE ESSAY

1. Is the real subject of "Dead Air" the death of the television? Rogers and Roommate Joe? Something else? Explain.
2. Rogers develops this essay through the use of an extended metaphor, implying a comparison between a television and a woman. Explain whether this metaphor is a paradox or personification. Point to evidence in the essay to support your answer. [*Harbrace* 14a(5); *Hodges'* 20a(4)]
3. How would you define the audience of this essay? What assumptions does Rogers make about the experiences or knowledge of his audience? Point to evidence from the essay to support your answer. [*Harbrace* 28a; *Hodges'* 32a]
4. Comment upon how Rogers achieves coherence in paragraph 11. [*Harbrace* 27b(3); *Hodges'* 31b(3)]
5. What strategy of development does Rogers choose for paragraph 2? Explain. [*Harbrace* 27c(2); *Hodges'* 31c(2)]
6. Consider the use of the pronouns *it* and *she* in the first paragraph of the essay. What rhetorical effect does Rogers achieve by delaying the pronoun references? [*Harbrace* 6b, 11e, and 27b(3); *Hodges'* 28, 29e, and 31b(3)]

ANALYZING THE ELEMENTS

Grammar

1. Explain why Rogers uses *is*, the present tense of *be*, rather than the past tense in the first sentence of paragraph 5. [*Harbrace* 7c; *Hodges'* 7c]
2. To what does *it* in the last sentence of paragraph 4 refer? Rewrite the sentence replacing *it* with the pronoun reference and compare this sentence to the original. What reason can you give for why Rogers wrote the sentence in this way? [*Harbrace* 6b; *Hodges'* 28]
3. What is the grammatical function of the last two phrases at the end of the third sentence of paragraph 9? [*Harbrace* 4; *Hodges'* 4]

Effective Sentences

1. How does Rogers create variety in the first paragraph? [*Harbrace* 12a and 12b; *Hodges'* 30a and 30b]
2. A series of grammatically parallel items usually implies that the items are of equal importance. Is this true of the series in the sentence in paragraph 3? What effect does Rogers achieve by writing the sentence this way? [*Harbrace* 10; *Hodges'* 26]
3. Justify Rogers' omission of the conjunction *that* in the first sentence of paragraph 6. [*Harbrace* 16a(2); *Hodges'* 22a(2)]

Punctuation and Mechanics

1. Explain the use of ellipsis points in the second sentence of paragraph 4. Try to explain the effect that Rogers achieves by punctuating the sentence in this way. [*Harbrace* 21i; *Hodges'* 17i]

2. Explain the use of single and double quotation marks in the second sentence of paragraph 13. [*Harbrace* 20a(4); *Hodges'* 16a(4)]
3. In the second sentence of the paragraph 14, *Oh* is followed by a comma. Explain this use of the comma. [*Harbrace* 17b; *Hodges'* 12b]

Diction

1. *Webster's Collegiate Dictionary* offers several meanings for the preposition *like*. What does the preposition *like* mean in the second sentences of paragraphs 5, 6, 7, and 10? Do any of these uses of *like* constitute similes? Explain. [*Harbrace* 14a(5); *Hodges'* 20a(4)]
2. In the second sentence of paragraph 11, Rogers uses the euphemism *dearly departed*. What does this euphemism mean? Can you think of alternative words or phrases that Rogers could have used? How would they affect the overall meaning of the sentence? [*Harbrace* 14c; *Hodges'* 20c]

BUILDING VOCABULARY

1. The word *interlude* has been borrowed from the Latin roots *inter* and *ludus*. Define *interlude* and the Latin roots from which the English word is borrowed.
2. Make a list of four words that derive from the Latin root *inter* and write sentences using each of the words you have listed.

SUGGESTIONS FOR WRITING

1. Write a narrative essay that reveals the comic or absurd side of your reaction to the loss of some inanimate object, such as the remote control, a computer, a doll or stuffed animal, or a car. (The essay need not be factual; you may exaggerate or even invent certain details to achieve the effect you want.)
2. Write a short narrative essay about a time when you were forced to replace or repair your television, stereo, computer, or car.

Momma, the Dentist, and Me
Maya Angelou

Born Marguerite Johnson in St. Louis in 1928, Maya Angelou was raised
with her brother, Bailey, in Stamps, Arkansas, by her grandmother, who, with
Uncle Willie, operated a country store. After leaving Stamps, she lived in Los
Angeles, where she had a dancing career, and in New York, where she became an active worker in the civil rights movement. She has produced a series on Africa for PBS-TV and written three books of poetry as well as four
volumes of her autobiography. This selection is from the first of those autobiographical volumes, *I Know Why the Caged Bird Sings*.

The angel of the candy counter had found me out at last, and was ex- 1
acting excruciating penance for all the stolen Milky Ways, Mounds, Mr. Good-
bars and Hersheys with Almonds. I had two cavities that were rotten to the
gums. The pain was beyond the bailiwick of crushed aspirins or oil of cloves.
Only one thing could help me, so I prayed earnestly that I'd be allowed to sit
under the house and have the building collapse on my left jaw. Since there
was no Negro dentist in Stamps, nor doctor either, for that matter, Momma
had dealt with previous toothaches by pulling them out (a string tied to the
tooth with the other end looped over her fist), pain killers and prayer. In this
particular instance the medicine had proved ineffective; there wasn't enough
enamel left to hook a string on, and the prayers were being ignored because
the Balancing Angel was blocking their passage.

I lived a few days and nights in blinding pain, not so much toying with 2
as seriously considering the idea of jumping in the well, and Momma decided
I had to be taken to a dentist. The nearest Negro dentist was in Texarkana,
twenty-five miles away, and I was certain that I'd be dead long before we
reached half the distance. Momma said we'd go to Dr. Lincoln, right in Stamps,
and he'd take care of me. She said he owed her a favor.

I knew there were a number of whitefolks in town that owed her favors. 3
Bailey and I had seen the books which showed how she had lent money to
Blacks and whites alike during the Depression, and most still owed her. But
I couldn't aptly remember seeing Dr. Lincoln's name, nor had I ever heard of
a Negro's going to him as a patient. However, Momma said we were going,
and put water on the stove for our baths. I had never been to a doctor, so she
told me that after the bath (which would make my mouth feel better) I had
to put on freshly starched and ironed underclothes from inside out. The ache

failed to respond to the bath, and I knew then that the pain was more serious than that which anyone had ever suffered.

Before we left the Store, she ordered me to brush my teeth and then wash my mouth with Listerine. The idea of even opening my clamped jaws increased the pain, but upon her explanation that when you go to a doctor you have to clean yourself all over, but most especially the part that's to be examined, I screwed up my courage and unlocked my teeth. The cool air in my mouth and the jarring of my molars dislodged what little remained of my reason. I had frozen to the pain, my family nearly had to tie me down to take the toothbrush away. It was no small effort to get me started on the road to the dentist. Momma spoke to all the passers-by, but didn't stop to chat. She explained over her shoulder that we were going to the doctor and she'd "pass the time of day" on our way home. 4

Until we reached the pond the pain was my world, an aura that haloed me for the three feet around. Crossing the bridge into whitefolks' country, pieces of sanity pushed themselves forward. I had to stop moaning and start walking straight. The white towel, which was drawn under my chin and tied over my head, had to be arranged. If one was dying, it had to be done in style if the dying took place in whitefolks' part of town. 5

On the other side of the bridge the ache seemed to lessen as if a white-breeze blew off the whitefolks and cushioned everything in their neighborhood—including my jaw. The gravel road was smoother, the stones smaller and the tree branches hung down around the path and nearly covered us. If the pain didn't diminish then, the familiar yet strange sights hypnotized me into believing that it had. 6

But my head continued to throb with the measured insistence of a bass drum, and how could a toothache pass the calaboose, hear the songs of the prisoners, their blues and laughter, and not be changed? How could one or two or even a mouthful of angry tooth roots meet a wagonload of powhite-trash children, endure their idiotic snobbery and not feel less important? 7

Behind the building which housed the dentist's office ran a small path used by servants and those tradespeople who catered to the butcher and Stamps' one restaurant. Momma and I followed that lane to the backstairs of Dentist Lincoln's office. The sun was bright and gave the day a hard reality as we climbed up the steps to the second floor. 8

Momma knocked on the back door and a young white girl opened it to show surprise at seeing us there. Momma said she wanted to see Dentist Lincoln and to tell him Annie was there. The girl closed the door firmly. Now the humiliation of hearing Momma describe herself as if she had no last name to the young white girl was equal to the physical pain. It seemed terribly unfair to have a toothache and a headache and have to bear at the same time the heavy burden of Blackness. 9

It was always possible that the teeth would quiet down and maybe drop out of their own accord. Momma said we would wait. We leaned in the harsh sunlight on the shaky railings of the dentist's back porch for over an hour. 10

He opened the door and looked at Momma. "Well, Annie, what can I do for you?"   11

He didn't see the towel around my jaw or notice my swollen face.   12

Momma said, "Dentist Lincoln. It's my grandbaby here. She got two rotten teeth that's giving her a fit."   13

She waited for him to acknowledge the truth of her statement. He made no comment, orally or facially.   14

"She had this toothache purt' near four days now, and today I said, 'Young lady, you going to the Dentist.'"   15

"Annie?"   16

"Yes, sir, Dentist Lincoln."   17

He was choosing words the way people hunt for shells. "Annie, you know I don't treat nigra, colored people."   18

"I know, Dentist Lincoln. But this here is just my little grandbaby, and she ain't gone be no trouble to you . . . ."   19

"Annie, everybody has a policy. In this world you have to have a policy. Now, my policy is I don't treat colored people."   20

The sun had baked the oil out of Momma's skin and melted the Vaseline in her hair. She shone greasily as she leaned out of the dentist's shadow.   21

"Seem like to me, Dentist Lincoln, you might look after her, she ain't nothing but a little mite. And seems like maybe you owe me a favor or two."   22

He reddened slightly. "Favor or no favor. The money has all been repaid to you and that's the end of it. Sorry, Annie." He had his hand on the doorknob. "Sorry." His voice was a bit kinder on the second "Sorry," as if he really was.   23

Momma said, "I wouldn't press on you like this for myself but I can't take No. Not for my grandbaby. When you come to borrow my money you didn't have to beg. You asked me, and I lent it. Now, it wasn't my policy. I ain't no moneylender, but you stood to lose this building and I tried to help you out."   24

"It's been paid, and raising your voice won't make me change my mind. My policy . . ." He let go of the door and stepped nearer Momma. The three of us were crowded on the small landing. "Annie, my policy is I'd rather stick my hand in a dog's mouth than in a nigger's."   25

He had never once looked at me. He turned his back and went through the door into the cool beyond. Momma backed up inside herself for a few minutes. I forgot everything except her face which was almost a new one to me. She leaned over and took the doorknob, and in her everyday soft voice she said, "Sister, go on downstairs. Wait for me. I'll be there directly."   26

Under the most common of circumstances I knew it did no good to argue with Momma. So I walked down the steep stairs, afraid to look back and afraid not to do so. I turned as the door slammed, and she was gone.   27

Momma walked in that room as if she owned it. She shoved that silly nurse aside with one hand and strode into the dentist's office. He was sitting in his chair, sharpening his mean instruments and putting extra sting into his medicines. Her eyes were blazing like live coals and her arms had doubled   28 *themselves in length. He looked up at her just before she caught him by the collar of his white jacket.*

"Stand up when you see a lady, you contemptuous scoundrel." *Her tongue* 29
had thinned and the words rolled off well enunciated. Enunciated and sharp like little claps of thunder.

The dentist had no choice but to stand at R.O.T.C. attention. His head 30
dropped after a minute and his voice was humble. "Yes, ma'am, Mrs. Henderson."

"You knave, do you think you acted like a gentleman, speaking to me like 31
that in front of my granddaughter?" *She didn't shake him, although she had the power. She simply held him upright.*

"No, ma'am, Mrs. Henderson." 32

"No, ma'am, Mrs. Henderson, what?" *Then she did give him the tiniest* 33
of shakes, but because of her strength the action set his head and arms to shaking loose on the ends of his body. He stuttered much worse than Uncle Willie. "No, ma'am, Mrs. Henderson, I'm sorry."

With just an edge of her disgust showing, Momma slung him back in his 34
dentist's chair. "Sorry is as sorry does, and you're about the sorriest dentist I ever laid my eyes on." *(She could afford to slip into the vernacular because she had such eloquent command of English.)*

"I didn't ask you to apologize in front of Marguerite, because I don't want 35
her to know my power, but I order you, now and herewith. Leave Stamps by sundown."

"Mrs. Henderson, I can't get my equipment . . ." *He was shaking terri-* 36
bly now.

"Now, that brings me to my second order. You will never again practice 37
dentistry. Never! When you get settled in your next place, you will be a vegetarian caring for dogs with the mange, cats with the cholera and cows with the epizootic. Is that clear?"

The saliva ran down his chin and his eyes filled with tears. "Yes, ma'am. 38
Thank you for not killing me. Thank you, Mrs. Henderson."

Momma pulled herself back from being ten feet tall with eight-foot arms 39
and said, "You're welcome for nothing, you varlet, I wouldn't waste a killing on the likes of you."

On her way out she waved her handkerchief at the nurse and turned her 40
into a crocus sack of chicken feed.

Momma looked tired when she came down the stairs, but who wouldn't 41
be tired if they had gone through what she had. She came close to me and adjusted the towel under my jaw (I had forgotten the toothache; I only knew that she made her hands gentle in order not to awaken the pain). She took my hand. Her voice never changed. "Come on, Sister."

I reckoned we were going home where she would concoct a brew to elim- 42
inate the pain and maybe give me new teeth too. New teeth that would grow overnight out of my gums. She led me toward the drugstore, which was in

the opposite direction from the Store. "I'm taking you to Dentist Baker in Texarkana."

I was glad after all that I had bathed and put on Mum and Cashmere Bouquet talcum powder. It was a wonderful surprise. My toothache had quieted to solemn pain, Momma had obliterated the evil white man, and we were going on a trip to Texarkana, just the two of us.   43

On the Greyhound she took an inside seat in the back, and I sat beside her. I was so proud of being her granddaughter and sure that some of her magic must have come down to me. She asked if I was scared. I only shook my head and leaned over on her cool brown upper arm. There was no chance that a dentist, especially a Negro dentist, would dare hurt me then. Not with Momma there. The trip was uneventful, except that she put her arm around me, which was very unusual for Momma to do.   44

The dentist showed me the medicine and the needle before he deadened my gums, but if he hadn't I wouldn't have worried. Momma stood right behind him. Her arms were folded and she checked on everything he did. The teeth were extracted and she bought me an ice cream cone from the side window of a drug counter. The trip back to Stamps was quiet, except that I had to spit into a very small empty snuff can which she had gotten for me and it was difficult with the bus humping and jerking on our country roads.   45

At home, I was given a warm salt solution, and when I washed out my mouth I showed Bailey the empty holes, where the clotted blood sat like filling in a pie crust. He said I was quite brave, and that was my cue to reveal our confrontation with the peckerwood dentist and Momma's incredible powers.   46

I had to admit that I didn't hear the conversation, but what else could she have said than what I said she said? What else done? He agreed with my analysis in a lukewarm way, and I happily (after all, I'd been sick) flounced into the Store. Momma was preparing our evening meal and Uncle Willie leaned on the door sill. She gave her version.   47

"Dentist Lincoln got right uppity. Said he'd rather put his hand in a dog's mouth. And when I reminded him of the favor, he brushed it off like a piece of lint. Well, I sent Sister downstairs and went inside. I hadn't never been in his office before, but I found the door to where he takes out teeth, and him and the nurse was in there thick as thieves. I just stood there till he caught sight of me." Crash bang the pots on the stove. "He jumped just like he was sitting on a pin. He said, 'Annie, I done tole you, I ain't gonna mess around in no niggah's mouth.' I said, 'Somebody's got to do it then,' and he said, 'Take her to Texarkana to the colored dentist' and that's when I said, 'If you paid me my money I could afford to take her.' He said, 'It's all been paid.' I tole him everything but the interest been paid. He said ''Twasn't no interest.' I said, ''Tis now, I'll take ten dollars as payment in full.' You know, Willie, it wasn't no right thing to do, 'cause I lent that money without thinking about it.   48

"He tole that little snippity nurse of his'n to give me ten dollars and make me sign a 'paid in full' receipt. She gave it to me and I signed the papers. Even   49 though by rights he was paid up before, I figger, he gonna be that kind of nasty, he gonna have to pay for it."

Momma and her son laughed and laughed over the white man's evilness and her retributive sin.   50

I preferred, much preferred, my version.   51

✸

RESPONDING TO THE WHOLE ESSAY

1. How would you describe Angelou's purpose in "Momma, the Dentist, and Me"? Is it mainly to share an experience, to move her reader to indignation, or both? Point to evidence in the essay. [*Harbrace* 28a; *Hodges'* 32a]
2. Comment on the difference in tone between the account of Momma's confrontation with the dentist given in italics and that given at the end of the essay. [*Harbrace* 29a; *Hodges'* 33a]
3. Although Angelou narrates the events involved in a trip to two dentists, the account deals with more than just the pain of a toothache. Explain.
4. What is Angelou's main point? How do you know? [*Harbrace* 28d; *Hodges'* 32d]
5. In what kind of order does Angelou relate the event? Why is this organization appropriate? [*Harbrace* 27c; *Hodges'* 31c]
6. Identify and account for any changes in the point of view Angelou uses in this essay.

ANALYZING THE ELEMENTS

Grammar

1. Why is *Negro's* in sentence 3 of paragraph 3 in the possessive case? [*Harbrace* 5d]
2. The last sentence of paragraph 29 is elliptical; that is, an important grammatical element is implied rather than stated. Supply the omitted part and comment on the difference in the effect. [*Harbrace* 2; *Hodges'* 2]
3. The first sentence of "Momma, the Dentist, and Me" contains the verb *had found,* the fifth sentence contains the verb *had dealt,* and the second sentence of paragraph 3 contains the verb *had lent.* To what time sequence do these verbs refer? What would be the effect of rewriting each sentence using *found, dealt,* and *lent* instead? [*Harbrace* 7c; *Hodges'* 7c]

Effective Sentences

1. This essay contains what appear to be two serious grammatical errors. One of these occurs in the fifth sentence of paragraph 1, and the other can be found in the second sentence of paragraph 5. Identify these errors and explain why you think they were not corrected. [*Harbrace* 5 and 6b; *Hodges'* 25 and 28]
2. Observe the parallelism Angelou uses in the third sentence of paragraph 28 and the fourth sentence of paragraph 37 (beginning "When you get settled"). Try to rewrite the second sentence of paragraph 6 so that all three elements described

are parallel. What difficulties do you encounter? How would you resolve them? [*Harbrace* 10; *Hodges'* 26]
3. Comment upon how Angelou achieves sentence variety in paragraph 45. [*Harbrace* 12; Hodges' 30]

Punctuation and Mechanics

1. Account for why, in the second sentence of paragraph 3, *Blacks* is capitalized, whereas *whites* is not. Why is *Store* capitalized in sentence 1 of paragraph 4? [*Harbrace* 23; *Hodges'* 9]
2. Justify the lack of a comma following the introductory adverb clause in the first sentence of paragraph 5 and before the last element of a series in the final sentence of paragraph 7. [*Harbrace* 17; *Hodges'* 12]
3. Explain the use of single and double quotation marks in paragraph 15. [*Harbrace* 20; *Hodges'* 16]

Diction

1. Angelou uses two kinds of vocabulary in "Momma, the Dentist, and Me." Dictionaries attach labels to words that are not in Edited American English. Use your dictionary to check for labels on the following words: *bailiwick* (paragraph 1), *calaboose* and *powhitetrash* (paragraph 7), *nigger* (paragraph 25), *knave* (paragraph 31), *sorriest* (paragraph 34), *epizootic* (paragraph 37), *varlet* (paragraph 39), *crocus* (paragraph 40), *peckerwood* (paragraph 46), *snippety* (paragraph 49), *retributive* (paragraph 50). If a word is not listed, what do you think that indicates? [*Harbrace* 14c; *Hodges'* 20c]
2. Paragraphs 13 through 24 contain a number of expressions that would be grammatically incorrect in most written English. Why are they acceptable here? Are there any other instances in which these expressions might be acceptable in writing? Explain. [*Harbrace* 13; *Hodges'* 19]
3. "Momma, the Dentist, and Me" contains several similes. Find three and explain why each is appropriate. [*Harbrace* 14a; *Hodges'* 20a]

BUILDING VOCABULARY

1. Define *humiliate*. List and define two synonyms and two antonyms for *humiliate*. Write sentences using each of these words.
2. The verb *concoct* has two related meanings. What are they? List and define one synonym for each of the meanings of *concoct*.

SUGGESTIONS FOR WRITING

1. Write an essay about an event where someone was unthinkingly and unnecessarily cruel.
2. Write an essay in which you give two versions of a single event, each from a different point of view. You might do as Angelou did and write about the event as you wanted it to be and also as it actually was, or you might write about how you could look at a single event in two different ways depending upon external influences.

God in the Doorway
Annie Dillard

Annie Dillard, a writer and a naturalist, was born in 1945 in Pittsburgh, Pennsylvania. She has published several volumes of essays, among them *Pilgrim at Tinker Creek,* for which she received the Pulitzer Prize for non-fiction (1974), *Holy the Firm* (1978), and *Teaching a Stone to Talk* (1982). Leaving Virginia, where she had written *Pilgrim at Tinker Creek,* she taught writing at Western Washington University. She now makes her home in Connecticut and is a frequent contributor to *Atlantic, Harper's, Science,* and other magazines.

One cold Christmas Eve I was up unnaturally late because we had all 1 gone out to dinner—my parents, my baby sister, and I. We had come home to a warm living room, and Christmas Eve. Our stockings dropped from the mantel; beside them, a special table bore a bottle of ginger ale and a plate of cookies.

I had taken off my fancy winter coat and was standing on the heat reg- 2 ister to bake my shoe soles and warm my bare legs. There was a commotion at the front door; it opened, and cold wind blew around my dress.

Everyone was calling me. "Look who's here! Look who's here!" I looked. 3 It was Santa Claus. Whom I never—ever—wanted to meet. Santa Claus was looming in the doorway and looking around for me. My mother's voice was thrilled: "Look who's here!" I ran upstairs.

Like everyone in his right mind, I feared Santa Claus, thinking he was 4 God. I was still thoughtless and brute, reactive. I knew right from wrong, but had barely tested the possibility of shaping my own behavior, and then only from fear, and not yet from love. Santa Claus was an old man whom you never saw, but who nevertheless saw you; he knew when you'd been bad or good. He knew when you'd been bad or good! And I had been bad.

My mother called and called, enthusiastic, pleading; I wouldn't come 5 down. My father encouraged me; my sister howled. I wouldn't come down, but I could bend over the stairwell and see: Santa Claus stood in the doorway with night over his shoulder, letting in all the cold air of the sky; Santa Claus stood in the doorway monstrous and bright, powerless, ringing a loud bell and repeating Merry Christmas, Merry Christmas. I never came down. I don't know who ate the cookies.

For so many years now I have known that this Santa Claus was actu- 6 ally a rigged-up Miss White, who lived across the street, that I confuse the

71

dramatis personae in my mind, making of Santa Claus, God, and Miss White an awesome, vulnerable trinity. This is really a story about Miss White.

Miss White was old; she lived alone in the big house across the street. She   7
liked having me around; she plied me with cookies, taught me things about the world, and tried to interest me in finger painting, in which she herself took great pleasure. She would set up easels in her kitchen, tack enormous slick soaking papers to their frames, and paint undulating undersea scenes: horizontal smears of color sparked by occasional vertical streaks which were understood to be fixed kelp. I liked her. She meant no harm on earth, and yet half a year after her failed visit as Santa Claus, I ran from her again.

That day, a day of the following summer, Miss White and I knelt in her   8
yard while she showed me a magnifying glass. It was a large, strong hand lens. She lifted my hand and, holding it very still, focused a dab of sunshine on my palm. The glowing crescent wobbled, spread, and finally contracted to a point. It burned; I was burned; I ripped my hand away and ran home crying. Miss White called after me, sorry, explaining, but I didn't look back.

Even now I wonder: if I meet God, will he take and hold my bare hand   9
in his, and focus his eye on my palm, and kindle that spot and let me burn?

But no. It is I who misunderstood everything and let everybody down. Miss   10
White, God, I am sorry I ran from you. I am still running, running from that knowledge, that eye, that love from which there is no refuge. For you meant only love, and love, and I felt only fear, and pain. So once in Israel love came to us incarnate, stood in the doorway between two worlds, and we were all afraid.

✳

RESPONDING TO THE WHOLE ESSAY

1. The first paragraph establishes the time and place of the action as well as introducing some of the actors—information commonly offered in introductions to narratives. How does Dillard make this information interesting and immediate for the reader? [*Harbrace* 29b, c, and d; *Hodges'* 33a, b, c, and d]
2. What time is being spoken of in each of paragraphs 5, 6, and 7? How does Dillard signal the time changes? [*Harbrace* 27b; *Hodges'* 31b]
3. How does Dillard integrate the magnifying glass incident with the Santa Claus incident? What details tie them together? What do the two events have in common? What does she see as the meaning of the two events?
4. Is Dillard's conclusion effective? Why or why not? What is the effect of the final sentence of the essay? [*Harbrace* 29b, c, and d; *Hodges'* 33b, c, and d]
5. Identify as clearly as you can Dillard's primary purpose in "God in the Doorway." Then examine the essay to see whether other purposes might also be involved and how they might interact in the essay. [*Harbrace* 28a; *Hodges'* 32a]
6. In paragraph 6, Dillard says, "This is really a story about Miss White." Is it really a story about Miss White? Explain your answer.

ANALYZING THE ELEMENTS

Grammar

1. In the second sentence of paragraph 2, Dillard coordinates main clauses in two ways. Explain what relationships among the three clauses are established by this handling of coordination. [*Harbrace* 1e; *Hodges'* 1e]
2. In the third sentence of paragraph 4, the coordinating conjunctions *but* and *and* help to establish certain relationships among a group of related ideas. Identify the ideas Dillard is presenting here, and explain the relationships among them. How are these relationships reflected in the rest of the essay? [*Harbrace* 1c; *Hodges'* 1c]
3. In the last sentence of paragraph 8, what do *sorry* and *explaining* modify? Explain why they are separated from the word they modify. [*Harbrace* 4 and 11f; *Hodges'* 4 and 29f]

Effective Sentences

1. What is the effect of the repetition in the fourth and fifth sentences of paragraph 4? [*Harbrace* 11e; *Hodges'* 29e]
2. Comment on Dillard's use of sentence variety in paragraph 5. [*Harbrace* 12a; *Hodges'* 30a]
3. In the fifth sentence of paragraph 8, does "It burned; I was burned" achieve more than the mere repetition of an idea? If so, what?

Punctuation and Mechanics

1. What is the purpose of the dashes in the fifth sentence of paragraph 3? [*Harbrace* 21e; *Hodges'* 17e]
2. Dillard makes frequent use of the semicolon throughout her essay. Explain her use of the semicolon in the first three sentences of paragraph 5, the second sentence of paragraph 7, and the next-to-last sentence of paragraph 8. [*Harbrace* 18; *Hodges'* 14]
3. Explain the commas in the third sentence of paragraph 10. [*Harbrace* 17; *Hodges'* 12]

Diction

1. In the third sentence of paragraph 5, Dillard combines the seemingly contradictory adjectives *monstrous, bright,* and *powerless* to describe Santa Claus. In paragraph 6 she combines *awesome* and *vulnerable.* Explain how this juxtaposition of seemingly contradictory qualities expands her meaning. [*Harbrace* 14a(2); *Hodges'* 23e(2)]
2. In the final sentence of the essay, Dillard uses the word *incarnate.* Look the word up in a good dictionary, and then explain what connotations it brings to the sentence.[*Harbrace* 14a(2); *Hodges'* 23e(2)]
3. Also in the last sentence of the essay, Dillard tells us that love "stood in the doorway between two worlds." What kind(s) of figurative language does this phrase contain? What does she mean by "doorway between two worlds"? [*Harbrace* 14a(5); *Hodges'* 20a(4)]

BUILDING VOCABULARY

1. *The American Heritage Dictionary* offers two distinct meanings for *kindle*. Dillard uses *kindle* as a transitive verb meaning "ignite or arouse." Explain the origin of this verb. How is it related to the intransitive verb *kindle,* meaning "to give birth to young?"
2. List and define two synonyms for the verb *try*. Write a sentence using each of these synonyms.

SUGGESTIONS FOR WRITING

1. Narrate an experience which you did not fully understand at the time it occurred but which you came to understand later.
2. Narrate an experience in which an irrational fear influenced your behavior.

Writing "God in the Doorway"

Ten years ago, a magazine editor asked me to describe Christmas memo- 1
ries. At first I refused, thinking I couldn't come up with anything more original than the usual "we-all-sat-around-the-big-table-at-Grandma's," with its
usual overwritten descriptions of platters of food. Writing is tough. I don't
like to take pains to come up with the usual. I told the editor I was sorry.

But I no sooner got off the phone than I recalled this scene, this old, sore 2
business of Miss White's playing Santa Claus. I'd run from Miss White because, when I was small, I was afraid of the wrathful, omnipotent God: who
wants to meet the God who'll make you fry in hell for your sins? (My parents didn't give me these notions; I must have picked them up from the world
at large.) Now, when I was thirty, I saw I was still afraid of the forgiving God:
who wants to be on the receiving end of undeserved love? I was still running
from the vulnerable God whose love I'd refused, the God people hurt as I'd
hurt Miss White. Miss White forgave me, I believe, just as Santa Claus forgives bad children by bringing them presents anyway, and just as God, I'd
heard, forgives people. The trouble was, I hadn't forgiven myself. I was still
brooding over it all when I was thirty.

I began roughing out a draft of the incidents. First I'd tell the Santa Claus 3
story, then the magnifying glass story; at the end I'd swiftly make the point,
that we are still running from God's love, God's "eye." As I write this now,
at forty, it's still hard to see which is worse: God's eye which sees your sins
(all the times you've hurt people), or God's eye which seeks you out with its
forgiveness, when you haven't forgiven yourself.

The first draft started abstractly: "Like everyone in his right mind, I 4
feared Santa Claus. Maybe this is the beginning of every child's wisdom.
Of course I thought he was God. He was unseen but real and somehow
omnipresent." . . .

Reading this over I saw how appallingly boring it was. Who would want 5
to read something that practically begins with the word "omnipresent"? Who
would want to read something so vague and drippy it uses the word "somehow"? Where are we, anyhow? What, if anything, is happening? So I chucked
all this and began with the scene: it's Christmas Eve, some time ago, in a living room.

Even so, my description of this scene wandered off the point right away. 6
In the second draft there was extraneous speculation about what restaurant
the family might have gone to that night. There was extraneous description

of how my lined coat felt on my bare arms on the drive home from the restaurant. That's the trouble with writing about your life: you keep babbling because you're so marvelously interested. You're always tempted to indulge yourself. The babbling does no real harm if you have sense enough to drag yourself back on course from time to time, and, more important, if you have sense enough to recognize and cut out all the babble before you let anyone read the thing.

In the course of the second or third draft I'd gotten interested not only in   7
my own irrelevant memories, but also in an abstract side issue: how a child shapes behavior. I went on for a page about this. Again I saw how boring readers would find it; it had little to do with the matter at hand, which was an image: Santa Claus in the doorway. I tossed this page and later used the ideas in another essay.

Almost everything I cut from the early drafts was too abstract. You don't   8
say, I was eagerly awaiting Santa Claus. You say, We'd set out ginger ale and cookies. When you're telling any kind of story, every sentence should be full of things to see, hear, smell, or touch.

It's important to cut out weak parts; it's even more important to strengthen   9
strong parts. I revised to strengthen the central image. Images are more powerful than ideas. They stick in the imagination. If they are good symbolic images, they carry ideas with them; they embody and vivify ideas.

The essay describes Santa Claus in the doorway twice. First it gives the   10
setting and lays out the picture plainly: Santa Claus was looming in the doorway and looking around for me. Then it explains why I was afraid of Santa Claus. Then it describes Santa Claus again (once more with feeling), hoping that the second time the same image would resound with multiple meanings: Santa Claus is like the omnipotent God we fear as we fear the cold abyss of eternal night, etc. To make an occasion for describing it twice, I had the narrator take another look at Santa Claus from upstairs.

This business of describing something more than once is effective. I learned   11
it from Faulkner. You give the picture, stop the action and fill in some background which invests the picture with a wealth of feeling and meaning, and then give the picture again. If I were writing this piece now, I'd go over it a third time, bringing out the contrast between the two worlds—the cold eternal night, and the warm bright room (like a stable with a manger) here on earth where loving people love imperfectly and Christmases are not always merry. There's a lot of meaning packed too tightly here; I didn't really develop it all.

The details of the second description suggest various aspects of the idea: 12
Santa Claus stood in the doorway with night over his shoulder, letting in all the cold air of the sky; Santa Claus monstrous and bright, powerless, ringing a loud bell and repeating Merry Christmas, Merry Christmas. I wanted the image to be paradoxical, nagging unresolved in the mind. "Bright" is usually a positive word, and ringing bells are usually cheerful things; together they set up a weird tension (a *frisson*) with "monstrous"—which in turn usually

doesn't go with "powerless." Good description doesn't moronically insist on one simple mood—the lyric flowery meadow, the terrifying avalanche. Interesting feelings are complex and contradictory; I try to evoke complex feelings by shading things with their opposites. (And of course good writing doesn't *describe* feelings at all; it evokes them in the reader by describing the observable world with vivid language.)

Miss White is an innocent. She gives cookies to a neighbor child; she enjoys finger painting. We hurt innocent people (or gods) because we are wrongly afraid they'll hurt us. I ran from Miss White as Santa Claus; I ran from her again when I fancied she'd burned me with her magnifying glass. In both cases the essay likens her to the omnipotent, angry God. But in both cases, it turns out, she is more like the innocent, vulnerable, forgiving God whose love we refuse—by crucifying Christ, you could say, or by hurting our innocent neighbor. 13

The essay draws parallels between Santa Claus and the omnipotent God through logic: He's an old man who knows when you've been bad or good. It draws parallels between Miss White and the omnipotent God through language: After describing the magnifying glass incident (with as many active verbs as I could muster), I skipped a few lines and used the same imagery to imagine God's burning me in hell. At its very end, the essay draws parallels between Miss White and the vulnerable God (of whom the familiar symbol is Christ) through the inner logic of imagery: So Santa Claus powerless in the doorway with night over his shoulder invokes (at least subconsciously) two other images: the infant Jesus in Bethlehem, and Christ crucified. Both are standard representations of love's vulnerability and ultimate triumph. 14

Note how remarkably less interesting all this is than the anecdotal essay itself. This is why no one reads literary criticism. This is also why writers are well advised to keep mum about what they've written. If they can please us with vivid little bits of story, who cares what weird ideas drove them to their typewriters in the first place? 15

The essay's last paragraph is crucial. It brings it all together nicely: So once in Israel love came to us incarnate, stood in the doorway between two worlds, and we were all afraid. The omnipotent God/Santa Claus becomes the vulnerable Christ/Miss White, the neighbor whom I failed to love. The fearful little girl on Christmas Eve becomes by implication the loud crowd on Good Friday crying "crucify him." And the adult who's writing the essay converges on past themes and writes in the present: I am still running. 16

But its tone is worrisome. It suddenly sounds too solemn; it sounds preachy and pious. It still bothers me. It sounds like an evangelist making a pitch" "You ever feel this way? You need Jesus Christ." 17

I thought a little intellectual Christianity wouldn't hurt a magazine's Christmas issue—but that's no excuse. More profoundly I hoped that the phrase "stood in the doorway between two worlds" would bring it all down to earth, and back to the essay's narrative surface. Right then, I fondly hoped, 18 the reader would see in a flash how well the essay works; the metaphor holds. The reader would be so pleased, so positively stunned, he'd forgive the pompous tone of "So once in Israel love came to us incarnate." I hoped he'd forgive it—but now, ten years later, I don't really think it's forgivable.

Annie Dillard, Easter Week, 1984

✳

RESPONDING TO THE WHOLE ESSAY

1. In paragraph 5, Dillard considers her original opening from the point of view of a reader. As a reader, do you agree with Dillard's judgments about the opening? Why or why not? What else do you see in it that you find either effective or ineffective? Note that Dillard says that she "chucked all this . . . ," but in fact she saved some of it and used it elsewhere in the final version. Is what she saved effective as she finally used it? [*Harbrace* 29b, c and d; *Hodges'* 33b, c, and d]

2. In retrospect, Dillard finds the final sentence of "God in the Doorway" pompous and doesn't "really think it's forgivable." On what grounds might a reader agree with her? Disagree with her?

3. Describe Dillard's intended audience for this essay. How is it different from the audience for "God in the Doorway"? What statements does Dillard make that show she is aware of both audiences? [*Harbrace* 28a; *Hodges'* 32a]

4. How does Dillard's purpose in this essay differ from that of "God in the Doorway"? What is her purpose in this essay? [*Harbrace* 28a; *Hodges'* 32a]

SUGGESTIONS FOR WRITING

1. Write an account of the process you used in writing an essay for your composition course or one of your other courses. If possible, choose an essay or paper you worked especially hard on. Here are a few questions to help you get started: What prompted you to write that particular essay on that particular subject, and to write it as you did? As you worked on it, did you encounter problems that were especially difficult to solve? What, if anything, came easily? As you re-read the essay now, do you find things in it that especially please you? What parts, if any, do you now wish you'd written differently, and why? Attach a copy of the essay or paper you are writing about to your account of writing it.

2. Write an evaluation of one of the other narrative essays printed in this section. Consider the writer's apparent purpose and intended audience, and, in light of those, comment on such matters as the choice and ordering of events, the beginning and ending, the writer's attitude (tone), and words, phrases, or sentences that strike you as especially effective.

The Harlem Renaissance: One Facet of an Unturned Kaleidoscope
Darwin Turner

Holding bachelor's (1947) and master's (1949) degrees from the University of Cincinnati, Darwin Turner earned a Ph.D. from the University of Chicago. He taught English at several universities, including North Carolina Agricultural and Technical State, Indiana University, and the University of Michigan, and from 1980 until his death in 1992 served as chair of Afro-American Studies at the University of Iowa. His publications include *A Guide to Composition* (1960), and *In a Minor Chord: Three African American Writers and Their Search for Identity* (1971); and he edited *Black Drama in America: An Anthology* (1971) and, with J. Sekona, *The Art of the Slave Narrative* (1983). Turner was born in Cincinnati, Ohio, in 1931.

Geraldine's brash cry, "What you see is what you get," is appropriate comment on the tendency of many Americans to fix their attention on only a particular aspect of Black life in America—usually the most spectacular aspect. If they would twist the base of the kaleidoscope of Black life, the multicolored fragments would rearrange themselves into different patterns, some of them startlingly different. But few viewers choose to adjust the kaleidoscope. 1

As a result, out of the many patterns of Black life during the 1920's, the dominant image emblazoned on the vision of America is the Harlem Renaissance. By the same process, from the Harlem Renaissance itself, a Jazzed Abandon has become the most memorable spectacle. James Weldon Johnson's description of reactions to Harlem summarizes the legend of the Harlem Renaissance: 2

It is known in Europe and the Orient, and it is talked about by natives in the interior of Africa. It is farthest known as being exotic, colourful [*sic*], and sensuous; a place of laughing, singing, and dancing; a place where life wakes up at night. This phase of Harlem's fame is most widely known because, in addition to being spread by ordinary agencies, it has been proclaimed in story and song. And certainly this is Harlem's most striking and fascinating aspect. New Yorkers and people visiting New York from the world over go to the night-clubs of Harlem and dance to such jazz music as can be heard nowhere else; and they get an exhilaration impossible to duplicate. Some of these seekers after new sensations go beyond the gay night-clubs; they peep in under the more seamy side of things; they nose down into lower strata of life. A visit to Harlem at night—the principal streets never deserted, gay crowds skipping from one place of amusement to another, lines of taxicabs and limousines standing under the sparkling lights of the entrances to the famous nightclubs, the subway kiosks swallowing and disgorging crowds all night long—gives the impression that Harlem never sleeps and that the inhabitants thereof jazz through existence.[1]

Johnson continued, "But, of course, no one can seriously think that the two hundred thousand and more Negroes in Harlem spend their nights on any such pleasance."[2] So we too can say, "Surely, no one seriously thinks that this picture or even the entire 'Renaissance' constitutes the totality of the patterns housed in the kaleidoscope of Black life during the 1920's, the decade of the 'New Negro.'"   3

Even if one examines only the literary portraiture of the decade, one discerns more than a single image as the minute, tinted mirrors arrange and rearrange themselves into diverse patterns reflecting the actuality of Black life or reflecting the psyches of the Black and white artists who depicted that life. A knowledgeable individual twists the instrument to view the primitivism depicted by such white authors as Julia Peterkin, Eugene O'Neill, Sherwood Anderson, Dubose Heyward, Mary Wiborg, and William Faulkner, or the exotic abandon simulated by Carl Van Vechten. But a slight adjustment reshapes those images into the cultural elitism revealed by Van Vechten and cherished by W. E. B. DuBois. Another adjustment reveals the integrationist optimism of Langston Hughes, or the pan-Africanism of W. E. B. DuBois, or the Black nationalism of Marcus Garvey. Examine rural southern Blacks from the perspectives of Peterkin, Heyward, Faulkner, and Jean Toomer; or scrutinize the urban northerners of Toomer, Claude McKay, Rudolph Fisher, Langston Hughes, and Countée Cullen. Smile at the enthusiastic and naive Carl Van Vechtens, Mabel Dodges, and other white patrons as they prance about with their trophies collected on safaris into the Black jungles; then scowl at the lynchers painted by Claude McKay and photographed by Walter White. Admire the "patient endurance," with which William Faulkner colored his Dilsey; but do not overlook the militant impatience that inflames McKay's poetic voice. Consider the African nationalism vaguely sketched by Cullen, Hughes, and McKay; but compare it with Hughes' poetic demands for American integration and McKay's impressionistic sketches of the damnable siren, America, that fascinates, challenges, and captivates Blacks. Excite yourselves with sexual abandon garishly painted by Van Vechten, Anderson, McKay, and Toomer; but study also the conservative, often frustrated Blacks portrayed by Jessie Fauset and Toomer. Weep for the impotent failures depicted by O'Neill and Paul Green; but rejoice with the bold, determined aspirants of Fauset and Fisher. . . .   4

[1]James W. Johnson, *Black Manhattan* (New York, 1968; originally published, 1930), pp. 160–161. [Author's note]

[2]Ibid., p. 161. [Author's note]

Such awareness of the multiplicity of patterns of Black life during the 1920's justifies a reexamination, necessarily brief and somewhat superficial, of the Harlem Renaissance, particularly the literary Renaissance—to determine the reasons for its image as Jazzed Abandon, to trace more closely the more serious themes of the literature, and to reassess the significance of the Renaissance.

If we of the 1970's picture Black life in the 1920's as a riotous night-club tour, we cannot blame the best-known white writers for our misconception. Ironically, although Blacks became so popular as a subject that almost every prominent American author of the decade featured them in at least one major work, most of these authors ignored the Harlem scene in their literature. Such obvious neglect prompts speculation about the reasons: Were the authors describing the Afro-Americans they knew best? Or were they deliberately creating Black characters who would contrast with, and perhaps obscure, the image of the proud Renaissance Blacks?

Of course, in 1920, when O'Neill's *Emperor Jones* appeared, the Harlem Renaissance was less than a flutter in the heart of Alain Locke, the Black philosopher and cultural historian who named that era. O'Neill cannot be accused of ignoring what he could not have been expected to see. Situating his Black on a Caribbean island, O'Neill showed how fear, stripping away civilized veneer, reduces a man—in this instance, a southern Black—to a primitive.

The contrast between the Renaissance and O'Neill's work, however, appears in *All God's Chillun Got Wings* (1924). This drama, necessarily set in the North, describes the pathetic relationship between a Black man, who aspires to be a lawyer, and the "fallen" white woman whom he marries. The woman, betrayed and deserted by a white lover, marries the Black but becomes insane—or more insane, according to your view. The Black fails to become a lawyer partly because his wife, not wanting him to succeed, interferes with his study. The more crucial reason for his failure, however, is that whenever he is examined by whites, he forgets whatever he knows. In 1924, the year the play appeared, Jessie Fauset and Walter White published the first Black novels of the decade: *There Is Confusion,* which centers on the lives of middle-class Blacks in Philadelphia, among them a Black graduate of a white medical school, and *The Fire in the Flint,* a protest against lynching. For three years, Black musicals had been the rage of Broadway theater. BLACK was in, by 1924. The next year *Survey Graphic* would focus an entire issue on the "New Negro," James Weldon Johnson would hail Harlem as the capital of Black America, others would call it "Mecca." Despite these events, O'Neill provided New York theatergoers with a Black protagonist whose aspirations exceed his ability. Whatever O'Neill's reasons for the theme, the choice of an actor to portray the protagonist could not have been more ironic. The Black who panics when examined by whites was played by Paul Robeson, all-American football player (I believe that he was the first Black selected by

Walter Camp as an all-American), a twelve-letter man in athletics, and a Phi Beta Kappa graduate, who earned one of the highest academic averages in the history of Rutgers University.

The spectacle of Black failure was continued by Paul Green, a North Carolinian who wrote more plays about Blacks than any other white person during the decade. In 1926 Green won the Pulitzer Prize for *In Abraham's Bosom*, a drama in which Black Abe McCrannie, during Reconstruction, tries futilely to establish a school for Blacks. In the same year, 1926, W. E. B. DuBois, editor of *The Crisis*, the voice of the N.A.A.C.P., continuing a practice intended to encourage Black scholarship, published the pictures of the year's Black college graduates. Within a few years, DuBois would proudly announce that the large number of graduates prohibited his publishing the pictures of all.   9

Another memorable drama of the decade was Dubose Heyward's *Porgy*, now an American "classic," a story of a Black and crippled junk dealer, who strives to win Bess, a fallen woman, from Crown, a bad, bad man. Perhaps the most appropriate evaluation of the drama comes from W. E. B. DuBois, who insisted that he did not object to the play. Then, sniffing delicately from the rarified atmosphere surrounding a New England Brahmin who was a Ph.D. graduate from Harvard and had been a graduate student at Heidelberg, DuBois explained that, although he did not doubt that Heyward's Blacks existed in Charleston, South Carolina, he regretted Heyward's failure to portray the educated Blacks DuBois associated with when he visited that city.   10

During the 1920's William Faulkner foreshadowed his future stature with *The Sound and the Fury*, located primarily in Mississippi, with a glance at Cambridge, Massachusetts. Faulkner's major Black character in this novel is Dilsey, prototype of "the Black who endures." Like Green and O'Neill, Faulkner probably had not read Alain Locke's introduction to *The New Negro* (1925). Locke asserted: "Sentimental interest in the Negro has ebbed. We used to lament this as the falling off of our friends; now we rejoice and pray to be delivered both from self-pity and condescension. The mind of each racial group has had a better weaning, apathy or hatred on one side matching disillusionment or resentment on the other; but they face each other today with the possibility at least of entirely new mutual attitudes."[3]   11

The decade ended with a production of the extraordinarily popular *Green Pastures* (1930) by Marc Connelly. Based on Roark Bradford's *Ol' Man Adam and His Chillun*, the drama seems to retell the Old Testament from the perspective of a Black child at a church fish-fry. The narrator is not a child, however; he is an adult.   12

However distorted their vision of Blacks may have been, well-known white American authors of the 1920's cannot be blamed for the exotic image of the nightclub Black. That image comes from Blacks themselves   13

[3]Locke, "The New Negro," *The New Negro* (New York, 1968). [Author's note]

and from a few whites who identified themselves as promoters of Blacks or as sympathizers.

The image may have begun with *Shuffle Along* (1921), a brilliant and popular musical, written and directed by four Blacks—Flournoy Miller, Eubie Blake, Noble Sissel, and Aubrey Lyles. In the same year, *Shuffle Along* was succeeded by *Put and Take,* another musical by a Black—Irving C. Miller, who also produced *Liza* (1923), which was followed in the same year by *Runnin' Wild* by Miller and Lyles. The beauty of Afro-American chorus girls such as Florence Mills and Josephine Baker, the exotic foreign settings, the gaiety and the frenzy of these musicals and their successors may have cultivated in Broadway audiences a taste for particular depictions of Black life. Furthermore, these musicals may have created an image difficult to change.   14

Although it is located in the South, Sherwood Anderson's *Dark Laughter* (1925) conjures up the image of a joyful, untroubled people who, themselves freed from the need to read Freud, laugh gently at frustrated whites, who repress their own sexual desires. The image of joy continues in Carl Van Vechten's novel, *Nigger Heaven* (1926), set in Harlem. Although Van Vechten later proclaimed his desire to familiarize white readers with a cultural Black society which gives soirées and speaks French, he glamorized the Scarlet Creeper, a "sweetman" (gigolo), and he depicted Black night life with an excitement certain to allure readers.   15

The exoticism and gaiety appear in the works of Black writers themselves. Even Countée Cullen, known to subsequent generations as a somewhat prim purveyor of high art, contrasted the warmth of Blacks with the coldness of whites, wrote atavistically of the African rhythm inherent in the walk of a Black waiter (in *Color,* 1925), and rhapsodized the wildness of the African heritage.   16

In his first collection, *The Weary Blues* (1926), Langston Hughes not only created jazz/blues poems but also wrote with an exuberance tending to promote the image of an uninhibited people: 17

DREAM VARIATION

To fling my arms wide
In some place of the sun,
To whirl and to dance
Till the white day is done.
Then rest at cool evening
Beneath a tall tree
While night comes on gently,
    Dark like me,—
That is my dream!

> *To fling my arms wide*
> *In the face of the sun,*
> *Dance! whirl! whirl!*
> *Till the quick day is done.*
> *Rest at pale evening. . . .*
> *A tall, slim tree. . . .*
> *Night coming tenderly*
> *Black like me.*[4]

Black novelists also contributed to the image of an uninhibited people whose lives are exotic whirls. In *Home to Harlem* (1928), Claude McKay, a Black West Indian, drowned social protest in a flood of night life—prostitutes, sweetmen, jazz, nightclub fights—as he told the story of a Black deserter from the armed services who searches through Harlem for the prostitute whom he loves. Succeeding novelists, such as Rudolph Fisher (*The Walls of Jericho*, 1928) and Wallace Thurman (*The Blacker the Berry*, 1929), seemed almost compelled to include irrelevant nightclub scenes as though they had become clichés of Black life.

It should not be wondered then that W. E. B. DuBois, editor of *The Crisis*, reserved sections of several issues to question whether writers and publishers shared his fear that Black writers were being encouraged to create derogatory pictures of Blacks. Seriously concerned about respectable images of Blacks, DuBois, more than two decades earlier, had rationalized their enthusiasm as a primitivism promoted by the experience of slavery, a primitivism which would be modified when Black Americans matured into the sophistication of Euro-American society. Now that his "Talented Tenth" seemed to promote spectacles of frenzy, however, DuBois suspected that their desire to publish persuaded them to ignore the truth of Black life and to pander to whites by creating images designed to titillate.   18

Beneath the surfaces of gay abandon during the 1920's, however, are more somber issues, more sober themes which should be examined more closely. The same writers who seem to rejoice in the enthusiasm of Black life also sounded what Langston Hughes described as "the sob of the jazz band"—the melancholy undertone of Black life, ever present but sometimes unheard by those who failed to listen carefully.   19

Claude McKay pictured a Harlem dancer who guards her soul from the lascivious image suggested by her dance (*Harlem Shadows*, 1922), and Langston Hughes described the weariness of a jazz pianist (*The Weary Blues*, 1926). In *The Walls of Jericho* (1928) Fisher overshadowed the scenes of night life with a quieter depiction of the romance of two working people of Harlem. Thurman tempered his scenes of night life and dances in *The Blacker the Berry* by revealing that some Blacks visited dance halls not to gorge themselves with gaiety but to discover companionship to ease their loneliness. In the same   20

---

[4]Hughes, *The Weary Blues* (New York, 1926). [Author's note]

novel a white Chicagoan confirms his impression that the exotic savagery of Harlemites is grossly exaggerated by their white press agents. While his actress-sister revels in what she considers the barbaric splendor of the Black club they visit, the Chicagoan sees a generally decorous behavior which assures him that Harlemites are no wilder than the Blacks he has known in Chicago (and perhaps not as wild as the whites in either city). Countée Cullen asserted that he wrote *One Way to Heaven* (1932) to counter Carl Van Vechten's *Nigger Heaven* by showing the humanity of Black life in Harlem. In scene after scene, Cullen balances superficial exuberance with sober explanation: The enthusiasm of a religious revival does not obscure the fact that in attendance also are some morally respectable Blacks who are not swept away by the emotion. The heroine, a morally circumspect, hard-working woman, has attended several revivals to which she has been indifferent. A male's illicit love affair is ascribed partly to the nature of the wandering male and partly to a desire to find companionship because his wife, who has become a religious fanatic, is engaged in an affair with Jesus.

These more serious vestiges of Black life in America should not be ignored when one considers the literature of the Renaissance; for, far from being mere entertainers, many Black writers regarded literature as a means of seriously examining problems of living. Moreover, they did not restrict their examinations to problems of Blacks in an adversary relationship with white society. Almost from the first they were concerned with issues which might be considered universal if American critics were more willing to discover universality in the lives of Black people.   21

The interest in human conditions appears in Jean Toomer's *Cane* (1923), the work of the Renaissance which is the best known and the most highly respected in academic circles. Toomer delineates many protagonists whose difficulties do not depend primarily upon their ancestry: Karintha has matured too soon sexually; Carma lives in a society which pretends that a woman should become sexless if her husband does not live with her; Esther cannot reconcile her sexual urges with the education by a society which has taught her that "good" girls do not feel such urges; John, in "Theater," cannot adapt his idealized romanticizing into a satisfactory relationship with an actual woman; Dorris, in "Theater," dreams of a companionship that will provide a real substitute for the artificiality of the theater; Muriel, in "Box Seat," fears to defy the little-minded, social regulators of the world; Avery finds it more pleasurable to be supported by men than to labor as a teacher in a normal school. The problems of these individuals may be complicated or intensified by their condition as Blacks in America, but the problems would exist regardless of their race.   22

Jessie Fauset, the too little-known author of *There Is Confusion* (1924), *Plum Bun* (1929), *The Chinaberry Tree* (1933), and *Comedy: American Style* (1933), contrived her novels to focus on the problems of Blacks whose lives are not continuously affected by their interrelationships with whites. Most often their problems derive from their ambition or from a society excessively   23 willing to evaluate individuals according to false criteria. In *There Is Confusion,* for example, an ambitious young Black protagonist disrupts and nearly destroys the people around her because she tries to regulate their lives according to her delusions. Because she believes that people should not marry outside their class, she interferes with her brother's romance with a young woman whose family background is different. Doing "the right thing," by withdrawing from the relationship, the second young woman then rushes into an unfortunate marriage. Because the protagonist believes that suitors must be trained into suitably devoted servants, she refused to apologize to the man she loves even though she is wrong. After he apologizes in order to effect a reconciliation, she delays a response with the deliberate intention of causing him to learn that he cannot win her too easily. She begins to realize her error only when he, jolted by her rebuff, proposes to a woman who offers him affection without reservation.

In stories which she published during the 1920's, Zora Neale Hurston of   24 Florida explores such an "in-group" issue as the manner in which townspeople affect individuals by forcing them to act out of character in order to maintain the respect of the mob ("Spunk"). In addition, she vividly revealed the problems which disturb male-female relationships: the alienation which develops when a naive wife is seduced by a traveling salesman ("The Gilded Six-Bits"); the tragic consequences when a self-centered husband who has exploited his wife tries to replace her ("Sweat").

Black dramatists, such as Willis Richardson and Georgia D. Johnson, pre-   25 pared domestic dramas for the Black community: the tensions between a man and his improvident brothers-in-law ("The Broken Banjo"); the pathos of a situation in which a child is permitted to die because the mother favors the healing power of faith above that of man's medicine.

In such ways as these, Black people of the Renaissance explored serious   26 issues involving Black people but not deriving primarily from the racial ancestry or from their relationship with whites. This statement, however, should not encourage a fallacious assumption that the Black writers evaded their racial identity or ignored problems which do derive from interracial conflict. To the contrary, Black Renaissance writers frequently expressed concerns which strikingly anticipate major themes identified with the revolutionary Black Arts writers of the 1960's: a search for and affirmation of ancestral heritage, a feeling of alienation from the white Euro-American world; a presentation of and protest against oppression; and even militant defiance of oppression. . . .

The serious themes that Renaissance writers explored most frequently,   27 as might be expected, are protests against oppression. The presence of such themes has been obscured by three facts: (1) many readers remember the glamorous gaiety and forget the serious comments; (2) some protests appear as brief asides rather than fully developed explanations; (3) some protests seem mild because, rather than directly assaulting whites, they adumbrate the manner in which external oppression causes Blacks to oppress themselves.

The way that serious protest can be ignored is evidenced by the customary reactions of casual readers to McKay's *Home to Harlem* (1928), which appears, even in this paper, as a prototype of a Black work that promotes exoticism. The vividly exotic spectacles blind many readers to McKay's presentation of such facts as the following: During World War I many Black soldiers who enlisted to fight for democracy were restricted to service as laborers; during the 1920's some Harlem clubs, whether owned by whites or Blacks, discriminated against Blacks by refusing them admission—except as entertainers or waiters; in many occupations Black workers surrendered their dignity to the caprice of white supervisors.

It is true that no *Native Son* burst from the Renaissance to denounce American oppression. But Walter White's novel *The Fire in the Flint* (1924) decries the brutality of lynchings, as does Claude McKay's "The Lynching." Toomer's "Blood-Burning Moon" and "Kabnis" (*Cane*) reveal the powerlessness of Blacks to protect themselves from white brutality: a successful self-defense summons the lynch mob as quickly as a murder would.

Much more prevalent is the Renaissance writers' tendency to attack oppression indirectly by showing how it causes Blacks to turn against themselves. Because color, as an evidence of African ancestry, was a shibboleth of whites against Blacks, many Blacks used color as a criterion of intra-group evaluation. In *The Blacker the Berry* the protagonist, because of her dark skin, suffers within her family, in school and college, and in efforts to secure employment. Yet pathetically, as Thurman shows, the heroine cherishes the same criteria which have victimized her. She desires only men who are of lighter complexion and Caucasian appearance; and she undervalues herself, believing for a time at least that her Blackness is an ineradicable blot upon her record. In *Comedy: American Style* (1933), Fauset censured a Negro mother who values her children according to the degree of their approximation to Caucasian appearance. Walter White's *Flight* (1928) and Nella Larsen's *Passing* (1929) show the dilemmas of heroines who, repressed by the conditions of life as Blacks, attempt to improve their lot by passing for white.

In ironic repudiation of the images of Blacks as amoral beings, Jean Toomer repeatedly stressed the necessity for middle-class Negroes to liberate themselves from conscious imitation of the restrictive morality of Anglo-Saxons. "Esther," "Theater," and "Box-Seat" all reveal the frustrations of Black people who, desiring social approval, repress their emotions, their humanness. In "Kabnis" Carrie K., fearing censure by others, represses her instinctual attraction to Lewis. Paul ("Rona and Paul," *Cane*) loses a female companion because of his self-conscious desire to explain to a bystander that the relationship is not lustful. Toomer's most fully developed attack on middle-class morality appears in the unpublished drama "Natalie Mann." Mert, a school teacher, dies because she perceives too late that she must enjoy passion fully without concern for society's censure. Natalie, the protagonist, develops to this awareness only through the assistance of a Christ-like male who himself has experienced the rebukes of the middle class.

Toomer was not the only writer to question the excessive effort of Blacks   31
to conform to the standards presumed to be those of whites. The protagonist
in Walter White's *Flight* is forced to leave town and, temporarily, to deny her
race because Blacks will not permit her to forget that she has had a child out
of wedlock: her lover's proposal of abortion so diminished him in her esteem
that she refused his subsequent efforts to marry her.

During the 1920's few writers reacted militantly to oppression with the   32
kind of rhetoric for which Black revolutionary literature became notorious
during the 1960's. There are several reasons. A generally optimistic faith that
talented Blacks soon would emerge with the mainstream muted rhetorical violence and violent rhetoric. Furthermore, publishers during the 1920's did not
permit the kind of language and the explicit description of violent action which
became almost commonplace in later decades. Third, the publishing houses
were controlled by whites. It should be remembered that much of the Black
revolutionary literature of the 1960's issued from Black publishers of poetry
and in Black community drama.

Under the circumstances it is not surprising that the militant reaction of-   33
ten was expressed as self-defense, as in Claude McKay's well-known "If We
Must Die" (*Harlem Shadows*). Less frequently came prayers for destruction,
as in McKay's "Enslaved" (*Harlem Shadows*). Most often the militancy is a
proud hostility toward whites. At the end of *Flight* the male protagonist learns
why his father abhorred whites: they had deprived him of inheritance by refusing to recognize him as their offspring. In turn he refuses to permit an elderly white to ease his own conscience by making a monetary donation while
continuing to ignore the blood relationship.

I cannot conclude without reassessing the significance of the literary   34
Harlem Renaissance. If it is remembered for expression of gaiety rather than
for the serious concerns of the Black authors; if it was a movement which involved only talented artists in one segment of the Black American population;
if it reflects primarily the life of only one part of one city inhabited by Blacks;
if it evidences little awareness of such a significant issue for Blacks as DuBois'
dreams and promotions of Pan-Africanism and even less awareness of or respect for Marcus Garvey's Back-to-Africa movement—if the literary Renaissance is so limited, does it merit serious study? Was it, as Harold Cruse has
suggested, an era to be examined only as a pathetic example of a time when
Black artists might have established criteria for their art but failed to do so?
Was it, as W. E. B. DuBois stated and as LeRoi Jones insisted more forcefully
later, a movement that lost validity as it became a plaything of white culture?
In fact, is the very attention given to it by historians of Black culture evidence
of the willingness of Blacks and whites to glorify, or permit glorification of,
inferior art by Blacks?

Each of these allegations has partial validity. But such objections based   35
on idealistic absolutes fail to consider the actual significances of the literary
Renaissance. First, in no other decade had Black novelists been afforded such
opportunity for publication. If fewer than twenty original, non-vanity-press

novels appeared between 1924 and 1933, that figure nevertheless exceeded the number published by American commercial houses in all the years since the publication of the first Black American novel, Williams Wells Brown's *Clotel* (1853). Even the Depression and the closing of some outlets could not dispel the new awareness that possibilities existed for Blacks who wished to write novels. The field was open to many writers, not merely to the individual geniuses—the Paul Dunbar or the Charles Chesnutt of an earlier decade. This productivity, as well as the later success of Richard Wright, undoubtedly encouraged such novelists as Chester Hines, Ann Petry, Frank Yerby, and William G. Smith, who developed during the late 1930's and early 1940's.

The literary examples and inspirations were not limited to the novel. Only a few serious Black dramas reached Broadway, but the enthusiastic establishment of Black community theaters during the 1920's furthered the creation of a Black audience for drama and promoted awareness of the need for writers to create material for that audience. 36

Perhaps the productivity in poetry had less significant influence because Blacks previously had found outlets for poetry—the national reputation of Paul Laurence Dunbar was known by Blacks. Moreover, poetry was still to be considered an avocation which one supported by revenue derived from a stable vocation. But there was hope that Black writers might be able to sustain themselves partly through grants, for Countée Cullen had established a precedent by winning a Guggenheim fellowship for his proposal of a poetry-writing project. 37

Of final benefit to future writers was the mere fact that entrées had been established. A Langston Hughes or Wallace Thurman or Countée Cullen or, later, an Arna Bontemps knew publishers and knew other people who might be able to assist prospective authors. In all these senses, the Renaissance was not a rebirth but, in very significant ways, a first birth for Black Americans in literature. 38

A second significance of the literary Renaissance is its inspiration for African and Caribbean poets such as Léopold Senghor, Aimé Césaire, and Léon Damas who, a generation later in the 1930's and 1940's, promoted Negritude, a literary-cultural movement which emphasized consciousness of African identity and pride in the Black heritage. More than a decade after the Negritude writers, newer Black American writers of the 1960's looked to African Negritude for inspiration. Thus, both directly and circuitously, the Renaissance promoted Black American literature and Black consciousness of future decades. 39

Finally, the Renaissance has importance as a symbol. In many respects, the actuality of a culture is less important than the myth which envelops and extends from that culture. The memory that Black Americans had been recognized and respected for literary achievements, as well as other artistic achievements, established awareness that there could be a literary culture among Blacks. If the memory faded rapidly from the consciousness of white America, it did not fade from the minds of Blacks responsible for continuing 40 the culture among their people. Marcus Garvey did not succeed in restoring Black Americans to Africa; consequently, he is remembered as a dream that faded. But the Renaissance, for Black Americans and others, has gained strength as the mythic memory of a time when Blacks first burst into national consciousness as a talented group that was young, rebellious, proud, and beautiful.

*

RESPONDING TO THE WHOLE ESSAY

1. What is Turner's purpose in "The Harlem Renaissance"? Is the essay primarily an expression of Turner's feelings about the movement, a report detailing the main features of the movement, or an argument that the movement should be seen as reflecting the realities of Black life? [*Harbrace* 28a; *Hodges'* 32a]
2. What does Turner assume his audience already knows? This essay may be difficult for readers who have a limited understanding of twentieth-century American literature. Is it, therefore, also ineffective for those readers? Why or why not? Assess and account for your own response to the essay. [*Harbrace* 28a; *Hodges'* 32a]
3. Notice that Turner maintains a third-person point of view throughout the essay. What is the relationship between that point of view and the purpose of the essay?
4. Explain how, in his introduction, Turner engages the reader's interest. [*Harbrace* 28f; *Hodges'* 32f]
5. Explain Turner's use of the kaleidoscope image as an organizing principle. [*Harbrace* 28c; *Hodges'* 32c]
6. Explain how the conclusion, beginning with paragraph 38, ties together the various views of the Renaissance that Turner has offered. [*Harbrace* 28f; *Hodges'* 32f]

ANALYZING THE ELEMENTS

Grammar

1. Explain why, in the second sentence of paragraph 8, Turner uses *who* and *whom* as he does. Why does he not say "man, whom" or "woman who"? [*Harbrace* 6d; *Hodges'* 5b and 5c]
2. Identify all of the verbs in the second sentence of paragraph 22. Then justify Turner's choice of singular or plural for each verb. [*Harbrace* 7a; *Hodges'* 6a]
3. Why does Turner use the past perfect in sentence 7 of paragraph 8, the simple past in sentence 8, the future in sentence 9, and the present in sentence 10? Explain. [*Harbrace* 7c; *Hodges'* 7c]

Effective Sentences

1. In the first sentence of paragraph 1, the subject and verb are divided by a parenthetical quotation. Is the effectiveness of the sentence increased or diminished? Explain. [*Harbrace* 12d; *Hodges'* 30d]

2. Explain how Turner keeps the large number of details in paragraph 30 from appearing to be excessive. [*Harbrace* 8b; *Hodges'* 23b]
3. Explain why the second sentence in paragraph 34 is periodic and comment upon its rhetorical effect. [*Harbrace* 11b; *Hodges'* 29b]

Punctuation and Mechanics

1. Explain why Turner uses a colon before the long quotation in paragraph 2. [*Harbrace* 20; *Hodges'* 16]
2. Comment upon Turner's use of italics and parentheses in paragraph 20. [*Harbrace* 24 and 21f; *Hodges'* 10 and 17f]
3. The second sentence of paragraph 27 is long, but Turner makes it clear with careful punctuation. Explain the use of the following in that sentence: colon, semicolon, comma, and parentheses. [*Harbrace* 17d, 18a, 21d, and 21f; *Hodges'* 12d, 14a, 17d and 17f]

Diction

1. Why are *non-vanity-press* (sentence 4, paragraph 35) and *poetry-writing* (sentence 3, paragraph 37) hyphenated? [*Harbrace* 22f; *Hodges'* 18f]
2. Paragraph 4 contains a long catalogue of "literary portraiture . . . reflecting the actuality of Black life." Using more than a dozen synonyms for "look at," Turner ingeniously relates the items in the catalogue while maintaining the reader's interest. Write a paragraph of your own in which you supply at least five synonyms for an action you want your reader to perform repeatedly. [*Harbrace* 14a; *Hodges'* 23e(2)]
3. Turner uses a rich and varied vocabulary in this essay. Look up the following words in your dictionary: *protagonist* (paragraph 8), *soirée* and *gigolo* (paragraph 15), *atavistically* (paragraph 16), *pander* (paragraph 18), *vestige* (paragraph 21), *improvident* (paragraph 25), *fallacious* (paragraph 26), *censure* (paragraph 30), *notorious* (paragraph 32). Explain how the connotations and denotations of these words are appropriate. [*Harbrace* 14a; *Hodges'* 20a and 23e(2)]

BUILDING VOCABULARY

1. Define *abhor*. From what Latin roots is *abhor* borrowed? What do they mean?
2. Identify and define the Latin roots that *circumspect* comes from. Write a sentence using a word derived from one of these Latin roots.

SUGGESTIONS FOR WRITING

1. Choose a particularly interesting recent event (a crime, a political confrontation or a significant event in the life of a celebrity, for example) and read at least three articles about the event in such sources as *Time, Newsweek,* or the *New York Times.* Then write your own account of the event, maintaining an objective, third-person point of view. Be careful to give credit when quoting from your sources. (see *Harbrace* 33, 34a, and 34b; *Hodges'* 37, 38a, and 38b for help with handling sources.)

2. You are an editor for a popular magazine that prints condensed books and articles. You have been assigned to condense Turner's article to fewer than 1,000 words—that is, boil it down while retaining the author's own words and organization. Carry out the assignment. (You may make small changes and insertions for coherence since the author will be asked to approve your version before it is published.)

✳
Chapter 3

Description

Description uses language to re-create for a reader what is experienced through the senses—sight, sound, taste, touch, and smell. Because it is grounded in the senses, description relies especially on concrete images. (For a discussion of concreteness, see [*Harbrace* 14a(4); *Hodges'* 20a(3)].) This *p·22* (3) emphasis on concreteness and specificity is one of the things that make description so effective in bringing a story to life or making an argument persuasive. Indeed, description most often occurs in combination with other strategies, particularly narration; description can explain and expand a comparison, a process, a definition, an argument, a classification—any of the other strategies.

Whatever your purpose for writing, description helps you and your reader share an experience or an impression. If your purpose is to express your feelings, description can make those feelings tangible for your reader. This kind of description, often called *subjective,* emphasizes the personal response to an object rather than the characteristics of the object itself. In contrast to expressive writing, informative writing usually employs *objective* description, which relies on sensory data uncolored by the writer's feelings and attitudes. For example, if you were to write, "Pitted with tiny depressions, the skin of the orange exudes a pungent odor when scraped," you would have written an objective description. If, on the other hand, you were to write, "The scraped skin of the orange is redolent of lazy summer mornings," you would have a subjective description.

Sometimes the difference between objective and subjective description is mainly a matter of the connotations of the words the writer chooses: "The skin under her eyes crinkled into fine networks when she laughed, and delicate traces of powder dusted her withered cheeks" has a more subjective quality than "The skin under her eyes was crossed and recrossed by tiny lines, and her cheeks, which bore traces of powder, had lost their former firm roundness." Notice how words like *crinkled, networks, dusted,* and *withered* contribute to the subjective quality of the first description.

The main task in writing successful description is to make sure that all of the details you select will contribute to a single *dominant impression* that fulfills your purpose. If you are writing about your grandmother's face, you must decide whether you want to show her as she would appear in a harsh light to a stranger or whether you want to allow your feelings for her to soften the portrait. In either case, you would not include details of her dress or the timbre of her voice because they would tell the reader nothing about her face. Nor would you include every detail of her face. When describing, select only the best and most relevant details to convey the impression you want.

Your purpose will govern not only your selection of details but also your arrangement of them. You might arrange them spatially—near to far, top to bottom, left to right, and so forth—or in order of importance, or moving from larger to smaller or more general to more specific (or vice versa). But whatever pattern you choose, follow through with it; jumping back and forth without reason between different principles or arrangement can blur the impression you are trying to build.

A good way to begin a description is to jot down, either from observation or from recollection, as many details, however tiny or seemingly unimportant, as you can. Then, according to your purpose, you can select the most significant details and arrange them in the most effective pattern. As you read the description essay by Lisa Garrett, a student, notice that Garrett structures her description within an argumentative frame. Notice also the kinds of details she has chosen to convey her corollary point that natural beauty is one important way that nature feeds the senses and augments the reader's experience of scenery.

The Fragility of Natural Wonders

Introduction establishes context	My home state of Oregon is known for a kind of scenic beauty that is protected by its very grandeur. It is hard to credit that the carelessness and greed of humans could damage such beauty writ
Details set broad initial perspective	large: the majesty of Mount Hood, the splendor of the Columbia Gorge, the grandeur of the rugged coastline. Complacency is easy in the face of such hugeness.
Narrows perspective	Mere scale disguises the fragility of diminutive gems such as Multnomah Falls, a ruined beauty nestled within the larger magnificence of the Gorge. Here the
Specific detail	careless enthusiasm of tourists supports a blatant commercialism that mars the ethereal natural beauty formed by delicate waterfall traceries. Other gems have so far been more fortunate, but they are threatened by air, water, and people pollution. Where will we
Thesis	find the rare peace that only nature offers when these places are gone? Each time I visit one of my favorite spots I become acutely aware of this threat.
Visual images	Here below the waterfall in Oneonta Gorge, the sunlight is diffused and the sky is just a thin blue strip between the black basalt walls of the gorge. At first the one-hundred-foot walls of the narrow gorge

Spatial perspective Visual images	with their seventy-five-foot crowns of majestic old-growth Douglas fir seem to lean ominously over me. As I sit on my water-rounded basalt boulder a while longer, the walls of the gorge seem to offer protection rather than threat. To outsiders, this place seems iso-
Reference to thesis	lated from things that might endanger it, but it is frighteningly attached to the polluted world and is precariously easy to spoil.
Olfactory and tactile images	I breathe in the clean, cool air filtered through the mist from the falls and mingled with the scents
Perspective narrows	of fir trees, rhododendron flowers, and clean soil. I listen to the gurgle of the water, the singing of robins,
Auditory images	and rustle of the trees and shrubs above me as they are brushed by the breeze. I observe a nearby trout
Visual images and very specific details	plucking its lunch of mayfly nymphs from the rocks, a few wild birds chasing mosquitoes, and a spider repairing its web. The bright, clear water of Oneonta Creek squeezes through thick cushions of moss and swirls through gracefully wavering strands of green algae.
Adjusts temporal perspective	On my way here I walked through a magnifi-cent stand of Douglas fir, where each regal tree seemed to protect its small section of forest. I rested
Visual image	in a quiet and radiant meadow where the dead trees, gnarled and silvery, proudly guarded the sweetly fra-
Olfactory image	grant huckleberry and wildflowers of the meadow.
Visual image	Now, as I watch the water surge over the falls and into the gorge below, I wonder at the immense power of the countless raindrops that it took to carve this deep, narrow crevasse into the hard Oregon basalt. The uniqueness of this gorge is in its dimen-
Specific details	sions. It is only two miles in length and only thirty feet wide. But unfortunately, even this narrow opening
Perspective narrows	cannot prevent pollutants borne by the air, the rain, and the groundwater from entering the gorge. and these pollutants jeopardize several species of plant life
Refers to thesis	that flourish in this gorge and are found nowhere else on earth.
Return to frame established in first paragraph	I am calmed and refreshed by this powerful and lovely place, but at the same time I am fright-ened for my Oneonta Creek and for the many un-usual places around the world that are similarly threatened. Will they remain the pure and vigorous
Conclusion echoes thesis	places they are now or will polluted air and water destroy them?

Commentary. In the first paragraph, Garrett creates a frame for the de-scription that follows, her expression of ecological concern. This frame also establishes the context that sparked the essay, her appreciation of the natural beauty of her home and her concern that it is in jeopardy. Garrett narrows the reader's view from the panoramic perspective of the introductory paragraph to the very minute focus on the trout catching a mayfly.

Throughout the essay, she emphasizes sensory details that show the reader exactly what she fears to lose, the clean air, the scents of flowers and trees, the sounds of water and wild life. In addition to her effective use of visual and auditory images, Garrett takes advantage of rarely used tactile and olfactory images that lend immediacy and richness to the picture she paints.

Her movement through the essay is not only a movement from large to small and near to far. She also includes a suggestion of chronological movement: what she saw on her way to Oneonta Creek, how time changed her perception of the brooding quality of the gorge, the eons it took to create this special place.

She also works at keeping her thesis before the reader by twice referring to the danger she senses and by giving additional specific details to muster the reader's concern as well, details such as the references to the unique plant life the gorge shelters. To conclude, Garrett recalls the sensory details by referring to their effects ("I am calmed and refreshed") and then reestablishes the environmental frame issue she established in the first paragraph.

The Way to Rainy Mountain
N. Scott Momaday

N. Scott Momaday (1934–   ) was awarded a Guggenheim Fellowship in 1966 and won a Pulitzer Prize in 1969 for his first novel, *House Made of Dawn*. Born in Lawton, Oklahoma, of Kiowa and Cherokee ancestry, Momaday graduated from the University of New Mexico and received a Ph.D. from Stanford University. Momaday has taught English and comparative literature at the University of California–Santa Barbara and at Stanford and has also published two collections of poetry. *The Way to Rainy Mountain*, his second book and the one from which this essay is taken, is a collection of legendary Kiowa tales. In this essay, using time as an organizing principle for his description, Momaday evokes a sense of both the immediate past and the remote past.

A single knoll rises out of the plain in Oklahoma, north and west of the   1
Wichita range. For my people, the Kiowas, it is an old landmark, and they gave it the name Rainy Mountain. The hardest weather in the world is there. Winter brings blizzards, hot tornadic winds arise in the spring, and in summer the prairie is an anvil's edge. The grass turns brittle and brown, and it cracks beneath your feet. There are green belts along the rivers and creeks, linear groves of hickory and pecan, willow and witch hazel. At a distance in July or August the steaming foliage seems almost to writhe in fire. Great green and yellow grasshoppers are everywhere in the tall grass, popping up like corn to sting the flesh, and tortoises crawl about on the red earth, going nowhere in the plenty of time. Loneliness is an aspect of the land. All things in the plain are isolate; there is no confusion of objects in the eye, but *one* hill or *one* tree or *one* man. To look upon that landscape in the early morning, with the sun at your back, is to lose the sense of proportion. Your imagination comes to life, and this, you think, is where Creation was begun.

I returned to Rainy Mountain in July. My grandmother had died in the   2
spring, and I wanted to be at her grave. She had lived to be very old and at last infirm. Her only living daughter was with her when she died, and I was told that in death her face was that of a child.

I like to think of her as a child. When she was born, the Kiowas were   3
living the last great moment of their history. For more than a hundred years they had controlled the open range from the Smoky Hill River to the Red,

97

from the headwaters of the Canadian to the fork of the Arkansas and Cimarron. In alliance with the Comanches, they had ruled the whole of the Southern Plains. War was their sacred business, and they were the finest horsemen the world has ever known. But warfare for the Kiowas was preeminently a matter of disposition rather than of survival, and they never understood the grim, unrelenting advance of the U.S. Cavalry. When at last, divided and ill provisioned, they were driven onto the Staked Plains in the cold of autumn, they fell into panic. In Palo Duro Canyon they abandoned their crucial stores to pillage and had nothing then but their lives. In order to save themselves, they surrendered to the soldiers at Fort Sill and were imprisoned in the old stone corral that now stands as a military museum. My grandmother was spared the humiliation of those high gray walls by eight or ten years, but she must have known from birth the affliction of defeat, the dark brooding of old warriors.

Her name was Aho, and she belonged to the last culture to evolve in North   4
America. Her forebears came down from the high country in western Montana nearly three centuries ago. They were a mountain people, a mysterious tribe of hunters whose language has never been classified in any major group. In the late seventeenth century they began a long migration to the south and east. It was a journey toward the dawn, and it led to a golden age. Along the way the Kiowas were befriended by the Crows, who gave them the culture and religion of the Plains. They acquired horses; and their ancient nomadic spirit was suddenly free of the ground. They acquired Tai-me, the sacred sun-dance doll, from that moment the object and symbol of their worship, and so shared in the divinity of the sun. Not least, they acquired the sense of destiny, therefore courage and pride. When they entered upon the Southern Plains they had been transformed. No longer were they slaves to the simple necessity of survival; they were a lordly and dangerous society of fighters and thieves, hunters and priests of the sun. According to their origin myth, they entered the world through a hollow log. From one point of view, their migration was the fruit of an old prophecy, for indeed they emerged from a sunless world.

Though my grandmother lived out her long life in the shadow of Rainy   5
Mountain, the immense landscape of the continental interior lay like memory in her blood. She could tell of the Crows, whom she had never seen, and of the Black Hills, where she had never been. I wanted to see in reality what she had seen more perfectly in the mind's eye, and drove fifteen hundred miles to begin my pilgrimage.

A dark mist lay over the Black Hills, and the land was like iron. At the   6
top of a ridge I caught sight of Devil's Tower upthrust against the gray sky as if in the birth of time the core of the earth had broken through its crust and the motion of the world was begun. There are things in nature that engender an awful quiet in the heart of man; Devil's Tower is one of them. Two centuries ago, because of their need to explain it, the Kiowas made a legend at the base of the rock. My grandmother said:

Eight children were there at play, seven sisters and their brother. Suddenly the boy was struck dumb; he trembled and began to run upon his hands and feet. His fingers became claws, and his body was covered with fur. There was a bear where the boy had been. The sisters were terrified; they ran, and the bear after them. They came to the stump of a great tree, and the tree spoke to them, It bade them climb upon it, and as they did so, it began to rise into the air. The bear came to kill them, but they were just beyond its reach. It reared against the tree and scored the bark all around with its claws. The seven sisters were borne into the sky, and they became the stars of the Big Dipper.

From that moment, and so long as the legend lives, the Kiowas have kinsmen in the night sky. Whatever they were in the mountains, they could be no more. However tenuous their well-being, however much they had suffered and would suffer again, they had found a way out of the wilderness.

My grandmother had a reverence for the sun, a holy regard that now   7
is all but gone out of mankind. There was a wariness in her, and an ancient awe. She was a Christian in her later years, but she had come a long way about, and she never forgot her birthright. As a child she had been to the sun dances; she had taken part in that annual rite, and by it she had learned the restoration of her people in the presence of Tai-me. She was about seven when the last Kiowa sun dance was held in 1887 on the Washita River above Rainy Mountain Creek. The buffalo were gone. In order to consummate the ancient sacrifice—to impale the head of a buffalo bull upon the Tai-me tree—a delegation of old men journeyed into Texas, there to beg and barter for an animal from the Goodnight herd. She was ten when the Kiowas came together for the last time as a living sun-dance culture. They could find no buffalo; they had to hang an old hide from the sacred tree. Before the dance could begin, a company of soldiers rode out from Fort Sill under orders to disperse the tribe. Forbidden without cause the essential act of their faith, having seen the wild herds slaughtered and left to rot upon the ground, the Kiowas backed away forever from the tree. That was July 20, 1890, at the great bend of the Washita. My grandmother was there. Without bitterness, and for as long as she lived, she bore a vision of deicide.

8

Now that I can have her only in memory, I see my grandmother in the several postures that were peculiar to her: standing at the wood stove on a winter morning and turning meat in a great iron skillet; sitting at the south window, bent above her beadwork and afterwards, when her vision failed, looking down for a long time into the fold of her hands; going out upon a cane, very slowly as she did when the weight of age came upon her; praying. I remember her most often at prayer. She made long, rambling prayers out of suffering and hope, having seen many things. I was never sure that I had the right to hear, so exclusive were they of all mere custom and company. The last time I saw her she prayed standing by the side of her bed at night, naked to the waist, the light of a kerosene lamp moving upon her dark skin. Her long black hair, always drawn and braided in the day, lay upon her shoulders and against her breasts like a shawl. I do not speak Kiowa, and I never understood her prayers, but there was something inherently sad in the sound, some merest hesitation upon the syllables of sorrow. She began in a high and descending pitch, exhausting her breath to silence; then again and again—and always the same intensity of effort, of something that is, and is not, like urgency in the human voice. Transported so in the dancing light among the shadows of her room, she seemed beyond the reach of time. But that was illusion; I think I knew then that I should not see her again.

Houses are like sentinels in the plain, old keepers of the weather watch.   9 There, in a very little while, wood takes on the appearance of great age. All colors wear soon away in the wind and rain, and then the wood is burned gray and the grain appears and the nails turn red with rust. The window panes are black and opaque; you imagine there is nothing within, and indeed there are many ghosts, bones given up to the land. They stand here and there against the sky, and you approach them for a longer time than you expect. They belong in the distance; it is their domain.

Once there was a lot of sound in my grandmother's house, a lot of com-   10 ing and going, feasting and talk. The summers there were full of excitement and reunion. The Kiowas are a summer people; they abide the cold and keep to themselves, but when the season turns and the land becomes warm and vital they cannot hold still; an old love of going returns upon them. The aged visitors who came to my grandmother's house when I was a child were made of lean and leather, and they bore themselves upright. They wore great black hats and bright ample shirts that shook in the wind. They rubbed fat upon their hair and wound their braids with strips of colored cloth. Some of them painted their faces and carried the scars of old and cherished enmities. They were an old council of warlords, come to remind and be reminded of who they were. Their wives and daughters served them well. The women might indulge themselves; gossip was at once the mark and compensation of their servitude. They made loud and elaborate talk among themselves, full of jest and gesture, fright and false alarm. They went abroad in fringed and flowered shawls, bright beadwork and German silver. They were at home in the kitchen, and they prepared meals that were banquets.

There was frequent prayer meetings, and nocturnal feasts. When I was   11 a child I played with my cousins outside, where the lamplight fell upon the ground and the singing of the old people rose up around us and carried away into the darkness. There were a lot of good things to eat, a lot of laughter and surprise. And afterwards, when the quiet returned, I lay down with my grandmother and could hear the frogs away by the river and feel the motion of the air.

Now there is a funeral silence in the rooms, the endless wake of some   12 final word. The walls have closed in upon my grandmother's house. When I returned to it in morning, I saw for the first time in my life how small it was. It was late at night, and there was a white moon, nearly full. I sat for a long time on the stone steps by the kitchen door. From there I could see out across the land; I could see the long row of trees by the creek, the low light upon the rolling plains, and the stars of the Big Dipper. Once I looked at the moon and caught sight of a strange thing. A cricket had perched upon the handrail, only a few inches away. My line of vision was such that the creature filled the moon like a fossil. It had gone there, I thought, to live and die, for there, of all places, was its small definition made whole and eternal. A warm wind rose up and purled like the longing within me.

The next morning, I awoke at dawn and went out on the dirt road to Rainy Mountain. It was already hot, and the grasshoppers began to fill the air. Still, it was early in the morning, and birds sang out of the shadows. The long yellow grass on the mountain shone in the bright light, and a scissortail hied above the land. There, where it ought to be, at the end of a long and legendary way, was my grandmother's grave. She had at last succeeded to that holy ground. Here and there on the dark stones were ancestral names. Looking back once, I saw the mountain and came away. 13

❋

RESPONDING TO THE WHOLE ESSAY

1. Discuss how "The Way to Rainy Mountain" is at once a memoir of Momaday's grandmother, a history of the Kiowas, and a chronicle of the author's own literal and spiritual journey. Using your discussion as a basis for judgment, point out where Momaday informs or persuades the reader, and where he expresses personal feelings. [*Harbrace* 28a; *Hodges'* 32a]
2. Find evidence in "The Way to Rainy Mountain" that suggests what kinds of readers Momaday was writing for. [*Harbrace* 28a; *Hodges'* 32a]
3. Descriptive details communicate by appealing to the senses: sight, sound, touch, taste, and smell. Comment on Momaday's use of concrete, sensory details to describe not only a place—the open range of Oklahoma—but also his grandmother and the Kiowas as a people. Which sense does Momaday rely on most frequently? What other senses does he invoke? (Look particularly at paragraphs 1 and 9.)
4. The concept of time is ever-present in "The Way to Rainy Mountain." Discuss Momaday's use in the essay of the present, the recent past, the historical past, and legendary time.
5. Is Momaday's discussion of Devil's Tower a digression, or is it relevant to the point of the essay? If it is a digression, why does he include it? If it is relevant to the point of the essay, explain how. [*Harbrace* 27a; *Hodges'* 31a]
6. In his conclusion, Momaday says, "There, where it ought to be, at the end of a long and legendary way, was my grandmother's grave." How does this sentence summarize the essay? [*Harbrace* 28f(2); *Hodges'* 32f(2)]

ANALYZING THE ELEMENTS

Grammar

1. Explain what time relationships are indicated by uses of the simple past and past perfect tenses in paragraph 2. [*Harbrace* 7c; *Hodges'* 7c]
2. In the eighth sentence of paragraph 3 (beginning "In Palo Duro Canyon . . ."), the phrase "to pillage" could formally be either an infinitive or a prepositional phrase. Explain how the reader knows which was intended. [*Harbrace* 1d; *Hodges'* 1d]

Effective Sentences

1. Comment on some of the various ways Momaday makes the fourth sentence of paragraph 1 effective. [*Harbrace* 14a(5), 10a, and 11d(2); *Hodges'* 20a(4), 26a, 29d(2)]
2. In paragraph 4, Momaday uses the work *acquired* near the beginning of three sentences—the seventh, eighth, and ninth. Comment on the effect of this repetition. [*Harbrace* 11e and 27b; *Hodges'* 29e and 31b]
3. Explain what makes the eleventh sentence in paragraph 7 (beginning "Forbidden without cause . . .") and the next-to-last sentence in paragraph 8 effective. [*Harbrace* 12c; *Hodges'* 30c]

Punctuation and Mechanics

1. Explain Momaday's use of the semicolon in the following sentences: the eleventh sentence of paragraph 4 (beginning "No longer . . ."); the first sentence of paragraph 8; the third sentence of paragraph 10. [*Harbrace* 18a; *Hodges'* 14a]
2. How is the colon used in the first sentence of paragraph 8? Could any other mark of punctuation have been used? If so, what? [*Harbrace* 21d; *Hodges'* 17d]

Diction

1. Comment on how figurative language contributes to the tone and the meaning of the essay. [*Harbrace* 14a(5); *Hodges'* 20a(4)]
2. Look up the following words in your dictionary: *preeminently* and *pillage* (paragraph 3), *tenuous* (after the block quotation in paragraph 6), *consummate* and *deicide* (paragraph 7), *inherently* (paragraph 8), *nocturnal* (paragraph 11), *hied* (paragraph 13). With the aid, if necessary, of a dictionary of synonyms, find possible substitutes for as many of these words as you can; you may have to use a phrase instead of a single word. Then explain either why the word Momaday uses is more precise than the substitute or why the substitute is more precise. [*Harbrace* 14a(3); *Hodges'* 20a(2)]

BUILDING VOCABULARY

1. Explain the origin of *imagine*. Does *imagine* come from a Latin or Greek root? If so, what is the root, what does it mean, and from which of these two languages does it originate? Can you find any indication of when this root was imported into the English language?

2. From what Old English word does *gossip* derive? What does this Old English word mean? What is the British meaning of the noun *gossip?* Can you find an American definition of *gossip* similar to that of the British definition? What is it? What is the meaning of *gossip* most often used in American English?

SUGGESTIONS FOR WRITING

1. Write an essay describing an elderly person and the place where he or she lives. Strive to show a relationship between the person and the place.
2. Using as many sensory details as you can muster, describe a natural (or urban) landscape that sticks in your memory. In your description, try to *show* rather than *tell* why the scene is memorable.

The Courage of Turtles
Edward Hoagland

Born in New York City, Edward Hoagland (1932–   ) was raised in Con-
necticut and educated at Harvard University. Hoagland has written for such
periodicals as *Harper's, Commentary, The New Yorker,* and *Esquire.* Among
the literary awards he has received are a Guggenheim Fellowship, an O. Henry
Award, and an American academy of Arts and Letters Travelling Fellowship.
His books include *The Courage of Turtles, Walking the Dead Diamond River,
Red Wolves and Black Bears,* and *African Calliope: A Journey to the Sudan.*
A careful observer, Hoagland often exploits the dramatic quality of the strug-
gle for survival, as he does in "The Courage of Turtles."

Turtles are a kind of bird with the governor turned low. With the same   1
attitude of removal, they cock a glance at what is going on, as if they need
only to fly away. Until recently they were also a case of virtue rewarded, at
least in the town where I grew up, because, being humble creatures, there
were plenty of them. Even when we still had a few bobcats in the woods the
local snapping turtles, growing up to forty pounds, were the largest carnivores. You would see them through the amber water, as big as green wash
basins at the bottom of the pond, until they faded into the inscrutable mud
as if they hadn't existed at all.

When I was ten I went to Dr. Green's Pond, a two-acre pond across the   2
road. When I was twelve I walked a mile or so to Taggart's Pond, which was
lusher, had big water snakes and a waterfall; and shortly after that I was bi-
cycling way up to the adventuresome vastness of Mud Pond, a lake-sized body
of water in the reservoir system of a Connecticut city, possessed of cat-backed
little islands and empty shacks and a forest of pines and hardwoods along the
shore. Otters, foxes and mink left their prints on the bank; there were pike
and perch. As I got older, the estates and forgotten back lots in town were
parceled out and sold for nice prices, yet, though the woods had shrunk, it
seemed that fewer people walked in the woods. The new residents didn't know
how to find them. Eventually, exploring, they did find them, and it required
some ingenuity and doubling around on my part to go for eight miles without meeting someone. I was grown by now, I lived in New York, and that's
what I wanted on the occasional weekends when I came out.

Since Mud Pond contained drinking water I had felt confident nothing   3
untoward would happen there. For a long while the developers stayed away,
until the drought of the mid-1960s. This event, squeezing the edges in,

convinced the local water company that the pond really wasn't a necessity as a catch basin, however; so they bulldozed a hole in the earthen dam, bulldozed the banks to fill in the bottom, and landscaped the flow of water that remained to wind like an English brook and provide a domestic view for the houses which were planned. Most of the painted turtles of Mud Pond, who had been inaccessible as they sunned on their rocks, wound up in boxes in boys' closets within a matter of days. Their footsteps in the dry leaves gave them away as they wandered forlornly. The snappers and the little musk turtles, neither of whom leave the water except once a year to lay their eggs, dug into the drying mud for another siege of hot weather, which they were accustomed to doing whenever the pond got low. But this time it was low for good; the mud baked over them and slowly entombed them. As for the ducks, I couldn't stroll in the woods and not feel guilty, because they were crouched beside every stagnant pothole, or were slinking between the bushes with their heads tucked into their shoulders so that I wouldn't see them. If they decided I had, they beat their way up through the screen of trees, striking their wings dangerously, and wheeled about with that headlong, magnificent velocity to locate another poor puddle.

I used to catch possums and black snakes as well as turtles, and I kept   4
dogs and goats. Some summers I worked in a menagerie with the big personalities of the animal kingdom, like elephants and rhinoceroses. I was twenty before these enthusiasms began to wane, and it was then that I picked turtles as the particular animal I wanted to keep in touch with. I was allergic to fur, for one thing, and turtles need minimal care and not much in the way of quarters. They're personable beasts. They see the same colors we do and they seem to see just as well, as one discovers in trying to sneak up on them. In the laboratory they unravel the twists of a maze with the hot-blooded rapidity of a mammal. Though they can't run as fast as a rat, they improve on their errors just as quickly, pausing at each crossroads to look left and right. And they rock rhythmically in place, as we often do, although they are hatched from eggs, not the womb. (A common explanation psychologists give for our pleasure in rocking quietly is that it recapitulates our mother's heartbeat *in utero*.)

Snakes, by contrast, are dryly silent and priapic. They are smooth movers,   5
legalistic, unblinking, and they afford the humor which the humorless do. But they make challenging captives; sometimes they don't eat for months on a point of order—if the light isn't right, for instance. Alligators are sticklers too. They're like war-horses, or German shepherds, and with their bar-shaped, vertical pupils adding emphasis, they have the *idée fixe* of eating, eating, even when they choose to refuse all food and stubbornly die. They delight in tossing a salamander up towards the sky and grabbing him in their long mouths as he comes down. They're so eager that they get the jitters, and they're too much of a proposition for a casual aquarium like mine. Frogs are depressingly defenseless: that moist, extensive back, with the bones almost sticking through. Hold a frog and you're holding its skeleton. Frogs' tasty legs are the staff of life to many animals—herons, raccoons, ribbon snakes—though they

themselves are hard to feed. It's not an enviable role to be the staff of life, and after frogs you descend down the evolutionary ladder a big step to fish.

Turtles cough, burp, whistle, grunt and hiss, and produce social judg- 6
ments. They put their heads together amicably enough, but then one drives the other back with the suddenness of two dogs who have been conversing in tones too low for an onlooker to hear. They pee in fear when they're first caught, but exercise both pluck and optimism in trying to escape, walking for hundreds of yards within the confines of their pen, carrying the weight of the cumbersome box on legs which are cruelly positioned for walking. They don't feel that the contest is unfair; they keep plugging, rolling like sailorly souls— a bobbing, infirm gait, a brave, sea-legged momentum—stopping occasionally to study the lay of the land. For me, anyway, they manage to contain the rest of the animal world. They can stretch out their necks like a giraffe, or loom underwater like an apocryphal hippo. They browse on lettuce thrown on the water like a cow moose which is partly submerged. They have a penguin's alertness, combined with a build like a Brontosaurus when they rise up on tiptoe. Then they hunch and ponderously lunge like a grizzly going forward.

Baby turtles in a turtle bowl are a puzzle in geometrics. They're as deco- 7
rative as pansy petals, but they are also self-directed building blocks, prop- ping themselves on one another in different arrangements, before upending the tower. The timid individuals turn fearless, or vice versa. If one gets a bit arrogant he will push the others off the rock and afterwards climb down into the water and cling to the back of one of these he has bullied, tickling him with his hind feet until be bucks like a bronco. On the other hand, when this same milder-mannered fellow isn't exerting himself, he will stare right into the face of the sun for hours. What could be more lionlike. And he's at home in or out of the water and does lots of metaphysical tilting. He sinks and rises, with an infinity of levels to choose from; or, elongating himself, he climbs out on the land again to perambulate, sits boxed in his box, and finally slides back in the water, submerging into dreams.

I have five of these babies in a kidney-shaped bowl. The hatchling, who 8
is a painted turtle, is not as large as the top joint of my thumb. He eats chicken gladly. Other foods he will attempt to eat but not with sufficient perseverance to succeed because he's so little. The yellow-bellied terrapin is probably a year- ling, and he eats salad voraciously, but no meat, fish or fowl. The Cumber- land terrapin won't touch salad or chicken but eats fish and all of the meats except for bacon. The little snapper, with a black crenelated shell, feasts on any kind of meat, but rejects greens and fish. The fifth of the turtles is African. I acquired him only recently and don't know him well. A mottled brown, he unnerves the green turtles, dragging their food off to his lairs. He doesn't seem to want to be green—he bites the algae off his shell, hanging meanwhile at daring, steep, head-first angles.

The snapper was a Ferdinand until I provided him with deeper water. 9
Now he snaps at my pencil with his downturned and fearsome mouth, his

swollen face like a napalm victim's. The Cumberland has an elliptical red mark on the side of his green-and-yellow head. He is benign by nature and ought to be as elegant as his scientific name (*Pseudemys scripta elegans*), except he has contracted a disease of the air bladder which has permanently inflated it; he floats high in the water at an undignified slant and can't go under. There may have been internal bleeding, too, because his carapace is stained along its ridge. Unfortunately, like flowers, baby turtles often die. Their mouths fill up with a white fugus and their lungs with pneumonia. Their organs clog up from the rust in the water, or diet troubles, and, like a dying man's, their eyes and heads become too prominent. Toward the end, the edge of the shell becomes flabby as felt and folds around them like a shroud.

While they live they're like puppies. Although they're vivacious, they would be a bore to be with all the time, so I also have an adult wood turtle about six inches long. Her shell is the equal of any seashell for sculpturing, even a Cellini shell; it's like an old, dusty, richly engraved medallion dug out of a hillside. Her legs are salmon-orange bordered with black and protected by canted, heroic scales. Her plastron—the bottom shell—is splotched like a margay cat's coat, with black ocelli on a yellow background. It is convex to make room for the female organs inside, whereas a male's would be concave to help him fit tightly on top of her. Altogether, she exhibits every camouflage color on her limbs and shells. She has a turtleneck neck, a tail like an elephant's, wise old pachydermatous hind legs and the face of a turkey—except that when I carry her she gazes at the passing ground with a hawk's eye and mouth. Her feet fit to the fingers of my hand, one to each one, and she rides looking down. She can walk on the floor in perfect silence, but usually she lets her shell knock portentously, like a footstep, so that she resembles some grand, concise, slow-moving id. But if an earthworm is presented, she jerks swiftly ahead, poises above it and strikes like a mongoose, consuming it with wild vigor. Yet she will climb on my lap to eat bread or boiled eggs.

If put into a creek, she swims like a cutter, nosing forward to intercept a strange turtle and smell him. She drifts with the current to go downstream, maneuvering behind a rock when she wants to take stock, or sinking to the nether levels, while bubbles float up. Getting out, choosing her path, she will proceed a distance and dig into a pile of humus, thrusting herself to the coolest layer at the bottom. The hole closes over her until it's as small as a mouse's hole. She's not as aquatic as a musk turtle, not quite as terrestrial as the box turtles in the same woods, but because of her versatility she's marvelous, she's everywhere. And though she breathes the way we breathe, with scarcely perceptible movements of her chest, sometimes instead she pumps her throat ruminatively, like a pipe smoker sucking and puffing. She waits and blinks, pumping her throat, turning her head, then sets off like a loping tiger in slow motion, hurdling the jungly lumber, the pea vine and twigs. She estimates angles so well that when she rides over the rocks, sliding down a drop-off with her rugged front legs extended, she has the grace of a rodeo mare.

But she's well off to be with me rather than at Mud Pond. The other tur- 12
tles have fled—those that aren't baked into the bottom. Creeping up the brooks
to sad, constricted marshes, burdened as they are with that box on their backs,
they're walking into a setup where all their enemies move thirty times faster
than they. It's like the nightmare most of us have whimpered through, where
we are weighted down disastrously while trying to flee; fleeing our home
ground, we try to run.

I've seen turtles in still worse straits. On Broadway, in New York, there 13
is a penny arcade which used to sell baby terrapins that were scrawled with
bon mots in enamel paint, such as KISS MY BABY. The manager turned out to
be a wholesaler as well, and once I asked him whether he had any larger turtles to sell. He took me upstairs to a loft room devoted to the turtle business.
There were desks for the paper work and a series of racks that held shallow
tin bins atop one another, each with several hundred babies crawling around
in it. He was a smudgy-complexioned, serious fellow and he did have a few
adult terrapins, but I was going to school and wasn't actually planning to buy;
I'd only wanted to see them. They were aquatic turtles but here they went
without water, presumably for weeks, lurching about in those dry bins like
handicapped citizens, living on gumption. An easel where the artist worked
stood in the middle of the floor. She had a palette and a clip attachment for
fastening the babies in place. She wore a smock and a beret, and was homely,
short and eccentric-looking, with funny black hair, like some of the ladies who
show their paintings in Washington Square in May. She had a cold, she was
smoking, and her hand wasn't very steady, although she worked quickly
enough. The smile that she produced for me would have looked giddy if she
had been happier, or drunk. Of course the turtles' doom was sealed when she
painted them, because their bodies inside would continue to grow but their
shells would not. Gradually, invisibly, they would be crushed. Around us their
bellies—two thousand belly shells—rubbed on the bins with a mournful, mo-
mentous hiss.

Somehow there were so many of them I didn't rescue one. Years later, 14
however, I was walking on First Avenue when I noticed a basket of living turtles in front of a fish store. They were as dry as a heap of old bones in the
sun; nevertheless, they were creeping over one another gimpily, doing their
best to escape. I looked and was touched to discover that they appeared to
be wood turtles, my favorites, so I bought one. In my apartment I looked
closer and realized that in fact this was a diamondback terrapin, which was
bad news. Diamondbacks are tidewater turtles from brackish estuaries, and I
had no sea water to keep him in. He spent his days thumping interminably
against the baseboards, pushing for an opening through the wall. He drank
thirstily but would not eat and had none of the hearty, accepting qualities of
wood turtles. He was morose, paler in color, sleeker and more Oriental in the
carved ridges and rings that formed his shell. Though I felt sorry for him, finally I found his unrelenting presence exasperating. I carried him, struggling
in a paper bag, across town to the Morton Street Pier on the Hudson. It was

August but gray and windy. He was very surprised when I tossed him in; for the first time in our association, I think, he was afraid. He looked afraid as he bobbed about on top of the water, looking up at me from ten feet below. Though we were both accustomed to his resistance and rigidity, seeing him still pitiful, I recognized that I must have done the wrong thing. At least the river was salty, but it was also bottomless; the waves were too rough for him, and the tide was coming in, bumping him against the pilings underneath the pier. Too late, I realized that he wouldn't be able to swim to a peaceful inlet in New Jersey, even if he could figure out which way to swim. But since, short of diving in after him, there was nothing I could do, I walked away.

✳

RESPONDING TO THE WHOLE ESSAY

1. Is Hoagland's purpose chiefly to give his reader information about turtles, to convey his own feelings toward them, or to persuade the reader to adopt his view of them? Support your answer with evidence. Whichever aim is primary, can you point to evidence of the others? [*Harbrace* 28a; *Hodges'* 32a]
2. What audience is Hoagland writing for? What elements of diction, tone, and organization help you to characterize the audience? [*Harbrace* 28a and 29a; *Hodges'* 32a and 33a]
3. Descriptive writing is usually found in combination with other methods of development. What other methods does Hoagland rely on in "The Courage of Turtles"? Point to instances of each. [*Harbrace* 27d; *Hodges'* 31d]
4. Who is the turtle's greatest enemy? How does that idea inform the entire essay? [*Harbrace* 28d; *Hodges'* 32d]
5. Explain how "bucks like a bronco" and "What could be more lionlike?" in the fourth and sixth sentences of paragraph 7 establish a connection between that paragraph and the previous one. Find several other examples of Hoagland's picking up a thread from an earlier part of the essay and weaving it in. What quality does the essay gain from this technique? [*Harbrace* 27b; *Hodges'* 31b]
6. Comment on the tone of this essay: How does Hoagland manage to convey his love of and admiration for turtles without falling into sentimentality? What keeps the conclusion from becoming maudlin? [*Harbrace* 29a and 28f; *Hodges'* 33a and 32f]

ANALYZING THE ELEMENTS

Grammar

1. In the third sentence of paragraph 1, what does the phrase "being humble creatures" modify? What does it add to the sentence? [*Harbrace* 1d and 4; *Hodges'* 1d and 4]
2. Explain why no coordinating conjunction is necessary between the last two independent clauses of the fifth sentence of paragraph 11. [*Harbrace* 3a; *Hodges'* 3a]

Effective Sentences

1. In the third sentence of paragraph 3 Hoagland repeats the word *bulldozed*. What is the effect of this repetition? How is repetition used for effect in the fifth sentence of paragraph 5? [*Harbrace* 11e; *Hodges'* 29e]
2. In the seventh sentence of paragraph 3 (beginning "But this time . . ."), how does coordination contribute to the force of the paragraph?
3. What effect does beginning the fourth sentence of paragraph 8 with the object rather than the subject have? Would the sentence have been as effective if it had been written in the normal order? Why or why not? [*Harbrace* 11f; *Hodges'* 29f]
4. Explain how the participial phrases in the third sentence of paragraph 12 contribute to sentence variety. [*Harbrace* 12b; *Hodges'* 30b]

Punctuation and Mechanics

1. Why is the last sentence of paragraph 4 in parentheses? Does the sentence contribute to the development of Hoagland's description of turtles' intelligence? How? What, if anything, would be lost by omitting the sentence? [*Harbrace* 21f; *Hodges'* 17f]
2. Explain Hoagland's use of the colon in the eighth sentence of paragraph 5. [*Harbrace* 21d; *Hodges'* 17d]
3. Why are italics used in the fourth sentence of paragraph 9? [*Harbrace* 24a; *Hodges'* 10a]

Diction

1. In the last sentence of paragraph 3, how does the phrase "another poor puddle" contrast with the rest of the sentence? What is the effect of this contrast?
2. Figurative language plays a large part in creating the tone of Hoagland's essay. Explain how the following examples of figurative language contribute to the tone: "with the suddenness of two dogs who have been conversing in tones too low for an onlooker to hear," "rolling like sailorly souls—a bobbing, infirm gait, a brave, sea-legged momentum" (paragraph 6); "as decorative as pansy petals" (paragraph 7); "The snapper was a Ferdinand," "like a napalm victim's," "like flowers, baby turtles often die," "like a dying man's, their eyes and heads become too prominent," "folds around them like a shroud" (paragraph 9); "swims like a cutter" (paragraph 11); "It's like the nightmare most of us have whimpered through" (paragraph 12); "lurching about in those dry bins like handicapped citizens, living on gumption," "like some of the ladies who show their paintings in Washington Square in May" (paragraph 13); "as dry as a heap of old bones in the sun" (paragraph 14). [*Harbrace* 14a(5); *Hodges'* 20a(4)]
3. Comment on the meaning and appropriateness of the following words: *carnivores* and *inscrutable* (paragraph 1, last two sentences); *untoward* (paragraph 3, first sentence); *cumbersome* and *apocryphal* (paragraph 6, third and sixth sentences); *metaphysical* (paragraph 7, next-to-last sentence); *carapace* (paragraph 9, fifth sentence); *canted, ocelli, portentously,* and *id* (paragraph 10, fourth, fifth, and tenth sentences); *ruminatively* (paragraph 11, sixth sentence); *gimpily, interminably,* and *morose* (paragraph 14, third, seventh, and ninth sentences). [*Harbrace* 14a(3); *Hodges'* 20a(2)]

BUILDING VOCABULARY

1. Define *voracious*. What Latin root does *voracious* come from? What does it mean?
2. List and define three synonyms for *voracious*. Write sentences using each of these synonyms.

SUGGESTIONS FOR WRITING

1. Write an essay describing some kind of creature you find especially appealing (for example, birds, cats, spiders, armadillos, dinosaurs). If no creature appeals to you, write on one you especially dislike. Try to write your description, as Hoagland does, with both facts and feelings, finding some personal perspective or angle that will help you achieve the tone you want.
2. Write an essay describing some occasion when, perhaps by accident or inattention, you unwittingly violated some principle you believed in strongly. Strive to maintain as matter-of-fact an approach as Hoagland does in his conclusion.

Creation Stories
Barbara Kingsolver

Barbara Kingsolver (1955–   ) is the author of four best-selling and award-winning novels, *The Bean Trees, Homeland, Animal Dreams,* and *Pigs in Heaven.* Along with writing novels, Kingsolver writes poetry and short stories, and she has published two nonfiction works, including *Holding the Line* and *High Tide in Tucson,* a collection of twenty-five essays in which "Creation Stories" appears. In "Creation Stories," Kingsolver draws from her training as a biologist and her deep understanding of the mythological stories that hold together the culture to create a distinct picture of the landscape and people of southern Arizona.

June is the cruelest month in Tucson, especially when it lasts till the end 1
of July. This is the season when every living thing in the desert swoons south toward some faint salt dream of the Gulf of Mexico: tasting the horizon, waiting for the summer storms. This year they are late. The birds are pacing the ground stiff-legged, panting, and so am I. Waiting. In this blind, bright still-June weather the shrill of the cicadas hurts your eyes. Every plant looks pitiful and, when you walk past it, moans a little, envious because you can walk yourself to a drink and it can't.

The water that came last winter is long gone. "Female rain," it's called 2
in Navajo: the gentle, furtive rains that fall from overcast skies between November and March. That was weather to drink and to grow on. But not to remember, anymore than a child remembers last birthday's ice cream, once the months have passed without another drop. In June there is no vital sign, not so much as a humid breath against a pane of glass, till the summer storms arrive. What we're waiting for now is male rain. Big, booming wait-till-your-father-gets-home cloudbursts that bully up from Mexico and threaten to rip the sky.

The Tohono O'odham have lived in the Sonoran Desert longer than any- 3
one else who's still living; their answer to this season is to make frothy wine from the ripe saguaro fruits; and drink it all day and all night in a do-or-die ceremony to bring down the first storm. When it comes, the answer to a desert's one permanent question, that first storm defines the beginning of the Tohono O'odham new year. The storms themselves are enough to get drunk on: ferocious thunder and raindrops splatting so hard on the cooked ground you hear the thing approaching like mortar fire.

112

I saw my first of these summer storms in 1978. I hadn't been in Arizona   4
long enough to see the calendar open and close, so I spent the early summer
in a state of near panic, as the earliest people in any place must have done
when they touched falling snow or the dry season's dust and asked each time:
This burning cold, these dying plants—is this, then, the end of the world?

I lived in a little stuccoed house in a neighborhood of barking dogs and   5
front-yard shrines to the Virgin of Guadalupe. One sweltering afternoon I
heard what I believed must be kids throwing gravel at the houses, relentlessly
and with feeling. It was hot enough so that the neighborhood, all of it, dogs
and broken glass on the sidewalks included, had murder in mind. I knew I
was risking my neck to go outside and scold kids for throwing rocks, but I
went anyway. What I saw from the front stoop arrested me in my footprints:
not a troop of juvenile delinquents, but a black sky and a wall of water as
high as heaven, moving up the block. I ran into the street barefoot and danced
with my mouth open. So did half my neighbors. Armistice Day.

Now I live on the outskirts of town, in the desert at the foot of the Tuc-   6
son Mountains, where waiting for the end of the drought becomes an obsession. It's literally 110 degrees in the shade today, the kind of weather real
southwesterners love to talk about. We have our own kind of Jack London
thing, in reverse: Remember that year (swagger, thumbs in the belt) when it
was 122 degrees and planes couldn't land at the airport?

This is actually true. For years I held the colorful impression that the tar-   7
mac had liquefied, so that aircraft would have plowed into it like mammoth
flies bellying into ointment. Eventually an engineer gave me a pedestrian, probably accurate, explanation about heat interfering with the generation of lift
above the wings. Either way, weather that stops modern air traffic is high
drama in America.

We revel in our misery only because we know the end, when it comes, is   8
so good. One day there will be a crackling, clean, creosote smell in the air
and the ground will be charged and the hair on your arms will stand on end
and then BOOM, you are thrillingly drenched. All the desert toads crawl out
of their burrows, swell out their throats, and scream for sex while the pud-
dles last. The ocotillos leaf out before your eyes, like a nature show on fast
forward. There is so little time before the water sizzles back to thin air again.
So little time to live a whole life in the desert. This is elemental mortality, the
root of all passion.

Since I moved to this neighborhood of desert, I've learned I have other   9
writers for neighbors. Unlike the toads, we're shy—we don't advertise our
presence to each other quite so ostentatiously. In fact, I only found out I'd
joined a literary commune when my UPS man—I fancy him a sort of manly
Dorothy Parker in uniform—began giving me weekly updates. Visitors up at
Silko's had been out looking for wild pigs, and Mr. Abbey had gone out in
his backyard and shot the TV, again. (Sad to say, that doesn't happen anymore. We all miss Ed.)

I imagine other neighbors: that Georgia O'Keeffe, for example, is out there   10
walking the hills in sturdy shoes, staring down the UPS man with such a fierce
eye that he will never dare tell.

What is it that draws creators to this place? Low rent, I tell my friends   11
who ask, but it's more than that. It's the Southwest: a prickly land where
mountain lions make bets with rabbits, and rabbits can win. Where nature
rubs belly to belly with subdivision and barrio, and coyotes take shortcuts
through the back alleys. Here even the rain has gender, the frogs sing carpe
diem, and fast teenage girls genuflect quickly toward the door of the church,
hedging their bets, as they walk to school in tight skirts and shiny high heels.

When I drive to the post office every few days to pick up my mail, it's   12
only about twelve miles round trip, but I pass through at least half-a-dozen
neighborhoods that distinguish themselves one from the other by architecture
and language and even, especially, creation myth. First among them is the
neighborhood of jackrabbits and saguaros, who imperiously tolerate my home,
though I can't speak their language or quite understand their myths.

Then, just inside the city limits, a red cobble of just-alike roofs—paved   13
air—where long strands of exurban condominiums shelter immigrants from
Wisconsin, maybe, or Kansas, who dream in green and hug small irrigated
lawns to their front doors.

Next I cross the bridge over the Santa Cruz, whose creation story bub-   14
bles from ephemeral springs in the mountains of southern Arizona and Mexico. In these lean days she's a great blank channel of sand, but we call her a
river anyway, and say it with a straight face too, because in her moods this
saint has taken out bridges and houses and people who loved their lives.

Then I pass under the artery of Interstate 10, which originates in Los An-   15
geles or Jacksonville, Florida, depending on your view of destiny; and the railroad track, whose legend is a tale tasting of dynamite, the lives and deaths of
immigrants who united a continent and divided in twain the one great original herd of American bison.

Then without warning I am smack in the middle of a Yaqui village that   16
is fringe-edged and small like a postage stamp, and every bit alive. Despite its
size, Pascua Yaqui is a sovereign world; I come here every Easter to watch an
irresistible pageant combining deer dances with crucifixion. Like the Tohono
O'odham singing down the rain, the masked Yaqui dancers listen for the heartbeat of creation, and keep a promise with every vernal equinox to hold the
world to its rightful position. On this small patch of dusty ground, the religion of personal salvation is eclipsed by a faith whose question and answer
are matters of order in the universe. Religion of that kind can crack your mind
open the way lightning splits a pine, leaving the wind to howl through the
scorched divide. I can hardly ever even drive through here, in my serviceable
old Toyota, without biting my lip and considering immensity.

Calle Ventura marks the entrance to another state, where on a fine, still   17
day your nose can compare the goods from three tortilla factories. From here

the sidewalks roll, the walls crumble and shout with territorial inscription, brown dogs lie under cherry Camaros and the Virgin of Guadalupe holds court in the parking lot of the Casa Rey apartments.

Across the street stands the post office, neutral territory: mailboxes all 18 identical, regardless of the keyholder's surname, as physically uniform as a table of contents. We are all equals in the eyes of the USPO, containing our secrets. I grab mine and scuttle away. The trip home takes me right back through all these lands again, all these creation stories, and that's enough culture for one day, usually.

I close the door, breathless, and stare out my window at a landscape of 19 wonders thrown together with no more thought than a rainstorm or a volcano can invoke on its own behalf. It's exactly as John Muir said, as if "nature in wildest extravagance held her bravest structures as common as gravelpiles."

From here I begin my story. I can't think of another place like it. 20

✳

RESPONDING TO THE WHOLE ESSAY

1. Throughout "Creation Stories," Kingsolver develops a connection between humans and nature. What evidence can you find in the essay suggesting that nature influences human creations? that humans influence the creation of natural phenomena?
2. Does Kingsolver assume her readers may already be acquainted with the cultures or traditions of the Native American nations in the Southwest? Find specifics in the essay to support your answer. What else can you say about the audience Kingsolver had in mind? [*Harbrace* 28a; *Hodges'* 32a]
3. How does Kingsolver achieve coherence in paragraph 11? Explain. [*Harbrace* 27b(2); *Hodges'* 31b(2)]
4. Comment upon the linking of paragraphs 14 and 15. [*Harbrace* 27b(6); *Hodges'* 31b(6)]
5. Consider the first sentence of the final paragraph. How might this statement influence the reader's expectations about the essay? Explain.

ANALYZING THE ELEMENTS

Grammar

1. Comment upon the grammatical function of the two phrases separating the subject and verb of the third sentence of paragraph 5. Why do you think Kingsolver chooses to include both of these phrases here? [*Harbrace* 1d; *Hodges'* 1d]
2. *Webster's Collegiate Dictionary* indicates that *pedestrian* functions as a noun or an adjective. What is the grammatical function of *pedestrian* in the third sentence of paragraph 7? [*Harbrace* 1c; *Hodges'* 1c]

Effective Sentences

1. The fourth statement in paragraph 2 is a fragment, but it is legitimate. What effect does Kingsolver achieve by using a fragment instead of a complete sentence here? Can you find other fragments in "Creation Stories"? Do they achieve similar rhetorical effects? Explain. [*Harbrace* 2; *Hodges'* 2]
2. Compare the third sentence of paragraph 9 (beginning "In fact, . . .") with the alternative: "In fact, I only found out I'd joined a literary commune when my UPS man began giving me weekly updates. I fancy him a sort of manly Dorothy Parker in uniform." How does this revision of the third sentence affect the coherence of paragraph 9? [*Harbrace* 27a and 27b; *Hodges'* 31a and 31b]
3. The fifth sentence of paragraph 8 could be rewritten: The water quickly sizzles back into thin air. What does Kingsolver achieve by beginning the sentence with the expletive *There is*? [*Harbrace* 7a(5) and 11f; *Hodges'* 6a(5) and 29f]
4. The second sentence of paragraph 3 includes an introductory clause and an appositive phrase. Does the appositive phrase explain, or identify, the introductory clause or the main subject or both? How might the sentence be rewritten to clarify the relationship between the appositive phrase and the element in supplements? [*Harbrace* 1d; *Hodges'* 1d]

Punctuation and Mechanics

1. Comment upon the use of commas in the last sentence of paragraph 1. How might this sentence be rewritten to eliminate the need for these commas? [*Harbrace* 17d; *Hodges'* 12d]
2. Explain the combination of the colon and dashes in the second sentence of paragraph 4. [*Harbrace* 21d and 21e; *Hodges'* 17d and 17e]
3. Why does Kingsolver capitalize *BOOM* in the second sentence of paragraph 8?

Diction

1. Explain the use of hyphens in *wait-till-your-father-gets-home* in the last sentence of paragraph 2 and *do-or-die* in the first sentence of paragraph 3. Can you find similar uses of the hyphen in this essay? [*Harbrace* 22f; *Hodges'* 18f]
2. Kingsolver makes use of several metaphors and similes in "Creation Stories." Comment upon the similes in the fifth sentence of paragraph 5 and the second sentence in paragraph 7. What metaphors can you find? [*Harbrace* 14a(5); *Hodges'* 20a(4)]

BUILDING VOCABULARY

1. From what Latin roots are *vernal* and *equinox* borrowed? What do they mean? Define *vernal equinox*.
2. What are the Greek roots from which the word *ephemeral* is derived? What do they mean? Write a sentence with a word derived from one of these Greek roots.

SUGGESTIONS FOR WRITING

1. Using concrete details, write a short essay describing your hometown or neighborhood.
2. Describe how an extremely hot summer ~~or unusually cold winter~~ influenced how you behaved or how you viewed your environment.

Borders

Barry Lopez

Since 1970, Barry Lopez has written of natural history and the environment for such publications as *The New York Times*, the *Washington Post, National Geographic,* and *Antaeus.* He is also a contributing editor to the *North American Review* and *Harper's.* His books include *Desert Notes* (1976), *Of Wolves and Men* (1978), *Giving Birth to Thunder* (1978), *River Notes* (1979), *Winter Count* (1981), *Arctic Dreams* (1986), *Crossing Open Ground* (1988), *Crow and Weasel* (1990), and *The Rediscovery of North America* (1991). In 1979 Lopez won the John Burroughs Medal, the Christopher Medal, and the Pacific Northwest Booksellers Award; in 1982, the Friends of American Writers Award for fiction; in 1986, the National Book Award and American Academy and Institute of Arts and Letters Award; in 1987, a John Simon Guggenheim Foundation Fellowship as well as a second Christopher Medal and Pacific Northwest Booksellers Award; and in 1990, the Governor's Award for the arts and the Lannan Foundation Award. Lopez's works have been translated into eleven languages. Born in Port Chester, New York, in 1945, Lopez holds BA and MA degrees from Notre Dame University and did graduate work at the University of Oregon. He is a member of the Author's Guild, PEN, and Poets and Writers. "Borders," from *Crossing Open Ground,* was first printed in *Country Journal.*

In early September, the eastern Arctic coast of Alaska shows several faces, 1
most of them harsh. But there are days when the wind drops and the sky is clear, and for reasons too fragile to explain—the overflight of thousands of migrating ducks, the bright, silent austerity of the Romanzof Mountains under fresh snow, the glassy stillness of the ocean—these days have an edge like no others. The dawn of such a clear and windless day is cherished against memories of late August snow squalls and days of work in rough water under leaden skies.

One such morning, a few of us on a biological survey in the Beaufort Sea 2
set that work aside with hardly a word and headed east over the water for the international border, where the state of Alaska abuts the Yukon Territory. The fine weather encouraged this bit of adventure.

There are no settlements along this part of the Arctic coast. We did not 3
in fact know if the border we were headed to was even marked. A northeast wind that had been driving loose pack ice close to shore for several days forced us to run near the beach in a narrow band of open water. In the lee of larger

pieces of sea ice, the ocean had begun to freeze, in spite of the strong sunlight and a benign feeling in the air. Signs of winter.

As we drove toward Canada, banking the open, twenty-foot boat in grace- 4
ful arcs to avoid pieces of drift ice, we hung our heads far back to watch migrating Canada geese and black brant pass over. Rifling past us and headed west at fifty miles an hour a foot off the water were flocks of old-squaw, twenty and thirty ducks at a time. Occasionally, at the edge of the seaward ice, the charcoal-gray snout of a ringed seal would break the calm surface of the ocean for breath.

We drew nearer the border, wondering aloud how we would know it. I 5
remembered a conversation of years before, with a man who had escaped from Czechoslovakia to come to America and had later paddled a canoe the length of the Yukon. He described the border where the river crossed into Alaska as marked by a great swath cut through the spruce forest. In the middle of nowhere, I said ruefully; what a waste of trees, how ugly it must have seemed. He looked silently across the restaurant table at me and said it was the easiest border crossing of his life.

I thought, as we drove on east, the ice closing in more now, forcing us to 6
run yet closer to the beach, of the geographer Carl Sauer and his concept of biologically distinct regions. The idea of bioregionalism, as it has been developed by his followers, is a political concept that would reshape human life. It would decentralize residents of an area into smaller, more self-sufficient, environmentally responsible units, occupying lands the borders of which would be identical with the borders of natural regions—watersheds, for example. I thought of Sauer because we were headed that day for a great, invisible political dividing line: 141 degrees western longitude. Like the border between Utah and Colorado, this one is arbitrary. If it were not actually marked— staked—it would not be discernible. Sauer's borders are noticeable. Even the birds find them.

On the shore to our right, as we neared the mouth of Demarcation Bay, 7
we saw the fallen remains of an Eskimo sod house, its meat-drying racks, made of driftwood, leaning askew. Someone who had once come this far to hunt had built the house. The house eventually became a dot on U.S. Coast and Geodetic Survey maps. Now its location is vital to the Inuit, for it establishes a politically important right of prior use, predating the establishment of the Arctic National Wildlife Refuge, within whose borders it has been included. I recall all this as we pass, from poring over our detailed maps the night before. Now, with the warmth of sunlight on the side of my face, with boyhood thoughts of the Yukon Territory welling up inside, the nearness of friends, with whom work has been satisfaction these past few weeks, I have no desire to see maps.

Ahead, it is becoming clear that the closing ice is going to force us right 8
up on the beach before long. The wedge of open water is narrowing. What there is is very still, skimmed with fresh slush ice. I think suddenly of my

brother, who lives in a house on Black Island, off the coast of Rhode Island. When I visit we walk and drive around the island. Each time I mean to ask him, does he feel any more ordered in his life for being able to see so clearly the boundary between the ocean and the land in every direction? But I am never able to phrase the question right. And the old and dour faces of the resident islanders discourage it.

Far ahead, through a pair of ten-power binoculars, I finally see what   9
appears to be a rampart of logs, weathered gray-white and standing on a bluff where the tundra falls off fifteen or twenty feet to the beach. Is this the border?

We are breaking ice now with the boat. At five miles an hour, the bow   10
wave skitters across the frozen surface of the ocean to either side in a hundred broken fragments. The rumbling that accompanies this shattering of solid ice is like the low-throttled voice of the outboard engines. Three or four hundred yards of this and we stop. The pack ice is within twenty feet of the beach. We cannot go any farther. That we are only a hundred feet from our destination seems a part of the day, divinely fortuitous.

We climb up the bluff. Arctic-fox tracks in the patchy snow are fresh.   11
Here and there on the tundra are bird feathers, remnants of the summer molt of hundreds of thousands of birds that have come this far north to nest, whose feathers blow inland and out to sea for weeks. Although we see no animals but a flock of snow geese in the distance, evidence of their residence and passage is everywhere. Within a few hundred feet I find caribou droppings. On a mossy tundra mound, like one a jaeger might use, I find two small bones that I know to be a ptarmigan's.

We examine the upright, weathered logs and decide on the basis of these   12
and several pieces of carved wood that this is, indeed, the border. No one, we reason, would erect something like this on a coast so unfrequented by humans if it were not. (This coast is ice-free only eight or ten weeks in the year.) Yet we are not sure. The bluff has a certain natural prominence, though the marker's placement seems arbitrary. But the romance of it—this foot in Canada, that one in Alaska—is fetching. The delightful weather and the presence of undisturbed animals has made us almost euphoric. It is, after days of bottom trawls in thirty-one-degree water, of cold hours of patient searching for seals, so clearly a holiday for us.

I will fly over this same spot a week later, under a heavy overcast, forced   13
down to two hundred feet above the water in a search for migrating bowhead whales. That trip, from the small settlement of Inuvik on the East Channel of the Mackenzie River in the Northwest Territories to Deadhorse, Alaska, will make this border both more real and more peculiar than it now appears. We will delay our arrival by circling over Inuvik until a Canadian customs officer can get there from the village of Tuktoyaktuk on the coast, though all we intend to do is to drop off an American scientist and buy gas. On our return trip we are required by law to land at the tiny village of Kaktovik to check through U.S. Customs. The entry through Kaktovik is so tenuous as to not

exist at all. One might land, walk the mile to town, and find or not find the customs officer around. Should he not be there, the law requires we fly 250 miles south to Fort Yukon. If no one is there we are to fly on to Fairbanks before returning to Deadhorse on the coast, in order to reenter the country legally. These distances are immense. We could hardly carry the fuel for such a trip. And to fly inland would mean not flying the coast to look for whales, the very purpose of being airborne. We fly straight to Deadhorse, looking for whales. When we land we fill out forms to explain our actions and file them with the government.

Here, standing on the ground, the border seems nearly whimsical. The view over tens of square miles of white, frozen ocean and a vast expanse of tundra which rolls to the foot of snow-covered mountains is unimpeded. Such open space, on such a calm and innocent day as this, gives extraordinary release to the imagination. At such a remove—from horrible images of human death on borders ten thousand miles away, from the press of human anxiety one feels in a crowded city—at such a remove one is lulled nearly to foundering by the simple peace engendered, even at the border between two nations, by a single day of good weather.

As we turn to leave the monument, we see two swans coming toward us. They are immature tundra swans, in steel-gray plumage. Something odd is in their shape. Primary feathers. They have no primary feathers yet. Too young. And their parents, who should be with them, are nowhere to be seen. They are coming from the east, from Canada, paddling in a strip of water a few inches deep right at the edge of the beach. They show no fear of us, although they slow and are cautious. They extend their necks and open their pink bills to make gentle, rattling sounds. As they near the boat they stand up in the water and step ashore. They walk past us and on up the beach. Against the gritty coarseness of beach sand and the tundra-stained ice, their smooth gray feathers and the deep lucidity of their eyes vibrate with beauty. I watch them until they disappear from view. The chance they will be alive in two weeks is very slim. Perhaps it doesn't exist at all.

In two weeks I am thousands of miles south. In among the letters and magazines in six weeks of mail sitting on the table is a thick voter-registration pamphlet. One afternoon I sit down and read it. I try to read it with the conscientiousness of one who wishes to vote wisely. I think of Carl Sauer, whose ideas I admire. And of Wendell Berry, whose integrity and sense of land come to mind when I ponder any vote and the effect it might have. I think of the invisible borders of rural landscapes, of Frost pondering the value of fences. I read in the pamphlet of referendums on statewide zoning and of the annexation of rural lands, on which I am expected to vote. I read of federal legislative reapportionment and the realignment of my county's border with that of an Indian reservation, though these will not require my vote. I must review, again, how the districts of my state representative and state senator overlap and determine if I am included now within the bounds of a newly created county commissioner's territory.

These lines blur and I feel a choking coming up in my neck and my face   17
flushing. I set the pamphlet on the arm of the chair and get up and walk outside. It is going to take weeks, again, to get home.

❋

RESPONDING TO THE WHOLE ESSAY

1. Does Lopez ever state his purpose for writing "Borders"? If so, where? If not,
    what do you think his purpose is? [*Harbrace* 28a; *Hodges'* 32a]
2. As nearly as you can, describe the audience you think Lopez is writing for. [*Har-
    brace* 28a; *Hodges'* 32a]
3. What sensory details does Lopez use in his description of the Alaskan wilderness,
    the border country, and borders themselves? What is the effect of such details on
    the reader? [*Harbrace* 27c; *Hodges'* 31c]
4. Comment on the title of Lopez's essay. Explain how borders as a metaphor uni-
    fies the essay. [*Harbrace* 27a and 28f(3); *Hodges'* 31a and 32f(3)]
5. Why does Lopez bring up the voter registration packet that awaited him in his
    mail? How does this packet help Lopez to make a comment on borders?
6. Consider the coherence of paragraph 16. What transitional devices help to link
    the sentences to each other? Do any of the sentences establish links to other para-
    graphs? [*Harbrace* 27b; *Hodges'* 31b]

ANALYZING THE ELEMENTS

Grammar

1. What is the function of the clause "What there is" in the third sentence of para-
    graph 8 and of the clause, "That we are only a hundred feet from our destina-
    tion" in the last sentence of paragraph 10? [*Harbrace* 1e; *Hodges'* 1e]
2. The fourth sentence of paragraph 10 is elliptical. Supply the missing element(s).
    Why do you think Lopez chose to make this sentence elliptical? [*Harbrace* 2;
    Hodges's 2]
3. Comment upon the agreement of subject and verb in the seventh sentence of para-
    graph 12. [*Harbrace* 7a; *Hodges'* 6a]

Effective Sentences

1. Paragraph 8 contains several sentences that some might describe as short and
    choppy. Why do you think Lopez chose to write them this way? What effect do
    they convey? [*Harbrace* 9a; *Hodges'* 24a]
2. Lopez uses two periodic sentences, one in paragraph 6 and another in paragraph
    7. Identify which are the periodic sentences and comment upon why they are or
    are not effective. [*Harbrace* 11b; *Hodges'* 29b]
3. Comment upon the inversion of subject and verb in sentence two of paragraph
    11. [*Harbrace* 11f; *Hodges'* 29f]

Punctuation and Mechanics

1. Justify the punctuation of the fourth sentence of paragraph 5. [*Harbrace* 17 and 18; *Hodges'* 12 and 14]
2. Comment upon Lopez's use of dashes in the second sentence of paragraph 1, the third and sixth sentences of paragraph 6, the sixth sentence of paragraph 12, and the fourth sentence of paragraph 14. Are they all used for the same reason? If so, what is it? If not, what are the different reasons? Could any of the dashes be replaced by other marks of punctuation? What would be the effect? [*Harbrace* 21e; *Hodges'* 17e]
3. In the sixth sentence of paragraph 8, why does Lopez not enclose the question he means to ask his brother in quotation marks? [*Harbrace* 20a; *Hodges'* 14a]

Diction

1. Much of the effect of Lopez's description results from his careful use of vocabulary. Identify three sentences in which the vocabulary Lopez uses contributes to a sharp visual image. Find a sentence in which the vocabulary contributes to an auditory image. [*Harbrace* 14c; *Hodges'* 20c]
2. Why do you think Lopez chose to repeat the phrase "at such a remove" in the fourth sentence of paragraph 14? How do you justify this usage with the instructions given in Harbrace chapter 21? [*Harbrace* 15c and 11e; *Hodges'* 21c and 29e]
3. Look up the following words in your dictionary: *austerity* (paragraph 1), *abuts* (paragraph 2), *benign* (paragraph 3), *dour* (paragraph 8), *rampart* (paragraph 9), *fortuitous* (paragraph 10), *jaeger* (paragraph 11), *fetching* and *euphoric* (paragraph 12), *tenuous* (paragraph 13), and *unimpeded* (paragraph 14). [*Harbrace* 14c; *Hodges'* 20c]

BUILDING VOCABULARY

1. From what Latin roots is *abut* borrowed? What do they mean? Write a sentence with a word derived from one of these Latin roots.
2. Identify and define the Latin roots that *discern* comes from. Write a sentence using a word derived from one of these Latin roots.

SUGGESTIONS FOR WRITING

1. Think of a time when a scene you were viewing or a place you were visiting encouraged you to ponder the meaning of a particular feature of the place. Describe that place so that your reader can understand its significance to you.
2. Describe your feelings upon returning home from a lengthy trip. Some variations of this suggestion might be to describe how it feels to return to your family home after being away at school or after having established your own home, or even how you feel when you return to your own place after being at your family's home.

Loma Prieta
John McPhee

John McPhee (1931–   ) has been recognized as a key innovator of nonfiction writing. McPhee brought to nonfiction writing the objectivity of a journalist, a keen eye for detail, and an ability to arrange information so that it shows a story rather than tells it. His distinction as a writer became apparent as early as 1965, when *The New Yorker* published McPhee's creative profile of basketball player Bill Bradley. Shortly after the publication of this article, McPhee, then a writer for *Time* magazine, accepted the position of staff writer at *The New Yorker*. McPhee continues to write for *The New Yorker* and teaches a course entitled "The Literature of Fact" as Ferris Professor of Journalism at Princeton University. In addition, McPhee has written a number of best-selling books, including *Coming into the Country* and his four-book series about geology, collectively known as *Annals of the Former World*. In this selection, from *Assembling California*, the fourth book of the geology series, McPhee explains how the Loma Prieta earthquake of 1989 came to be and how it affected the people and landscape of California.

There is a swerve in the San Andreas Fault where it moves through the   1
Santa Cruz Mountains. It bends a little and then straightens again, like the track of a tire that was turned to avoid an animal. Because deviations in transform faults retard the sliding and help strain to build, the most pronounced ones are known as tectonic knots, or great asperities, or prominent restraining bends. The two greatest known earthquakes on the fault occurred at or close to prominent restraining bends. The little jog in the Santa Cruz Mountains is a modest asperity, but enough to tighten the lock. As the strain rises through the years, the scales of geologic time and human time draw ever closer, until they coincide. An earthquake is not felt everywhere at once. It travels in every direction—up, down, and sideways—from its place and moment of beginning. In this example, the precise moment is in the sixteenth second of the fifth minute after five in the afternoon, as the scales touch and the tectonic knot lets go.

The epicenter is in the Forest of Nisene Marks, a few hundred yards from   2
Trout Creek Gulch, five miles north of Monterey Bay. The most conspicuous nearby landmark is the mountain called Loma Prieta. In a curving small road in the gulch are closed gates and speed bumps. PRIVATE PROPERTY. KEEP OUT. This is steep terrain—roughed up, but to a greater extent serene. Under the redwoods are glades of maidenhair. There are fields of pampas grass, stands

of tan madrone. A house worth two million dollars is under construction, and will continue when this is over. BEWARE OF DOG.

Motion occurs fifty-nine thousand eight hundred feet down—the deepest hypocenter ever recorded on the San Andreas Fault. No drill hole made anywhere on earth for any purpose has reached so far. On the San Andreas, no earthquake is ever likely to reach deeper. Below sixty thousand feet, the rock is no longer brittle.   3

The epicenter, the point at the surface directly above the hypocenter, is four miles from the fault trace. Some geologists will wonder if the motion occurred in a blind thrust, but in the Santa Cruz Mountains the two sides of the San Andreas Fault are not vertical. The Pacific wall leans against the North American wall at about the angle of a ladder.   4

For seven to ten seconds, the deep rockfaces slide. The maximum jump is more than seven feet. Northwest and southeast, the slip propagates an aggregate twenty-five miles. This is not an especially large event. It is nothing like a plate-rupturing earthquake. Its upward motion stops twenty thousand feet below the surface. Even so, the slippage plane—where the two great slanting faces have moved against each other—is an irregular oval of nearly two hundred square miles. The released strain turns into waves, and they develop half a megaton of energy. Which is serious enough. In California argot, this is not a tickler—it's a slammer.   5

The pressure waves spread upward and outward about three and a half miles a second, expanding, compressing, expanding, compressing the crystal structures in the rock. The shear waves that follow are somewhat slower. Slower still (about two miles a second) are the surface waves: Rayleigh waves, in particle motion like a rolling sea, and Love waves, advancing like snakes. Wherever things shake, the shaking will consist of all these waves. Half a minute will pass before the light towers move at Candlestick Park. Meanwhile, dogs are barking in Trout Creek Gulch. Car alarms and house alarms are screaming. If, somehow, you could hear all such alarms coming on throughout the region, you could hear the spread of the earthquake. The redwoods are swaying. Some snap like asparagus. The restraining bend has forced the rock to rise. Here, west of the fault trace, the terrain has suddenly been elevated a foot and a half—a punch delivered from below. For some reason, it is felt most on the highest ground.   6

On Summit Road, near the Loma Prieta School, a man goes up in the air like a diver off a board. He lands on his head. Another man is thrown sideways through a picture window. A built-in oven leaves its niche and shoots across a kitchen. A refrigerator walks, bounces off a wall, and returns to its accustomed place. As Pearl Lake's seven-room house goes off its foundation, she stumbles in her kitchen and falls to the wooden floor. In 1906, the same house went off the same foundation. Her parents had moved in the day before. Lake lives alone and raises prunes. Ryan Moore, in bed under the covers, is still under the covers after his house travels a hundred feet and ends up in ruins around him.   7

People will come to think of this earthquake as an event that happened   8
in San Francisco. But only from Watsonville to Santa Cruz—here in the region of the restraining bend, at least sixty miles south of the city—will the
general intensity prove comparable to 1906. In this region are almost no freeway overpasses, major bridges, or exceptionally tall buildings. Along the narrow highland roads, innumerable houses are suddenly stoop-shouldered,
atwist, bestrewn with splinters of wood and glass, even new ones "built to
code." Because the movement on the fault occurs only at great depth, the surface is an enigma of weird random cracks. Few and incongruous, they will
not contribute to the geologic record. If earthquakes like Loma Prieta are il-
legible, how many of them took place through the ages before the arrival of
seismographs, and what does that do to geologists' frequency calculations?

Driveways are breaking like crushed shells. Through woods and fields, a   9
ripping fissure as big as an arroyo crosses Morrill Road. Along Summit Road,
a crack three feet wide, seven feet deep, and seventeen hundred feet long runs
among houses and misses them all. Roads burst open as if they were being
strafed. Humps rise. Double yellow lines are making left-lateral jumps. (Left-
lateral: either way you look at it, the far side of the jump appears to have
moved to the left.)

||
 ||

Cracks, fissures, fence posts are jumping left as well. What is going on? The
San Andreas is the classic right-lateral fault. Is country going south that
should be going north? Is plate tectonics going backward? Geologists will
figure out an explanation. With their four-dimensional minds, and in their
interdisciplinary ultraverbal way, geologists can wiggle out of almost anything. They will say that while the fault motion far below is absolutely right
lateral, blocks of rock overhead are rotating like ball bearings. If you look
down on a field of circles that are all turning clockwise, you will see what
the geologists mean.

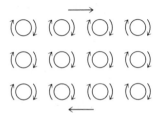

Between one circle and the next, the movement everywhere is left lateral. But
the movement of the field as a whole is right lateral. The explanation has legerdemain. Harry Houdini had legerdemain when he got out of his ropes,
chains, and handcuffs at the bottom of the Detroit River.

All compression resulting from the bend is highest near the bend, and the   10
compression is called the Santa Cruz Mountains. Loma Prieta, near four thousand feet, is the highest peak. The words mean Hill Dark. This translation
will gain in the shaking, and appear in the media as Dark Rolling Mountain.

At the University of California, Santa Cruz, three first-year students from   11
the East Coast sit under redwoods on the forest campus. As the shock waves
reach them and the trees whip overhead, the three students leap up and spon-
taneously dance and shout in a ring. Near the edge of town, a corral disinte-
grates, horses run onto a highway, a light truck crashes into them and the driver is killed. Bicyclists are falling to the streets and automobiles are bouncing.
Santa Cruz has been recovering from severe economic depression, in large part
through the success of the Pacific Garden Mall, six blocks of old unreinforced
brick buildings lately turned into boutiques. The buildings are contiguous and
are of different heights. As the shock waves reach them, the buildings react
with differing periods of vibration and knock each other down. Twenty-one
buildings collapse. Higher ones fall into lower ones like nesting boxes. Ten
people die. The Hotel Metropol, seventy years old, crashes through the ceiling of the department store below it. The Pacific Garden Mall is on very-
young-floodplain river silts that amplify the shaking—as the same deposits
did in 1906.

Landslides are moving away from the epicenter in synchrony with the car   12
alarms. As if from explosions, brown clouds rise into the air. A hundred and
eighty-five acres go in one block slide, dozens of houses included. Hollister's
clock tower falls. Coastal bluffs fall. Mountain cliffs and roadcuts fall.

The shock waves move up the peninsula. Reaching Los Gatos, they give   13
a wrenching spin to houses that cost seven hundred and fifty thousand dollars and have no earthquake insurance. A man is at work in a bicycle shop.
In words that *Time* will print in twenty-four-point type, he will refer to the
earthquake as "my best near-death experience." (For a number of unpublished
fragments here, I am indebted to editors at Time Warner, who have shared
with me a boxful of their correspondents' files.)

Thirteen seconds north of the epicenter is Los Altos, where Harriet and   14
David Schnur live. They grew up in New York City and have the familiar
sense that an I.R.T. train is passing under their home. It is a "million-dollar
Cape Cod," and glass is breaking in every room. This is scarcely their first
earthquake.

David: "Why is it taking so long?"   15

Harriet: "This could be the last one. Thank God we went to *shul* during   16
the holidays."

The piano moves. Jars filled with beans shatter. Wine pours from break-   17
ing bottles. A grandfather clock, falling—its hands stopping at 5:04—lands
on a metronome, which begins to tick.

The shock reaches Stanford University, and sixty buildings receive a hun-   18
dred and sixty million dollars' worth of damage. The university does not have
earthquake insurance.

The waves move on to San Mateo, where a woman in a sixteenth-floor   19
apartment has poured a cup of coffee and sat down to watch the third game
of the World Series. When the shock arrives, the apartment is suddenly like
an airplane in a wind shear. The jolt whips her head to one side. A lamp
crashes. Books fall. Doors open, Dishes fall. Separately, the coffee and the cup
fly across the room.

People are dead in Santa Cruz, Watsonville has rubble on the ground, and   20
San Francisco has yet to feel anything. The waves approach the city directly
from the hypocenter and indirectly via the Moho. Waves that begin this deep
touch the Moho—the geophysical boundary between crust and mantle—at so
slight an angle that they carom upward, a phenomenon known as critical reflection. As the shaking begins in San Francisco, it is twice as strong as would
generally be expected for an earthquake of this magnitude at that distance
from the epicenter.

Two men are on a motor scooter on Sixteenth Street. The driver, glanc-   21
ing over his shoulder, says, "Michael, stop bouncing." A woman walking on
Bush Street sees a Cadillac undulating like a water bed. She thinks, What are
those people *doing* in there? Then the windows fall out of a nearby café. The
sidewalks are moving. Chimneys fall in Haight-Ashbury, landing on cars. In
Asbury Heights, a man is watering his patch of grass. He suddenly feels faint,
his knees weaken, and his front lawn flutters like water under wind. Inside,
his wife is seated at her seven-foot grand. The piano levitates, comes right up
off the floor as she plays. She is thinking, I'm good but not this good. A blimp
is in the air above. The pilot feels vibration. He feels four distinct bumps.

In Golden Gate Park, high-school girls are practicing field hockey. Their   22
coach sees the playing field move, sees "huge trees . . . bending like wind-
shield wipers." She thinks, This is the end, I'm about to fall into the earth,
this is the way to go. Her players freeze in place. They are silent. They just
look at one another.

In the zoo, the spider monkeys begin to scream. The birdhouse is full of   23
midair collisions. The snow leopards, lazy in the sun with the ground shaking, are evidently unimpressed. In any case, their muscles don't move. Pachy,
the approximately calico cat who lives inside the elephant house, is outside
the elephant house. She refused to enter the building all day yesterday and all
day today. When someone carried her inside to try to feed her, she ran outside, hungry.

At Chez Panisse, in Berkeley, cupboard doors open and a chef's personal   24
collection of pickles and preserves crashes. The restaurant, renowned and
booked solid, will be half full this evening. Those who come will order exceptionally expensive wine. Meanwhile, early patrons at a restaurant in Oakland suddenly feel as if they were in the dining car of a train that has lurched
left. When it is over, they will all get up and shake hands.

In the San Francisco Tennis Club, balls are flying without being hit. Play-   25
ers are falling down. The ceilings and the walls seem to be flowing. Nearby,

at Sixth and Bluxome, the walls of a warehouse are falling. Bricks crush a car and decapitate the driver. Four others are killed in this avalanche as well.

In the hundred miles of the San Andreas Fault closest to San Francisco, no energy has been released. The accumulated strain is unrelieved. The U.S. Geological Survey will continue to expect within thirty years an earthquake in San Francisco as much as fifty times as powerful. In the Survey's offices in Menlo Park, a seismologist will say, "This was not a big earthquake, but we hope it's the biggest we deal with in our careers." The Pacific Stock Exchange, too vital to suffer as much as a single day off, will trade by candlelight all day tomorrow. 26

Passengers on a rapid-transit train in a tube under the bay feel as if they had left the rails and were running over rocks. The Interstate 80 tunnel through Yerba Buena Island moves like a slightly writhing hose. Linda Lamb, in a sailboat below the Bay Bridge, feels as if something had grabbed her keel. Cars on the bridge are sliding. The entire superstructure is moving, first to the west about a foot, and then back east, bending the steel, sending large concentric ripples out from the towers, and shearing through bolts thicker than cucumbers. This is the moment in which a five-hundred-ton road section at one tower comes loose and hinges downward, killing the driver of a car below and breaking open the lower deck, so that space gapes to the bay. Heading toward Oakland on the lower deck, an Alameda County Transit driver thinks that all his tires have blown, fights the careening bus for control, and stops eight feet from a plunge to the water. Smashed cars vibrate on the edge but do not fall. Simultaneously, the Golden Gate Bridge is undulating, fluctuating, oscillating, pendulating. Daniel Mohn—in his car heading north, commuting home—is halfway across. From the first tremor, he knows what is happening, and his response to his situation is the exact opposite of panic. He feels very lucky. He thinks, as he has often thought before, If I had the choice, this is where I would be. Reporters will seek him later, and he will tell them, "We never close down." He is the current chief engineer of the Golden Gate Bridge. 27

Peggy Iacovini, having crossed the bridge, is a minute ahead of the chief engineer and a few seconds into the Marin Headlands. In her fluent Anglo-Calif she will tell the reporters, "My car jumped over like half a lane. It felt like my tire blew out. Everybody opened their car doors or stuck their heads out their windows to see if it was their tires. There were also a couple of girls holding their chests going oh my God. All the things on the freeway were just blowing up and stuff. It was like when you light dynamite—you know, on the stick—it just goes down and then it blows up. The communication wires were just sparking. I mean my heart was beating. I was like oh my God. But I had no idea of the extent that it had done." 28

At Candlestick Park, the poles at the ends of the foul lines throb like fishing rods. The overhead lights are swaying. The upper deck is in sickening motion. The crowd stands as one. Some people are screaming. Steel bolts fall. 29

Chunks of concrete fall. A chunk weighing fifty pounds lands in a seat that a fan just left to get a hot dog. Of sixty thousand people amassed for the World Series, not one will die. Candlestick is anchored in radiolarian chert.

The tall buildings downtown rise out of landfill but are deeply founded   30
in bedrock, and, with their shear walls and moment frames and steel-and-rubber isolation bearings, they sway, shiver, sway again, but do not fall. A woman forty-six floors up feels as if she were swinging through space. A woman twenty-nine floors up, in deafening sound, gets under her desk in fetal position and thinks of the running feet of elephants. Cabinets, vases, computers, and law books are flying. Pictures drop. Pipes bend. Nearly five minutes after five. Elevators full of people are banging in their shafts.

On the high floors of the Hyatt, guests sliding on their bellies think of it   31
as surfing.

A quick-thinking clerk in Saks herds a customer into the safety of a door-   32
jamb and has her sign the sales slip there.

Room service has just brought shrimp, oysters, and a bucket of cham-   33
pagne to Cybill Shepherd, on the seventh floor of the Campton Place Hotel. Foot of Nob Hill. Solid Franciscan sandstone. Earthquakes are not unknown to Shepherd. At her home in Los Angeles, pictures are framed under Plexiglas, windowpanes are safety glass, and the water heater is bolted to a wall. Beside every bed are a flashlight, a radio, and a hard hat. Now, on Nob Hill, Shepherd and company decide to eat the oysters and the shrimp before fleeing, but to leave the champagne. There was a phone message earlier, from her astrologer. Please call. Shepherd didn't call. Now she is wondering what the astrologer had in mind.

A stairway collapses between the tenth and eleventh floors of an office   34
building in Oakland. Three people are trapped. When they discover that there is no way to shout for help, one of them will dial her daughter in Fairfax County, Virginia. The daughter will dial 911. Fairfax County Police will teletype the Oakland police, who will climb the building, knock down a wall, and make the rescue.

Meanwhile, at sea off Point Reyes, the U.S. Naval Ship Walter S. Diehl is   35
shaking so violently that the officers think they are running aground. Near Monterey, the Moss Landing Marine Laboratory has been destroyed. A sea cliff has fallen in Big Sur—eighty-one miles south of the epicenter. In another minute, clothes in closets will be swinging on their hangers in Reno. Soon thereafter, water will form confused ripples in San Fernando Valley swimming pools. The skyscrapers of Los Angeles will sway.

After the earthquake on the Hayward Fault in 1868, geologists clearly   36
saw that dangers varied with the geologic map, and they wrote in a State Earthquake Investigation Commission Report, "The portion of the city which suffered most was . . . on made ground." In one minute in 1906, made ground in San Francisco sank as much as three feet. Where landfill touched natural terrain, cable-car rails bent down. Maps printed and distributed well before 1989—stippled and cross-hatched where geologists saw the greatest violence

to come—singled out not only the Nimitz Freeway in Oakland but also, in San Francisco, the Marina district, the Embarcadero, and the Laocoönic freeways near Second and Stillman. Generally speaking, shaking declines with distance from the hypocenter, but where landfill lies on loose sediment the shaking can amplify, as if it were an explosion set off from afar with a plunger and a wire. If a lot of water is present in the sediment and the fill, they can be changed in an instant into gray quicksand—the effect known as liquefaction. Compared with what happens on bedrock, the damage can be something like a hundredfold, as it was on the lakefill of Mexico City in 1985, even though the hypocenter was far to the west, under the Pacific shore.

In a plane that has just landed at San Francisco International Airport, passengers standing up to remove luggage from the overhead racks have the luggage removed for them by the earthquake. Ceilings fall in the control tower, and windows break. The airport is on landfill, as is Oakland International, across the bay. Sand boils break out all over both airfields. In downtown San Francisco, big cracks appear in the elevated I-280, the Embarcadero Freeway, and U.S. 101, where they rest on bayfill and on filled-in tidal creek and filled-in riparian bog. They do not collapse. Across the bay, but west of the natural shoreline, the Cypress section of the Nimitz Freeway—the double-decked I-880—is vibrating at the same frequency as the landfill mud it sits on. This coincidence produces a shaking amplification near eight hundred percent. Concrete support columns begin to fail. Reinforcing rods an inch and a half thick spring out of them like wires. The highway is not of recent construction. At the tops of the columns, where they meet the upper deck, the joints have inadequate shear reinforcement. By a large margin, they would not meet present codes. This is well known to state engineers, who have blueprinted the reinforcements, but the work has not been done, for lack of funds. 37

The under road is northbound, and so is disaster. One after the last, the slabs of the upper roadway are falling. Each weighs six hundred tons. Reinforcing rods connect them, and seem to be helping to pull the highway down. Some drivers on the under road, seeing or sensing what is happening behind them, stop, set their emergency brakes, leave their cars, run toward daylight, and are killed by other cars. Some drivers apparently decide that the very columns that are about to give way are possible locations of safety, like doorjambs. They pull over, hover by the columns, and are crushed. A bank customer-service representative whose 1968 Mustang has just come out of a repair shop feels the jolting roadway and decides that the shop has done a terrible job, that her power steering is about to fail, and that she had better get off this high-speed road as fast as she can. A ramp presents itself. She swerves onto it and off the freeway. She hears a huge sound. In her rearview mirror she sees the upper roadway crash flat upon the lower. 38

As the immense slabs fall, people in cars below hold up their hands to try to stop them. A man eating peanuts in his white pickup feels what he thinks are two flat tires. A moment later, his pickup is two feet high. Somehow, he survives. In an airport shuttle, everyone dies. A man in another 39 car guns his engine, keeps his foot to the floor, and races the slabs that are successively falling behind him. His wife is yelling, "Get out of here! Get out of here!" Miraculously, he gets out of here. Many race the slabs, but few escape. Through twenty-two hundred yards the slabs fall. They began falling where the highway leaves natural sediments and goes onto a bed of landfill. They stop where the highway leaves landfill and returns to natural sediments.

Five minutes after five, and San Francisco's Red Cross Volunteer Disaster   40
Services Committee is in the middle of a disaster-preparedness meeting. The Red Cross Building is shivering. The committee has reconvened underneath its table.

In yards and parks in the Marina, sand boils are spitting muds from ori-   41
fices that resemble the bell rims of bugles. In architectural terminology, the Marina at street level is full of soft stories. A soft story has at least one open wall and is not well supported. Numerous ground floors in the Marina are garages. As buildings collapse upon themselves, the soft stories vanish. In a fourth-floor apartment, a woman in her kitchen has been cooking Rice-A-Roni. She has put on long johns and a sweatshirt and turned on the television to watch the World Series. As the building shakes, she moves with experience into a doorway and grips the jamb. Nevertheless, the vibrations are so intense that she is thrown to the floor. When the shaking stops, she will notice a man's legs, standing upright, outside her fourth-story window, as if he were floating in air. She will think that she is hallucinating. But the three floors below her no longer exist, and the collapsing building has carried her apartment to the sidewalk. Aqueducts are breaking, and water pressure is falling. Flames from broken gas mains will rise two hundred feet. As in 1906, water to fight fires will be scarce. There are numbers of deaths in the Marina, including a man and woman later found hand in hand. A man feels the ground move under his bicycle. When he returns from his ride, he will find his wife severely injured and his infant son dead. An apartment building at Fillmore and Bay has pitched forward onto the street. Beds inside the building are standing on end.

The Marina in 1906 was a salt lagoon. After the Panama Canal opened,   42
in 1914, San Francisco planned its Panama-Pacific International Exposition for the following year, not only to demonstrate that the city had recovered from the great earthquake to end all earthquakes but also to show itself off as a golden destination for shipping. The site chosen for the Exposition was the lagoon. To fill it up, fine sands were hydraulically pumped into it and mixed with miscellaneous debris, creating the hundred and sixty-five dry acres that flourished under the Exposition and are now the Marina. Nearly a minute has passed since the rock slipped at the hypocenter. In San Francisco, the tremors this time will last fifteen seconds. As the ground violently shakes and the sand boils of the Marina discharge material from the liquefying depths, the things they spit up include tarpaper and bits of redwood—the charred remains of houses from the earthquake of 1906.

❋

RESPONDING TO THE WHOLE ESSAY

1. Would you say that McPhee's purpose in this essay is primarily expressive, informative, or persuasive? Cite evidence to support your answer. [*Harbrace* 28a; *Hodges'* 32a]
2. What kinds of readers does McPhee seem to have in mind? Is he writing for people with knowledge of geology and the geological workings of earthquakes? Does he expect that his readers have experienced an earthquake? Use evidence in the essay to comment on the assumptions he appears to make about his audience. [*Harbrace* 28a; *Hodges'* 32a]
3. Comment upon paragraph 2 as an example of a description arranged spatially. [*Harbrace* 27b(2); *Hodges'* 31b(2)]
4. How does McPhee link the first five sentences of paragraph 6 and the last five sentences of paragraph 27? [*Harbrace* 27b(3); *Hodges'* 31b(3)]
5. Analyze paragraph 9 as an example of question-answer development. Does McPhee answer these questions or are they rhetorical questions? What does McPhee achieve by developing the paragraph in this way? [*Harbrace* 27b(2); *Hodges'* 31b(2); Glossary of Usage]
6. Notice that the verb tense in paragraph 41 is not consistent. Present, past perfect, and future tenses are all present in this paragraph. Explain whether the shifts in verb tense in sentences 1–6 are necessary. Be as specific as you can. [*Harbrace* 7c; *Hodges'* 7c]

ANALYZING THE ELEMENTS

Grammar

1. Explain the grammatical function of *whose* in the eighth sentence of paragraph 38. To what does *whose* refer? [*Harbrace* 6; *Hodges'* 5b and 28]
2. What does the phrase *One after the last* modify in the sentence of paragraph 38? Why? [*Harbrace* 4a; *Hodges'* 4a]
3. What is the mood of *come* in the third sentence of paragraph 24? How can you tell? [*Harbrace* 6d(1) and 7d; *Hodges'* 5b(1) and 7d]

Effective Sentences

1. The third sentence of paragraph 8 could be rewritten: Almost no freeway overpasses, major bridges, or exceptionally tall buildings are in this region. What does McPhee achieve by writing the sentence as he does? Explain as well as you can. [*Harbrace* 11f; *Hodges'* 29f]
2. McPhee makes effective use of parallel structure of several kinds, including balanced parts, repeated words, correlatives. Find at least one example of each. [*Harbrace* 10; *Hodges'* 26]
3. How does McPhee achieve emphasis in the seventh sentence of paragraph 27 and the first sentence of paragraph 30? How do these sentences add to the emphatic tone of the essay? [*Harbrace* 11c; *Hodges'* 29c]

4. Throughout the essay, McPhee uses fragments for emphasis. The two fragments in paragraph 33 could be added to the sentence that precedes them: Room service has just brought shrimp, oysters, and a bucket of champagne to Cybill Shepherd, on the seventh floor of the Campton Place Hotel, a hotel made of solid Franciscan sandstone and located at the foot of Nob Hill. Does this sentence retain the urgency conveyed by McPhee's use of fragments? Try to explain why or why not. [*Harbrace* 2; *Hodges'* 2]

5. Notice that the seventh sentence of paragraph 9 and the last sentence of paragraph 13 are enclosed in parentheses. Try to explain the purpose of each of these sentences. Why does McPhee choose to enclose them in parentheses? [*Harbrace* 21f; *Hodges'* 17f]

Punctuation and Mechanics

1. Comment upon the use of the apostrophe in *dollars'* in the first sentence of paragraph 18. How might the sentence be rewritten to clarify the relationship indicated by this apostrophe? [*Harbrace* 19; *Hodges'* 15]

2. Explain the capitalization of *Franciscan* in the first sentence of paragraph 33; *Plexiglas* in the fifth sentence of paragraph 33, and *San Francisco's Red Cross Volunteer Disaster Services Committee* in the first sentence of paragraph 40. Why do you think McPhee capitalizes each word in the fragments that make up the fourth, fifth, and last sentences of paragraph 2? [*Harbrace* 23; *Hodges'* 9]

3. Explain why McPhee chooses commas, rather than semicolons, to separate the main clauses that make up the fourth sentence of paragraph 13. [*Harbrace* 18a; *Hodges'* 14a]

4. Double quotation marks generally set off thoughts from other text. Why do you think McPhee avoids using double quotation marks in the fourth and twelfth sentences of paragraph 21, the third sentence of paragraph 22, and the thirteenth sentence of paragraph 27? How might this choice have influenced McPhee to italicize *doing* in the fourth sentence of paragraph 21? Explain. [*Harbrace* 20a(5) and 24; *Hodges'* 16a(5) and 10]

5. The second sentence of paragraph 28 ("In her fluent . . .") begins a quotation that extends throughout the remainder of the paragraph. If this essay were written in the MLA style of documentation, how would this quotation be handled? in APA style of documentation? Write a paraphrase of this long quotation. Is the paraphrase as effective as McPhee's original use of direct quotation? Why or why not? [*Harbrace* 20b and 33h(4); *Hodges'* 16b and 37h(4)]

Diction

1. Throughout the essay, McPhee uses words that are exact, idiomatic, and fresh. Comment upon the effectiveness of each of the following words: *stoop-shouldered, atwist, bestrewn* in the fourth sentence of paragraph 8 and *undulating, fluctuating, oscillating, pendulating* in the ninth sentence of paragraph 27. [*Harbrace* 14c; *Hodges'* 20c]

2. Paragraph 20 includes several technical terms: *hypocenter, geophysical boundary, crust, mantle, critical reflection,* and *epicenter.* Justify this use of jargon and ex-

plain how it contributes to the overall tone of the essay. [*Harbrace* 13c and 29; *Hodges'* 19g and 33]

3. Why does McPhee use *lies* instead of *lays* in the fifth sentence of paragraph 36? Explain. [*Harbrace* 13c(3); *Hodges'* 7b]

BUILDING VOCABULARY

1. From what Greek roots do the words *epicenter* and *hypocenter* originate? What do these roots mean? List two words derived from each of these roots and write sentences using each.

2. Explain the meanings and origin of the prefixes *super-*, *ultra-*, and *trans-*. Make a list of six words, including two words beginning with each of these prefixes. Write a sentence with each of the words you have listed.

SUGGESTIONS FOR WRITING

1. Using concrete details, describe an earthquake or other natural disaster that you have witnessed (for example, a blizzard, a tornado, a heat wave, a flood, a hurricane, a thunderstorm).

2. Write a short essay describing your anticipation of or preparation for a natural disaster or extreme change in the weather.

Chapter 4

Process

Process explanations are of two kinds: those that tell a reader how to perform some task and those that simply explain how something works. In both kinds, a writer describes a sequence of steps, generally in chronological order, one step leading to the next. As you might suppose, therefore, process is closely related both to narration and to cause and effect.

In this section, Alexander Petrunkevitch's "The Spider and the Wasp" explains a process that occurs in nature, a process humans cannot duplicate. Garrison Keillor's "How to Write a Letter" humorously describes letter writing from the point of view of a shy person, encouraging his readers to make their marks upon the world through letters. Patricia Brooks makes an effort to teach readers about evaluating dining establishments in "Do-It-Yourself Restaurant Reviewing." In "The Maker's Eye: Revising Your Own Manuscripts," Donald M. Murray aims to give his readers practical advice, as his subtitle indicates, though the process Murray writes about is not straightforward and varies greatly from writer to writer and from project to project, so its steps cannot be set down in any firm order. Mummifying a corpse is a process more clearly structured: you *must* do some things before others. Adam Goodheart, in "Mummy Arts," gives step-by-step directions (don't try this at home).

In writing about a process, be very careful to explain the steps in the proper order and to omit no steps that are necessary. An awareness of your reader is supremely important in writing about processes—especially if you are giving directions. As you write, continually ask yourself what your readers already know and what they need to be told. Must terms be defined, parts described, steps illustrated? Crucial, too, is the way you make time relationships clear for the reader. Special care with verb tenses [*Harbrace* 7c; *Hodges'* 7c] and transitional devices [*Harbrace* 27b; *Hodges'* 31b] is part of the key to success here. ↳ *Pg.* 311

In the following student essay, Maya Ramirez gives directions for playing the Irish bagpipes. Notice how she combines explanation with instructions, describing each part of the instrument before telling the reader exactly what to do. Notice, too, how she uses verb tenses and transitional expressions signaling time to keep the sequence of steps clear.

Playing the Irish Bagpipes

If you want to play the Irish bagpipes, you need a set of pipes, a lot of time and patience, and, if you live in an apartment building, neighbors who are hard of hearing. Since Irish pipes are bellows-blown rather than mouth-blown, you do not need the powerful lungs required for the more familiar Scottish bagpipes. There is an adage that it takes seven years to make a piper, and the first year or two can be a little excruciating; once the worst is over, however, the instrument is a joy to play.

Start with a practice set. You will have a chanter, bag, and bellows. The chanter is the part that actually makes sound. As you examine it, you will see that it is a long wooden tube with finger holes cut in it like a recorder, and it has a closed brass tube mounted on the end. Inside the brass tube is the reed, which vibrates to produce the sound, but the reed is very fragile and the brass tube should not be removed except with extreme caution. From the brass tube a smaller, shorter tube, called the input tube, protrudes at an angle. This is the part you will insert into the bag.

Now examine the bag. It is made of leather (or vinyl), usually covered with fabric, and is shaped like the letter P. In the end of the stem of the P you will find a fitting to receive the input tube of the chanter. Sticking out of the side of the fat part of the P is a tube called the blowstick, to which you will eventually attach the bellows.

Next, therefore, examine the bellows. It resembles a fireplace bellows without handles. One cheek of the bellows has a short leather strap and an air valve, through which air can enter the bellows as you pump. The other cheek has a long leather strap and a flexible tube (often made of a piece of bicycle inner tube). Air comes out of this tube when you pump.

Now you are ready to strap the thing on and begin to play. First, strap the bellows to your body. The long strap goes around your body at about rib height with the bellows itself on the right side, and the short strap goes around your right arm just above

the elbow. When the bellows is on in this fashion, the flexible tube will pass in front of your body extending about halfway across. Try pumping the bellows with

your elbow (the motion is rather like imitating a chicken flapping its wings). Next, tuck the bag under

your left arm with the fat part of the bag under the

	elbow and the long narrow part on top, jutting forward. If the bag is placed properly, the blowstick will
Fourth step	project halfway across in front of your body and be in just the right place to plug into the tube that sticks out of the bellows. Plug the blowstick into the tube.
How to prepare the pipes for making sound	If you now pump the bellows, air coming into the bellows on the upstroke of your right elbow will, on the downstroke, pass through the tube and blow-
Fifth step	stick in front of you into the bag under your left arm. Several strokes with the bellows should begin to fill
Sixth step	the bag, and if you then squeeze the bag with your left elbow, air will come out the long narrow neck that
Seventh step	sticks out in front of you. Into the fitting at the end of this neck, insert the input tube of the chanter. Now the air, instead of passing uselessly out of the bag, passes through the chanter, causing the reed to vibrate and make a horrible noise. As you master the instrument, this noise will gradually be transformed into music.
How to adjust sound quality	Sit down, if you are not already sitting, and place the open end of the chanter against your right
Eighth step	leg a couple of inches above the knee. Pump the bellows
Ninth step	with long, steady strokes and, as the bag fills, apply
Tenth step	steady gentle pressure to the bag with the left elbow.
Eleventh step	You can get a second, higher octave by forcing a little extra air from the bag through the chanter. Lifting the
Twelfth step	chanter off the knee gives a louder, wailing tone for variety. Closing the chanter against the knee and covering all the finger holes between notes stops the sound and allows you to play staccato. With a fingering chart
Conclusion	handy, you will be able to play different notes of the scale, and as you become accustomed to the simultaneous actions of pumping, squeezing, and fingering, you will soon be playing tunes. At that point, you will be well on your way to becoming a piper.

Commentary. Maya Ramirez begins her process essay with a nod to the convention of listing the equipment necessary—and brings a little humor to the subject as she does so. Her equipment list includes not only the requisite pipes, but also the necessary lifestyle (one with considerable free time), the best kind of personality (a patient one), and the right kind of neighbors (ones who are hard of hearing). To allay any apprehensions the reader may have developed through a minimal familiarity with Scottish pipes, she also points out, again with some levity, that Irish pipes require no extraordinary physical ability.

Ramirez assumes that her audience knows little about the Irish pipes—a fairly exotic instrument. Accordingly, she makes her description unusually detailed. If one had never seen a set of these pipes, one could readily recognize them from having read her description. Furthermore, she makes the description a part of the process of learning to play the pipes. Essentially Ramirez is saying, "Familiarize yourself with this instrument. Look at the parts and let me explain what those parts do," defining the function of each part of the instrument so that when she actually sets forth the steps involved in playing the pipes, the reader can more readily follow the instructions.

When she has described the form and the function of each part of the instrument (and also told the reader how to handle each part and which parts to be especially careful with), Ramirez begins her instructions: "Now you are ready to strap the thing on and begin to play." It is worth noting that these instructions are organized into three sets. First she tells the reader how to put the instrument on and connect the bellows and the bag. Next she explains how to ready the instrument so that it can make a sound: pump air into the bag with the bellows and fit the chanter to the bag. Finally, she tells the reader how to adjust the quality of the sound that comes out of the instrument. Her conclusion suggests that the reader use a fingering chart and practice the motions required to play the pipes.

This process essay is especially clear and direct, providing all the information the rank novice needs to begin with. But Ramirez did not simply sit down and produce this kind of clarity and simplicity straight off. As the rough draft which follows will show, she had to do considerable cutting and simplifying for her uninformed audience, and she also radically reorganized the essay. Originally, she did not give step-by-step directions, nor did she take an encouraging approach. For example, the second paragraph of the draft would be enough to scare any prospective piper, and so she simplified it by deleting her explanation of the difference between a full set of pipes and a practice set. She also deleted extraneous (though interesting) information about the name of the pipes, and transferred to the introduction the information about how Irish pipes are blown.

To avoid getting the reader tangled in all the information about what the straps do and where to put them, she separated those ideas, explaining the bellows and the bag before addressing what to do with the straps. She also separated the instructions about how to manipulate the instrument from those about how it works and amplified the information about the chanter.

First Draft of "Playing the Irish Bagpipes"
by Maya Ramirez

If you want to play the Irish bagpipes, you need a set of pipes, a lot of time and patience, and, if you live in an apartment building, neighbors who are hard of hearing. There is an adage that it takes seven years to make a piper, and the first one or two can be somewhat excruciating; once the worst is over, however, the instrument is a joy to play.

Irish bagpipes are blown with a bellows, rather than by mouth. In fact, there are those who believe that "Uilleann" pipes, the Gaelic term, means "elbow pipes" because it is with the elbow that the bellows is pumped. Because there is so much to coordinate, with the bellows being pumped with the right arm, the bag being squeezed with the left arm, and the chanter, which is the melody pipe, being played with the fingers, it is best to start with a practice set, composed only of these pieces. A full set also includes drones, low pipes that play a steady note behind the melody, and regulators, which play chords when their metal keys are pressed with the right wrist—usually while both hands are being used on the chanter. A practice set is quite enough to wrestle with in the beginning.

There is a long strap on one face of the bellows. This strap goes around your waist, to hold the contraption stationary against your right side, nestled against the bottom of your ribs. A shorter strap on the other face buckles around your upper arm. You can practice pumping the bellows with your right elbow. (If there isn't any padding for your elbow on the bellows, add some, or your elbow will be extremely sore in no time at all.)

Now take the bag and tuck it under your left elbow. Protruding from one side of the bag is a hollow stick, called the blowstick. The blowstick is inserted into the tube that protrudes from the inner face of the bellows, so that air pumped by the bellows passes through the tube in front of you into the bag under your left arm. Pump the bellows a few times and make sure there are no leaks in the connections of the bellows to blowstick, and blowstick to bag. As you pump, you should feel the bag fill with air.

Now you are ready for the chanter. In the end of the narrow neck of the bag, there is a round piece of wood with a hole in it. This is called the chanter-stock. Near the top end of the chanter itself there is a narrow angled tube, usually made of brass, that fits into the holes. Again, make sure there is no leak in the joint, or much of your laborious bellows-pumping will be wasted. Once you are sure everything is more or less airtight, you are ready to play music.

Sit down, if you are not already sitting, and place the open end of the chanter against your right leg a couple of inches above the knee. With the chanter thus closed, you can get a second, higher octave by forcing a little extra air from the bag through the chanter. Popping the chanter off the knee gives a louder, wailing sound for variety. You will need a chart for the fingering, but with a fingering chart handy you can begin exploring notes and scales.

At first, the sensation will be like wrestling with an octopus, but soon you will get the hang of pumping in long, steady strokes with the right arm, maintaining pressure on the bag with the left arm and raising and lowering the chanter off your knee as you finger the notes. You will find that by closing the chanter entirely between notes, with all fingers down and the end of the pipe against your leg, you can play staccato, or put rests in the music for phrasing. By rolling your fingers off the holes, rather than just lifting them, you can "bend" notes, sliding from one pitch to another. If the chanter is slightly out of tune, and nearly all of them are, you can sometimes keep the notes truer by varying the pressure of your left arm. When all that finally becomes second nature, you will be well on your way to becoming a piper.

How to Write a Letter
Garrison Keillor

Writer and broadcaster Garrison Keillor was born in Anoka, Minnesota, in 1942. A graduate of the University of Minnesota, Keillor published his first story in 1969 in *The New Yorker.* Keillor is best known as the host of the popular National Public Radio program *Prairie Home Companion,* which aired between 1974 and 1987, when Keillor left the program to write. Keillor has also published *Happy to Be Here* (1982), *Lake Wobegon Days* (1985), and *Leaving Home: A Collection of Lake Wobegon Stories* (1987). "How to Write a Letter," which Keillor wrote as an advertisement for the International Paper Company, offers humorous, but insightful, advice to help shy people make their mark upon the world.

1   We shy persons need to write a letter now and then, or else we'll dry up and blow away. It's true. And I speak as one who loves to reach for the phone, dial the number, and talk. I say, "Big Bopper here—what's shakin', babes?" The telephone is to shyness what Hawaii is to February, it's a way out of the woods, *and yet:* a letter is better.

2   Such a sweet gift—a piece of handmade writing, in an envelope that is not a bill, sitting in our friend's path when she trudges home from a long day spent among yahoos and savages, a day our words will help repair. They don't need to be immortal, just sincere. She can read them twice and again tomorrow: *You're someone I care about, Corinne, and think of often and every time I do you make me smile.*

3   We need to write, otherwise nobody will know who we are. They will have only a vague impression of us as A Nice Person, because frankly, we don't shine at conversation, we lack the confidence to thrust our faces forward and say, "Hi, I'm Heather Hooten, let me tell you about my week." Mostly we say "Uh-huh" and "Oh really." People smile and look over our shoulder, looking for someone else to talk to.

4   So a shy person sits down and writes a letter. To be known by another person—to meet and talk freely on the page—to be close despite distance. To escape from anonymity and be our own sweet selves and express the music of our souls.

5   Same thing that moves a giant rock star to sing his heart out in front of 123,000 people moves us to take ballpoint in hand and write a few lines to our dear Aunt Eleanor. *We want to be known.* We want her to know that we have fallen in love, that we quit our job, and we're moving to New York, and

we want to say a few things that might not get said in casual conversation: *thank you for what you've meant to me, I am very happy right now.*

The first step in writing letters is to get over the guilt of *not* writing. You don't "owe" anybody a letter. Letters are a gift. The burning shame you feel when you see unanswered mail makes it harder to pick up a pen and makes for a cheerless letter when you finally do. *I feel bad about not writing, but I've been so busy,* etc. Skip this. Few letters are obligatory, and they are *Thanks for the wonderful gift* and *I am terribly sorry to hear about George's death* and *Yes, you're welcome to stay with us next month,* and not many more than that. Write those promptly if you want to keep your friends. Don't worry about the others, except love letters, of course. When your true love writes *Dear Light of My Life, Joy of My Heart, O Lovely Pulsating Core of My Sensate Life,* some response is called for.

Some of the best letters are tossed off in a burst of inspiration, so keep your writing stuff in one place where you can sit down for a few minutes and *Dear Roy, I am in the middle of an essay for International Paper but thought I'd drop you a line. Hi to your sweetie too* dash off a note to a pal. Envelopes, stamps, address book, everything in a drawer so you can write fast when the pen is hot.

A blank white 8" × 11" sheet can look as big as Montana if the pen's not so hot—try a smaller page and write boldly. Or use a note card with a piece of fine art on the front; if your letter ain't good, at least they get the Matisse. Get a pen that makes a sensuous line, get a comfortable typewriter, a friendly word processor—whichever feels easy to the hand.

Sit for a few minutes with the blank sheet in front of you, and meditate on the person you will write to, let your friend come to mind until you can almost see her or him in the room with you. Remember the last time you saw each other and how your friend looked and what you said and what perhaps was unsaid between you, and when your friend becomes real to you, start to write.

Write the salutation—*Dear You*—and take a deep breath and plunge in. A simple declarative sentence will do, followed by another and another and another. Tell us what you're doing and tell it like you were talking to us. Don't think about grammar, don't think about lit'ry style, don't try to write dramatically, just give us your news. Where did you go, who did you see, what did they say, what do you think?

If you don't know where to begin, start with the present moment: *I'm sitting at the kitchen table on a rainy Saturday morning. Everyone is gone and the house is quiet.* Let your simple description of the present moment lead to something else, let the letter drift gently along.

The toughest letter to crank out is one that is meant to impress, as we all know from writing job applications; if it's hard work to slip off a letter to a friend, maybe you're trying too hard to be terrific. A letter is only a report to someone who already likes you for reasons other than your brilliance. Take it easy.

Don't worry about form. It's not a term paper. When you come to the   13
end of one episode, just start a new paragraph. You can go from a few lines
about the sad state of rock 'n roll to the fight with your mother to your fond
memories of Mexico to your cat's urinary tract infection to a few thoughts
on personal indebtedness to the kitchen sink and what's in it. The more you
write, the easier it gets, and when you have a True True Friend to write to, a
compadre, a soul sibling, then it's like driving a car down a country road, you
just get behind the keyboard and press on the gas.

Don't tear up the page and start over when you write a bad line—try to   14
write your way out of it. Make mistakes and plunge on. Let the letter cook
along and let yourself be bold. Outrage, confusion, love—whatever is in your
mind, let it find a way to the page. Writing is a means of discovery, always,
and when you come to the end and write *Yours ever* or *Hugs and Kisses,*
you'll know something you didn't when you wrote *Dear Pal.*

Probably your friend will put your letter away, and it'll be read again a   15
few years from now—and it will improve with age. And forty years from now,
your friend's grandkids will dig it out of the attic and read it, a sweet and
precious relic of the ancient Eighties that gives them a sudden clear glimpse
of you and her and the world we old-timers knew. You will then have created
an object of art. Your simple lines about where you went, who you saw, what
they said, will speak to those children and they will feel in their hearts the
humanity of our times.

You can't pick up a phone and call the future and tell them about our   16
times. You have to pick up a piece of paper.

✹

RESPONDING TO THE WHOLE ESSAY

1. Keillor wrote this essay as an advertisement for International Paper Company. Use
    evidence in the essay to comment on Keillor's assumptions about his audience.
    [*Harbrace* 28a; *Hodges'* 32a]
2. Would you say Keillor's purpose in writing this essay is mainly to express his feel-
    ings about writing, to inform the reader, or to persuade the reader? Can you find
    evidence of aims other than the one you chose as primary? Explain. [*Harbrace*
    28a; *Hodges'* 32a]
3. Could a reader use this essay as a guide for writing a personal letter? Why or
    why not?
4. Explain what Keillor accomplishes in his introduction. Where does he establish a
    context for the essay? [*Harbrace* 28f(1); *Hodges'* 32f(1)]
5. Keillor's conclusion accomplishes more than simply telling how to end a personal
    letter. Explain what else it accomplishes and how it does so. [*Harbrace* 28f(2);
    Hodges' 32f(2)]
6. Comment on the use of humor in this essay. [*Harbrace* 29a; *Hodges'* 33a]

ANALYZING THE ELEMENTS

Grammar

1. Notice that most of the verbs in Keillor's essay are present-tense verbs. What does he accomplish by using the present tense throughout the essay? Try converting the verbs in one paragraph to past tense. In what ways does the past tense change the effect of the essay? [*Harbrace* 7c; *Hodges'* 7c]
2. The first sentence in paragraph 7 begins with a passive construction. Try to rewrite the sentence so that both independent clauses are in the active voice. What difficulties do you encounter? [*Harbrace* 7; *Hodges'* 7]
3. Keillor uses a fragment as the last sentence of paragraph 7. Explain why this fragment is justifiable. [*Harbrace* 2; *Hodges'* 2]

Effective Sentences

1. The second sentence of paragraph 9 consists of a number of coordinate clauses linked by *and*. What keeps this sentence from being "stringy"? [*Harbrace* 9b; *Hodges'* 24b]
2. Comment on the parallel structure of sentence three of paragraph 5. [*Harbrace* 10; *Hodges'* 26]
3. Find three examples of sentences in which Keillor has used forceful verbs and comment on the effect of those verbs. [*Harbrace* 11d; *Hodges'* 29d]

Punctuation and Mechanics

1. Justify Keillor's use of commas to link independent clauses in the fifth sentence of paragraph 1. [*Harbrace* 3a; *Hodges'* 3a]
2. Why is "A Nice Person" capitalized in the second sentence of paragraph 3? What would be the effect of not capitalizing the phrase? [*Harbrace* 23; *Hodges'* 9]
3. What is the function of the italics in the first sentence of paragraph 7? [*Harbrace* 24; *Hodges'* 10]

Diction

1. Keillor uses a word (*ain't*, second sentence of paragraph 8) referred to in the *American Heritage Dictionary* as "nonstandard" and "beyond rehabilitation." What justification can you find for his using this word? [*Harbrace* 13; *Hodges'* 19]
2. Paragraph 8 begins with a simile. Explain why the comparison is humorous. [*Harbrace* 14c; *Hodges'* 20c]

BUILDING VOCABULARY

1. List and define three synonyms of the present tense verb *read*. Write sentences using each of these synonyms.
2. What is the Greek root from which *letter* is derived? What does it mean? Through what other languages and roots can *letter* be traced?

SUGGESTIONS FOR WRITING

1. Take Keillor's advice as you write a personal letter.
2. Using Keillor as a loose model, write an essay explaining how to accomplish some common, but unpleasant, daily task that requires mainly mental effort, such as paying bills, planning menus, scheduling appointments.

Mummy Arts
Adam Goodheart

Adam Goodheart is the senior editor of and columnist for the Library of Congress's *Civilization,* a magazine devoted to the discussion of history, culture, social issues, and literature. In his column, "Lost Arts," Goodheart explores such historical and cultural phenomena as witch-hunting and dueling. Writing from a twentieth-century perspective, Goodheart creates, in "Mummy Arts," a humorous yet informative account of the ancient Egyptians' method of preparing corpses for the afterlife. Through his combination of detailed instructions and witty commentary, Goodheart emphasizes the religious and cultural significance of the ancient Egyptians' ritual of mummification.

Old pharaohs never died—they just took long vacations. Ancient Egyptians believed that at death a person's spirit, or *ka,* was forcibly separated from the body. But it returned now and then for a visit, to snack on the food that had been left in the tomb. It was crucial that the body stay as lifelike as possible for eternity—that way, the *ka* (whose life was hard enough already) would avoid reanimating the wrong corpse. These days, dead pharaohs are admittedly a bit hard to come by. If you decide to practice mummification on a friend or relative, please make sure that the loved one in question is fully deceased before you begin.

1. Evisceration Made Easy. The early stages of the process can be a bit malodorous, so it's recommended that you follow the ancient custom of relocating to a well-ventilated tent. (You'll have trouble breathing anyway, since tradition also prescribes that you wear a jackal-head mask in honor of Anubis, god of the dead.) After cleansing the body, break the nose by pushing a long iron hook up the nostrils. Then use the hook to remove the contents of the skull. You can discard the brain (the ancient Egyptians attributed no special significance to it).

Next, take a flint knife and make a long incision down the left side of the abdomen. Actually, it's best to have a friend do this, since the person who cuts open the body must be pelted with stones to atone for the profanation. After you've stoned your friend, use a bronze knife to remove the internal organs through the incision. Wash them in palm wine as a disinfectant and set them aside to inter later in separate alabaster jars. Leave the heart in place (Egyptians believed it was the seat of consciousness).

2. Salting and Stuffing. Once the abdominal cavity is empty, fill it with
natron, a natural salt found at the Wadi Natrun in the western Nile delta. Heap
more natron on top of the body until it is completely covered. According to a
papyrus in the Louvre, it should then be left for 42 days, after which it will be
almost totally desiccated. Having removed the natron, anoint the head with
frankincense and the body with sacred oil. Pack the skull and abdomen with
myrrh and other spices, and cover the incision with a sheet of gold.

For an extra-lifelike effect, you can stuff the corpse's skin with a compound of sawdust, butter, and mud. Don't overdo it, though. Queen Henettowey, wife of Pinedjem I, was so overstuffed that when archaeologists found
her, her face had split open like an old sofa.

3. Wrapping Up. If you thought mummies wrapped in bedsheets were the
stuff of B movies, think again: Even pharaohs were usually wound in strips
cut from household linens. Pour molten pine resin over the body; in the course
of centuries this will turn the flesh black, glassy, and rock-hard. While the
resin's still tacky, bandage each of the extremities separately, including fingers and toes. Then brush on another coat and repeat. (Go easy on the resin—
Tutankhamen stuck to his coffin and had to be chipped out piece by piece.)
Amulets can be placed between the layers of bandages; a scarab over the heart
is the minimum. The last layers should secure the arms and legs to the body.
Your mummy is now ready to be entombed in grand style.

A note on sarcophagi: Careful labeling will prevent embarrassing mix-ups
later on. A mummy long thought to be Princess Mutemhet of the 21st dynasty was recently x-rayed and found to be a pet baboon.

✳

RESPONDING TO THE WHOLE ESSAY

1. What is Goodheart's primary purpose in "Mummy Arts"? Does he focus mainly
   on the information itself, on amusing his readers, or on moving his audience to a
   particular action or point of view? Does he have a secondary purpose? If so, how
   is it revealed? [*Harbrace* 28a; *Hodges'* 32a]
2. Explain how Goodheart unifies paragraph 4 and makes it coherent. [*Harbrace*
   27b; *Hodges'* 31b]
3. For what audience does Goodheart appear to write? What evidence can you muster
   to support your answer? [*Harbrace* 28a; *Hodges'* 32a]

ANALYZING THE ELEMENTS

Grammar

1. What kind of verbal phrase is *reanimating the wrong corpse* in the fourth sentence of paragraph 1? How does it function in this sentence? [*Harbrace* 1d;
   Hodges' 1d]

2.   What advantage does Goodheart's use of *can* rather than *may* bring to the first sentence of paragraph 2 and the first sentence of paragraph 5? Would *may* be a better choice in either of these sentences? Why or why not? [*Harbrace* 7; *Hodges'* 7]

Effective Sentences

1.   Compare the use of *it* in the third sentence of paragraph 1 with the use of *it* in the following sentence. What does *it* refer to in the third sentence? How is *it* used in the fourth sentence? [*Harbrace* 6b; *Hodges'* 28c and 28d]
2.   Explain why the participial phrase in the fourth sentence of paragraph 4 is not a dangling modifier. [*Harbrace* 1d and 5b; *Hodges'* 1d and 25b]
3.   In what ways does Goodheart add variety to the sentences of paragraph 1? Find and discuss at least two ways. [*Harbrace* 12; *Hodges'* 30]

Punctuation and Mechanics

1.   Explain Goodheart's use of the semicolon in the second and sixth sentences of paragraph 6. Rewrite these sentences without using the semicolon. [*Harbrace* 18; *Hodges'* 14]
2.   What purpose is served by using a colon in the first sentence of paragraph 6 rather than punctuating the clauses as separate sentences? [*Harbrace* 21d; *Hodges'* 17d]
3.   Comment upon the use of the apostrophe in *you'll* in the second sentence of paragraph 2, *it's* in the second sentence of paragraph 3, *corpse's* in the first sentence of paragraph 5, and *resin's* in the third sentence of paragraph 6. [*Harbrace* 19; *Hodges'* 15]

Diction

1.   The last sentence of paragraph 5 contains figurative language. Comment upon how the splitting of an overstuffed corpse might resemble the splitting of an old sofa. [*Harbrace* 14a(1); *Hodges'* 20a(1)]
2.   The first sentence of this essay alludes to a well-known pattern of expression (old . . . never die—they just . . .). How does this opening cliché influence the overall tone of the essay? [*Harbrace* 14c and 29; *Hodges'* 20c and 11]

BUILDING VOCABULARY

1.   What are the Latin roots from which the word *evisceration* is derived? What do they mean? Write a sentence using a word derived from one of the Latin roots you identified.
2.   What are the Greek roots from which the words *sarcophagus* and *scarab* are borrowed? What do each of these roots mean? How do the meanings of the Greek and Latin roots differ from the meanings of the words derived from them? Are the English borrowings more or less descriptive?

SUGGESTIONS FOR WRITING

1. Think of something that you do or have done that most people have little experience in doing (for example, coloring hair, rebuilding an engine, catering a party, skydiving). Using plenty of specific details, explain to a stranger how to perform this activity.

2. Write a process essay giving instructions for preparing a food or beverage you enjoy (for example, baking bread, cooking spaghetti, making cocoa, broiling steak).

Do-It-Yourself Restaurant Reviewing
Patricia Brooks

As a restaurant critic for the Connecticut section of *The New York Times,* Patricia Brooks has evaluated numerous dining establishments. Brooks is the author of *Connecticut's Best Dining & Wining* (1995) and several cookbooks. In "Do-It-Yourself Restaurant Reviewing," she encourages her readers to try their hand at evaluating the restaurants at which they are patrons, and she offers her readers advice that can help them become proficient restaurant reviewers.

1   Wanted: a discerning palate, a penchant for dining out, and long experience as a schmecker and voilà, you have the makings of a restaurant critic.

2   Who needs those restaurant guides telling you what's good or not? If you can tell the difference between pamplemousse and charlotte russe, samosas and mimosas, porcini and zucchini, Hollandaise and Lyonnaise, crème brulée and salsa molé, well, you're on your way. No doctorate in Restaurant Critiquing required (or available).

3   Here are a few tips to help you hone your skills at evaluating unfamiliar dining establishments.

THE RESTAURANT

4   Welcome to our happy haven. A maître d' or hostess who greets you with a smile, instead of a "who-the-hell-are-you" look, doesn't guarantee a great meal, but it's a gracious start. Inadequate or churlish service can ruin a good meal, while friendly attentiveness can make an ordinary meal tolerable. But discount the too-friendly "Hi, I'm Sebastian, your waiter for tonight" approach. Look instead for cordial professionalism, staffers who can describe each dish accurately, are knowledgeable about wines, can pronounce the foreign names on the menu, refill water glasses before you have to ask, and serve drinks promptly with a quick menu and wine list follow-up. These touches suggest the wait staff has been trained, which offers promise for the kitchen staff as well.

5   Beauty is as beauty does. A restaurant can be modest, but it needn't look like Rick's Place in "Casablanca." Good lighting can do wonders for a diner's mood, as can well-spaced tables and comfortable chairs. Rule of fork: the more expensive a place, the better it should look. This doesn't mean a Cecil B. DeMille production (which often masks weakness in the

kitchen), but attractive, often understated elegance. Dining out at a pricey place is usually an event; the restaurant's decor should set the stage.

Cleanliness: next to godliness? No, but it shows that attention is being paid. Look for evidence of hands-on management: clean tablecloth or table, fresh (not faded) flowers, pristine menus, spotless glassware and silverware. Anything less is not a happy harbinger of edible meals to come.   6

Is it a menu or a United Nations roster? The larger the menu, the higher the potential for failure. It's a rare kitchen that can turn out twenty different appetizers and twenty entrées with equal success. A menu with a dozen entrées from as many different countries sends this signal loud and clear: cherchez the Birds-Eye packaged meals.   7

Save the poetry for books, not menus. A menu that is brief and states each dish succinctly without seductive asides ("caressed by a fragrant lemon grass coulis") offers greater promise than one that wallows in imagery ("lovingly marinated") that often doesn't translate into reality on the plate. A short menu suggests that the chef is experienced and confident enough to limit his repertoire to his specialties. Be wary of a menu awash with misspelled foreign names. If they can't get the name right, what's the dish going to taste like?   8

THE FOOD

Look for "Short Cuts" the movie, not "short cuts" the restaurant. Bread alone does not a restaurant make, but it's the first indicator of what to expect. Soft, commercial bread or stale rolls, served with foil-wrapped butter pats (tolerable at a casual eatery, unforgivable at an upscale restaurant), are not good omens. Other red flags: too many salad dressing choices (indicating they are commercially bottled); soups that taste canned; sauces that smack of Gravymaster; genie-style whipped cream (straight from the bottle or canister); oil that tastes rancid or re-used; canned vegetables; untrimmed salad greens brown at the edges; fish that left its home waters days ago. Fresh food looks and tastes fresh and has real flavor.   9

Say what? Listen up. Rare is rare, whether in lamb, beef, liver, salmon or tuna, and should be served that way if you requested it. Al dente means "to the tooth," barely cooked (meat) or not overcooked (pasta). A good wait person records your request; a good kitchen honors it.   10

No excuses. The chef's day off is not your problem. Consistent performance is often what separates a fine restaurant from an ordinary one, and that means day in and day out. As a customer, you don't want alibis for a poor meal; you've paid for one as good as you had in the same place last week.   11

A rose is a rose is a rose, but risotto ain't always what it's supposed to be. Sometimes it seems as though the chef is meeting a dish for the first time. Whether a simple quiche, cassoulet or teriyaki, food should meet the expectations of the diner and be at least a kissing cousin of the dish whose name it bears. If it isn't, the restaurant should give it a different name, like Chef Paul's Surprise, perhaps.   12

Dining out can be a terrific experience. Just keep your palate honed, your   13
eyes sharp and your sense of humor fine-tuned.

✳

RESPONDING TO THE WHOLE ESSAY

1. Instead of narrating step-by-step the process of restaurant dining, Brooks phrases
    the explanation of the process as advice. By doing so, she is able to establish two
    main categories of the dining experience that a restaurant reviewer should evalu-
    ate. What are they? How does Brooks indicate these categories to the reader?
    Make a list of the things in each of these categories that Brooks advises her read-
    ers to consider when evaluating a dining establishment. Can the items for your
    list be found easily? Why? Explain.
2. Does Brooks ever explicitly state her thesis? If so, where? What is her thesis? [*Har-
    brace* 28d; *Hodges'* 32d]
3. Analyze paragraph 5 as an example of comparison and contrast development.
    Which method of comparison and contrast organization does Brooks choose? Cite
    evidence from the paragraph to support your answer. [*Harbrace* 27b(2); *Hodges'*
    31b(2)]
4. What kind of audience do you think Brooks has in mind for this essay? Cite ev-
    idence from the essay to support your answer. [*Harbrace* 28a; *Hodges'* 32a]
5. Identify and discuss the ways Brooks creates sentence variety in paragraph 11.
    [*Harbrace* 2, 12a, and 12b; *Hodges'* 2, 30a, and 30b]

ANALYZING THE ELEMENTS

Grammar

1. Brooks uses the dialogue in the fourth sentence of paragraph 4 in a unique way.
    What grammatical function does *"Hi, I'm Sebastian, your waiter for tonight"*
    serve in this sentence? What does *too-friendly* modify in this sentence? [*Harbrace*
    1c(4) and 1c(5); *Hodges'* 1c(4) and 1c(5)]
2. Comment upon *which* as an example of broad reference in the last sentence of
    paragraph 4. [*Harbrace* 6b; *Hodges'* 28c]

Effective Sentences

1. The fifth sentence of paragraph 4 could be rewritten: Look instead for cordial
    professionalism; in other words, look for staffers who can describe each dish ac-
    curately, who are knowledgeable about wines, who can pronounce the foreign
    names on the menu, who refill water glasses before you have to ask, and who
    serve drinks promptly with a quick menu and wine list follow-up. What does
    Brooks achieve by writing the sentence as she does? [*Harbrace* 15d; *Hodges'* 21d]
2. What does Brooks achieve by allowing *No excuses* to stand as a fragment at the
    beginning of paragraph 11? Rewrite the fragment as a complete sentence. Is the
    revision as effective as the fragment? [*Harbrace* 2; *Hodges'* 2]

3. What is the function of the parenthetical material in the second sentence of paragraph 8?

Punctuation and Mechanics

1. Brooks introduces several French words, including *cherchez, maître d', crème brulée, quiche,* and *cassoulet.* Explain why these foreign words are not italicized. [*Harbrace* 24b; *Hodges'* 10b]
2. Explain the use of the colon in the first and third sentences of paragraph 6. [*Harbrace* 21d; *Hodges'* 17d]

Diction

1. Paragraph 9 contains several hyphenated words. Make a list of these words and state the reason why each is hyphenated. [*Harbrace* 22f; *Hodges'* 18f]
2. Throughout this essay, Brooks uses idiomatic expressions. Find at least two of the many idiomatic expressions she uses and explain why they are effective. [*Harbrace* 14b and 14c; *Hodges'* 20b and 20c]
3. What effect does Brooks achieve by using *ain't* instead of *is not* in the first sentence of paragraph 12? What does this suggest about the tone of the essay? [*Harbrace* 13b(4) and 29a; *Hodges'* 19e and 33a]

BUILDING VOCABULARY

1. The words *cleanliness* and *weakness* share the suffix *-ness.* What is the meaning of the suffix *-ness?* What are the meanings of *cleanliness* and *weakness?* What is the grammatical form of these words? Make a list of three more words ending in *-ness* and write sentences using each of them.
2. Is the suffix *-ness* borrowed from a foreign language? If not, what is the origin of this suffix?

SUGGESTIONS FOR WRITING

1. Write a short process essay explaining how to evaluate fast-food restaurants or restaurants that deliver meals, such as pizzas.
2. Write an essay to a stranger explaining what he or she can do to find a suitable apartment, roommate, or degree program.

The Maker's Eye: Revising Your Own Manuscripts

Donald M. Murray

Donald M. Murray (1924–) teaches writing at the University of New Hampshire. Before entering teaching, he was a professional journalist, serving as an editor for *Time* and winning the Pulitzer Prize for his editorials in the *Boston Globe.* In recent years Murray has published several books that have influenced the teaching of writing: *A Writer Teaches Writing* and *Learning by Teaching* are both addressed to his fellow teachers; *Write to Learn* is a textbook for students. In "The Maker's Eye: Revising Your Own Manuscripts," Murray focuses on revising as a part of the writing process.

When students complete a first draft, they consider the job of writing done—and their teachers too often agree. When professional writers complete a first draft, they usually feel that they are at the start of the writing process. When a draft is completed, the job of writing can begin.

That difference in attitude is the difference between amateur and professional, inexperience and experience, journeyman and craftsman. Peter F. Drucker, the prolific business writer, calls his first draft "the zero draft"— after that he can start counting. Most writers share the feeling that the first draft, and all of those which follow, are opportunities to discover what they have to say and how best they can say it.

To produce a progression of drafts, each of which says more and says it more clearly, the writer has to develop a special kind of reading skill. In school we are taught to decode what appears on the page as finished writing. Writers, however, face a different category of possibility and responsibility when they read their own drafts. To them the words on the page are never finished. Each can be changed and rearranged, can set off a chain reaction of confusion or clarified meaning. This is a different kind of reading, which is possibly more difficult and certainly more exciting.

Writers must learn to be their own best enemy. They must accept the criticism of others and be suspicious of it; they must accept the praise of others and be even more suspicious of it. Writers cannot depend on others. They must detach themselves from their own pages so that they can apply both their caring and their craft to their own work.

Such detachment is not easy. Science fiction writer Ray Bradbury supposedly puts each manuscript away for a year to the day and then rereads it

156

as a stranger. Not many writers have the discipline or the time to do this. We must read when our judgment may be at its worst, when we are close to the euphoric moment of creation.

Then the writer, counsels novelist Nancy Hale, "should be critical of every- 6 thing that seems to him most delightful in his style. He should excise what he most admires, because he wouldn't thus admire it if he weren't . . . in a sense protecting it from criticism." John Ciardi, the poet, adds, "The last act of the writing must be to become one's own reader. It is, I suppose, a schizophrenic process, to begin passionately and to end critically, to begin hot and to end cold; and, more important, to be passion-hot and critic-cold at the same time."

Most people think that the principal problem is that writers are too proud 7 of what they have written. Actually, a greater problem for most professional writers is one shared by the majority of students. They are overly critical, think everything is dreadful, tear up page after page, never complete a draft, see the task as hopeless.

The writer must learn to read critically but constructively, to cut what is 8 bad, to reveal what is good. Eleanor Estes, the children's book author, explains: "The writer must survey his work critically, coolly, as though he were a stranger to it. He must be willing to prune, expertly and hard-heartedly. At the end of each revision, a manuscript may look . . . worked over, torn apart, pinned together, added to, deleted from, words changed and words changed back. Yet the book must maintain its original freshness and spontaneity."

Most readers underestimate the amount of rewriting it usually takes to 9 produce spontaneous reading. This is a great disadvantage to the student writer, who sees only a finished product and never watches the craftsman who takes the necessary step back, studies the work carefully, returns to the task, steps back, returns, steps back, again and again. Anthony Burgess, one of the most prolific writers in the English-speaking world, admits, "I might revise a page twenty times." Roald Dahl, the popular children's writer, states, "By the time I'm nearing the end of a story, the first part will have been reread and altered and corrected at least 150 times. . . . Good writing is essentially rewriting. I am positive of this."

Rewriting isn't virtuous. It isn't something that ought to be done. It is 10 simply something that most writers find they have to do to discover what they have to say and how to say it. It is a condition of the writer's life.

There are, however, a few writers who do little formal rewriting, primarily 11 because they have the capacity and experience to create and review a large number of invisible drafts in their minds before they approach the page. And some writers slowly produce finished pages, performing all the tasks of revision simultaneously, page by page, rather than draft by draft. But it is still possible to see the sequence followed by most writers most of the time in rereading their own work.

Most writers scan their drafts first, reading as quickly as possible to catch 12 the larger problems of subject and form, then move in closer and closer as they read and write, reread and rewrite.

The first thing writers look for in their drafts is *information*. They know   13
that a good piece of writing is built from specific, accurate, and interesting
information. The writer must have an abundance of information from which
to construct a readable piece of writing.

Next writers look for *meaning* in the information. The specifies must build   14
to a pattern of significance. Each piece of specific information must carry the
reader toward meaning.

Writers reading their own drafts are aware of *audience*. They put them-   15
selves in the reader's situation and make sure that they deliver information
which a reader wants to know or needs to know in a manner which is easily
digested. Writers try to be sure that they anticipate and answer the questions
a critical reader will ask when reading the piece of writing.

Writers make sure that the *form* is appropriate to the subject and the au-   16
dience. Form, or genre, is the vehicle which carries meaning to the reader, but
form cannot be selected until the writer has adequate information to discover
its significance and an audience which needs or wants that meaning.

Once writers are sure the form is appropriate, they must then look at the   17
structure, the order of what they have written. Good writing is built on a solid
framework of logic, argument, narrative, or motivation which runs through
the entire piece of writing and holds it together. This is the time when many
writers find it most effective to outline as a way of visualizing the hidden spine
by which the piece of writing is supported.

The element on which writers may spend a majority of their time is *de-*   18
velopment. Each section of a piece of writing must be adequately developed.
It must give readers enough information so that they are satisfied. How much
information is enough? That's as difficult as asking how much garlic belongs
in a salad. It must be done to taste, but most beginning writers underdevelop,
underestimating the reader's hunger for information.

As writers solve development problems, they often have to consider ques-   19
tions of *dimension*. There must be a pleasing and effective proportion among
all the parts of the piece of writing. There is a continual process of subtract-
ing and adding to keep the piece of writing in balance.

Finally, writers have to listen to their own voices. *Voice* is the force which   20
drives a piece of writing forward. It is an expression of the writer's authority
and concern. It is what is between the words on the page, what glues the piece
of writing together. A good piece of writing is always marked by a consistent,
individual voice.

As writers read and reread, write and rewrite, they move closer and closer   21
to the page until they are doing line-by-line editing. Writers read their own
pages with infinite care. Each sentence, each line, each clause, each phrase,
each word, each mark of punctuation, each section of white space between
the type has to contribute to the clarification of meaning.

Slowly the writer moves from word to word, looking through language   22
to see the subject. As a word is changed, cut, or added, as a construction is

rearranged, all the words used before that moment and all those that follow that moment must be considered and reconsidered.

Writers often read aloud at this stage of the editing process, muttering or whispering to themselves, calling on the ear's experience with language. Does this sound right—or that? Writers edit, shifting back and forth from eye to page to ear to page. I find I must do this careful editing in short runs, no more than fifteen or twenty minutes at a stretch, or I become too kind with myself. I begin to see what I hope is on the page, not what actually is on the page. 23

This sounds tedious if you haven't done it, but actually it is fun. Making something right is immensely satisfying, for writers begin to learn what they are writing about by writing. Language leads them to meaning, and there is the joy of discovery, of understanding, of making meaning clear as the writer employs the technical skills of language. 24

Words have double meanings, even triple and quadruple meanings. Each word has its own potential for connotation and denotation. And when writers rub one word against the other, they are often rewarded with a sudden insight, an unexpected clarification. 25

The maker's eye moves back and forth from word to phrase to sentence to paragraph to sentence to phrase to word. The maker's eye sees the need for variety and balance, for a firmer structure, for a more appropriate form. It peers into the interior of the paragraph, looking for coherence, unity, and emphasis, which make meaning clear. 26

I learned something about this process when my first bifocals were prescribed. I had ordered a larger section of the reading portion of the glass because of my work, but even so, I could not contain my eyes within this new limit of vision. And I still find myself taking off my glasses and bending my nose towards the page, for my eyes unconsciously flick back and forth across the page, back to another page, forward to still another, as I try to see each evolving line in relation to every other line. 27

When does this process end? Most writers agree with the great Russian writer Tolstoy, who said, "I scarcely ever reread my published writings, if by chance I come across a page, it always strikes me: all this must be rewritten; this is how I should have written it." 28

The maker's eye is never satisfied, for each word has the potential to ignite new meaning. This article has been twice written all the way through the writing process, and it was published four years ago. Now it is to be republished in a book. The editors make a few small suggestions, and then I read it with my maker's eye. Now it has been re-edited, re-revised, re-read, re-re-edited, for each piece of writing to the writer is full of potential and alternatives. 29

A piece of writing is never finished. It is delivered to a deadline, torn out of the typewriter on demand, sent off with a sense of accomplishment and shame and pride and frustration. If only there were a couple more days, time for just another run at it, perhaps then . . . 30

✳

RESPONDING TO THE WHOLE ESSAY

1. Is Murray writing primarily for college students or for anyone who wants to improve as a writer? How do you know? How useful is the essay for college students? For others? [*Harbrace* 28a; *Hodges'* 32a]
2. Is Murray's purpose in "The Maker's Eye" primarily to express himself about writing, to provide information about writing, or to persuade the reader to adopt certain writing procedures? If the essay has more than one of these aims, point to evidence of each one. [*Harbrace* 28a; *Hodges'* 32a]
3. What characteristics of a good introduction does Murray's first paragraph display? Explain. [*Harbrace* 28f(1); *Hodges'* 32f(1)]
4. Explain why Murray's conclusion is effective. [*Harbrace* 33f(2); *Hodges'* 37f(2)]
5. After rereading paragraph 20, explain what methods Murray uses to define *voice*. [*Harbrace* 27d(7); *Hodges'* 31d(7)]
6. What are the steps in the writing process that Murray describes? Will the process work if some steps are performed out of sequence? Which steps (if any) can be omitted? Will following these steps guarantee better writing? Why or why not?

ANALYZING THE ELEMENTS

Grammar

1. Identify the subordinate clauses in the second sentence of paragraph 15 and explain specifically how each one functions in the sentence. [*Harbrace* 1d; *Hodges'* 1d]
2. In paragraphs 16, 17, and 18 (and in a number of other paragraphs as well) Murray uses the passive voice. In each of these paragraphs, find the sentence in which the verb is passive, and rewrite the sentence with an active verb. What problems do you encounter? In each sentence, what problem did Murray's choice of the passive solve? Explain. [*Harbrace* 7c; *Hodges'* 7c]

Effective Sentences

1. Comment on at least two ways in which Murray makes the first sentence in paragraph 3 effective. [*Harbrace* 11b and 11e; *Hodges'* 29b and 29e]
2. Examine the second sentence of paragraph 4. Explain its structure and the effect. [*Harbrace* 10a; *Hodges'* 26a]

Punctuation and Mechanics

1. Explain the uses of the commas, quotation marks, and ellipsis points in the first two sentences of paragraph 6. [*Harbrace* 17, 20a, and 21i; *Hodges'* 12, 16a, and 17i]
2. Explain the uses of the commas, colon, and quotation marks in the second sentence of paragraph 8. [*Harbrace* 17, 21d, and 20a; *Hodges'* 12, 17d, and 16a]

Diction

1. Examine Murray's use of figurative language—for example, "the hidden spine" (paragraph 17) and "writers rub one word against the other" (paragraph 25). Point to several instances of figurative language and explain what each one adds to the essay. [*Harbrace* 14a(5); *Hodges'* 20a(4)]
2. Murray repeats the word *each* seven times in the last sentence in paragraph 21. What is gained by the repetition? Is the repetition necessary? Why do we not perceive it as wordy? [*Harbrace* 15a and 15b; *Hodges'* 21a and 21b]

BUILDING VOCABULARY

1. From what Latin roots is *manuscript* derived? What do they mean? Write a sentence using a word derived from one of these Latin roots.
2. List and define two synonyms for *revise*. Write sentences using each of these synonyms.

SUGGESTIONS FOR WRITING

1. Write a process essay explaining how to acquire a certain skill (such as riding a bicycle or skateboard, windsurfing, skiing, swimming, playing a certain musical instrument, juggling).
2. Write a process essay explaining how to solve a particular problem (selecting a course of study, overcoming stage fright, breaking a bad habit).

The Spider and the Wasp
Alexander Petrunkevitch

Born in Russia and educated there and in Germany, Petrunkevitch (1875–1964) emigrated to America in 1903. He taught for many years at Yale University, and while on that faculty published the books that made him an internationally recognized authority on spiders: *Index Catalogue of Spiders of North, Central, and South America* (1911) and *An Inquiry into the Natural Classification of Spiders* (1933). Petrunkevitch was also well known for his translations of English and Russian poetry, and he was a historian and philosopher as well as a scientist. This essay, written for *Scientific American,* reflects his lifelong interest in insects and his gifts as a writer.

In the feeding and safeguarding of their progeny insects and spiders exhibit some interesting analogies to reasoning and some crass examples of blind instinct. The case I propose to describe here is that of the tarantula spiders and their arch-enemy, the digger wasps of the genus Pepsis. It is a classic example of what looks like intelligence pitted against instinct—a strange situation in which the victim, though fully able to defend itself, submits unwittingly to its destruction.

Most tarantulas live in the tropics, but several species occur in the temperate zone and a few are common in the southern U.S. Some varieties are large and have powerful fangs with which they can inflict a deep wound. These formidable looking spiders do not, however, attack man; you can hold one in your hand, if you are gentle, without being bitten. Their bite is dangerous only to insects and small mammals such as mice; for man it is no worse than a hornet's sting.

Tarantulas customarily live in deep cylindrical burrows, from which they emerge at dusk and into which they retire at dawn. Mature males wander about after dark in search of females and occasionally stray into houses. After mating, the male dies in a few weeks, but a female lives much longer and can mate several years in succession. In a Paris museum is a tropical specimen which is said to have been living in captivity for 25 years.

A fertilized female tarantula lays from 200 to 400 eggs at a time; thus it is possible for a single tarantula to produce several thousand young. She takes no care of them beyond weaving a cocoon of silk to enclose the eggs. After they hatch, the young walk away, find convenient places in which to dig their burrows and spend the rest of their lives in solitude. The eyesight of tarantulas is poor, being limited to a sensing of change in the intensity of light and to the perception of moving objects. They apparently have little or no sense of hearing, for a hungry tarantula will pay no attention to a loudly chirping cricket placed in its cage unless the insect happens to touch one of its legs.

But all spiders, and especially hairy ones, have an extremely delicate sense 5
of touch. Laboratory experiments prove that tarantulas can distinguish three types of touch: pressure against the body wall, stroking of the body hair, and riffling of certain very fine hairs on the legs called trichobothria. Pressure against the body, by the finger or the end of a pencil, causes the tarantula to move off slowly for a short distance. The touch excites no defensive response unless the approach is from above where the spider can see the motion, in which case it rises on its hind legs, lifts its front legs, opens its fangs and holds this threatening posture as long as the object continues to move.

The entire body of a tarantula, especially its legs, is thickly clothed with 6
hair. Some of it is short and wooly, some long and stiff. Touching this body hair produces one of two distinct reactions. When the spider is hungry, it responds with an immediate and swift attack. At the touch of a cricket's antennae the tarantula seizes the insect so swiftly that a motion picture taken at the rate of 64 frames per second shows only the result and not the process of capture. But when the spider is not hungry, the stimulation of its hairs merely causes it to shake the touched limb. An insect can walk under its hairy belly unharmed.

The trichobothria, very fine hairs growing from disclike membranes on 7
the legs, are sensitive only to air movement. A light breeze makes them vibrate slowly, without disturbing the common hair. When one blows gently on the trichobothria, the tarantula reacts with a quick jerk of its four front legs. If the front and hind legs are stimulated at the same time, the spider makes a sudden jump. This reaction is quite independent of the state of its appetite.

These three tactile responses—to pressure on the body wall, to moving of 8
the common hair, and to flexing of the trichobothria—are so different from one another that there is no possibility of confusing them. They serve the tarantula adequately for most of its needs and enable it to avoid most annoyances and dangers. But they fail the spider completely when it meets its deadly enemy, the digger wasp Pepsis.

These solitary wasps are beautiful and formidable creatures. Most species 9
are either a deep shiny blue all over, or deep blue with rusty wings. The largest have a wing span of about four inches. They live on nectar. When excited, they give off a pungent odor—a warning that they are ready to attack. The sting is much worse than that of a bee or common wasp, and the pain and swelling last longer. In the adult stage the wasp lives only a few months. The female produces but a few eggs, one at a time at intervals of two or three days. For each egg the mother must provide one adult tarantula, alive but paralyzed. The mother wasp attaches the egg to the paralyzed spider's abdomen. Upon hatching from the egg, the larva is many hundreds of times smaller than

its living but helpless victim. It eats no other food and drinks no water. By the time it has finished its single Gargantuan meal and become ready for wasp-hood, nothing remains of the tarantula but its indigestible chitinous skeleton.

The mother wasp goes tarantula-hunting when the egg in her ovary is al-   10
most ready to be laid. Flying low over the ground late on a sunny afternoon, the wasp looks for its victim or for the mouth of a tarantula burrow, a round hole edged by a bit of silk. The sex of the spider makes no difference, but the mother is highly discriminating as to species. Each species of Pepsis requires a certain species of tarantula, and the wasp will not attack the wrong species. In a cage with a tarantula which is not its normal prey, the wasp avoids the spider and is usually killed by it in the night.

Yet when a wasp finds the correct species, it is the other way about. To   11
identify the species the wasp apparently must explore the spider with her an-tennae. The tarantula shows an amazing tolerance to this exploration. The wasp crawls under it and walks over it without evoking any hostile response. The molestation is so great and so persistent that the tarantula often rises on all eight legs, as if it were on stilts. It may stand this way for several minutes. Meanwhile the wasp, having satisfied itself that the victim is of the right species, moves off a few inches to dig the spider's grave. Working vigorously with legs and jaws, it excavates a hole 8 to 10 inches deep with a diameter slightly larger than the spider's girth. Now and again the wasp pops out of the hole to make sure that the spider is still there.

When the grave is finished, the wasp returns to the tarantula to complete   12
her ghastly enterprise. First she feels it all over once more with her antennae. Then her behavior becomes more aggressive. She bends her abdomen, pro-truding her sting, and searches for the soft membrane at the point where the spider's legs join its body—the only spot where she can penetrate the horny skeleton. From time to time, as the exasperated spider slowly shifts ground, the wasp turns on her back and slides along with the aid of her wings, trying to get under the tarantula for a shot at the vital spot. During all this maneu-vering, which can last for several minutes, the tarantula makes no move to save itself. Finally the wasp corners it against some obstruction and grasps one of its legs in her powerful jaws. Now at last the harassed spider tries a desperate but vain defense. The two contestants roll over and over on the ground. It is a terrifying sight and the outcome is always the same. The wasp finally manages to thrust her sting into the soft spot and holds it there for a few seconds while she pumps in the poison. Almost immediately the taran-tula falls paralyzed on its back. Its legs stop twitching; its heart stops beat-ing. Yet it is not dead, as is shown by the fact that if taken from the wasp it can be restored to some sensitivity by being kept in a moist chamber for sev-eral months.

After paralyzing the tarantula, the wasp cleans herself by dragging her   13
body along the ground and rubbing her feet, sucks the drop of blood oozing

from the wound in the spider's abdomen, then grabs a leg of the flabby, help-less animal in her jaws and drags it down to the bottom of the grave. She stays there for many minutes, sometimes for several hours, and what she does all that time in the dark we do not know. Eventually she lays her egg and at-taches it to the side of the spider's abdomen with a sticky secretion. Then she emerges, fills the grave with soil carried bit by bit in her jaws, and finally tramples the ground all around to hide any trace of the grave from prowlers. Then she flies away, leaving her descendant safely started in life.

In all this the behavior of the wasp evidently is qualitatively different from that of the spider. The wasp acts like an intelligent animal. This is not to say that instinct plays no part or that she reasons as man does. But her actions are to the point; they are not automatic and can be modified to fit the situa-tion. We do not know for certain how she identifies the tarantula—probably it is by some olfactory or chemo-tactile sense—but she does it purposefully and does not blindly tackle a wrong species.   14

On the other hand, the tarantula's behavior shows only confusion. Evi-dently the wasp's pawing gives it no pleasure, for it tries to move away. That the wasp is not simulating sexual stimulation is certain because male and fe-male tarantulas react in the same way to its advances. That the spider is not anesthetized by some odorless secretion is easily shown by blowing lightly at the tarantula and making it jump suddenly. What, then, makes the tarantula behave as stupidly as it does?   15

No clear, simple answer is available. Possibly the stimulation by the wasp's antennae is masked by a heavier pressure on the spider's body, so that it re-acts as when prodded by a pencil. But the explanation may be much more complex. Initiative in attack is not in the nature of tarantulas; most species fight only when cornered so that escape is impossible. Their inherited patterns of behavior apparently prompt them to avoid problems rather than attack them. For example, spiders always weave their webs in three dimensions, and when a spider finds that there is insufficient space to attach certain threads in the third dimension, it leaves the place and seeks another, instead of fin-ishing the web in a single plane. This urge to escape seems to arise under all circumstances, in all phases of life, and to take the place of reasoning. For a spider to change the pattern of its web is as impossible as for an inexperi-enced man to build a bridge across a chasm obstructing his way.   16

In a way the instinctive urge to escape is not only easier but often more efficient than reasoning. The tarantula does exactly what is most efficient in all cases except in an encounter with a ruthless and determined attacker de-pendent for the existence of her own species on killing as many tarantulas as she can lay eggs. Perhaps in this case the spider follows its usual pattern of trying to escape, instead of seizing and killing the wasp, because it is not aware of its danger. In any case, the survival of the tarantula species as a whole is protected by the fact that the spider is much more fertile than the wasp.   17

❋

RESPONDING TO THE WHOLE ESSAY

1.   What kind of audience is Petrunkevitch writing for in this essay? What evidence in the essay reveals the audience Petrunkevitch envisions? [*Harbrace* 28a; *Hodges'* 32a]
2.   "The Spider and the Wasp" is primarily a minutely observed factual account, but its power as an essay depends on the author's fascination with his subject. What evidence of this personal involvement can you point to? Are Petrunkevitch's feelings ever explicitly stated? If so, where? [*Harbrace* 28a; *Hodges'* 32a]
3.   Analyze paragraph 12 for ways in which Petrunkevitch links sentences to make time relationships clear and form a coherent sequence. Mark the kinds of transitional devices you discover in the paragraph. [*Harbrace* 27b; *Hodges'* 31b]
4.   Point throughout the essay to examples of inductive reasoning. [*Harbrace* 31e; *Hodges'* 35e]
5.   What kinds of transitions does Petrunkevitch use to move from paragraph to paragraph? Explain the transition from paragraph 15 to paragraph 16. [*Harbrace* 27b(4); *Hodges'* 31b(4)]
6.   What central idea gives unity to the essay? Show how the essay is unified. [*Harbrace* 27a; *Hodges'* 31a]

ANALYZING THE ELEMENTS

Grammar

1.   In the first sentence of paragraph 1, what is the grammatical function of each of these words: *feeding, safeguarding, interesting, reasoning*? [*Harbrace* 1c and 4a; *Hodges'* 1c and 4a]
2.   What is the grammatical function of each *which* in the first sentence of paragraph 3? What is the antecedent? What reasons can you give for preferring the sentence as it is written rather than writing it as follows: "burrows which they emerge from at dusk and which they retire into at dawn"? [*Harbrace* 1c; *Hodges'* 1c]
3.   What reason can you give for the use of the passive voice in the final sentence in paragraph 10? Try rewriting the sentence so that the verbs are all in the active voice. What difficulties do you encounter? [*Harbrace* 1b and 7; *Hodges'* 1b and 7]
4.   What is the subject of each of the following verbs in the first sentence of paragraph 13: *cleans, sucks, grabs, drags*? [*Harbrace* 1a and 1b; *Hodges'* 1a and 1b]

Effective Sentences

1.   In the first sentence of the essay, how does Petrunkevitch let the reader know which kinds of characteristics insects exhibit and which kinds spiders exhibit? [*Harbrace* 10a; *Hodges'* 26a]
2.   The last sentence in paragraph 3 is inverted. Why? [*Harbrace* 11f; *Hodges'* 29f]
3.   In the first sentence of paragraph 8, are the elements of the series contained within the dashes parallel? If so, explain why. If not, how could the sentence be written to make them parallel? [*Harbrace* 10a; *Hodges'* 26a]

Punctuation and Mechanics

1. Explain the uses of the dash and the commas in the final sentence of paragraph 1. Would other punctuation have served as well? Why or why not? [*Harbrace* 21e and 17d; *Hodges'* 17e and 12d]
2. What use of the semicolon is found in the last two sentences of paragraph 2? How are the parts of the sentences on either side of each semicolon related to each other? [*Harbrace* 18a; *Hodges'* 14a]
3. Why is the colon in the second sentence of paragraph 5 appropriate? What other marks of punctuation could have been used? Which is most effective? Why? [*Harbrace* 21d; *Hodges'* 17d]

Diction

1. What is the meaning of the following words: *progeny, crass,* and *unwittingly* (paragraph 1); *riffling* (paragraph 5); *tactile* (paragraph 8); *formidable* and *pungent* (paragraph 9); *tramples* (paragraph 13)? Explain how these words are more exact choices than their synonyms would be. [*Harbrace* 14a(1); *Hodges'* 20a(1)]
2. Find examples of technical vocabulary in the essay. What reasons did Petrunkevitch probably have for using these words? Do they interfere with your understanding of the essay? Why or why not? [*Harbrace* 13c(1); *Hodges'* 19g]
3. Throughout the essay, Petrunkevitch uses several informal words and expressions. How do they contribute to or detract from the success of the essay? [*Harbrace* 13b(1); *Hodges'* 19b]
4. Petrunkevitch uses an allusion, *Gargantuan,* in the final sentence of paragraph 9. To what does he allude? Is the allusion effective? Why or why not? [*Harbrace* 13a; *Hodges'* 19a]

BUILDING VOCABULARY

1. A secondary definition offered in *The American Heritage Dictionary* describes the tarantula as "a large wolf spider (*Lycosa tarentula*) of southern Europe, once thought to cause tarantism." Look up the word *tarantism* in your dictionary. What does it mean? What is the primary definition of *tarantula*?
2. The word *cylindrical* is the adjectival form of *cylinder.* Notice that *cylinder* is defined according to three different academic disciplines. What are they? How is *cylinder* defined within each of these disciplines?

SUGGESTIONS FOR WRITING

1. Consider the ritual of the spider and the wasp, as Petrunkevitch reports it. Then, as a detached but fascinated observer, write a short process essay (under 1,000 words) describing in meticulous detail some human ritual. Here are a few suggestions:

Commuting

Going to the laundromat

Celebrating a birthday

Eating a lobster or an artichoke

High school graduation

College registration

Calling for a date

Shopping at the supermarket

2. Closely observe your pet or another animal in some typical behavior, such as eating, begging, or stalking, and write a short process essay describing the behavior in great detail.

Writing the First-Person Article
Mary Alice Kellogg

Living in New York, Mary Alice Kellogg works as a writer and editor, and she has published numerous essays in such popular magazines as the *Ladies' Home Journal, GQ, Sports Illustrated, Newsweek,* and *Travel & Leisure.* Along with the Lowell Thomas Journalism Award, Kellogg has received the ASJA Article of the Year Award for her first-person essay published in *Glamour,* "The Search for My Father." In "Writing the First-Person Article," originally published in *The Writer,* Kellogg uses excerpts from her award-winning essay about the search for her father and anecdotes from her twenty-five years of experience as a professional writer to explain how anyone can write a successful first-person essay.

When does someone become a writer? How do you know that that's what you want to do? Everyone has some particular, pivotal moment when the answer to that question becomes clear, and for me, it was at the tender age of ten. I wrote a letter to the editor of *The Western Horseman,* recounting in my best ten-year-old prose what it was like to ride horses in the desert outside my hometown, and how happy it made me. To my delight—and total surprise—the magazine published my effort, and my writing course was set.

Without realizing it, I had published my first first-person story. And, also without knowing it, I had followed one of the most important rules of writing: "Write what you know." That's what we do, after all, when we write an essay or first-person piece. But even with no characters to invent, no endless interviewing, the first-person piece, ironically, is one of the hardest things to write. But in twenty-five years of professional writing, I've found that the first-person form is the one place I can be myself as a writer, let my thoughts and observations go where they will. It's the form I love the most, but it's also, even after all these years, still difficult.

Why? Because having a great first-person story to tell is only the beginning. Take the story I'm working on now: a first-person piece about my Aunt Mary, who recently died. For 35 years we'd exchanged letters—I saved every one—and I wanted to do a story about what she taught me through our correspondence. While the experience meant a great deal to me, would people who didn't know me or my Aunt Mary want to read it? That's the first question I ask myself when thinking about writing any essay. In this case, I decided that the key to the piece would be how generations can reach out to

1

2

3

169

one another, learn from one another—an element that would touch many families, not just mine.

Your first-person essay is on solid ground if you follow three basic rules: 4
1) You should feel passionately about the subject; it should make you laugh, see red, contemplate the human condition in ways large or small. Passion— an enthusiasm for what you are saying—is not only *a* starting point, it's the *only* place to begin. You must have a point of view, and sell that point of view, that particular experience, to others.

2) Your first-person piece must have a point that is applicable to others,   5
a focus that gives what happened to you a universal quality. It's not enough, for example, to experience being discriminated against because you're over fifty; you have to take that experience and make others feel what you felt, and along the way offer some insight into how others might react or change. Yes, you have something you want to say, but *why* do you want to say it? Whom do you want to reach? What do you passionately want to tell them?

And 3) you must write in your own voice. That's the whole point of any   6
first-person effort. If you admire Dave Barry's prose, the worst thing you can do is try to write like him. Writers who succeed do so because they have something to say in a way that can't be said by anyone else. Listen to how you speak, the phrases you use that mark your speech, the way you organize your thought patterns, the way you tell a story or anecdote. Then sit down and write that way, and continue to do so. No one finds his or her writing voice right off the bat; the key is to stick with it so your first-person style is as natural as your being there in person. The highest compliment readers can give me is to say that in reading an article of mine, they can *hear* my voice.

As with any article, the first-person piece must tell a story, with a begin-   7
ning (including a grabbing lead), a middle to develop your views, and a strong end. Last year, I did a first-person piece about growing older (something I feel passionately about). I decided to have a makeup artist age me 25 years, then spent a day as an older woman to see what fears about aging might crop up (the universal here: many members of my generation are afraid of getting gray). Here's how I began the piece:

> As a member of the baby-boom generation, I've tried not to think about growing older. When I am old and gray, I will be blonde, I trill. But if truth be told, at 45 I am frightened of growing old, which is why I decided to conduct this generation-bending experiment.

My experiences that day made up the middle of the piece: people's reac-   8
tions to me, how I felt in my new "skin." And, at the end, I told what I had learned:

> I was encouraged by what the woman within had shown me: that I am invisible only if I allow myself to be. . . . I look forward to meeting that woman in the mirror again. I know now how very much I will enjoy being her someday, for real.

It's true that life is the best source material. It is for me. And there are as 9
many opportunities for first-person expression, as many places to begin, as
there are experiences to relate. It's up to you to decide which way to go. Here
are some basic jumping-off points that I use to get started:

- *An incident that happened to you.* Make the reader care about it. Did the
airline lose your luggage? It happened to me a few years ago, and not only did
I get mad, I got even, writing an essay about what was in that suitcase, how
much I felt the loss, and what I learned about taking irreplaceable items on the
road in the future.

- *A unique experience you've had:* Surviving a plane crash or earthquake; helping a loved one through an illness or divorce; raising a Down's Syndrome child;
or learning to write with your left hand after breaking your right arm—all perfect first-person material. The key is to examine in a personal way not just the
experience itself, but the aftermath. How did it change you? Your loved ones?
What did you learn that might help others? In my case, searching for and finding my father after many years and discovering I had an entirely new batch of
relatives gave me the opportunity to examine the issues of tolerance, forgiveness, and personal growth. The article appeared in *Glamour* and received a
national writing award.

It also taught me a lot about patience, which is important when writing
in the first person about a life-altering event. I had tried for years to write this
story—in first person, as a reporting piece, and as third-person fiction. But it
never quite worked out the way I wanted it to. Finally, when the time was
right, first-person won out. I joked with my editor that the story took me
15 years and an afternoon to write, but in this case, I simply needed time
to put all the issues—and my thoughts—into perspective:

> I've learned to accept things. I saw that finding someone is never a sim-
> ple proposition, even on the best of terms. Nothing is the same. I can
> accept my father, too. When his father died recently, he called me and
> we settled down to talk as I had always hoped a father and daughter
> could. Our exchange wasn't an insight-filled sensitivity session, but it
> was something basic and of value. And, at the end of it, he signed off
> as he always does: "I love you, hon. Thanks for finding me."

- *Life stages.* Turning 40, being a newly divorced dad with custody of the kids,
losing your job. If Gail Sheehy can make a career out of this, surely you can
find a new angle in the tale you have to tell others going through the same
thing.

- *Humor.* Say you're a klutz? A bad housekeeper and proud of it? The only
one whose dog flunked obedience class? Then tell it with a smile.

- *A trend that touches you.* I broke into *TV Guide* by noticing that there were
few blonde role models on television (I'm blonde), then I not only wrote about
how that made me feel, but also interviewed and took to task the programming
executives who create TV shows. (No surprise: They were all brunette.) We're

all touched by societal issues, from blaring radios in cars, to worries about health care, to kids who behave badly in restaurants. Take a trend or issue, show how it affects your life, and offer some first-person observation and advice along the way.

• *Family.* Everyone's got 'em; the trick is to find something unique that makes your reminiscence of interest to the reader. My recent essay in *Diversion* was a tribute to my mother, who taught me from childhood how to travel "first class." I spoke of what I learned from her, what made our trips memorable, and how her legacy lives in me in a particularly special way. I'm a travel writer who's reported from 64 countries so far; much of my interest in the world came from my mother's enthusiasm about new places.

Once you have the subject and framework for your first-person piece, *know your market.* A lively or moving first-person piece can never see the light of day, no matter how well-written, unless it finds the appropriate publisher. And there are more outlets today than ever before: the editorial pages of your local newspaper (yes, a reasoned and passionate letter to the editor is a good start, and could lead to an op-ed piece; or in my case, to a career); general magazines; magazines for men and women; publications for every hobby and special interest. I turned my experience of breaking my foot and being in a cast into a light piece for *Weight Watchers Magazine.* I wrote about how the experience taught me patience, not to mention ingenious ways of keeping the weight off when I couldn't jog. 10

Marketing is all-important. A careful reading of several issues of the magazine you are aiming for will tell you the kinds of subjects and treatment they give to first-person pieces. Check the length (a 2,000-word piece won't fly if the magazine runs only 750-word, one-page essays), note whether all the first-person pieces are by men or women, and if the magazine is hospitable to humor or never uses it. 11

But in your marketing, be careful not to try to adapt your writing *voice* to those that have appeared in the magazine. Your unique voice is your key to selling; your research will simply tell you what magazines publish first-person and what kinds of subjects are of interest to them. If you want to write a piece on being a klutz in your all-woman aerobics class, *Family Circle,* for example, would be a better place to submit than *Esquire.* Your experiences working in a senior center would find a more receptive home in *Ladies' Home Journal* or *Modern Maturity* than in a Generation X-type publication like *Details.* 12

Writing the first-person piece can be one of the most satisfying and rewarding—and yes, *fun*—writing you may do. Just keep your own voice and perspective in the forefront, and remember that what happens to you is important and may be important to a reader as well, if written with passion and enthusiasm. 13

✳

RESPONDING TO THE WHOLE ESSAY

1. Point to evidence of expressive, informative, and persuasive purposes in "Writing the First-Person Article." Is one purpose dominant? Explain. [*Harbrace* 28a; *Hodges'* 32a]
2. What strategy for developing ideas does Kellogg choose for paragraph 1? What effect does she achieve by opening the essay in this way? [*Harbrace* 27b(2); *Hodges'* 31b(2)]
3. Reread "Writing the First-Person Article," marking places where Kellogg uses examples. Comment on the effect these examples produce. [*Harbrace* 27b(2); *Hodges'* 31b(2)]
4. Kellogg presents herself as an authority whose advice readers should accept. Where and how does she do so? Is her claim convincing? Explain. [*Harbrace* 31d; *Hodges'* 35d]
5. Notice that Kellogg uses two different series of lists in this essay. Where do each of these lists begin and end? How can you tell? What purpose is served by developing the essay in this way? [*Harbrace* 21d, 21f, and 24; *Hodges'* 17d, 17f, and 10]

ANALYZING THE ELEMENTS

Grammar

1. The first sentence after "*Life stages*" in paragraph 9 is a fragment, but it is justifiable. To see how Kellogg makes this fragment work, try connecting it to the sentence that follows it. What happens in this case? Is this revision grammatically effective? Why or why not? Explain. What is the effect of allowing the fragment to stand alone? [*Harbrace* 2 and 21f; *Hodges'* 2 and 17f]
2. Why does Kellogg use *who's* rather than *whose* in the last sentence after "*Family*" in paragraph 9? Explain. [*Harbrace* 19a; *Hodges'* 13a]

Effective Sentences

1. What is achieved by the parallel structures of the first and second sentences of paragraph 2? [*Harbrace* 10a and 27b(3); *Hodges'* 26a and 31b(3)]
2. In the third sentence of paragraph 10, Kellogg uses a correlative, but it is incomplete. What correlative does Kellogg use? What word is omitted? How does Kellogg compensate for this omission? [*Harbrace* 1c(7); *Hodges'* 1c(7)]
3. Explain why Kellogg uses the *there are* construction in the main clause of the third sentence of paragraph 10. Be as specific as you can. [*Harbrace* 7a(5) and 11f; *Hodges'* 6a(5) and 29f]
4. Rewrite the fifth sentence of paragraph 6 by replacing the comma following *speak* with a colon. Now rewrite the sentence replacing the comma after *speak* with a dash. Which of these sentences, including Kellogg's original, most clearly shows

the relationship between the main clause and the following series of phrases? Why do you think Kellogg chose to use the comma? [*Harbrace* 21d and 21e; *Hodges'* 17d and 17e]

Punctuation and Mechanics

1. Comment upon Kellogg's use of the semicolon in the following sentences: the seventh sentence of paragraph 6, the last sentence after "*Family*," and the third sentence of paragraph 9. [*Harbrace* 18; *Hodges'* 14]
2. Explain Kellogg's use of the dash in paragraph 9 after "breaking your right arm." [*Harbrace* 21e; *Hodges'* 17e]
3. How does Kellogg use italics in paragraph 9? Try to explain why Kellogg italicizes the one word or phrasal openings that follow the bullets (•). [*Harbrace* 24; *Hodges'* 10]
4. Kellogg uses parentheses throughout "Writing the First-Person Article." Explain the use of parentheses in paragraphs 4, 5, and 6. Why do you think Kellogg chooses to use only one half of the parentheses in paragraphs 4–6? Does this partial punctuation confuse the reader? Why or why not? [*Harbrace* 21f; *Hodges'* 17f]

Diction

1. Kellogg uses idiomatic expressions in the following sentences: the first sentence of paragraph 4, the seventh sentence of paragraph 6, and the parenthetical sentence in paragraph 11. Identify and discuss these expressions. Are any of these expressions metaphorical? Explain what they mean in the context of the sentences. [*Harbrace* 14b and 14c; *Hodges'* 20b and 20c]
2. Explain why Kellogg chooses to use the adjective *jumping-off* rather than *starting* in the fifth sentence of paragraph 9. [*Harbrace* 15c; *Hodges'* 21c]
3. In the third sentence of paragraph 10, Kellogg introduces the term *op-ed*. From what two words does this abbreviated term derive? [*Harbrace* 13; *Hodges'* 19]

BUILDING VOCABULARY

1. The suffixes -*ation* and -*ence* are often added to verbs to create nouns, as in *generation, observation, publication, correspondence,* and *reminiscence.* What are the verbs from which these words derive?
2. Define each of the nouns in question 1 and the verbs from which they derive. Write sentences using each of these nouns and verbs.

SUGGESTIONS FOR WRITING

1. Think of an intellectual or artistic activity which you enjoy and at which you excel. Write an essay explaining how you came to discover this activity and how a person unfamiliar with that activity could do it successfully.
2. Pretend that a younger member of your family is setting up housekeeping alone for the first time. Offering some examples from your own experiences, write an essay giving directions for a survival skill (for example, balancing a checkbook, doing laundry, cleaning a bathroom).

✳

Chapter 5

Cause and Effect

C*ause* and *effect* are complementary terms: *cause* refers to what makes things happen (reasons); *effect* refers to what happens (results). A cause always presupposes one or more effects; an effect has one or more causes. Cause-and-effect essays can focus on exploring either causes or effects, or they may analyze a causal chain, in which an effect becomes the cause of an effect that in turn also is a cause, and so on. In this chapter, for example, Rachel L. Jones's "The Price of Hate: Thoughts on Covering a Ku Klux Klan Rally" and Carl Sagan's "The Nuclear Winter" predict effects, and Maurice Shadbolt's "Who Killed the Bog Men of Denmark? And Why?" explores a causal chain.

Although cause-and-effect essays occasionally have a mainly expressive aim, emphasizing the writer's personal responses, usually they are intended to be informative or persuasive. An informative essay focuses on causal relationships objectively, simply as facts the reader will find useful or interesting. A persuasive essay explores causal relationships in order to sway the reader to the writer's point of view or to move the reader to some kind of action—for instance, to correct some condition that has undesirable effects. (For further discussion of purpose, see *Harbrace* 28a; *Hodges'* 32a.)

Causal relationships are rarely simple. Any given effect is likely to have several causes, some more immediate than others, and of course each of those causes may have produced a variety of effects besides the one under consideration. Consider all of the following statements:

I'm cold because it's only 30 degrees Fahrenheit.

I'm cold because it's winter.

I'm cold because I left my coat on the bus.

I'm cold because a friend was talking to me on the bus and made me forget my coat.

I'm cold because I live in Bemidji, Minnesota, rather than near the equator.

I'm cold because heat is being exchanged between my body and the atmosphere in accordance with the second law of thermodynamics.

I'm cold because the metabolic processes of human beings do not produce enough heat to keep them warm in Bemidji.

I'm cold because I don't have fur.

All of these causes can be true simultaneously. And note that every one of them has effects besides making me cold. Even leaving my coat on the bus has other effects: I'll have to go to the bus company's lost-and-found room (a nuisance that will cause me to miss doing something else), and if the coat hasn't been turned in I'll have to buy another one (which in turn will cause me to forgo something else I could have bought with the money). Yet this example, my shivering in Bemidji, is a very simple one. Imagine, then, how long a possible list might be constructed for something really complicated, such as the causes of crime.

So writers must guard against oversimplifying. Discovering the immediate cause of an event may be easy, but other more remote causes may be more important. The firing on Fort Sumter is often seen as the immediate cause of the Civil War. But of course the issue of slavery was far more basic, and slavery was in turn causally related to economic factors such as Northern control of banking and Southern control of cotton supplies for the Northern fabric mills, as well as to political factors such as the Southern championship of states' rights and the Northern commitment to federalism. All of these things contributed to the conflict, though some more immediately and more visibly than others.

The complexity of events is not the only difficulty the writer faces in cause-and-effect analysis. Vested interests sometimes deliberately obscure causal relationships for their own benefit. For instance, when the Warren Commission investigated the causes of President John F. Kennedy's assassination, one of the obstacles it met was that certain government agencies pointed the finger of blame at each other to avoid having it pointed in their own direction.

Finally, in assigning causes to effects, writers must be not only objective but rational. It is all too easy to ignore evidence that points to a cause we do not wish to consider. And even the most fair-minded writer can still fall into those logical traps, to which we are all vulnerable, called fallacies. (See *Harbrace* 31; *Hodges'* 35.)

In the following essay, Nandina Brownell, a student, develops her analysis of causes and effects into an effective argument. Note especially how Brownell addresses both the immediate and remote causes.

Control

Establishes context

A family boards a transport shuttle at the Orlando airport. Mother, father, son, and daughter chatter animatedly about their day at Disneyworld. Ten-year-old Ray Junior wears a Donald Duck sweatshirt and is laden with Disney souvenirs. His six-year-old sister, Amy, wears a hat with Mickey ears and clutches her own small bag of memorabilia. All the seats are filled, so the four of them stand around the chromium support poles in the car, smiling, happy, and tired. As the car lurches to a start, Amy stumbles. Her father shoots a disapproving glance and thunders, "Watch what you're doing, you clumsy fool!" Amy silently grabs the support pole, and her large eyes sweep the carful of strangers now staring at her. She blinks once, twice, three times as the tears well in her eyes and her face flushes scarlet. She lowers her head, and her Mickey ears tumble to the floor of the car. Clutching the pole, she picks up the hat and puts it back on her head akimbo. The family, and the entire car, falls silent. Finally, the family reaches its stop and gets off. The incident is over. The family walks in silence to their departure gate, their Disney regalia now a bizarre counterpoint.

Analysis of causes

You have all witnessed an Amy. Most of you have done nothing. And most of you regret it long after. Interestingly, Amy's case is not strictly child abuse. The casual observer may rightly interpret this as a single act of a loving but tired father at the end of a long day. Nevertheless, Amy <u>is</u> a victim of something that may be far more insidious than overt abuse. Amy is clearly a victim of inappropriate control. And she is not alone. Like Amy we have all been victims of inappropriate control. Worse, we have all been perpetrators.

Transition to argument

At a time when issues such as child and spousal abuse, sexual harassment, police brutality, and human rights violations are at the American fore, it may seem frivolous to talk about such a minor issue as control. Nevertheless, it is clearly time to talk, because each of those larger issues, each of these incursions into the well-being of another, is clearly the result of inappropriate control.

Even more than the stuff of media events—children and spouses not interactively part of a family, students disenfranchised from their own learning process, a national work force made up of the robotically disempowered—the result of inappropriate control is the death of personal, social, and political autonomy. We are at least nominally a nation where <u>all</u> are created equal and <u>all</u> are entitled to "life, liberty, and the pursuit of happiness." To begin to turn these constitutional guarantees into a personal reality, we need to find solutions to the problem of inappropriate control, solutions that may lie in the causes.

Illustration

Ben is a 34-year-old systems analyst. Raised alternately by an occasionally institutionalized schizophrenic mother, then his domineering father and acquiescent stepmother, Ben had had to make his own

Remote causes

way for as long as he could remember: he set his own bedtimes, took his baths, packed his own peanut butter sandwiches for school, ordered his own existence. Following in his father's footsteps, he worked as a roofer for ten years after high school and just recently graduated with a B.S. degree. He has gladly turned in his hard hat for a white shirt and dark tie. He has been married for about a year to Lisa, who quit her job at Ben's request. For the first month or so, Lisa spent time decorating their new home and

Immediate causes

enjoying her unstructured time. Ben would often make what seemed like simple requests: don't tuck the sheets in at the foot of the bed, keep the thermostat at 70 degrees at all times. On their three-month anniversary, Ben joined Lisa in the shower—to explain the waste involved in shampooing her hair twice every time she washed it. Ben now insists that his shirts be laundered once a week and all hung with the second button buttoned and fronts facing left in the closet. He insists that Lisa have a hot meal on the table at 6 p.m. but chides her when she uses more than one pan to prepare the meal—one-pot meals are more efficient. He wants Lisa to finish the dishes by 7 so she can sit beside him in front of the television. They go to bed at 11 because they have to be up at 6:30—Ben to get dressed for work, Lisa to fix his breakfast and pack his mid-morning snack: peanut butter and honey sandwiches without the crusts. Every Saturday, they go to the mall, where Ben looks for office attire, soliciting Lisa's opinion, but seldom buying. When they argue, Ben frequently compares Lisa to his mentally ill mother and attacks her competency as a wife and potential mother. He always makes up the next day with flowers.

Effect

Lisa, after a year, is abjectly unhappy. It's obvious in many ways that Ben loves her, and she's sure she loves him. She wants to please and to do right by him as a wife. His requests are simple, but she just can't seem to keep them all straight. She's confused and occasionally thinks she may be losing her mind.

Immediate cause

But as any counselor can tell her, she's not losing her mind, she's lost control over her own life.

Remote causes

The causes of that lost control—and the concomitant loss of power and self-esteem—lie in both Lisa and Ben. First, out of a sense of love and wifely duty, Lisa has abdicated control, and her attempts at regaining control erupt into arguments, recriminations, and then a return to the established controller-controlled roles. Second, Ben's need for control has two causes: he thinks he is making an honest attempt to keep the chaos of the world out of his home, <u>and</u> he needs to feel important.

Many deny they could ever be like Ben or Lisa. However, each one of us dons and doffs these roles often: we become the obsequious pleaser to avoid rocking the boat; we see the world as a dangerous and chaotic place and order our existences accordingly; and we often put ourselves and others through strange psychological gyrations so we can feel important.

But when we slip into these roles, what can we do? First, do a control-check periodically. Looking at the large picture, do you still feel in control of your own existence? If not, quickly find the source. Is it your job? your family? yourself? If you can push the control reset button yourself, do so: talk to your supervisor about your need to feel some ownership over your projects; talk to your spouse and family about your need to do a fair share of things "your way"; convince yourself that making your own decisions benefits you and those around you. If the reset button seems inaccessible, seek professional help: the office industrial psychologist, a family counselor, a personal psychologist. Clearly the longer you give up control, the more difficult it is to regain it.

What about those occasions when we slip into the controller role: when we are on the verge of ridiculing our child, of blabbing an embarrassing anecdote about a co-worker, of badgering our spouse, of imposing order on others? The first step is to stop before speaking or acting. The next step is to think. Will there be any losers if I say or do what I'm planning? If the answer is <u>yes</u>, don't do it. Rather, begin searching for win-win strategies. Does your five-year-old have an affinity for matches? Supervise his or her candle-lighting at dinner time. Are two valuable employees always battling for power? Make them co-leaders on a project and reward them equally. Does your near-perfect spouse's lip-smacking during meals drive you crazy? Focus on the half-full glass, count your blessings, count to ten, and think of his or her last act of kindness to you.

Granted, stamping out child and spousal abuse, sexual harassment, police brutality, and human rights violations may seem a near impossibility. And it may

be. But we can't eliminate national and global woes when the seeds of them thrive in our own homes and communities. If each of us learns to give and take

control appropriately, we may, in a small and important way, make this a better, more egalitarian world.

Commentary.   Nandina Brownell's essay is both an analysis of cause and effect and an argument proposing a solution to the problem. She begins with a calculated bid for the reader's sympathy: she tells a tale of a father's callous and public criticism of his young daughter—an event which she sees as the effect of an inappropriate exercise of control, the primary cause she analyzes in the essay. Following the narrative, Brownell analyzes its causes: potential, immediate, and remote. She makes a transition to her argument by claiming that several national, social, and political issues also result from the same cause and that dealing with that cause as individuals may reduce its effect nationally.

To illustrate her point and to make the problem more immediate for the general reader, Brownell devotes the next three paragraphs to a narrative of events occurring in the lives of a newly married couple, Ben and Lisa, presenting a chain of causes and effects. Brownell then generalizes the causes of such marital disruptions to all people, who seek to please, to impose order on our own lives, and to feel important. Next, she offers a way to take control of our own lives and suggests how to relinquish control of others' lives. Her conclusion derives directly from this proposal: by controlling ourselves rather than others we may begin to take small steps toward resolving some of our major social problems—a new set of causes and effects.

Brownell's essay is an ambitious effort, but it suffers from oversimplification, though she is apparently aware of that problem and attempts to handle it in her conclusion. She is to be commended, however, for taking the risk and for maintaining enough distance from her own writing to notice and attempt to correct a potential problem which would qualify her success.

Who Killed the Bog Men of Denmark? And Why?

Maurice Shadbolt

A New Zealander, Maurice Shadbolt (1932–) has worked as a freelance writer and journalist since the 1950s. He is the author of several collections of short stories and a number of novels, including *An Ear of the Dragon, Danger Zone,* and *The Lovelock Version.* Shadbolt also contributes magazine articles to such publications as *National Geographic, The New Yorker,* and *New Zealand Listener.* "Who Killed the Bog Men of Denmark? And Why?" was first published in *Reader's Digest.*

Every year in the Danish town of Silkeborg, thousands of visitors file past 1
the face of a murder victim. No one will ever know his name. It is enough to know that 2000 years ago he was as human as ourselves. That face has moved men and women to poetry, and to tears.

Last summer I journeyed to the lake-girt Danish town and, peering at that 2
face behind glass in a modest museum, I felt awe—for his every wrinkle and whisker tell a vivid and terrible tale from Denmark's distant past. The rope which choked off the man's breath is still around his neck. Yet it is a perplexingly peaceful face, inscrutable, one to haunt the imagination.

This strangest of ancient murder mysteries began 27 years ago, on May 8, 3
1950, when two brothers, Emil and Viggo Højgaard, were digging peat in Tollund Fen, near Silkeborg. Their spring sowing finished, the brothers were storing up the umber-brown peat for their kitchen range, and for warmth in the winter to come. It was a peaceful task on a sunny morning. Snipe called from the aspens and firs fringing the dank bowl of the fen, where only heather and coarse grass grew. Then, at the depth of nine feet, their spades suddenly struck something.

They were gazing, with fright and fascination, at a face underfoot. The 4
corpse was naked but for a skin cap, resting on its side as if asleep, arms and legs bent. The face was gentle, with eyes closed and lips lightly pursed. There was stubble on the chin. The bewildered brothers called the Silkeborg police.

Quick to the scene, the police did not recognize the man as anyone listed 5
missing. Shrewdly guessing the brothers might have blundered into a black hole in Europe's past, the police called in archeologists.

Enter Prof. Peter Glob, a distinguished scholar from nearby Aarhus Uni- 6
versity, who carefully dislodged a lump of peat from beside the dead man's

head. A rope made of two twisted hide thongs encircled his neck. He had been strangled or hanged. But when, and by whom? Glob ordered a box to be built around the corpse and the peat in which it lay, so nothing might be disturbed.

Next day, the box, weighing nearly a ton, was manhandled out of the bog   7 onto a horse-drawn cart, on its way for examination at Copenhagen's National Museum. One of Glob's helpers collapsed and died with the huge effort. It seemed a dark omen, as if some old god were claiming a modern man in place of a man from the past.

Bog bodies were nothing new—since records have been kept, Denmark's   8 bogs have surrendered no fewer than 400—and the preservative qualities of the humic acid in peat have long been known. But not until the 19th century did scientists and historians begin to glimpse the finds and understand that the bodies belonged to remote, murky recesses of European prehistory. None survived long: the corpses were either buried again or crumbled quickly with exposure to light and air.

When peat-digging was revived during and after World War II, bodies   9 were unearthed in abundance—first in 1942 at Store Arden, then in 1946, 1947 and 1948 at Borre Fen. Artifacts found beside them positively identified them as people of Denmark's Early Iron Age, from 400 B.C. to A.D. 400. None, then, was less than 1500 years old, and some were probably much older. The first of the Borre Fen finds—a full-grown male—was to prove especially significant: Borre Fen man, too, had died violently, with a noose about his neck, strangled or hanged. And his last meal had consisted of grain.

Peter Glob, alongside his artist father (a portraitist and distinguished am-   10 ateur archeologist), had been digging into Denmark's dim past since he was a mere eight years old. For him, the Tollund man, who had by far the best-preserved head to survive from antiquity, was a supreme challenge. Since 1936, Glob had been living imaginatively with the pagan hunters and farmers of 2000 years ago, fossicking among their corroded artifacts, foraging among the foundations of their simple villages; he knew their habits, the rhythms of their lives. Suddenly, here was a man of that very time. "Majesty and gentleness," he recalls, "seemed to stamp his features as they did when he was alive." What was this enigmatic face trying to tell him?

Glob was intrigued by the fact that so many of the people found in bogs   11 had died violently: strangled or hanged, throats slit, heads battered. Perhaps they had been travelers set upon by brigands, or executed criminals. But there might be a different explanation. These murder victims all belonged to the Danish Iron Age. If they were to be explained away as victims of robber bands, there should be a much greater spread in time—into other ages. Nor would executed criminals all have had so many common traits.

Glob considered the body with care. X rays of Tollund man's vertebrae,   12 taken to determine whether he had been strangled or hanged, produced inconclusive results. The condition of the wisdom teeth suggested a man well over 20 years old. An autopsy revealed that the heart, lungs and liver were well preserved; most important, the alimentary canal was undisturbed, containing the dead man's last meal—a 2000-year-old gruel of hand-milled grains and seeds: barley, linseed, flaxseed, knotgrass, among others. Knowledge of prehistoric agriculture made it possible to determine that the man had lived in the first 200 years A.D. The mixture of grains and seeds suggested a meal prepared in winter or early spring.

Since Iron Age men were not vegetarians, why were there no traces of   13
meat? Glob also marveled that the man's hands and feet were soft; he appeared to have done little or no heavy labor in his lifetime. Possibly, then, he was high-ranking in Iron Age society.

Then, on April 26, 1952, peat-digging villagers from Grauballe, 11 miles   14
east of Tollund, turned up a second spectacularly well-preserved body, and again Glob was fast to the scene. Unmistakably another murder victim, this discovery was, unlike Tollund man, far from serene. The man's throat had been slashed savagely from ear to ear. His face was twisted with terror, and his lips were parted with a centuries-silenced cry of pain.

Glob swiftly removed the body—still imbedded in a great block of peat—   15
for preservation and study. Carbon-dating of body tissue proved Grauballe man to be about 1650 years old, a contemporary of Constantine the Great. Grauballe man was in extraordinary condition; his fingerprints and footprints came up clearly. Tallish and dark-haired, Grauballe man, like Tollund man, had never done any heavy manual work. He had been slain in his late 30s. Another similarity came to light when Grauballe man's last meal was analyzed: it had been eaten immediately before death and, like Tollund man's, like Borre Fen man's too, it was a gruel of grains and seeds, a meal of winter, or early spring. All three had perished in a similar season.

Who had killed these men of the bogs? Why in winter, or early spring?   16
Why should they—apparently—have led privileged lives? And why the same kind of meals before their sudden ends?

The bodies had told Glob all they could. Now he turned to one of his   17
favorite sources—the Roman historian Tacitus. Nearly 2000 years ago Tacitus recorded the oral traditions of Germanic tribes who inhabited northwest Europe. Tacitus' account of these wild, brave and generous blue-eyed people often shed light into dark corners of Denmark's past. Glob found these lines: "At a time laid down in the distant past, all peoples that are related by blood meet in a sacred wood. Here they celebrate their barbarous rites with a human sacrifice."

Elsewhere, Tacitus wrote: "These people are distinguished by a common   18
worship of Nerthus, or Mother Earth. They believe that she interests herself in human affairs." Tacitus confirmed early spring as a time among the Germanic tribes for offerings and human sacrifice. They were asking the goddess to hasten the coming of spring, and the summer harvest. Men chosen for sacrifice might well have been given a symbolic meal, made up of plant seeds, before being consecrated through death to the goddess—thus explaining the

absence of meat. The sacrificial men, with their delicate features, neat hands and feet, might have been persons of high rank chosen by lot for sacrifice, or priests, ritually married to Nerthus.

Tacitus supplied another essential clue: the symbol of Nerthus, he   19 recorded, was a twisted metal "torque," or neck ring, worn by the living to honor the goddess. The leather nooses about the necks of Tollund man and the body from Borre Fen and some earlier bodies were replicas of those neck rings. Glob concluded that it was Nerthus—Mother Earth herself—who had preserved her victims perfectly in her peaty bosom long after those who had fed them into the bogs were dust.

Peter Glob was satisfied. He had found the killer and identified the vic-   20 tims. The centuries-old mystery of Denmark's bog bodies was no more.

✹

RESPONDING TO THE WHOLE ESSAY

1. Is Shadbolt's purpose in the essay chiefly expressive, informative, or persuasive? Is there evidence of a secondary purpose? [*Harbrace* 28a; *Hodges'* 32a]
2. If you didn't know that the essay on the bog men first appeared in *Reader's Digest,* a mass-circulation magazine with an exceedingly diverse audience, what elements in the essay might lead you to assume that Shadbolt wrote for such an audience? [*Harbrace* 28a; *Hodges'* 32a]
3. What strategy does Shadbolt use to capture and hold the attention of his readers? Do you find any similarities between this essay and fiction you have read? If so, what kind of fiction? What are the similarities? [*Harbrace* 28e; *Hodges'* 32e]
4. Shadbolt develops the essay by analyzing the causes of the bog men's deaths. Show where and how he treats both the direct (immediate) causes and the indirect (remote) causes.
5. What different chains of causes and effects can you find in the essay? How does each chain provide clues to the mystery?

ANALYZING THE ELEMENTS

Grammar

1. Examine the grammatical relationships and the pronoun reference in the second sentence of paragraph 4. Could the sentence be rewritten to make them clearer? Explain. [*Harbrace* 1d and 6b; *Hodges'* 1d and 28]
2. What are the grammatical functions of the words *glimpse* and *finds* in the second sentence of paragraph 8? Can you invent sentences in which the functions of the two words are reversed? [*Harbrace* 1c; *Hodges'* 1c]
3. Paragraph 16 contains a series of questions, some of which contain subjects and verbs, some of which do not. Can the omissions be justified? Explain. [*Harbrace* 2; *Hodges'* 2]

Effective Sentences

1. Explain the use of *enter* in the first sentence of paragraph 6, and comment on how it contributes to the effectiveness of the sentence. [*Harbrace* 11f, 11h, and 12d; *Hodges'* 29f, 29h, and 30]
2. Comment on the effect Shadbolt achieves by varying sentence length in paragraph 9. [*Harbrace* 11h; *Hodges'* 29h]

Punctuation and Mechanics

1. Do you feel that the comma in the last sentence of the first paragraph is justified? Why or why not? [*Harbrace* 17; *Hodges'* 12]
2. Explain the use of dashes in the first sentence of paragraph 8. [*Harbrace* 21e; *Hodges'* 17e]

Diction

1. What is the meaning of the following words: *umber-brown* (paragraph 3); *humic* (paragraph 8); *fossicking, artifacts,* and *enigmatic* (paragraph 10); *brigands* (paragraph 11); *alimentary, gruel* (paragraph 12); *barbarous* (paragraph 17). Could synonyms be conveniently substituted for any of these words? Why or why not? [*Harbrace* 14a(3); *Hodges'* 20a(2)]
2. Explain Shadbolt's use of figurative language in the fourth sentence of paragraph 17. [*Harbrace* 14a(5); *Hodges'* 20a(4)]

BUILDING VOCABULARY

1. One way English makes new words is to combine two existing words, joining them with a hyphen. Find as many examples of such words in "Who Killed the Bogmen of Denmark? And Why?" as you can. Then, define three.
2. What vocabulary elements make up the word *perplexingly?* Explain what each element contributes to the meaning of the word.

SUGGESTIONS FOR WRITING

1. Using cause and effect as a mode of development, analyze a mystery you have solved or been keenly aware of—for example, strange sounds emanate from the attic of your home (caused by squirels); a lost piece of jewelry is found (in a most unusual place, such as the refrigerator); your automobile refuses to run on rainy days (a problem with its electrical system).
2. Write an essay analyzing the causes and/or effects of an unusual custom or tradition of which you are aware (for example, the Southern custom of eating black-eyed peas on New Year's Day, traditions surrounding your family's annual reunion, the custom of wearing new clothing at Easter).

The Price of Hate: Thoughts on Covering a Ku Klux Klan Rally

Rachel L. Jones

Rachel Jones was born in 1961 in Cairo, Illinois, and attended Northwestern University and Southern Illinois University. Having served internships at *The New York Times* and the *Washington Post*, she writes for the *Miami Herald*. Jones explains that she has always been fascinated with words "and the images they could evoke, how they could make you feel, hear, smell and taste power there," and so she chose writing as a profession to "translate events—everyday and extraordinary—into digestible bites" so that people become aware that "their world is growing and changing." "The Price of Hate" chronicles one event which resulted in the world changing for Jones herself.

1   I was sitting at my computer terminal when I overheard someone in the office mention his concern because he thought a black couple was moving into a house on his street.

2   He was standing only four feet away from me, yet lacked a mechanism that would prevent him from making racist statements in front of a black person. I stopped typing and stared at his back. He froze momentarily, and the woman he was talking to glanced at me.

3   I didn't confront him. I had to transmit copy to St. Petersburg and then leave to cover a graduation. Besides, my stomach was churning. Just seven days earlier, at a Ku Klux Klan rally in Clearwater, I had stood only four feet away from a Tarpon Springs man who told me he was tired of "the n-----s getting everything."

4   I'd be lying if I said that the possibility of covering a Ku Klux Klan rally didn't cause me a few moments' concern about my physical well-being. But when another reporter came over to tell me about the May 28th Klan rally in front of Clearwater City Hall, I reasoned, "It's just another assignment. I am a reporter, and I know my life isn't all budget meetings."

5   I must also admit to a curiosity about the Klan, and it seemed a good opportunity to take a look at that sideshow of human nature. Now, I *could* have asked to be excused from that particular assignment. As a police reporter, my Saturdays are sometimes very busy. Had I approached my editor to delicately decline, we could have both made ourselves believe it was only natural to send a burly young man into the fray. Anthing could have happened that day—traffic accidents, drownings, first-degree murders at the jail.

I couldn't be two places at once, could I?   6

But two days before the event, I turned to my editor and asked, "I AM   7
covering the rally on Saturday, aren't I?"

She didn't miss a beat. Yes, of course. Just a short story, unless the streets   8
were running with blood or something.

I jokingly told her about the only slightly feigned horror of my older sister,   9
who shrieked into the phone, "They're letting a black reporter cover the KLAN?"

At the Klan rally, the man from Tarpon Springs saw my press badge and   10
figured I was a part of something he called the "Black Associated Press,"
which he swore was denying white journalism graduates jobs. Mr. Tarpon told
me that n-----s weren't qualified to get the jobs they were getting through affirmative action, and that America is for white people.

I paused momentarily and asked what he thought should be done about   11
black people. He didn't know or care.

"Send 'em all to hell," he said, while I took notes.   12

It's funny—it was all so clinical. My voice held an even tone, and while   13
he talked I searched his contorted face for some glimmer of recognition on his
part that *I* was a human being, and the words that he spat just might hurt me.

Just as I later waited for Mr. Welcome Wagon to turn around and apol-   14
ogize for his blunder, I waited for the Tarpon Springs man to show some spark
of humanity, but he finished his conversation and walked away.

My stomach was still churning hours later as I relived that rally. The whole   15
experience was like being scalded, like having something sharp raked over my
flesh until it was raw.

After it was over I went home and drank a shot from the bottle of brandy   16
I'd bought last Christmas. In Harlequin romances, handsome princes always
proffered hard liquor to soothe the jangled nerves of a distraught heroine.

But I was alone, and I was no heroine. That night, every noise from the   17
apartment upstairs made me jump, and the pattern of trees against the cur-
tains frightened me as I tossed and turned. I called three of my siblings, but
other than offering sympathy, they felt helpless to ease my trauma.

I had been so naive about the whole assignment. The thing is, I never   18
thought it would change me. I figured it would be difficult, but I didn't want
it to *change* me.

What you must understand about the Klan is that its members and sup-   19
porters have been stripped of their humanity. I gained that insight and feel
stronger for it. It was easy enough on one level to say, "These people are stupid, so I shouldn't be bothered by what they say."

But that was cold comfort as I walked across the City Hall parking lot,   20
feeling a numbness creep through my arms and legs. I thought I must have
been walking like the Scarecrow in *The Wizard of Oz*, but figured if I could
just make it to the church across the street, I'd be fine.

At the church, I asked to use the phone and was sent down a hall and to   21
the left. My fingers felt like sausages as I tried to use the rotary dial, muttering

curses as I fouled up several times. Finally managing to reach an editor, I was coherent enough to give her information for a brief summary of the rally.

But when the next editor picked up the phone, I dissolved in tears after three words. He was puzzled, and I think unaware of what was wrong at first. I whimpered that I was sorry and didn't know what was wrong, either. I gasped and caught a few breaths before describing in a wavering voice what had happened.   22

He tried calming me down to discuss the facts. How many people attended? Had there been any clashes? What did police have to say? I planned to write a full story.   23

The editor said maybe we should just ignore the event. He asked if any of the Klan members had been abusive to me. I mumbled, "Uh hum," and the tears flowed fresh. He told me to get as much police information as I could and to call him back later.   24

I placed the phone on the hook and buried my face in my hands, letting the sobs come freely. The man who had let me use the church phone brought me a box of tissues and a Coke.   25

After I splashed my face with cold water and controlled the sobs, I headed back to the rally, just as the Klansmen were loading up to leave. Shouts of "white supremacy" rang through the air as they rolled out, and my photographer walked over to give me the Klansmen's names. I turned away, telling her that I probably wouldn't use them anyway.   26

"I didn't think it would affect me," I whispered.   27

"Don't cry. They aren't worth it, Rachel," she said.   28

But even then, it had started to change me . . .   29

When you have stared into the twisted face of hate, you *must* change. I remember watching the documentary *Eyes on the Prize,* in particular the segment on the desegregation of Little Rock High School in 1957, and being disturbed by the outpouring of rage against those nine students.   30

The whites who snarled into the camera back then had no explanation for their vitriol and violence other than that the students were black, and they didn't care who knew it. They weren't going to let those n-----s into the school, no matter what.   31

I've struggled all my life against a visceral reaction to that kind of racism. I have been mistreated because of my color, but nothing ever came near to what those students went through on a daily basis.   32

That and countless other examples let me know what I'd been spared, and I decided to choose the path of understanding, realizing that some people are always going to fear or even hate me because of my color alone.   33

It's a burden blacks must carry no matter how high a level of achievement they reach, and I sought to incorporate that into my own striving. Watching films of what hate turned those people into made me choose to reject it, to deal with people individually and not tarnish all whites with the same obscene images. *I would not hate.*   34

But as one Klan supporter muttered, "N----- b----," at me as I weaved my way through the crowd, that resolve crumbled. It stung as much as if he *had* slapped me or thrown something. 35

The leader shouted taunts and epithets at a black woman who was infuriated by the proceedings, and who had even lunged at several people in the small group of supporters. 36

As the black woman walked away, the leader shouted, "Why don't you go back to Nee-gor Africa where you came from!" I laughed because he sounded foolish, but he saw me and sent a fresh stream of obscenity my way. 37

A Jewish woman who came to protest was heaped with stinging abuse, and the rabble was ingenious in its varied use of sexual and racial obscenities directed toward her. 38

Other reporters and photographers eyed me warily throughout the rally, watching for my reactions to the abuse. When the leader started passing out leaflets and avoided my outstretched hand, a photographer asked for two and brought me one. 39

I said thank you. He said quietly, "You're very, very welcome," and was embarrassed when I caught his eye. 40

When it was all over, several police officials called me brave. But I felt cold, sick and empty. I felt like such a naive fool. I felt bitter. So this is what it feels like, I thought. Why *shouldn't* I just hate them right back, why couldn't I diffuse this punch in the gut? 41

What is noble about not flinching in the face of hate? Slavery, lynchings, rape, inequality, was that not enough? If they want to send me to hell, shouldn't I want to take them along for the ride? 42

But I still couldn't hate. I was glad I had cried, though. It defied their demented logic. It meant I was human. 43

✳

RESPONDING TO THE WHOLE ESSAY

1. What is Jones's primary purpose in writing "The Price of Hate: Thoughts on Attending a Ku Klux Klan Rally"? How can you discern that purpose? Is there evidence of a secondary purpose? If so, what? [*Harbrace* 28a; *Hodges'* 32a]
2. What audience is Jones writing for? Marshal evidence to support your answer. [*Harbrace* 28a; *Hodges'* 32a]
3. What is Jones's basic plan of organization? Is she concerned with both immediate and remote causes? If so, what are they and where are they mentioned?
4. Jones introduced her essay by briefly relating an incident that occurred at her office. How is that incident related to the rest of the essay? [*Harbrace* 28a and 28f; *Hodges'* 32a and 32f]
5. The paragraphs in "The Price of Hate" are very short. Explain why these paragraphs are so short and comment on how Jones links them so that her essay flows smoothly. [*Harbrace* 27b; *Hodges'* 31b]

6. Jones divided her essay into four sections. Why? [*Harbrace* 27a and 27b; *Hodges'* 31a and 31b]

ANALYZING THE ELEMENTS

Grammar

1. The second sentence of paragraph 8 is a virtual sentence. Rewrite the sentence supplying the missing element(s). Which is more effective? Why? [*Harbrace* 2; *Hodges'* 2]
2. Examine the tenses of the verbs in the final sentence of paragraph 10 and compare with the tenses of the verbs in the preceding sentences. Why do you think Jones changed the tense? Is the change effective? [*Harbrace* 7c; *Hodges'* 7c]

Effective Sentences

1. What elements in the second sentence of paragraph 15 are parallel? How else might the sentence be written? Which is more effective? Why? [*Harbrace* 10; *Hodges'* 26]
2. The first sentence of paragraph 33 begins with the relative pronoun *that*. What does *that* refer to? How do you know? [*Harbrace* 6b; *Hodges'* 28c]
3. Comment on the structure of the second sentence of paragraph 42. Is it effective? Why or why not? [*Harbrace* 12; *Hodges'* 30]

Punctuation and Mechanics

1. Comment on Jones's use of italics in the second sentence of paragraph 5. [*Harbrace* 24; *Hodges'* 10]
2. Justify the omission of the comma following the introductory adverbial clause in the first sentence of paragraph 16. [*Harbrace* 17; *Hodges'* 12]

Diction

1. In the first sentence of paragraph 35 Jones uses *weaved* rather than *wove*. Explain this usage. Consult your dictionary if necessary. [*Harbrace* 13b(5); *Hodges'* 19f]
2. Jones uses the phrase "on a daily basis" in paragraph 32. Explain why this phrase could be considered wordy and rewrite the sentence. [*Harbrace* 15a and 15b; *Hodges'* 21a and 21b]
3. The first sentence of paragraph 30 contains a personification. Explain. [*Harbrace* 14c; *Hodges'* 20c]

BUILDING VOCABULARY

1. Find two synonyms for *proffer*. How is *proffer* different from *offer*?
2. What is the source of the word *jangle*?

SUGGESTIONS FOR WRITING

1. Write an essay about an event that made you change your view of yourself or your world, explaining why you changed.
2. Write an essay about an event or circumstance in your life (or the life of someone you know) that resulted in a chain of causes.

On Warts
Lewis Thomas

Born in New York in 1913, Lewis Thomas was educated at Princeton University and Harvard Medical School. He has served on the faculties of several medical schools and is still engaged in the practice of medicine as president of the Memorial Sloan-Kettering Cancer Clinic. Since 1971 he has been writing columns for the *New England Journal of Medicine,* many of which have been collected in three books: *The Lives of a Cell: Notes of a Biology Watcher,* for which Thomas won the National Book Award in 1974; *The Medusa and the Snail: More Notes of a Biology Watcher,* for which he won the American Book Award in 1979; and *Late Night Thoughts on Listening to Mahler's Ninth Symphony* (1983). These collections have established Thomas's reputation as an essayist of extraordinary lucidity and grace—qualities exemplified in the essay that follows, "On Warts."

Warts are wonderful structures. They can appear overnight on any part   1
of the skin, like mushrooms on a damp lawn, full grown and splendid in the
complexity of their architecture. Viewed in stained sections under a micro-
scope, they are the most specialized of cellular arrangements, constructed as
though for a purpose. They sit there like turreted mounds of dense, impene-
trable horn, impregnable, designed for defense against the world outside.

In a certain sense, warts are both useful and essential, but not for us. As   2
it turns out, the exuberant cells of a wart are the elaborate reproductive apparatus of a virus.

You might have thought from the looks of it that the cells infected by the   3
wart virus were using this response as a ponderous way of defending themselves against the virus, maybe even a way of becoming more distasteful, but
it is not so. The wart is what the virus truly wants; it can flourish only in cells
undergoing precisely this kind of overgrowth. It is not a defense at all; it is
an overwhelming welcome, an enthusiastic accommodation meeting the needs
of more and more virus.

The strangest thing about warts is that they tend to go away. Fully grown,   4
nothing in the body has so much the look of toughness and permanence as a
wart, and yet, inexplicably and often very abruptly, they come to the end of
their lives and vanish without a trace.

And they can be made to go away by something that can only be called   5
thinking, or something like thinking. This is a special property of warts which
is absolutely astonishing, more of a surprise than cloning or recombinant DNA

or endorphin or acupuncture or anything else currently attracting attention in the press. It is one of the great mystifications of science: warts can be ordered off the skin by hypnotic suggestion.

Not everyone believes this, but the evidence goes back a long way and is   6
persuasive. Generations of internists and dermatologists, and their grand-mothers for that matter, have been convinced of the phenomenon. I was once told by a distinguished old professor of medicine, one of Sir William Osler's original bright young men, that it was his practice to paint gentian violet over a wart and then assure the patient firmly that it would be gone in a week, and he never saw it fail. There have been several meticulous studies by good clinical investigators, with proper controls. In one of these, fourteen patients with seemingly intractable generalized warts on both sides of the body were hypnotized, and the suggestion was made that all the warts on one side of the body would begin to go away. Within several weeks the results were indis-putably positive; in nine patients, all or nearly all of the warts on the sug-gested side had vanished, while the control side had just as many as ever.

It is interesting that most of the warts vanished precisely as they were in-   7
structed, but it is even more fascinating that mistakes were made. Just as you might expect in other affairs requiring a clear understanding of which is the right and which the left side, one of the subjects got mixed up and destroyed the warts on the wrong side. In a later study by a group at the Massachusetts General Hospital, the warts on both sides were rejected even though the in-structions were to pay attention to just one side.

I have been trying to figure out the nature of the instructions issued by   8
the unconscious mind, whatever that is, under hypnosis. It seems to me hardly enough for the mind to say, simply, get off, eliminate yourselves, without pro-viding something in the way of specifications as to how to go about it.

I used to believe, thinking about this experiment when it was just pub-   9
lished, that the instructions might be quite simple. Perhaps nothing more de-tailed than a command to shut down the flow through all the precapillary ar-terioles in and around the warts to the point of strangulation. Exactly how the mind would accomplish this with precision, cutting off the blood supply to one wart while leaving others intact, I couldn't figure out, but I was satis-fied to leave it there anyhow. And I was glad to think that my unconscious mind would have to take the responsibility for this, for if I had been one of the subjects I would never have been able to do it myself.

But now the problem seems much more complicated by the information   10
concerning the viral etiology of warts, and even more so by the currently plau-sible notion that immunologic mechanisms are very likely implicated in the rejection of warts.

If my unconscious can figure out how to manipulate the mechanisms   11
needed for getting around that virus, and for deploying all the various cells in the correct order for tissue rejection, then all I have to say is that my un-conscious is a lot further along than I am. I wish I had a wart right now, just to see if I am that talented.

There ought to be a better word than "Unconscious," even capitalized, 12 for what I have, so to speak, in mind. I was brought up to regard this aspect of thinking as a sort of private sanitarium, walled off somewhere in a suburb of my brain, capable only of producing such garbled information as to keep my mind, my proper Mind, always a little off balance.

But any mental apparatus that can reject a wart is something else again. 13 This is not the sort of confused, disordered process you'd expect at the hands of the kind of Unconscious you read about in books, out at the edge of things making up dreams or getting mixed up on words or having hysterics. Whatever, or whoever, is responsible for this has the accuracy and precision of a surgeon. There almost has to be a Person in charge, running matters of meticulous detail beyond anyone's comprehension, a skilled engineer and manager, a chief executive officer, the head of the whole place. I never thought before that I possessed such a tenant. Or perhaps more accurately, such a landlord, since I would be, if this is in fact the situation, nothing more than a lodger.

Among other accomplishments, he must be a cell biologist of world class, 14 capable of sorting through the various classes of one's lymphocytes, all with quite different functions which I do not understand, in order to mobilize the right ones and exclude the wrong ones for the task of tissue rejection. If it were left to me, and I were somehow empowered to call up lymphocytes and direct them to the vicinity of my wart (assuming that I could learn to do such a thing), mine would come tumbling in all unsorted, B cells and T cells, suppressor cells and killer cells, and no doubt other cells whose names I have not learned, incapable of getting anything useful done.

Even if immunology is not involved, and all that needs doing is to shut 15 off the blood supply locally, I haven't the faintest notion how to set that up. I assume that the selective turning off of arterioles can be done by one or another chemical mediator, and I know the names of some of them, but I wouldn't dare let things like these loose even if I knew how to do it.

Well, then, who does supervise this kind of operation? Someone's got to, 16 you know. You can't sit there under hypnosis, taking suggestions in and having them acted on with such accuracy and precision, without assuming the existence of something very like a controller. It wouldn't do to fob off the whole intricate business on lower centers without sending along a quite detailed set of specifications, way over my head.

Some intelligence or other knows how to get rid of warts, and this is a 17 disquieting thought.

It is also a wonderful problem, in need of solving. Just think what we 18 would know, if we had anything like a clear understanding of what goes on when a wart is hypnotized away. We would know the identity of the cellular and chemical participants in tissue rejection, conceivably with some added information about the ways that viruses create foreignness in cells. We would know how the traffic of these reactants is directed, and perhaps then be able to understand the nature of certain diseases in which the traffic is being conducted in wrong directions, aimed at the wrong cells. Best of all, we would be finding out about a kind of superintelligence that exists in each of us, infinitely smarter and possessed of technical know-how far beyond our present understanding. It would be worth a War on Warts, a Conquest of Warts, a National Institute of Warts and All.

✳

RESPONDING TO THE WHOLE ESSAY

1. What can you say about the audience for whom Thomas wrote "On Warts"? Can you point to evidence that he was writing for his fellow physicians? Does anything in the essay seem to indicate that Thomas also had a wider audience in mind? [*Harbrace* 28a; *Hodges'* 32a]

2. How would you characterize Thomas's purpose or purposes in "On Warts"? Is his aim chiefly expressive, informative, or persuasive? Can you point to evidence of all three aims? [*Harbrace* 28a; *Hodges'* 32a]

3. Where in the essay does Thomas state causes? What effects does he assign to those causes? Which are immediate (direct) causes? How does Thomas deal with remote causes?

4. Point to examples of inductive reasoning in the essay. Would you expect to find inductive reasoning in many essays that involve cause and effect? Why or why not? [*Harbrace* 31e; *Hodges'* 35e]

5. Where does Thomas make clear what his thesis is? [*Harbrace* 28d; *Hodges'* 32d]

6. How is Thomas's conclusion (paragraph 18) related to the rest of the essay? Does it summarize the essay? Does it indicate new directions for exploration? Point out how each sentence in the conclusion is prepared for earlier in the essay. [*Harbrace* 28f(2); *Hodges'* 32f]

7. How would you describe the tone of "On Warts"? How is the tone related to Thomas's audience and purpose? [*Harbrace* 29a; *Hodges'* 33a]

ANALYZING THE ELEMENTS

Grammar

1. Explain why the correlatives *both . . . and* are appropriate to link *useful* and *essential* in the first sentence of paragraph 2. [*Harbrace* 1c; *Hodges'* 1c]

2. Can the sentence fragment that follows the first sentence in paragraph 9 be justified? Would Thomas have done better to attach it to the preceding sentence? How else might he have rewritten it? Would one tactic have been better than the other? [*Harbrace* 2; *Hodges'* 2]

Effective Sentences

1. Analyze the first sentence in paragraph 3. How does the imbalance in the length of the two main clauses contribute to the effectiveness of the sentence? Compare the third sentence of paragraph 9. [*Harbrace* 12a; *Hodges'* 30a]

2. The final sentence of paragraph 14 contains many details. Explain how Thomas establishes the relationships among those details and thus keeps them from overpowering the sentence. [*Harbrace* 9a; *Hodges'* 24a]

Punctuation and Mechanics

1. Thomas uses semicolons to separate independent clauses in the last two sentences in paragraph 3, but a colon to separate the independent clauses in the last sentence of paragraph 5. Account for the differences. [*Harbrace* 18a and 21d; *Hodges'* 14a and 17d]
2. Thomas capitalized *unconscious* in the first sentence of paragraph 12, and *mind* in the last. What does this capitalization indicate about how Thomas wants the reader to understand the sentence? [*Harbrace* 23a; *Hodges'* 9a]

Diction

1. Thomas makes frequent and effective use of similes and metaphors. Find as many as you can, and explain why each is appropriate. [*Harbrace* 14a(5); *Hodges'* 20a(4)]
2. Thomas occasionally uses medical terms in "On Warts" and also words that are not part of most people's everyday vocabulary. Look up the following medical terms (using a medical dictionary if necessary): *cloning, recombinant DNA,* and *endorphin* (paragraph 5); *gentian violet* (paragraph 6); *precapillary arterioles* (paragraph 9); *etiology* (paragraph 10); and *lymphocytes* (paragraph 14). Then explain the probable reason Thomas used *impregnable* (paragraph 1) instead of *unconquerable; ponderous* (paragraph 3) instead of *heavy; meticulous* instead of *careful,* and *intractable* instead of *stubborn* (paragraph 6); and *plausible* instead of *believable* (paragraph 10). [*Harbrace* 13c(1) and 14a(3); *Hodges'* 19g and 20a(2)]

BUILDING VOCABULARY

1. What elements is the word *architecture* made up of? List as many words as you can think of using the first two roots.
2. What are the sources of the words *meticulous, exuberant,* and *fob?* What does each mean?

SUGGESTIONS FOR WRITING

1. Select some illness or other unwelcome condition, and in a short essay explain the cause(s). Consider both immediate and (if possible) remote causes. Some possibilities: sunburn, near- (or far-) sightedness, tooth decay, a hangover, sneezing, yawning, snoring, blushing, hiccups.
2. Write a short essay exploring probable effects, taking as your topic "If _____ could be cured by hypnosis. . . ." (You fill in the blank, possibly with one of the conditions referred to in question 1.)
3. Write a cause-and-effect essay explaining how current medical thinking validates some old-fashioned explanation of illness or cure for illness. (For example, the old-fashioned belief that chicken soup is good for what ails you has been validated by the discovery of minute amounts of penicillin in chicken soup.)

The Nuclear Winter

Carl Sagan

A distinguished astronomer, Carl Sagan (1934–1996) was a prolific writer of books and articles explaining modern science in layperson's language. Educated at the University of Chicago, where he received his doctorate in 1960, he was professor of astronomy and space science at Cornell University. Sagan won the Pulitzer Prize in 1978 for *The Dragons of Eden: Speculations on the Evolution of Human Intelligence*. Among his other well-known books are *Broca's Brain: Reflections on the Romance of Science* and *Cosmos*, which presents in book form the content of Sagan's popular television series for PBS. "The Nuclear Winter" was first published in *Parade*, a Sunday supplement to many major newspapers. Although the threat between East and West has receded, many people fear that the risk of holocaust is even greater today because small nations possess nuclear arms which they might not hesitate to use. In this carefully reasoned essay, Sagan postulates the results of nuclear war with frightening effect.

Into the eternal darkness, into fire, into ice.

—Dante, *The Inferno*

1   Except for fools and madmen, everyone knows that nuclear war would be an unprecedented human catastrophe. A more or less typical strategic warhead has a yield of 2 megatons, the explosive equivalent of 2 million tons of TNT. But 2 million tons of TNT is about the same as all the bombs exploded in World War II—a single bomb with the explosive power of the entire Second World War but compressed into a few seconds of time and an area 30 or 40 miles across. . . .

2   In a 2-megaton explosion over a fairly large city, buildings would be vaporized, people reduced to atoms and shadows, outlying structures blown down like matchsticks and raging fires ignited. And if the bomb were exploded on the ground, an enormous crater, like those that can be seen through a telescope on the surface of the Moon, would be all that remained where midtown once had been. There are now more than 50,000 nuclear weapons, more than 13,000 megatons of yield, deployed in the arsenals of the United States and the Soviet Union—enough to obliterate a million Hiroshimas.

3   But there are fewer than 3000 cities on the Earth with populations of 100,000 or more. You cannot find anything like a million Hiroshimas to

obliterate. Prime military and industrial targets that are far from cities are comparatively rare. Thus, there are vastly more nuclear weapons than are needed for any plausible deterrence of a potential adversary.

Nobody knows, of course, how many megatons would be exploded in a real nuclear war. There are some who think that a nuclear war can be "contained," bottled up before it runs away to involve many of the world's arsenals. But a number of detailed analyses, war games run by the U.S. Department of Defense and official Soviet pronouncements, all indicate that this containment may be too much to hope for: Once the bombs begin exploding, communications failures, disorganization, fear, the necessity of making in minutes decisions affecting the fates of millions and the immense psychological burden of knowing that your own loved ones may already have been destroyed are likely to result in a nuclear paroxysm. Many investigations, including a number of studies for the U.S. government, envision the explosion of 5000 to 10,000 megatons—the detonation of tens of thousands of nuclear weapons that now sit quietly, inconspicuously, in missile silos, submarines and long-range bombers, faithful servants awaiting orders.

The World Health Organization, in a recent detailed study chaired by Sune K. Bergstrom (the 1982 Nobel laureate in physiology and medicine), concludes that 1.1 billion people would be killed outright in such a nuclear war, mainly in the United States, the Soviet Union, Europe, China and Japan. An additional 1.1 billion people would suffer serious injuries and radiation sickness, for which medical help would be unavailable. It thus seems possible that more than 2 billion people—almost half of all the humans on Earth—would be destroyed in the immediate aftermath of a global thermonuclear war. This would represent by far the greatest disaster in the history of the human species and, with no other adverse effects, would probably be enough to reduce at least the Northern Hemisphere to a state of prolonged agony and barbarism. Unfortunately, the real situation would be much worse.

In technical studies of the consequences of nuclear weapons explosions, there has been a dangerous tendency to underestimate the results. This is partly due to a tradition of conservatism which generally works well in science but which is of more dubious applicability when the lives of billions of people are at stake. In the Bravo test of March 1, 1954, a 15-megaton thermonuclear bomb was exploded on Bikini Atoll. It had about double the yield expected, and there was an unanticipated last-minute shift in the wind direction. As a result, deadly radioactive fallout came down on Rongelap in the Marshall Islands, more than 200 kilometers away. Almost all the children on Rongelap subsequently developed thyroid nodules and lesions, and other long-term medical problems, due to the radioactive fallout.

Likewise, in 1973, it was discovered that high-yield airbursts will chemically burn the nitrogen in the upper air, converting it into oxides of nitrogen; these, in turn, combine with and destroy the protective ozone in the Earth's stratosphere. The surface of the Earth is shielded from deadly solar ultraviolet radiation by a layer of ozone so tenuous that, were it brought down to sea level, it would be only 3 millimeters thick. Partial destruction of this ozone layer can have serious consequences for the biology of the entire planet.

These discoveries, and others like them, were made by chance. They were largely unexpected. And now another consequence—by far the most dire—has been uncovered, again more or less by accident.   8

The U.S. Mariner 9 spacecraft, the first vehicle to orbit another planet, arrived at Mars in late 1971. The planet was enveloped in a global dust storm. As the fine particles slowly fell out, we were able to measure temperature changes in the atmosphere and on the surface. Soon it became clear what had happened: 9

The dust, lofted by high winds off the desert into the upper Martian atmosphere, had absorbed the incoming sunlight and prevented much of it from reaching the ground. Heated by the sunlight, the dust warmed the adjacent air. But the surface, enveloped in partial darkness, became much chillier than usual. Months later, after the dust fell out of the atmosphere, the upper air cooled and the surface warmed, both returning to their normal conditions. We were able to calculate accurately, from how much dust there was in the atmosphere, how cool the Martian surface ought to have been.   10

Afterwards, I and my colleagues, James B. Pollack and Brian Toon of NASA's Ames Research Center, were eager to apply these insights to the Earth. In a volcanic explosion, dust aerosols are lofted into the high atmosphere. We calculated by how much the Earth's global temperature should decline after a major volcanic explosion and found that our results (generally a fraction of a degree) were in good accord with actual measurements. Joining forces with Richard Turco, who has studied the effects of nuclear weapons for many years, we then began to turn our attention to the climatic effects of nuclear war. [The scientific paper, "Global Atmospheric Consequences of Nuclear War," is writted by R. P. Turco, O. B. Toon, T. P. Ackerman, J. B. Pollack and Carl Sagan. From the last names of the authors, this work is generally referred to as "TTAPS."]   11

We knew that nuclear explosions, particularly groundbursts, would lift an enormous quantity of fine soil particles into the atmosphere (more than 100,000 tons of fine dust for every megaton exploded in a surface burst.) Our work was further spurred by Paul Crutzen of the Max Planck Institute for Chemistry in Mainz, West Germany, and by John Birks of the University of Colorado, who pointed out that huge quantities of smoke would be generated in the burning of cities and forests following a nuclear war.   12

Groundbursts—at hardened missile silos, for example—generate fine dust. Airbursts—over cities and unhardened military installations—make fires and therefore smoke. The amount of dust and soot generated depends on the conduct of the war, the yields of the weapons employed and the ratio of groundbursts to airbursts. So we ran computer models for several dozen different nuclear war scenarios. Our baseline case, as in many other studies, was a 5000-megaton war with only a modest fraction of the yield (20 percent)   13 expended on urban or industrial targets. Our job, for each case, was to follow the dust and smoke generated, see how much sunlight was absorbed and by how much the temperatures changed, figure out how the particles spread in longitude and latitude, and calculate how long before it all fell out of the air back onto the surface. Since the radioactivity would be attached to these same fine particles, our calculations also revealed the extent and timing of the subsequent radioactive fallout.

Some of what I am about to describe is horrifying. I know, because it horrifies me. There is a tendency—psychiatrists call it "denial"—to put it out of our minds, not to think about it. But if we are to deal intelligently, wisely, with the nuclear arms race, then we must steel ourselves to contemplate the horrors of nuclear war.   14

The results of our calculations astonished us. In the baseline case, the amount of sunlight at the ground was reduced to a few percent of normal— much darker, in daylight, than in a heavy overcast and too dark for plants to make a living from photosynthesis. At least in the Northern Hemisphere, where the great preponderance of strategic targets lies, an unbroken and deadly gloom would persist for weeks.   15

Even more unexpected were the temperatures calculated. In the baseline case, land temperatures, except for narrow strips of coastline, dropped to minus 25° Celsius (minus 13° Fahrenheit) and stayed below freezing for months— even for a summer war. (Because the atmospheric structure becomes much more stable as the upper atmosphere is heated and the lower air is cooled, we may have severely *under*estimated how long the cold and the dark would last.) The oceans, a significant heat reservoir, would not freeze, however, and a major ice age would probably not be triggered. But because the temperatures would drop so catastrophically, virtually all crops and farm animals, at least in the Northern Hemisphere, would be destroyed, as would most varieties of uncultivated or undomesticated food supplies. Most of the human survivors would starve.   16

In addition, the amount of radioactive fallout is much more than expected. Many previous calculations simply ignored the intermediate time-scale fallout. That is, calculations were made for the prompt fallout—the plumes of radioactive debris blown downwind from each target—and for the long-term fallout, the fine radioactive particles lofted into the stratosphere that would descend about a year later, after most of the radioactivity had decayed. However, the radioactivity carried into the upper atmosphere (but not as high as the stratosphere) seems to have been largely forgotten. We found for the baseline case that roughly 30 percent of the land at northern midlatitudes could receive a radioactive dose greater than 250 rads, and that about 50 percent of northern midlatitudes could receive a dose greater than 100 rads. A 100-rad dose is the equivalent of about 1000 medical X-rays. A 400-rad dose will, more likely than not, kill you.   17

The cold, the dark and the intense radioactivity, together lasting for months, represent a severe assault on our civilization and our species. Civil   18 and sanitary services would be wiped out. Medical facilities, drugs, the most rudimentary means for relieving the vast human suffering, would be unavailable. Any but the most elaborate shelters would be useless, quite apart from the question of what good it might be to emerge a few months later. Synthetics burned in the destruction of the cities would produce a wide variety of toxic gases, including carbon monoxide, cyanides, dioxins and furans. After the dust and soot settled out, the solar ultraviolet flux would be much larger than its present value. Immunity to disease would decline. Epidemics and pandemics would be rampant, especially after the billion or so unburied bodies began to thaw. Moreover, the combined influence of these severe and simultaneous stresses on life are likely to produce even more adverse consequences—biologists call them synergisms—that we are not yet wise enough to foresee.

So far, we have talked only of the Northern Hemisphere. But it now   19 seems—unlike the case of a single nuclear weapons test—that in a real nuclear war, the heating of the vast quantities of atmospheric dust and soot in northern midlatitudes will transport these fine particles toward and across the Equator. We see just this happening in Martian dust storms. The Southern Hemisphere would experience effects that, while less severe than in the Northern Hemisphere, are nevertheless extremely ominous. The illusion with which some people in the Northern Hemisphere reassure themselves—catching an Air New Zealand flight in a time of serious international crisis, or the like— is now much less tenable, even on the narrow issue of personal survival for those with the price of a ticket.

But what if nuclear wars *can* be contained, and much less than 5000 mega-   20 tons is detonated? Perhaps the greatest surprise in our work was that even small nuclear wars can have devastating climatic effects. We considered a war in which a mere 100 megatons were exploded, less than one percent of the world arsenals, and only in low-yield airbursts over cities. This scenario, we found, would ignite thousands of fires, and the smoke from these fires alone would be enough to generate an epoch of cold and dark almost as severe as in the 5000-megaton case. The threshold for what Richard Turco has called the Nuclear Winter is very low.

Could we have overlooked some important effect? The carrying of dust   21 and soot from the Northern to the Southern Hemisphere (as well as more local atmospheric circulation) will certainly thin the clouds out over the Northern Hemisphere. But, in many cases, this thinning would be insufficient to render the climatic consequences tolerable—and every time it got better in the Northern Hemisphere, it would get worse in the Southern.

Our results have been carefully scrutinized by more than 100 scientists in   22 the United States, Europe, and the Soviet Union. There are still arguments on points of detail. But the overall conclusion seems to be agreed upon: There are severe and previously unanticipated global consequences of nuclear war— subfreezing temperatures in a twilit radioactive gloom lasting for months or longer.

Scientists initially underestimated the effects of fallout, were amazed that 23 nuclear explosions in space disabled distant satellites, had no idea that the fireballs from high-yield thermonuclear explosions could deplete the ozone layer and missed altogether the possible climatic effects of nuclear dust and smoke. What else have we overlooked?

Nuclear war is a problem that can be treated only theoretically. It is not 24 amenable to experimentation. Conceivably, we have left something important out of our analysis, and the effects are more modest than we calculate. On the other hand, it is also possible—and, from previous experience, even likely— that there are further adverse effects that no one has yet been wise enough to recognize. With billions of lives at stake, where does conservatism lie—in assuming that the results will be better than we calculate, or worse?

Many biologists, considering the nuclear winter that these calculations de- 25 scribe, believe they carry somber implications for life on Earth. Many species of plants and animals would become extinct. Vast numbers of surviving humans would starve to death. The delicate ecological relations that bind together organisms on Earth in a fabric of mutual dependency would be torn, perhaps irreparably. There is little question that our global civilization would be destroyed. The human population would be reduced to prehistoric levels, or less. Life for any survivors would be extremely hard. And there seems to be a real possibility of the extinction of the human species.

It is now almost 40 years since the invention of nuclear weapons. We have 26 not yet experienced a global thermonuclear war—although on more than one occasion we have come tremulously close. I do not think our luck can hold forever. Men and machines are fallible, as recent events remind us. Fools and madmen do exist, and sometimes rise to power. Concentrating always on the near future, we have ignored the long-term consequences of our actions. We have placed our civilization and our species in jeopardy.

Fortunately, it is not yet too late. We can safeguard the planetary civi- 27 lization and the human family if we so choose. There is no more important or more urgent issue.

✳

RESPONDING TO THE WHOLE ESSAY

1. What is Sagan's chief purpose in writing "The Nuclear Winter"? How do you know? What secondary purpose is evident? How are the two purposes related? [*Harbrace* 28a; *Hodges'* 32a]

2. How do the details and the vocabulary of "The Nuclear Winter" reveal what kind of audience Sagan is writing for? What kind of audience reads *Parade?* Is there a discrepancy between the audience Sagan intended to address and the audience he reached? How is the question of audience related to Sagan's purpose? [*Harbrace* 28a; *Hodges'* 32a]

3. What is the cause from which Sagan reasons the effects described in "The Nuclear Winter"? Is this an immediate or a remote cause? Explain. What causal chain can be found in the essay? Trace the chain.
4. Compare Sagan's introduction and conclusion. What is repeated? Why? What is the effect of Sagan's conclusion? Is it effective? Why or why not? [*Harbrace* 28f; *Hodges'* 32f]
5. Evaluate Sagan's use of evidence. What problem is inherent in the evidence he presents? How does that affect his purpose? [*Harbrace* 31b, 31c, and 28a; *Hodges'* 35b, 35c, and 32a]
6. What is the main idea of "The Nuclear Winter"? How is the information about *Mariner 9*'s visit to Mars related to the main idea? How is the information about volcanic eruptions related to it? [*Harbrace* 28d and 28e; *Hodges'* 32d and 32e]
7. What kind of organization does Sagan use for arranging his ideas in paragraph 6? In paragraph 20? Explain. [*Harbrace* 27b; *Hodges'* 31b]
8. What kind of development strategy does Sagan use in paragraph 6? In paragraph 25? [*Harbrace* 27d; *Hodges'* 31d]
9. Explain the kinds of transitions Sagan uses between paragraphs. [*Harbrace* 27b(4); *Hodges'* 31b(4)]

ANALYZING THE ELEMENTS

Grammar

1. Explain why the passive verbs in paragraph 7 are more appropriate than active verbs would be. [*Harbrace* 7c; *Hodges'* 7c]
2. The sixth sentence of paragraph 13 contains a string of infinitives, some of which lack the *to*. Explain how these infinitives are used in the sentence, and account for the omission of the *to*. [*Harbrace* 1d; *Hodges'* 1d]
3. Why is the verb in the third sentence of paragraph 20 *were* rather than *was*? [*Harbrace* 7d; *Hodges'* 7d]

Effective Sentences

1. To what does *this* refer in the next-to-last sentence of paragraph 5? Is the reference clear enough? Could it be made clearer? If so, how? [*Harbrace* 6b; *Hodges'* 28c]
2. Could any of the questions Sagan asks in paragraphs 20, 21, 23, and 24 have been phrased instead as statements? What would have been the difference in the effect?

Punctuation and Mechanics

1. Justify the use of numerals in paragraph 1. [*Harbrace* 25f; *Hodges'* 11f]
2. Explain the use of quotation marks to set off *contained* in the second sentence of paragraph 4. [*Harbrace* 20d; *Hodges'* 16d]
3. Explain the use of the colon in the third sentence of paragraph 4. [*Harbrace* 21d; *Hodges'* 17d]
4. Explain why, in paragraph 19, *Northern Hemisphere* and *Southern Hemisphere* are capitalized but not *northern midlatitudes*. [*Harbrace* 23a; *Hodges'* 9a]

Diction

1. Explain why *2-megaton* is hyphenated in the first sentence of paragraph 2. [*Harbrace* 22f; *Hodges'* 18f]
2. Explain the omission in the first sentence of paragraph 2 of *would be* in the verbs *reduced, blown,* and *ignited.* [*Harbrace* 15d; *Hodges'* 21d]
3. Throughout the essay, Sagan uses technical and military jargon. Find examples of this jargon. Does it diminish the effectiveness of the essay? Why or why not? [*Harbrace* 13c(1); *Hodges'* 19g]
4. In the first two sentences of paragraph 13, Sagan uses the words *hardened* and *unhardened* in a particular sense. He also uses the term *baseline case* in the fifth sentence. What is meant by these terms, and how do you know? [*Harbrace* 13c(1); *Hodges'* 19g]

BUILDING VOCABULARY

1. Units of measurement are often combined with the prefixes *mega-, milli-, centi-,* and *kilo-.* What does each of these prefixes mean? Can you think of any others?
2. What does *paroxysm* mean? What is its source?
3. What is the root word of *tenuous?* What does it mean? List two other words that share the same root and state their meanings.

SUGGESTIONS FOR WRITING

1. Write an essay tracing the various effects of some hypothetical disaster in an area where you live or have lived—for instance, a flood, tornado or hurricane, fire, epidemic, drought, blight on crops. If you've lived through a real disaster, you can write on that, explaining the real effects.
2. Emphasizing effects, argue for or against some policy decision (for example, elimination of social security or the minimum wage, establishment of subsidized child care at colleges and universities, reestablishment of the 55-miles-per-hour speed limit.)

Growing Up in Black and White
Jack E. White

Jack White, author of the "Dividing Line" column and National Correspondent for *Time* magazine, is the first African-American journalist to rise to the high-ranking positions of Nation Editor with *Time* and Senior Producer for domestic news for ABC News *World News Tonight,* as well as the first to become a columnist for a national newsweekly. Beginning in 1972, White's career with *Time* exceeds a quarter of a century and is marked by increasingly responsible posts: Nairobi bureau chief in 1980, correspondent for the presidential campaign and member of the panel of journalists at the 1984 vice-presidential debate, Midwest bureau chief in 1985, and deputy chief of correspondents in 1987, with responsibility for supervising 51 correspondents in the magazine's ten domestic bureaus across the U.S.

Before joining *Time,* White was a general assignments reporter for the *Washington Post* and later for Tennessee's *Race Relations Reporter.* His articles have appeared in the *Columbia Journalism Review,* the *Progressive, Ebony Magazine,* and *Our World News,* an online version of a forthcoming black-controlled national newspaper. Among his numerous journalism awards is the National Association of Black Journalists' First Place for Magazines, the Griot Award from the New York Association of Black Journalists, and the Unity Award from Lincoln University for commentary. He has also appeared on NBC's *Today Show,* PBS's *Washington Week in Review* and *Charlie Rose* shows, BET's *Our Voices* and *Lead Story,* CNBC's *Equal Time* and CNN's *Both Sides with Jesse Jackson* and the *McLaughlin Group.*

A native of North Carolina, White attended Swarthmore College and in 1976–77 was a Nieman Fellow at Harvard University with a concentration on African affairs and American ethnic politics. He is married and the father of three sons and a daughter.

"Mommy, I want to be white." 1

Imagine my wife's anguish and alarm when our beautiful brown-skinned 2 three-year-old daughter made that declaration. We thought we were doing everything right to develop her self-esteem and positive racial identity. We overloaded her toy box with black dolls. We carefully monitored the racial content of TV shows and videos, ruling out *Song of the South* and *Dumbo,* two classic Disney movies marred by demeaning black stereotypes. But we saw no harm in *Pinocchio* which seemed as racially benign as *Sesame Street* or *Barney* and a good deal more engaging. Yet now our daughter was saying she wanted to be white, to be like the puppet who becomes a real boy in the movie. How had she got that potentially soul-destroying idea and, even more important, what should we do about it?

That episode was an unsettling reminder of the unique burden that haunts black parents in America: helping their children come to terms with being black in a country where the message too often seems to be that being white is better. Developing a healthy self-image would be difficult enough for black children with all the real-life reminders that blacks and whites are still treated differently. But it is made even harder by the seductive racial bias in TV, movies and children's books, which seem to link everything beautiful and alluring with whiteness while often treating blacks as afterthoughts. Growing up in this all-pervading world of whiteness can be psychologically exhausting for black children just as they begin to figure out who they are. As a four-year-old boy told his father after spending another day in the overwhelmingly white environment of his Connecticut daycare facility, "Dad, I'm tired of being black." 3

In theory it should now be easier for children to develop a healthy sense of black pride than it was during segregation. In 1947 psychologists Kenneth and Mamie Clark conducted a famous experiment that demonstrated just how much black children had internalized the hatred that society directed at their race. They asked 253 black children to choose between four dolls, two black and two white. The result: two-thirds of the children preferred white dolls. 4

The conventional wisdom had been that black self-hatred was a by-product of discrimination that would wither away as society became more tolerant. Despite the civil rights movement of the 1960s, the black-is-beautiful movement of the '70s, the proliferation of black characters on television shows during the '80s and the renascent black nationalist movement of the '90s, the pro-white message has not lost its power. In 1985 psychologist Darlene Powell-Hopson updated the Clarks' experiment using black and white Cabbage Patch dolls and got a virtually identical result: 65% of the black children preferred white dolls. "Black is dirty," one youngster explained. Powell-Hopson thinks the result would be the same if the test were repeated today. 5

Black mental-health workers say the trouble is that virtually all the progress the U.S. has made toward racial fairness has been in one direction. To be accepted by whites, blacks have to become more like them, while many whites have not changed their attitudes at all. Study after study has shown that the majority of whites, for all the commitment to equality they espouse, still consider blacks to be inferior, undesirable and dangerous. "Even though race relations have changed for the better, people maintain those old stereotypes," says Powell-Hopson. "The same racial dynamics occur in an integrated environment as occurred in segregation; it's just more covert." 6

Psychiatrists say children as young as two can pick up these damaging messages, often from subtle signals of black inferiority unwittingly embedded in children's books, toys and TV programs designed for the white mainstream. There are many more positive images about black people in the media than there used to be, but there's still a lot that says that white is more beautiful 7 and powerful than black, that white is good and black is bad, says James P. Comer, a Yale University psychiatrist who collaborated with fellow black psychiatrist Alvin F. Poussaint on *Raising Black Children* (Plume).

The bigotry is not usually as blatant as in Roald Dahl's *Charlie and the Chocolate Factory.* When the book was published in 1964, *The New York Times* called it a "richly inventive and humorous tale." Blacks didn't see anything funny about having the factory staffed by "Oompaoompas," pygmy workers imported in shipping cartons from the jungle where they had been living in the trees.   8

Today white-controlled companies are doing a better job of erasing racially loaded texts from children's books and movies. But those messages still get through, in part because they are at times so subtle even a specialist like Powell-Hopson misses them. She recently bought a book about a cat for her six-year-old daughter, who has a love of felines. Only when Powell-Hopson got home did she discover that the beautiful white cat in the story turns black when it starts behaving badly. Moreover, when the products are not objectionable, they are sometimes promoted in ways that unintentionally drive home the theme of black inferiority. Powell-Hopson cites a TV ad for dolls that displayed a black version in the background behind the white model "as though it were a second-class citizen."   9

Sadly, black self-hatred can also begin at home. Even today, says Powell-Hopson, "many of us perpetuate negative messages, showing preference for lighter complexions, saying nappy hair is bad and straight hair is good, calling other black people 'niggers,' that sort of thing." This danger can be greater than the one posed by TV and the other media because children learn so much by simple imitation of the adults they are closest to. Once implanted in a toddler's mind, teachers and psychologists say, such misconceptions can blossom into a full-blown racial identity crisis during adolescence, affecting everything from performance in the classroom to a youngster's susceptibility to crime and drug abuse. But they can be neutralized if parents react properly.   10

In their book, Comer and Poussaint emphasize a calm and straightforward approach. They point out that even black children from affluent homes in integrated neighborhoods need reassurance about racial issues because from their earliest days they sense that their lives are "viewed cheaply by white society." If, for example, a black little girl says she wishes she had straight blond hair, they advise parents to point out "in a relaxed and unemotional manner . . . that she is black and that most black people have nice curly black hair, and that most white people have straight hair, brown, blond, black. At this age what you convey in your voice and manner will either make it O.K. or make it a problem."   11

Powell-Hopson, who along with her psychologist husband Derek has written *Different and Wonderful: Raising Black Children in a Race-Conscious Society* (Fireside), takes a more aggressive approach, urging black parents in effect to inoculate their children against negative messages at an early age. For example, the authors suggest that African-American parents whose chil-   12 dren display a preference for white dolls or action figures should encourage them to play with a black one by "dressing it in the best clothes, or having it sit next to you, or doing anything you can think of to make your child sense that you prefer that doll." After that, the Hopsons say, the child can be offered a chance to play with the toy, on the condition that "you promise to take the very best care of it. You know it is my favorite." By doing so, the Hopsons claim, "most children will jump at a chance to hold the toy even for a second."

White children are no less vulnerable to racial messages. Their reactions can range from a false sense of superiority over blacks to an identification with sports superstars like Michael Jordan so complete that they want to become black. But if white parents look for guidance from popular child-care manuals, they won't find any. "I haven't included it because I don't feel like an expert in that area," says T. Berry Brazelton, author of *Infants and Mothers* and other child-care books. "I think it's a very, very serious issue that this country hasn't faced up to." Unless it does, the U.S. runs the risk of rearing another generation of white children crippled by the belief that they are better than blacks and black children who agree.   13

As for my daughter, we're concerned but confident. As Comer says, "In the long run what children learn from their parents is more powerful than anything they get from any other source." When my little girl expressed the wish to be white, my wife put aside her anguish and smilingly replied that she is bright and black and beautiful, a very special child. We'll keep telling her that until we're sure she loves herself as much as we love her.   14

*

RESPONDING TO THE WHOLE ESSAY

1. White establishes the context for "Growing Up in Black and White" in paragraph 1. What event occasioned the essay and what were the circumstances surrounding that event?

2. What is White's main point and where does he state it? How is information about the relative numbers of positive black and white images related to the main idea? How is information about approaches to parenting related to the main idea? [*Harbrace* 28d; *Hodges'* 32d]

3. Pointing to specific evidence in the essay, comment on White's purpose in "Growing Up in Black and White." To what extent can the essay be said to be expressive, informative, or persuasive? [*Harbrace* 28a; *Hodges'* 32a]

4. White indicates a number of causes, both immediate and remote, that contribute to the negative image African-Americans internalize about blackness. What are three of these causes? Which does White identify as immediate and which as remote causes?

5. For what kind of audience would you say White is writing? Does anything in the essay reveal or suggest the intended audience? Be specific. Might any particular

group or groups find the essay offensive? If so, which, and why? [*Harbrace* 28a; *Hodges'* 32a]

6. What devices does White use to achieve coherence in paragraph 6? paragraph 12? [*Harbrace* 27b; *Hodges'* 31b]

ANALYZING THE ELEMENTS

Grammar

1. What is the grammatical function of the infinitive phrase *To be accepted by whites* in the second sentence of paragraph 6? Of *embedded* in the first sentence of paragraph 7? [*Harbrace* 1d(2) and (3); *Hodges'* 1d(2) and (3)]
2. In the second sentence of paragraph 7 the subject and the verb appear not to agree. Is there in fact a problem? If so, what is it? If not, why not? [*Harbrace* 7a; *Hodges'* 6a]
3. How many separate simple sentences can you derive from the fourth sentence of paragraph 11? Has White gained anything by combining all of these ideas in a single sentence? If so, what? If not, why not? [*Harbrace* 1f; *Hodges'* 1f]

Effective Sentences

1. Rewrite the first sentence of paragraph 4 removing both instances of *it* as the subject. What would you say is accomplished by this revision? Which is better, the revision or the sentence as White wrote it? Explain. [*Harbrace* 15a(3); *Hodges'* 21a(3)]
2. In the second sentence of paragraph 5, White employs two techniques that contribute to sentence effectiveness. Identify each technique and explain what it offers. [*Harbrace* 10a and 12e; *Hodges'* 26a and 30e]
3. The fourth sentence of paragraph 9 is inverted. Explain what this inversion contributes to the effectiveness of the sentence. [*Harbrace* 11f; *Hodges'* 29f]

Punctuation and Mechanics

1. Explain why White uses a colon in sentence 1 of paragraph 3, the final sentence of paragraph 4, and sentence 3 of paragraph 5. What other mark could he have used? [*Harbrace* 21d; *Hodges'* 17d]
2. In paragraph 5, White uses two different styles to refer to dates. He also spells out some numbers but states others using Arabic numerals. Explain these practices. [*Harbrace* 25f; *Hodges'* 11f]
3. In the first sentence of paragraph 6, the words following *say* are not enclosed in quotation marks. What reason can you give for that? [*Harbrace* 20a; *Hodges'* 16a]

Diction

1. The word *virtual* is becoming quite common as a result of the contemporary interest in virtual reality. Dilbert once introduced his virtual girlfriend to his mother,

philosophers of the Internet refer to virtual machines, and one wag wrote "virtual" when asked to state his place of employment. White uses *virtually* twice in "Growing Up in Black and White." Look the word up in a recent dictionary. Which meaning does White intend for *virtually* in paragraph 5? In paragraph 6? [*Harbrace* 14a; *Hodges'* 20a]

2. Look up *O.K.* in at least three different dictionaries (such as *Webster's Collegiate Dictionary*, 10th edition, the *American Heritage Dictionary*, 3rd edition, or the *Random House Dictionary*). What does each give as its origin? Do any of the dictionaries comment on usage? If so, which one(s) and what do they say? [*Harbrace* 13a; *Hodges'* 19a]

3. In "Growing Up in Black and White" three different terms refer to black people. Identify each of these terms and justify its use in its context. Is this usage racist? Why or why not?

BUILDING VOCABULARY

1. Look up the following words and note their etymology: *demeaning* (paragraph 2), *espouse* (paragraph 6), *covert* (paragraph 6), and *blatant* (paragraph 8). Comment on the role of the prefix or suffix (if any) in determining the meaning of the word.

2. Look carefully through "Growing Up in Black and White" to find at least three words formed using each of the following suffixes: *-ance*, *-ation*, *-ity*, and *-ment*. What are the words from which these are created? What class of words (part of speech) do these suffixes create?

SUGGESTIONS FOR WRITING

1. Write an essay in which you identify at least two influences in society that positively or negatively affected your own upbringing.

2. White describes how subtle elements in our society conspire to foster an unhealthy self-image in children. Write an essay in which you identify, describe, and explain the effect of such an element or combination of elements in your own life or in that of a person you know well. (The emphasis on slenderness or on keeping a stiff upper lip could be examples of such elements.)

Chapter 6

Comparison and Contrast

Should you walk or take the bus? Vote Democratic or Republican (or not vote)? Major in classics or accounting? Watch the news or a comedy rerun? Order a pizza or cook? Such decisions—and hosts of others both trivial and important that you confront every day—require you to *compare* and *contrast* alternatives. You continually set objects, ideas, or possible courses of action side by side in your mind and consider their similarities and their differences in order to understand them better and make wise choices. And since understanding and intelligent decision making are two of the most important goals of writing, comparison and contrast are important in your writing—especially college writing—as well as in your other activities.

Comparing, which focuses on similarities, and contrasting, which focuses on differences, may sound like contrary tasks, but in practice the two cannot be divorced (and so they are often referred to by the single term *comparison*, as we shall do in the following discussion). The reason is that only things that are likely to exhibit both similarities and differences are worth considering in a side-by-side, comparative way. What could be the point of enumerating the similarities of two things that are known to be identical, whether they are two identical spoons in a drawer or identical positions on a social issue? Conversely, why examine the differences between two things known to have *nothing* in common? Examining the merits of the electric shaver versus the "safety" razor can be productive because both are devices for separating hair from skin; exploring whether to shave with a blade or with a banana is not likely to be, shall we say, fruitful (except, perhaps, in the hands of an absurdist such as Steve Martin or Woody Allen). There must be some significant similarity in order for differences to be meaningful. In short, there must be a *basis for comparison*. When writing a comparison-and-contrast paper, always ask yourself, "Have I chosen for comparison two things whose similarities and differences are sufficient to make the comparison worthwhile for me and my readers?" The basis for comparison need not be obvious, however; you can *make* it clear. Separated by five hundred years, Christopher Columbus and the U.S. astronauts may seem to have little in common; yet in "Columbus and the Moon," in this section, Tom Wolfe finds and develops a strong basis for comparison in the fact that both were explorers and especially in the public response to the adventures of both. When the basis for comparison is not obvious, involving two essentially unlike things, it is a special kind of comparison called *analogy*. Analogy depends on pointing out uncommon or uncanny likenesses between two dissimilar things, usually one familiar and one unfamiliar.

Comparison can be useful for many purposes, as we have already hinted. Certainly it is an important tool for clarifying decisions for oneself: "Shall I major in classics or accounting? Let's see: here are the advantages of the one, here of the other. But on the other hand, these are the disadvantages of the one, and these of the other." But a decision need not be at stake; writers often engage in comparison because what may be revealed is interesting or important in itself. When you consider two objects side by side, each emphasizes certain features of the other that would not be as evident if you examined the objects individually. That is why instructors in college courses so often give assignments that are comparative: compare two poems or two characters in a story or play; compare two biological specimens; compare two historic documents, such as the Magna Carta and the Constitution, or two figures, such as Ben Franklin and Thomas Jefferson, or conditions in the North and those in the South; and so forth. (Notice in chapter 11, "The Essay Examination," that all three of Anne Nishijima's essay examination answers—in literature, history, and zoology—involve comparison to a significant degree.) Comparison can also be a powerful persuasive strategy: for example, a writer might contrast the conditions of life of a wealthy person with those of a poor or homeless person to dramatize the plight of the latter.

Basically, a comparison paper can be organized in either of two ways—*subject by subject* or *point by point*—or a combination of the two. A subject-by-subject comparison (also called a "whole-by-whole" or "block" comparison) is divided into two major blocks (plus, usually, an introduction and conclusion): the first block considers one of the items (ideas, courses of action) being compared and examines all the pertinent points; the second block then does the same for the other item (idea, course of action). A point-by-point (also called "part-by-part") comparison reverses this pattern; the points of comparison rather than the items themselves are the main basis or organization. One point or feature is raised at a time, and the items are compared in relation to that point before the next point is raised. An illustration will help to make this clear: a comparison of typical families in the 1950s with those in the nineties. We can use either a block structure or a point-by-point structure. Thus a general outline of block structure would look something like the one on the left below. For point-by-point structure, the outline would look like the one on the right.

Subject by Subject	*Point by Point*
Fifties families [1st subj.]	Mothers' role [point 1]
Mothers' role [point 1]	Fifties families [1st subj.]
Fathers' role [point 2]	Nineties families [2nd subj.]

Children's role [point 3]   Fathers' role [point 2]
  Nineties families [2nd subj.]   Fifties families [1st subj.]
  Mothers' role [point 1]   Nineties families [2nd subj.]
  Fathers' role [point 2]   Children's role [point 3]
  Children's role [point 3]   Fifties families [1st subj.]
                                   Nineties families [2nd subj.]

Each of these arrangements has its advantages and disadvantages. The subject-by-subject organization has the advantage of helping the reader keep each subject in mind *as a whole*. But if this organization is used in a long, complex comparison, one with many points, the reader may have a hard time keeping all the points in mind until it is time to turn from one subject to the other. So the subject-by-subject arrangement is usually best suited to short, simple comparisons involving only a few points. The disadvantage of the point-by-point arrangement has already been implied: the reader tends to lose sight of the whole while focusing on the parts; but when the parts being examined are numerous, point-by-point is usually the practical choice. You can greatly diminish the drawbacks of either strategy if you include appropriate transitional devices to keep your reader "on the track" and if you supply reminders from time to time to help the reader keep in mind exactly how your various points are related.

Subject-by-subject and point-by-point strategies can sometimes be combined in the same essay, as they are in Bruce Catton's "Grant and Lee: A Study in Contrasts." Catton employs a subject-by-subject approach in revealing the numerous differences between the two great Civil War generals—presenting first a full-length picture of Lee, then one of Grant. But he then shifts to a point-by-point approach in showing their similarities.

Balance is very important in writing comparisons. This does not mean that you are obliged to devote equal space and emphasis to every point or even to both of your subjects; your purpose will determine what should be emphasized. But your reader is certain to be puzzled, and perhaps confused, if you raise points about one subject that you ignore altogether in writing about the other.

In the following essay, notice how Louise Keene establishes fundamental similarities—a basis for comparison—as well as fundamental differences—a basis for contrast—before she develops each, using a subject-by-subject approach.

Heroes: Past and Present

	The hero's role in society is to stand as a surrogate for the ordinary citizen and fulfill his or her needs, desires, and dreams. In this larger-than-life quality the heroes of today are similar to those of the
Basis for comparison	past, no doubt because basic human desires and needs change little over the centuries. The ordinary citizen

today, much like the ordinary citizen of yesterday, needs such a figure to admire and to serve as a model for behavior. But the values of John Q. Public

Basis for contrast may be significantly different from those of Everyman. Although heroes both past and present have displayed great strength, been endowed with remarkable abilities, and engaged in extraordinary exploits, those

Thesis of the past were admired for their physical and moral strength, whereas contemporary heroes are known primarily for their star quality.

Rationale for The difference may be attributable to cultural
difference differences between the past and the present. Whereas Everyman personally provided food and shelter and made war with sword and spear, John Q. Public does it all with technology. Thus it was logical for Everyman to admire extraordinary physical and moral courage and strength, whereas it is logical for John Q. Public to admire status and celebrity, distanced as we are from getting our hands dirty and our bodies sweaty (unless we want to). A medieval hero was chaste, loyal, honest, and humble before duty and before God, better, more virtuous than the average person. The true hero might even die for the people, thereby gaining their respect and becoming immortal through lasting fame.

Subject: medieval Two warrior kings typify the medieval hero.
hero—King King Arthur and his Round Table perfectly expressed
Arthur the ideals of heroism. Their code of chivalry, chastity, and courtesy reflected medieval ideal values as did their lack of vanity and personal arrogance. Values were relatively simple in those days and heroism involved a certain mystique. So much was unknown, danger was ever-present, and mystery motivated existence. Arthur and his knights sought to distinguish themselves by daring exploits in the fight against evil. They felt a sense of duty and went out of their way to gain honor.

Medieval hero— Another exemplary hero-king is Beowulf, who
Beowulf came to rescue the Danish people from the horrible monster, Grendel. But it was not only because of his success in slaying Grendel that Beowulf was a hero—a giant among men. When Beowulf gave his life for the people, he became immortal because his great sacrifice and achievement was chronicled by the poets.

Transition There are also heroes today, yet those whose achievements are sung loudest are not those who have given their all for their fellows. Today's heroes are chosen differently and exhibit different requirements and characteristics. Hard work, tenacity, enterprise,

Difference:
medieval vs.
modern

and firmness in the face of odds are still admired,
but heroism today turns upon personality as much
as upon achievement. Those people most admired are
those with "star" quality—in sports, movies, music,
politics, business and other fields.

Subject: modern
hero—Dirty
Harry

Today, music, motion picture, and sports stars
are idolized as heroes, even if their personal qualities
are antithetical to the generally accepted ideals of the
society. For example, the movie character Dirty Harry
is a violent man to whom the end justifies the means
in his fight against evil. He shows no humility in
duty, yet many regard Dirty Harry as a hero.

Modern heroes—
sports and music
stars

In the same way, music and sports stars are
looked upon as heroes. Millions of young people idolize
Michael Jackson, treating him as a superstar—a hero
by virtue of publicity. Vanilla Ice, another music star,
is viewed with awe, yet he leads a troubled life. In
sports, Bo Jackson, a football and baseball player, was
treated as a hero solely because of his daring exploits
on the playing field. Michael Jordan, a basketball
player, is accorded hero and celebrity status entirely
because of his abilities on the court.

Exceptions

Many modern heroes display vanity and personal arrogance, traits unacceptable in antiquity; some
exploit themselves for monetary gain. But not all.
Some superstars serve as excellent role models by
virtue of their strong character and selfless devotion
to principle. Unfortunately they are few, but that is
nothing new. For every Robin Hood, there are a dozen
Sheriffs of Nottingham, and for every Quincy Jones,
there are a dozen Jim Morrisons.

Summary

Many similarities exist between the heroes of
today and those of medieval times—great powers and
abilities, dignity, daring, and integrity. Nevertheless,
many differences also exist. Many of today's heroes
are not humble, chaste, or loyal; some are egocentric
and self-concerned, with little concern for social values. Today's interpretation of what it means to be a
hero varies considerably from that of medieval times.
Clearly, cultural values determine who is a hero and
who is not. The world has changed. Thus, our heroes
have changed.

Commentary. Keene introduces her essay by telling us what she thinks a
hero is supposed to be and that she has noticed similarities and differences in
the medieval and modern perceptions of a hero. This is her basis for comparison. (In her conclusion she will sum up this cultural view.) She then states
her thesis: modern heroes are different from medieval heroes because cultural

values have changed. She devotes the next paragraph to making a point about why cultural values are reflected in society's view of the hero.

Keene then focuses on the medieval hero, offering two examples of typical warrior-kings—King Arthur and Beowulf. She outlines how they reflect the values of the Middle Ages before she moves on to take up the modern hero.

She devotes a paragraph to explaining what she sees as the most basic difference between the medieval and the modern view of the hero—the modern focus upon "star quality" rather than actual integrity. She then gives one example—Dirty Harry—of the hero who not only does not have the medieval virtues, but seems to actively oppose them. She follows that example with several other modern heroes who have star quality—Michael Jackson, Vanilla Ice, Bo Jackson, Michael Jordan—but little else to recommend them as heroes. All are either musical stars or sports figures.

Keene then sets the typical modern hero in contrast to the typical medieval hero but grants that the picture is not one of unrelieved superficiality. There are a few admirable modern heroes. Her final paragraph sums up the argument that she has made and ends with a restatement of the thesis.

Grant and Lee: A Study
in Contrasts
Bruce Catton

Bruce Catton (1899–1978) began his career as a journalist and worked for several newspapers, including the *Cleveland Plain Dealer.* His abiding interest in history, however, led to his becoming a noted authority on the Civil War, about which he published more than a dozen books. In 1954 he received both the Pulitzer Prize and the National Book Award for one of these, *A Stillness at Appomattox.* Among the others—all good reading for the nonspecialist as well as the historian—are *Mr. Lincoln's Army* (1960), *Never Call Retreat* (1965), *Terrible Swift Sword* (1967), *This Hallowed Ground* (1969), and *Gettysburg: The Final Fury* (1974). The essay that follows, "Grant and Lee: A Study in Contrasts," first appeared in a collection of historical essays written by prominent historians, *The American Story* (1956), and has been widely reprinted since. In it Catton compares and contrasts the two greatest Civil War generals in terms of the different traditions they represented.

When Ulysses S. Grant and Robert E. Lee met in the parlor of a modest house at Appomattox Court House, Virginia, on April 9, 1865, to work out the terms for the surrender of Lee's Army of Northern Virginia, a great chapter in American life came to a close, and a great new chapter began. 1

These men were bringing the Civil War to its virtual finish. To be sure, other armies had yet to surrender, and for a few days the fugitive Confederate government would struggle desperately and vainly, trying to find some way to go on living now that its chief support was gone. But in effect it was all over when Grant and Lee signed the papers. And the little room where they wrote out the terms was the scene of one of the poignant, dramatic contrasts in American history. 2

They were two strong men, these oddly different generals, and they represented the strengths of two conflicting currents that, through them, had come into final collision. 3

Back of Robert E. Lee was the notion that the old aristocratic concept might somehow survive and be dominant in American life. 4

Lee was tidewater Virginia, and in his background were family, culture, and tradition . . . the age of chivalry transplanted to a New World which was making its own legends and its own myths. He embodied a way of life that had come down through the age of knighthood and the English country squire. America was a land that was beginning all over again, dedicated to nothing 5 much more complicated than the rather hazy belief that all men had equal rights, and should have an equal chance in the world. In such a land Lee stood for the feeling that it was somehow of advantage to human society to have a pronounced inequality in the social structure. There should be a leisure class, backed by ownership of land; in turn, society itself should be keyed to the land as the chief source of wealth and influence. It would bring forth (according to this ideal) a class of men with a strong sense of obligation to the community; men who lived not to gain advantage for themselves, but to meet the solemn obligations which had been laid on them by the very fact that they were privileged. From them the country would get its leadership; to them it could look for the higher values—of thought, of conduct, of personal deportment—to give it strength and virtue.

Lee embodied the noblest elements of this aristocratic ideal. Through him,   6
the landed nobility justified itself. For four years, the Southern states had fought a desperate war to uphold the ideals for which Lee stood. In the end, it almost seemed as if the Confederacy fought for Lee; as if he himself was the Confederacy . . . the best thing that the way of life for which the Confederacy stood could ever have to offer. He had passed into legend before Appomattox. Thousands of tired, underfed, poorly clothed Confederate soldiers, long-since past the simple enthusiasm of the early days of the struggle, somehow considered Lee the symbol of everything for which they had been willing to die. But they could not quite put this feeling into words. If the Lost Cause, sanctified by so much heroism and so many deaths, had a living justification, its justification was General Lee.

Grant, the son of a tanner on the Western frontier, was everything Lee   7
was not. He had come up the hard way, and embodied nothing in particular except the eternal toughness and sinewy fiber of the men who grew up beyond the mountains. He was one of a body of men who owed reverence and obeisance to no one, who were self-reliant to a fault, who cared hardly anything for the past but who had a sharp eye for the future.

These frontier men were the precise opposites of the tidewater aristocrats.   8
Back of them, in the great surge that had taken people over the Alleghenies and into the opening Western country, there was a deep, implicit dissatisfaction with a past that had settled into grooves. They stood for democracy, not from any reasoned conclusion about the proper ordering of human society, but simply because they had grown up in the middle of democracy and knew how it worked. Their society might have privileges, but they would be privileges each man had won for himself. Forms and patterns meant nothing. No man was born to anything, except perhaps to a chance to show how far he could rise. Life was competition.

Yet along with this feeling had come a deep sense of belonging to a na-   9
tional community. The Westerner who developed a farm, opened a shop or set up in business as a trader, could hope to prosper only as his own community prospered—and his community ran from the Atlantic to the Pacific and from Canada down to Mexico. If the land was settled, with towns and highways and accessible markets, he could better himself. He saw his fate in

terms of the nation's own destiny. As its horizons expanded, so did his. He had, in other words, an acute dollars-and-cents stake in the continued growth and development of his country.

And that, perhaps, is where the contrast between Grant and Lee becomes   10
most striking. The Virginia aristocrat, inevitably, saw himself in relation to his own region. He lived in a static society which could endure almost anything except change. Instinctively, his first loyalty would go to the locality in which that society existed. He would fight to the limit of endurance to defend it, because in defending it he was defending everything that gave his own life its deepest meaning.

The Westerner, on the other hand, would fight with an equal tenacity for   11
the broader concept of society. He fought so because everything he lived by was tied to growth, expansion, and a constantly widening horizon. What he lived by would survive or fall with the nation itself. He could not possibly stand by unmoved in the face of an attempt to destroy the Union. He would combat it with everything he had, because he could only see it as an effort to cut the ground out from under his feet.

So Grant and Lee were in complete contrast, representing two diametri-   12
cally opposed elements in American life. Grant was the modern man emerging; beyond him, ready to come on the stage, was the great age of steel and machinery, of crowded cities and a restless, burgeoning vitality. Lee might have ridden down from the old age of chivalry, lance in hand, silken banner fluttering over his head. Each man was the perfect champion of his cause, drawing both his strengths and his weaknesses from the people he led.

Yet, it was not all contrast, after all. Different as they were—in back-   13
ground, in personality, in underlying aspiration—these two great soldiers had much in common. Under everything else, they were marvelous fighters. Furthermore, their fighting qualities were really very much alike.

Each man had, to begin with, the great virtue of utter tenacity and fi-   14
delity. Grant fought his way down the Mississippi Valley in spite of acute personal discouragement and profound military handicaps. Lee hung on in the trenches at Petersburg after hope itself had died. In each man there was an indomitable quality . . . the born fighter's refusal to give up as long as he can still remain on his feet and lift his two fists.

Daring and resourcefulness they had, too; the ability to think faster and   15
move faster than the enemy. These were the qualities which gave Lee the dazzling campaigns of Second Manassas and Chancellorsville and won Vicksburg for Grant.

Lastly, and perhaps greatest of all, there was the ability, at the end, to turn   16
quickly from war to peace once the fighting was over. Out of the way these two men behaved at Appomattox came the possibility of a peace of reconciliation. It was a possibility not wholly realized in the years to come, but which did, in the end, help the two sections to become one nation again . . . after a war whose bitterness might have seemed to make such a reunion wholly impossible. No part of either man's life became him more than the part he played in their brief meeting in the McLean house at Appomattox. Their behavior

there put all succeeding generations of Americans in their debt. Two great Americans, Grant and Lee—very different, yet under everything very much alike. Their encounter at Appomattox was one of the great moments of American history.

✳

RESPONDING TO THE WHOLE ESSAY

1. Is Catton's purpose in "Grant and Lee: A Study in Contrasts" primarily expressive, informative, or persuasive? What evidence can you find to support your answer? Is there evidence of all three purposes? [*Harbrace* 28a; *Hodges'* 32a]
2. What kind of audience do the details in "Grant and Lee: A Study in Contrasts" lead you to imagine Catton had in mind? In what way(s) are you or are you not a member of that audience? [*Harbrace* 28a; *Hodges'* 32a]
3. What advantage does Catton gain by contrasting the two generals before he compares them? What would have been the effect of approaching the subject the other way?
4. Analyze Catton's use of both subject-by-subject (whole-by-whole or block) organization and point-by-point (part-by-part) organization (explained in the introduction to this section). Where, and for what kind of information, is each pattern used? Might alternative arrangements have been as effective? Why or why not?
5. Analyze Catton's use of various transitional devices throughout the essay to help readers keep their bearings. In particular, comment on the functions of paragraphs 12 and 13 within the whole essay and on the transition between these two paragraphs. [*Harbrace* 27b; *Hodges'* 31b]
6. Explain how the introduction and conclusion frame the essay, providing and reinforcing the basis for Catton's comparison. [*Harbrace* 28f; *Hodges'* 32f]

ANALYZING THE ELEMENTS

Grammar

1. In the third sentence of paragraph 6, Catton writes "for which Lee stood." Would the meaning of the sentence change if Catton had instead written "which Lee stood for"? To what does *which* refer in both versions? What is the probable reason Catton preferred the former? Is that choice obligatory? [*Harbrace* 1c and 1d; *Hodges'* 1c and 1d]
2. The next-to-last sentence of the essay is a deliberate fragment. What reason might Catton have had for using it? Had Catton written a complete sentence instead, what would it have been? How would the effect have been different? [*Harbrace* 2; *Hodges'* 2]

Effective Sentences

1. Comment on the use and effectiveness of parallel structure in the last sentence of paragraph 5. [*Harbrace* 10a; *Hodges'* 26a]

2. Explain how Catton's inversion of normal sentence order in the first sentence of paragraph 15 contributes to the effectiveness of the sentence. [*Harbrace* 11f; *Hodges'* 29f]

Punctuation and Mechanics

1. Explain the use of the semicolon in the sixth sentence of paragraph 5 and the fourth sentence of paragraph 6. What other mark of punctuation could have been used? Explain what advantage(s) the semicolon offers. [*Harbrace* 18b; *Hodges'* 14b]
2. Explain Catton's use of ellipsis points in paragraphs 5, 6, 14, and 16. What other kinds of punctuation might he have used? Would other punctuation have made the sentences more or less effective? Why? [*Harbrace* 21i; *Hodges'* 17i]

Diction

1. Explain the meaning (both the denotation and connotations) of *tidewater* in the first sentences of paragraph 5 and paragraph 8. [*Harbrace* 14a(1) and 14a(3); *Hodges'* 20a(1) and 20a(2)]
2. Examine the ways in which Catton's use of images and figurative language contributes to the effectiveness of the essay—for example, the image of Lee "lance in hand, silken banner fluttering over his head" (paragraph 12) and of Grant embodying "the eternal toughness and sinewy fiber of the men who grew up beyond the mountains" (paragraph 7). [*Harbrace* 14a(5); *Hodges'* 20a(4)]

BUILDING VOCABULARY

1. Look up *static, sinewy, fidelity,* and *daring* and state the meaning of each. What are their antonyms?
2. What are the sources of *poignant* and *chivalry*? Approximately when did each word come into the English language?

SUGGESTIONS FOR WRITING

1. Write an essay comparing and contrasting two professionals you know (for instance, teachers, ministers, doctors) who represent different professional styles but who are both excellent in their work.
2. Report an imaginary encounter between two figures who have something in common but whose differences are striking enough to make the meeting interesting to observe. Locate your characters wherever it suits you: at a party, in adjacent airplane seats on a long flight, in the dentist's waiting room, or even in a chance encounter in heaven (or elsewhere, as may be appropriate). A few possibilities: Citizen Kane and Mike Wallace; George Washington and Yasser Arafat; John Lennon and Caruso; Charlie Brown and Doonesbury; General Patton and Barry Switzer; Babe Ruth and Nolan Ryan; Beethoven and Mozart; Wyatt Earp and J. Edgar Hoover.

Columbus and the Moon
Tom Wolfe

A Virginian who attended Washington and Lee University and then earned a
Ph.D. in American studies from Yale University, Tom Wolfe turned to journalism instead of the academic world, working first as a reporter for the
Washington Post and then as a feature writer for *Esquire* and *New York*
(when it was still the Sunday magazine of the late *New York Herald Tribune*
and also afterward). He is a frequent contributor to *Harper's* and other magazines. Wolfe is one of the most gifted practitioners of "the new journalism"—a style of reporting in which the writer's personality is given full sway.
His books (whose titles reflect his unusual style) include *The Kandy-Colored
Tangerine-Flake Streamline Baby, The Electric Kool-Aid Acid Test,* and *The
Pump House Gang* (all 1968); *Radical Chic and Maumauing the Flak Catch-
ers* (1970); *The Bonfire of the Vanities* (1985); two books on art and architecture, *The Painted Word* (1975) and *From Bauhaus to Our House* (1981);
and *The Right Stuff* (1979), which won him the American Book Award. In
"Columbus and the Moon," Wolfe traces the similarities and differences between the space explorations through the 1970s and the explorations of
Columbus in the fifteenth century.

The National Aeronautics and Space Administration's moon landing 10
years ago today was a Government project, but then so was Columbus's voyage to America in 1492. The Government, in Columbus's case, was the Spanish Court of Fedrinand and Isabella. Spain was engaged in a sea race with
Portugal in much the same way that the United States would be caught up in
a space race with the Soviet Union four and a half centuries later.

The race in 1492 was to create the first shipping lane to Asia. The Portuguese expeditions had always sailed east, around the southern tip of Africa.
Columbus decided to head due west, across open ocean, a scheme that was
feasible only thanks to a recent invention—the magnetic ship's compass. Until then ships had stayed close to the great land masses even for the longest
voyages. Likewise, it was only thanks to an invention of the 1940's and early
1950's, the high-speed electronic computer, that NASA would even consider
propelling astronauts out of the Earth's orbit and toward the moon.

Both NASA and Columbus made not one but a series of voyages. NASA
landed men on six different parts of the moon. Columbus made four voyages to different parts of what he remained convinced was the east coast of
Asia. As a result both NASA and Columbus had to keep coming back to the
Government with their hands out, pleading for refinancing. In each case the

reply of the Government became, after a few years: "This is all very impressive, but what earthly good is it to anyone back home?"

Columbus was reduced to making the most desperate claims. When he 4 first reached land in 1492 at San Salvador, off Cuba, he expected to find gold, or at least spices. The Arawak Indians were awed by the strangers and their ships, which they believed had descended from the sky, and they presented them with their most prized possessions, live parrots and balls of cotton. Columbus soon set them digging for gold, which didn't exist. So he brought back reports of fabulous riches in the form of manpower; which is to say, slaves. He was not speaking of the Arawaks, however. With the exception of criminals and prisoners of war, he was supposed to civilize all natives and convert them to Christianity. He was talking about the Carib Indians, who were cannibals and therefore qualified as criminals. The Caribs would fight down to the last unbroken bone rather than endure captivity, and few ever survived the voyages back to Spain. By the end of Columbus's second voyage, in 1496, the Government was becoming testy. A great deal of wealth was going into voyages to Asia, and very little was coming back. Columbus made his men swear to return to Spain saying that they had not only reached the Asian mainland, they had heard Japanese spoken.

Likewise by the early 1970's, it was clear that the moon was in economic 5 terms pretty much what it looked like from Earth, a gray rock. NASA, in the quest for appropriations, was reduced to publicizing the "spinoffs" of the space program. These included Teflon-coated frying pans, a ballpoint pen that would write in a weightless environment, and a computerized biosensor system that would enable doctors to treat heart patients without making house calls. On the whole, not a giant step for mankind.

In 1493, after his first voyage, Columbus had ridden through Barcelona 6 at the side of King Ferdinand in the position once occupied by Ferdinand's late son, Juan. By 1500, the bad-mouthing of Columbus had reached the point where he was put in chains at the conclusion of his third voyage and returned to Spain in disgrace. NASA suffered no such ignominy, of course, but by July 20, 1974, the fifth anniversary of the landing of Apollo 11, things were grim enough. The public had become gloriously bored by space exploration. The fifth anniversary celebration consisted mainly of about 200 souls, mostly NASA people, sitting on folding chairs underneath a camp meeting canopy on the marble prairie outside the old Smithsonian Air Museum in Washington listening to speeches by Neil Armstrong, Michael Collins, and Buzz Aldrin and watching the caloric waves ripple.

Extraordinary rumors had begun to circulate about the astronauts. The 7 most lurid said that trips to the moon, and even into earth orbit, had so traumatized the men, they had fallen victim to religious and spiritualist manias or plain madness. (Of the total 73 astronauts chosen, one, Alrdin, is known to have suffered from depression, rooted, as his own memoir makes clear, in matters that had nothing to do with space flight. Two teamed up in an evangelical organization, and one set up a foundation for the scientific study of psychic phenomena—interests the three of them had developed long before they flew in space.) The NASA budget, meanwhile, had been reduced to the light-bill level.

Columbus died in 1590, nearly broke and stripped of most of his honors   8
as Spain's Admiral of the Ocean, a title he preferred. It was only later that history began to look upon him not as an adventurer who had tried and failed to bring home gold—but as a man with a supernatural sense of destiny, whose true glory was his willingness to plunge into the unknown, including the remotest parts of the universe he could hope to reach.

NASA still lives, albeit in reduced circumstances, and whether or not his-   9
tory will treat NASA like the admiral is hard to say.

The idea that the exploration of the rest of the universe is its own reward   10
is not very popular, and NASA is forced to keep talking about things such as bigger communications satellites that will enable live television transmission of European soccer games at a fraction of the current cost. Such notions as "building a bridge to the stars for mankind" do not light up the sky today—but may yet.

✳

RESPONDING TO THE WHOLE ESSAY

1. To what extent is Wolfe concerned here with informing and to what extent with persuading the reader? Which aim is dominant? How does Wolfe's choice of subjects to compare serve this aim? Is that an expressive dimension in the essay as well? Point to evidence. [*Harbrace* 28a; *Hodges'* 32a]
2. Wolfe takes pains to provide background information about his two subjects. What does this effort tell us about the audience he had in mind as he wrote? [*Harbrace* 28a; *Hodges'* 32a]
3. What is Wolfe's basis for comparing Columbus and NASA? How is the essay organized? How else might it have been organized? What advantage did arranging the essay as it appears offer?
4. Comment on the title of Wolfe's essay. What does it promise the reader? How does it reflect the approach Wolfe takes in the essay? [*Harbrace* 28f(3); *Hodges'* 32f(3)]
5. How does Wolfe accomplish transitions between paragraphs? Explain, giving specific examples. [*Harbrace* 27b; *Hodges'* 31b]
6. Explain how Wolfe's introduction arouses the reader's interest at the same time that it announces the subject of the essay. What is the effect of Wolfe's conclusion? [*Harbrace* 28f; *Hodges'* 32f]

ANALYZING THE ELEMENTS

Grammar

1. The third sentence in paragraph 4 and the first sentence in paragraph 10 are both compound-complex sentences. Explain what a compound-complex sentence is,

and, as fully as you can, comment on what rhetorical advantages these sentences offer Wolfe. [*Harbrace* 1e; *Hodges'* 1e]

2. The final sentence in paragraph 4 may appear at first glance to be a comma splice; however, it is not. Explain why a comma between *mainland* and *they* is sufficient and why it is unnecessary to add a coordinating conjunction. How does handling the sentence this way make it more effective? [*Harbrace* 3a; *Hodges'* 3a]

3. The last sentence of paragraph 5 is a fragment. What reason might Wolfe have had for using it here? [*Harbrace* 2; *Hodges'* 2]

Effective Sentences

1. How does parallel structure contribute to the effectiveness of the final sentence in paragraph 6? [*Harbrace* 10a; *Hodges'* 26a]

2. Wolfe could have begun the second sentence of paragraph 8 as follows: "Only later did history begin to look upon him. . . ." Is Wolfe's actual beginning better? Why or why not?

Punctuation and Mechanics

1. Justify Wolfe's capitalization of *Government* in the first sentence of paragraph 1 and *Court* in the second. [*Harbrace* 23a; *Hodges'* 9a]

2. Explain why it is unnecessary to use quotation marks in the second sentence of paragraph 7. What advantage does this method of quotation offer Wolfe? What disadvantage would the use of quotation marks have entailed? [*Harbrace* 20a; *Hodges'* 16a]

Diction

1. Explain how the following words and phrases contribute to the tone Wolfe establishes in the essay: *their hands out* (paragraph 3), *testy* (paragraph 4), *bad-mouthing* (paragraph 6), *light-bill level* (paragraph 7), *broke* (paragraph 8). [*Harbrace* 14a(3); *Hodges'* 20a(2)].

2. Wolfe uses two different kinds of allusions in "Columbus and the Moon." Explain what "a giant step for mankind" (paragraph 5) alludes to. Then explain what "in reduced circumstances" (paragraph 9) alludes to. How do these allusions differ? How does each expand the meaning of the essay?

BUILDING VOCABULARY

1. List at least five other words that are derived from the same root word as *expedition*.

2. What does the prefix *circum-* mean? List at least three words that begin with it.

SUGGESTIONS FOR WRITING

1. Considering either your college career or your working career as a kind of voyage, think of two different directions in which you could go and contrast them.

2. Both explorations Wolfe describes consumed enormous sums of money that conceivably could have been used for human benefit in other ways. Think of an alternative program the United States could establish with the vast funds it spends on the space program, or that it spends on some particular aspect of the space program, and compare and contrast the space program and your alternative in terms of the benefits and sacrifices entailed. For example, you might think of medical or educational programs, economic subsidies of various kinds, and so forth.

The Decline of the Front Porch
David Dawson

David Dawson (1954–   ) was born in Memphis, Tennessee, attended the
University of St. Thomas in Houston, and graduated from Memphis State
University, from which he holds a bachelor's degree in English and a master's degree in history. A full-time writer, his work has appeared in *The New
York Times Book Review, Time,* and *Life* as well as in *Memphis Magazine,*
for which he is a senior writer, and *Southern Magazine,* from which this essay comes. Having been asked by *Merian,* a magazine similar to *National
Geographic* and published in Hamburg, Germany, to explain the Elvis phenomenon and Graceland for a German audience, Dawson is bemused by the
phenomenon of seeing his own work translated into another language: "I
wish I knew how they handled such phrases as 'down home.'" Although he
enjoys volleyball and walking, he claims parenting as his current major
hobby.

This is an evening of slightly anemic breezes, feeble but persistent gusts   1
that whisper high in the trees but lack the energy to come down and get in
your hair. The season doesn't matter: It could be spring, it could be summer,
or perhaps fall. What counts instead is the fact that tonight I have the opportunity to sit awhile, forget the day, and study the sky as it runs through
its twilight palette.

At times like this—which is to say, any pleasant evening—you'll find me   2
out back on the deck. I could just as easily be on the front porch—our house
is blessed with both—but, invariably, when the weather is right and the dim-
ming of the day is at hand, I migrate to the deck. For no matter how honored or how highly recollected the traditional Southern porch remains, the
deck has virtues to which the porch could never aspire.

This evening, I happen to be in one of the wrought iron chairs we're still   3
paying for, leaning back into the cushions, my bare feet propped insolently
on the splintery rail. Other times you might find me slung low in the ham-
mock draped across the end of the deck—looking, my wife tells me, like a
basketball stuck in a net—admiring the effortless manner in which the highest branches of the elm above me acquiesce to the gentle demands of the
breeze. I am not dressed for company, clad in a T-shirt with some unfortunate holes in it and a pair of shorts with one leg cut longer than the other, as
sloppy as can be. This rickety wooden deck is my place, and I'll be damned
if I'll ever dress up to be lazy.

227

Surrounding me are items that testify to the informality of the deck: a 4
barbecue grill, several pots filled with ailing geraniums, a few piles of mis-
creant leaves, a rusting harmonica, the dog's dishes, a neglected rake—things
you'd never leave out on the front porch for a minute.

Yet the deck is much more than a setting in which to become a slob. Its 5
main virtue is that it is an altogether private domain. Because of its inherent
isolation, tucked away behind the house, the deck is a wondrously meditative
platform, a secret sanctuary as serene in its own disreputable way as any Zen
garden. Unlike the porch, the deck is a perfect place to settle down after a
hard day and, quite simply, to hide.

This privacy is reinforced even in the deck's very rusticity. In its splintery, 6
weather-bitten informality lies an intimate, casual sort of comfort that is not
to be found on any porch. Add to this the deck's natural clutter and you have,
in essence, a permanent invitation to stop your caring for a few moments, a
promise that any sort of behavior short of the criminal is not only tolerated,
but encouraged.

The same can't be said for the front porch. Being open, as it is, to the 7
gaze of any who happen to walk or drive by, the porch is an altogether more
formal place: As much as anything else, it is a room, a kind of airy extension
of the parlor. Because of this, the front porch is not a place that lends itself
to the kind of serious, unfettered loafing required in the modern world.

Let me assert that I'm not merely taking pot-shots at yet another slightly 8
clichéd bastion of Old Southern gentility just for the sake of being trendy. Like
anyone in this region old enough to have lived without the blessings of the ar
conditioner, I, too, have fond memories of the vital function the porch once
served.

Each summer when I was small, my parents used to deposit me at my 9
grandmother's house near Overton Park in Memphis to spend a few weeks
while they went off for their (no doubt) much needed respite. There, I spent
my days and evenings on the porch. In the morning, the porch became a classroom where I was awarded gold stars for each Curious George or Tom Swift
book I waded through. In the afternoon, given a few items of furniture and
my child's imagination, the porch was transformed by turns into a fortress, a
spaceship, or a submarine.

But then, after supper, this versatile playground assumed an altogether 10
different mission. There, dressed to meet the evening's callers, we would sit
and wait to greet any and all of the neighbors who came by. Never was an
invitation issued, nor was one needed. Like a grown-up version of trick or
treat, a parade of strollers—the ladies in dresses and gloves, the men in
Panama hats and ties—would make they way up and down the street. When
they encountered an occupied porch, they would pause to share a few moments of conversation about such pressing topics as the ferocity of the mosquitoes, the scrawniness of the tomatoes at the curb market, or the particular beauty of Mr. Crawford's roses. And then they would move on to another
porch and another segment of their night's conversation. My grandmother

knew all of her neighbors' names, and usually she knew a good bit more about them than that.

Of course, what ended this ritual was the advent of the air conditioner. 11 Before that, during the long summer months the porch was quite simply the coolest place to be. Shady, open to whatever breezes decided to blow, the porch was an architectural stepchild of the plantation house's sweeping veranda, offering a modicum of relief from the stuffiness which welled up inside even the best ventilated houses.

So pervasive was the impact of the air conditioner that homes built after 12 its arrival rarely even *have* porches. From the mid-1950s on, the "gallery" porch—that is, one big enough to put a chain on—by and large disappeared from the face of Southern houses. What replaced the porch in very short order was the backyard deck. Now that we rely so heavily on air conditioning, there is no longer a real need to have a shady place—like a porch—on which to escape the heat. What we have opted for instead is a sunny place—like a deck—on which to escape the pressures of the world without.

Sure, knowing your neighbors is a definite amenity, and the evening 13 porch visits were once the means by which neighborhoods were bound into real communities. Today, however, we have the block club, the neighborhood association, and the community center to accomplish that—not quite as spontaneous or as intimate as the porch visit, perhaps, but effective nonetheless.

The decline of the front porch is but a symbol of a more fundamental 14 change that has nothing whatever to do with porches or decks. Back when porch sitting and evening visits were in vogue, we never felt the need to keep loaded shotguns next to our beds or, in most cases, to even lock our doors at night. Crime, TV, the increasingly frenetic pace of urban life, and the lure of the air conditioner—these are but a few of the things that have chased us indoors. The front porch has been a victim of the disease, not the cause.

While much has been lost in the decline of the porch, much more has 15 been gained with the emergence of the deck. For the deck offers us everything the porch once did, only without the requisite bother and sweaty formality.

On the deck, we are able to be outside, and yet, at the same time, be entirely concealed, saved from the necessity of maintaining appearances merely for appearances' sake. Nature—in the form of our own little plot of backyard and our own little patch of sky above—belongs only to us when we are on the deck. We have, in essence, the perfect venue to be alone with ourselves— or with our friends and families.

For those not of a mystical bent, the deck is also a more utilitarian ob- 17 ject than the porch. On the deck, we can grill our burgers, eat dinner in our shorts, put our feet on the table, and let ice cream run down our chins, should we so desire. We have the opportunity to be genuinely and effectively lazy, for never do we have to worry about jumping up between each forkful to hastily wipe our mouths and spend time earnestly discussing mosquitoes or the humidity with a covey of wandering neighbors.

So, on evenings like this one, with the scant breezes moving high in the   18
trees and the first stars of the night winking through the urban haze, don't
look for me on the porch. I'll be out back, slowly letting go of the pressures
of the day in my own private way, my mind focused only on the play of the
breeze in the top branches of the elm, confident that the night will proceed
according to its own particular rhythm.

❋

RESPONDING TO THE WHOLE ESSAY

1. What basis does Dawson use for contrasting porches and decks? Comment upon
    the basic similarity between the two that leads the author to note the contrasts.
    [*Harbrace* 27a; *Hodges'* 31a]
2. Examine the essay paragraph by paragraph, noting the subject of each. Then ex-
    plain the organization Dawson has chosen and comment on what may (or may
    not) make that organization effective. [*Harbrace* 27d; *Hodges'* 31d]
3. Analyze Dawson's introductory paragraphs. Where does he state what he will com-
    pare? How does he limit and focus his subject? Explain why the first paragraph
    establishes a context for the essay and how it helps Dawson focus the essay and
    then conclude it. [*Harbrace* 28d and 28f; *Hodges'* 32d and 32f]
4. Is Dawson's purpose for writing "The Decline of the Front Porch" primarily to
    meditate upon the various virtues of porches and decks, to inform readers about
    the differences between them, or to persuade readers to prefer decks to porches?
    Is more than one of these aims present? Cite evidence from the essay to support
    your answer. [*Harbrace* 28a; *Hodges'* 32a]
5. What are the main characteristics of Dawson's audience? What details in the es-
    say help you to define the audience Dawson was probably writing for? Does he
    make an effort to anticipate the reader's questions and answer them? If so, where?
    [*Harbrace* 28a; *Hodges'* 32a]
6. What kinds of transitional devices does Dawson use to move from point to point
    in this essay? Are they effective? Why or why not? [*Harbrace* 27b; *Hodges'* 31b]

ANALYZING THE ELEMENTS

Grammar

1. Comment on the grammatical structure of "What counts instead" in sentence 3
    of paragraph 1. Find at least two other occurrences of that structure in this essay.
    [*Harbrace* 1d; *Hodges'* 1d]
2. What is the function of *pervasive* in the first sentence of paragraph 12? How might
    the sentence be rewritten to reveal the grammatical function more clearly? Which
    sentence is the better choice for this essay? Why? [*Harbrace* 4b; *Hodges'* 4b]

Effective Sentences

1. Comment on Dawson's placement of the phrase "clad in a T-shirt . . . sloppy as can
    be" after the verb in the third sentence of paragraph 3. [*Harbrace* 5b; *Hodges'* 25b]

2. Explain what makes the third sentence of paragraph 10 effective. [*Harbrace* 11f; *Hodges'* 29f]

Punctuation and Mechanics

1. Explain why dashes are used in the first and second sentences of paragraph 2. What other mark of punctuation could have been used? Would the sentences be more or less effective if the other mark were used? Why? [*Harbrace* 21e; *Hodges'* 17e]
2. Explain the use of the colon and the dash in paragraph 4. Rewrite the sentence so that neither is necessary. Which version is clearer? Why? [*Harbrace* 21d and 21f; *Hodges'* 17d and 17f]

Diction

1. Examine the vocabulary of paragraph 5, paying particular attention to the following words: *altogether, inherent, meditative, sanctuary.* Are these the kind of words a reader expects to encounter in the same paragraph with the word *slob*? Explain your answer. [*Harbrace* 14a; *Hodges'* 20a]
2. Comment on the expression "splintery, weather-bitten informality" in the second sentence of paragraph 6. What, exactly, does "weather-bitten" mean? What more common phrase is it similar to? [*Harbrace* 14c; *Hodges'* 20c]

BUILDING VOCABULARY

1. English has been immensely enriched by words borrowed from other languages. Such words are used in English for a time as foreign words, and then they are frequently Anglicized. Look up the following words and identify which have been assimilated into the English vocabulary and which are still considered foreign: *barbecue, bastion, cliché, covey, veranda.*
2. English treats slang words in a similar way to the way it treats borrowed words: they are used for a time and then some of them become a part of the general vocabulary and others either disappear or remain slang. All of the following words have been slang at some time or another. Look them up, define them, state (if possible) when they were first used, and identify whether they are still considered slang: *booze, mob, O.K., slob, scrawny.*

SUGGESTIONS FOR WRITING

1. Compare and/or contrast the sense of place of two groups—or two individuals—with whom you are familiar (for example, the young and the old, city people and country people, those who move about frequently and those who have always lived in the same place).
2. Compare and/or contrast some kind of behavior people don't observe today as rigorously as they did in the past with how people behave today (for instance, dressing up for dinner and dressing down for dinner, calling older adults by their surnames and calling them by their given names, eating the main meal at midday and eating the main meal in the evening).

The Knight and the Jester
Anna Quindlen

Born in 1952 in Philadelphia, Pennsylvania, Anna Quindlen graduated from
Barnard College in 1974 and went to work for *The New York Times* in 1977
where she was a reporter and an editor. Author of the syndicated columns,
"Life in the Thirties" and "Old Enough to Kill," Quindlen has collected many
of her best columns in *Living Out Loud*. The oldest of five children and
mother of four, she blends memories of her childhood and observations of
adulthood in humorous, thought-provoking essays. She received a Pulitzer
Prize for her novel, *Object Lessons*, published in 1991 by Random House.

Sometimes I think you can tell everything about my two children by watch- 1
ing them sleep at night. One lies flat on his back, the quilt tucked neatly under his armpits, his arms at his side, as though he were a child miming
perfect sleep for an advertisement for cocoa or pajamas. No matter what
time it is, you will find him so.

The other will be sprawled in some corner of the bed, and on the floor 2
will be his quilt, his sheets, his pillow and, if he's feeling particularly froggy,
his pajamas. Sometimes he is at the head and sometimes he is at the foot, and
sometimes half of him is hanging over the side. For the sake of futile moth-
ering gestures, I will often cover him up, but if I return 15 minutes later the
quilt will be on the floor again. I look from one bed to the other and think:
the knight and the jester; the gentleman and the wild man; the parson and the
gambler.

I like to think there are no particular value judgments to these assess- 3
ments, but that is not true. I try to suppress them sometimes, to think in terms
of body temperature as I straighten one set of perfectly straight blankets and
untangle another from the floor. It is not fair to make two children foils for
one another, although it is common and, I suppose, understandable to do so.
It can also turn to poison faster than you can say Cain and Abel, for sometimes the the unconscious assessments become sharper: the good child and the
bad one; the smart one and the stupid one; the success and the failure. And
sometimes thinking makes it so.

Perhaps I am overly sensitive on this subject, since I grew up with its 4
shadow. I have a brother barely a year younger than I am, and I suspect that
both of us were thoroughly sick, after a while, of the comparisons. Deep down
we were not so different, but it was inevitable that in finding his own way
around the world, one of the things he wanted was to find a way that was

232

different from mine. By high school, I had become the circle-pin princess of the junior class. My brother, meanwhile, had begun to affect black leather jackets and shoes with pointed toes. If we had had a buck for every teacher who was incredulous that we shared the same parents, we could have started a small business together.

It was not as bad for me as it was for him, since I got the prime position at the starting gate, and he got the "on the other hand." Sometimes I think it turned him into some things he wasn't, just for the sake of living out the contrast.

Now I know how easily it happens, as we play out our liking for proto- types here, in the little bedrooms and the playgrounds and at the kitchen table. At some point after the first child is born, we ditch the books and learn the lessons of eating, sleeping and talking by doing. And in the process what we come to know about children is what the first child teaches us. We use that to measure the progress of the next child. And quietly, subtly, without malice or bad intentions, begins the process of comparison.

Some say that this is the nature of being second, and that the person a second child becomes has more to do with filling in the spaces that haven't been claimed yet than with some innate difference of temperament. It's easy sometimes for me to believe that. My children are quite different. The eldest had staked out early the territory of being sensitive, sweet, thoughtful and ea- ger to please. There were openings in the areas of independence, confidence, creative craziness and pure moxie, and whether by coincidence or design, the second child has all those things.

Yet when I think of the theory of filling in the family blanks I think, too, of two babies in utero, one slow and languorous and giving no trouble, the other a real pistol, pounding the pavement, dancing the fandango, throwing his sheets on the floor even while floating in amniotic fluid. And I remember that in every knight there is something of the jester; in every wild man, a bit of the gentleman. The danger in making our children take roles on opposite sides of the family room is that the contradictions in their own characters, the things that make humans so interesting, get flattened out and hidden away. The other danger is that they will hate one another.

So far, I think we are doing all right. Certainly there's little hatred, for which I am deeply grateful. But in my attempts to make our chaotic lives or- derly, I have to battle constantly against the urge to pigeonhole each of them, to file away the essentials of their personalities as one thing I've finally got- ten down, once and for all. I have never said to either, "Why can't you be more like your brother?" I have never compared them aloud. I am always mindful of my mother's will, in which she noted that I was everything she was not; this happened to be true, but since at the time I thought everything she was was wonderful, it left me little doubt about my own inadequacies.

And in truth one boy is not everything the other is not. Both of them are everything—obedient, willful, sensitive, tough, wild, pacific—in different mea- sures. Both look like angels when they are asleep, although neither is anything quite so two-dimensional as angelic. Children are not easy, no matter what mothers sometimes like to think in their attempts to turn all this tortured family calculus into plain arithmetic.

✳

RESPONDING TO THE WHOLE ESSAY

1. To what extent does Quindlen allow her feelings about each boy to find expression in this essay? Do you think she prefers one of the children to the other? If so, which one? How do you know? If not, how do you know?
2. How would you describe the audience Quindlen writes for? What evidence can you marshal to support your position? [*Harbrace* 28a; *Hodges'* 32a]
3. In "The Knight and the Jester" Quindlen does more than simply compare her two sons. What other comparisons does she imply? What are we to understand from her comparison?
4. Consider Quindlen's title. What qualities of a good title does it have? Explain which child is referred to as the knight and which as the jester. [*Harbrace* 28f(3); *Hodges'* 32f(3)]
5. Paragraph 10 begins Quindlen's conclusion. Explain how her conclusion summarizes her main points. [*Harbrace* 28f(2); *Hodges'* 32f(2)]

ANALYZING THE ELEMENTS

Grammar

1. Briefly explain the grammatical function of each subordinate clause in the final sentence of paragraph 9. What are the main clauses? As fully as you can, comment on Quindlen's choice of which ideas to present in the main clauses and which to put in the subordinate structures. [*Harbrace* 1e and 1f; *Hodges'* 1e and 1f]
2. Comment on the use of *for* in the fourth sentence of paragraph 3. [*Harbrace* 1f; *Hodges'* 1f]
3. What is the grammatical function of the final clause of the last sentence of paragraph 8? [*Harbrace* 1e; *Hodges'* 1e]

Effective Sentences

1. To what does the *it* that begins the third sentence and the one that begins the fourth sentence of paragraph 3 refer? How are they different? Do you think most readers would find the references clear enough? Why or why not? [*Harbrace* 6b; *Hodges'* 28]
2. What rhetorical effect does Quindlen achieve by beginning two sentences in paragraph 6 with *and*? [*Harbrace* 12b; *Hodges'* 30b]

Punctuation and Mechanics

1. What does Quindlen probably intend the reader to understand by her use of dashes in the second sentence of paragraph 10? [*Harbrace* 21e; *Hodges'* 17e]

2. Justify the omission of a comma between *craziness* and *and* in the fifth sentence of paragraph 7. [*Harbrace* 17; *Hodges'* 12]
3. What is the reason for using *15* instead of *fifteen* in the third sentence of paragraph 2? [*Harbrace* 25f; *Hodges'* 11f]

Diction

1. Quindlen refers to herself as the "circle-pin princess of the junior class." What does she mean? [*Harbrace* 14; *Hodges'* 20]
2. Comment on the metaphor with which Quindlen concludes her essay: "turn all this tortured family calculus into plain arithmetic." [*Harbrace* 14c; *Hodges'* 20c]
3. Quindlen uses the word *buck* in the last sentence of paragraph 4. Look the word up in your dictionary. Are there any labels attached to it? Explain why Quindlen uses it here, [*Harbrace* 14c; *Hodges'* 20c]

BUILDING VOCABULARY

1. The noun *foil* has two quite different meanings. What are they? Which meaning is related to the verb, *to foil*?
2. Identify the source of each of the following: *cocoa, pajamas, moxie*. What does each word mean?

SUGGESTIONS FOR WRITING

1. Choose two people that you know (or know about) and write an essay comparing and contrasting them to reveal what seem to you the most important differences.

Cyberpunk R.I.P.
Paul Saffo

Paul Saffo delves into recent literary and social history to explore the similarities he notes between the cyberpunk movement of the early 1990s and the
beatnik movement of the late 1950s. In each movement, Saffo sees the seeds
of a coming revolution in mass culture, and indeed, if his analysis is correct,
we might all want to heed Bette Davis's command in *All About Eve:* "Fas-
ten your seatbelts! It's going to be a bumpy night." A frequent contributor
to such computer magazines as *Wired, Windows,* and *PC Computing,* Saffo
(psaffo@MCImail.com) is a research fellow at the Institute for the Future in
Menlo Park, California.

Like a sun-grazing comet on a deep-space trajectory, the cyberpunk move- 1
ment is disappearing as quickly as it arrived just a few years ago. Moreover,
the movement was hardly more substantial than a comet's fuzzy tail when it
came to numbers—there were never more than 100 hardcore cyberpunks at
any time before the term hit the mainstream press.

But don't sell cyberpunks's social impact short, for insubstantial comets 2
have long served as messengers. I suspect that cyberpunks are to the 1990s
what the beatniks were to the '60s—harbingers of a mass movement waiting
in the wings. Just as the beatniks anticipated the hippies, cyberpunks are setting the stage for a coming digital counterculture that will turn the '90s zeitgeist utterly on its head. This movement in the making has yet to be described,
much less named, but eerie parallels between the beatnik and cyberpunk movements offer strong hints of what is to come.

For starters, both movements were given focus by literary fiction. The 3
beatniks took their cue from a handful of "beat writers" (Jack Kerouac, Alan
Ginsberg, Gregory Corso, and William S. Burroughs), while cyberpunks found
their identity in the cyberpunk science fiction genre defined by writers such
as William Gibson, Rudy Rucker, Bruce Sterling, and John Shirley. Moreover,
the lead works in both traditions orbited emerging infrastructures: Kerouac's
On the Road played off the concrete mobility enabled by the Interstate Highway Act, while Gibson's *Neuromancer* portrayed a future world wrapped
around vast information highways. Eager readers never realized that neither
writer was really one of them: Kerouac disliked driving; Gibson banged out
Neuromancer on a 1927 Hermes typewriter.

Like the cyberpunks, there were never more than a handful of true 4
beatniks—less than 120 in all before the movement hit the media in the late

1950s, according to essayist George Leonard. Leonard's descriptions of the North Beach beatnik milieu parallel today's cyberpunk culture. Word got out on the grapevine of parties at people's "pads," and, like raves, these happenings quickly evolved into underground quasi-commercial events. Just as cyberpunks carry their network identities into the physical world, the beatniks were fond of pseudonyms. "Everyone had a name, like in a Damon Runyon novel," observes Leonard. Ironically, neither group named its own movement, for just as the cyberpunks were so dubbed by a literary interloper, the term "beatnik" was coined by *San Francisco Chronicle* columnist Herb Caen.

Once labeled, both movements quickly surrendered their visual archetypes to the cultural mainstream. In 1960, youths the world over were aping the goateed, cool-shades beatnik look, while today, PDBs (people dressed in black) affecting electronic lifestyles are more numerous than network nodes. This surrender would send both movements into the black hole of history, but not before they inspired larger movements to come. Just five years after the beatniks's demise in 1960, the hippies emerged from the Haight Ashbury to change our cultural landscape forever.

Like cyberpunks, the beatniks were for the most part low-key, slightly mournful loners. Beatnik individualism was a sullen and stubborn reaction to the optimistic company-man materialism of the Eisenhower era, just as the cyberpunks stand in stark contrast to the antiseptic military-industrial orderliness of the Reagan-Bush years.

But Kerouac later concluded that beat also meant beatific—imbued with joy or blessedness—and it was this aspect of the beatniks that became the germ of the hippie movement, according to Leonard. "It was a time of grace," he told me, referring to the early days of the Haight-Ashbury, when it seemed that a new age of cultural consciousness truly was dawning.

Optimism and a sense of community distinguished the hippies from the beatniks, and will also distinguish the cyberpunks from the coming digital counterculture. The cyberpunk world is starkly non-utopian, serving up the same sort of intimate but uneasy accommodation with technology portrayed in the movie *Blade Runner*. I will bet that the digital counterculture will reject this bleak vision of a future in which technology enlarges the human spirit as a new tool for consciousness in much the same way that the hippies appropriated the psychoactive chemical spin-offs of the military-industrial complex. This new movement will be cyberpunk imbued with human warmth, substituting a deep sense of interdependence in place of lone wolf isolationism. Cyberpunks envision humans as electronic cyber-rats lurking in the interstices of the information mega-machine; the gospel of the post-cyberpunk movement will be one of machines in the service of enlarging our humanity.

It is too early to tell what the digital counterculture will call itself, but the history of the hippies offers a clue. "Hippie" traces its origins to "hipster," slang for a cruel and cynical 1950s subculture that predated the beats. The digital counterculture thus is likely to appropriate an older term for its own, in the same way that the hippies appropriated and turned "hipster" into something entirely new. I'll bet that they call themselves something like "tekkies," consciously adopting the scornful '80s slang for nerds, stripping the word of its industrial coldness and making it synonymous with the human control of technology.

Hippies appeared in 1965, several years after the beatnik movement had   10
gone public. Given this chronology, the tekkies will arrive sometime in the mid-1990s, if not sooner. Watch the skies for a new comet—it will be digital, and its tail is likely to glow in Technicolor swirls. Its arrival will change our lives forever.

✳

RESPONDING TO THE WHOLE ESSAY

1. What basis for comparison does Saffo use for this essay? Does he state it? If so, where? [*Harbrace* 27c; *Hodges'* 31c]
2. With what literary device does Saffo introduce and conclude this essay? Why is this kind of device particularly appropriate in a comparison-contrast essay? [*Harbrace* 14a(5); *Hodges'* 20a(4)]
3. Comment upon the organization of this essay—part by part, whole by whole, or a combination? [*Harbrace* 28e; *Hodges'* 32e]
4. Analyze sentence by sentence the organizational strategy used in paragraph 3. [*Harbrace* 27c; *Hodges'* 31c]

ANALYZING THE ELEMENTS

Grammar

1. Why is the first sentence of paragraph 2 not a comma splice? [*Harbrace* 3; *Hodges'* 3]
2. Explain what makes the first sentence in paragraph 8 a grammatically simple sentence. [*Harbrace* 1f; *Hodges'* 1f]
3. Comment upon the use of the infinitive in the final sentence of paragraph 5. [*Harbrace* 7c; *Hodges'* 7c]
4. The final sentence in paragraph 9 is a complex sentence. Explain what a complex sentence is and find at least one more in this essay. Then, as fully as you can, comment on what rhetorical advantages these sentences offer Saffo. [*Harbrace* 1e; *Hodges'* 1e]

Effective Sentences

1. How does parallel structure contribute to the effectiveness of the second sentence of paragraph 6? [*Harbrace* 10; *Hodges'* 26]
2. Saffo could have begun the second sentence of paragraph 8 as follows: "Starkly non-utopian, the cyberpunk world serves up the same sort of intimate . . . " Is Saffo's actual beginning better? Why or why not? [*Harbrace* 12b; *Hodges'* 30b]

Punctuation and Mechanics

1. There is a small difference in meaning between "a sullen and stubborn reaction," as Saffo writes in paragraph 6, and the more common approach of separating these coordinate adjectives with a comma—"a sullen, stubborn reaction." What does Saffo gain by separating them with a conjunction? [*Harbrace* 17c; *Hodges'* 12c]

2. Justify the use of a semicolon in the last sentence in paragraph 8. What do you think was Saffo's reason for not making separate sentences? [*Harbrace* 18a; *Hodges'* 14a]

3. Why are the following italicized: *Neuromancer* (paragraph 3), *On the Road* (paragraph 3), *Blade Runner* (paragraph 8)? [*Harbrace* 24a; *Hodges'* 10a]

4. Comment upon Saffo's use of numbers in paragraph 2. [*Harbrace* 25f; *Hodges'* 11f]

Diction

1. What is the origin of the phrase *to sell something short* (paragraph 2)? What does it mean? [*Harbrace* 14c; *Hodges'* 20c]

2. Look up the following words in a good desk dictionary, write down the etymology (history) of each one, and then write an explanation of how the meaning of each word is probably related to its history: *harbinger* (paragraph 2), *dubbed* (paragraph 4), *milieu* (paragraph 4), *interloper* (paragraph 4), *archetype* (paragraph 5). [*Harbrace* 13a; *Hodges'* 19a]

BUILDING VOCABULARY

1. *Zeitgeist* (paragraph 2) is a German word made by combining the words *Zeit* and *Geist*. Look each word up in a German-English dictionary and write down the meanings. Then, considering the meanings of those two words as well as the way the word is used in the essay, explain the meaning of *Zeitgeist*.

2. *Goateed* is used as an adjective in paragraph 5. The word is easily recognizable as a relative of the noun, *goatee*, but what steps had to occur for it to be used as an adjective?

SUGGESTIONS FOR WRITING

1. Write a short essay in which you compare behaviors and attitudes in high school with those in college. For instance, you might compare the behaviors of students studying for final exams or their attitudes toward homework.

2. Write an essay in which you suggest a new term for the coming cyberculture, comparing and contrasting it to Saffo's term, *tekkies*.

Anglo vs. Chicano: Why?

Arthur L. Campa

Arthur L. Campa (1905–1975) was the author of more than seventy mono-
graphs and articles for professional journals as well as of several books:
Acquiring Spanish, Spanish Folk-Poetry in New Mexico, and *Treasure of
the Sangre de Cristos.* Born in Guaymas, Mexico, he was educated at the
University of New Mexico and Columbia University and for many years
he was chairman of the modern language department at the University of
Denver and directed the Center for Latin American Studies there. He also
served as a U.S. State Department lecturer in Spain, as cultural attaché to
the U.S. Embassy in Peru, and as training project director in Denver for
the Peace Corps. Among his many awards were a Rockefeller research
grant and a Guggenheim fellowship. First published in *Western Review,*
"Anglo vs. Chicano: Why?" takes an anthropological view of the conflict
between the two cultures.

1   The cultural differences between Hispanic and Anglo-American people
have been dwelt upon by so many writers that we should all be well informed
about the values of both. But audiences are usually of the same persuasion as
the speakers, and those who consult published works are for the most part
specialists looking for affirmation of what they believe. So, let us consider the
same subject, exploring briefly some of the basic cultural differences that cause
conflict in the Southwest, where Hispanic and Anglo-American cultures meet.

2   Cultural differences are implicit in the conceptual content of the languages
of these two civilizations, and their value systems stem from a long series of
historical circumstances. Therefore, it may be well to consider some of the
English and Spanish cultural configurations before these Europeans set foot
on American soil. English culture was basically insular, geographically and
ideologically; was more integrated on the whole, except for some strong theological differences; and was particularly zealous of its racial purity. Spanish
culture was peninsular, a geographical circumstance that made it a catchall of
Mediterranean, central Europe and north African peoples. The composite nature of the population produced a marked regionalism that prevented close
integration, except for religion, and led to a strong sense of individualism.
These differences were reflected in the colonizing enterprise of the two cultures. The English isolated themselves from the Indians physically and culturally; the Spanish, who had strong notions about *pureza de sangre* [purity
of blood] among the nobility, were not collectively averse to adding one more
strain to their racial cocktail. Cortés led the way by siring the first *mestizo* in

North America, and the rest of the conquistadores followed suit. The ultimate products of these two orientations meet today in the Southwest.

Anglo-American culture was absolutist at the onset; that is, all the dom- 3 inant values were considered identical for all, regardless of time and place. Such values as justice, charity, honesty were considered the superior social order for all men and were later embodied in the American Constitution. The Spaniard brought with him a relativistic viewpoint and saw fewer moral implications in man's actions. Values were looked upon as the result of social and economic conditions.

The motives that brought Spaniards and Englishmen to America also dif- 4 fered. The former came on an enterprise of discovery, searching for a new route to India initially, and later for new lands to conquer, the fountain of youth, minerals, the Seven Cities of Cíbola and, in the case of the missionaries, new souls to win for the Kingdom of Heaven. The English came to escape religious persecution, and once having found a haven, they settled down to cultivate the soil and establish their homes. Since the Spaniards were not seeking a refuge or running away from anything, they continued their explorations and circled the globe 25 years after the discovery of the New World.

This peripatetic tendency of the Spaniard may be accounted for in part 5 by the fact that he was the product of an equestrian culture. Men on foot do not venture far into the unknown. It was almost a century after the landing on Plymouth Rock that Governor Alexander Spotswood of Virginia crossed the Blue Ridge Mountains, and it was not until the nineteenth century that the Anglo-American began to move west of the Mississippi.

The Spaniard's equestrian role meant that he was not close to the soil, as 6 was the Anglo-American pioneer, who tilled the land and built the greatest agricultural industry in history. The Spaniard cultivated the land only when he had Indians available to do it for him. The uses to which the horse was put also varied. The Spanish horse was essentially a mount, while the more robust English horse was used in cultivating the soil. It is therefore not surprising that the viewpoints of these two cultures should differ when we consider that the pioneer is looking at the world at the level of his eyes while the *caballero* [horseman] is looking beyond and down at the rest of the world.

One of the most commonly quoted, and often misinterpreted, character- 7 istics of Hispanic peoples is the deeply ingrained individualism in all walks of life. Hispanic individualism is a revolt against the incursion of collectivity, strongly asserted when it is felt that the ego is being fenced in. This attitude leads to a deficiency in those social qualities based on collective standards, an attitude that Hispanos do not consider negative because it manifests a measure of resistance to standardization in order to achieve a measure of individual freedom. Naturally, such an attitude has no *reglas fijas* [fixed rules].

Anglo-Americans who achieve a measure of success and security 8 through institutional guidance not only do not mind a few fixed rules but demand them. The lack of a concerted plan of action, whether in business or in politics, appears unreasonable to Anglo-Americans. They have a sense of individualism, but they achieve it through action and self-determination. Spanish individualism is based on feeling, on something that is the result not of rules and collective standards but of a person's momentary, emotional reaction. And it is subject to change when the mood changes. In contrast to Spanish emotional individualism, the Anglo-American strives for objectivity when choosing a course of action or making a decision.

The Southwestern Hispanos voiced strong objections to the lack of courtesy of the Anglo-Americans when they first met them in the early days of the Santa Fe trade. The same accusation is leveled at the *Americanos* today in many quarters of the Hispanic world. Some of this results from their different conceptions of polite behavior. Here too one can say that the Spanish have no *reglas fijas* because for them courtesy is simply an expression of the way one person feels toward another. To some they extend the hand, to some they bow and for the more *íntimos* there is the well-known *abrazo*. The concepts of "good or bad" or "right and wrong" in polite behavior are moral considerations of an absolutist culture.   9

Another cultural contrast appears in the way both cultures share part of their material substance with others. The pragmatic Anglo-American contributes regularly to such institutions as the Red Cross, the United Fund and a myriad of associations. He also establishes foundations and quite often leaves millions to such institutions. The Hispano prefers to give his contribution directly to the recipient so he can see the person he is helping.   10

A century of association has inevitably acculturated both Hispanos and Anglo-Americans to some extent, but there still persist a number of culture traits that neither group has relinquished altogether. Nothing is more disquieting to an Anglo-American who believes that time is money than the time perspective of Hispanos. They usually refer to this attitude as the *"mañana* psychology." Actually, it is more of a "today psychology," because Hispanos cultivate the present to the exclusion of the future; because the latter has not arrived yet, it is not a reality. They are reluctant to relinquish the present, so they hold on to it until it becomes the past. To an Hispano, nine is nine until it is ten, so when he arrives at nine-thirty, he jubilantly exclaims: *"¡Justo!"* [right on time]. This may be why the clock is slowed down to a walk in Spanish while in English it runs. In the United States, our future-oriented civilization plans our lives so far in advance that the present loses its meaning. January magazine issues [including ID's] are out in December; 1973 cars have been out since October; cemetery plots and even funeral arrangements are bought on the installment plan. To a person engrossed in living today the very idea of planning his funeral sounds like the tolling of the bells.   11

It is a natural corollary that a person who is present oriented should be compensated by being good at improvising. An Anglo-American is told in advance to prepare for an "impromptu speech," but an Hispano usually can improvise a speech because *"Nosotros lo improvisamos todo"* [we improvise everything].   12

Another source of cultural conflict arises from the difference between *being* and *doing*. Even when trying to be individualistic, the Anglo-American achieves it by what he does. Today's young generation decided to be themselves, to get away from standardization, so they let their hair grow, wore ragged clothes and even went barefoot in order to be different from the Establishment. As a result they all ended up doing the same things and created another stereotype. The freedom enjoyed by the individuality of *being* makes it unnecessary for Hispanos to strive to be different. 13

In 1963 a team of psychologists from the University of Guadalajara in Mexico and the University of Michigan compared 74 upper-middle-class students from each university. Individualism and personalism were found to be central values for the Mexican students. This was explained by saying that a Mexican's value as a person lies in his *being* rather than, as is the case of the Anglo-Americans, in concrete accomplishments. Efficiency and accomplishments are derived characteristics that do not affect worthiness in the Mexican, whereas in the American it is equated with success, a value of highest priority in the American culture. Hispanic people dissociate themselves from material things or from actions that may impugn a person's sense of being, but the Anglo-American shows great concern for material things and assumes responsibility for his actions. This is expressed in the language of each culture. In Spanish one says, *"Se me cayó la taza"* [the cup fell away from me] instead of "I dropped the cup." 14

In English, one speaks of money, cash and all related transactions with frankness because material things of this high order do not trouble Anglo-Americans. In Spanish such materialistic concepts are circumvented by referring to cash as *efectivo* [effective] and when buying or selling as something *al contado* [counted out], and when without it by saying *No tengo fondos* [I have no funds]. This dissociation from material things is what produces *sobriedad* [sobriety] in the Spaniard according to Miguel de Unamuno, but in the Southwest the dissociation from materialism leads to *dejadez* [lassitude] and *desprendimiento* [disinterestedness]. A man may lose his life defending his honor but is unconcerned about the lack of material things. *Desprendimiento* causes a man to spend his last cent on a friend, which when added to lack of concern for the future may mean that tomorrow he will eat beans as a result of today's binge. 15

The implicit differences in words that appear to be identical in meaning are astonishing. Versatile is a compliment in English and an insult in Spanish. An Hispano student who is told to apologize cannot do it, because the word doesn't exist in Spanish. *Apología* means words in praise of a person. The Anglo-American either apologizes, which is a form of retraction abhorrent in Spanish, or compromises, another concept foreign to Hispanic culture. *Compromiso* means a date, not a compromise. In colonial Mexico City, two hidalgos once entered a narrow street from opposite sides, and when they could not go around, they sat in their coaches for three days until the viceroy 16 ordered them to back out. All this because they could not work out a compromise.

It was that way then and to some extent now. Many of today's conflicts in the Southwest have their roots in polarized cultural differences, which need not be irreconcilable when approached with mutual respect and understanding.   17

✸

RESPONDING TO THE WHOLE ESSAY

1. What primary purpose can you ascertain for Campa's writing "Anglo vs. Chicano: Why?" What features in the essay make the purpose clear? [*Harbrace* 28a; *Hodges'* 32a]
2. How does the essay reveal the nature of the audience Campa was writing for? Does knowing that the essay was written twenty or more years ago influence your understanding of Campa's audience? Would the essay need to be modified to appeal to the same group of readers today? If so, how and why? If not, why not? [*Harbrace* 28a; *Hodges'* 32a]
3. Does Campa organize this essay subject-by-subject or point-by-point? What advantages does his chosen method offer? What would be the effect of using the other method?
4. Campa makes frequent use of examples to develop his ideas. Explain how examples develop the ideas in paragraphs 4, 10, 11, 13, and 16. [*Harbrace* 27d; *Hodges'* 31d]
5. Where does Campa make clear that he is focusing on *why* there are cultural differences between Hispanic and Anglo-American cultures? Explain how the rest of the essay maintains that focus. [*Harbrace* 28d; *Hodges'* 32d]
6. What solution to the problems raised in the essay does Campa's concluding paragraph suggest? Comment on the effectiveness of this strategy for a conclusion. [*Harbrace* 28f(2); *Hodges'* 32f(2)]

ANALYZING THE ELEMENTS

Grammar

1. Explain how the phrase "the superior social order for all men" is used in the second sentence of paragraph 3. [*Harbrace* 4b; *Hodges'* 4b]
2. Campa uses a fragment to conclude paragraph 16. Why? [*Harbrace* 2; *Hodges'* 2]

Effective Sentences

1. Explain the probable reason for Campa's use of the passive in the first sentence of the essay. How does this sentence establish a pattern for the rest of the essay? Is the use of passive voice here effective? Why or why not? [*Harbrace* 11d(1); *Hodges'* 29d(1)]

2. In the fourth sentence of paragraph 14, to what does *it* refer? Explain why the reference is clear and the antecedent need not be repeated. [*Harbrace* 6b; *Hodges'* 28c]

Punctuation and Mechanics

1. Examine the use of commas in the last sentence of paragraph 1 and the seventh sentence of paragraph 2 (beginning "The English isolated . . . "). Is each comma necessary? Why or why not? Would the meaning of the sentence change if the comma(s) were eliminated from the sentence in paragraph 1? In paragraph 2? [*Harbrace* 17d and 17f; *Hodges'* 12d and 13]
2. Explain the use of semicolons in the third sentence of paragraph 2. What other method of punctuation could have been used, if any? [*Harbrace* 18b; *Hodges'* 14b]

Diction

1. Campa incorporates a number of Spanish words and expressions into "Anglo vs. Chicano: Why?" Considering Campa's audience, comment on whether these expressions contribute to or detract from the essay.
2. Campa's vocabulary is varied and precise. Check your dictionary for the meanings of the following words and explain how each is appropriate in its context: *insular* and *peninsular* (paragraph 2), *absolutist* (paragraph 3), *peripatetic* (paragraph 5), *incursion* and *collective* (paragraph 7), *pragmatic* (paragraph 10), *acculturated* (paragraph 11), *corollary* (paragraph 12). [*Harbrace* 14a(3); *Hodges'* 20a(2)]

BUILDING VOCABULARY

1. What is the meaning of the prefix, *pen-*? How does it alter the meaning of the word *insular*? List at least two other words beginning with the prefix *pen-*. Explain the way it alters the root word in each case.
2. The following words are frequently confused: *disinterested* and *uninterested*, *pragmatic* and *practical*, *prevaricate* and *procrastinate*. Look up each word and state its meaning.

SUGGESTIONS FOR WRITING

1. Write an essay in which you compare and contrast two families you know well.
2. Contrast two culturally different communities from your own region as Campa does for the Southwest. These communities need not be ethnically different, but may be socially or religiously different, or different for other reasons. Take care to maintain, as Campa does, a spirit of fairness and objectivity as you account for the cultural differences you discuss.

Chapter 7

Classification and Division

When you group ideas or objects into categories, you are classifying. When you separate ideas or objects into parts, you are dividing. Classifying and dividing are complementary. They are both important strategies in writing, but they are far more than that; they are fundamental to how people understand and organize information to make it useful. For instance, if you have to buy grapes, hamburger, cheese, tomatoes, milk, chicken, and butter at the supermarket, you'll proceed most efficiently through the store if you consider the categories into which the management has classified those items: produce, meats, and dairy products. But at the dairy counter you will also want to consider whether to buy whole, lowfat, or skimmed milk.

Classification is important in every field, but perhaps especially in science, which often progresses by refining categories and establishing new ones. Think of the great classification systems that enable botanists and zoologists to find order in, and write intelligibly about, the staggering diversity of living things on the earth. Or consider, for that matter, how astronomers classify the earth itself, as a *planet,* one of several classes of heavenly bodies that make up our solar system, which in turn belongs to a larger star system we call a *galaxy;* galaxies themselves are classified in four categories on the basis of their form: elliptical, spiral (ours is spiral, as is Andromeda), barred spiral, and irregular.

Classification, obviously, involves recognizing common characteristics that diverse items share (and therefore is closely related to comparison and contrast, dealt with in chapter 6). Galaxies, as we noted, are normally classified on the basis of shape. Stars, however, can be classified on many different bases—for instance, size, composition, color, brightness, age, distance; the choice of a basis depends on the classifier's immediate purpose. The point is that in writing an essay or other paper you may be able to classify your subject in several different ways, some of which will serve your purpose better than others; you must choose the *basis of classification* that is best for your purpose. To return to the supermarket for a moment, the management (though it might not remain the management very long) could choose an alphabetical basis of classification and arrange everything on the shelves accordingly—the apples next to the antacids, the bread between the beans and the brooms, and so forth. Such an arrangement works fine, after all, in the telephone directory, where "your fingers do the walking." Or the merchandise could be classified according to the type of package: bottled things in aisle 1, canned things in aisle 2, boxed things in aisle 3, bagged things in aisle 4, loose things in aisle 5. Obviously, not all bases of classification are equally valuable. To return from shopping to writing, if you were writing with the purpose of showing that certain types of folk legends are found over and over again in many different cultures, you might classify legends by their content: creation legends, flood legends, and so on. For a different purpose—for instance, to emphasize the distinctive qualities of legends from different cultures—you might classify legends according to where they originated—Greek legends, American Indian legends, Japanese legends, and so on. Whenever you classify, have a clear idea of your purpose and your *basis* for classifying.

Once you have a basis clearly in mind, make sure that all of your categories stick to that basis. It is all too easy to fall into the trap of creating overlapping, illogical categories. Do not, that is, classify dogs as large, medium, small, and unfriendly. The last is a category formed on a different basis from the others—degree of friendliness rather than size. (Friendliness could, of course, be the basis for a classification—in, for example, an entertaining essay on the dogs you have known; friendly to a fault, affable but reserved, indifferent, and downright hostile.) All of this may seem too obvious—and indeed, if you were writing about newspapers, you probably would not fall into the error of classifying them as conservative, moderate, liberal, or weekly. But it's not hard to imagine a writer's illogically grouping newspapers into two classes such as these: papers interested in promoting the good of the public and papers interested in making a profit for themselves—as if these two interests could not be combined. When you classify, be sure your categories are consistent, established on the same basis.

Finally, be sure your classification does not omit any important categories. This does not mean that you must give equal attention to every category as you write; that decision will depend on your purpose. It does mean that your readers are likely to wonder whether you have both oars in the water if you appear to have overlooked a category they regard as significant in the context of your discussion. For instance, if you were writing about the ways in which oppressed people might respond to oppression, as Martin Luther King, Jr., does in this chapter, and you failed to consider the possibility of people's simply giving in to oppression, accepting their situation as hopeless, readers who have given in and lost all hope might be justified in feeling that your essay was not intended for them—that you do not understand or perhaps even care about their plight.

Division (also called analysis) is a mode of thought—and of writing—that breaks things down into their parts for a purpose, usually to understand them better, and often in preparation for putting the elements together again in new ways (called synthesis). As a user of this book, you have continually been engaged in division, analyzing elements of the essays printed here in order to understand what makes the essays successful. Having analyzed the many individual choices the various writers have made, you will be prepared to put this information together in a new synthesis: your own, unique writing. Division helps us understand almost any subject—objects, ideas, emotions, processes, texts, and so forth. Consider, for example, the diverse subjects of the analyses that follow in this chapter: good writing, a honey bee colony, our response to music.

For analytical essays, as for other kinds, purpose and audience may vary greatly. For instance, the audience for an analysis might be exclusively oneself—as in a diary entry written to sort out the writer's feelings or ideas about some experience. It should be stressed that analytical writing does not merely report the findings of finished investigations; even when you begin your writing with the sense that you have already investigated your subject thoroughly, you are quite likely to make further discoveries as you write about it. That is the nature of analysis, and is the reason analytical writing is so often called for in college courses, where the objective is learning. You might divide a poem into its parts for a literature course, consider the various parts that make up the structure of a bridge for an engineering course, or analyze a business situation for a management course. Beyond the campus, analysis usually serves very immediate practical ends; nurses and doctors analyze patients; lawyers analyze briefs; politicians analyze voters; coaches analyze teams; business people analyze products, competitors, problems; and so forth.

Division is a powerful tool not only for discovering but also for explaining—and here, of course, is where the question of audience becomes crucial. Consider, for example, "How We Listen to Music" by Aaron Copland, printed in this chapter. Though Copland, one of America's most distinguished symphonic composers, certainly is capable of writing at an extremely high level of technical sophistication, notice how his purpose in this essay requires that he write in simple, nontechnical language that will be understood by an audience of nonmusicians.

Especially if you are writing on a subject that is complex, you may need to give considerable thought to the *basis* of your analysis—your reason for dividing it in a particular way. For example, Jacqueline Berke's essay in this chapter seeks to discover the qualities of good writing. To proceed, however, Berke finds that she must first establish what she means by *good:* "pungent, vital, moving, memorable." This definition, focusing on the effect of the writing on the reader, provides the basis for an investigation that leads Berke to certain qualities in the writing itself: economy, simplicity, and clarity. However, the story editor of a television soap opera might define good writing in a quite different way: writing for which sponsors will pay a high price in order to sell their products during the commercial breaks. An analysis on this basis might reveal the qualities of "good" writing to be that it always keeps the viewers wondering what will happen next so they'll stay tuned, punishes the bad characters and rewards the good ones, and has plenty of romance—and plenty of breaks for commercials.

Five of the seven essays reprinted in this chapter illustrate classification, and two illustrate analysis. One of the essays is by a scientist writing with a primarily informative aim: Desmond Morris's "Territorial Behavior" examines the ways in which human beings establish and protect three types of "territories"—tribal, familial, and personal. In contrast, William Golding's "Thinking as a Hobby" classifies types of thinking. Martin Luther King, Jr., makes classification a powerful tool for persuasion, arguing to his readers that nonviolent resistance in the face of oppression is the only choice that can work. Russell Baker and Scott Adams—both humorists with widely different temperaments and styles—demonstrate still other uses of classification. Jacqueline Berke and Aaron Copland—a writer and a musician, respectively—analyze their arts for the purpose of explaining them to novices.

Two student essays illustrate the principles expressed in this section. Both students were given complete freedom of subject, but Lauren Reismann's assignment was to write a classification paper and Timothy Ellis's was to write an analytical essay. Reismann chose a subject she was familiar with, one which she could assume any reader would have at least a glancing acquaintance. She shows her reader how the various kinds of houses fall into clear categories related to how the features of each category fit her family. Ellis takes a different approach. He assumes the reader knows virtually nothing about his subject. As you read each of the essays and the commentary that follows, consider how these writers attempt to adhere to the principles just explained.

A House Is Not a Home

Introduction—
reason for
classifying

My family's recent move from Omaha to Dallas revealed to me that houses come in three main categories—houses that my family can afford but wouldn't live in, houses that we can't afford but would die to live in, and houses that will do. I base my observation upon the fact that we looked at over a hundred houses, but we never saw any that would not fit into one of these classifications. I am a little nervous, however, because one of the categories—houses that will do—is very small, whereas the other two categories are very large.

Identification of
classes

Completeness

First class—
implies basis for
classification

We found a large number of houses we cannot afford but which we absolutely love. After exhausting the real estate agent, my family and I generally spent the rest of the afternoon looking at model homes in elegant subdivisions. We contended that doing so would give us many ideas about what we really wanted in the home we would eventually live in; and we were right. We got hundreds of ideas, none of which we could afford. We particularly like the houses with elevated ceilings and large, elaborate leaded windows. Those windows sparkled in the afternoon sun like jewels. Built-in Jacuzzi tubs and private saunas in the master bathrooms sang a siren's song to my father, and my mother was enamored of the large, separate walk-in closets and the fireplaces in the master bedrooms. I, myself, was partial to the upstairs arrangements—large book-lined game rooms from which enough bedrooms with private bathrooms for me and each of my sisters and brothers opened. My brothers were enchanted by the swimming pools and the mirrored exercise rooms. Nobody cared much about the kitchens, although they were large, contained built-in barbecue grills, silent dishwashers and sub-zero refrigerators, not to mention enough cabinets to store dishes for a large restaurant and a pantry that would hold enough food for a small army.

Implies basis for classification

Second class

The real estate agent, a nice woman named Loretta, tirelessly showed us used houses. Although we expressed to her our desires for saunas, pools, fireplaces, and lots of bathrooms, she insisted upon showing us houses that did not meet those simple requirements (except that we could afford them). The typical house sat on what she insisted upon calling a "sunlight" lot which was distinguished by lacking any shade whatsoever. Not only that, but my brothers were discouraged by the large expanses of grass these houses displayed. My sister and I found the bathroom arrangements unacceptable—one for my parents, one for my brothers, and one for my sister and me. Not only that, but Eileen and I would have to share a bedroom—a small bedroom, the closet to which would not hold all of my clothes let alone hers. (Besides, the single closet would make it all too easy for her to raid my wardrobe.) The undersized two-car garages couldn't hold a wrench to the spacious garage with workbench that my Dad longed for. And the kitchens! Their only virtue is that they would accommodate only one person at a time, thus protecting my siblings and me from KP. My parents were only induced to look at these shacks for two reasons: the school district was reputed to be a good one and they were concerned about my younger brothers and sister getting a decent education and the locations were within easy reach of my parents' offices.

Third class— implies basis for classification

Finally, Loretta got wise. She showed us some houses in a suburb where the prices were only about two-thirds of those in the fancy school district but where the education was adequately maintained thanks to the presence of two state universities in the town (one of which I now attend). My parents would have to commute only about an hour each way. There were two acceptable houses, although they lacked what my sister and I had come to think of as basic luxuries. We bought the cheaper one. My sister and I still have to share a bathroom, but we each have our own bedroom; my brothers lack a pool, but the yard has plenty of trees. My parents got the Jacuzzi in the master bathroom and separate closets, but had to forgo the sauna and the fireplace in the bedroom. Although my brothers still have to share a bedroom, the kitchen has two pantries so that they won't starve, and there is enough cabinet space for my grandmother's china and crystal which my mother has kept packed away most of my life. Dad has an oversized two-car garage to play in, and there's lots

Conclusion of storage space in the attic. It will do.

Commentary.   In her introduction, Reismann comments briefly on why she wants to classify the kinds of houses that are for sale—to explain why her family bought the house they did. She first identifies houses that her family cannot afford as a class—mainly houses that are expensively built with many high-priced options. She then further divides this category by explaining what each family member liked about the expensive houses.

Then she identifies the class of houses which her family can affording but which are unsuitable. Again, she applies her test—how does this house fit the way the family lives? Although she had referred to location in her discussion of the previous category (elegant subdivisions), she makes a stronger point about location in her discussion of this category. It is, after all, the reason that the real estate agent shows them houses that are unsuitable even though the family makes their desires known.

In discussing her final category, Reismann takes up only those elements about which the family has had to compromise, thus fulfilling her focus on the category of "houses that will do." She concludes her essay with a curt statement emphasizing that point.

A Brief Beginner's Guide to Reference Sources

Introduction   Recently, I was required to write a lengthy paper for my history class, and after much deliberation, I decided to write about the events that prompted the Germans to destroy the Berlin Wall. Because I had not currently seen news on this subject in popular publications, I realized that my topic would require a great deal of research. Unfortunately, I had no idea where to begin my study; therefore, this project became very intimidating. Then at the suggestion of a friend, I asked a reference librarian for assistance. The librarian told me about reference materials available at most libraries that aid in the location of published documents and learning aids on a variety of subjects. The librarian's suggestions reduced my research time—time that I, otherwise, would have spent searching aimlessly through magazines and books for information. Consequently, I became interested in learning more about reference materials that could make my college and business research more efficient.

Thesis

Reference sources offer a wealth of information, and are helpful tools for beginning any study. Reference sources are available in print and microfilm formats as well as in on-line formats. They are divided into two categories: control-access and information sources. Control-access sources, primarily bibliographies and indexes, direct the researcher to documents and materials necessary for extensive study.

Primary division

First major part

For most people, the mention of bibliographies brings to mind a list of books; however, bibliographies also inventory audiovisual materials, periodicals, software programs, movies, reports, and studies. Due to the recent information explosion, bibliographies play a vital role in research because they compile available resources and offer necessary facts for finding these items for further research.

First minor part

Bibliographies that contain information not restricted by time, territory, language, subject, or form are referred to as universal bibliographies. One example of a universal bibliography is the <u>National Union Catalog</u> compiled by the Library of Congress. This catalog describes information sources held by libraries throughout the United States. Obviously, universal bibliographies are difficult to compile; therefore, most bibliographies are limited in scope. Often these bibliographies are limited to a particular subject, country, or trade. These limited bibliographies are generally good sources to use for studies in a particular discipline such as history, the humanities, and science.

Further subdivision

Indexes are also good sources for locating information on a particular subject, especially information published in current magazines. Indexes contain listings that are analyzed by the name and subject of the document and then listed under the author's name and all other subject headings that apply. Indexes are traditionally divided into periodical indexes, newspaper indexes, and serial indexes which provide citations including the name of the author, the subject of the document, and the name of the publisher.

Second minor part

<u>The Reader's Guide to Periodical Literature</u> is an index consisting of periodical citations in broad

Further subdivision

and specific subject fields. This annually published reference guide is useful in locating magazine articles published on current social issues and events. To locate information in particular subject areas such as the humanities or science, subject indexes are also available. Historical Abstracts is one such publication; it offers a short brief summary of journals, books, and other related materials concentrating on world history.

Second major part

Although bibliographies and indexes are essential tools for beginning research, many factual questions arise that can easily be answered by the second type of reference source, the information source or ready-reference. Most people have used a ready-reference source sometime in their life. Ready-reference sources are divided into encyclopedias, dictionaries, geographical sources, fact sources and government documents. Ready-reference sources are necessary materials for the better understanding of the subject studied. While researching a subject, most people encounter new terms that they must understand before they can continue their study. New words may be found quickly in a dictionary—an alphabetical listing of words, pronunciations, and meanings. Geographical sources such as atlases and guidebooks offer information about place names that the researcher has never before encountered, and statistics and other factual information is available in fact sources such as yearbooks, almanacs, and directories.

Further subdivision

Conclusion

The collection and synthesis of information are two of the greatest challenges of the college experience. Knowledge of both control-access and ready-reference materials makes the collection of information much easier and significantly reduces research time. In fact, just knowing that these materials are available increases the researcher's confidence in his or her ability to complete a project and, as a result, allows the researcher more time for synthesizing the information located.

Commentary.   Tim Ellis sets an ambitious agenda for himself by proposing to analyze basic reference sources. His clear sense of audience contributes much to the accomplishment of that purpose. He views his readers as those who feel lost when they walk into a library, and so he assumes that they know virtually nothing of how to find information on a subject.

To identify with his audience, Ellis begins with an account of how he was overwhelmed by the prospect of trying to locate information for a history paper he had to write, explaining that all he knew to do was to page through magazines trying to find something on his subject. But with the help of a reference librarian he learns how to start.

His guide breaks the subject—reference sources—into parts and analyzes each of those parts so that the neophyte researcher knows where to begin. For instance, in the second paragraph he divides reference sources into two groups and then defines those groups—those which enable access to sources and so give the researcher some control over the process, and those which furnish information.

Ellis subdivides his first group of sources into bibliographies and indexes and describes some bibliographies and indexes available to search for specific kinds of information. He then takes up the next group and suggests some general information sources in particular fields. He concludes by reemphasizing the value of knowing how to handle sources.

Three Types of Resistance to Oppression

Martin Luther King, Jr.

Martin Luther King, Jr., was born in Atlanta, Georgia, in 1929, and assassinated in Memphis, Tennessee, in 1968—four years after he was awarded the
Nobel Peace Prize. The son of a Baptist minister, he himself was ordained to
the ministry at the age of eighteen and subsequently graduated from More-
house College and Crozer Theological Seminary. He received a Ph.D. in systematic philosophy from Boston University in 1954. King became nationally
prominent as a result of his activities in the Montgomery, Alabama, bus boy-
cott in 1955, and for the rest of his life was an advocate of nonviolent resistance to racial injustice and a powerful voice for the civil rights movement—as president of the Southern Christian Leadership Conference and as
a charismatic and persuasive speaker. Among his writings are *Why We Can't
Wait* (1964) and *Where Do We Go From Here? Chaos or Community* (1968).
The following selection is from his first book, *Stride toward Freedom* (1958).

Oppressed people deal with their oppression in three characteristic ways. 1
One way is acquiescence: the oppressed resign themselves to their doom. They
tacitly adjust themselves to oppression, and thereby become conditioned to it.
In every movement toward freedom some of the oppressed prefer to remain
oppressed. Almost 2800 years ago Moses set out to lead the children of Israel from the slavery of Egypt to the freedom of the promised land. He soon
discovered that slaves do not always welcome their deliverers. They become
accustomed to being slaves. They would rather bear those ills they have, as
Shakespeare pointed out, than flee to others that they know not of. They prefer the "fleshpots of Egypt" to the ordeals of emancipation.

There is such a thing as the freedom of exhaustion. Some people are so 2
worn down by the yoke of oppression that they give up. A few years ago in
the slum areas of Atlanta, a Negro guitarist used to sing almost daily: "Ben
down so long that down don't bother me." This is the type of negative freedom and resignation that often engulfs the life of the oppressed.

But this is not the way out. To accept passively an unjust system is to co- 3
operate with that system; thereby the oppressed become as evil as the oppressor. Noncooperation with evil is as much a moral obligation as is cooperation with good. The oppressed must never allow the conscience of the
oppressor to slumber. Religion reminds every man that he is his brother's
keeper. To accept injustice or segregation passively is to say to the oppressor
that his actions are morally right. It is a way of allowing his conscience to fall

asleep. At this moment the oppressed fails to be his brother's keeper. So acquiescence—while often the easier way—is not the moral way. It is the way of the coward. The Negro cannot win the respect of his oppressor by acquiescing; he merely increases the oppressor's arrogance and contempt. Acquiescence is interpreted as proof of the Negro's inferiority. The Negro cannot win the respect of the white people of the South or the peoples of the world if he is willing to sell the future of his children for his personal and immediate comfort and safety.

A second way that oppressed people sometimes deal with oppression is   4
to resort to physical violence and corroding hatred. Violence often brings about momentary results. Nations have frequently won their independence in battle. But in spite of temporary victories, violence never brings permanent peace. It solves no social problem; it merely creates new and more complicated ones.

Violence as a way of achieving racial justice is both impractical and im-   5
moral. It is impractical because it is a descending spiral ending in destruction for all. The old law of an eye for an eye leaves everybody blind. It is immoral because it seeks to humiliate the opponent rather than win his understanding; it seeks to annihilate rather than to convert. Violence is immoral because it thrives on hatred rather than love. It destroys community and makes brotherhood impossible. It leaves society in monologue rather than dialogue. Violence ends by defeating itself. It creates bitterness in the survivors and brutality in the destroyers. A voice echoes through time saying to every potential Peter, "Put up your sword." History is cluttered with the wreckage of nations that failed to follow this command.

If the American Negro and other victims of oppression succumb to the   6
temptation of using violence in the struggle for freedom, future generations will be the recipients of a desolate night of bitterness, and our chief legacy to them will be an endless reign of meaningless chaos. Violence is not the way.

The third way open to oppressed people in their quest for freedom is the   7
way of nonviolent resistance. Like the synthesis in Hegelian philosophy, the principle of nonviolent resistance seeks to reconcile the truths of two opposites—acquiescence and violence—while avoiding the extremes and immoralities of both. The nonviolent resister agrees with the person who acquiesces that one should not be physically aggressive toward his opponent; but he balances the equation by agreeing with the person of violence that evil must be resisted. He avoids the nonresistance of the former and the violent resistance of the latter. With nonviolent resistance, no individual or group need submit to any wrong, nor need anyone resort to violence in order to right a wrong.

It seems to me that this is the method that must guide the actions of the   8
Negro in the present crisis in race relations. Through nonviolent resistance the Negro will be able to rise to the noble height of opposing the unjust system while loving the perpetrators of the system. The Negro must work passionately and unrelentingly for full stature as a citizen, but he must not use inferior methods to gain it. He must never come to terms with falsehood, malice, hate, or destruction.

Nonviolent resistance makes it possible for the Negro to remain in the   9
South and struggle for his rights. The Negro's problem will not be solved by
running away. He cannot listen to the glib suggestion of those who would
urge him to migrate en masse to other sections of the country. By grasping
his great opportunity in the South he can make a lasting contribution to the
moral strength of the nation and set a sublime example of courage for generations yet unborn.

By nonviolent resistance, the Negro can also enlist all men of good will   10
in his struggle for equality. The problem is not a purely racial one, with Negroes set against whites. In the end, it is not a struggle between people at all,
but a tension between justice and injustice. Nonviolent resistance is not aimed
against oppressors but against oppression. Under its banner consciences, not
racial groups, are enlisted.

If the Negro is to achieve the goal of integration, he must organize him-   11
self into a militant and nonviolent mass movement. All three elements are
indispensable. The movement for equality and justice can only be a success
if it has both a mass and militant character; the barriers to be overcome
require both. Nonviolence is an imperative in order to bring about ultimate
community.

A mass movement of militant quality that is not at the same time com-   12
mitted to nonviolence tends to generate conflict, which in turns breeds anarchy. The support of the participants and the sympathy of the uncommit-
ted are both inhibited by the threat that bloodshed will engulf the
community. This reaction in turn encourages the opposition to threaten and
resort to force. When, however, the mass movement repudiates violence
while moving resolutely toward its goal, its opponents are revealed as the
instigators and practitioners of violence if it occurs. Then public support is
magnetically attracted to the advocates of nonviolence, while those who employ violence are literally disarmed by overwhelming sentiment against their
stand.

✳

RESPONDING TO THE WHOLE ESSAY

1. What categories does King establish? What is the basis of the classification? Has
    King omitted any categories that ought to appear in this particular classification?
    If so, what? If not, show how the classification is complete.
2. What is King's primary purpose in the essay? How does classification help him
    accomplish that purpose? [*Harbrace* 28a; *Hodges'* 32a]
3. From evidence in the essay, try to describe the audience King was writing for.
    What kinds of language help you to identify that audience? What allusions does
    King make in the essay, and how do they contribute to your understanding of
    King's audience? You are now also part of King's audience. How successful
    are King's rhetorical strategies for you? Explain. [*Harbrace* 28a; *Hodges'* 32a]

4. Paragraphs 1 and 2 are similar in two ways: both are arranged according to the topic-restriction-illustration pattern, and both are developed by examples. In each paragraph, what is the topic? The restriction? How do the examples develop the ideas? [*Harbrace* 27b; *Hodges'* 31b]
5. Comment upon King's use of transitional devices to ensure coherence in paragraph 3. [*Harbrace* 27b; *Hodges'* 31b]
6. King's skillful use of various devices to establish clear transitions between paragraphs makes the reader's task of following the essay almost effortless. Show how King achieves this coherence. [*Harbrace* 27b(6); *Hodges'* 31b(6)]

ANALYZING THE ELEMENTS

Grammar

1. In the third sentence of paragraph 2, what is the subject of the clause " 'that down don't bother me' "? Usually, what part of speech is that word? What does this use tell you about rigid classifications of parts of speech? In standard English, the verb here would be *doesn't* rather than *don't*. How can *don't* be justified in this context? Do the same considerations apply to the deliberate misspelling of *been*? [*Harbrace* 1c and 13b(1); *Hodges'* 1c and 19b]
2. The final sentence of paragraph 7 summarizes King's discussion to that point. Analyze the sentence to show how the various grammatical elements contribute to the summary.
3. What is the mood of the verb in the last sentence of paragraph 7? What reason might King have had for choosing that mood? What is the grammatical function of *individual, group,* and *anyone*? [*Harbrace* 1b and 7d; *Hodges'* 1b and 7d]
4. In the second sentence of paragraph 8, King uses a series of prepositional phrases to clarify what he means by "noble height." Show how each prepositional phrase contributes to this classification. What part of speech is the object of each preposition? [*Harbrace* 1c and 1d; *Hodges'* 1c and 1d]

Effective Sentences

1. Compare the ninth sentence of paragraph 3 with the tenth, and the first sentence of paragraph 6 with the second. What strategies for making sentences effective do these comparisons reveal? [*Harbrace* 10b, 11e, and 11h; *Hodges'* 26b, 29e, and 29h]
2. Analyze King's use of parallel structure in paragraph 5. Point to effective uses of parallelism elsewhere in the essay. [*Harbrace* 10a and 10b; *Hodges'* 26a and 26b]

Punctuation and Mechanics

1. Explain the use of the colon in the second sentence of paragraph 1. Could King have used a semicolon? Why or why not? What would be the effect of using a semicolon rather than a colon? [*Harbrace* 18 and 21d; *Hodges'* 14 and 17d]
2. Explain the use of the semicolon in the third sentence of paragraph 11. How would the effect have been different had King used a period and then started a new sentence instead? [*Harbrace* 18; *Hodges'* 14]

Diction

1. Check the meaning of the following words in your dictionary: *tacitly* and *acquiescence* (paragraph 1), *corroding* (paragraph 4), *desolate* and *legacy* (paragraph 6), *synthesis* (paragraph 7), *malice* (paragraph 8), *sublime* (paragraph 9), *imperative* (paragraph 11), *anarchy, inhibited,* and *repudiates* (paragraph 12). Explain how each word helps to make precise the meaning of the sentence in which it appears. In each instance, can you think of any other word that would have served as well? [*Harbrace* 14a(1); *Hodges'* 20a(1)]
2. Explain the effect of the figurative language King uses in the first sentence of paragraph 6. [*Harbrace* 14a(5); *Hodges'* 20a(4)]
3. King makes an allusion to the philosophy of Hegel in the second sentence of paragraph 7. Must the reader be familiar with Hegelian philosophy to grasp the meaning of this sentence? Why or why not? Why do you suppose King included the allusion?

BUILDING VOCABULARY

1. Identify the elements from which each of the following is derived: *tacit, acquiesce, corrode, overwhelm.* What does each word mean? What other word or words are derived from the same root?
2. What words are derived from the root *-hibit?* What does each mean? What does *-hibit* mean?

SUGGESTIONS FOR WRITING

1. Consider some obstacle, limiting circumstance, or other frustration with which you are (or have been) confronted in your life—for instance, at work, at school, or at home—and write an essay in which you classify the possible responses and then argue that one of these is best. If you prefer, or if your life seems to have been free of obstacles and frustrations, write the same kind of essay about possible responses to some opportunity.
2. Write an essay classifying the kinds of action that may be taken to accomplish a purpose (such as purchasing a car or a home, getting a raise in pay, changing someone's attitude toward you).

Territorial Behavior
Desmond Morris

Desmond Morris, noted British zoologist, is the author of several widely acclaimed studies aimed at the general reader explaining human behavior from a zoological perspective: *The Naked Ape, The Human Zoo, Intimate Behavior,* and *Manwatching.* A graduate of Oxford University, Morris has taught at Oxford and worked as a research fellow of the university; he is presently affiliated with the department of psychology. He has contributed to a number of journals, among them *Behavior, British Birds, New Scientist,* and *Zoo Life.* "Territorial Behavior," from *Manwatching,* describes man's behavior by classifying it according to the kinds of territory being defended.

A territory is a defended space. In the broadest sense, there are three kinds 1
of human territory: tribal, family and personal.

It is rare for people to be driven to physical fighting in defense of these 2
"owned" spaces, but fight they will, if pushed to the limit. The invading army encroaching on national territory, the gang moving into a rival district, the trespasser climbing into an orchard, the burglar breaking into a house, the bully pushing to the front of a queue, the driver trying to steal a parking space, all of these intruders are liable to be met with resistance varying from the vigorous to the savagely violent. Even if the law is on the side of the intruder, the urge to protect a territory may be so strong that otherwise peaceful citizens abandon all their usual controls and inhibitions. Attempts to evict families from their homes, no matter how socially valid the reasons, can lead to siege conditions reminiscent of the defence of a medieval fortress.

The fact that these upheavals are so rare is a measure of the success of 3
Territorial Signals as a system of dispute prevention. It is sometimes cynically stated that "all property is theft," but in reality it is the opposite. Property, as owned space which is *displayed* as owned space, is a special kind of sharing system which reduces fighting much more than it causes it. Man is a co-operative species, but he is also competitive, and his struggle for dominance has to be structured in some way if chaos is to be avoided. The establishment of territorial rights is one such structure. It limits dominance geographically. I am dominant in my territory and you are dominant in yours. In other words, dominance is shared out spatially, and we all have some. Even if I am weak and unintelligent and you can dominate me when we meet on neutral ground, I can still enjoy a thoroughly dominant role as soon as I retreat to my private base. Be it ever so humble, there is no place like a home territory.

Of course, I can still be intimidated by a particularly dominant individual who enters my home base, but his encroachment will be dangerous for him and he will think twice about it, because he will know that here my urge to resist will be dramatically magnified and my usual subservience banished. Insulted at the heart of my own territory, I may easily explode into battle— either symbolic or real—with a result that may be damaging to both of us.   4

In order for this to work, each territory has to be plainly advertised as such. Just as a dog cocks its leg to deposit its personal scent on the trees in its locality, so the human animal cocks its leg symbolically all over his home base. But because we are predominantly visual animals we employ mostly visual signals, and it is worth asking how to do this at the three levels: tribal, family, and personal.   5

First: The Tribal Territory. We evolved as tribal animals, living in comparatively small groups, probably of less than a hundred, and we existed like that for millions of years. It is our basic social unit, a group in which everyone knows everyone else. Essentially, the tribal territory consisted of a home base surrounded by extended hunting grounds. Any neighboring tribe intruding on our social space would be repelled and driven away. As these early tribes swelled into agricultural super-tribes, and eventually into industrial nations, their territorial defence systems became increasingly elaborate. The tiny, ancient home base of the hunting tribe became the great capital city, the primitive warpaint became the flags, emblems, uniforms, and regalia of the specialized military, and the war-chants became national anthems, marching songs and bugle calls. Territorial boundary-lines hardened into fixed borders, often conspicuously patrolled and punctuated with defensive structures—forts and lookout posts, checkpoints and great walls, and, today, customs barriers.   6

Today each nation flies its own flag, a symbolic embodiment of its territorial status. But patriotism is not enough. The ancient tribal hunter lurking inside each citizen finds himself unsatisfied by membership in such a vast conglomeration of individuals, most of whom are totally unknown to him personally. He does his best to feel that he shares a common territorial defence with them all, but the scale of the operation has become inhuman. It is hard to feel a sense of belonging with a tribe of fifty million or more. His answer is to form sub-groups, nearer to his ancient pattern, smaller and more personally known to him—the local club, the teenage gang, the union, the specialist society, the sports association, the political party, the college fraternity, the social clique, the protest group, and the rest. Rare indeed is the individual who does not belong to at least one of these splinter groups, and take from it a sense of tribal allegiance and brotherhood. Typical of all these groups is the development of Territorial Signals—badges, costumes, headquarters, banners, slogans, and all the other displays of group identity. This is where the action is, in terms of tribal territorialism, and only when a major war breaks out does the emphasis shift upwards to the higher group level of the nation.   7

Each of these modern pseudo-tribes sets up its own special kind of home base. In extreme cases non-members are totally excluded, in others they are   8 allowed in as visitors with limited rights and under a control system of special rules. In many ways they are like miniature nations, with their own flags and emblems and their own border guards. The exclusive club has its own "customs barrier": the doorman who checks your "passport" (your membership card) and prevents strangers from passing in unchallenged. There is a government: the club committee; and often special displays of the tribal elders: the photographs or portraits of previous officials on the walls. At the heart of the specialized territories there is a powerful feeling of security and importance, a sense of shared defence against the outside world. Much of the club chatter, both serious and joking, directs itself against the rottenness of everything outside the club boundaries—in that "other world" beyond the protected portals.

In social organizations which embody a strong class system, such as military units and large business concerns, there are many territorial rules, often unspoken, which interfere with the official hierarchy. High-status individuals, such as officers or managers, could in theory enter any of the regions occupied by the lower levels in the peck order, but they limit this power in a striking way. An officer seldom enters a sergeant's mess or a barrack room unless it is for a formal inspection. He respects those regions as alien territories even though he has the power to go there by virtue of his dominant role. And in businesses, part of the appeal of unions, over and above their obvious functions, is that with their officials, headquarters, and meetings they add a sense of territorial power for the staff workers. It is almost as if each military organization and business concern consists of two warring tribes: the officers versus the other ranks, and the management versus the workers. Each has its special home base within the system, and the territorial defence pattern thrusts itself into what, on the surface, is a pure social hierarchy. Negotiations between managements and unions are tribal battles fought out over the neutral ground of a boardroom table, and are as much concerned with territorial display as they are with resolving problems of wages and conditions. Indeed, if one side gives in too quickly and accepts the other's demands, the victors feel strangely cheated and deeply suspicious that it may be a trick. What they are missing is the protracted sequence of ritual and counter-ritual that keeps alive their group territorial identity.

Likewise, many of the hostile displays of sports fans and teenage gangs are primarily concerned with displaying their group image to rival fan-clubs and gangs. Except in rare cases, they do not attack one another's headquarters, drive out the occupants, and reduce them to a submissive, subordinate condition. It is enough to have scuffles on the borderlands between the two rival territories. This is particularly clear at football matches, where the fan-club headquarters becomes temporarily shifted from the club-house to a section of the stands, and where minor fighting breaks out at the unofficial boundary line between the massed groups of rival supporters. Newspaper reports play up the few accidents and injuries which do occur on such occasions, but when these are studied in relation to the total numbers of displaying fans involved it is clear that the serious incidents represent only a tiny fraction of the overall group behavior. For every actual punch or kick there are a thousand war-cries, war-dances, chants, and gestures.

Second: The Family Territory. Essentially, the family is a breeding unit   11
and the family territory is a breeding ground. At the center of this space, there is the next—the bedroom—where, tucked up in bed, we feel at our most territorially secure. In a typical house the bedroom is upstairs, where a safe nest should be. This puts it farther away from the entrance hall, the area where contact is made, intermittently, with the outside world. The less private reception rooms, where intruders are allowed access, are the next line of defence. Beyond them, outside the walls of the building, there is often a symbolic remnant of the ancient feeding grounds—a garden. Its symbolism often extends to the plants and animals it contains, which cease to be nutritional and become merely decorative—flowers and pets. But like a true territorial space it has a conspicuously displayed boundary-line, the garden fence, wall, or railings. Often no more than a token barrier, this is the outer territorial demarcation, separating the private world of the family from the public world beyond. To cross it puts any visitor or intruder at an immediate disadvantage. As he crosses the threshold, his dominance wanes, slightly but unmistakably. He is entering an area where he senses that he must ask permission to do simple things that he would consider a right elsewhere. Without lifting a finger, the territorial owners exert their dominance. This is done by all the hundreds of small ownership "markers" they have deposited on their family territory: the ornaments, the "possessed" objects positioned in the rooms and on the walls; the furnishings, the furniture, the colors, the patterns, all owner-chosen and all making this particular home base unique to them.

It is one of the tragedies of modern architecture that there has been a stan-   12
dardization of these vital territorial living units. One of the most important aspects of a home is that it should be similar to other homes only in a general way, and that in detail it should have many differences, making it a *particular* home. Unfortunately, it is cheaper to build a row of houses, or a block of flats, so that all the family living-units are identical, but the territorial urge rebels against this trend and house-owners struggle as best they can to make their mark on their mass-produced properties. They do this with garden-design, with front-door colors, with curtain patterns, with wallpaper and all the other decorative elements that together create a unique and different family environment. Only when they have completed this nest-building do they feel truly "at home" and secure.

When they venture forth as a family unit they repeat the process in a   13
minor way. On a day-trip to the seaside, they load the car with personal belongings and it becomes their temporary, portable territory. Arriving at the beach they stake out a small territorial claim, marking it with rugs, towels, baskets, and other belongings to which they can return from their seaboard wanderings. Even if they all leave it at once to bathe, it retains a characteristic territorial quality and other family groups arriving will recognize this

by setting up their own "home" bases at a respectful distance. Only when the whole beach has filled up with these marked spaces will newcomers start to position themselves in such a way that the inter-base distance becomes reduced. Forced to pitch between several existing beach territories they will feel a momentary sensation of intrusion, and the established "owners" will feel a similar sensation of invasion, even though they are not being directly inconvenienced.

The same territorial scene is being played out in parks and fields and on 14 riverbanks, wherever family groups gather in their clustered units. But if rivalry for spaces creates mild feelings of hostility, it is true to say that, without the territorial system of sharing and space-limited dominance, there would be chaotic disorder.

Third: The Personal Space. If a man enters a waiting-room and sits at one 15 end of a long row of empty chairs, it is possible to predict where the next man to enter will seat himself. He will not sit next to the first man, nor will he sit at the far end, right away from him. He will choose a position about halfway between these two points. The next man to enter will take the largest gap left, and sit roughly in the middle of that, and so on, until eventually the latest newcomer will be forced to select a seat that places him right next to one of the already seated men. Similar patterns can be observed in cinemas, public urinals, airplanes, trains, and buses. This is a reflection of the fact that we all carry with us, everywhere we go, a portable territory called a Personal Space. If people move inside this space, we feel threatened. If they keep too far outside it, we feel rejected. The result is a subtle series of spatial adjustments, usually operating quite unconsciously and producing ideal compromises as far as this is possible. If a situation becomes too crowded, then we adjust our reactions accordingly and allow our Personal Space to shrink. Jammed into an elevator, a rush-hour compartment, or a packed room, we give up altogether and allow body-to-body contact, but when we relinquish our Personal Space in this way, we adopt certain special techniques. In essence, what we do is to convert these other bodies into "nonpersons." We studiously ignore them, and they us. We try not to face them if we can possibly avoid it. We wipe all expressiveness from our faces, letting them go blank. We may look up at the ceiling or down at the floor, and we reduce body movements to a minimum. Packed together like sardines in a tin, we stand dumbly still, sending out as few social signals as possible.

Even if the crowding is less severe, we still tend to cut down our social 16 interactions in the presence of large numbers. Careful observations of children in play groups revealed that if they are high-density groupings there is less social interaction between the individual children, even though there is theoretically more opportunity for such contacts. At the same time, the high-density groups show a higher frequency of aggressive and destructive behavior patterns in their play. Personal Space—"elbow room"—is a vital commodity for the human animal, and one that cannot be ignored without risking serious trouble.

Of course, we all enjoy the excitement of being in a crowd, and this re-   17
action cannot be ignored. But there are crowds and crowds. It is pleasant
enough to be in a "spectator crowd," but not so appealing to find yourself in
the middle of a rush-hour crush. The difference between the two is that the
spectator crowd is all facing in the same direction and concentrating on a distant point of interest. Attending a theatre, there are twinges of rising hostility toward the stranger who sits down immediately in front of you or the one
who squeezes into the seat next to you. The shared armrest can become a polite, but distinct territorial boundary-dispute region. However, as soon as the
show begins, these invasions of Personal Space are forgotten and the attention is focused beyond the small space where the crowding is taking place.
Now, each member of the audience feels himself spatially related, not to his
cramped neighbors, but to the actor on the stage, and this distance is, if anything, too great. In the rush-hour crowd, by contrast, each member of the
pushing throng is competing with his neighbors all the time. There is no escape to a spatial relation with a distant actor, only the pushing, shoving bodies all around.

Those of us who have to spend a great deal of time in crowded condi-   18
tions become gradually better able to adjust, but no one can ever become completely immune to invasions of Personal Space. This is because they remain
forever associated with either powerful hostile or equally powerful loving feelings. All through our childhood we will have been held to be loved and held
to be hurt, and anyone who invades our Personal Space when we are adults
is, in effect, threatening to extend his behavior into one of these two highly
charged areas of human interaction. Even if his motives are clearly neither
hostile nor sexual, we still find it hard to suppress our reactions to his close
approach. Unfortunately, different countries have different ideas about exactly
how close is close. It is easy enough to test your own "space reaction": when
you are talking to someone in the street or in any open space, reach out with
your arm and see where the nearest point on his body comes. If you hail from
western Europe, you will find that he is at roughly fingertip distance from
you. In other words, as you reach out, your fingertips will just about make
contact with his shoulder. If you come from eastern Europe you will find you
are standing at "wrist distance." If you come from the Mediterranean region
you will find that you are much closer to your companion, at little more than
"elbow distance."

Trouble begins when a member of one of these cultures meets and talks   19
to one from another. Say a British diplomat meets an Italian or an Arab diplomat at an embassy function. They start talking in a friendly way, but soon
the fingertips man begins to feel uneasy. Without knowing quite why, he starts
to back away gently from his companion. The companion edges forward
again. Each tries in his way to set up a Personal Space relationship that suits
his own background. But it is impossible to do. Every time the Mediterranean
diplomat advances to a distance that feels comfortable for him, the British
diplomat feels threatened. Every time the Briton moves back, the other feels

rejected. Attempts to adjust this situation often lead to a talking pair shifting slowly across a room, and many an embassy reception is dotted with western-European fingertip-distance men pinned against the walls by eager elbow-distance men. Until such differences are fully understood and allowances made, these minor differences in "body territories" will continue to act as an alienation factor which may interfere in a subtle way with diplomatic harmony and other forms of international transaction.

If there are distance problems when engaged in conversation, then there are clearly going to be even bigger difficulties where people must work privately in a shared space. Close proximity of others, pressing against the invisible boundaries of our personal body-territory, makes it difficult to concentrate on non-social matters. Flat-mates, students sharing a study, sailors in the cramped quarters of a ship, and office staff in crowded work-places, all have to face this problem. They solve it by "cocooning." They use a variety of devices to shut themselves off from the others present. The best possible cocoon, of course, is a small private room—a den, a private office, a study, or a studio—which physically obscures the presence of other nearby territory-owners. This is the ideal situation for non-social work, but the space-sharers cannot enjoy this luxury. Their cocooning must be symbolic. They may, in certain cases, be able to erect small physical barriers, such as screens and partitions, which give substance to their invisible Personal Space boundaries, but when this cannot be done, other means must be sought. One of these is the "favored object." Each space-sharer develops a preference, repeatedly expressed until it becomes a fixed pattern, for a particular chair, or table, or alcove. Others come to respect this, and friction is reduced. This system is often formally arranged (this is my desk, that is yours), but even where it is not, favored places soon develop. Professor Smith has a favorite chair in the library. It is not formally his, but he always uses it and others avoid it. Seats around a mess-room table, or a boardroom table, become almost personal property for specific individuals. Even in the home, father has his favorite chair for reading the newspaper or watching television. Another device is the blinkers-posture. Just as a horse that over-reacts to other horses and the distractions of the noisy race-course is given a pair of blinkers to shield its eyes, so people studying privately in a public place put on pseudo-blinkers in the form of shielding hands. Resting their elbows on the table, they sit with their hands screening their eyes from the scene on either side.

A third method of reinforcing the body-territory is to use personal markers. Books, papers, and other personal belongings are scattered around the favored site to render it more privately owned in the eyes of companions. Spreading out one's belongings is a well-known trick in public-transport situations, where a traveller tries to give the impression that seats next to him are taken. In many contexts carefully arranged personal markers can act as an effective-territorial display, even in the absence of the territory owner. Experiments in a library revealed that placing a pile of magazines on the table in one seating position successfully reserved that place for an average of 77 minutes. If a

20

21

sports-jacket was added, draped over the chair, then the "reservation effect" lasted for over two hours.

In these ways, we strengthen the defences of our Personal Spaces, keeping out intruders with the minimum of open hostility. As with all territorial be-havior, the object is to defend space with signals rather than with fists and at all three levels—the tribal, the family, and the personal—it is a remarkably ef-ficient system of space-sharing. It does not always seem so, because newspa-pers and newscasts inevitably magnify the exceptions and dwell on those cases where the signals have failed and wars have broken out, gangs have fought, neighboring families have feuded, or colleagues have clashed, but for every ter-ritorial signal that has failed, there are millions of others that have not. They do not rate a mention in the news, but they nevertheless constitute a domi-nant feature of human society—the society of a remarkably territorial animal.   22

✳

RESPONDING TO THE WHOLE ESSAY

1. What purpose is most evident in "Territorial Behavior"? Explain with evidence from the essay. What evidence of a secondary purpose, if any, does the essay con-tain? [*Harbrace* 28a; *Hodges'* 32a]
2. What evidence in "Territorial Behavior" indicates the audience for which Morris was writing? Describe that audience. [*Harbrace* 28a; *Hodges'* 32a]
3. What is the tone of the essay? Does the tone influence the reader's perception of the information the essay provides? If so, how? [*Harbrace* 29a; *Hodges'* 33a]
4. What basis for classification does Morris use? Where does he state it? What kinds of background information does he offer for his classification?
5. Explain how Morris introduces his subject and arouses the reader's interest in it in the first five paragraphs of the essay [*Harbrace* 28f(1); *Hodges'* 32f(1)]
6. Morris develops paragraph 11, paragraph 17, paragraph 18, and paragraph 20 in different ways. Comment on his use of these different patterns of development. [*Harbrace* 27d; *Hodges'* 31d]

ANALYZING THE ELEMENTS

Grammar

1. What form of the verb is used in the first clause of the final sentence of paragraph 3? Why is this form used? [*Harbrace* 7d; *Hodges'* 7d]
2. The phrase following *unit* in the second complete sentence of paragraph 6 is an appositive. Check the glossary, "Grammatical and Rhetorical Terms," in *Harbrace* for an explanation of appositives, and then comment on what this appositive adds to *unit,* the noun it is in apposition to. Do the modifiers of *unit* need to be taken into consideration?
3. Justify the use of a comma to separate the independent clauses in the second sen-tence of paragraph 8. [*Harbrace* 3a; *Hodges'* 3a]

Effective Sentences

1. Analyze the techniques for ensuring sentence variety that Morris uses in each main clause of the first sentence of paragraph 2. [*Harbrace* 15; *Hodges'* 21]
2. How does the absolute phrase that begins the fifth sentence of paragraph 17 contribute to its effectiveness? [*Harbrace* 12b; *Hodges'* 30b]

Punctuation and Mechanics

1. Explain the use of a comma after *space* in the second sentence of paragraph 2. What other mark of punctuation could have been used? What is the difference in effect between the two marks of punctuation in this context? [*Harbrace* 17d and 21e; *Hodges'* 12d and 17e]
2. Explain why the three independent clauses in the sixth complete sentence of paragraph 6 are separated by commas. [*Harbrace* 17c; *Hodges'* 12c]
3. Explain the difference between the ways Morris uses quotation marks (as in the first sentence of paragraph 2) and italics (as in the third sentence of paragraph 3). Is this distinction maintained throughout the essay? [*Harbrace* 24e and 20d; *Hodges'* 10e and 16c]

Diction

1. Examine the use of hyphenated words in the last sentence of paragraph 11 and throughout paragraph 12. Why are these words hyphenated? Do all of them need to be? Why or why not? [*Harbrace* 22f(1); *Hodges'* 18f(1)]
2. In the last sentence of paragraph 15, Morris uses a cliché: "like sardines in a tin." Explain why this cliché is or is not effectively used. [*Harbrace* 14c; *Hodges'* 20c]

BUILDING VOCABULARY

1. In Great Britain, the following words have meanings different from those they have in the United States: *bathe, football, cinema, flat, garden.* What are the American equivalents?
2. What is the source of the word *fan* in its informal meaning? List at least two other words with the same source.

SUGGESTION FOR WRITING

1. Classify and describe the kinds of territorial behavior you have observed at one or more events (for example, at basketball games, in classrooms, in elevators, in your living quarters, at parties, in meetings, and so on).

The Plot against People
Russell Baker

After graduating from Johns Hopkins University, Russell Baker worked as a reporter for the *Baltimore Sun* and *The New York Times*. Since 1962, he has written "The Observer," a syndicated newspaper column of humorous social criticism, which appears several times a week. He was awarded the Pulitzer Prize in 1979 for distinguished commentary. He has also contributed to a number of magazines including *Ladies' Home Journal, McCall's, Saturday Evening Post,* and *The New York Times Magazine.* In addition to collections of his columns—*Poor Russell's Almanac, The Upside Down Man,* and *So This Is Depravity*—Baker has published two autobiographical works, *Growing Up* and *The Rescue of Miss Yaskell and Other Pipe Dreams.* Typical of Baker's wry view of the world, "The Plot against People" is a humorous classification of inanimate objects according to a very surprising principle.

Inanimate objects are classified scientifically into three major categories— those that break down, those that get lost, and those that don't work. 1

The goal of all inanimate objects is to resist man and ultimately to defeat 2 him, and the three major classifications are based on the method each object uses to achieve its purpose. As a general rule, any object capable of breaking down at the moment when it is most needed will do so. The automobile is typical of the category.

With the cunning peculiar to its breed, the automobile never breaks down 3 while entering a filling station which has a large staff of idle mechanics. It waits until it reaches a downtown intersection in the middle of the rush hour, or until it is fully loaded with family and luggage on the Ohio Turnpike. Thus it creates maximum inconvenience, frustration, and irritability, thereby reducing its owner's lifespan.

Washing machines, garbage disposals, lawn mowers, furnaces, TV sets, 4 tape recorders, slide projectors—all are in league with the automobile to take their turn at breaking down whenever life threatens to flow smoothly for their enemies.

Many inanimate objects, of course, find it extremely difficult to break 5 down. Pliers, for example, and gloves and keys are almost totally incapable of breaking down. Therefore, they have had to evolve a different technique for resisting man.

They get lost. Science has still not solved the mystery of how they do 6 it, and no man has ever caught one of them in the act. The most plausible theory is that they have developed a secret method of locomotion which they are able to conceal from human eyes.

It is not uncommon for a pair of pliers to climb all the way from the cel-   7
lar to the attic in its single-minded determination to raise its owner's blood pressure. Keys have been known to burrow three feet under mattresses. Women's purses, despite their great weight, frequently travel through six or seven rooms to find hiding space under a couch.

Scientists have been struck by the fact that things that break down virtu-   8
ally never get lost, while things that get lost hardly ever break down. A furnace, for example, will invariably break down at the depth of the first winter cold wave, but it will never get lost. A woman's purse hardly ever breaks down; it almost invariably chooses to get lost.

Some persons believe this constitutes evidence that inanimate objects are   9
not entirely hostile to man. After all, they point out, a furnace could infuriate a man even more thoroughly by getting lost than by breaking down, just as a glove could upset him far more by breaking down than by getting lost.

Not everyone agrees, however, that this indicates a conciliatory attitude.   10
Many say it merely proves that furnaces, gloves and pliers are incredibly stupid.

The third class of objects—those that don't work—is the most curious of   11
all. These include such objects as barometers, car clocks, cigarette lighters, flashlights and toy-train locomotives. It is inaccurate, of course, to say that they *never* work. They work once, usually for the first few hours after being brought home, and then quit. Thereafter, they never work again.

In fact, it is widely assumed that they are built for the purpose of not   12
working. Some people have reached advanced ages without ever seeing some of these objects—barometers, for example—in working order.

Science is utterly baffled by the entire category. There are many theories   13
about it. The most interesting holds that the things that don't work have attained the highest state possible for an inanimate object, the state to which things that break down and things that get lost can still only aspire.

They have truly defeated man by conditioning him never to expect any-   14
thing of them. When his cigarette lighter won't light or his flashlight fails to illuminate, it does not raise his blood pressure. Objects that don't work have given man the only peace he receives from inanimate society.

✳

RESPONDING TO THE WHOLE ESSAY

1. What is Baker's purpose in "The Plot against People"? Is there evidence of a secondary purpose? Explain. [*Harbrace* 28a; *Hodges'* 32a]
2. Comment on the appropriateness of the essay for an audience of college students, giving reasons for your view. What other groups would find the essay appealing?

Is there any group of readers who would not be likely to appreciate this essay? If so, which group and why? If not, why not? [*Harbrace* 28a; *Hodges'* 32a]

3. Baker intends to be illogical in certain ways in this essay, yet in other ways he is rigorously logical. Point to examples and explain the effect. [*Harbrace* 31; *Hodges'* 35]

4. A standard method of organizing a classification essay is to begin by stating the categories that will be discussed and then to establish the basis for classification used to arrive at those categories. Explain how Baker's use of this method helps to establish the tone of his essay.

5. In a successful classification, categories must be exclusive rather than overlapping; in other words, items in one category may not also be placed in another category within the same classification. How well does Baker fulfill this requirement?

6. What do things that break down, things that get lost, and things that don't work have in common? Is the order in which Baker discusses these categories meaningful? Explain. [*Harbrace* 27b; *Hodges'* 31b]

ANALYZING THE ELEMENTS

Grammar

1. Explain the grammatical function of *scientifically* in the first sentence of paragraph 1 and explain how the word influences the reader's expectations about how the essay will proceed. [*Harbrace* 4a; *Hodges'* 4a]

2. In the first sentence of paragraph 12, what purpose is served by the use of the passive voice? [*Harbrace* 7c; *Hodges'* 7c]

Effective Sentences

1. Explain the parallel structure of the second sentence of paragraph 9. How does the parallelism contribute to the tone? [*Harbrace* 10a and 10b; *Hodges'* 26a and 26b]

2. To what does *it* in the second sentence of the final paragraph refer? Can this broad reference be justified? Explain. [*Harbrace* 6b; *Hodges'* 28c]

Punctuation and Mechanics

1. What use of the dash is illustrated by the first sentence of paragraph 4? Could the sentence be structured more effectively any other way? Explain your answer. [*Harbrace* 21e; *Hodges'* 17e]

2. What justification can be given for the italics in the third sentence of paragraph 11? [*Harbrace* 24f; *Hodges'* 10e]

Diction

1. Notice the combination of an inanimate object as subject with a verb of action in paragraph 7. Explain the effect of this incongruity.

2. How does Baker's imitation of scientific language (even of jargon) contribute to the effect of the essay? Find several examples of this kind of parody.

BUILDING VOCABULARY

1. Words with sources in Old English are so common that we rarely notice them. Look up the following words and state the meaning of the Old English word from which they are descended: *blood, breed, cunning, guest, light, work, woman.*
2. Words for objects are borrowed from other languages at least as often as they derive from earlier English words. Which of the following are borrowed and which are native: *pliers, furnace, purse, luggage, glove, couch, mattress?*

SUGGESTIONS FOR WRITING

1. Classify some ordinary group of people or things (for example, automobile drivers, retail clerks, grocery store paperbacks, horror movies, fast foods) into categories, and write a humorous essay showing how each category represents a different approach in a secret plot to destroy our sanity, our digestion, or even our lives.
2. Write an essay (either serious or humorous) classifying the different varieties of an emotion or attitude—for example, different kinds of frustration, anger, happiness, love, envy, or excitement.

Computer Skills Mean Sex Appeal
Scott Adams

Scott Adams was an applications engineer at Pacific Bell in the Bay Area when he created his very successful comic strip, "Dilbert," which satirizes modern office life. Certainly the fact that, like Dilbert, most of us have had to deal with incompetent authority figures accounts for at least part of the success of the strip. Dilbert is Everyman (as Dogbert is Everydog); he's an ordinary guy who does what we do, and occasionally what we would like to do. In this essay, by equating Dilbert's nerdiness with the sexual mystique most of us would like to have—a nerdiness with which most of us fear we may be overly well endowed—Adams lends substance to daydreams we may have of becoming fabulously attractive to potential significant others.

1   I get about a hundred e-mail messages a day from readers of my comic strip "Dilbert." Most are from disgruntled office workers, psychopaths, stalkers, comic-strip fans—that sort of person. But a growing number are from women who write to say they think Dilbert is sexy. Some say they've already married someone like Dilbert and couldn't be happier.

2   If you're not familiar with Dilbert, he's an electrical engineer who spends most of his time with his computer. He's a nice guy but not exactly Kevin Costner.

3   Okay, Dilbert is polite, honest, employed, and educated. These are good traits, but they don't explain the incredible sex appeal. So what's the attraction?

4   I think it's a Darwinian thing. We're attracted to people who have the best ability to survive and thrive. In the old days it was important to be able to run down an antelope and kill it with a single blow to the forehead. But that skill is becoming less important every year. Now all that matters is if you can install your own Ethernet card without having to call tech support and confess your inadequacies to a stranger.

5   It's obvious that the world today has three distinct classes of people, each with its own evolutionary destiny:

- KNOWLEDGEABLE COMPUTER USERS who will evolve into godlike noncorporeal beings who rule the universe (except for those who work in tech support).

- COMPUTER OWNERS who try to pass as knowledgeable but secretly use hand calculators to add totals to their Excel spreadsheets. This group will gravitate toward jobs as high school principals and operators of pet crematoriums. Eventually they will become extinct.

- NON-COMPUTER USERS who will grow tails, sit in zoos, and fling dung at tourists.

Obviously, if you're a woman and you're trying to decide which evolu- 6
tionary track you want your offspring to take, you don't want them on the luge ride to the dung-flinging Olympics. You want a real man. You want a knowledgeable computer user with real evolutionary potential.

And women prefer men who listen. Computer users are excellent listen- 7
ers because they can look at you for long periods of time without saying anything. Granted, early in a relationship it's better if the guy actually talks. But men use up all the stories they'll ever have after six months. If a woman marries a guy who's in, let's say, retail sales, she'll get repeat stories starting in the seventh month and lasting forever. Marry a computer programmer and she gets a great listener for the next 70 years.

Plus, with the ozone layer evaporating, it's good strategy to mate with 8
somebody who has an indoor hobby. Outdoorsy men are applying suntan lotion with SPF 10,000 and yet by the age of 30 they still look like dried chili peppers in trousers. Compare that with the healthy glow of a man who spends 12 hours a day in front of a video screen.

It's also well established that computer users are better lovers. If you doubt 9
the sexiness of male PC users, consider their hair. They tend to have either (1) male pattern baldness—a sign of elevated testosterone—or (2) unkempt jungle hair—the kind you see only on people who just finished a frenzied bout of lovemaking.

In less enlightened times, the best way to impress women was to own a 10
hot car. But women wised up and realized it was better to buy their own hot cars so they wouldn't have to ride around with such jerks. Information technology has replaced hot cars as the new symbol of robust manhood. Men know that unless they get a digital line to the Internet no woman is going to look at them twice.

Finally there is the issue of mood lighting. Nothing looks sexier than a 11
man in boxer shorts illuminated only by a 15-inch SVGA monitor. If we agree that this is every woman's dream scenario, then I think we can also agree that it's best if the guy knows how to use the computer. Otherwise, he'll just look like a loser sitting in front of a PC in his underwear.

In summary, it's not that I think non–PC users are less attractive. It's just 12
that I'm sure they won't read this article.

✳

RESPONDING TO THE WHOLE ESSAY

1. Adams uses the first four paragraphs of his essay to establish a context—the occasion, place, or intellectual climate influencing a piece of writing. What does he give as the occasion for writing this essay? [*Harbrace* 28a; *Hodges'* 32a]

2. What is Adams's main purpose in writing "Computer Skills Mean Sex Appeal"? Is there evidence of other aims? Is there a relationship between the occasion and the purpose of this essay? Explain. [*Harbrace* 28a; *Hodges'* 32a]
3. Comment on the audience Adams probably envisioned for this essay, which was originally published in *Windows Magazine,* a publication dedicated to news and commentary regarding the Windows computer operating system. [*Harbrace* 28a; *Hodges'* 32a]
4. Adams identifies "three distinct classes of people, each with its own evolutionary destiny." What basis for classification does Adams use here? Does it make useful distinctions? Explain. [*Harbrace* 27d; *Hodges'* 31d]

ANALYZING THE ELEMENTS

Grammar

1. In the second sentence of paragraph 1, what is the grammatical function of the phrase "that sort of person"? Comment on Adams's use of this phrase to achieve his purpose. [*Harbrace* 1d(2); *Hodges'* 1d(2)]
2. In the first sentence of paragraph 9, Adams comments that computer users are "better lovers." How can this incomplete comparison be justified? [*Harbrace* 4c; *Hodges'* 4c]

Effective Sentences

1. Success in telling jokes often depends upon the ability to know just how long to pause before saying the punch line. Similarly, in written humor much depends upon making two incongruous statements appear to be related. Comment on how Adams accomplishes this feat with the final phrase of the second sentence in paragraph 1 and with the third and fourth sentences of paragraph 4.
2. What does the parallel structure in the third sentence of paragraph 11 contribute to the humor of the essay? [*Harbrace* 10; *Hodges'* 26]

Punctuation and Mechanics

1. What reasons can you give for Adams's omitting a comma after *Internet* in the last sentence of paragraph 10? [*Harbrace* 21b; *Hodges'* 17b]
2. Comment upon Adams's use of abbreviations and acronyms in paragraph 11. [*Harbrace* 25; *Hodges'* 11]

Diction

1. Adams uses casual, informal language in this essay. What does he gain (or lose) by doing so? Give two examples of casual language. [*Harbrace* 13; *Hodges'* 19]
2. What is a *luge ride* (paragraph 6)? What does it mean in the context of the rest of the sentence and of the last sentence of paragraph 5? [*Harbrace* 14c; *Hodges'* 20c].

BUILDING VOCABULARY

1. Look up *frenzy* (*frenzied,* paragraph 9) in a desk or unabridged dictionary. Write one sentence in which you use the word as a noun and another in which you use it as an adjective.
2. According to *Webster's Collegiate Dictionary,* 10th edition, the word *robust* (paragraph 10) derives from a Latin word for "the strength of an oak." What are the modern meanings for the word?

SUGGESTIONS FOR WRITING

1. Write an essay classifying people you have met while doing something you enjoy. Make sure you state your basis for classification clearly.
2. Write an essay concerning college life that might have a title such as "Three (or Four) Kinds of _____."

Thinking as a Hobby
William Golding

William Golding (1911–1993) received a bachelor's degree from Oxford University. Except during the years of World War II, he was active in the London theater from the late 1930s through the 1950s—writing, producing, and acting in experimental drama. Golding's reputation rests mainly on his novels, including *Pincher Martin* (1962), *The Pyramid and the Spire* (1964), *The Scorpion God* (1971), *Darkness Visible* (1979), *Rites of Passage* (1980), and *Paper Work* (1984), although he has also written poetry. But it is for his masterpiece on the manifestation of evil even in children, *Lord of the Flies* (1954), that Golding will probably be best remembered. Golding was awarded the Nobel Prize for Literature in 1983. In "Thinking as a Hobby," originally published in *Harper's Magazine*, Golding classifies three levels of thinking.

While I was still a boy, I came to the conclusion that there were three grades of thinking; and since I was later to claim thinking as my hobby, I came to an even stranger conclusion—namely, that I myself could not think at all.

I must have been an unsatisfactory child for grownups to deal with. I remember how incomprehensible they appeared to me at first, but not, of course, how I appeared to them. It was the headmaster of my grammar school who first brought the subject of thinking before me—though neither in the way, nor with the result he intended. He had some statuettes in his study. They stood on a high cupboard behind his desk. One was a lady wearing nothing but a bath towel. She seemed frozen in an eternal panic lest the bath towel slip down any farther; and since she had no arms, she was in an unfortunate position to pull the towel up again. Next to her, crouched the statuette of a leopard, ready to spring down at the top drawer of a filing cabinet labeled A–AH. My innocence interpreted this as the victim's last, despairing cry. Beyond the leopard was a naked, muscular gentleman, who sat, looking down, with his chin on his fist and his elbow on his knee. He seemed utterly miserable.

Some time later, I learned about these statuettes. The headmaster had placed them where they would face delinquent children, because they symbolized to him the whole of life. The naked lady was the Venus of Milo. She was Love. She was not worried about the towel. She was just busy being beautiful. The leopard was Nature, and he was being natural. The naked, muscular gentleman was not miserable. He was Rodin's Thinker, an image of pure thought. It is easy to buy small plaster models of what you think life is like.

I had better explain that I was a frequent visitor to the headmaster's study, 4
because of the latest thing I had done or left undone. As we now say, I was
not integrated. I was, if anything, disintegrated; and I was puzzled. Grownups
never made sense. Whenever I found myself in a penal position before the
headmaster's desk, with the statuettes glimmering whitely above him, I would
sink my head, clasp my hands behind my back and writhe one shoe over the
other.

The headmaster would look opaquely at me through flashing spectacles. 5

"What are we going to do with you?" 6

Well, what were they going to do with me? I would writhe my shoe some 7
more and stare down at the worn rug.

"Look up, boy! Can't you look up?" 8

Then I would look up at the cupboard, where the naked lady was frozen 9
in her panic and the muscular gentleman contemplated the hindquarters of
the leopard in endless gloom. I had nothing to say to the headmaster. His
spectacles caught the light so that you could see nothing human behind them.
There was no possibility of communication.

"Don't you ever think at all?" 10

No, I didn't think, wasn't thinking, couldn't think—I was simply waiting 11
in anguish for the interview to stop.

"Then you'd better learn—hadn't you?" 12

On one occasion the headmaster leaped to his feet, reached up and plonked 13
Rodin's masterpiece on the desk before me.

"That's what a man looks like when he's really thinking." 14

I surveyed the gentleman without interest or comprehension. 15

"Go back to your class." 16

Clearly there was something missing in me. Nature had endowed the rest 17
of the human race with a sixth sense and left me out. This must be so, I mused,
on my way back to the class, since whether I had broken a window, or failed
to remember Boyle's Law, or been late for school, my teachers produced me
one, adult answer: "Why can't you think?"

As I saw the case, I had broken the window because I had tried to hit 18
Jack Arney with a cricket ball and missed him; I could not remember Boyle's
Law because I had never bothered to learn it; and I was late for school because I preferred looking over the bridge into the river. In fact, I was wicked.
Were my teachers, perhaps, so good that they could not understand the depths
of my depravity? Were they clear, untormented people who could direct their
every action by this mysterious business of thinking? The whole thing was incomprehensible. In my earlier years, I found even the statuette of the Thinker
confusing. I did not believe any of my teachers were naked, ever. Like someone born deaf, but bitterly determined to find out about sound, I watched my
teachers to find out about thought.

There was Mr. Houghton. He was always telling me to think. With a mod- 19
est satisfaction, he would tell me that he had thought a bit himself. Then why
did he spend so much time drinking? Or was there more sense in drinking

than there appeared to be? But if not, and if drinking were in fact ruinous to health—and Mr. Houghton was ruined, there was no doubt about that—why was he always talking about the clean life and the virtues of fresh air? He would spread his arms wide with the action of a man who habitually spent his time striding along mountain ridges.

"Open air does me good, boys—I know it!"   20

Sometimes, exalted by his own oratory, he would leap from his desk and   21
hustle us outside into a hideous wind.

"Now, boys! Deep breaths! Feel it right down inside you—huge draughts   22
of God's good air!"

He would stand before us, rejoicing in his perfect health, an open-air man.   23
He would put his hands on his waist and take a tremendous breath. You could hear the wind, trapped in the cavern of his chest and struggling with all the unnatural impediments. His body would reel with shock and his ruined face go white at the unaccustomed visitation. He would stagger back to his desk and collapse there, useless for the rest of the morning.

Mr. Houghton was given to high-minded monologues about the good life,   24
sexless and full of duty. Yet in the middle of one of these monologues, if a girl passed the window, tapping along on her neat little feet, he would interrupt his discourse, his neck would turn of itself and he would watch her out of sight. In this instance, he seemed to me ruled not by thought but by an invisible and irresistible spring in his nape.

His neck was an object of great interest to me. Normally it bulged a   25
bit over his collar. But Mr. Houghton had fought in the First World War alongside both Americans and French, and had come—by who knows what illogic?—to a settled detestation of both countries. If either country happened to be prominent in current affairs, no argument could make Mr. Houghton think well of it. He would bang the desk, his neck would bulge still further and go red. "You can say what you like," he would cry, "but I've thought about this—and I know what I think!"

Mr. Houghton thought with his neck.   26

There was Miss Parsons. She assured us that her dearest wish was our   27
welfare, but I knew even then, with the mysterious clairvoyance of childhood, that what she wanted most was the husband she never got. There was Mr. Hands—and so on.

I have dealt at length with my teachers because this was my introduction   28
to the nature of what is commonly called thought. Through them I discovered that thought is often full of unconscious prejudice, ignorance and hypocrisy. It will lecture on disinterested purity while its neck is being remorselessly twisted toward a skirt. Technically, it is about as proficient as most businessmen's golf, as honest as most politicians' intentions, or—to come near my own preoccupation—as coherent as most books that get written. It is what I came to call grade-three thinking, though more properly, it is feeling, rather than thought.

True, often there is a kind of innocence in prejudices, but in those days I   29
viewed grade-three thinking with an intolerant contempt and an incautious
mockery. I delighted to confront a pious lady who hated the Germans with
the proposition that we should love our enemies. She taught me a great truth
in dealing with grade-three thinkers; because of her, I no longer dismiss lightly
a mental process which for nine-tenths of the population is the nearest they
will ever get to thought. They have immense solidarity. We had better respect
them, for we are outnumbered and surrounded. A crowd of grade-three
thinkers, all shouting the same thing, all warming their hands at the fire of
their own prejudices, will not thank you for pointing out the contradictions
in their beliefs. Man is a gregarious animal, and enjoys agreement as cows
will graze all the same way on the side of a hill.

Grade-two thinking is the detection of contradictions. I reached grade two   30
when I trapped the poor, pious lady. Grade-two thinkers do not stampede easily, though often they fall into the other fault and lag behind. Grade-two thinking is a withdrawal, with eyes and ears open. It became my hobby and brought
satisfaction and loneliness in either hand. For grade-two thinking destroys
without having the power to create. It set me watching the crowds cheering
His Majesty and King and asking myself what all the fuss was about, without giving me anything positive to put in the place of that heady patriotism.
But there were compensations. To hear people justify their habit of hunting
foxes and tearing them to pieces by claiming that the foxes liked it. To hear
our Prime Minister talk about the great benefit we conferred on India by jail-
ing people like Pandit Nehru and Gandhi. To hear American politicians talk
about peace in one sentence and refuse to join the League of Nations in the
next. Yes, there were moments of delight.

But I was growing toward adolescence and had to admit that Mr.   31
Houghton was not the only one with an irresistible spring in his neck. I, too,
felt the compulsive hand of nature and began to find that pointing out contradiction could be costly as well as fun. There was Ruth, for example, a serious and attractive girl. I was an atheist at the time. Grade-two thinking is
a menace to religion and knocks down sects like skittles. I put myself in a position to be converted by her with an hypocrisy worthy of grade three. She
was a Methodist—or at least, her parents were, and Ruth had to follow suit.
But, alas, instead of relying on the Holy Spirit to convert me, Ruth was foolish enough to open her pretty mouth in argument. She claimed that the Bible
(King James Version) was literally inspired. I countered by saying that the
Catholics believed in the literal inspiration of Saint Jerome's *Vulgate*, and the
two books were different. Argument flagged.

At last she remarked that there were an awful lot of Methodists, and they   32
couldn't be wrong, could they—not all those millions? That was too easy, said
I restively (for the nearer you were to Ruth, the nicer she was to be near to)
since there were more Roman Catholics than Methodists anyway; and they
couldn't be wrong, could they—not all those hundreds of millions? An awful

flicker of doubt appeared in her eyes. I slid my arm around her waist and murmured breathlessly that if we were counting heads, the Buddhists were the boys for my money. But Ruth had *really* wanted to do me good, because I was so nice. She fled. The combination of my arm and those countless Buddhists was too much for her.

That night her father visited my father and left, red-cheeked and indignant. I was given the third degree to find out what had happened. It was lucky we were both of us only fourteen. I lost Ruth and gained an undeserved reputation as a potential libertine. 33

So grade-two thinking could be dangerous. It was in this knowledge, at the age of fifteen, that I remember making a comment from the heights of grade two, on the limitations of grade three. One evening I found myself alone in the school hall, preparing it for a party. The door of the headmaster's study was open. I went in. The headmaster had ceased to thump Rodin's Thinker down on the desk as an example to the young. Perhaps he had not found any more candidates, but the statuettes were still there, glimmering and gathering dust on top of the cupboard. I stood on a chair and rearranged them. I stood Venus in her bath towel on the filing cabinet, so that now the top drawer caught its breath in a gasp of sexy excitement. "A-ah!" The portentous Thinker I placed on the edge of the cupboard so that he looked down at the bath towel and waited for it to slip. 34

Grade-two thinking, though it filled life with fun and excitement, did not make for content. To find out the deficiencies of our elders bolsters the young ego but does not make for personal security. I found that grade two was not only the power to point out contradictions. It took the swimmer some distance from the shore and left him there, out of his depth. I decided that Pontius Pilate was a typical grade-two thinker. "What is truth?" he said, a very common grade-two thought, but one that is used always as the end of an argument instead of the beginning. There is still a higher grade of thought which says, "What is truth?" and sets out to find it. 35

But these grade-one thinkers were few and far between. They did not visit my grammar school in the flesh though they were there in books. I aspired to them, partly because I was ambitious and partly because I now saw my hobby as an unsatisfactory thing if it went no further. If you set out to climb a mountain, however high you climb, you have failed if you cannot reach the top. 3•

I *did* meet an undeniably grade-one thinker in my first year at Oxford. I was looking over a small bridge in Magdalen Deer Park, and a tiny mustached and hatted figure came and stood by my side. He was a German who had just fled from the Nazis to Oxford as a temporary refuge. His name was Einstein. 3•

But Professor Einstein knew no English at that time and I knew only two words of German. I beamed at him, trying wordlessly to convey by my bearing all the affection and respect that the English felt for him. It is possible—and I have to make the admission—that I felt here were two grade-one thinkers 3•

standing side by side; yet I doubt if my face conveyed more than a formless awe. I would have given my Greek and Latin and French and a good slice of my English for enough German to communicate. But we were divided; he was as inscrutable as my headmaster. For perhaps five minutes we stood together on the bridge, undeniable grade-one thinker and breathless aspirant. With true greatness, Professor Einstein realized that my contact was better than none. He pointed to a trout wavering in midstream.

He spoke: *"Fisch."*   39

My brain reeled. Here I was, mingling with the great, and yet helpless as   40
the veriest grade-three thinker. Desperately I sought for some sign by which I might convey that I, too, revered pure reason. I nodded vehemently. In a brilliant flash I used up half of my German vocabulary.

"Fisch. Ja Ja."   41

For perhaps another five minutes we stood side by side. Then Professor   42
Einstein, his whole figure still conveying good will and amiability, drifted away out of sight.

I, too, would be a grade-one thinker. I was irreverent at the best of times.   43
Political and religious systems, social customs, loyalties and traditions, they all came tumbling down like so many rotten apples off a tree. This was a fine hobby and a sensible substitute for cricket, since you could play it all the year round. I came up in the end with what must always remain the justification for grade-one thinking, its sign, seal and charter. I devised a coherent system for living. It was a moral system, which was wholly logical. Of course, as I readily admitted, conversion of the world to my way of thinking might be difficult, since my system did away with a number of trifles, such as big business, centralized government, armies, marriage. . . .

It was Ruth all over again. I had some very good friends who stood by   44
me, and still do. But my acquaintances vanished, taking the girls with them. Young women seemed oddly contented with the world as it was. They valued the meaningless ceremony with a ring. Young men, while willing to concede the chaining sordidness of marriage, were hesitant about abandoning the organizations which they hoped would give them a career. A young man on the first rung of the Royal Navy, while perfectly agreeable to doing away with big business and marriage, got as rednecked as Mr. Houghton when I proposed a world without any battleships in it.

Had the game gone too far? Was it a game any longer? In those prewar   45
days, I stood to lose a great deal, for the sake of a hobby.

Now you are expecting me to describe how I saw the folly of my ways   46
and came back to the warm nest, where prejudices are so often called loyalties, where pointless actions are hallowed into custom by repetition, where we are content to say we think when all we do is feel.

But you would be wrong. I dropped my hobby and turned professional.   47

If I were to go back to the headmaster's study and find the dusty stat-   48
uettes still there, I would arrange them differently. I would dust Venus and put her aside, for I have come to love her and know her for the fair thing she

is. But I would put the Thinker, sunk in his desperate thought, where there were shadows before him—and at his back, I would put the leopard, crouched and ready to spring.

✳

RESPONDING TO THE WHOLE ESSAY

1. Would you say Golding's purpose in "Thinking as a Hobby" is primarily expressive, informative, or persuasive? Support your answer with evidence. [*Harbrace* 28a; *Hodges'* 32a]

2. An author who sets out to classify levels of thinking runs the risk of appearing arrogant to the reader. Does Golding avoid giving the impression of arrogance? If so, how?

3. Though Golding's main method of development here is classification, he also makes extensive use of the strategies of example and narration (see chapters 1 and 2). Find instances of both these strategies, and show how they are related to Golding's classification. [*Harbrace* 27d; *Hodges'* 31d]

4. How does Golding use the statuettes as a structural device for his essay? What does each statuette represent? What does each arrangement of the statuettes indicate? What are the implications of the final arrangement of the statuettes?

5. In paragraphs 37 through 42, Golding recounts his encounter with Einstein on a bridge in Magdalen Deer Park. How is that encounter foreshadowed in paragraph 18? In paragraph 18, how does each of the "sins" Golding committed relate to the three kinds of thinking?

6. What kinds of transitional devices does Golding use to achieve coherence in paragraphs 32 and 44? Mark the paragraphs to show how the sentences are linked. [*Harbrace* 27b; *Hodges'* 31b]

ANALYZING THE ELEMENTS

Grammar

1. In the fifth sentence of paragraph 4, Golding uses *glimmering* and *whitely* as modifiers. What kinds of modifiers are these, and what do they contribute to the sentence? [*Harbrace* 4a and 4b; *Hodges'* 4a and 4b]

2. Golding begins the fifth sentence of paragraph 4 with *Whenever*. As a result, some of the verbs that follow (even in paragraph 9) take the form of *would sink* rather than *sank*. Explain why these verbs take this form. [*Harbrace* 7c; *Hodges'* 7c]

3. Justify Golding's use of the fragments at the end of paragraph 30. [*Harbrace* 2; *Hodges'* 2]

Effective Sentences

1. Golding frequently makes use of short, two- to four-word sentences. Explain how that contributes to the effectiveness of these sentences. [*Harbrace* 11h; *Hodges'* 29h]

2.   In paragraph 29, Golding uses the personal pronoun *we* to refer to those who are grade-two (or grade-one) thinkers. Why?

Punctuation and Mechanics

1.   Comment on the use of quotation marks, short paragraphs, and end punctuation in paragraphs 5 through 16 and paragraphs 20 through 22. [*Harbrace* 20a; *Hodges'* 16a]
2.   Justify Golding's use of ellipses in the final sentence of paragraph 43. [*Harbrace* 21i; *Hodges'* 17i]

Diction

1.   Look up the following words in your dictionary: *penal* and *writhe* (paragraph 4), *depravity* (paragraph 18), *draughts* (paragraph 22), *impediments* and *visitation* (paragraph 23), *clairvoyance* (paragraph 27), *skittles* (paragraph 31), and *libertine* (paragraph 33). What words can you think of that Golding might have used instead? Why do you think he made the particular choices he did? [*Harbrace* 14a(3); *Hodges'* 20a(2)]
2.   In the first sentence of paragraph 4, Golding makes an allusion to the general confession from the *Book of Common Prayer* ("We have left undone those things which we ought to have done; and we have done those things which we ought not to have done"). What does this allusion suggest about Golding's childhood state of mind when he was called to the headmaster's study? How is this notion reemphasized in paragraph 18? [*Harbrace* 14a(5); *Hodges'* 20a(4)]
3.   Golding uses figurative language in the last sentences of paragraphs 18 and 29. Explain the meaning and the effect of these similes. What other figurative language does the essay contain? [*Harbrace* 14a(5); *Hodges'* 20a(4)]

BUILDING VOCABULARY

1.   What is the meaning of the suffix *-ette*? Is there a difference between using it in a word such as *statuette* and in a word such as *usherette*? What is the difference?
2.   Look up *ruinous* and *ruined*. How do they differ in meaning?

SUGGESTIONS FOR WRITING

1.   Write a short essay comparing Banesh Hoffmann's description of Einstein's thinking processes and intellectual attitudes ("My Friend, Albert Einstein," pp. 17–23) with Golding's definition of grade-one thinking.
2.   Write an essay classifying three or four kinds of "intelligence" or aptitude in some special area (for example, types of scholastic ability, artistic or musical talent, athletic ability, spatial understanding, facility in dealing with people, and so forth).

The Qualities of Good Writing
Jacqueline Berke

Jacqueline Berke is professor of English at Drew University, where she teaches both introductory and advanced writing courses and various courses in literature. A widely published writer herself, she has contributed to many journals and magazines, has been a fellow of the MacDowell Colony for artists and writers, and is the author of a widely used writing textbook, *Twenty Questions for the Writer*. "The Qualities of Good Writing" is reprinted here from that book. (The speech by Patrick Henry from which Berke quotes in her first two paragraphs is printed in full in chapter 13 of *The Resourceful Reader*.)

Even before you set out, you come prepared by instinct and intuition to make certain judgments about what is "good." Take the following familiar sentence, for example: "I know not what course others may take, but as for me, give me liberty or give me death." Do you suppose this thought of Patrick Henry's would have come ringing down through the centuries if he had expressed this sentiment not in one tight, rhythmical sentence but as follows:

> It would be difficult, if not impossible, to predict on the basis of my limited information as to the predilections of the public, what the citizenry at large will regard as action commensurate with the present provocation, but after arduous consideration I personally feel so intensely and irrevocably committed to the position of social, political, and economic independence, that rather than submit to foreign and despotic control which is anathema to me, I will make the ultimate sacrifice of which humanity is capable—under the aegis of personal honor, ideological conviction, and existential commitment, I will sacrifice my own mortal existence.

How does this rambling, "high-flown" paraphrase measure up to the bold "Give me liberty or give me death"? Who will deny that something is "happening" in Patrick Henry's rousing challenge that not only fails to happen in the paraphrase but is actually negated there? Would you bear with this long-winded, pompous speaker to the end? If you were to judge this statement strictly on its rhetoric (its choice and arrangement of words), you might aptly call it more boring than brave. Perhaps a plainer version will work better:

286

Liberty is a very important thing for a person to have. Most people—at least the people I've talked to or that other people have told me about—know this and therefore are very anxious to preserve their liberty. Of course I can't be absolutely sure about what other folks are going to do in this present crisis, what with all these threats and everything, but I've made up my mind that I'm going to fight because liberty is really a very important thing to me; at least that's the way I feel about it.

This flat, "homely" prose, weighted down with what Flaubert called "fatty deposits," is grammatical enough. As in the pompous paraphrase, every verb agrees with its subject, every comma is in its proper place; nonetheless it lacks the qualities that make a statement—of one sentence or one hundred pages—pungent, vital, moving, memorable. 3

Let us isolate these qualities and describe them briefly. . . . The first quality of good writing is *economy*. In an appropriately slender volume entitled *The Elements of Style,* authors William Strunk and E. B. White stated concisely the case for economy: "A sentence should contain no unnecessary words, a paragraph no unnecessary sentences, for the same reason that a drawing should have no unnecessary lines and a machine no unnecessary parts. This requires not that the writer make all his sentences short or that he avoid all detail . . . but that every word tell." In other words, economical writing is *efficient* and *aesthetically satisfying*. While it makes a minimum demand on the energy and patience of readers, it returns to them a maximum of sharply compressed meaning. You should accept this as your basic responsibility as a writer: that you inflict no unnecessary words on your readers—just as a dentist inflicts no unnecessary pain, a lawyer no unnecessary risk. Economical writing avoids strain and at the same time promotes pleasure by producing a sense of form and right proportion, a sense of words that fit the ideas that they embody—with not a line of "deadwood" to dull the reader's attention, not an extra, useless phrase to clog the free flow of ideas, one following swiftly and clearly upon another. 4

Another basic quality of good writing is *simplicity*. Here again this does not require that you make all your sentences primerlike or that you reduce complexities to bare bone, but rather that you avoid embellishment or embroidery. The natural, unpretentious style is best. But, paradoxically, simplicity or naturalness does not come naturally. By the time we are old enough to write, most of us have grown so self-conscious that we stiffen, sometimes to the point of rigidity, when we are called upon to make a statement in speech or in writing. It is easy to offer the kindly advice "Be yourself," but many people do not feel like themselves when they take a pencil in hand or sit down at a typewriter. Thus during the early days of the Second World War, when air raids were feared in New York City and blackouts were instituted, an anonymous writer—probably a young civil service worker at City Hall—produced and distributed to stores throughout the city the following poster: 5

Illumination
is Required
to be
Extinguished
on These Premises
After Nightfall

What this meant, of course, was simply "Lights Out After Dark"; but ap-   6
parently that direct imperative—clear and to the point—did not sound "official" enough; so the writer resorted to long Latinate words and involved syntax (note the awkward passives "*is* Required" and "*to be* Extinguished") to
establish a tone of dignity and authority. In contrast, how beautifully simple
are the words of the translators of the King James Version of the Bible, who
felt no need for flourish, flamboyance, or grandiloquence. The Lord did not
loftily or bombastically proclaim that universal illumination was required to
be instantaneously installed. Simply but majestically "God said, Let there be
light: and there was light. . . . And God called the light Day, and the darkness he called Night."

Most memorable declarations have been spare and direct. Abraham   7
Lincoln and John Kennedy seemed to "speak to each other across the span
of a century," notes French author André Maurois, for both men embodied noble themes in eloquently simple terms. Said Lincoln in his second Inaugural Address: "With malice towards none, with charity for all, with
firmness in the right as God gives us the right, let us strive on to finish the
work we are in. . . ." One hundred years later President Kennedy made his
Inaugural dedication: "With a good conscience our only sure reward, with
history the final judge of our deeds, let us go forth to lead the land we
love. . . ."

A third fundamental element of good writing is *clarity*. Some people ques-   8
tion whether it is always possible to be clear; after all, certain ideas are inherently complicated and inescapably difficult. True enough. But the responsible writer recognizes that writing should not add to the complications nor
increase the difficulty; it should not set up an additional roadblock to understanding. Indeed, the German philosopher Wittgenstein went so far as to say
that "whatever can be said can be said clearly." If you understand your own
idea and want to convey it to others, you are obliged to render it in clear, or-
derly, readable, understandable prose—else why bother writing in the first
place? Actually, obscure writers are usually confused, uncertain of what they
want to say or what they mean; they have not yet completed that process of
thinking through and reasoning into the heart of the subject.

Suffice it to say here that whatever the topic, whatever the occasion, ex-   9
pository writing should be readable, informative, and, wherever possible, engaging. At its best it may even be poetic, as Nikos Kazantzakis suggests in

Zorba the Greek, where he draws an analogy between good prose and a beautiful landscape:

> To my mind the Cretan countryside resembled good prose, carefully ordered, sober, free from superfluous ornament, powerful and restrained. It expressed all that was necessary with the greatest economy. It had no flippancy nor artifice about it. It said what it had to say with a manly austerity. But between the severe lines one could discern an unexpected sensitiveness and tenderness; in the sheltered hollows the lemon and orange trees perfumed the air, and from the vastness of the sea emanated an inexhaustible poetry.

Even in technical writing, where the range of styles is necessarily limited (and poetry is neither possible nor appropriate), you must always be aware of "the reader over your shoulder." Take such topics as how to follow postal regulations for overseas mail, how to change oil in an engine, how to produce aspirin from salicylic acid. Here are technical expository descriptions that defy a memorable turn of phrase; here is writing that is of necessity cut and dried, dispassionate, and bloodless. But it need not be difficult, tedious, confusing, or dull to those who want to find out about mailing letters, changing oil, or making aspirin. Those who seek such information should have reasonably easy access to it, which means that written instructions should be clear, simple, spare, direct, and most of all, *human:* for no matter how technical a subject, all writing is done *for* human beings *by* human beings. Writing, in other words, like language itself, is a strictly human enterprise. Machines may stamp letters, measure oil, and convert acids, but only human beings talk and write about these procedures so that other human beings may better understand them. It is always appropriate, therefore, to be human in one's statement.   10

Part of this humanity must stem from your sense of who your readers are. You must assume a "rhetorical stance." Indeed this is a fundamental principle of rhetoric: *nothing should ever be written in a vacuum.* You should identify your audience, hypothetical or real, so that you may speak to them in an appropriate voice. A student, for example, should never "just write," without visualizing a definite group of readers—fellow students, perhaps, or the educated community at large (intelligent nonspecialists). Without such definite readers in mind, you cannot assume a suitable and appropriate relationship to your material, your purpose, and your audience. A proper rhetorical stance, in other words, requires that you have an active sense of the following: 11

1. Who you are as a writer.
2. Who your readers are.
3. Why you are addressing them and on what occasion.
4. Your relationship to your subject matter.
5. How you want your readers to relate to the subject matter.

✳

RESPONDING TO THE WHOLE ESSAY

1. Would you say that Berke's primary purpose in "The Qualities of Good Writing" is expressive, informative, or persuasive? Does knowing that the selection comes from a textbook on writing influence your judgment? Why or why not? What evidence can you find of purposes other than the one you named as primary? [*Harbrace* 28a; *Hodges'* 32a]

2. Reread Berke's final paragraph, which concludes with a list of five things the writer must have actively in mind in order to have a "rhetorical stance." What do you suppose Berke's own answers to these five questions were as she wrote "The Qualities of Good Writing"?

3. Analyze Berke's essay for its use of examples. Are any important points made that are not illustrated?

4. From a consideration of Berke's first two paragraphs, how would you describe Berke's attitude toward her reader and the kind of relationship she wishes to establish with the reader? [*Harbrace* 28c; *Hodges'* 32c]

5. Analyze the use of transitional devices in paragraph 8. You may find it helpful to mark the paragraph as is done in the examples in *Harbrace* 32b and *Hodges'* 36b.

6. Find and discuss examples in Berke's own writing of the qualities of good writing she identifies: economy, simplicity, clarity.

ANALYZING THE ELEMENTS

Grammar

1. The third sentence of paragraph 8 is actually an intentional sentence fragment. How might Berke justify using the fragment? [*Harbrace* 2; *Hodges'* 2]

2. The first sentence of paragraph 9 is a complex sentence, comprising a main clause and a subordinate clause. What is the verb of the main clause? Comment on the verb's number, tense, voice, and mood. [*Harbrace* 7, especially 7d; *Hodges'* 7, especially 7d]

Effective Sentences

1. Consider the second sentence of paragraph 4 and the first sentences of paragraph 5 and paragraph 8:

   The first quality of good writing is *economy*.
   Another basic quality of good writing is *simplicity*.
   A third fundamental element of good writing is *clarity*.

   In the context of the essay, how would the effect be different if these three sentences had been written as follows?

   Economy is the first quality of good writing.
   Simplicity is another basic quality of good writing.
   Clarity is a third fundamental element of good writing.

2. Analyze the use of parallelism in the last three sentences of paragraph 4, and comment on its effectiveness. [*Harbrace* 10a; *Hodges'* 26a]

Punctuation and Mechanics

1. Give reasons for Berke's uses of italics in paragraph 4. Are any of the italics optional (that is, not required by rules of correctness)? Might the fact that this selection was written for a textbook have any bearing on Berke's use of italics? [*Harbrace* 24a and 24f; *Hodges'* 10a and 10e]
2. The use of capital letters in the first sentence of paragraph 6 is unusual. Normally it would not be necessary to capitalize all the words in a phrase such as "Lights Out After Dark," or to capitalize "Required" and "Extinguished" in such phrases as "is required" and "to be extinguished." Why has Berke done so here?

Diction

1. Paragraph 4 contains several striking comparisons that lend force to points being made—both in the quotation from Strunk and White (drawing, machine) and in Berke's own subsequent discussion (dentist, lawyer). Comment on the appropriateness and effect of each comparison.
2. Using your dictionary if necessary, comment on the meaning and appropriateness of *Latinate, grandiloquence,* and *bombastically* in paragraph 6 and of *spare* in the first sentence of paragraph 7. [*Harbrace* 14a(2); *Hodges'* 23e(2)]

BUILDING VOCABULARY

1. What is the usual meaning of the word *homely*? What word do we generally use to mean "having the qualities of home"?
2. Look up the meaning of the prefix *para-*. Find three words in Berke's essay that begin with this prefix. What is the meaning of each?

SUGGESTIONS FOR WRITING

1. Analyze some academic field of study—perhaps the one you expect to choose as your major—dividing it into its main parts or subfields, and write an essay explaining it for a reader (such as a friend or parent or some other relative) who knows little about it. Unless your instructor prefers otherwise, such an essay could be in the form of a letter, which you might actually wish to send (thus getting a double benefit) after it has served its purpose in your writing course.
2. Write an essay analyzing in detail the wordiness and other weaknesses in Berke's long, windy paraphrase in paragraph 1 of Patrick Henry's statement, "Give me liberty or give me death." (You may find it helpful first to review *Harbrace* 13, 14, and 15; *Hodges'* 19, 20, and 21. If you need assistance with the mechanics of quoting, see *Harbrace* 20; *Hodges'* 16]

How We Listen to Music
Aaron Copland

Pianist and composer of music for orchestra, ballet, stage, films, and voice, Aaron Copland (1900–1990) was the first composer to receive a Guggenheim fellowship, and has been awarded the Pulitzer Prize in music, twice the New York Music Critics Circle Award, and an Oscar for his musical score for *The Heiress.* He received the Gold Medal of the American Academy of Arts and Letters in 1956. Copland holds honorary degrees from many colleges and universities, including Brandeis University, the University of Hartford, Harvard University, Illinois Wesleyan University, Oberlin College, Princeton University, and Temple University. He has appeared extensively in this country and in Europe as a lecturer and as a conductor, and has also taught musical composition at Harvard and the New School for Social Research. Among his books are *What to Listen for in Music, Our New Music, Music and Imagination,* and *Copland on Music.* "How We Listen to Music" is from *What to Listen for in Music* (1957).

We all listen to music according to our separate capacities. But, for the sake of analysis, the whole listening process may become clearer if we break it up into its component parts, so to speak. In a certain sense we all listen to music on three separate planes. For lack of a better terminology, one might name these: (1) the sensuous plane, (2) the expressive plane, (3) the sheerly musical plane. The only advantage to be gained from mechanically splitting up the listening process into these hypothetical planes is the clearer view to be had of the way in which we listen.

The simplest way of listening to music is to listen for the sheer pleasure of the musical sound itself. That is the sensuous plane. It is the plane on which we hear music without thinking, without considering it in any way. One turns on the radio while doing something else and absent-mindedly bathes in the sound. A kind of brainless but attractive state of mind is engendered by the mere sound appeal of the music.

You may be sitting in a room reading this book. Imagine one note struck on the piano. Immediately that one note is enough to change the atmosphere of the room—proving that the sound element in music is a powerful and mysterious agent, which it would be foolish to deride or belittle.

The surprising thing is that many people who consider themselves qualified music lovers abuse that plane in listening. They go to concerts in order to lose themselves. They use music as a consolation or an escape. They enter an ideal world where one doesn't have to think of the realities of everyday life. Of course they aren't thinking about the music either. Music allows them to leave it, and they go off to a place to dream, dreaming because of and apropos of the music yet never quite listening to it.

Yes, the sound appeal of music is a potent and primitive force, but you must not allow it to usurp a disproportionate share of your interest. The sensuous plane is an important one in music, a very important one, but it does not constitute the whole story.

There is no need to digress further on the sensuous plane. Its appeal to every normal human being is self-evident. There is, however, such a thing as becoming more sensitive to the different kinds of sound stuff as used by various composers. For all composers do not use that sound stuff in the same way. Don't get the idea that the value of music is commensurate with its sensuous appeal or that the loveliest sounding music is made by the greatest composer. If that were so, Ravel would be a greater creator than Beethoven. The point is that the sound element varies with each composer, that his usage of sound forms an integral part of his style and must be taken into account when listening. The reader can see, therefore, that a more conscious approach is valuable even on this primary plane of music listening.

The second plane on which music exists is what I have called the expressive one. Here, immediately, we tread on controversial ground. Composers have a way of shying away from any discussion of music's expressive side. Did not Stravinsky himself proclaim that his music was an "object," a "thing," with a life of its own, and with no other meaning than its own purely musical existence? This intransigent attitude of Stravinsky's may be due to the fact that so many people have tried to read different meanings into so many pieces. Heaven knows it is difficult enough to say precisely what it is that a piece of music means, to say it definitely, to say it finally so that everyone is satisfied with your explanation, but that should not lead one to the other extreme of denying to music the right to be "expressive."

My own belief is that all music has an expressive power, some more and some less, but that all music has a certain meaning behind the notes and that that meaning behind the notes constitutes, after all, what the piece is saying, what the piece is about. This whole problem can be stated quite simply by asking, "Is there a meaning to music?" My answer to that would be, "Yes." And "Can you state in so many words what the meaning is?" My answer to that would be, "No." Therein lies the difficulty.

Simple-minded souls will never be satisfied with the answer to the second of these questions. They always want music to have a meaning, and the more concrete it is the better they like it. The more the music reminds them of a train, a storm, a funeral, or any other familiar conception the more expressive it appears to be to them. This popular idea of music's meaning—stimulated and abetted by the usual run of musical commentator—should be discouraged wherever and whenever it is met. One timid lady once confessed to me that she suspected something seriously lacking in her appreciation of music because of her inability to connect it with anything definite. That is getting the whole thing backward, of course.

Still, the question remains, How close should the intelligent music lover   10 wish to come to pinning a definite meaning to any particular work? No closer than a general concept, I should say. Music expresses, at different moments, serenity or exuberance, regret or triumph, fury or delight. It expresses each of these moods, and many others, in a numberless variety of subtle shadings and differences. It may even express a state of meaning for which there exists no adequate word in any language. In that case, musicians often like to say that it has only a purely musical meaning. They sometimes go farther and say that *all* music has only a purely musical meaning. What they really mean is that no appropriate word can be found to express the music's meaning and that, even if it could, they do not feel the need of finding it.

But whatever the professional musician may hold, most musical novices   11 still search for specific words with which to pin down their musical reactions. That is why they always find Tschaikovsky easier to "understand" than Beethoven. In the first place, it is easier to pin a meaning-word on a Tschaikovsky piece than on a Beethoven one. Much easier. Moreover, with the Russian composer, every time you come back to a piece of his it almost always says the same thing to you, whereas with Beethoven it is often quite difficult to put your finger right on what he is saying. And any musician will tell you that that is why Beethoven is the greater composer—because music which always says the same thing to you will necessarily soon become dull music, but music whose meaning is slightly different with each hearing has a greater chance of remaining alive.

Listen, if you can, to the forty-eight fugue themes of Bach's *Well Tem-*   12 *pered Clavichord.* Listen to each theme, one after another. You will soon realize that each theme mirrors a different world of feeling. You will also soon realize that the more beautiful a theme seems to you the harder it is to find any word that will describe it to your complete satisfaction. Yes, you will certainly know whether it is a gay theme or a sad one. You will be able, in other words, in your own mind, to draw a frame of emotional feeling around your theme. Now study the sad one a little closer. Try to pin down the exact quality of its sadness. Is it pessimistically sad; is it fatefully sad or smilingly sad?

Let us suppose that you are fortunate and can describe to your own sat-   13 isfaction in so many words the exact meaning of your chosen theme. There is still no guarantee that anyone else will be satisfied. Nor need they be. The important thing is that each one feel for himself the specific expressive quality of a theme or, similarly, an entire piece of music. And if it is a great work of art, don't expect it to mean exactly the same thing to you each time you return to it.

Themes or pieces need not express only one emotion, of course. Take such   14 a theme as the first main one of the *Ninth Symphony,* for example. It is clearly made up of different elements. It does not say only one thing. Yet anyone hearing it immediately gets a feeling of strength, a feeling of power. It isn't a power that comes simply because the theme is played loudly. It is a power inherent in the theme itself. The extraordinary strength and vigor of the theme results in the listener's receiving an impression that a forceful statement has been made. But one should never try to boil it down to "the fateful hammer of life," etc. That is where the trouble begins. The musician, in his exasperation, says it means nothing but the notes themselves, whereas the nonprofessional is only too anxious to hang on to any explanation that gives him the illusion of getting closer to the music's meaning.

Now, perhaps, the reader will know better what I mean when I say that music does have an expressive meaning but that we cannot say in so many words what that meaning is.   15

The third plane on which music exists is the sheerly musical plane. Besides the pleasurable sound of music and the expressive feeling that it gives off, music does exist in terms of the notes themselves and of their manipulation. Most listeners are not sufficiently conscious of this third plane.   16

Professional musicians, on the other hand, are, if anything, too conscious of the mere notes themselves. They often fall into the error of becoming so engrossed with their arpeggios and staccatos that they forget the deeper aspects of the music they are performing. But from the layman's standpoint, it is not so much a matter of getting over bad habits on the sheerly musical plane as of increasing one's awareness of what is going on, in so far as the notes are concerned.   17

When the man in the street listens to the "notes themselves" with any degree of concentration, he is most likely to make some mention of the melody. Either he hears a pretty melody or he does not, and he generally lets it go at that. Rhythm is likely to gain his attention next, particularly if it seems exciting. But harmony and tone color are generally taken for granted, if they are thought of consciously at all. As for music's having a definite form of some kind, that idea seems never to have occurred to him.   18

It is very important for all of us to become more alive to music on its sheerly musical plane. After all, an actual musical material is being used. The intelligent listener must be prepared to increase his awareness of the musical material and what happens to it. He must hear the melodies, the rhythms, the harmonies, the tone colors in a more conscious fashion. But above all he must, in order to follow the line of the composer's thought, know something of the principles of musical form. Listening to all of these elements is listening on the sheerly musical plane.   19

Let me repeat that I have split up mechanically the three separate planes on which we listen merely for the sake of greater clarity. Actually, we never listen on one or the other of these planes. What we do is to correlate them—listening in all three ways at the same time. It takes no mental effort, for we do it instinctively.   20

Perhaps an analogy with what happens to us when we visit the theater   21
will make this instinctive correlation clearer. In the theater, you are aware of
the actors and actresses, costumes and sets, sounds and movement. All these
give one the sense that the theater is a pleasant place to be in. They constitute the sensuous plane in our theatrical reactions.

The expressive plane in the theater would be derived from the feeling that   22
you get from what is happening on the stage. You are moved to pity, excitement, or gayety. It is this general feeling, generated aside from the particular
words being spoken, a certain emotional something which exists on the stage,
that is analogous to the expressive quality in music.

The plot and plot development is equivalent to our sheerly musical plane.   23
The playwright creates and develops a character in just the same way that a
composer creates and develops a theme. According to the degree of your
awareness of the way in which the artist in either field handles his material
will you become a more intelligent listener.

It is easy enough to see that the theatergoer never is conscious of any of   24
these elements separately. He is aware of them all at the same time. The same
is true of music listening. We simultaneously and without thinking listen on
all three planes.

In a sense, the ideal listener is both inside and outside the music at the   25
same moment, judging it and enjoying it, wishing it would go one way and
watching it go another—almost like the composer at the moment he composes
it; because in order to write his music, the composer must also be inside and
outside his music, carried away by it and yet coldly critical of it. A subjective
and objective attitude is implied on both creating and listening to music.

What the reader should strive for, then, is a more *active* kind of listening.   26
Whether you listen to Mozart or Duke Ellington, you can deepen your understanding of music only by being a more conscious and aware listener—not
someone who is just listening, but someone who is listening *for* something.

✳

RESPONDING TO THE WHOLE ESSAY

1. From reading the essay, how would you characterize the audience for whom it
    was written? Point to evidence in support of your answer. [*Harbrace* 28c;
    Hodges' 32c]
2. What is Copland's primary purpose in "How We Listen to Music"? Where does
    he state or strongly imply this purpose? [*Harbrace* 28a; *Hodges'* 32a]
3. Copland announces in his introduction the strategy he will use to develop his es-
    say. Explain how the introduction reflects the organization of the essay as a whole.
    [*Harbrace* 28f(1); *Hodges'* 32f(1)]
4. What is Copland's basis for division in "How We Listen to Music"?
5. What problem with his analysis does Copland acknowledge? Why does he bring
    it up where he does?

6. How does Copland establish the conversational tone of the essay? [*Harbrace* 29a; *Hodges'* 33a]

ANALYZING THE ELEMENTS

Grammar

1. The fourth sentence of paragraph 11 is an intentional sentence fragment. What reason might Copland have had for using it? [*Harbrace* 2; *Hodges'* 2]
2. In paragraph 13 Copland uses verbs with three different moods—imperative, indicative, and subjunctive. Point to the shifts, and explain what Copland accomplishes by this variation. [*Harbrace* 7c; *Hodges'* 7c]
3. The last sentence of paragraph 19 contains two gerund phrases. What are they, and how does each function in the sentence? [*Harbrace* 1d(1)] *Hodges'* 1d(1)]

Effective Sentences

1. Explain how parallelism helps to make the last sentence of paragraph 4 effective. [*Harbrace* 10; *Hodges'* 26]
2. In paragraph 14 a number of the sentences could be combined to make longer sentences. Which ones lend themselves easily to combination? What rhetorical purpose is served by not combining them? [*Harbrace* 9a and 9b; *Hodges'* 24a and 24b]

Punctuation and Mechanics

1. Explain why the first sentence of paragraph 10 ends with a question mark rather than a period. [*Harbrace* 21b; *Hodges'* 17b]
2. Explain the function of the dash in the last sentence of paragraph 11. [*Harbrace* 21e; *Hodges'* 17e]

Diction

1. Look up the following words in your dictionary and consider their appropriateness in the essay: *sensuous* (paragraph 1), *deride* (paragraph 3), *apropos* (paragraph 4), *usurp* (paragraph 5), *commensurate* and *integral* (paragraph 6), *intransigent* (paragraph 7), and *arpeggios* and *staccatos* (paragraph 17). [*Harbrace* 13a and 14a(1); *Hodges'* 19a and 20a(1)]
2. Comment on whether, in the fifth sentence of paragraph 6, the connotations of *commensurate* fit with the tone established by "Don't get the idea. . . ." [*Harbrace* 14a(2) and 28c; *Hodges'* 23e(2) and 32c]

BUILDING VOCABULARY

1. What are the three meanings of the adjective *sheer*?
2. *Concert, compose,* and *commensurate* all use the same prefix. What is that prefix? Why is this prefix sometimes spelled *com-* and sometimes *con-*?

SUGGESTIONS FOR WRITING

1. Consider carefully your own response to some work of art other than a musical work—a painting, statue, or work of architecture, a poem or short story, a film or play—and write an essay in which you analyze your response, dividing it into different aspects or levels. Alternatively, write such an essay analyzing your response to a person—either a real person or a character in a book or film—toward whom your attitude is complex. (Caution: Do not choose your composition instructor, no matter what your feelings may be; this is never successful.)

2. Although Copland excludes no kind of music, he focuses on classical music. Write a brief "listening guide" to another kind of music you like—such as jazz (or a particular kind of jazz), country, rock (either soft rock or heavy metal), or folk—analyzing it for a reader who has little or no knowledge of it. Or instead you may write such a guide to appreciating the music of a particular instrument—guitar, trombone, flute, whatever.

✸
Chapter 8

Definition

When you say, "I mean . . . ," you are defining. A definition, whether it is a short dictionary definition or an entire essay, explains what something is. Formal definitions—the kind you most often find in your dictionary—follow a classic three-part pattern, naming the object or concept to be defined, placing it in a class, and then differentiating it from other members of that class. See *Harbrace* 13a or *Hodges'* 19a for some samples, or refer to your own dictionary.

You will find that you often need to use formal definitions in your writing. But the dictionary does not restrict itself to such definitions, and you need not do so either. In fact, a definition essay may involve many of the strategies *(mod* discussed in this book, as the essays in this chapter show. Kathleen Murphy defines *romantic hero* by giving examples. John R. Erickson begins his definition of *cowboy* with a short narrative, compares and contrasts the cowboy with the rancher and with other workers, and also relies on examples and description.

Since you write a definition to explain some concept or object to your reader, obviously you must consider what the reader already knows before you can decide what kinds of details and examples you need to supply and what kind of vocabulary you should use—or whether you need to define at all. For instance, if you were writing about a *rumble seat,* you would have to give much more explanation for readers under 60 than for readers who are older, since such open passenger seats were not used in cars manufactured much after World War II. And older readers could simply be expected to know what a rumble seat is without explanation—very likely having sat in the rumble seat as a child or as a teenager out on a double date.

An awareness not only of your readers' background and interests but also of your purpose in writing for those readers is crucial to the decisions you will make. Are you writing primarily to convey information to a reader who you can safely assume is interested in learning more about your subject? If so, you may have the luxury of taking time and space to explore your subject in considerable depth, as Kathleen Murphy does in "The Good, The Bad, & The Ugly: Clint Eastwood as Romantic Hero." On the other hand, you might be writing with a strongly persuasive aim, hoping to win over skeptical readers to your point of view—and you might therefore try to be as brief as possible and to rely on a few striking examples and carefully chosen details so as not to exhaust your readers' patience while you make your case.

As you write definitions, a few special cautions are worth bearing in mind. Be careful with your logic; one of the most frequent traps writers fall into with definition is circularity. You don't help your reader much when you define a Cistercian monk as a monk belonging to the Cistercian order. Also avoid the awkward and illogical use of *is when* or *is where* in definitions that do not involve time or place. For instance, do not write "Terrorism *is where* [or *is when*] violence and intimidation are used for some political purpose." Terrorism is neither a place (*is where*) nor a time (*is when*). Instead, write "Terrorism is the use of violence and intimidation for some political purpose."

In the following essay, a freshman student, Carol Johnson, defines "feminist." As you read the essay, notice the kinds of information Johnson provides and the various development strategies she employs.

What Is a Feminist?

<table>
<tr><td>Term to be
defined</td><td>The term "feminist" has been used to batter or applaud so many women and movements in our society that it is easily one of the most misunderstood adjectives of the century. So, what is a feminist? Is it a woman who hates men? Is it a woman who wants only women to run the country? Is it a woman with short cropped hair wearing comfortable shoes? I don't</td></tr>
<tr><td>Reason for
definition</td><td>think there is an easy answer; an understanding of the word "feminist," I believe, requires an understanding of the political, social, and economic issues that form its origination.</td></tr>
<tr><td>Historical context Process</td><td>First, historically and politically speaking, there were some women who saw the role women played in society and were concerned; they felt women needed the right to vote. These women questioned why society, at that time almost entirely represented by men, did not consider them equal to men. These women interpreted the United States Constitution to affirm that it was not God's intention to enslave men, so they wanted to know why women were being enslaved. Also, these women knew that if they ever hoped to influence the laws that oppressed them, women must have the right to vote.</td></tr>
<tr><td>Historical
definition</td><td>Narration For women in this country in the early part of this century were pitifully oppressed both economically and socially. Because they were not allowed to receive the same education men were given, if a woman had to earn her living, she was forced into low-paying service jobs or low-level factory positions that required long hours of tedious labor under</td></tr>
</table>

horrendous conditions. The majority of women lacked the ability to exercise any control over their circumstances. These women were not women of influence, but women of the working class, overworked, underpaid, and without a voice—the majority of women!

Political definition

Women from all classes protested these abusive and discriminatory practices. These protesters banded together and marched through the streets of their country demanding equality with men. And these women were labeled feminists. They wanted the right to vote, they wanted the right to fair working conditions and fair wages, and they wanted the right to live their lives in the manner they chose without ostracism from society. Yes, these women (and a few like-minded men) were called feminists.

Modern feminist agenda

Today, feminists come in all shapes, sizes, races, ages, and sexes. Today, the word "feminist" still implies a political agenda. But do we really need to have feminists and a feminist agenda today? The answer is a definite yes. Why? Because women still make only 70 cents on the dollar men earn doing similar jobs; because women single heads of households and their children are the fastest growing segment of the homeless population; because abuse of women by their fathers, husbands, and boyfriends is still happening and on the increase—the truth is, feminists must continue to work every day to make equality a reality.

Term and class differentia

These feminists are men and women who actively promote the political, economic, and social equality of women. Some feminists may be gay; far more are heterosexual. But all feminists believe in the undeniable fact that men and women are equal under

Expansion of class

our Constitution.

Commentary. Johnson sets up the essay as a question to be answered by the definition. She begins by presenting several commonly held, but patently false, views of what a feminist is and notes that the true definition must be understood in a historical and political context; hence her essay is also an argument for feminism.

The body of her essay first offers a historical context, giving background information about the plight of ordinary women at the turn of the century and about the early feminists who protested against discrimination against women. This information leads to her historical definition of a feminist.

However, since her purpose is to present a definition of the modern feminist, she then identifies how a feminist looks and follows that information with a statement of how a feminist thinks. To justify the need for feminists, Johnson states several ways in which women are oppressed today.

Her essay concludes with her statement of term, class and differentiating characteristics—the elements of a formal definition. The term is *feminist;* the class is *men* and *women;* and the differentiating characteristic is *who actively promote the political, economic, and social equality of women.*

Johnson's strategy is interesting. Because the essay is an argument as well as a definition essay, Johnson defers her strongest evidence. As she draws to a close, she points out how in several ways life has changed little for the working-class woman. She also deflects a standard, but ignorant, criticism of feminists by pointing out that sexual preference is not relevant. Structuring the essay in this way allows Johnson to make her point strongly.

Breaking the Hungry Teen Code
Ellen Goodman

Winner of a 1980 Pulitzer Prize for distinguished commentary for her syndicated column, "At Large," which she writes for the *Boston Globe*, Ellen Goodman was born in Massachusetts in 1941. She graduated with honors from Radcliffe College. Her books include a collection of interviews, *Turning Points* (1979), and three collections of her essays, *Close to Home* (1979), *At Large* (1981), and *Keeping in Touch* (1985).

As a parent who works with words for a living, I have prided myself over 1 many years for a certain skill in breaking the codes of childspeak. I began by interpreting babytalk, moved to more sophisticated challenges like "chill out" and graduated with "wicked good."

One phrase, however, always stumped me. I was unable to crack the mean- 2 ing of the common cry echoing through most middle-class American households: "There's Nothing to Eat in This House!"

This exclamation becomes a constant refrain during the summer months 3 when children who have been released from the schoolhouse door grow attached to the refrigerator door. It is during the summer when the average taxpayer realizes the true cost-effectiveness of school: It keeps kids out of the kitchen for roughly seven hours a day. A feat no parent is able to match.

At first, like so many others, I assumed that "NETH!" (as in "Nothing 4 to Eat in This House") was a straightforward description of reality. If there was NETH, it was because the children had eaten it all. After all, an empty larder is something you come to expect when you live through the locust phase of adolescence.

I have one friend with three teenage sons who swears that she doesn't 5 even have to unload her groceries anymore. Her children feed directly from the bags, rather like ponies. I have other friends who only buy ingredients for supper on the way home so that supper doesn't turn into lunch.

Over the years, I have considered color-coding food with red, yellow and 6 green stickers. Green for eat. Yellow for eat only if you are starving. Red for "touch this and you die."

However, I discovered that these same locusts can stand in front of a rel- 7 atively full refrigerator while bleating the same pathetic choruses of "NETH! NETH!" By carefully observing my research subjects, I discovered that the demand of "NETH!" has little to do with the supply.

What then does the average underage eater mean when he or she bleats 8
"NETH! NETH!" You will be glad to know that I have finally broken the
code for the "nothing" in NETH and offer herewith my translation.

NETH includes: 9

1. Any food that must be cooked, especially in a pan or by convectional heat. This covers boiling, frying or baking. Toasting is acceptable under dire conditions.
2. Any food that is in a frozen state with the single exception of ice cream. A frozen pizza may be considered "something to eat" only if there is a microwave oven on hand.
3. Any food that must be assembled before eaten. This means tuna that is still in a can. It may also mean a banana that has to be peeled, but only in extreme cases. Peanut butter and jelly are exempt from this rule as long as they are on the same shelf beside the bread.
4. Leftovers. Particularly if they must be re-heated. (See 1.)
5. Plain yogurt or anything else that might have been left as a nutrition trap.
6. Food that must be put on a plate, or cut with a knife and fork, as opposed to ripped with teeth while watching videos.
7. Anything that is not stored precisely at eye level. This includes:
8. Any item on a high cupboard shelf, unless it is a box of cookies and:
9. Any edible in the back of the refrigerator, especially on the middle shelf.

While divining the nine meanings of "NETH!" I should also tell you that 10
I developed an anthropological theory about the eating patterns of young
Americans. For the most part, I am convinced, Americans below the age of
20 have arrested their development at the food-gathering stage.

They are intrinsically nomadic. Traveling in packs, they engage in noth- 11
ing more sophisticated than hand-to-mouth dining. They are, in effect, strip
eaters who devour the ripest food from one home, and move on to another.

Someday, I am sure they will learn about the use of fire, not to mention 12
forks. Someday, they will be cured of the shelf-blindness, the inability to imagine anything hidden behind a large milk carton. But for now, they can only
graze. All the rest is NETH-ing.

✳

RESPONDING TO THE WHOLE ESSAY

1. What is Goodman's purpose in "Breaking the Hungry Teen Code"—expressive, informative, or persuasive? What evidence leads you to decide? Is there evidence of more than one purpose? If so, what? [*Harbrace* 28a; *Hodges'* 32a]
2. In this definition essay, where does Goodman state what is to be defined (NETH), assign it to a class in which it belongs, and distinguish it from other members of that class? What is the class to which it belongs? What are other members of that class? How is NETH different from the other members?
3. Definition essays frequently make use of a variety of development strategies. What other strategies can you find evidence of and how does Goodman make each con- tribute to the definition? [*Harbrace* 27d and 28c(1); *Hodges'* 31d and 32c(1)]

4.   Short essays, like Goodman's, require smooth transitions just as do longer ones. Examine Goodman's essay to see how she uses transitions between parts of the essay, paragraphs, and between sentences. [*Harbrace* 27b; *Hodges'* 31b]

5.   In her conclusion, Goodman offers an "anthropological" description of teens. How does she make this description consistent with her definition? [*Harbrace* 28f; *Hodges'* 32f]

ANALYZING THE ELEMENTS

Grammar

1.   The second sentence of paragraph 1 is a simple sentence, but it contains three verbs. What is the grammatical function of these verbs and what do they contribute to the content of the essay? [*Harbrace* 1a; *Hodges'* 1a]

2.   In the ninth "meaning" of NETH (paragraph 9), Goodman refers to food as an *edible*. Comment on why this word is a noun rather than an adjective. [*Harbrace* 1c; *Hodges'* 1c]

Effective Sentences

1.   The second sentence of paragraph 3 contains two clauses beginning with *it*. How is the first *it* used? The second? Is this a balanced sentence? Why or why not? How does each contribute to the effectiveness of the sentence? [*Harbrace* 6b and 12; *Hodges'* 28 and 30]

2.   Comment on the effect Goodman gains by using parallel structure in sentences 1 and 2 of paragraph 12. [*Harbrace* 10; *Hodges'* 26]

Punctuation and Mechanics

1.   Comment on Goodman's use of the acronym, NETH, throughout the essay. Why does it not contain periods? [*Harbrace* 25; *Hodges'* 11]

2.   Explain why Goodman does not use parentheses to enclose the numbers in paragraph 9. [*Harbrace* 21f; *Hodges'* 17f]

Diction

1.   Comment on Goodman's use of the slang terms *chill out* and *wicked good*. [*Harbrace* 13b(2); *Hodges'* 19c]

2.   Goodman refers to *locusts* in paragraph 7. Explain. [*Harbrace* 14c; *Hodges'* 20c]

BUILDING VOCABULARY

1.   An acronym is a word constructed from the initial letters or parts of several words; for example, NETH comes from "N(othing to) E(at in) T(his) H(ouse)," and sonar from SO(und) NA(vigation) R(anging). List at least five other acronyms, showing the complete phrase each is made up of. Include at least one acronym formed from the initial letters of words in a phrase (like NETH) and at least one formed from the initial parts of such words (like sonar).

2. Explain how words such as childspeak and shelf-blind are created. What do they mean?

SUGGESTIONS FOR WRITING

1. In a brief essay, define a slang term that you use (or hear) frequently.
2. Consider a particular kind of behavior that you find bizarre. Write an essay defining the group that engages in that behavior *entirely on the basis of your observation*. If you wish, write the essay in the *persona* of an anthropologist visiting from another planet (and invisible, perhaps) who is observing the behavior for the first time, without any preconceptions about it.

Is It Reverse Discrimination?
Ruben Navarrette, Jr.

Born in 1967 in Fresno, California, Ruben Navarrette was valedictorian of his high school class in Sanger, California, the small town in the San Joaquin Valley where he has lived all his life except for the years he spent pursuing a bachelor's degree at Harvard University and graduate study at UCLA. Navarrette taught briefly at Fresno State University, and teaching also provided him with what he calls the "most humbling experience of my life"— teaching kindergarten. Now a full-time writer, Navarrette is editor of *Hispanic Student,* a magazine for high school students. He writes regularly for the *Los Angeles Times,* the *Arizona Republic,* the *San Antonio Light,* and occasionally for the *San Francisco Chronicle.* He has also authored a book about being a Mexican-American at Harvard, *The Darker Shade of Crimson: Reflections of a Harvard Chicano,* published in 1993 by Bantam.

Their young eyes stare at me with a hint of skepticism, and perhaps a bit 1 of anger I have come as a guest speaker to a government class at the high school in Sanger, Calif., I attended not long ago. Invited to defend an educational program that is continually under siege by those who want racial equity without sacrifice, I have come to confront an old friend—Allan Bakke.

It was six years ago, as a high-school senior, that I first met the spirit of 2 the 33-year-old NASA engineer who, a decade earlier, had decided to become a doctor. After being rejected by 12 medical schools, he had challenged the admissions policy at the University of California, Davis' medical school. Bakke charged that the school's special admissions program, which reserved 16 of 100 places for "economically and educationally disadvantaged" applicants, violated his 14th Amendment right to equal protection.

Though, in 1978, the U.S. Supreme Court, by 5-4, eventually ordered his 3 admission to Davis, it also allowed—indeed encouraged—colleges and universities to consider the race and sex of its applicants in order to bring diversity and racial parity to U.S. higher education.

None of this seemed important to me at the beginning of my senior year 4 in high school, when I was setting my sights on applying to some of the top colleges in the United States.

Not everyone shared my confidence. In the middle of the application 5 process, my high school principal counseled me that it was "fine" that I was applying to schools like Harvard, Yale and Princeton, but that I should also consider applying to Fresno State nearby "just in case." I thanked him for his concern and promptly disregarded his advice.

Rebuffed, he cast the first spear of a bitter attack that was to be taken   6
over by my Anglo classmates and maintained through spring. "You may be
right," he conceded with insincerity. "After all, your race should help you a
lot. . . ." In five minutes, he had dismissed four years of hard work and perfect grades.

My white classmates, many of them with grades not as good as mine and   7
reeling from rejections by the schools that were admitting me, were far more
direct. "Now, you know if you hadn't been Mexican. . . ." one of them said.
And it was then that I met Allan Bakke.

He was there in the eyes of my classmates, clutching in their fists letters   8
of rejection from Stanford. "It's not fair," I remember one of them saying.
"They turned me down because I was white."

I half-expected to find huge clusters of Mexican students at Harvard, but   9
I was one of only 35 Mexican-Americans in the school. Did this signify the
alleged "darkening" of higher education?

This is the legacy with which I entered the high school government class   10
and confronted Bakke. "Granted, racial discrimination was wrong back then
(presumably pre-civil rights movement)," a student conceded "But now that
that's over with, shouldn't we get rid of affirmative action?"

The first time I'd heard this line was from Nathan Glazer, a professor of   11
mine at Harvard, who some say coined the phrase "reverse discrimination."
Once a society has liberated its employment and educational opportunities
and fully met the burden of its democratic principles, Glazer argues, any further tampering with the laws of appropriation through race-preference programs constitutes impermissible "reverse discrimination."

My dispute with my old professor is that U.S. society has not yet reached   12
Glazer's window of equal opportunity.

I suggested to the students that they needed only to look at their im-   13
mediate surroundings. Sanger is, I reminded them, 72.8 percent Mexican-
American. The fire chief, the police chief, the mayor, the city attorney, the
city manager and the majority of the City Council are white. The dropout
rate of Latino students from the school system that produced me is consistent with the distressing national figure of 50 percent to 60 percent.

Clearly, no matter how slick and seductive the rhetoric about the suffer-   14
ing of "new victims," the reality of American society is that, as we enter the
year 2000, we have not yet ended the suffering of our old victims.

✳

RESPONDING TO THE WHOLE ESSAY

1. Does the fact that this essay first appeared in a newspaper help you to explain
    why Navarrette's paragraphs are so short? How? [*Harbrace* 27; *Hodges'* 31]

2. Is Navarrette's purpose in "Is It Reverse Discrimination?" predominantly expressive, informative, or persuasive? Explain how the essay reveals Navarrette's purpose. [*Harbrace* 28a; *Hodges'* 32a]
3. In paragraph 1 Navarrette explains the situation that motivated his definition of *reverse discrimination*. Does this explanation provide necessary information—for example, would the essay be as effective if it began with the information in paragraph 3? Why or why not?
4. To define *reverse discrimination*, Navarrette uses both functional and stipulative kinds of definition. From evidence in the essay, what part(s) of the definition are functional, and what part(s) stipulative? You may need to look up *stipulative* in your dictionary. [*Harbrace* 27d; *Hodges'* 31d]
5. Comment on how the rhetorical situation and the occasion influence the reader's understanding of Navarrette's essay. [*Harbrace* 28a; *Hodges'* 32a]

ANALYZING THE ELEMENTS

Grammar

1. Explain the time relationships among the tenses of the verbs in the first sentence of paragraph 1. [*Harbrace* 7; *Hodges'* 7]
2. What is the grammatical function of the clause "that U.S. society has not yet reached Glazer's window of equal opportunity" in paragraph 12? What are the implications of equating that clause with the subject of the sentence? [*Harbrace* 1b; *Hodges'* 1b]

Effective Sentences

1. Comment on how Navarrette achieves sentence variety in paragraph 7. [*Harbrace* 11; *Hodges'* 29]
2. To what does *this* in the first sentence of paragraph 4 refer? Is the reference clear? Explain. [*Harbrace* 6b; *Hodges'* 28]

Punctuation and Mechanics

1. Comment on Navarrette's use of numbers in paragraph 2. Which, if any, need not be spelled out because the essay appeared in a newspaper but should be under other circumstances? [*Harbrace* 25; *Hodges'* 11]
2. Explain what Navarrette probably intended to convey by his use of ellipsis points in paragraphs 6 and 7. [*Harbrace* 21i; *Hodges'* 17i]

Diction

1. In paragraph 11 Navarrette significantly changes tone. How does he accomplish this change? What do you think Navarrette's reason for the change was? [*Harbrace* 14; *Hodges'* 20]
2. What is the "spear" that Navarrette says his principal "cast"? Comment on any similar similes or metaphors in the rest of the essay. [*Harbrace* 14a; *Hodges'* 20a]

BUILDING VOCABULARY

1. A euphemism is an inoffensive word that substitutes for one that might be considered offensive. Traditionally, euphemisms have referred to body functions and parts: a hundred years ago, tables were said to have *limbs* rather than *legs*—a body part that might give rise to salacious thought. Today, euphemisms often refer to two kinds of potentially offensive language: words that identify various ethnic groups (as *minority* replaces *Native American,* for example) and words that refer to deplorable social conditions (as *disadvantaged* replaces *poor*). List at least five euphemisms that you encounter in one 24-hour period and state the word that each replaces.

2. What is the meaning of *equity*? of *parity*? In what discipline are they most commonly used?

SUGGESTIONS FOR WRITING

1. Write a brief essay (500–750 words) defining a kind of behavior (procrastination, prevarication, exaggeration, and so on).

2. Define an object according to what it *does* (for example, nuclear warhead, computer, automobile).

The Art of the Crush
Zach Parsi

For most of the last twenty years or so, the images that have assaulted us on
television and in print have privileged youth and sexuality. In response to
these shallow perceptions of the eighties, the early nineties saw efforts to make
people aware that true beauty exists more in what people are than in what
they look like. At the turn of the century, we are urged to appreciate the less
visible beauties of age, sincerity, intelligence, and honesty—among others. As
a result, and lacking any approved category for such responses, some people
are becoming uncomfortable with acknowledging physical beauty. Zach Parsi
defines such a category and makes a case for responding to the physical allure of both men and women.

1　What would you call someone who derives a vital thrill from the beauty
of passing strangers? Before you answer, consider this: a perfect body, waiting at a corner for the light to change. Consider the faultless, curving neck,
tan and strong and graceful. Or think of a well-muscled forearm, two bar
stools down from you. Or a beautiful accent floating over from a stranger's
flickering tongue, twisting familiar words into music.

2　You see someone on the street or across the room in a restaurant or crowded
into the corner of a subway car, and from a body or a face or the sound of a
laugh a beautiful fiction develops. You nearly trip in admiration at the coyly
blinking belly eye of a strolling stranger—a wayward prince or princess from
the fabled land of Ab whose favorite sexual position is the sit-up crunch. You
sip your beer and make cat-eyes across the dining room at a young poetess
with poems by Swinburne circling inside her head like chicken hawks. You
wonder when the tiny creature crowded by the rush-hour throng into the corner of the downtown express will call out your name, because surely those little hands were meant to be held by you and you alone.

3　What is the word for the active pursuit of erotic reveries inspired by random faces? Your granddad might have called it girl-watching, but granddad
was a sexually constipated, tonic-slurping old deacon; his characterization
strikes me as much too pathetic a term for what one hopes is, at least occasionally, a two-way interaction. Girl-watching is something greasy-haired math
majors do during chess-club breaks.

4　My friend Sabine describes the phenomenon as "anonymous flirting" and
considers the fleeting but powerful erotic tension between passing strangers
to be as normal a part of urban life as hailing cabs or looking both ways before crossing the street.

Less charitable critics might say that my admiration of unknown beauties   5
approaches a form of stalking—an objectification of humans that betrays a
bubbling psychosis. But really this is an exaggeration. If I turned and followed
the objects of my fascination after they passed, then perhaps. If my fascination persisted and grew dire; if I followed them home and waited outside their
doors with fistfuls of shabby Korean-deli roses—well, then, yes. If I took photographs of them with a telescopic lens and wrote them love letters that I
never mailed, if I trailed them when they went out on dates, keeping a discreet distance, consumed with jealous rage, thumbing the honed edge of a
mail-order hunting knife, weeping quietly and humming "Mi Cielito Lindo"
into an ether-soaked handkerchief—now *that* would be stalking.

To me, though, my deep appreciation of sundry shopkeepers, sidewalk   6
strollers, café dawdlers and waitstaff has always seemed much more complicated, astounding, and innocent than the unsubtle characterizations I have
heard people propound. I've come to think of it as an art—the art of the
crush—and it is the closest thing to a transcendent experience I have ever felt.

Like many metaphysical notions, the art of the crush is easier to define   7
by what it is not. The art of the crush does not concern the pickup game, that
vulgar wolf's pissing contest. It is not about belt-notching. Nor does it have
anything to do with doe-eyed infatuation.

The art of the crush is not about sex. Sex too is easy— . . . generally re-   8
stricted only to the extent that public enjoyment of it is prohibited. Sex is easy,
and even the best sex is always a letdown.

The crush, in contrast, is a spell that, because it remains unconsummated,   9
is never broken by reality's inevitable anticlimax. There is no meeting. There
is no first date. There is no awkward, hairless-ape first copulation, no pillow
talk; no rocky times, no ups and downs. There is no depressingly inevitable
conclusion, when the relationship dissolves like a bankrupt corporation. There
is only the crush—part nostalgia and part hope; the figure approaching from
afar and then receding; the infinite possibility contained within a pouting lip
or a grin, within blue eyes or brown or green, within that billowing skirt or
tight blue jeans.

The truly accomplished crush artist is a grinning celibate.   10

For the phylogenetically minded, I separate crushes into two broad cate-   11
gories. There are constant crushes (*Eros perennis*)—landmarks of beauty that
dot the urban landscape to which you return as often as you dare to recharge
your soul's batteries and breathe in the sweet laughing gas of the crush. They
are the shops where beautiful men and women work behind plate-glass windows like pastries on display. They are the coffee girls and espresso-jerking,
cool-eyed caffeine boys. The violet-eyed bank tellers and pert-breasted waitresses. The fitness center's dreamy, cocksure muscle boys. The fourth-row-
center, always-late, sleepy-eyed lit-class deity. The city's hothouse flowers.

The second category is passing crushes (*Eros peripateticus*). These are   12
to constant crushes what charcoal sketches are to full-blown oil paintings—
perhaps more freely and unconsciously rendered (more purely artistic),

but for that less fully realized. They are the short, sweet biographies of urban fate. The parade of unknown lovelies: Samantha Flatbelly, Billy Bungus, High-heel Jane, Roundbottom, Button-Eyes, Pouty Doherty— urban seraphim!

In summer the art of the crush flourishes in this peripatetic form. Every- 13 one is outside. The streets are full. Office dwellers linger in the sunshine during their lunch breaks.

Strolling through the farmers' market in Union Square or drinking a sweet, 14 cinnamon-dusted latte in Soho, I am the happiest of men. Walking through the farmers' stands I harvest the ripe fruit of Manhattan with my eyes. Beautiful strangers approach, and I salute each one with a thousand beats of my palpitating heart. She of the short, short skirt. He of the tattered overalls. She of the jaunty stride. He with the doomed black eyes. I slurp my java, smile a cinnamon-crusted smile, and wonder what lies beyond those dark glasses reading *Figaro*.

*

RESPONDING TO THE WHOLE ESSAY

1. Parsi uses two main development strategies to define crush: definition and cause and effect. Identify each of these strategies in the essay and explain what each contributes to the definition of *crush*. [*Harbrace* 28e; *Hodges'* 32e]
2. What techniques does Parsi use to make paragraph 5 coherent? Is one technique used more frequently than another? If so, which one and why? [*Harbrace* 27b; *Hodges'* 31b]
3. What elements in "The Art of the Crush" suggest the rhetorical situation for this essay—audience, purpose, situation, occasion? Explain. Describe the rhetorical situation for this essay. Does the essay give enough information to determine all of these? Explain. [*Harbrace* 28a; *Hodges'* 32a]

ANALYZING THE ELEMENTS

Grammar

1. Paragraph 11 concludes with four fragments. Justify this usage. [*Harbrace* 2; *Hodges'* 2]
2. Comment upon the use of the passive voice in the final sentence of paragraph 2. Rewrite the sentence using active voice for all verbs. Which is better, active or passive? Why? [*Harbrace* 7; *Hodges'* 7]

Effective Sentences

1. What does Parsi gain by writing the second and third sentences of paragraph 13 as he does instead of "The streets are full because everyone is outside"? [*Harbrace* 12a; *Hodges'* 30a]

2. How does Parsi achieve emphasis in the second sentence of paragraph 12? Explain. [*Harbrace* 11; *Hodges'* 29]

Punctuation and Mechanics

1. Comment upon the use of dashes and parentheses in the second sentence of paragraph 12. How else might Parsi have punctuated this sentence? [*Harbrace* 21e and 21f; *Hodges'* 17e and 17f]
2. What advantage does Parsi gain by punctuating the second sentence of paragraph 3 with a semicolon? [*Harbrace* 18a; *Hodges'* 14a]

Diction

1. In the third sentence of paragraph 2, Parsi uses the word *poetess* and in the fifth sentence of paragraph 11, *waitresses*. Is this sexist usage? Why or why not? What do you make of Parsi's use of *waitstaff* in the first sentence of paragraph 6? [*Harbrace* 13c(2); *Hodges'* 19h]
2. What does the simile *like chicken hawks* (paragraph 2, sentence 3) accomplish? [*Harbrace* 14a(5); *Hodges'* 20a(4)]
3. What does Parsi accomplish by his allusion to Swinburne in paragraph 2? [*Harbrace* 14a(5); *Hodges'* 20a(4)]

BUILDING VOCABULARY

1. What are the Greek roots from which the word *phylogenetically* is borrowed? What do they mean?
2. Write a sentence using a word derived from one of the Greek roots identified in question 1.

SUGGESTIONS FOR WRITING

1. Write an essay analyzing a crush you have had and explaining the basis for the crush.
2. Write an essay in which you classify several kinds of friendships or other kinds of personal relationships.

What Is a Cowboy?

John R. Erickson

John R. Erickson (1943–) wrote "What Is a Cowboy?" in a barn in Beaver County, Oklahoma, in January, wearing gloves, a down vest, and a coat. In addition to battling the cold, Erickson fought daily with the barn mice over possession of his typewriter, which the mice found ideal to build nests in. The essay was published as the first chapter of Erickson's book *The Modern Cowboy* (1981), which grew out of Erickson's two years' experience working on an Oklahoma ranch, as did another book, *Panhandle Cowboy*. He is also author of *Through Time and the Valley* and other works of Western nonfiction, as well as a series of humorous novelettes about Hank the Cow Dog—spoofs of both detective fiction and old-fashioned Westerns. In "What Is a Cowboy?" Erickson shows how the real modern cowboy differs from the myth.

In 1978 and 1979 I was working as a cowboy on a ranch in Beaver County, Oklahoma. In the depths of January, I drove over to the next ranch and found my good friend and cowboy companion, Jake Parker. "Jake," I said, "we're about to starve out. We just can't make it on six hundred dollars a month. Inflation is killing us and I'm so danged tired of feeding cattle seven days a week that I could scream." Jake nodded.

In February I caught Jake as he was coming in from his feed run. "Jake," I said, "we're just barely getting by. If everyone stays healthy and the car doesn't break down, we'll make it. But if something goes wrong . . . I guess I'd better start looking around for another line of work."

Jake nodded. He understood.

In March I helped Jake do some cattle work. It was the first time we had been a-horseback since January. The day was warm and most of the snow had melted off the sandhills. Our horses felt good and so did we. "Parker," I said, "I'm looking forward to spring roundup season, aren't you?" He smiled and said, "You bet."

In April we were riding on a roundup crew, laughing and joking with the other cowboys, drinking in the spring air, working our horses, and playing with our ropes. And I said, "You know, Parker, we're damned lucky that somebody will pay us money for doing this." Jake laughed and said, "Yalp."

I have met the American cowboy on ranches in the Texas and Oklahoma Panhandles. I have ridden with him and worked beside him. I have eaten lunch with him on the ground and drunk water from his cup. I am tempted to describe him as I have seen him described in several books: "Merely folks, just a plain everyday bowlegged human." It is a marvelous description, and very quotable. However, the temptation to use it merely points out the degree to which, on the subject of cowboys, we have come to rely on books and observations of the past. The fact is—and I rather hate to admit this—that I have known only one bowlegged cowboy, and I think he was born that way. Legend tells us that cowboys are supposed to have legs warped by long days in the saddle, and maybe fifty years ago they did. Today they don't. We can begin our description of the modern cowboy with the observation that, at least on one point of anatomy, he ain't what he used to be.

The cowboy I know is a workingman. He is defined by his work, which   7
should not be confused with the term "job." Cowboy work is more than a job; it is a life-style and a medium of expression. Remove the cowboy from his working environment and you have someone else, someone who resembles a cowboy in outward appearance but who, to one degree or another, is an imposter. Standing on a street corner, the cowboy is just an ordinary human. But out in the pasture, when he's a-horseback and holds a rope in his hands, he assumes the qualities that have made him a legend.

The fact that the cowboy is defined by his work has made him a difficult   8
subject to study. To see him at his best, you almost have to work with him day after day, and to understand what he does in his work, you almost have to possess a fundamental knowledge of the skills of his profession. Perhaps the people who are in the best position to observe and discuss the working cowboy are the men who work with him every day—other cowboys. Unfortunately, most cowboys don't write, and most writers don't work on ranches.

The cowboy does not own property. Owners of ranchland go by various   9
titles, among them rancher, cattleman, and stockman. The rancher owns the land, manages the operation, and makes decisions about buying and selling. Of course you can find instances where the two roles overlap. Some ranchers work beside their cowboys, and some cowboys are permitted to make management decisions, and in small ranching operations family members function in both capacities. But as a general rule it is safe to say that ranchers and cowboys are not the same breed. The term *cowboy*, as I use it, means a workingman who has mastered the skills needed in working around cattle, while the term *rancher* implies ownership and management.

In the cow lot or on a roundup crew the social differences between rancher   10
and cowboy don't mean much, but elsewhere they are clearly defined. Ranchers are often prominent leaders in the community; cowboys are not. Ranchers often sit on governing boards of businesses, churches, and schools; cowboys do not. Ranchers are frequently the subject of articles in livestock journals, while the cowboys are rarely mentioned. The rancher and his wife may belong to the country club, but the cowboy and his wife won't. The rancher has his circle of friends, the cowboy has his, and they do not often overlap.

There is one difference between them that goes right to the heart of the   11
matter: the rancher can take the day off or go into town whenever he wishes, but the cowboy can't. The cowboy's life is tied to the rhythms and patterns

of animals: a cow that must be milked twice a day, chickens that must be turned out in the morning and shut up at night, horses that must be fed and watered, pregnant heifers that must be watched, and, in winter, cows that must be fed seven days a week. The rancher and the cowboy may dress alike, talk alike, and even think alike, but at six o'clock in the evening, one goes down to the milking barn while the other attends a meeting in town.

The cowboy is a workingman, yet he has little in common with the ur-   12
ban blue-collar worker. In the first place, as we have already observed, cow-
boy work is not just a job, with established work days, certain hours, and guaranteed holidays. Since he lives where he works, and since he deals with animals instead of machines, the cowboy is never really off work. He is on call 24 hours a day, 7 days a week, 365 days a year. The work is not always hard, but as a friend once observed to me, "It's damned sure steady." A calv-
ing heifer, a prairie fire, a sick horse may have him up at any hour of the day or night, and in this business there is no such thing as time-and-a-half for overtime.

In the second place, cowboys, unlike urban blue-collar workers, do not   13
belong to a union, and they probably never will. The cowboy life attracts a special type of individual, one who can shift for himself and endure isolation, and one who thrives on physical hardship, a certain amount of danger, and low wages. These are not the qualities of a joiner, but of a loner. You might even go so far as to say that there is little bit of outlaw in most of them—
not that they are dishonest or deceitful, but rather that they are incorrigible like a spirited horse that is never quite broke and gentle, even though he may take the bit and saddle. Some cowboys stay in the profession simply because they don't fit anywhere else. They tried other jobs and couldn't adapt, or they went into business for themselves and failed. They returned to cowboying because it was in their bones and blood.

This stubborn, independent quality of the cowboy has fascinated the   14
American public and has contributed to his status as a myth and a legend. We like to think of ourselves as a free and independent people, ready at any moment to tell the boss, the mayor, or the president himself to go straight to hell. Of course this is more a dream than a reality. Most of us are inden-
tured to mortgage payments and car payments and live in terror of an IRS audit. Perhaps the cowboy, riding his horse across an endless prairie, has be-
come a symbol of what we used to be—or at least what we *think* we used to be—and of what we would be if we could. He doesn't have to punch a time clock, drive through snarls of traffic every morning and afternoon, shave or wear a tie to work, or participate in hollow rituals in order to gain ad-
vancement. When he gets tired of the scenery, or if the boss crowds him too close, he packs his few possessions in a pickup and horse trailer and moves on to another ranch. In the American cowboy we find qualities we deeply admire—simplicity, independence, physical strength, courage, peace of mind, and self-respect—but which, to one degree or another, we have surrendered in order to gain something else. These qualities have made the cowboy the

most powerful mythical character in our folklore, and one which reaches to the very core of our identity as a people.

The typical cowboy, if we may speak of such an animal, does not carry   15
a pistol, strum a guitar, or burst into song at the end of the day. He has never rescued a maiden in distress or cleaned the outlaws out of a saloon. He can ride a bucking horse, but he can also get piled. He can rope a calf in the pasture, but he can also burn three loops before he makes the catch. In his working environment, he is dressed in blue jeans, a long-sleeved shirt, boots, western hat, and a vest. He looks good in these clothes, like an animal in its skin. In his work he moves with ease and grace, and sitting astride his horse he exudes confidence and authority. We are tempted to say that he is handsome, even though he might lack the physical endowments that we usually associate with that term.

But take him off his horse, throw him into a bathtub, scrub him down,   16
put him in a set of "good" clothes, and send him to town, and we will meet an entirely different man. All at once he becomes graceless and awkward. He isn't wearing his work hat and we see that he is getting bald, or if he has a good head of hair, it looks as though he has plastered it with lard and run a rake through it. His eyes, which outside are naturally set into a squint, seem puffy in the fluorescent light, and they do not sparkle. His "good" clothes are appalling, and we can hardly keep from laughing at him.

The mythology and legend of the Cowboy begin in this humble human   17
vessel. But the working cowboy is neither a myth nor a legend. He is an ordinary mortal. If we stopped at this point, we would have performed the ritual known as debunking, wherein a notable figure is taken like a buck deer, strung up, skinned and gutted, and held up naked for all to see. But I'm not setting out to debunk the cowboy. If he sometimes falls short of our expectations, he will surpass them when we see him at his best. And he is at his best when he is at his work. Ultimately, the cowboy *is* what he *does*.

So what is a cowboy? Is he a heroic figure or just a common laborer? It's   18
hard to say. I've seen both sides, and I think it would be a mistake to place too much emphasis on one side or the other. If we view him only as a symbol and a mythical figure, then we lose contact with his humanness and fall into the kind of sentimentality that allows some observers to ignore the poverty, the loneliness, the exploitation of cowboys, and to gloss over the darker side of the cattle industry with little homilies about the "honor" of being a cowboy. But neither do we want to strip him down to enzymes and electrons or to present him as just another human fop doomed to mediocrity and failure, for this view would deny that he can rise above himself through displays of skill, strength, and courage. And that would be false.

If the cowboy is a hero, then we will want to know the price he pays for   19
this honor. If he is a common man, then we will want to know why he has fascinated our people for a hundred years. For the moment let us content ourselves with this definition: The cowboy is a common laborer with heroic tendencies and a sense of humor.

✴

RESPONDING TO THE WHOLE ESSAY

1. Is Erickson's purpose mainly to inform the reader about cowboy life, to express his own feelings about the cowboy, or to persuade the reader to adopt a more realistic view? To what extent are all three purposes present? [*Harbrace* 28a; *Hodges'* 32a]
2. Describe the audience Erickson appears to have had in mind. Use evidence from the essay to support your assumptions about Erickson's intended audience. [*Harbrace* 28a; *Hodges'* 32a]
3. "What Is a Cowboy?" can be viewed as an expansion of the classic three-part formal definition, which names the thing to be defined, puts it into a class, and then differentiates it from the rest of the class. Analyze the essay, showing where each kind of information appears.
4. What rhetorical purpose is served by beginning with a series of examples illustrating the lifestyle of the cowboy? Is this an effective introduction to a definition of a cowboy? Why or why not? [*Harbrace* 28f(1); *Hodges'* 32f(1)]
5. Extended definitions often make use of several strategies of development: examples, narration, comparison, description, classification, and so forth. How many different development strategies can you find at work in "What Is a Cowboy"? [*Harbrace* 27d and 28c(1); *Hodges'* 31d and 32c(1)]
6. Erickson offers what might be called a negative definition of *cowboy* in paragraph 6. Is the technique effective? Why or why not?
7. Comment on how coherence is achieved in paragraph 10. [*Harbrace* 27b; *Hodges'* 31b]

ANALYZING THE ELEMENTS

Grammar

1. In the third sentence of paragraph 6, why does Erickson use *drunk* rather than *drank*? [*Harbrace* 7b; *Hodges'* 7a]
2. The second sentence of paragraph 11 contains a passive construction. Try rewriting this sentence in the active voice. What are the difficulties? Which sentence is more effective? Why? [*Harbrace* 7c; *Hodges'* 7c]

Effective Sentences

1. Compare the second sentence and the last sentence of paragraph 8. In what way are the sentences alike? In what way do the two sentences differ? What makes each of them effective? [*Harbrace* 10a and 10b; *Hodges'* 26a and 26b]
2. Explain how coordination and subordination contribute to the effectiveness of the first sentence in paragraph 11. [*Harbrace* 9; *Hodges'* 24]
3. To what does *one* in the last sentence of paragraph 14 refer? Try reading the sentence without the *and* before *one*. How does the meaning change?

Punctuation and Mechanics

1. Explain the use of the dash in the fourth sentence of paragraph 13. Is that use of the dash different from the way the dash is used in paragraph 6? Explain. What

other kind of punctuation might be used in place of these dashes? Which would be more effective? Why? [*Harbrace* 21e; *Hodges'* 17e]

2. Why is *Cowboy* capitalized in the first sentence of paragraph 17? Does it need to be? Why or why not? [*Harbrace* 23a; *Hodges'* 9a]

Diction

1. In the final sentence of paragraph 6, Erickson writes, "he ain't what he used to be." Does Erickson's language throughout the rest of the essay indicate that this use of *ain't* is the result of ignorance, or does he have a rhetorical purpose for its use? Explain. [*Harbrace* 13 and 28a; *Hodges'* 19 and 32a]
2. Explain why *blue-collar* in the first sentence of paragraph 12 and *long-sleeved* in the fifth sentence of paragraph 15 are hyphenated. [*Harbrace* 22f; *Hodges'* 18f]
3. Erickson uses cowboy jargon in paragraph 15. Explain what *piled, burn,* and *catch* mean as he uses them and why their use is justifiable. [*Harbrace* 13c(1); *Hodges'* 19g]
4. Explain Erickson's figurative definition of debunking in paragraph 17. Why is it effective here? [*Harbrace* 14a(5); *Hodges'* 20a(4)]

BUILDING VOCABULARY

1. In a sentence or two, write down a plausible origin for the word *cowboy*. Take into consideration both parts of the word. What do you make of the use of *boy*?
2. What is the origin of the word *fop* and what does it mean? Of *job*?

SUGGESTIONS FOR WRITING

1. Write an essay in which you define the practitioner of an occupation that you think has been overvalued, undervalued, or misunderstood (for example, physician, nurse, teacher, minister, salesperson, farmer, waiter, taxi driver, soldier, flight attendant, housekeeper).
2. Write an essay in which you use examples to define the popular view of a cowboy, senator, astronaut, police officer, movie star, sports hero, or other "larger than life" figure.

The Good, The Bad, & The Ugly:
Clint Eastwood as Romantic Hero
Kathleen Murphy

Formerly head of a cinema studies program at the University of Washington, film critic Kathleen Murphy is writer-in-residence at the Film Society of Lincoln Center. Her work as a film critic has been collected in several book-length studies and regularly appears in *Film Comment,* to which she is a contributing editor, as well as in various periodicals. The essay which follows was written upon the occasion of Eastwood's being honored by the Film Society of Lincoln Center. In it, Murphy attempts to define what a romantic hero is by giving examples of the various kinds of such heroes played by veteran actor/director/writer Clint Eastwood during his long and successful career.

Topped by an assertive crest of tawny hair, a lanky cowboy edges his way   1
to the head of the chow-line for the lion's share of grub. It's 1959, the first
episode of "Rawhide," a TV series debuting in a season that favors Westerns,
and the hungry young man is, of course, Clint Eastwood as Rowdy Yates,
trail boss Gil Favor's sidekick. "Rawhide" would run for seven seasons, but
before its demise the brash, fresh-faced Rowdy had already metamorphosed
into a Man with No Name, the burnt-out hardcase who shot a trilogy of Ser-
gio Leone's famously bloody Westerns into the money. And by 1968, little
more than a decade into his accidental acting career, Clint Eastwood had
formed Malpaso, his own production company, cannily taking early control
of his filmmaking destiny.

From the first, Eastwood demonstrated a remarkable shrewdness, a tal-   2
ent for the kind of focused observation that has translated into a consistently
enlarging vision of a potent off- and on-screen persona. At 13, he taught himself to write music and play the piano; Eastwood the man clearly kept an eye
out for anything—narrative motif, directorial style, genre convention, character components—that might be taken in and reconceived to expedite his ambitious ascent up the Hollywood foodchain. He saw the vein that worked for
him as a performer, and mined it, sculpting variations for the better part of
four decades. He's aimed that same control and cinematic intelligence at the
business of directing. Eastwood's craft and art have always derived from informed, instinctive taste, most notably in the fabrication of an idiosyncratic,
strangely durable romantic hero—a lover whose masks have been that of artist,
angel, demon, death, holy fool, and even, on occasion, endearing dolt.

That first "Rawhide" episode, "Incident of the Tumbleweed Wagon," fea- 3
tured a paradigmatic Fifties sexpot, pouting, curvaceous Terry Moore, wearing heels, low-cut blouse, and manacles for her transport by prison wagon
through the wilderness. Dallas has exacted revenge—"an eye for an eye"—on
a townful of people who hanged her innocent, half-blind father: "There were
a lot of empty chairs at the dinnertable before I was through . . . ." At first
glimpse of this cactus Antigone, Rowdy Yates whistles wholehearted appreciation, prompting a caveat from Favor: "You haven't seen a woman in trouble yet that you haven't fallen for." Redemption for past-haunted Dallas is
death, taking a bullet meant for the good guys. One wonders if somewhere
in the babydoll vulgarity of Moore's expressions of vengeance lies recombinant DNA for Eastwood's innocent man hanged for rustling, resurrected for
revenge, and mirrored by Inger Stevens's raped and widowed huntress in *Hang
'Em High* (Ted Post, '68). Or for Evelyn Draper (Jessica Walter), Clint's mur-
derously outraged castoff in *Play Misty for Me* (Eastwood, '71). Or for the
coven of betrayed bacchantes in *The Beguiled* (Don Siegel, '74). Or even for
the actor's first full-fledged revenant, carrier of hellish retribution to a whole
guilty town in *High Plains Drifter* (CE, '73). Or Sondra Locke's violated Fury,
Harry's Dirty Harriet, in *Sudden Impact* (CE, '83).

In seminal collaboration with Leone, Eastwood forged a masculine pres- 4
ence predicated on the strictest conservation of energy and emotion, a con-
traction of character so severe that its *primum mobile* must remain mystery. As
with Robert Mitchum, that deep reserve is a come-on, provoking the desire—
in men and women—to agitate, to assault the still, unmoved flesh. Disengaged
and deracinated, he is given to intense watchfulness from some inner coign of
vantage—hell, grave, or madness. Confronted, his head turns slowly, eyes narrowing into scorched-earth fury, as steady and deadly as a swiveling gun tur-
ret. The thin lower lip curls upward to sign dismay or disgust, like a cat gri-
macing at a bad smell.* Fine lines already ray out from the corners of the early
Eastwood's fierce eyes, his forehead is vertically furrowed and veined, and the
very shock of his hair seems to spring thickly up along those same rising vec-
tors. It's as though whatever imploded the soul of the Man with No Name
scarred permanent blastlines into the desiccated landscape of his face.

His gait is that of a ghost or a predator, his poncho'd torso remaining 5
strangely still, propelled ahead by the long legs, as though swimming upright
in slowmotion. Paradoxically, the hands of the remorseless gunfighter are those
of a musician or a painter: elegant, long-fingered, with graceful wrists. In these
formative stages of the Eastwood persona, his often nearly whispered vocal
tones seem too pressured for ordinary speech. The silky, then increasingly
abrasive sibilance of his drawl, like sand or gravel shifting in water, works
best for epigrams, cryptic ripostes, up-close seduction.

---

*Twenty-eight years later, in Wolfgang Petersen's *In the Line of Fire*, Eastwood plays at being Bogart, whose teeth-baring, berserker rages may have inspired his "spaghetti Western" variation. Sharing his piano bench with Rene Russo, he faces down his soon-to-be-lover by kidding
his own style: "Sometimes a glare is as good as a gun."

In Leone's *A Fistful of Dollars* ('64), Eastwood is enigma but not yet a 6
dead man walking: he concentrates and reflects the town's amorality, as well
as incarnating the unspoken prayer of Marisol (Marianne Koch), the faithful
wife and mother held prisoner by the worst of a wolfish lot (Gian Maria
Volonté). Riding down *Fistful's* main drag on his mule, this cold Christ come
to harrow hell pauses to pass a dim smile on to the woman jailed for her de-
sirability. A past crucifixion is hinted: when he takes the time to rescue
Marisol, he recalls that "I knew someone like you once . . . there was no one
to help her."

Similarly, there is no one to help the young sheriff (Eastwood) whipped 7
to death in *High Plains Drifter,* a Grand Guignol Golgotha witnessed by two
very different "Marys." When the lawman's unquiet shade returns to paint
the town red, he uses his allure as demon lover to strip each woman down to
her true soul, damning the pretty, young creature of vicious appetite (Mari-
ana Hill) and saving the earthy, older Verna Bloom. Before disappearing into
a horizon of shimmering heat waves, he stops to share that complicit smile—
born of more than carnal knowledge—with Bloom, the only distaff survivor
of his retribution. Later, in *Pale Rider* (CE, '85), Eastwood's supernatural
Shane materializes in his funereal *Drifter* frock coat to protect both virgin and
a last Western paradise from rape, to renew and confirm Carrie Snodgress's
abandoned womanhood as well as miner Michael Moriarty's uncertain mas-
culinity.

In *Coogan's Bluff* ('68) and *The Beguiled,* Eastwood took tutelage under 8
director Don Siegel, his American film-father. Interestingly, in both films, The
Man with No Name's existential arrogance shades into specific sexual inso-
lence, erotic allure used as lethally as a gun. Arizona stud Coogan, abroad in
the Big Apple, seduces with too-practiced ease a social worker (Susan Clark)
committed to a program of "self-regeneration" for bad girls. Gentling her
body as he might a skittish horse, whispering her into sensual trance, Coogan
doesn't miss a beat when, having rifled her files of the information he's after,
he walks out—without a word—on his unsuspecting prey. Scarcely hours later,
he deliberately beds down a sociopathic hippie to con her into giving up a
killer's whereabouts. It's probable that Siegel and Eastwood aren't consciously
exposing manipulative machismo as a species of whoring. Still, when a slutty
hotel-tart, way past her prime, tries to run an obvious scam on Coogan, his
response is excessively ugly: there's a cruel, cracked mirror here, but the rest
of *Coogan's Bluff* doesn't really support such reflections.

No question, though, that *The Beguiled,* the third film by Siegel and East- 9
wood, does—with a vengeance. In this Grimm fairy tale, Corporal John
McBurney is a wounded Yankee deserter who stumbles on to a Southern seminary housing a tribe of girls and women as perversely neurasthenic as any
out of Tennessee Williams's imagining. McBurney's first act is to passionately
soul-kiss 12-year-old Amy (Pamelyn Ferdin), diverting her attention from an
approaching Confederate column. An adept sexual performer, he plays to each
seminarian's script: Geraldine Page's bisexual headmistress, seething with hot

memories of incestuous lovemaking with her brother; Elizabeth Hartman's repressed virgin, man-shy courtesy of a promiscuous father; Jo Ann Harris's self-serving Lolita; and little Amy's budding bad seed. "I wonder," he purrs into spinster Hartman's ear, "if you don't think of yourself as a Sleeping Beauty in a castle waiting for a handsome prince to free you with a kiss."

Could be a 19th century Coogan, working his main chance, but *Beguiled* has more in common with *Boxing Helena*, genders reversed. The dominant POV keeps shifting between McBurney and his avid auditors. When the young soldier is first brought in, unconscious, Page gazes hungrily down at the handsome head at her breast, savoring eyelashes on cheek, fine mouth relaxed in almost feminine curves, unruly blonde mane. It's the kind of titillating shot that in most movies (especially soft-porn and splatter flicks) would frame the face of a beautiful sleeping woman, helpless and vulnerable to rape.   10

Later, much recovered, McBurney leans back smiling, smug in his sexual power, to indulge in a fantasy that stars him as each woman's lover. This rather conventional casting segues into Page's more outré dream: she, McBurney, and Hartman in a sexual romp, climaxing with his naked body sprawled across her lap in perfect reflection of the painting of a Pietà that hangs beside her bed.   11

Though he's the source of reawakened fertility (in women and chickens), the ravaged McBurney ends up a symbolically castrated gigolo, "planted"— in parts—by *The Beguiled's* convent of twisted sisters. Not until *The Rookie* (CE, '90) will such physical violation by a woman be visited on an Eastwood hero. Amazonian Sonia Braga, bad guy Raul Julia's second in command, cuts and caresses the handcuffed Eastwood's bared flesh with a razor blade; moving down toward his groin: "I hate anything useless," she growls. "Something is no good to me, I cut it off and throw it away." In this truly disturbing sequence, echoed many times over in a bank of video monitors, the sadistic Braga mounts and rides the unblinking Eastwood to climax. It's as though he's trying the experience on for size—playing the role from which he's rescued so many virgins and hookers in his films (*Two Mules for Sister Sara, The Outlaw Josey Wales, The Gauntlet, Sudden Impact, Tightrope, Pale Rider, Bronco Billy*). Braga is unfettered succubus, and her genealogy leads straight back to nightmare Evelyn Draper in *Play Misty for Me*, the film that followed hard upon *The Beguiled*, and Eastwood's directorial debut.   12

As The Man with No Name seemed a fatal projection of his enemies' own amorality, so too is Evelyn Draper a Dantean retribution for the casual promiscuity practiced by Eastwood's Carmel disc jockey. She comes out of nowhere, her only I.D. "Annabel Lee," a Poe poem about two lovers so attached not even death can separate them. Like Eastwood's gunfighter revenant in *High Plains Drifter*, this unforgiving one-night stand lives to send those who sinned against her to hell. Despite Eastwood's soft-focus vision of Carmel's paradisiacal landscape through which he and the blonde artist who settles him down (Donna Mills) walk, swim, and make love, it's Walter's dark, unrelenting Lilith who steals the show until her directorial doppelgänger rubs her out.   13

There's something of unregenerate Evelyn abroad in *Tightrope* (Richard   14
Tuggle, '84), a film in which Eastwood's bitterly divorced cop, father of two
little girls (the older played by his own daughter Alison), takes a dangerous
dive into the belly of the sexual beast. Eastwood acts out his authentic, am-
biguous rage at the woman who abandoned him, handcuffing hookers in kinky,
sado-masochistic psychodramas. Shadowed, even directed, by a clown-masked
serial killer–rapist, the cop's dangerous play brings his darkside home, into
his girls' lives—despite the framed unicorn that guards their chaste beds. (In
Sudden Impact, shot just the year before *Tightrope*, the trauma caused by brutal sexual assault in her youth brings a woman round to an antique carousel,
on which she is stalked by her old tormentors. The most psychotic of the
rapists is ultimately impaled on the horn of a maddened unicorn.)

Tightrope is punctuated by genuinely disquieting moments, suggestive of   15
deeper sexual waters than are usually plumbed in the traditional cop story.
Eastwood lounges in a doorway, eyeing Geneviève Bujold—a woman who sees
through his conflicted psyche—as she demonstrates to a class how to disable
a rapist. When she kicks the dummy in the crotch, its eyes light up, its tongue
pops out, and tennis balls shoot across the gym straight at her male audience
of one. It's grotesque slapstick, and draws real blood from wounded manhood. Later, Eastwood's daughter finds her dead-drunk dad sprawled face-
down on the livingroom couch, a wedding photograph clutched in his hand.
Her delicate features very grave, the prepubescent child climbs aboard her father, warming with her tomgirl body the man her mother has rejected.

Not much later, the cop's crazed-clown alter ego deposits this same child,   16
bound and gagged, in her father's bed, and her violation there is barely
thwarted. In the aftermath of her rescue, Eastwood explodes in purgative rage,
tearing up the offending bed and bellowing "You mother . . . !" at his own—
possessed—reflection. By film's end, the sexually shattered cop's reformation
is signaled when he flings away a severed arm, all that remains of the creature that acted out what Eastwood only dreamed of.

Sudden Impact introduced Dirty Harry Callahan to his vigilante coun-   17
terpart (Sondra Locke), a woman taking revenge on the thugs who raped her
and her younger sister years ago. As director and star, Eastwood can be remarkably generous with actresses in his films, and here he mostly steps back
to give the steely Locke, her hairstyle verging on Veronica Lake, room to play
out her version of *The Bride Wore Black*. What's of particular interest in *Sudden Impact* is its mating of illness and creativity—the obsessed Locke paints
anguished self-portraits when she's not aiming crotch-shots at the men who
fractured her own innocence and her fragile sister's sanity. During the Eighties, in *Bronco Billy* ('80), *Honky Tonk Man* ('82), *Sudden Impact*, TV's
"Vanessa in the Garden" ('85), and *Bird* ('88), director Eastwood signposted
intriguing intersections between assault on the mind or body and the generation of some form of art, between muses and mirrored selves, between mostly
male artists or performers and their enabling lovers.

Eastwood directed "Vanessa in the Garden" for Steven Spielberg's short-   18
lived TV series *Amazing Stories*. Written by Spielberg and featuring Harvey
Keitel as a 19th century impressionist, Sondra Locke as his wife, and Beau
Bridges as agent and family friend, this half-hour effort suffers from woeful
miscasting and awkward performances by the two male leads. But at the heart
of its oddly hallucinatory narrative lies a striking evocation of the power of
the imagination and the nature of the creative process.

Wife, subject, and muse, Vanessa is truly the artist's "godsend," an Eve   19
who composes his real and painted gardens and makes them fruitful. After
her accidental death, Keitel burns every canvas that bears her likeness—with
the inadvertent exception of the garden portrait—and sinks into drunken despair. One morning he wakes to a painting emptied of its central figure, and
Vanessa's sweet humming outside his window. In a stunning elision, the camera moves rightward from the abandoned canvas to catch Keitel's reflection
in a mirror; then tracks into the mirror to frame—through window panes—
the white-clad woman posed among her flowers; then, using the edge of the
actual painting as a wipe, drives leftward to confirm the scene in reality; returns to the artist's reflection, followed by a reprise of the ghost in the garden. When Keitel plunges outdoors, the vision dissolves away. (In *Sudden
Impact*, made just two years before, Locke played the despairing artist—as
well as murderess—firing her gun into a glass that mirrors her own face and
one of the grotesque self-portraits she has painted.)

It's irrelevant whether Keitel has gone mad, conjured his very own "pale   20
rider," or somehow found a way back to the spiritual source of his creativity: that audacious camera sequence precisely diagrams a syntax of the imagination at work. "It cannot be unless you create it," Vanessa whispers, and
through the art of making pictures, Keitel resurrects his wife and all their past
and future times. That phrase—"making pictures"—is Robert Kincaid's from
The Bridges of Madison County ('95), Eastwood's celebration of love as an
expression of passionate creativity. Kincaid explicitly identifies the aesthetic
impulse to make pictures with "making his way" to Francesca (Meryl Streep),
and takes into exile the faith that they "are hardly two separate people now."
Through the looking-glass of "Vanessa in the Garden," Francesca and her
godsend can be seen creating a durable illusion to sustain them for the rest
of their separated lives.

At the beginning of *Bronco Billy*, Eastwood's camera locates a circus big-   21
top in the middle of heartland fields, and time-dissolving ever deeper into
evening, closes slowly in on the set where a New Jersey shoe salesman directs
a sweetly communal fantasy of an heroic Wild West. The brightly lighted island inside the tent where Billy and his crew present their *tableaux vivants*
often seems to float in an ocean of darkness—indeed, at film's end, Billy and
his "family" of costumed misfits disappear into that darkness. As long as "or-
phaned" heiress-on-the-run Antoinette Lilly (Sondra Locke) insists on poking
holes in Billy's creation, she's the author of "bad luck" that literally brings

down the show. This gentle screwball comedy is a remarkably self-aware take on Eastwood's career, and the art of the Western: even the director's reputed need and ability to control every aspect of a shoot may be referenced in Billy's hot-tempered insistence on being "head ramrod." Eastwood's contemporary "Western" shapes up as a much lighter, self-reflexive version of *The Outlaw Josey Wales* (CE, '76): both Billy and Josey lose their wives under traumatic conditions, turning outlaw as a result; collect a ragtag family of mixed race, gender, and age; save from rape a girl (Sondra Locke, in both cases) who redeems the outsider—or is herself redeemed—through love and enlistment in the hero's cause; and find a home in unexpected "paradise," Billy's American Flag circus tent and Josey's democratic ranch.

In the richly imagined *Bird*, a well-meaning psychiatrist recommends shock therapy for lifetime drug-addict Charlie Parker (Forest Whitaker), who, recently confronted by his sorry soul in a bathroom mirror, has downed a bottle of iodine. When Chan (Diane Venora), the jazzman's wife and best audience, expresses concern about the effect of ECT on Bird's creativity, the doctor suggests that she may have to choose either husband or musician. Venora's red-hot Chan lays it on the line: "Husband *and* musician—they do not separate!" As though her words called up a home-movie memory, the space behind camera-facing Chan slowly blacks out. In that darkness materializes a "street of dreams," a neon-lit big-city strip of pulsing jazz joints down which a young, vibrant woman strides on her way to fall for Bird and his music. Chan's remembrance of a (flawed) paradise lost is as potent and seductive as Bronco Billy's Wild West bigtop, as Red Stovall's Grand Ole Opry, the "heart's desire" of a country singer in *Honky Tonk Man,* and yes, even Vanessa in her quiet garden.

That garden has turned nearly Fordian grave in *Unforgiven,* Eastwood's masterpiece. William Munny's lost wife, marrying beneath her, reformed a devil of a man. In turn, after Claudia Feathers dies of smallpox, Munny makes her his guardian angel, an internalized ethic. Her chaste and aging knight— "I don't miss it much"—is drawn into a rather lowdown quest, inspired more by money than a lady's honor. But William Munny rises from pigshit to apotheosis when he lays his ghostly superego long enough to exact terrible revenge on men for whom slashing a woman's face or whipping a good man to death count less than civic peace and prosperity. (Shades of guilty Lago in *High Plains Drifter.*)

Wracked by fever-chills and a brutal beating by Sheriff Daggett (Gene Hackman), Munny passes through the little death that often precedes the transformation of an Eastwood hero into a killing-machine. That transformation is triggered by a spiritual dissolve of three visages into one: his hallucinated vision of Claudia, her face eaten by worms; the white-blonde whore (Anna Thomson), her face crisscrossed by scars; and his own, its marred flesh skinned back to show a true death's head. "I thought you was an angel," says Munny to the woman who set this story in motion. Then: "I must look kinda like you."

It's not that William Munny reverts to his former drunken, demonic state, 25 during which he annihilated "everything that walked or crawled." Wearing the "colors" of both Claudia Feathers, "a comely young woman . . . not without prospects," and Delilah Fitzgerald, "damaged property," he becomes a force for something like divine retribution. Drifter, pale rider, barest bones of Bronco Billy's fairy tale, William Munny reshapes the ignominious stuff of actuality (Little Bill's eyewitness account of how English Bob came to kill Two-Gun Corky Corcoran) and cheap fiction (dime-novelist Beauchamp's Duke of Death, avenger of a woman's slighting) into purely clarifying myth. Afterwards, Claudia Feathers's faithful husband disappears into vague, mundane history: "There was nothing on [her grave] marker to explain why [she] had married William Munny. . . . "

Reportedly, Eastwood planned early on to make a "romance" for his fifti- 26 eth film. *The Bridges of Madison County* stands as a love story for adults, unreeling in brave slowness (given contemporary popcult pulse rates). As in *Bird,* his lovers talk their way toward touching, exploring each other—mostly during and after meals at a kitchen table—through easy, sometimes heated conversational rhythms. A convention of many previous Eastwood films is the hero's uncanny ability to establish immediate, wordless rapport with women of all ages; here and in 1993's *In the Line of Fire,* he reveals a truly irresistible gift for gab and self-revelation. The intensely focused, yet mercilessly impersonal, attention with which he has always seared his enemies becomes, in *Bridges,* generous, erotic apprehension of Otherness. Always unusually partial to less-than-conventional beauty, more idiosyncratic, authentically lived-in faces—Jessica Walter, *Breezy's* Kay Lenz, Verna Bloom, Sondra Locke, Alexa Kenin (*Honky Tonk Man*), Carrie Snodgress, Diane Venora, Rene Russo—*Bridges'* director virtually celebrates the seasoned character and flesh of Meryl Street's earthy Francesca.

In *The Bridges of Madison County,* Eastwood once more plays a sexual 27 savior of sorts, but through some alchemy of imagination and style, transubstantiates a four-day love affair between an Iowa farmwife and a footloose photographer, played by two stars beyond their physical prime, into the kind of newness we yearn to confer on sexual—and emotional—experience, if only for the space of a movie. As director and actor, Eastwood has rarely rested on his laurels, has always pushed toward new ground: when he turns his haggard visage to the camera in his last scene in *Bridges,* his hair lankly plastered down by pouring rain, his face is as open in its naked age and pain as any seen in the cinema. It's a courageous exposure, an opening of the soul, something few could have visualized when he was The Man with No Name. But this late divestiture of the mystery he took to the bank for so long, of any mask and armor, has been earned by four decades of accumulating assurance and self-knowledge as director, star, and man. They do not separate in this shootist for all seasons.

✳

RESPONDING TO THE WHOLE ESSAY

1. In an allusion to the title of Eastwood's early hit, the title of Murphy's essay suggests that some of Eastwood's romantic heroes are good, some are bad, and some are ugly. Identify which of Eastwood's heroes fit each of these categories and explain the contribution of each to Murphy's definition of "romantic hero."
2. What technique does Murphy use to catch the reader's attention in her introductory paragraph? Why does this technique work? [*Harbrace* 28f(1); *Hodges'* 32f(1)]
3. What kinds of assumptions does Murphy appear to have made about the background, interests, and needs of her intended audience? Point to evidence in the essay. [*Harbrace* 28a; *Hodges'* 32a]
4. What is the purpose of Murphy's essay? Does she appear to be primarily concerned with exploring her own perceptions about her subject, with exploring the subject itself, or with attempting to sway the reader to a particular point of view or course of action? Can you discern several purposes? [*Harbrace* 28a; *Hodges'* 32a].
5. Murphy employs a number of different development strategies in this essay. Find and discuss examples of each [*Harbrace* 28c(1) and 28d; *Hodges'* 32c(1) and 32d]
6. What transitional devices does Murphy use to make paragraph 21 coherent? Which device is most frequently used? [*Harbrace* 27b; *Hodges'* 31b]

ANALYZING THE ELEMENTS

Grammar

1. Explain the use of "erotic allure used as lethally as a gun" in the second sentence of paragraph 8. [*Harbrace* 1d(1); *Hodges'* 1d(1)]
2. Determine the function of each clause in the final sentence of paragraph 8. Rewrite the sentence as two separate sentences. Which is better, the sentence as Murphy wrote it or the revised sentence? Why? [*Harbrace* 1e; *Hodges'* 1e]
3. The first sentences of both paragraph 9 and paragraph 10 are elliptical; what is understood? Should either sentence have been rewritten? Why or why not? [*Harbrace* 2; *Hodges'* 2]
4. Explain what completes the comparison in the first sentence of paragraph 15. [*Harbrace* 4c]

Effective Sentences

1. Comment on whether the passive voice used in the last sentence of paragraph 6 does or does not contribute to the effectiveness of the sentence. [*Harbrace* 11d; *Hodges'* 29d]
2. Explain the advantages Murphy gains from repetition in the last sentence of paragraph 17. [*Harbrace* 11e; *Hodges'* 29e]

3. What makes each of the following sentences effective: sentence 4 in paragraph 19, sentence 6 in paragraph 22, the final sentence of paragraph 26, and the second sentence of paragraph 27. [*Harbrace* 10a, 11g, and 12a; *Hodges'* 26a, 29g, and 30a]

Punctuation and Mechanics

1. What reason may Murphy have had for capitalizing *Fury* in the last sentence of paragraph 3? [*Harbrace* 23a; *Hodges'* 9a]
2. Murphy uses two acronyms without giving the full form first: *POV* in sentence 2 of paragraph 10 and *I.D.* in sentence 2 of paragraph 13. What does each of these stand for? What reason can you think of for not first giving the full form? [*Harbrace* 25e; *Hodges'* 11e]
3. Explain the use of semicolons in sentence 4 of paragraph 19. [*Harbrace* 18a and 18b; *Hodges'* 14a and 14b]
4. What do the brackets in the last sentence of paragraph 25 indicate? [*Harbrace* 21g; *Hodges'* 17g]
5. Explain the use of commas in the next-to-last sentence in paragraph 27. [*Harbrace* 17c; *Hodges'* 12c]

Diction

1. What is meant by the following phrases borrowed from other languages: *primum mobile* (paragraph 4), *tableaux vivants* (paragraph 21)? [*Harbrace* 13a; *Hodges'* 19a]
2. Write two sentences, one using *predicate* (paragraph 4) as a verb, the other using it as a noun. [*Harbrace* 14a; *Hodges'* 20a]
3. Murphy uses a rich vocabulary peppered with words not commonly encountered. Look up the following terms and find a synonym for each: *caveat* (paragraph 3), *revenant* (paragraph 3), *seminal* (paragraph 4), *coign* (paragraph 4), *tutelage* (paragraph 8), *elision* (paragraph 19). [*Harbrace* 14c; *Hodges'* 20c]
4. Explain the following allusions: *Grand Guignol* and *Golgotha* (paragraph 7), *Grimm* and *Tennessee Williams* (paragraph 9), *Pietà* (paragraph 11). [*Harbrace* 14a(5); *Hodges'* 20a(4)]
5. *Flick* appears in the last sentence of paragraph 10. Check the current edition of a good desk dictionary to determine whether this word is slang or has come into common usage. [*Harbrace* 13b(2); *Hodges'* 19c]

BUILDING VOCABULARY

1. The following words have been borrowed from other languages. Look up each word in an unabridged dictionary and state its language of origin and its meaning: *segue* and *outré* (paragraph 11), and *doppelgänger* (paragraph 13).
2. Look up *deracinate* and *desiccate* in a good desk dictionary. What are the roots of each word? What does each root mean? What does the prefix *de-* mean?

SUGGESTIONS FOR WRITING

1. You are a reporter for a small cable company magazine that features commentary on actors starring in films that will be shown in the coming week. Do some research (see *Harbrace* 33 and 34; *Hodges'* 37 and 38) and write an essay of about 1,000–1,200 words presenting a particular actor (male or female) as the virtual definition of a role (for example, tough cop, wise mother, wisecracking juvenile delinquent).

2. Write an essay in which you begin with a commonly accepted definition (such as a definition for friend) which you reject in favor of a more meaningful one.

Chapter 9

Argument

Argument can be difficult to write well—in fact, it may be the most difficult of the many kinds of writing considered in this book (partly because it can include all those other kinds). But, although difficult, argument is worth the trouble; it is a kind of writing that very directly aims to make a difference, that gets things done.

By *argument* we do not mean quarreling or bickering—the meaning often given the term in everyday speech. Rather, argument is a method (or set of methods) for convincing readers of the rightness of an opinion or of a course of action that the writer considers desirable. Any or all of the other development strategies discussed in this book may be employed in writing arguments.

An argument may rely on several different kinds of appeals: appeals to the writer's own credibility or authority (sometimes called ethical appeals); appeals to reason (logical appeals); and appeals to the reader's emotions, values, or attitudes (pathetic or affective appeals). Writers appeal to their own credibility by demonstrating that they are knowledgeable about the subject and fair-minded in their argumentative approach, that they understand and respect the reader's viewpoint. They appeal to reason by being logical—that is, by reasoning properly themselves and supporting their assertions with good evidence—and by using development strategies appropriate to the material they are presenting. They appeal to emotions, values, and attitudes by choosing examples and raising issues about which the reader is likely to have strong feelings and by using language with connotations that are favorable to the writer's purpose (see *Harbrace* 14a[3]; *Hodges'* 20a[2]).

As you plan an argument, consider how each kind of appeal can help you achieve your purpose. Often it is useful to emphasize one kind more than the others. For example, Mike Godwin's "The Wrong Spin" appeals to the emotions and values of his audience as well as to logic. In contrast, Wallace Stegner, in "The Gift of Wilderness," stresses the appeal to his own credibility or authority: because he has experience, he expects his reader to grant that he knows what he's talking about.

Be careful, however, not to rely on one appeal too heavily. Too great a reliance on an appeal to your own credibility can give the impression that you are indifferent to the reader's values or that you have doubts about the reader's ability to reason logically. Relying exclusively on logical appeals may make you seem cold-blooded, heartless. Relying too much on appeals to the reader's emotions may make you seem unreasonable or softheaded.

The reasoning processes underlying an argument may be either inductive or deductive; more often they are both. Induction draws conclusions from amassed evidence; deduction applies a general truth to a particular case to reach a conclusion. Either method, if pursued carelessly, can lead the unwary writer into reasoning errors called fallacies. (See *Harbrace* 31a through 31g or *Hodges'* 35a through 35g for discussions of induction, deduction, and common fallacies.)

The basic formal elements of most arguments are the *thesis,* a statement of the position or proposition the reader is being urged to accept (see *Harbrace* 28d; *Hodges'* 32d); the presentation of *evidence* supporting the thesis; consideration of *opposing arguments* (if appropriate); and a *conclusion* emphasizing the thesis. These elements can be organized in various ways, depending on the situation and the writer's purpose. One classic pattern, often useful, begins by stating the thesis (and, if necessary, establishing the writer's credentials) in the introduction, goes on to present the evidence in favor of the thesis, next raises and refutes any likely objections, and concludes with a restatement of the thesis or perhaps with a recommendation or call to action based upon it. However, you may not always wish to open with a statement of your thesis. For example, if—as may often occur—you are arguing in response to someone else's argument, it may be best to begin by summarizing the other person's position and then presenting your own. Or if you are arguing in favor of some policy or course of action that you believe will solve a problem, you may need to begin by showing that there *is* a problem before you go on to present and defend your solution. Sometimes—especially if your thesis is one your reader might find distasteful enough to dismiss without giving you a chance to defend it—you may be wise to postpone a direct statement of the thesis until the end of your essay, after you have presented your evidence. Wherever you decide to state the thesis itself, the case you build for it will usually be most effective if you present your specific supporting points in increasing order of importance—strongest points last. (However, note the word "usually"; there are exceptions.)

The effectiveness of argument, perhaps more than of any other kind of writing you will do, depends on your consideration of the nature, needs, and interests of your intended audience, the reader (or readers) whom you are trying to convince. If you present too little evidence, the reader can justifiably dismiss your argument as weak. If you rely on evidence that the reader cannot understand or that is not pertinent to the reader's own interests, the reader can dismiss your argument as irrelevant. If you make mistakes in logical reasoning, the reader can dismiss your argument as false. If you adopt, or lapse into, an inappropriate tone, your reader can dismiss your argument as tactless, insensitive. Try hard to put yourself in your reader's place, to see your argument from the reader's point of view. (For help in analyzing audiences, see *Harbrace* 28a; *Hodges'* 32a.)

Not all arguments are serious. Argumentative writing can also be light-hearted, as Roxana Barry Robinson's "The Horse as Heater" demonstrates. Nevertheless, arguments often deal with matters of considerable gravity—even with issues of life and death, as a number of essays in this chapter do. In the following essay, student Oshunkentan Solomon argues movingly against capital punishment.

Death Penalty

Introduction: statement of the issue

The death penalty is not justice; this state-inflicted death is, rather, an act of hate and vengeance which chiefly succeeds in reminding us of how close we are to the jungle. The death penalty is retribution, and retribution is one of the most appealing arguments for the death penalty—so says Mencken. Yet, retribution cannot be considered a legitimate goal of criminal law.

Evidence: need for some remedy

We live in days of turbulence. Violence is common; murder is an hourly occurrence. Scarcely a day goes by that the evening news fails to report a tale of murder or other evidence of humankind's disdain for life.

Appeal to values

In the midst of all this anxiety and fear, perhaps our greatest need is reverence for life—mere life, our lives, the lives of others, and all life. Life is an end in itself. A humane and generous concern for every individual, for his safety, his health, and his fulfillment is and should be a legitimate goal of every law. It is this basic premise with which the concept of retribution—the death penalty—is at war.

Appeal to logic

Indeed, murder and capital punishment are not opposites that cancel one another, but similarities that breed their kind. From the perspective of reverence for life, how is the state's execution of mass-murderer Ted Bundy different from Bundy's own execution of dozens of women? And how can Bundy's state-inflicted death deter other murderers? When the state itself kills, the mandate "thou shalt not kill" loses the force of the absolute.

Evidence: an execution

Proposed remedy

Surely, the abolition of the death penalty is a major achievement in the long road up from barbarism. Earlier societies excused themselves by pleading that self-preservation necessitated the imposition of capital punishment and, as cruelty begets cruelty, the number of crimes deemed capital offenses increased. But it was for the public good; too bad if

Evidence: history

in the process of isolating dangerous persons from the public, some innocents were executed for crimes they did not commit. Modern civilization has no such excuse.

Appeal to credibility and call to action

Our difficult days call for rare courage, the willingness to disenthrall ourselves to think and act anew. There is no justification for the death penalty. It cheapens life. Its injustices and inhumanity raise basic questions about our institutions and our purpose as a people. Why must we kill? What do we fear? What do we accomplish beside our own embitterment? Why cannot we revere life and in doing so create in the hearts of our people a love for mankind that will finally still violence?

Conclusion: statement of position

A responsible society wants protection, not revenge. It does not need to avenge itself, nor should it want to do so. Punishment for punishment's sake is not justice and is repugnant to civilized peoples. The death penalty is not only unnecessary and futile; it is barbaric and brutal.

Commentary.   Oshunkentan Solomon's argument falls into three main parts. He introduces the essay by naming the issue and stating his position on it—the death penalty's most appealing justification is not a legitimate concern of the law. The body of the essay presents Solomon's argument that the death penalty could not exist if humankind valued life. His conclusion restates his position.

The most obvious kind of reasoning in Solomon's argument is deductive; he has read about the violence in society, seen the death penalty enacted, and noted that it is not effective in preventing further violence. This leads him to reason that the death penalty should be abolished. Beginning his argument with a commentary on the barbaric nature of the death penalty—that its chief value is reminding us "how close we are to the jungle"—Solomon makes the telling point that it is not a legitimate means for law to take. The rest of the essay explains why the death penalty is not a legitimate means for controlling violence in the society. Solomon uses several appeals, the most effective being the appeal to the reader's attitudes and values. He also appeals to the lessons of history and to credibility—and invites the reader to join him in his call for courage and commitment to think and act anew. Having stated his case and made an impassioned emotional appeal, though he has brought logic and history to bear, Solomon restates his position, this time not his alone but that of every civilized person.

Cinderella's Stepsisters
Toni Morrison

One of our most-honored contemporary writers is Toni Morrison, born in
Ohio in 1931. She won the Pulitzer Prize for fiction for *Beloved* (1988) and
the National Book Award for *Song of Solomon* (1977). Her other novels include *The Bluest Eye* (1970), *Tar Baby* (1981), and *Jazz* (1992). A graduate
of Cornell University (M.A., 1955), Morrison taught English and worked for
Random House as an editor before she began teaching fiction writing and
Black literature at Yale and at Barnard. She has also edited a collection of
commentaries upon the Clarence Thomas-Supreme Court confirmation hear-
ings (**Race-*ing* Justice, *En*-gender*ing* Power:** *Essays on Anita Hill, Clarence
Thomas, and the Construction of Social Reality,* 1992). This version of "Cinderella's Stepsisters," adapted from a commencement address Morrison delivered at Barnard College, was first published in *Ms.* magazine.

Let me begin by taking you back a little. Back before the days at college.   1
To nursery school, probably, to a once-upon-a-time time when you first heard,
or read, or, I suspect, even saw "Cinderella." Because it is Cinderella that I
want to talk about; because it is Cinderella who causes me a feeling of urgency. What is unsettling about that fairy tale is that it is essentially the story
of household—a world, if you please—of women gathered together and held
together in order to abuse another woman. There is, of course, a rather vague
absent father and a nick-of-time prince with a foot fetish. But neither has
much personality. And there are the surrogate "mothers," of course (god- and
step-), who contribute both to Cinderella's grief and to her release and happiness. But it is her stepsisters who interest me. How crippling it must have
been for those young girls to grow up with a mother, to watch and imitate
that mother, enslaving another girl.

I am curious about their fortunes after the story ends. For contrary to re-   2
cent adaptations, the stepsisters were not ugly, clumsy, stupid girls with out-
size feet. The Grimm collection describes them as "beautiful and fair in appearance." When we are introduced to them they are beautiful, elegant, women
of status, and clearly women of power. Having watched and participated in
the violent dominion of another woman, will they be any less cruel when it
comes their turn to enslave other children, or even when they are required to
take care of their own mother?

It is not a wholly medieval problem. It is quite a contemporary one: fem-   3
inine power when directed at other women has historically been wielded in

what has been described as a "masculine" manner. Soon you will be in a position to do the very same thing. Whatever your background—rich or poor—whatever the history of education in your family—five generations or one—you have taken advantage of what has been available to you at Barnard and you will therefore have both the economic and social status of the stepsisters *and* you will have their power.

I want not to *ask* you but to *tell* you not to participate in the oppression   4
of your sisters. Mothers who abuse their children are women, and another woman, not an agency, has to be willing to stay their hands. Mothers who set fire to school buses are women, and another woman, not an agency, has to tell them to stay their hands. Women who stop the promotion of other women in careers are women, and another woman must come to the victim's aid. Social and welfare workers who humiliate their clients may be women, and other women colleagues have to deflect their anger.

I am alarmed by the violence that women do to each other: professional   5
violence, competitive violence, emotional violence. I am alarmed by the willingness of women to enslave other women. I am alarmed by a growing absence of decency on the killing floor of professional women's worlds. You are the women who will take your place in the world where *you* can decide who shall flourish and who shall wither; you will make distinctions between the deserving poor and the undeserving poor, where you can yourself determine which life is expendable and which is indispensable. Since you will have the power to do it, you may also be persuaded that you have the right to do it. As educated women the distinction between the two is first-order business.

I am suggesting that we pay as much attention to our nurturing sensi-   6
bilities as to our ambition. You are moving in the direction of freedom and the function of freedom is to free somebody else. You are moving toward self-fulfillment, and the consequences of that fulfillment should be to discover that there is something just as important as you are and that just-as-important thing may be Cinderella—or your stepsister.

In your rainbow journey toward the realization of personal goals, don't   7
make choices based only on your security and your safety. Nothing is safe. That is not to say that anything ever was, or that anything worth achieving ever should be. Things of value seldom are. It is not safe to have a child. It is not safe to challenge the status quo. It is not safe to choose work that has not been done before. Or to do old work in a new way. There will always be someone there to stop you. But in pursuing your highest ambitions, don't let your personal safety diminish the safety of your stepsister. In wielding the power that is deservedly yours, don't permit it to enslave your stepsisters. Let your might and your power emanate from that place in you that is nurturing and caring.

Women's rights is not only an abstraction, a cause; it is also a personal   8
affair. It is not only about "us"; it is also about me and you. Just the two of us.

✳

RESPONDING TO THE WHOLE ESSAY

1.   What evidence do you see in "Cinderella's Stepsisters" that Morrison wrote it as a commencement address? Explain. [*Harbrace* 28a; *Hodges'* 32a]
2.   Explain the appropriateness of Morrison's title, "Cinderella's Stepsisters." [*Harbrace* 28f(3); *Hodges'* 32f(3)]
3.   Is the first sentence of paragraph 1 an effective introduction? Why or why not? [*Harbrace* 28f(1); *Hodges'* 32f(1)]
4.   Analyze Morrison's argument identifying her basic claim and the assumptions (stated or unstated) that she makes.
5.   What is Morrison's purpose in "Cinderella's Stepsisters"? [*Harbrace* 28a; *Hodges'* 32a]
6.   What would you say are the characteristics of the audience for whom Morrison is writing? What evidence within the essay helps you define the audience? [*Harbrace* 28a; *Hodges'* 32a]

ANALYZING THE ELEMENTS

Grammar

1.   Sentences 2, 3, and 4 of paragraph 1 are fragments. What rhetorical effect does Morrison achieve by using these fragments? [*Harbrace* 2; *Hodges'* 2]
2.   Comment on the agreement of the subject and verb in the first sentence of paragraph 8. [*Harbrace* 7a; *Hodges'* 6a]

Effective Sentences

1.   Find at least two groups of sentences in which Morrison uses parallel structure and comment on what contribution parallelism makes. [*Harbrace* 10; *Hodges'* 26]
2.   Explain why the phrase, *As educated women,* in the last sentence of paragraph 5 may be a dangling modifier, and justify its use. [*Harbrace* 5b; *Hodges'* 25b]

Punctuation and Mechanics

1.   Comment on Morrison's use of commas in the fourth sentence of paragraph 2. [*Harbrace* 17a, b, and c; *Hodges'* 12a, b, and c]
2.   What message does Morrison's use of the colon in the first sentence of paragraph 5 send the reader? [*Harbrace* 21d; *Hodges'* 17d]

Diction

1.   Explain why *once-upon-a-time* and *nick-of-time* in paragraph 1 are hyphenated. [*Harbrace* 22f; *Hodges'* 18f]
2.   In the fourth sentence of paragraph 5, Morrison says, "you can determine who shall flourish and who shall wither." Why do you think she uses *shall* here, rather than *will*? [*Harbrace* 14a; *Hodges'* 20a]

3. Morrison comments that it must have been *crippling* for the stepsisters to see Cinderella abused. What elements of the story does the word *crippling* evoke? [*Harbrace* 14a; *Hodges'* 20a]

BUILDING VOCABULARY

1. *Status quo* is a phrase borrowed from Latin. Look it up in a good desk dictionary. What do the Latin words mean? What does the phrase signify in English? What other phrases borrowed from other languages can you think of that have become commonly used English ones?
2. Find at least three hyphenated adjectives in Morrison's "Cinderella's Stepsisters." What does each mean? What single-word synonym (if any) exists for these adjectives?

SUGGESTIONS FOR WRITING

1. Imagine that you are giving an address to a group of people just beginning their chosen careers. Write an essay arguing for or against the "feminine" or "masculine" use of power.
2. Write an essay in which the basic claim for your argument is Morrison's statement that "the function of freedom is to free somebody else" (paragraph 6).

The Horse as Heater
Roxana Barry Robinson

Born in Pine Mountain, Kentucky, Roxana Barry Robinson (1946–) was educated at Bennington College and the University of Michigan, from which she holds a B.A. degree. A recipient of a creative writing fellowship from the National Endowment of the Arts, Robinson has published her first novel, *Summer Light* (1988), and a biography titled *Georgia O'Keeffe: A Life* (1989). Her work has appeared in such diverse publications as *The New Yorker, Southern Review, The New York Times, House and Garden, Arts, Artnews,* and *McCall's.* "The Horse as Heater" was first published in the *Patent Trader,* a newspaper serving Upper Westchester County, New York, where Robinson lives.

As fuel costs continue to spiral upwards, the householder must continue 1 his search for a reasonable and effective means of heating his establishment. Solar, or "passive," heating and woodburning stoves are popular alternatives to oil- and coal-burning systems; however, no discussion of modern heating methods would be complete without mention of the horse.

Horses may be used in a variety of ways as heating units. All of these are 2 simpler than existing mechanical methods, and surprisingly effective. The average 1,200-pound horse has a caloric production rate of 600 therms per minute, and double that if he is angry or unsettled. The fuel-calorie conversion rate is extremely favorable, being about one to eight, which means that the standard four-bedroom house, with snacking center and media room, can be heated by one healthy horse and eight bales of hay per week: an appealing statistic and a soothing prospect. As there are a number of horse-heating methods available, it is wise to examine each to determine which will fit your particular needs the best.

One common practice is the installation of a very large horse (a Percheron 3 or other heavy draft type is popular) in the basement of the house. Hot air ducts lead off the Percheron and act as conduits throughout the house. This is a safe and reliable method, as Percherons are mild and ruminative by nature, and fond of basements. In the event that your basement has been turned into a family recreation center, this should not adversely affect your Percheron system: many Percherons are ardent ping-pong spectators, and some are interested in taking up the game themselves. If the prospect of a blue-roan gelding playing round-robin in your basement unsettles you, remember this: even the most ineffectual efforts on the Percheron's part to join in family ping-pong games will raise the heat production in your home by a tremendous factor. Encouraging the horse in any sort of physical activity, even charades, should enable your entire family and the close neighbors of your choice to take hot showers as a result.

A drawback of the central-heating Percheron is that it heats the entire house regardless of which rooms are being used, and some homeowners prefer a more adaptable system which will heat only the rooms that are routinely occupied. Many people find that stationing Thoroughbred mares throughout the house is an attractive alternative to the heavy draft cellar horse. The Thoroughbred is an extremely energetic breed, and its heat production is enormous, owing to its highly developed capillary system, which is a relatively new feature in equine design. The dainty Thoroughbred foot, another hallmark of this fine breed, ensures minimum damage to your flooring and fine carpets. Thoroughbreds are, however, emotionally unstable, and more care and attention must be paid them than the placid draft horse. This maintenance may be more than the average homeowner is willing to provide: soothing words must be used, idle or vicious gossip must be eschewed, and a friendly greeting must be offered daily, incorporating the correct name of the horse (not some jocular substitute), to maintain psychic order. Failure to follow these rules may result in "sulk-outs," and a general lowering of temperature. Mares are more effusive than geldings, and they make particularly good heat producers, but they tend to shy at mice and violence, so geldings are recommended for kitchen and TV room use.

A third, and highly recommended, plan is to give each member of the family a Shetland pony of his own. These tiny ponies are docile creatures, with thick coats and long manes which will double as bathmats. If properly trained, these nimble creatures will follow their receptors eagerly and unselfishly about the house, producing a steady stream of therms. They can be trained as well to make beds and wash sweaters; the drawback is, of course, that they are such terrible liars.

Besides the practical attractions of the horse, there is his great aesthetic appeal. Durably made and skillfully designed, the horse is available in a handsome selection of coordinated earth tones, ranging from white to black and including brown. He also comes in a wide assortment of body styles, from the trim and compact Shetland, through the rugged, all-purpose Quarter horse, whose stylish white trim and abstract patterning make him a popular favorite with decorators, to the massive, heavy-duty Percheron or Clydesdale, who can heat an entire convention without moving a fetlock.

The horse is clean, docile, thrifty, and cheerful. He is biodegradable, noncarcinogenic, and produces no long-term side effects. His own needs are modest: he requires only sweet sun-cured timothy hay and a double-handful of dry oats daily. Clearly, the record of the horse as a reliable and valuable helpmate to man continues, and the horse takes his place beside the stove, the sun, and the furnace.

✳

RESPONDING TO THE WHOLE ESSAY

1. How and where does Robinson let her readers know exactly what she is arguing for in this essay?
2. Robinson defines her rhetorical situation for the reader in the first paragraph. Identify her announced audience, explain what her purpose is, and comment on what lets the reader know that she intends to make her point through humor. [*Harbrace* 28a; *Hodges'* 32a]
3. Comment on the tone of this essay and how Robinson's use of logic—or lack of it—contributes to the tone. [*Harbrace* 29a; *Hodges'* 33a]
4. Would you say that Robinson's method in this essay is mainly deductive or inductive? Explain. [*Harbrace* 31e and 31f; *Hodges'* 35e and 35f]
5. Does Robinson refute objections to her argument? If so, where and how? If not, why not?
6. Examine how Robinson connects paragraphs to give coherence to this essay, and comment on the techniques she uses. [*Harbrace* 27b; *Hodges'* 31b]

ANALYZING THE ELEMENTS

Grammar

1. In the first sentence of the essay, Robinson refers to "the householder" as *he.* Rewrite the sentence to make the language inclusive. [*Harbrace* 6b and 13c(2); *Hodges'* 28 and 19h]
2. In the third sentence of paragraph 3, what is the grammatical relationship between the clause beginning "as Percherons . . ." and the rest of the sentence? [*Harbrace* 4a; *Hodges'* 4a]

Effective Sentences

1. Writers generally try to avoid frequent use of the passive voice, but Robinson turns such usage to her advantage. Comment on how her use of passive constructions contributes to the effectiveness of the essay. [*Harbrace* 11d; *Hodges'* 29d]
2. Analyze Robinson's use of coordination and subordination in the third sentence of paragraph 4. What does subordination contribute to the general effectiveness of the sentence? [*Harbrace* 9; *Hodges'* 24]

Punctuation and Mechanics

1. Robinson uses colons in a number of sentences in "The Horse as Heater." Comment on her use of the colon in the fourth sentence of paragraph 2 and in the fourth and fifth sentences of paragraph 3. [*Harbrace* 21d; *Hodges'* 17d]
2. Explain Robinson's use of quotation marks in the next-to-last sentence of paragraph 4. What other method could Robinson have used to accomplish this effect? [*Harbrace* 20d; *Hodges'* 16d]

Diction

1. Explain the reason for each hyphen in *oil-* and *coal-burning* (paragraph 1), *fuel-calorie* (paragraph 2), *blue-roan* and *ping-pong* (paragraph 3), *central-heating* (paragraph 4), and *heavy-duty* (paragraph 6). [*Harbrace* 22f; *Hodges'* 18f]
2. Comment on how Robinson's choice of words contributes to the humorous effect of the essay, paying particular attention to the fifth sentence of paragraph 3 and the final sentence of paragraph 5.

BUILDING VOCABULARY

1. The terms *blue-roan*, *gelding*, and *fetlock* refer specifically to attributes of horses. What does each term mean? Can you think of instances in which you might use one or more of these terms to refer to something other than a horse? Explain.
2. The following words are not frequently used in most writing, but they all have the advantage of being exceedingly precise: *ruminative, hallmark, eschew, docile*. What does each mean? Write a sentence using each word.

SUGGESTIONS FOR WRITING

1. Reflect carefully on some problem that you think needs a solution, but for which ordinary solutions are not easily available. Write your own modest proposal in which you offer a startling—and potentially ridiculous—solution to the problem.
2. Write an essay in which your goal is to persuade an unbeliever of the value of some labor-saving gadget—microwave ovens, computers, power saws, battery-operated personal fans, and so on. Your essay might be serious or humorous, as you wish.

"'We can't dance together'"[1]
María Rosa Menocal

Born in 1953, María Rosa Menocal grew up along with rock and roll. She earned a Ph.D. in Romance philology, and she is a professor in the Department of Spanish and Portuguese at Yale University. Among her other academic writings, she has authored two books: *The Arabic Role in Medieval Literary History* (1987) and *Writing in Dante's Cult of Truth from Borges to Boccaccio* (1991). The original version of this essay, which was first published in *Profession 88*, a journal "of opinion about and for the modern language profession," contained a number of quotations from rock lyrics which could not be included because of copyright restrictions.

Maybe this small attachment to my past is only another case of what Frank Zappa calls a bunch of old guys sitting around playing rock 'n' roll. But as we all know, rock 'n' roll will never die, and education too, as Henry Adams always sez, keeps going on forever.

—Thomas Pynchon, Introduction to Slow Learner, *xxxiv*

Anyone who teaches Petrarch's lyric magnum opus, vulgarly known as the *Canzoniere*, is eventually bound to reveal to his or her students the rather delicious irony that Petrarch actually thought—or at least said, repeatedly—that writing in the vernacular, the language of the masses and the vulgar, was not a particularly worthwhile or dignified enterprise. I, at least, get a somewhat malicious pleasure from pointing out that it is, of course, because of his magnificently "vulgar" collection of love songs that Petrarch is at all remembered—and that he is such an integral part of canonical Western culture. The irony is a double one: first, if his statements can be taken at face value, Petrarch was terribly wrong in his assessments of the relative merits of his vernacular versus his "classical" writings; second, we have now, following his obviously misguided thinking on the matter and in blatant disregard of the historical lesson, "classicized" the love songs—which were so successful

---

This paper is written in memory of Clifton Cherpack, who did not quite make it to sixty-four. [Au.]

[1]Steely Dan, "Hey Nineteen."

precisely because they weren't "classical" in the first place.[2] When one reads Allan Bloom's derisive comments about music in *The Closing of the American Mind,* which are characterized by a remarkably similar disdain for popular love lyrics and the accompanying reverence for the "great tradition," one can't help but wonder, at least for a split second, if Bloom doesn't have a manuscript of rock lyrics stashed away someplace. Well, it was just a split second.

In fact, a first reading of Bloom, of the chapter entitled "Music" in particular, should logically lead one merely to shrug one's shoulders at his stereotypically retrograde views. I spent several months ticking off all the reasons why writing a response to Bloom's book was, is, even on the face of it, a waste of time and a somewhat self-indulgent exercise. It struck me as significant, however, that other reviewers, no matter how negative, rarely mentioned his ravings about music, tending to be concerned with more "serious" issues about education he raises. Even the witty and intelligent review in *Rolling Stone,* which lays many of Bloom's pretenses bare ("he is peddling fundamentalism for highbrows" [Greider 39]) essentially passes over Bloom's substantive comments about music—in great measure, no doubt, because for anyone reading that journal his comments are too ludicrous even to require a response, their silliness exposed just by their being quoted. But because, as the example of Petrarch so clearly indicates, the multiple and complex issues revolving around the question of "vulgar" love lyrics and the canonical literary tradition are much too important to and central in our profession to be left to the occasional college newspaper refutation by a student music reviewer, I decided to respond.

I do so acknowledging the following limitations. First, I do not pretend to be in any way comprehensive or systematic in my treatment of rock, and the examples I have chosen are idiosyncratic, personal, and relatively random, the music that happened to come to mind. I am not a scholar or an expert in this area, nor is this a research paper on rock.[3] I am a middling to average, at best, connoisseur of the genre. But my examples are not unrepresentative

----

[2]See Vickers's extraordinary article for a much fuller discussion of these issues. Her appreciation of the parallels between Petrarch's work and that of one rock group, Survivor, as well as her detailed and sensitive exploration of the complexities of the relationship between popular and "classical" culture is exemplary. I am indebted to her for allowing me to read a pre-publication version of the article. [Au.]

[3]Nevertheless, I have been asked to provide scholarly documentation for the songs and lyrics I quote. This is both perfectly reasonable and appropriate, given that I am, in part, claiming that much of rock and its lyrics is a cultural phenomenon to be treated like any other—and thus a song should be quoted as we would quote a poem. It is also true, however, and also part of my argument, that "everyone" knows that, for example, "When I'm Sixty-Four" is on the Beatles's *Sgt. Pepper* that came in 1967 and that the lyrics of a remarkable body of rock are part of the active memory of many people. Thus the citations and quotations that follow are representative of the communal knowledge and memory of rock—a reflection of the living lyrical tradition. The "Works Cited" listings reflect ex post facto documentation, in some cases incomplete. Note that many artists avoid putting dates on their albums. [Au.]

(although they in fact represent a minuscule selection of the full range), and someone else's personal sampling would have comparable validity. Second, I will not address in any great detail the much larger issues Bloom raises, although they are, perforce, the backdrop for the music chapter and, more important, they reflect an ideology within which his rejection of rock must be understood. But those are other reviews.[4] And for the sake of my argument—in sum, that Bloom is, from a scholarly point of view, wrong about what rock and roll is—I will attempt to suspend any sustained rebuttal that involves opinion as to what culture (and thus rock and roll) ought to be.

Bloom's argument about rock has three major elements: (1) that rock music and its lyrics are limited to "sex, hate and a smarmy, hypocritical version of brotherly love" (74), with an emphasis on sex: "rock music has one appeal only, a barbaric appeal, to sexual desire—not love, not *eros,* but sexual desire undeveloped and untutored" (73); (2) that rock's values (or lack thereof) are, at worst, antagonistic to fundamental cultural values and, at best, lie well outside other lasting cultural pursuits: "Rock music encourages passions and provides models that have no relation to any life the young people . . . can possibly lead, or to the kinds of admiration encouraged by liberal studies. . . . [A]s long as they have the Walkman on, they cannot hear what the great tradition has to say" (80–81); (3) that rock is a musical lyrical genre that concerns youth and children overwhelmingly: "Never was there an art form directed so exclusively to children" (74). Let's take these elements in that order.

Bloom's assertions about the poverty and limitations of rock's themes are perhaps the most excruciating in their simple lack of factualness—and there is such an embarrassment of riches available as counterargument that it is difficult to know where to start. What *is* true, certainly, is that the richest thematic mine is that of love—and more often than not, love that is in some way unsatisfying, unhappy, or unfulfilled. But many, if not most, of rock's classic love songs are about a great deal more—or less—than sex. From the Beatles' basically silly "Michelle" . . . (which reveals the metaliterary preoccupation of rock as well) to Dylan's charming ditty "You're Gonna Make Me Lonesome When You Go," which includes a refusal of other types of love poetry . . . , to the troubled and tortured love of Neil Young's "Now that you've made yourself love me . . . " there are few, if any, of the variations and variegations of "classical" love poetry that have not found lyrics in the rock canon.

Even if we limit ourselves to the writing of the artists mentioned above, Bloom's generalization not only crumbles but has to be replaced by the realization that rock's obsession with love and with its own expressions of the longing for love are next of kin to those same obsessions in all other lyrical schools. Thus, the Beatles's hymn to enduring, perfect, and as yet unfound love in "I Will" . . . is neatly counterbalanced by their wistful and hopeful

4

5

6

[4]See especially David Rieff's scathing comments about Bloom's cultural-ideological posture. [Au.]

projection about a perhaps nonexistent future in the classic "When I'm Sixty-Four." . . . Dylan's repertoire of love songs (although it is fair to say that he is far from being known as a love lyricist) is scarcely less representative of these ties to lyric antecedents. From the early, bittersweet "Don't Think Twice It's All Right" about the pain of failed love . . . to the famous "Just like a Woman" (satirized by Woody Allen in *Annie Hall*) to other, much more difficult and hermetic songs such as "Queen Jane Approximately" . . . , his long and varied career as a lyricist is reminiscent of a poetic ancestry he is quite conscious of following.[5] And the centrality of the broken heart to the lyric tradition is simply and touchingly reflected in Neil Young's "Only Love Can Break Your Heart." . . .

The interesting question, of course, is why and how the preoccupation   7
with love and its expression in rock is so reminiscent of other lyrical traditions, so like other schools and canons that are now studied, by and large, in a more rarefied atmosphere. From twelfth-century Persian courtly poetry to Petrarchism in Renaissance Europe to opera in the last century, love and its many problems—sometimes sexual, sometimes not—are of overwhelming and enduring fascination and are perhaps the ultimate inspiration for poetry and lyrics—an inspiration that all these lyrical schools are also explicitly conscious of and that is often the focus of metaliterary interest itself. Taken as a whole, rock exhibits, theme for theme, much the same concerns as those of the traditions we have now classicized. In one example, the preoccupation with unsatisfactory love becomes the subject or object of poetry and creates, in turn, the association between the lyricist or singer and the lover. Self-reflection and metalyrical concerns include the glory and fame that will be achieved through the singing or poetry: some examples are "So You Want to Be a Rock 'n' Roll Star," "Do You Believe in Magic?" and that early and enduring anthem of rock, "Johnny B. Goode." . . . Thus, what is critical is not merely that Bloom (and others) have got it wrong but that ignorance prevents them from seeing that rock is in so many ways like parts of the "great tradition." And one is then, indeed, led to the question of whether rock resembles these traditions because it is descended from them or because some sort of universal parallelism is at work—a question that, because of our Bloom-like prejudices, has scarcely been asked, let alone answered.[6] As for the sexuality, well, indeed, some rock lyrics are sexual, even, perhaps, exclusively and pointedly and vulgarly sexual. But sexuality, too, is far from uniquely modern, and Mick Jagger's "Satisfaction" and "Let's Spend the Night Together" pale, in both vulgarity and explicitness, beside some of the songs of the venerated William of Aquitaine.

---

[5]Dylan, who changed his name from Robert Zimmerman to one that linked him explicitly with the great tradition, has written dozens of songs whose lyrics explicitly harken back to all manner of poetic schools, from the Bible . . . to Petrarch . . . to the great poetic struggle of modernism. . . . [Au.]

[6]The one exception I know of is Vickers's article. [Au.]

But while rock may thus mimic earlier lyric schools in its fascination   8
with the generative power of unhappy love, it has exploited a much fuller
range of themes, including the historicopolitical one that Bloom dismisses as
"a smarmy, hypocritical version of brotherly love." Once again the generalization alarmingly misrepresents the remarkable range of topics covered and
views expressed. Many of rock's earliest masterpieces, written in the late six-
ties and early seventies, were, in fact, politically committed, and opposition
to the war (and the draft) and sympathy for the civil rights movements were
major conditioning and influential currents. But as often as not, the lyrics
produced in this climate were most conspicuously informed by and inter-
woven with the other musical and lyrical traditions that are such important
components of rock: black, particularly spiritual, music and the sort of folk
tradition that Joan Baez's songs rely on so heavily. Remnants of these strains,
pervasive in rock even today, explain the centrality of the Talking Heads's
"Take Me to the River" and Eric Clapton's (and others') recordings of "Swing
Low, Sweet Chariot." And while there are plenty of examples of virtually
unmediated protest (Country Joe and the Fish's "What are we fighting for?
. . ." is a classic, certainly, as is Dylan's even more famous "The Times They
Are a-Changin'"), much of the "political" lyrics of rock are infinitely more
complex.

The Band, for example, specialized in songs that reflected back on the   9
Civil War South, and by giving the poet a Confederate voice in "The Night
They Drove Old Dixie Down," they brilliantly underscored, without ever being explicit, the universal tragedy of war. The currently popular U2 plumbs
the complex problems and no-win situation of Northern Ireland in equally
subtle ways. Finally, many rock lyricists have made their points by merely taking over or only slightly rewriting "classics" from other traditions: Prince sings
the Lord's Prayer with remarkable effect; the Byrds sang Ecclesiastes in "Turn,
Turn, Turn." If these are smarmy versions of brotherly love, so be it. In fact,
what is stunning here is that rock's connections with the "great tradition" are
often quite explicit, markedly intertextual, and ultimately impossible to ignore. The extent to which Bloom's second major objection to rock—that it
has no cultural ties or links or avenues beyond itself—is simply mistaken comes
very much to the fore here.[7]

But above and beyond specific songs that are strictly and obviously tied,   10
intertextually, to any number of classic texts outside the rock tradition, rock's
place in contemporary society is a major link to a number of cultural phenomena that we now, from a safe distance, view as canonical. In fact, it is
telling that Bloom does acknowledge the great impact of rock: at the outset
of the chapter he goes on at some length, and with considerable accuracy,

---

[7]The British punk tradition, which I know scarcely at all and thus do not discuss more fully,
includes a number of "singings" of important texts. I am grateful to a student, Kirsten Thorne,
for bringing to my attention "The Wasteland," by the Mission U.K., and *In Dulce Decorum,*
by the Damned, where the text is a speech of Winston Churchill's. [Au.]

about the unique role rock plays in society and about rock's importance, un-paralleled in recent history. He begins the chapter, in fact, noting that "[n]oth-ing is more singular about this generation than its addiction to music. This is the age of music and the states of soul that accompany it. To find a rival to this enthusiasm, one would have to go back at least a century to Germany and the passion for Wagner's operas" (68). And, having remarked that one crucial difference between rock and the German passion of the last century is that rock is much less elitist (i.e., it cuts across class boundaries more), he goes on to note the great change that has occurred in the role music and its lyrics play in this century: "The power of music in the soul . . . has been re-covered after a long period of desuetude" (69). In acknowledging this rather remarkable turn of events, this existence in the late twentieth century of a sta-tus for music and its lyrics that did not always exist and when it did was a major cultural institution and a central part of the culture, Bloom is implic-itly recognizing what he will explicitly deny later on: the cultural centrality of the rock phenomenon. In fact, Bloom even goes on to note that this is the first generation he has taught that fully understand Plato's opposition to mu-sic, something earlier generations, for whom music was "background," were incapable of understanding. And since Bloom explicitly recognizes the enor-mous impact per se of the phenomenon, his refusal to see its cultural impact is grounded, explicitly, in what he sees as its failure to address issues other than sex—an opinion that, as I have tried to suggest, cannot be substantiated.

What can be substantiated is the perhaps radical-sounding assertion, al-   11
ready implicit in Bloom's comments, that the rock phenomenon is a twentieth-century version, in many if not in most of its details, of what at other times and in other places have been major lyrical schools with resounding impact in the cultures that produced them. Poetry, after all, had long ago ceased to be "lyrical" in the etymological sense of the word, an integral part of music. For most people—and many scholars—poetry is what was and is written down to be read and what is published in poetry journals or in the *New Yorker* or in anthologies. Poetry in that form not only is substantively different from lyrics but is rarely (and then only for a minuscule percentage of the population, now or in any other period of history) a living part of one's cultural or spiritual ex-perience. But rock is much like opera and even more like the phenomenon of the troubadours in twelfth- and thirteenth-century Europe, when lyricists started singing in the vernaculars rather than in the long-dead Latin. Rock is poetry that is aggressively and self-consciously a part of the living tradition that, in great measure because it is attached to music, plays a fundamental and vital cultural role for many more people. In this regard, as in various others, Bloom's assertion that rock makes it difficult for young people to have a pas-sionate relationship to the art and thought that are the substance of a liberal education is almost perversely skewed.

The truth is the opposite: the person, young or otherwise, for whom po-   12
etry is a living form that resonates daily in the mind and soul is quite capa-ble of appreciating not only the poetry of the troubadours or of Petrarch, so

similar in other ways, but, more important, the great lyrical power of poetry in and of itself. Members of this generation, as Bloom likes to put it, are the first in a long time, thanks to rock, to be in a position to understand the impact and repercussions of many earlier lyrical phenomena. They should be able to grasp, for example (particularly if we as mediators can simply pull out the parallels), what is moving, rather than dusty and mechanical and arcane, in a previous generation's songs—much more so, I would argue, than people who don't know why tears have been shed at Lennon's "Imagine" or who don't think of love in the haunting structures of "Here, There, and Everywhere," or who might not hear the ecstasy and triumph of the Grateful Dead's "Touch of Grey" . . . , so often sung last summer by Jerry Garcia, who could have been grandfather to many in the audience. For those whose poetic sensibilities have incubated in the heart and soul and tapping feet, Puccini's sentimental arias can be truly moving and Verdi's triumphal choruses can stir, vicariously if nothing else, the same sentiments stirred at Woodstock.[8] The list of ways in which the experience of rock is enlightening vis-à-vis the "great tradition" is seemingly endless: students who know full well that a strong lyric tradition thrives on the seemingly paradoxical combination of parameters and restraints, and the individual creativity that thrives within the tradition and the repetition of commonplaces, can eventually read the medieval and Renaissance lyric traditions with a fuller appreciation of their astonishing repetitiousness. And those same "students" of rock, because rock has included, and continues to include, a substantial "trobar clus"[9] strain, those students who have learned instinctively to appreciate everything from "Lucy in the Sky with Diamonds" . . . to "Third World Man," by Steely Dan . . . , bring an important background to the study of the myriad canonical schools of hermetic lyrics that have produced poets as varied as Arnaut Daniel, the Spanish mystics, Mallarmé, and that fellow splicer of lines from the Italian, Ezra Pound.

Bloom's third major misapprehension is actually rather touching—or pathetic: that rock's appeal is exclusively to the young, that rock is a phenomenon of a "generation," that it affects his "students," and so on. This notion is belied by the simple facts of chronologies, celebrated every year as one great rock star after another turns forty or fifty and as those who grew up on rock are now bringing up children of their own. Toward the end of this chapter Bloom depicts a pathetic scenario where the poor parents who have struggled to provide a good life and who wish only the best for their child watch on, terrified and helpless, as their thirteen-year-old boy is mesmerized by MTV and its attendant horrors. This is a remarkable fantasy; the parents are, likely as not, especially if they are highbrow and college-educated, the ones who

13

[8]Lest the connection appear farfetched I note that in the movie *The Killing Fields* the two most emotionally wrenching scenes are accompanied by Puccini's "Nessun dorma" and Lennon's "Imagine." [Au.]

[9]A complicated style used by some medieval Provençal poets.

watch MTV and who introduced rock to their child in the first place. And while they may care less for their child's currently preferred groups and lyrics than for their own classics, they are probably not much concerned since it has become clear that their classics are becoming *the* classics and that their child will be listening to the Beatles, as well as to the Beatles's progeny. But more telling than even those fundamentals are columns on contemporary music that now appear regularly in the *New Yorker,* that holy sanctum of haute culture, and articles in academic journals that reflect the extent to which the centrality of rock can no longer be defined in generational terms at all.[10]

In fact, many of Bloom's (and others') misapprehensions about rock and   14
its impact are rooted in remarkably clichéd notions about the general poverty of "youth culture" and a commensurate (and I believe equally illusory) aggrandizement of the degree of "high culture" in earlier societies and generations. Thus, to take but one example, Bloom dismisses the powerful argument that, in fact, there is a significant revival of interest in classical music by saying that even if there is, only 5 to 10 percent of the population is affected. Does he believe that much more than that has ever had a serious interest in classical music? The serious listener does, indeed, listen seriously to all sorts of music. And not only is "Roll Over, Beethoven" tongue-in-cheek, ultimately, but twenty or so years down the line it may well end up on the same shelf as the Ninth. Likewise, it is obvious that, as with all other schools or cultural phenomena, there is a lot of trash out there and a part of the audience at every concert has never heard of Ecclesiastes. So what else is new? Are we to pretend that everyone who listened avidly to Wagner knew all the allusions? Don't we all know that for every Mozart there were hundreds of Salieris? Rock is no better and probably no worse. There is little doubt that many people who listen to much that is marvelously lyrical in rock, that is poetic and moving, never get past the beat, and, also undoubtedly, much of what has been written and will continue to be written will never amount to anything in posterity.

But it is nonsense—or wishful thinking—to say, as Bloom does, that when   15
we take the Walkmans off after years of listening to rock there will be nothing left. *Au contraire.* It is a pity Bloom has listened so little, for, given the great concern for culture and the educational tradition he claims to be championing, he is thus almost perversely depriving himself of access to a richly variegated and (in the very cultural terms he wishes to see the "liberal tradition") an enormously influential phenomenon. We cannot afford to ignore Bloom's misapprehensions about music, because the nature of his misunderstanding is so intimately tied with the debates now raging, not just at Stanford but nearly everywhere, about what constitutes the canon of "Western civilization." And the educator, particularly in the field of literature and literary culture, who like Bloom walks about deaf to our living lyric tradition is a less able explicator and mediator of the literary traditions and canonized

---

[10]A recent issue of *Stanford French Review* contains an article entitled "The Grateful Dead: Corneille's Tragedy and the Illusion of History." [Au.]

poets that are the fundamental intertexts for the troubadours of our own time. It might alter both the tenor and the substance of these discussions considerably if we were to recognize that a great deal of what is being listened to on the Walkmans is the great tradition very much alive and well—and as Pynchon sez, rock 'n' roll will never die, and education keeps going on forever.

Works Cited

The Band. "The Night They Drove Old Dixie Down." *The Band.* Capitol, CDP 7 46493 2, n.d. on original album.

Beatles. "Here, There and Everywhere." *Revolver.* Capitol, CDP 7 46441 2, 1966.

———. "I Will." No title [*White Album*]. EMI-Capitol, CDP 7 46443 2, 1968.

———. "Michelle." *Rubber Soul.* EMI-Capitol, CDP 7 46440 2, 1965.

———. "When I'm Sixty-Four." "Lucy in the Sky with Diamonds." *Sgt. Pepper's Lonely Hearts Club Band.* EMI, CDP 7 46442 2, 1967.

Berry, Chuck. "Johnny B. Goode."

———. "Roll Over, Beethoven."

Bloom, Allan. *The Closing of the American Mind: How Higher Education Has Failed Democracy and Impoverished the Souls of Today's Students.* New York: Simon, 1987.

Byrds. "So You Want to Be a Rock 'n' Roll Star." *The Byrds.* Columbia, G 30127, n.d.

———. "Turn, Turn, Turn." *Turn, Turn, Turn.* Columbia, CG 33645, n.d.

Clapton, Eric. "Swing Low, Sweet Chariot." *Time Pieces,* RSO, 800 014-2, 1975.

Country Joe McDonald. "I-Feel-like-I'm-Fixin'-to-Die Rag." *Woodstock.* Atlantic-Cotillion, SD 3-500, 1970.

Dylan, Bob. "Don't Think Twice It's All Right." *The Freewheelin' Bob Dylan.* Columbia, CK 8786, n.d.

———. "Queen Jane Approximately." *Highway 61 Revisited.* Columbia, CK 9189, 1965.

———. "Just like a Woman." *Blonde on Blonde.* Columbia, CK 841, n.d.

———. "You're Gonna Make Me Lonesome When You Go." *Blood on the Tracks.* Columbia, X 698, 1974.

———. "The Times They Are a-Changin'."

Grateful Dead. "Touch of Grey." *In the Dark.* Arista, ARCD 8452, 1987.

Greider, William. "Bloom and Doom." *Rolling Stone* 8 Oct. 1987:39–40.

Lennon, John. "Imagine."

Lovin' Spoonful. "Do You Believe in Magic?"

Pynchon, Thomas. *Slow Learner.* New York: Bantam, 1984.

Rieff, David. "The Colonel and the Professor." *Times Literary Supplement* 4–11 Sept. 1987:950, 960.

Rolling Stones. "Let's Spend the Night Together." *Flowers.* Abkco, 75092, 1966.

———. "Satisfaction."

Steely Dan. "Hey Nineteen." "Third World Man." *Gaucho.* MCA Records, MCAD-37220, 1980.

Talking Heads. "Take Me to the River." *Stop Making Sense.* Sire, 25186-1, 1984.

Vickers, Nancy. "Vital Signs: Petrarch and Popular Culture." *Romanic Review* January 1988:184–95.

Young, Neil. "Only Love Can Break Your Heart." "I Believe in You." *After the Gold Rush.* Reprise, 2283-2, 1970.

✳

RESPONDING TO THE WHOLE ESSAY

1. Comment as fully as you can on Menocal's audience. What evidence can you find to show that she writes with her audience in mind? How might this essay be different if Menocal had written it for *Rolling Stone*? [*Harbrace* 28a; *Hodges'* 32a]
2. Why do you think Menocal begins her essay with a long paragraph discussing Petrarch's attitudes about his love poetry? What does this paragraph contribute to her argument? [*Harbrace* 28f; *Hodges'* 32f]
3. What is Menocal's purpose for writing "'We can't dance together'" and where does she state it? [*Harbrace* 28a; *Hodges'* 32a]
4. Analyze the structure of Menocal's argument in "'We can't dance together'" and answer the following: What case does she wish to make? How does she present her evidence? What concessions does she make, and why does she place them where she does? Does she refute possible objections? If so, where and how? What solution does she offer? Where does she state it? Does she urge the reader to take action? If so, what kind?
5. Is Menocal's reasoning in this essay primarily inductive or deductive? Support your answer with evidence from the essay. [*Harbrace* 31; *Hodges'* 35]
6. What are the premises on which Menocal bases her argument? Where and how does she make them clear to the reader? [*Harbrace* 31c; *Hodges'* 35c]
7. Paragraph 4 consists almost entirely of a single sentence. Justify both the length of the sentence and Menocal's choice to devote the entire paragraph to that sentence. [*Harbrace* 27c; *Hodges'* 31c]
8. Given the fact that Menocal uses footnotes in her essay, why are her sources indicated in parentheses rather than in footnotes? [*Harbrace* 34; *Hodges'* 38]

ANALYZING THE ELEMENTS

Grammar

1. In the first sentence of paragraph 2, Menocal writes "should logically lead one merely to shrug one's shoulders." Why do you think Menocal chose to write the sentence as she did, rather than to write "should logically lead a person merely to shrug his shoulders"? What other choices did she have? [*Harbrace* 6b; *Hodges'* 28]
2. The second sentence of footnote 3 contains the statement, "much of rock and roll and its lyrics is a cultural phenomenon." Comment on the agreement of subject and verb in this statement. [*Harbrace* 7a; *Hodges'* 6a]
3. Comment on the time relationships represented by the sequence of tenses in the sixth and seventh sentences of paragraph 10. [*Harbrace* 7c; *Hodges'* 7c]

Effective Sentences

1. Analyze the fourth sentence of paragraph 5 as a periodic sentence. [*Harbrace* 11b; *Hodges'* 29b]
2. The third sentence of paragraph 1 is very long and involved. Rewrite this sentence for a less academic audience. [*Harbrace* 12a; *Hodges'* 30a]
3. Rewrite the sixth sentence of paragraph 14 and the final sentence of paragraph 15 to remove expletive constructions. [*Harbrace* 12b; *Hodges'* 30b]

Punctuation and Mechanics

1. Why is each word of the title of this essay not capitalized? [*Harbrace* 23c; *Hodges'* 9c]
2. In view of the fact that some lyrics have been deleted from this version of Menocal's essay, what do you make of the use of ellipses in paragraph 6? Are all of the ellipses used to indicate the same kind of omission? [*Harbrace* 20a and 21i; *Hodges'* 16a and 17i]
3. Analyze the use of parentheses in paragraph 4. [*Harbrace* 21f; *Hodges'* 17f]
4. Why does Menocal place the *n* in brackets in the third sentence of paragraph 10? [*Harbrace* 21g; *Hodges'* 17g]

Diction

1. What is the plural of *Walkman* (sentences 1 and 6, paragraph 15)? [*Harbrace* 22; *Hodges'* 18]
2. Justify Menocal's misspelling, *sez,* in the final sentence of paragraph 15. [*Harbrace* 22; *Hodges'* 18]
3. Comment on Menocal's use of *back* with *reflected.* [*Harbrace* 15d; *Hodges'* 21d]
4. Look up the following words in your dictionary and comment on the appropriateness (or lack of appropriateness) of diction in "'We can't dance together'": *stashed* (paragraph 1), *retrograde* (paragraph 2), *perforce* (paragraph 3), *metaliterary* and *ditty* (paragraph 5), *hermetic* (paragraph 6), *historicopolitical* and *smarmy* (paragraph 8), *intertextual* (paragraph 9), *telling* and *desuetude* (paragraph 10), *vis-à-vis* (paragraph 12), *haute culture* (paragraph 13), *commensurate* and *aggrandizement* (paragraph 14), *explicator* (paragraph 15). Which expressions could accurately be termed "academic jargon"? Why? [*Harbrace* 13c(1) and 14; *Hodges'* 19g and 20]
5. Comment on whether "not unrepresentative" (sentence 5, paragraph 3) is a double negative. If so, is it justified? Why or why not? [*Harbrace* 15a; *Hodges'* 21a]

BUILDING VOCABULARY

1. What do *vulgar* and *vernacular* mean? What is the source of each word? What do they have in common?
2. Look up each of the following words and note (1) its source, (2) its meaning, (3) synonym(s), (4) usage notes, and (5) other words made from the same root: *blatant, ludicrous, smarmy, arcane, sanctum, canonical.*

SUGGESTIONS FOR WRITING

1. Write an essay in which you argue that the attitude(s) of a particular authority group (for instance, parents, supervisors, internal revenue agents) is based on unsubstantiated beliefs rather than fact.
2. Write an essay in which you argue for the appeal of a particular kind of music or performer (for instance, classical music or jazz, a specific "sound" like the Seattle sound or the Nashville sound, or a group like Soundgarden or the Oak Ridge Boys).

The Wrong Spin
Mike Godwin

In July of 1995 *Time* magazine published an article showcasing "a new study, *Marketing Pornography on the Information Superhighway,* purportedly by a team of researchers at Carnegie Mellon University"[1] and accepted for publication by the *Georgetown Law Journal.* As it turns out, the study was conducted primarily by an undergraduate at Carnegie Mellon, Marty Rimm. Donna Hoffman and Thomas Novak, associate professors of management at Vanderbilt University, claim that Rimm "grossly exaggerated the extent of pornography on the Internet by conflating findings from private adult-bulletin-board systems that require credit cards for payments (and are off limits to minors) with those from the public networks (which are not)." Hoffman and Novak argue further that Rimm's statistics, particularly his "claim that 83.5 percent of the images stored on the Usenet newsgroups are pornographic," are so inaccurate as to be meaningless, and they point out that pornographic files comprise "less than one half of one percent of all messages posted on the Internet." Three weeks after publication of the article, *Time* noted that Rimm himself may not be what he had seemed, apparently having conducted a questionable survey that concluded that nearly two-thirds of his former fellow high school students had gambled at Atlantic City casinos. *Time* also reported that Rimm authored two books: one titled *The Pornographer's Handbook: How to Exploit Women, Dupe Men & Make Lots of Money,* which Rimm says is a satire, and the other a privately published novel titled *An American Playground* and based on his casino experiences. Godwin's essay takes the position that since the *Time* article fueled the hysteria begun by the radical right using tainted data, the magazine has a responsibility to fulfill its stated mission to help readers "think clearly about the legal issues of online life." It is important to know that Godwin (mnemonic@well.com) is staff counsel for the Electronic Frontier Foundation in San Francisco, an organization dedicated to ensuring that new communications technologies have the benefit of constitutional civil liberties.

Here's an interesting experiment. Try combining the topics of sex, children, and the Net in a magazine or newspaper story, or even in an online discussion. Amazingly, this combination will almost invariably cause ostensibly intelligent people to shut down their higher thinking centers. Let's hope this column proves an exception to the rule.

[1] Quotations in this note are from *Time,* July 24, 1995.

For me, the most recent example of this rule appeared on America On- 2
line in *Time* magazine's online forum, Time Online. Generally, *Time* has done
a good job of creating a lively and interesting discussion forum, but sometimes the corporate interests of Time Warner skew the discussion. Take, for
example, the following post by RPTime (Robert Pondiscio, a public relations
person for *Time*) in the topic dedicated to discussion and criticism of the magazine's now-notorious "Cyberporn" cover story. Shortly after the national
press reported that the U.S. Justice Department had announced a dozen arrests in a two-year investigation into the use of commercial online services to
distribute child porn and seduce minors into sex, the following message appeared in the Cyberporn topic in Time Online:

Subj: Arrests 95-09-14 10:20:08 EDT
From: RPTime
Posted on: America Online

Looks like the FBI has arrested a dozen people in connection with the biggest
non-problem in cyberspace. The feds have reportedly seized digitized pornographic images of children as young as two years old from members of this
very online service.

I'll be interested in the reactions of our First Amendment absolutist friends.
Perhaps they will argue the arrested should be released, and the parents of
children involved should be charged with neglect for not adequately supervising their kids' online activities.

Robert

Analyzed rhetorically and legally, this is a fascinating post. In Pondis- 3
cio's defense, it must be said that he's had to work overtime in defending
Time's decision to hype the fraudulent "Carnegie Mellon" study authored
by Martin Rimm. Given the flood of criticism of both the story and the study
itself, you can understand if Pondiscio is feeling a bit fried. So you may be
able to forgive his over-the-top rhetorical strategy of classing critics of the
cover story as "First Amendment absolutists" who are blasé about child
pornography or the victimization of children.

From a legal standpoint, however, the post is even more interesting and far 4
less forgivable, given that Pondiscio, in both his public role and as a private individual, has touted *Time's* strength in explaining the issues to its readers. You
see, by posting this message in the topic dedicated to discussion of the "Cyberporn" cover story, Pondiscio is implying that the FBI raids somehow vindicate
Time's decision to run the story. Yet even if we accept the (false) implication
that the cover story was not primarily about Marty Rimm and his *Georgetown
Law Journal* article, Pondiscio's post demonstrates confusion about what the legal and factual issues relating to porn, the Net, and children really are.

Defining the Terms.   When talking about pornography and child safety on   5
the Net, you'll often see several different terms bandied about as if they were
interchangeable. They're not. Here are some basic definitions.

Pornography: In general, material that presents sexual content of some   6
sort, with the intent of being arousing. *Playboy* and *Penthouse* could be included under this definition, and, like any other uses of the press, such material is presumptively legal under the First Amendment. To be illegal, pornography either must be found to be "obscene" (see below) or "child
pornography" (see below).

Obscenity: To be "obscene," pornography must meet all parts of a three-   7
part test designed by then-Chief Justice Warren Burger in 1973 in a case called
Miller v. California. This is normally a question of *content.* The three parts
of the so-called "Miller test" are as follows:

- *State statute.* Normally, there must be a state statute in place that describes
  with specificity the particular sexual (or excretory) acts that cannot be depicted.
- *Community standards.* The depiction of the sexual acts must be "patently offensive" and "appeal to the prurient interest," as judged by a reasonable man
  applying the standards of the community.
- *The escape clause.* To be obscene, the material must fail to meet the requirements of the *Miller v. California* "escape clause." That is, it must lack "serious" literary, artistic, scientific, political, or other social value.

Child Pornography: This material is illegal regardless of whether it is ob-   8
scene, which means you don't even bother to ask any questions about "community standards." Under federal law, "child pornography" is any *visual* material that depicts a child either engaging in explicit sexual acts or posing in
a "lewd and lascivious" manner, when the manufacture of such material involves the actual use of a real child. Thus, verbal material can't be child porn
under federal law, although it could be obscene.

Similarly, computer-generated material that seems to depict children en-   9
gaged in sexual activity but does not use real children would not be child
porn, although it almost certainly would be obscene. In short, this category
is defined not primarily in terms of *content* ("offensive" depictions) but in
terms of *conduct* (the victimization of actual children).

Child Sexual Abuse: Sometimes children are abused sexually, yet no one   10
takes any pictures of it. This is not child porn, although of course it is illegal.

Child Seduction: Sometimes child abusers (see above) will attempt to se-   11
duce new victims. They may try to contact such victims via an online service.
Note: Despite the commonly repeated claim that pedophiles rely on pornography to seduce children, it is possible to engage in child seduction without
ever using pornography, obscenity, or child pornography.

Exposure to Inappropriate Materials. Most states make it illegal to ex-   12
pose minors to sexually explicit material—even when such material is otherwise legal. It is *this* issue that has been the primary subject of the "indecency"
legislation that we've seen so much of in Congress this year.

Indecency: This is a special term for content that, up to now, has been   13
regulated only in two special areas of federal jurisdiction—broadcasting
and so-called "dial-a-porn" services, both currently under the jurisdiction
of the Federal Communications Commission (FCC). In those contexts, "indecency" normally means "patently offensive" sexual content or profane
language.

When you're talking about media that are not under FCC jurisdiction—   14
newspaper and book publication, say, or the movie industry—the term "indecency" has no legal meaning. One of the strategies that lobbyists for the
Christian Coalition and associated groups have been employing to limit sexual content online has been to ask Congress to expand FCC jurisdiction (and
the FCC's definition of "indecency") to cover the Internet. In previous columns,
I've argued that this would be unconstitutional.

Children First.   With our primer in hand, we can return to Robert Pondis-   15
cio's posting above. And once you're clear on the different meanings of the
terms and concepts I've outlined here, you can note that the FBI raids primarily involve material described as child pornography.

Yet the critics of *Time*'s "Cyberporn" cover story have been addressing   16
issues under pornography, obscenity, child seduction, and exposure to inappropriate materials—and primarily as they relate to *Time*'s coverage or to
Martin Rimm's fraudulent study. What the critics were saying was a "non-
problem" was the *Time*/Rimm implication that children (and others) were routinely stumbling, unwittingly, across pornographic images, which *Time* had
described as "pervasive."

They were also arguing that, despite scary anecdotes about pedophiles   17
e-mailing pornography to children online, it's common for minors to spend
years online without ever encountering a child predator or having any inappropriate material sent to them.

It was this argument that Pondiscio transmuted into a claim that child   18
predation in cyberspace was a "non-problem"—an especially adroit rhetorical move, given that Philip Elmer-DeWitt's story for *Time* had said the danger was minimal. Elmer-DeWitt wrote, "While groups like the Family Research Council insist that online child molesters represent a clear and present
danger, there is no evidence that it is any greater than the thousand other
threats children face every day."

That consideration aside, no one has ever denied that child sexual abuse   19
is a problem, whether in cyberspace or out of it. And neither *Time* nor its PR
director are doing anyone any favors by distorting the arguments of the magazine's critics.

What *Time* could do, if Pondiscio and his employers were interested in   20
correcting the damage done by the "Cyberporn" article, would be to repeat
a few basic and irreducible facts that have gotten lost in all the sensational-
ism—such as the fact that there's arguably less of a threat to your child online than there is on the corner across from the schoolyard. After all, even the
most determined child predator can't reach through the screen.

Time also could underscore the fact that the National Center for Missing   21
and Exploited Children has developed some excellent guidelines for parents
and children. The NCMEC pamphlet entitled *Child Safety on the Information Superhighway* is available on America Online and just about everywhere
else in cyberspace. If you and your children follow those guidelines, the Internet is a far safer place than is Disney World.

Unfortunately, the Net still isn't a safe place for the Constitution. And that   22
won't change until we solve two problems. First, we've got to teach ourselves
to think clearly about the legal issues of online life, regardless of the willingness of anti-porn activists and the mainstream media—including *Time*—to confuse them. Secondly, we've got to remember, come election time, that we need
to protect ourselves against the "clear and present danger" of rogue senators
who've forgotten the meaning of the Constitution they've sworn to uphold.

✹

RESPONDING TO THE WHOLE ESSAY

1. What is Godwin's probable reason for including the seven definitions cited in para-
    graphs 6 through 13? What would be the effect of leaving them out?
2. Comment on the transition from paragraph 21 to 22. Is it effective? Why or why
    not? [*Harbrace* 27b; *Hodges'* 31b]
3. Where does Godwin let his readers know what his essay is about? How does he
    let us know his purpose? [*Harbrace* 28a; *Hodges'* 32a]
4. The essay was first published in *Internet World* magazine, a publication read by
    people interested in and knowledgeable about the Internet. With that in mind,
    comment on the characteristics of the audience Godwin was writing for. [*Har-
    brace* 28a; *Hodges'* 32a]

ANALYZING THE ELEMENTS

Grammar

1. Examine the uses of the past and past perfect tenses in the fourth sentence in para-
    graph 2. Which event referred to in the sentence happened first and which hap-
    pened last? How do you know? [*Harbrace* 7c; *Hodges'* 7c]
2. Comment upon the use of *you* as the word modified by the participial phrase
    When talking in the first sentence of paragraph 5. [*Harbrace* 5b; *Hodges'* 25b]
3. Can the sentence fragment that begins paragraph 6 be justified? Would Godwin
    have done better to insert an innocuous verb such as *is*? Why or why not? [*Har-
    brace* 2; *Hodges'* 2]
4. Why does Godwin use *are* instead of *is* to agree with *that* in the first sentence of
    paragraph 14? [*Harbrace* 7a; *Hodges'* 6a]
5. Rewrite the first sentence of paragraph 20 to remove all verbs in the subjunc-
    tive mood. What is the effect of rewriting the sentence this way? [*Harbrace* 7d;
    Hodges' 7d]

6. In the first sentence of paragraph 19, what is the grammatical function of the phrase "That consideration aside"? [*Harbrace* 1d(3); *Hodges'* 1d(3)]

Effective Sentences

1. Consider Godwin's use of the first person pronoun in paragraphs 2, 4, 14, 15, and 22 and of the second person pronoun in paragraphs 3, 4, 5, 14, 15, 20, and 21. Comment on how this practice contributes to or detracts from sentence effectiveness. [*Harbrace* 8e(2); *Hodges'* 27b]
2. To what does *this* in the last sentence of paragraph 14 refer? To understand clearly the effect of broad reference, first justify the sentence as Godwin wrote it, and then rewrite the sentence making the reference more specific. [*Harbrace* 6b; *Hodges'* 28c]
3. Examine the relationships between coordinate and subordinate clauses in sentence 2 of paragraph 16. Explain as well as you can how these relationships contribute to making the sentence effective. [*Harbrace* 11h; *Hodges'* 29h]
4. Comment upon what makes sentence 1 in paragraph 18 effective or not effective. [*Harbrace* 11c; *Hodges'* 29c]
5. What does repetition contribute to the effectiveness of the third and fourth sentences of paragraph 22? [*Harbrace* 11e; *Hodges'* 29e]

Punctuation and Mechanics

1. Is the final clause in the first sentence of paragraph 8 restrictive or nonrestrictive? How can you tell? What does it modify? [*Harbrace* 17d; *Hodges'* 12d]
2. Why does Godwin use the full name of the FCC in paragraph 13 but not in paragraph 14? [*Harbrace* 25e; *Hodges'* 11e]
3. What do you think the quotation marks around *Carnegie Mellon* in sentence 2 of paragraph 3 mean? What other choice did Godwin have? [*Harbrace* 20c; *Hodges'* 16c]

Diction

1. Using synonyms for the following words, rewrite the sentences in which each appears: *bandied* (paragraph 5), *presumptively* (paragraph 6), *prurient* (paragraph 7), *lascivious* (paragraph 8), *pedophile* (paragraph 11), *fraudulent* (paragraph 16), *adroit* (paragraph 28), *irreducible* (paragraph 20), *rogue* (paragraph 16). [*Hodges'* 22].
2. Is the use of words such as *hype* and *fried* (paragraph 3) appropriate in an essay in which words such as *bandied, prurient,* and *adroit* are also used? Why or why not? [*Harbrace* 13b and 28a; *Hodges'* 19b-e]

BUILDING VOCABULARY

1. Identify the base form (prefix + root) from which the adverb *presumptively* is made. How many other words can be made from the same base form? What are they?

2. What other words can be formed by combining various prefixes with the root form for *presumptively?* How does each prefix change the word?

SUGGESTIONS FOR WRITING

1. Identify an issue that you think has been irresponsibly reported. Write an essay arguing that the media have an obligation to make amends for the problems their irresponsibility has created.
2. Write an essay arguing for or against the proposition that one of the most pernicious effects of pornography is the way it demeans those who read (view) it.

The Gift of Wilderness
Wallace Stegner

Wallace Stegner (1909–93) has written an impressive body of fiction and non-fiction. Among his many novels are *The Big Rock Candy Mountain, All the Little Live Things, Angle of Repose,* for which he received the Pulitzer Prize for fiction, and *The Spectator Bird,* for which he received the National Book Award. He is also the author of many nonfiction works, including *The Writer in America, Wolf Willow: A History, a Story, and a Memory of the Last Plains Frontier, The Uneasy Chair: A Biography of Bernard DeVoto,* and *One Way to Spell Man.* Born in Iowa and educated at the University of Iowa and the University of Utah, Stegner most often writes—in his nonfiction as well as his fiction—of how the good person lives responsibly in this world. That theme is reflected in "The Gift of Wilderness," in which Stegner calls attention to the responsibility we have not only to ourselves and to each other, but also to future generations and to the land itself.

Once, writing in the interests of wilderness to a government commission, I quoted a letter from Sherwood Anderson to Waldo Frank, written in the 1920s. I think it is worth quoting again. "Is it not likely," Anderson wrote, "that when the country was new and men were often alone in the fields and forest they got a sense of bigness outside themselves that has now in some way been lost? . . . I am old enough to remember tales that strengthen my belief in a deep semireligious influence that was formerly at work among our people. . . . I can remember old fellows in my home town speaking feelingly of an evening spent on the big empty plains. It had taken the shrillness out of them. They had learned the trick of quiet."   1

I have a teenaged granddaughter who recently returned from a month's Outward Bound exposure to something like wilderness in Death Valley, including three days alone, with water but no food, up on a slope of the Panamints. It is a not-unheard-of kind of initiation—Christ underwent it; Indian youths on the verge of manhood traditionally went off alone to receive their visions and acquire their adult names. I don't know if my granddaughter had any visions or heard the owl cry her name. I do know *she* cried some; and I know also that before it was over it was the greatest experience of her young life. She may have greater ones later on, but she will never quite get over this one.   2

It will probably take more than one exposure to teach her the full trick of quiet, but she knows now where to go to learn it, and she knows the mood to go in. She has felt that bigness outside herself; she has experienced the birth   3 of awe. And if millions of Americans have not been so lucky as she, why, all the more reason to save intact some of the places to which those who are moved to do so may go, and grow by it. It might not be a bad idea to require that wilderness initiation of all American youth, as a substitute for military service.

I, too, have been one of the lucky ones. I spent my childhood and youth   4 in wild, unsupervised places, and was awed very early, and never recovered. I think it must have happened first when I was five years old, in 1914, the year my family moved to the remote valley of the Frenchman River, in Saskatchewan. The town was not yet born—we were among the first fifty or so people assembled to create it. Beaver and muskrat swam in the river, and ermine, mink, coyotes, lynx, bobcats, rabbits, and birds inhabited the willow breaks. During my half dozen years there, I shot the rabbits and trapped the fur-bearers, as other frontier boys have done, and I can remember buying Canadian Victory Bonds, World War I vintage, with the proceeds from my trapline. I packed a gun before I was nine years old. But it is not my predatory experiences that I cherish. I regret them. What I most remember is certain moments, revelations, epiphanies, in which the sensuous little savage that I then was came face to face with the universe. And blinked.

I remember a night when I was very new there, when some cowboys from   5 the Z-X hitched a team to a bobsled and hauled a string of us on our coasting sleds out to the Swift Current hill. They built a fire on the river ice above the ford, and we dragged our sleds to the top of the hill and shot down, blind with speed and snow, and warmed ourselves a minute at the fire, and plowed up the hill for another run.

It was a night of still cold, zero or so, with a full moon—a night of pure   6 magic. I remember finding myself alone at the top of the hill, looking down at the dark moving spots of coasters, and the red fire with black figures around it down at the bottom. It isn't a memory so much as a vision—I don't remember it, I *see* it. I see the valley, and the curving course of the river with its scratches of leafless willows and its smothered bars. I see the moon reflecting upward from a reach of wind-blown clear ice, and the white hump of the hills, and the sky like polished metal, and the moon; and behind or in front of or mixed with the moonlight, pulsing with a kind of life, the paled, washed-out green and red of the northern lights.

I stood there by myself, my hands numb, my face stiff with cold, my nose   7 running, and I felt very small and insignificant and quelled, but at the same time exalted. Greenland's icy mountains, and myself at their center, one little spark of suffering warmth in the midst of all that inhuman clarity.

And I remember that evening spent on the big empty plains that Sher-   8 wood Anderson wrote about. In June of 1915 my father took my brother and me with him in the wagon across fifty miles of unpeopled prairie to build a house on our homestead. We were heavily loaded, the wagon was heavy and the team light, and our mare Daisy had a young foal that had a hard time keeping up. All day we plodded across nearly trackless buffalo grass in dust and heat, under siege from mosquitoes and horseflies. We lunched beside a slough where in the shallow water we ignorantly chased and captured a couple of baby mallards. Before I let mine go, I felt the thumping of that wild little heart in my hands, and that taught me something too. Night overtook us, and we camped on the trail. Five gaunt coyotes watched us eat supper, and later serenaded us. I went to sleep to their music.

Then in the night I awoke, not knowing where I was. Strangeness flowed 9 around me; there was a current of cool air, a whispering, a loom of darkness overhead. In panic I reared up on my elbow and found that I was sleeping beside my brother under the wagon, and that night wind was breathing across me through the spokes of the wheel. It came from unimaginably far places, across a vast emptiness, below millions of polished stars. And yet its touch was soft, intimate, and reassuring, and my panic went away at once. That wind knew me. I knew it. Every once in a while, sixty-six years after that baptism in space and night and silence, wind across grassland can smell like that to me, as secret, perfumed, and soft, and tell me who I am.

It is an opportunity I wish every American could have. Having been 10 born lucky, I wish we could expand the opportunities I benefited from, instead of extinguishing them. I wish we could establish a maximum system of wilderness preserves and then, by a mixture of protection and education, let all Americans learn to know their incomparable heritage and their unique identity.

We are the most various people anywhere, and every segment of us 11 has to learn all anew the lessons both of democracy and conservation. The Laotian and Vietnamese refugees who in August 1980 were discovered poaching squirrels and pigeons in San Francisco's Golden Gate Park were Americans still suffering from the shock and deprivation of a war-blasted homeland, Americans on the road of learning how to be lucky and to conserve their luck. All of us are somewhere on a long arc between ecological ignorance and environmental responsibility. What freedom means is freedom to choose. What civilization means is some sense of *how* to choose, and among what options. If we choose badly or selfishly, we have, not always intentionally, violated the contract. On the strength of the most radical political document in human history, democracy assumes that all men are created equal and that given freedom they can learn to be better masters for themselves than any king or despot could be. But until we arrive at a land ethic that unites science, religion, and human feeling, the needs of the present and the claims of the future, Americans are constantly in danger of being what Aldo Leopold in an irritable moment called them: people remodeling the Alhambra with a bulldozer, and proud of their yardage.

If we conceive development to mean something beyond earth-moving, ex- 12 traction, and denudation, America is one of the world's most undeveloped nations. But by its very premises, learned in wilderness, its citizens are the only proper source of controls, and the battle between short-range and long-range goals will be fought in the minds of individual citizens. Though it is entirely proper to have government agencies—and they have to be federal—to manage the residual wild places that we set aside for recreational, scientific, and spiritual reasons, they themselves have to be under citizen surveillance, for government agencies have been known to endanger the very things they ought to protect. It was San Francisco, after all, that dammed Hetch Hetchy, it was the Forest Service that granted permits to Disney Enterprises for the resortification of Mineral King, it is Los Angeles that is bleeding the Owens Valley dry and destroying Mono Lake, it is the Air Force that wants to install the MX Missile tracks under the Utah-Nevada desert and in an ecosystem barely hospitable to man create an environment as artificial, sterile, and impermanent as a space shuttle.

We need to learn to listen to the land, hear what it says, understand what   13
it can and can't do over the long haul; what, especially in the West, it should not be asked to do. To learn such things, we have to have access to natural wild land. As our bulldozers prepare for the sixth century of our remodeling of this Alhambra, we could look forward to a better and more rewarding national life if we learned to renounce short-term profit, and practice working for the renewable health of our earth. Instead of easing air-pollution controls in order to postpone the education of the automobile industry; instead of opening our forests to greatly increased timber cutting; instead of running our national parks to please and profit the concessionaires; instead of violating our wilderness areas by allowing oil and mineral exploration with rigs and roads and seismic detonations, we might bear in mind what those precious places are: playgrounds, schoolrooms, laboratories, yes, but above all shrines, in which we can learn to know both the natural world and ourselves, and be at least half reconciled to what we see.

✴

RESPONDING TO THE WHOLE ESSAY

1. How do the first nine paragraphs of the essay contribute to Stegner's persuasive purpose? [*Harbrace* 28a; *Hodges'* 32a]

2. Who are the people Stegner aims to persuade in "The Gift of Wilderness"? Does he hope to move his audience to a change of attitude, to action, or to both? Explain. [*Harbrace* 28a; *Hodges'* 32a]

3. Where does Stegner reveal what he is arguing for? Is his logical strategy primarily inductive or deductive? Explain. [*Harbrace* 31e and 31f; *Hodges'* 35e and 35f]

4. Which kinds of appeals discussed in the introduction to this chapter does Stegner use in "The Gift of Wilderness"? Trace the appeals in the essay and explain how they strengthen the argument. [*Harbrace* 32d; *Hodges'* 36d]

5. Explain how Stegner uses a combination of methods to develop paragraph 11. [*Harbrace* 27d; *Hodges'* 31d]

6. How does the title of Stegner's essay fit the subject matter? What does the title reveal of Stegner's attitude about his approach to his subject: [*Harbrace* 28f(3); *Hodges'* 32f(3)]

ANALYZING THE ELEMENTS

Grammar

1. In paragraph 4, why has Stegner chosen to set off the final phrase as a deliberate sentence fragment rather than include it in the previous sentence? What considerations might help a writer decide whether this technique will be effective? [*Harbrace* 2; *Hodges'* 2]
2. Stegner uses an intentional sentence fragment in paragraph 7. What might his reason(s) have been? [*Harbrace* 2; *Hodges'* 2]

Effective Sentences

1. Discuss the effects of sentence length in paragraph 9. [*Harbrace* 12a; *Hodges'* 30a]
2. Analyze and explain the effectiveness of the last sentence of the essay. [*Harbrace* 10a, 12a, and 20b; *Hodges'* 26a, 30a, and 16b]

Punctuation and Mechanics

1. Explain how the dash and the semicolon in the second sentence of paragraph 2 help to make the sentence more emphatic than three separate sentences would be. [*Harbrace* 18a and 21e; *Hodges'* 14a and 17e]
2. Explain why the third sentence of paragraph 8 is punctuated with commas rather than with semicolons. [*Harbrace* 17c; *Hodges'* 12c]

Diction

1. Discuss Stegner's use of concrete details and of figurative language in paragraph 6. [*Harbrace* 14a(4) and 14a(5); *Hodges'* 20a(3) and 20a(4)]
2. What is the Alhambra that Stegner refers to in the last sentence of paragraph 11? Why is the idea of remodeling it with a bulldozer shocking? Explain Stegner's use of the Alhambra in paragraph 13.

BUILDING VOCABULARY

1. English converts nouns to verbs and to adjectives, and verbs and adjectives to nouns by using a variety of suffixes. The suffix *-ed* combined with a noun creates a verb, and *-less* combined with a noun produces an adjective. Similarly, a verb combined with *-tion* becomes a noun, as does an adjective combined with *-ness*. Create nouns, verbs, and adjectives from the following words: *leaf, track, dark, pollute, educate, explore, detonate, strange, dark, empty, big, shrill, initiate.* (All of the words to be created occur in Stegner's "The Gift of Wilderness.")
2. The words *breaks* (paragraph 4), referring to a geographical feature, and *packed* (paragraph 4) are particularly regional terms as Stegner uses them. What do they mean? Are they defined in your dictionary? Are they marked as regional or as informal?

SUGGESTIONS FOR WRITING

1. Strong convictions frequently develop out of personal experiences. Write an essay arguing for such a conviction of yours, recounting one or more personal experiences to support your argument.

2. Write an essay arguing for or against one of the issues Stegner raises in his final paragraph: automobile emission controls, liberalization of timber cutting in national forests, private concessions in public parks, allowing oil and mineral exploration in wilderness areas.

✳

Chapter 10

A Life-and-Death Issue Debated:
The Environment

Although the six essays that follow were not written in direct response to one another, they form a debate, offering differing arguments (as well as similar ones occasionally) on issues related to the environment—whether it is in danger; what, if anything, needs to be done to protect it; what may happen if nothing is done.

As you read the essays, you will notice that they often reach different conclusions because of the different assumptions on which they are based, and even when the essays agree, they differ in the emphasis they place on particular points. They differ in tone, as well, reflecting not only the different attitudes of the writers toward both their subjects and their audiences, but also how seriously the writers take the subject.

The essays afford excellent opportunities to see at work the several appeals discussed in the introduction to chapter 9: the appeal to reason, the appeal to the reader's emotions and values, and the appeal to the credibility or authority of the one making the argument. Some of the six writers depend heavily—and some hardly at all—upon language freighted with emotional connotations. Some explicitly present themselves, or others for whom they speak, as authorities, whose views therefore deserve at least our very serious consideration; others give us hardly a clue about themselves, relying entirely on the force of the points they make and the evidence they can present.

All, however, are writers of intelligence, skill, and stature, who deserve to be read with an open mind; try as you read to set aside any preconceptions you may have about the environment. Give each writer his or her "day in court," and then judge the case as wisely and thoughtfully as you can. Each essay is followed by questions designed to help you consider its individual merits (and perhaps weaknesses). The "Suggestions for Discussion and Writing" at the end of the chapter focus for the most part on issues raised in several of the essays.

Confessions of a Nature Hater
Eugene V. Weinstock

Born in 1927, Eugene V. Weinstock received a Ph.D. in physics from the University of Pennsylvania and is associated with Brookhaven National Laboratories. He has published a number of articles on experimental reactor physics and nuclear safeguards, his most recent being an article on arms control verification. He also write short stories, which are as yet unpublished. No stranger to nature, Weinstock has lived on a farm, backpacked, and canoed. When his leisure time is not occupied waging war on nature's annoyances, he enjoys tennis, music, and reading.

I have a terrible confession to make. I like man and his works better than 1 nature. No doubt this will condemn me in the eyes of those who gush over the limited, repetitious, and near-mechanical activities of birds while disdaining the infinitely more varied repertoire of human beings.

Theirs is an essentially misanthropic view. Personally, I would rather sit 2 in my car and watch the bustle of a busy supermarket parking lot than the flittings of birds in a salt marsh. A snatch of conversation overheard in a restaurant can engage my curiosity and arouse my imagination far more effectively than the mysteries of animal migration. And I find a promenade down Fifth Avenue incomparably more interesting than a safari in the Serengeti.

Oh, like everyone else I will watch Jacques Cousteau and his rubber-suited 3 minions propelling themselves through submarine canyons, and David Attenborough bounding from continent to continent till my eyes drop out. But I never kid myself that what I am watching is reality, or that I would ever want to be a participant rather than a spectator. Long ago I learned that there is a world of difference between watching nature on television and actually experiencing it. Almost always, TV is better.

The camera condenses and prettifies things for us. Television, by tele- 4 scoping a succession of seasons into 60 minutes and entire lives into a few climactic episodes—the charge of a lion or the mating of whales—cuts out the sheer tedium of "natural" existence. It selects those moments in life that dramatize it or seem to endow it with meaning, while discarding the rest, by far the bulk of it, as irrelevant or boring. Sometimes it achieves its effect by magnifying the microscopic—for example, by filling the screen with a close-up of a bee entering a flower—thereby transforming the humdrum into the wondrous. But an ordinary observer, unequipped with a macro zoom lens, is apt to find the same scene, in its true scale, surpassingly dull.

But there is more to my lack of enthusiasm for "unspoiled" nature (by which is meant, of course, nature unspoiled by man) than that. The truth is, as anyone with half an eye can see, the natural state of living things—that is, of things living in the wild—is to be diseased, undernourished, or hunted, and sometimes, all three. For both plants and animals life is a grim struggle for survival, one in which, until the rise of modern technology and medicine, man was as often a victim as a victor.

The view that nature is red in tooth and claw is no longer a fashionable one. Instead, we now take the Panglossian position that the natural world is the best of all possible worlds. So, as we watch the lioness tearing out the throat of a gazelle, the unctuous voice of the narrator, safe in his studio in Cambridge, assures us that this is merely nature's way of weeding out the sick and the weak, thus preventing overpopulation and improving the species. To appreciate fully the reality underlying this bland assurance one has only to imagine the savannah as Central Park, the lion as a mugger, and the bleating victim as an elderly woman. Since man is also a part of nature, is the mugger, in the larger view, also improving the species?

The fact is, we enjoy these scenes and can watch them with detached interest only because we ourselves, thanks to industrialization, are no longer threatened by nature in the raw. Munching potato chips, we sit entranced as the snake swallows the rat alive, inch by inch, and the voice from *Nova* drones on soothingly about the important role of predators in preserving the precious balance of nature. The last thing we want, however, is to become part of that balance ourselves. Nature may be neither cruel nor benign, but she most assuredly isn't merciful, either.

Of course, boredom and gore aren't all there is to nature. There are also mosquitoes and biting flies, those maddening spoilers of the wild that take such a consuming interest in whatever warm-blooded creature has the misfortune to wander into their particular corner of paradise and which, in the far North, can torment caribou into headlong, suicidal flight. Thoreau, in all his rhapsodizing about the wilderness, discreetly ignores them, but my theory is that they were what drove him out of Walden after only two years.

Don't get me wrong, though. I don't actually *hate* nature. There's nothing I like better than a stroll through a tree-lined park on a summer evening, observing young lovers passing by and children from the surrounding apartment houses chasing each other across the grass. Nature's fine, as long as you don't let her get the upper hand.

✳

ANALYZING THE ARGUMENT

1. What can the reader infer from Weinstock's first paragraph about the argument that will follow? Point to specifics in the paragraph that suggest the nature of the argument.

2. What is Weinstock's thesis? Summarize the main points Weinstock makes in support of this thesis, and show where each is presented in the essay.
3. Weinstock makes three points about why he thinks civilization is preferable to nature. What are they?
4. Weinstock makes a large concession toward the end of the essay. What is it, and why is it placed at the end? [*Harbrace* 32c and 32e; *Hodges'* 36c and 36e]
5. Show where Weinstock uses appeals primarily to the emotions and values of the reader, and where primarily to reason. [*Harbrace* 32d; *Hodges'* 36d]
6. What clues does the essay contain about the audience for whom Weinstock intended it? Are there indications Weinstock was not writing for those he says disdain the "varied repertoire of human beings"? Describe Weinstock's intended audience. [*Harbrace* 28a; *Hodges'* 32a]
7. In paragraph 6, Weinstock draws an analogy between a lion and a mugger. What similarities does Weinstock see? What differences between the lion and the mugger are essential from the point of view of the environmentalist?

Buying In
Eve Pell

Eve Pell, a native New Yorker, was born in 1937 and earned a bachelor's degree from Bryn Mawr College in 1958. She has been a staff reporter for the Center for Investigative Reporting and has authored articles for *Nation, New West,* and *In These Times.* In 1971 she co-edited *To Serve the Devil,* a two-volume history of ethnic groups in the United States, and in 1972 edited *Maximum Security,* a collection of letters by convicts describing conditions in California's prisons. She teaches English at the Sara Dix Hamlin School in San Francisco, California.

1   If the 1980s taught us anything, it is that almost everything is for sale. Even the environmental movement now risks slipping under the influence of some of the most powerful corporations in the United States.

2   As the public increasingly supports environmental activism, corporate executives are gaining access to environmental organizations. Governing boards of some major environmental groups now include the chair of the New York Stock Exchange as well as executives of such corporations as Exxon, Stroh Brewery, Philip Morris, and the giant paper and pulp maker, Union Camp Corporation. Moreover, as the competition for foundation grants intensifies, corporations are giving more and more money to conservation groups. Consider that:

- The World Wildlife Fund/Conservation Foundation, one of the top ten environmental groups in the country, now lists as major donors Chevron and Exxon, which each donated more than $50,000 in 1988, as well as Philip Morris, Mobil, and Morgan Guaranty Trust.
- The National Audubon Society, which in 1986 received only $150,000 in corporate contributions, expects to receive nearly $1 million in such funds in 1989.
- The National Wildlife Federation recently added three new members to its Corporate Council. It costs each company $10,000 to join. Among the fourteen members are Arco, DuPont, and Ciba-Geigy. The Council promotes cooperation between industry leaders and environmentalists.
- The Sierra Club, after considerable agonizing, turned down $700,000 from McDonald's, which wanted to sponsor an environmental education project. McDonald's sought another environmental organization to fund. The National Audubon Society turned down a similar offer shortly afterward.

Businesses say they are just being good citizens, and the environmental   3
groups claim they can remain independent while taking corporate money. But
critics charge that the reality is far more sinister. "These corporations claim
to be environmentalists, but they are buying off the groups who are opposing them," says David Rapaport of Greenpeace. "And the corporations are
buying legitimacy as well. Dow funds environmental groups and schools in
Michigan, and the chemical companies do the same in the Louisiana chemical corridor."

The relationship between Waste Management, Inc. (WMI) and the Envi-   4
ronmental Grantmakers Association (EGA) is a prime example of the growing connection between big business and the environmental movement. Perhaps the most sophisticated of the corporate infiltrators, WMI is a worldwide
conglomerate with an annual gross income of more than $3 billion and nearly
nine hundred subsidiaries. Although WMI is the nation's largest and most
advanced handler of wastes, it is also know for its leaky landfills, its conviction for price-fixing, and its violations of environmental regulations that resulted in more than $30 million in fines being assessed from 1982 to 1987.
For those reasons it has become a prime target for many grassroots activists
around the country.

Strange as it may seem, Waste Management has been admitted to the En-   5
vironmental Grantmakers Association, an association of foundation executives who have studied, worked with, and financially supported most of the
varied organizations that make up the U.S. environmental movement today.
The diversity of the funders mirrors the diversity of the environmental movement itself, which spans a wide spectrum of environmental policies and goals—
from simple preservation of rain forests to lawsuits against polluters. By deciding which organizations get money, the grant-makers help set the agenda
of the environmental movement and influence the programs and strategies that
activists carry out.

A latecomer to philanthropy, WMI, in the past three years, has donated   6
more than $900,000 to organizations such as the National Wildlife Federa-
tion, the National Audubon Society, and the Trust for Public Land. Because
of these contributions to environmental causes, WMI's public affairs director,
Dr. William Y. Brown, was invited to attend the EGA's 1988 meeting in Princeton; his presence there made several funders very uncomfortable.

Admission to the EGA gives the controversial WMI unusual access to the   7
inner sanctum of the environmental movement. Since the funders hold frank,
detailed discussions about the activists they are considering for support, EGA
members learn the movement's plans and tactics. As a major target of some
of those activist groups, WMI is now in the position that the fox might envy:
guarding, and even financing, the henhouse.

Dr. Brown says that his company likes to fund legislative advocacy, espe-   8
cially laws to strengthen regulations governing hazardous waste. If, for instance,

laws prohibit dumping waste at sea, that means more business for WMI. "Stricter legislation is environmentally good and it also helps our business," he says. Conceding that his company "is not perfect," he says that because of the nature of its operations, it can't have "a squeaky clean record as if we made yogurt." And Brown readily admits, "The EGA has been useful for me to share information about environmental groups."

That's just what some environmentalists fear. "We don't want to be worried about giving information to the enemy," says a funder who wishes to remain anonymous. The debate over WMI has polarized the EGA into groups roughly paralleling divisions in the environmental movement, where groups that favor compromising with polluters square off against those that favor confrontation. Some funders feel that to keep lines of communication open to all, WMI must be included. Others, who believe that the EGA should hew to higher standards, refuse to attend any meeting where Dr. Brown shows up. "I have met with the parents who come from the bedsides of kids in hospitals as a result of pollution," says another foundation officer. "It's a matter of conscience for me that if he is admitted, I will leave." 9

Greenpeace, which accepts neither corporate nor foundation money, took the unprecedented step of picketing the Environmental Grantmakers' November 1989 meeting in San Francisco. There, Greenpeace activists marched around with placards telling EGA members about the local groups across the United States that are currently battling to keep WMI landfills out of their communities. Among the signs: "People for Clean Air and Water Is Fighting WMI in Kettleman, CA"; "Dumpstoppers Are Fighting WMI, Inc., in Ft. Wayne, IN"; "Alabamans for a Clean Environment Is Fighting WMI, Inc., in Emelle, AL"; "Citizens United to Recover the Environment Is Fighting WMI, Inc., in Chicago, IL." 10

To many, the question of whether to exclude WMI from the EGA dramatizes the issues facing the environmental movement in the United States today: where is its soul? And can money buy that soul? 11

Grassroots groups, such as the Citizen's Clearinghouse for Hazardous Wastes, Inc., are already suspicious of the three-way revolving door connecting many large environmental organizations (like the National Wildlife Federation and the National Audubon Society), government regulatory agencies, and big business. For example, William Ruckelshaus, the Environmental Protection Agency's first director, now chairs Browning-Ferris Industries, second in size only to WMI in the waste disposal field. Ruckelshaus also sits on the governing board of the World Wildlife Fund/Conservation Foundation. The current EPA head, William Reilly, joined the Bush administration from the World Wildlife Fund/Conservation Foundation, which he headed. This revolving door allows established Beltway insiders to move so easily from one sector to another that it is not always clear just whose interests they are serving. 12

For those who say that the dangers of accepting corporate money are exaggerated, critics point to the way WMI appeared to benefit from its relationship with the National Wildlife Federation. In 1987, WMI began giving money to the NWF. That same year, WMI chief executive officer Dean Buntrock was appointed a director of the NWF, a development that caused considerable controversy. NWF director Jay D. Hair, a figure in the upper reaches of the environmental elite, defended Buntrock and, in letters to critics of the appointment, called WMI's environmental records "responsible."   13

Buntrock then parlayed his connection with Hair into a cozy breakfast meeting with EPA chief William Reilly. Afterward, Reilly softened an EPA position on waste disposal regulations, to the benefit of WMI.   14

The events leading up to that meeting illustrate the workings of the insider network. Last March, NWF director Hair, a friend of Reilly's, suggested that Reilly meet with him and Buntrock. The invitation was written on a newspaper clipping describing a South Carolina state regulation that spelled trouble for WMI's business practices—and which the EPA had the power to affect. In the note, Hair suggested that Reilly discuss the "national implications" of the South Carolina regulation and "get to know Dean." After the breakfast, Reilly said he was reversing the EPA policy WMI disliked, telling a reporter that Buntrock had lobbied him to make the change. However, Reilly later denied to in-house investigators that any lobbying had taken place.   15

Publicly, NWF director Hair opposed the EPA policy change, but the WMI breakfast controversy shows the difficulty of determining whose side environmentalists are on once the corporate nose enters the environmental tent.   16

While corporations wishing to improve their images are able to saturate the air waves with public-relations campaigns, corporate influence over environmental organizations through quiet funding is less easily detected. Chevron's "People Do" campaign—which gives the impression that Chevron is in the business of raising eagles rather than selling oil—may be offensive, but at least viewers recognize it as a paid message.   17

Why have businesses suddenly begun funding some of their most effective adversaries—groups that have cost them billions of dollars in government regulations, court actions, fines, and other headaches? The companies are buying credibility and access to insider networks because they cannot win a free and open war of ideas, and because nothing covers up depredations like large checks.   18

Not everyone agrees with the analysis. EGA president Joe Kilpatrick asserts, "Even if corporations have adopted what they call an 'enlightened strategy' to make grants to environmental groups in order to 'inject reason' into their tactics, the grantees have their eyes open."   19

Nevertheless, it seems naive to believe that environmental groups will act any differently than politicians or judges or journalists when confronted with gobs of cold cash.   20

Do people *really* respond to large amounts of money? People do.   21

✳

ANALYZING THE ARGUMENT

1. Does Pell oppose the funding of environmental groups by corporations, warn about the problems that may result, or both? Support your answer with evidence from the essay. In one sentence, state Pell's thesis as completely and exactly as you can.

2. Pell's thesis rests upon the premise that people do, indeed, respond to large amounts of money. What evidence of this assertion does she provide? [*Harbrace* 28d; *Hodges'* 32d]

3. According to Pell, what are some reasons that corporate funding of environmental groups is dangerous? Can you think of any way an environmental group might elude this danger?

4. Is Pell's method in this argumentative essay primarily inductive or deductive? Is the other kind of reasoning also apparent? Explain [*Harbrace* 31; *Hodges'* 35]

5. Which of the appeals—to reason, to emotion, to the writer's credibility or authority—does Pell rely on in this essay? Point to and discuss examples. [*Harbrace* 32d; *Hodges'* 36d]

6. Where, if at all, does Pell acknowledge possible objections to what she is saying? If she does make such acknowledgement, does she attempt to refute the objection(s)? [*Harbrace* 32c and 32e; *Hodges'* 36c and 36e]

7. This essay appeared first in *Mother Jones,* a publication that specializes in investigative reporting having a focus on progressive politics and the arts. What qualities of Pell's essay would appeal to the regular readers of a publication like *Mother Jones*? Would anything in the essay be likely to offend such readers? If so, what and why? If not, why not? [*Harbrace* 28a; *Hodges'* 32a]

8. Paragraph 2 of Pell's essay contains five examples of corporate gifts offered to environmental organizations. Could this paragraph be used in an argument defending the actions of corporations? If so, how? If not, why not?

Toward a Land Ethic
Aldo Leopold

Known as the "father of wildlife ecology," Aldo Leopold (1887–1948) is widely respected as a scientist, philosopher, teacher, and writer. After earning a degree in forestry from Yale University, Leopold served as the Deputy Forest Assistant for the U.S. Forestry Service in Arizona and was promoted to Associate Director of the U.S. Forestry Products Laboratory. In 1928, Leopold resigned from the national forestry service to conduct research in the Midwest and teach in, and later chair, the Game Management department of the University of Wisconsin. Along with his teaching and research, Leopold founded the Wilderness Society in 1934, and wrote *Game Management* and *A Sand County Almanac*, which are revered as literary landmarks in the evolution of conservation and environmentalism. "Toward a Land Ethic" originally appeared in *A Sand County Almanac*, published one year after Leopold's death.

1   When god-like Odysseus returned from the wars in Troy, he hanged all on one rope a dozen slave-girls of his household whom he suspected of misbehavior during his absence.

2   This hanging involved no question of propriety. The girls were property. The disposal of property was then, as now, a matter of expediency, not of right and wrong.

3   Concepts of right and wrong were not lacking from Odysseus' Greece: witness the fidelity of his wife through the long years before at last his black-prowed galleys clove the wine-dark seas for home. The ethical structure of that day covered wives, but had not yet been extended to human chattels. During the three thousand years which have since elapsed, ethical criteria have been extended to many fields of conduct, with corresponding shrinkages in those judged by expediency only. . . .

4   The first ethics dealt with the relation between individuals; the Mosaic Decalogue is an example. Later accretions dealt with the relation between the individual and society. The Golden Rule tries to integrate the individual to society; democracy to integrate social organization to the individual.

5   There is as yet no ethic dealing with man's relation to land and to the animals and plants which grow upon it. Land, like Odysseus' slave-girls, is still property. The land-relation is still strictly economic, entailing privileges but not obligations. . . .

6   **The Community Concept.** All ethics so far evolved rest upon a single premise: that the individual is a member of a community of interdependent

parts. His instincts prompt him to compete for his place in the community, but his ethics prompt him also to cooperate (perhaps in order that there may be a place to compete for).

The land ethic simply enlarges the boundaries of the community to include soils, waters, plants, and animals, or collectively: the land.   7

This sounds simple: do we not already sing our love for and obligation   8
to the land of the free and the home of the brave? Yes, but just what and whom do we love? Certainly not the soil, which we are sending helter-skelter downriver. Certainly not the waters, which we assume have no function except to turn turbines, float barges, and carry off sewage. Certainly not the plants, of which we exterminate whole communities without batting an eye. Certainly not the animals, of which we have already extirpated many of the largest and most beautiful species. A land ethic of course cannot prevent the alteration, management, and use of these "resources," but it does affirm their right to continued existence, and, at least in spots, their continued existence in a natural state.

In short, a land ethic changes the role of *Homo sapiens* from conqueror   9
of the land-community to plain member and citizen of it. It implies respect for his fellow members, and also respect for the community as such.

In human history, we have learned (I hope) that the conqueror role is   10
eventually self-defeating. Why? Because it is implicit in such a role that the conqueror knows, *ex cathedra,* just what makes the community clock tick, and just what and who is valuable, and what and who is worthless, in community life. It always turns out that he knows neither, and this is why his conquests eventually defeat themselves. . . .

Substitutes for a Land Ethic.   . . . One basic weakness in a conservation sys-   11
tem based wholly on economic motives is that most members of the land community have no economic value. Wildflowers and songbirds are examples. Of the 22,000 higher plants and animals native to Wisconsin, it is doubtful whether more than 5 percent can be sold, fed, eaten, or otherwise put to economic use. Yet these creatures are members of the biotic community, and if (as I believe) its stability depends on its integrity, they are entitled to continuance.

When one of these noneconomic categories is threatened, and if we hap-   12
pen to love it, we invent subterfuges to give it economic importance. At the beginning of the century songbirds were supposed to be disappearing. Ornithologists jumped to the rescue with some distinctly shaky evidence to the effect that insects would eat us up if birds failed to control them. The evidence had to be economic in order to be valid.

It is painful to read these circumlocutions today. We have no land ethic   13
yet, but we have at least drawn nearer the point of admitting that birds should continue as a matter of biotic right, regardless of the presence or absence of economic advantage to us.

A parallel situation exists in respect of predatory mammals, raptorial birds,   14
and fish-eating birds. Time was when biologists somewhat overworked the

evidence that these creatures preserve the health of game by killing weaklings, or that they control rodents for the farmer, or that they prey only on "worthless" species. Here again, the evidence had to be economic in order to be valid. It is only in recent years that we hear the more honest argument that predators are members of the community, and that no special interest has the right to exterminate them for the sake of a benefit, real or fancied, to itself. Unfortunately this enlightened view is still in the talk stage. In the field the extermination of predators goes merrily on. . . .

Some species of trees have been "read out of the party" by economics-minded foresters because they grow too slowly, or have too low a sale value to pay as timber crops: white cedar, tamarack, cypress, beech, and hemlock are examples. In Europe, where forestry is ecologically more advanced, the noncommercial tree species are recognized as members of the native forest community, to be preserved as such, within reason. Moreover some (like beech) have been found to have a valuable function in building up soil fertility. The interdependence of the forest and its constituent tree species, ground flora, and fauna is taken for granted.   15

Lack of economic value is sometimes a character not only of species or groups, but of entire biotic communities: marshes, bogs, dunes, and "deserts" are examples. Our formula in such cases is to relegate their conservation to government as refuges, monuments, or parks. The difficulty is that these communities are usually interspersed with more valuable private lands; the government cannot possibly own or control such scattered parcels. The net effect is that we have relegated some of them to ultimate extinction over large areas. If the private owner were ecologically minded, he would be proud to be the custodian of a reasonable proportion of such areas, which add diversity and beauty to his farm and to his community.   16

In some instances, the assumed lack of profit in these "waste" areas has proved to be wrong, but only after most of them had been done away with. The present scramble to reflood muskrat marshes is a case in point. . . .   17

To sum up: a system of conservation based solely on economic self-interest is hopelessly lopsided. It tends to ignore, and thus eventually to eliminate, many elements in the land community that lack commercial value, but that are (as far as we know) essential to its healthy functioning. It assumes, falsely, I think, that the economic parts of the biotic clock will function without the uneconomic parts. It tends to relegate to government many functions eventually too large, too complex, or too widely dispersed to be performed by government.   18

An ethical obligation on the part of the private owner is the only visible remedy for these situations.   19

The Land Pyramid.   An ethic to supplement and guide the economic relation to land presupposes the existence of some mental image of land as a biotic mechanism. We can be ethical only in relation to something we can see, feel, understand, love, or otherwise have faith in.   20

The image commonly employed in conservation education is "the balance of nature." For reasons too lengthy to detail here, this figure of speech fails to describe accurately what little we know about the land mechanism. A much truer image is the one employed in ecology: the biotic pyramid. I shall first sketch the pyramid as a symbol of land, and later develop some of its implications in terms of land-use. 21

Plants absorb energy from the sun. This energy flows through a circuit called the biota, which may be represented by a pyramid consisting of layers. The bottom layer is the soil. A plant layer rests on the soil, an insect layer on the plants, a bird and rodent layer on the insects, and so on up through various animal groups to the apex layer, which consists of larger carnivores. 22

The species of a layer are alike not in where they came from, or in what they look like, but rather in what they eat. Each successive layer depends on those below it for food and often for other services, and each in turn furnishes food and services to those above. Proceeding upward, each successive layer decreases in numerical abundance. Thus, for every carnivore there are hundreds of his prey, thousands of their prey, millions of insects, uncountable plants. The pyramidal form of the system reflects this numerical progression from apex to base. Man shares an intermediate layer with the bears, raccoons, and squirrels which eat both meat and vegetables. 23

The lines of dependency for food and other services are called food chains. Thus soil-oak-deer-Indian is a chain that has now been largely converted to soil-corn-cow-farmer. Each species, including ourselves, is a link in many chains. The deer eats a hundred plants other than oak, and the cow a hundred plants other than corn. Both, then, are links to a hundred chains. The pyramid is a tangle of chains so complex as to seem disorderly, yet the stability of the system proves to be a highly organized structure. Its functioning depends on the cooperation and competition of its diverse parts. 24

In the beginning, the pyramid of life was low and squat; the food chains short and simple. Evolution has added layer after layer, link after link. Man is one of thousands of accretions to the height and complexity of the pyramid. Science has given us many doubts, but it has given us at least one certainty: the trend of evolution is to elaborate and diversify the biota. 25

Land, then, is not merely soil; it is a fountain of energy flowing through a circuit of soils, plants, and animals. Food chains are the living channels which conduct energy upward; death and decay return it to the soil. The circuit is not closed; some energy is dissipated in decay, some is added by absorption from the air, some is stored in soils, peats, and long-lived forests; but it is a sustained circuit, like a slowly augmented revolving fund of life. There is always a net loss by downhill wash, but this is normally small and offset by the decay of rocks. It is deposited in the ocean and, in the course of geological time, raised to form new lands and new pyramids. 26

The velocity and character of the upward flow of energy depend on the complex structure of the plant and animal community, much as the upward flow of sap in a tree depends on its complex cellular organization. Without 27 this complexity, normal circulation would presumably not occur. Structure means the characteristic numbers, as well as the characteristic kinds and functions, of the component species. This interdependence between the complex structure of the land and its smooth functioning as an energy unit is one of its basic attributes.

When a change occurs in one part of the circuit, many other parts must   28
adjust themselves to it. Change does not necessarily obstruct or divert the flow of energy; evolution is a long series of self-induced changes, the net result of which has been to elaborate the flow mechanism and to lengthen the circuit. Evolutionary changes, however, are usually slow and local. Man's invention of tools has enabled him to make changes of unprecedented violence, rapidity, and scope.

One change is in the composition of floras and faunas. The larger preda-   29
tors are lopped off the apex of the pyramid; food chains, for the first time in history, become shorter than longer. Domesticated species from other lands are substituted for wild ones, and wild ones are moved to new habitats. In this world-wide pooling of faunas and floras, some species get out of bounds as pests and diseases, others are extinguished. Such effects are seldom intended or foreseen; they represent unpredicted and often untraceable readjustments in the structure. Agricultural science is largely a race between the emergence of new pests and the emergence of new techniques for their control.

Another change touches the flow of energy through plants and animals and   30
its return to the soil. Fertility is the ability of soil to receive, store, and release energy. Agriculture, by overdrafts on the soil, or by too radical a substitution of domestic for native species in the superstructure, may derange the channels of flow or deplete storage. Soils depleted of their storage, or of the organic matter which anchors it, wash away faster than they form. This is erosion.

Waters, like soil, are part of the energy circuit. Industry, by polluting wa-   31
ters or obstructing them with dams, may exclude the plants and animals necessary to keep energy in circulation.

Transportation brings about another basic change: the plants or animals   32
grown in one region are now consumed and returned to the soil in another. Transportation taps the energy stored in rocks, and in the air, and uses it elsewhere; thus we fertilize the garden with nitrogen gleaned by the guano birds from the fishes of seas on the other side of the equator. Thus the formerly localized and self-contained circuits are pooled on a world-wide scale.

The process of altering the pyramid for human occupation releases stored   33
energy, and this often gives rise, during the pioneering period, to a deceptive exuberance of plant and animal life, both wild and tame. These releases of biotic capital tend to becloud or postpone the penalties of violence.

This thumbnail sketch of land as an energy circuit conveys three basic   34
ideas:

1. That the land is not merely soil.
2. That the native plants and animals keep the energy circuit open; others may or may not.

3. That man-made changes are of a different order than evolutionary changes, and have effects more comprehensive than is intended or foreseen. . . .

Land Health and The A-B Cleavage.   A land ethic, then, reflects the exis-   35
tence of an ecological conscience, and this in turn reflects a conviction of individual responsibility for the health of the land. Health is the capacity of the
land for self-renewal. Conservation is our effort to understand and preserve
this capacity.

Conservationists are notorious for their dissensions. Superficially these   36
seem to add up to mere confusion, but a more careful scrutiny reveals a
single plane of cleavage common to many specialized fields. In each field
one group (A) regards the land as soil, and its function as a commodity-
production; another group (B) regards the land as a biota, and its function
as something broader. How much broader is admittedly in a state of doubt
and confusion.

In my own field, forestry, Group A is quite content to grow trees like cab-   37
bages, with cellulose as the basic forest commodity. It feels no inhibition
against violence; its ideology is agronomic. Group B, on the other hand, sees
forestry as fundamentally different from agronomy because it employs natural species, and manages a natural environment rather than creating an artificial one. Group B prefers natural reproduction on principle. It worries on
biotic as well as economic grounds about the loss of species like chestnut, and
the threatened loss of the white pines. It worries about a whole series of secondary forest functions: wildlife, recreation, watersheds, wilderness areas. To
my mind, Group B feels the stirrings of an ecological conscience.

In the wildlife field, a parallel cleavage exists. For Group A the basic com-   38
modities are sport and meat; the yardsticks of production are ciphers of take
in pheasants and trout. Artificial propagation is acceptable as a permanent as
well as a temporary recourse—if its unit costs permit. Group B, on the other
hand, worries about a whole series of biotic side-issues. What is the cost in
predators of producing a game crop? Should we have further recourse to ex-
otics? How can management restore the shrinking species, like prairie grouse,
already hopeless as shootable game? How can management restore the threatened rarities, like trumpeter swan and whooping crane? Can management
principles be extended to wildflowers? Here again it is clear to me that we
have the same A-B cleavage as in forestry. . . .

In all these cleavages, we see repeated the same basic paradoxes: man the   39
conqueror versus man the biotic citizen; science the sharpener of his sword
versus science the searchlight on his universe; land the slave and servant versus land the collective organism. . . .

The Outlook.   It is inconceivable to me that an ethical relation to land can   40
exist without love, respect, and admiration for land, and a high regard for its
value. By value, I of course mean something far broader than mere economic
value; I mean value in the philosophical sense.

Perhaps the most serious obstacle impeding the evolution of a land ethic   41
is the fact that our educational and economic system is headed away from,
rather than toward, an intense consciousness of land. Your true modern is
separated from the land by many middlemen, and by innumerable physical
gadgets. He has no vital relation to it; to him it is the space between cities on
which crops grow. Turn him loose for a day on the land, and if the spot does
not happen to be a golf links or a "scenic" area, he is bored stiff. If crops
could be raised by hydroponics instead of farming, it would suit him very
well. Synthetic substitutes for wood, leather, wool, and other natural land
products suit him better than the originals. In short, land is something he has
"outgrown."

Almost equally serious as an obstacle to a land ethic is the attitude of the   42
farmer for whom the land is still an adversary, or a taskmaster that keeps him
in slavery. Theoretically, the mechanization of farming ought to cut the farmer's
chains, but whether it really does is debatable. . . .

The "key-log" which must be moved to release the evolutionary process   43
for an ethic is simply this: quit thinking about decent land-use as solely an
economic problem. Examine each question in terms of what is ethically and
esthetically right, as well as what is economically expedient. A thing is right
when it tends to preserve the integrity, stability, and beauty of the biotic community. It is wrong when it tends otherwise.

It of course goes without saying that economic feasibility limits the tether   44
of what can or cannot be done for land. It always has and it always will.
The fallacy the economic determinists have tied around our collective neck,
and which we will now need to cast off, is the belief that economics determines *all* land-use. This is simply not true. An innumerable host of actions
and attitudes, comprising perhaps the bulk of all land relations, is determined by the land-users' tastes and predilections, rather than by his purse.
The bulk of all land relations hinges on investments of time, forethought,
skill, and faith rather than on investments of cash. As a land-user thinketh,
so is he. . . .

The evolution of a land ethic is an intellectual as well as emotional   45
process. Conservation is paved with good intentions which prove to be futile, or even dangerous, because they are devoid of critical understanding
either of the land, or of economic land-use. I think it is a truism that as
the ethical frontier advances from the individual to the community, its intellectual content increases.

The mechanism of operation is the same for any ethic: social approbation   46
for right actions: social disapproval for wrong actions.

By and large, our present problem is one of attitudes and implements. We   47
are remodeling the Alhambra with a steam shovel, and we are proud of our
yardage. We shall hardly relinquish the shovel, which after all has many good
points, but we are in need of gentler and more objective criteria for its successful use.

✳

ANALYZING THE ARGUMENT

1. What does Leopold's opening anecdote accomplish? How is it related to the rest of the essay? [*Harbrace* 28f(1); *Hodges'* 32f(1)]
2. How does Leopold define the "land ethic"? What alternative motive for conservation does Leopold discuss? How does he characterize this viewpoint? Support your answer with evidence from the essay.
3. From paragraphs 21 through 34, the essay is given over to Leopold's description of the land pyramid and how he believes it works. Briefly summarize how this system works. What consequences does Leopold attribute to the introduction of man-made changes into this ecosystem?
4. On which of these appeals—to reason, to emotion, to personal credibility or authority—does Leopold's essay chiefly rely? On which does it least rely? Explain. [*Harbrace* 32d; *Hodges'* 36d]
5. Reread paragraphs 36 through 39, in which Leopold discusses the dissension among conservationists, and determine whether Leopold favors one group of conservationists more than the other. How can you tell?
6. Leopold identifies several obstacles to the evolution of a land ethic. What are they? Explain how Leopold proposes that his readers begin to eliminate these impediments.
7. Does Leopold object to the economic motive for conservation, warn about the problems that may result from this basis for conservation, or both? Point to evidence from the essay to support your answer. In one sentence, state Leopold's thesis as completely and exactly as you can. [*Harbrace* 28d(1); *Hodges'* 32d(1)]
8. What basic assumptions does Leopold make about his audience? Explain. [*Harbrace* 28a; *Hodges'* 32a]

Environment for Sale
Brian Tokar

An activist for two decades in the peace, anti-nuclear, and environmental movements, Brian Tokar was born in Brooklyn, New York, in 1955 and holds degrees from MIT in biology and physics (1976) and from Harvard University in biophysics (M.S., 1981). A neurophysiologist, Tokar is also an adjunct faculty member in social ecology at Goddard College. He is the author of *The Great Alternative: Creating an Ecological Future*, and of numerous articles in such publications as *The Ecologist*, the *Utne Reader, New Age Journal*, the *New Internationalist, Alternatives, The Guardian*, and *Z Magazine*, where "Environment for Sale" first appeared. Tokar lectures and consults throughout the country on technical and political aspects of environmental issues and is a founding member of the regional Green Confederation in New England and of the Central Vermont Greens. He lives on an organic vegetable farm in Plainfield, Vermont.

Few international environmental issues in recent years have raised as much 1
widespread concern or as much passion as the fate of the world's tropical forests. Tropical forests are the earth's greatest reservoir of biological diversity, housing up to three-quarters of all living species. They hold massive amounts of organic carbon and release globally-significant quantities of oxygen. Their human inhabitants include many of the last remaining tribal people whose traditional ways have not been compromised by the intrusion of civilization. The crippling indebtedness of many tropical nations, especially Brazil, has brought pressure for a wave of new development schemes, in which vast tracts of rainforest are being destroyed to satisfy the demands of international banks. Rainforest activists predict that if the destruction continues at present rates, there will be no tropical forests left in just 20 or 30 years.

In the 1980s, several Third World countries began to resist continuing 2
debt payments. Citing the effects of foreign debt on their national economies and the fact that many loans have already been paid several times over in exorbitant interest payments, several countries have threatened to default on their loans. Others have slowed debt payments to a trickle, forcing banks to admit that many Third World loans will simply never be repaid.

Anxious to keep these countries "in the system," the banks continue to 3
loan countries money to support debt payments, while proposing new, more destructive development projects and imposing ever-stricter austerity measures. In an effort to squeeze some tangible benefit from these increasingly dubious loans, banks have become increasingly involved in international

debt-swapping. They are directly trading portions of various countries' debt for equity in debtor countries, stakes in future development and, most significantly for environmentalists, commitments for the preservation and "sustainable management" of parcels of tropical forest land. Organizations like the World Wildlife Fund, Conservation International, and the Nature Conservancy are actively sponsoring so-called "debt-for-nature swaps," promoting them as vehicles for "The Greening of International Finance."

Vehicle for Exploitation.   The first, and by far the best publicized, of all these   4
"swaps" was launched in 1987 when the Frank Weeden Foundation of Connecticut granted $100,000 to Conservation International for the purchase of $650,000 in unpaid debt from a Citibank affiliate in Bolivia. In exchange, the Bolivian government had agreed to support the expansion of the Beni Biological Reserve, an ecologically unique area containing some of the world's largest remaining reserves of mahogany and tropical cedar. The Reserve itself would become protected "to the maximum extent possible under Bolivian law," according to CI, and would be surrounded by a much larger "multiple use and conservation" buffer zone, for a total of almost 4 million acres. The Bolivian government agreed to allocate $250,000 (mostly from funds generated through US-sponsored food aid) toward the management of the project. CI would provide training, technical support and other forms of international assistance for the project, and advise local agencies on the "sustainable use" of the precious mahogany forests.

Supporters of the project assert that the entire area might have been stripped   5
of trees before the next century had Conservation International not intervened, while critics argue that the entire project is merely a vehicle for the more rational exploitation of the area. Some accounts report that logging in the buffer zone has increased tremendously since the project began: twice as many mahogany trees were removed in 1988 as in 1987, for example. Contracts for several new sawmills in the area were approved immediately before the debt swap went into effect. Residents of the area were not consulted before the debt-swap agreement was signed, even though much of the land was already in dispute between logging companies and the area's 5,000 native inhabitants.

Experts in so-called "sustainable development"—one of the key catch-   6
phrases of corporate environmentalism—have carved the land up into experimental parcels which will experience varying degrees of tree harvesting, from the most limited to the most intensive. For the native people, these are trees that would have been used to build homes and canoes, and to shelter local wildlife for countless generations to come. The Moxeno and Chimane people have seen environmentalists thwart their efforts to manage the land as a community—the project's needs were apparently better served by continuing the Bolivian government's practice of maintaining native lands in isolated private plots, the preferred model in much of Latin America.

Debt-for-nature swaps, like the equity swaps upon which they were mod-   7
eled, raise serious questions about both local and national sovereignty. The

land ostensibly remains under the host country's control, but patterns of use are determined by international organizations. . . . Of course, most of the countries involved remain indebted to international banks to the tune of many billions of dollars.

African Concerns.   Concerns about the impact of such schemes have arisen   8
in Africa, where several countries are discussing plans for future debt-for-nature arrangements. Africans have already had some difficult experiences with North American conservationists. In 1909 Teddy Roosevelt went there and reportedly shot a third of the rhinos in Uganda. Groups like the World Wildlife Fund, with encouragement from wealthy big game hunters and safari enthusiasts, have been involved in the creation of National Parks in several African countries. The parks, conceived on the American model, are seen as pristine places where wild animal habitats can be preserved without human disturbance. This often happens at the expense of native peoples, who have been living alongside wild animals for countless generations and, in many cases, fought to keep slave traders, poachers and colonialists out of these areas. Without native protection wildlife habitats might be designated for preservation today, but can be eliminated tomorrow at the stroke of a pen or the roll of a bulldozer. The damage could be done before international wildlife groups knew what was happening.

In Kenya and Tanzania, the pastoral Masaai people have protected ele-   9
phants and other animals from hunters since the beginnings of European colonialism, but are being systematically excluded from National Parks planned with support from U.S. environmentalists. Moringe Parkipuny, a Masaai elder who represents his people in the national parliament of Tanzania, explains: "To us in Africa, the disappearance of the elephant is just one aspect of the major problem of colonialism. . . . The conflict, as we see it, is between indigenous peoples and the policies imposed on them by foreign governments. These policies discriminate against us by making wild animals more important than indigenous peoples. They have also turned our people against wild animals, because they feel that wildlife is now being used as a weapon to destroy us."

By blinding themselves to underlying political factors, US-based environ-   10
mental organizations become unwitting agents of imperialism overseas, just as they sometimes help to rationalize polluting practices at home.

✸

ANALYZING THE ARGUMENT

1.   What purpose is served by Tokar's opening with a discussion of tropical forests? How is it related to the rest of the essay? [*Harbrace* 28f(1); *Hodges'* 32f(1)]
2.   How would you described Tokar's tone in this essay? For example, does it reveal strong feelings on his part about the issue he is discussing, or is the tone more

dispassionate, objective? Would you say he addresses his reader in a voice that is formal, conversational, or something in between? Does he seem to assume an audience hostile to his views, sympathetic with them, or perhaps undecided but willing to hear him out? Point to specifics in the essay that support your answer. [*Harbrace* 29a; *Hodges'* 33a]

3. What is Tokar's thesis? Does he state it explicitly? If so, where? [*Harbrace* 28d; *Hodges'* 32d]

4. On which of the three appeals—to reason, to emotion, to personal credibility or authority—does Tokar's essay chiefly rely? On which does it least rely? Explain. [*Harbrace* 32d; *Hodges'* 36d]

5. What basic assumptions does Tokar make about U.S. corporations? What is the relationship of the final sentence of paragraph 3 to those assumptions? Explain.

6. What does Tokar say are the real objections to "debt-for-nature swaps"? Would you say that his distrust of financial interests is more important to him than his defense of the environment itself? Why or why not?

7. Does Tokar offer any alternatives to "debt-for-nature swaps"? If so, what are they? If not, why not?

Government Intervention Can Protect the Environment
Robert Gottlieb and Helen Ingram

Robert Gottlieb and Helen Ingram are both professors—Gottlieb in the Urban Planning Program at UCLA and Ingram at the University of Arizona. Gottlieb is well known for his writing on public policy issues and is author of several books, among them *A Life of Its Own: The Politics and Power of Water*. Ingram holds a bachelor's degree from Oberlin College (1959) and a Ph.D. from Columbia University (1967). Professor Ingram has taught at the University of New Mexico as well as the University of Arizona, and she has directed the Udall Center for Studies in Public Policy. She is the author of several books and is book review editor for the *American Political Science Review*.

Environmental policy today is at a crossroads. Attempts . . . to undo 1 the legislation and regulatory policies established during the 1970s have backfired. Environmental groups have grown in numbers and reach, and Congressional initiatives have increased. In some cases, this has led to more legislation, greater funding for environmental programs, and increased regulations.

Yet environmental problems have, for the most part, remained intractable. 2 Legislative and regulatory approaches have often been inadequate in addressing a growing set of concerns that touch the very fabric of our urban and industrial society. Target dates, such as those established by the Clean Air Act, have come and gone, without anticipated goals having been reached. While the current regulatory approaches look to tradeoffs, cost-benefit analysis, and risk assessment procedures, among others, to try to reduce or at least contain the degradation at hand, it is not even clear whether such goals will ever be met for particular contaminants, such as ozone, in those cities, such as Los Angeles or Denver, where dirty air appears to have become a permanent fixture of the urban design.

The basis for environmental policy continues to evolve around how best 3 to accommodate the dual objectives of environmental protection and economic growth. Government policymakers are continually beset by the apparently conflicting pressures regarding environmental degradation, reindustrialization (whether high tech or old tech), job creation, and community fears regarding environmental and/or economic decline. Policy questions frequently are posed as a choice between contrasting objectives: jobs versus community versus environment. Those environmental groups who accept such a framework are faced with either selecting the route of tradeoffs and compromise, and accepting some level of degradation as an inevitable byproduct of industrialization, or choosing the environment over jobs and economic growth; that is, either enter the corridors of power and likely alienate part of the environmental constituency or be considered marginal in terms of the present political discourse. It is an unhappy predicament somehow incommensurate with the overwhelming public sentiment in favor of large-scale and more definitive action to address hazardous wastes, air and water contamination, pesticide use, solid waste disposal, and countless other environmental problems of our contemporary urban/industrial society.

Protective Laws.   The established environmental movement of the 1970s and   4
1980s prided itself on developing a legislative and regulatory agenda over the years. This consisted of specific initiatives in a range of policy areas, much of which translated into laws and administrative programs designed to protect the natural environment. Efforts, such as the 1985 *Environmental Agenda for the Future* put together by the ten largest established environmental groups, represented an elaboration of this already developed program. Their approach, furthermore, has been dictated by the politics of the lobbyist, where agreements are crafted by various interest groups in a give-and-take process in which the giving often exceeds the taking when the power of money is involved.

There is, however, a more grassroots-oriented environmentalism on both   5
a more local and unyielding basis. These movements will frequently insist that a particular project such as an incinerator or a power plant be stopped. They exhibit less willingness to compromise, although their focus is usually limited to the specific matter at hand. Thus, they develop little by way of national program or agenda. Still, many of these movements have begun to make tentative efforts toward developing networks and coalitions. In the process, they have established the outlines of a statewide or national approach, albeit one confined to particular issues.

A national environmental strategy and set of policy goals and objectives   6
remain imperative in face of a declining environment and untempered forms of industrialization. Between the political constraints of the national lobbyist and the limits of a localized campaign, there needs to emerge a form of action—and theory—that links grassroots mobilization with attacking the structure of the problem on the state, national, and even international levels. Such an approach—a new environmental politics—would indeed entail the obvious ("think globally, act locally"), as well as the less obvious ("think globally, act globally") and the most immediate ("think locally, act locally").

Programs and improvements come about largely through the influence   7
of social movements and community action. Legislative initiatives, regulatory

actions, and court interventions have been framed in part by the public's concern and activity; such is likely to be the case in the future as well. Environmental "improvements" in this light reflect the state of environmental politics. . . .

Government Acts.   During the 1970s, environmental organizations were successful in establishing what came to be called the "environmental agenda," aided largely by the enormous swelling of public environmental sentiment. This included the major legislative initiatives of the decade such as the Clean Air Act, Safe Drinking Water Act, the Endangered Species Protection Act, the Resource Recovery and Conservation Act, and the Comprehensive Environmental Response, Conservation, and Liabilities Act (better known as Superfund). These bills and several others signed into law during the 1970s sought to address the problems of pollution and contamination as well as the protection of scenic and natural resources.

Environmental organizations also developed a series of complex and interactive relationships with a host of new administrative bureaucracies such as the Environmental Protection Agency and the Council on Environmental Quality, complementing the relations established by the previous generation of conservationists and preservationists with such agencies as the National Park Service, the Soil Conservation Service, and the U.S. Forest Service. Environmental groups were also successful in transforming a range of legal rulings and legislative initiatives, such as the California Friends of Mammoth ruling in 1972 and the 1969 National Environmental Policy Act, into a whole new field of environmental law where, for example, the production and review of environmental impact statements became an industry unto itself.

The election of Ronald Reagan seemed to threaten that agenda. The new administration, under the banner of deregulation, attempted to either reduce or restructure bureaucracies, limit spending levels for "clean up" legislation, and separate certain key constituencies such as hunters and fishermen and the tourism trade as a whole from the scenic protectionists among the environmental groups. While Jimmy Carter had overestimated the clout and reach of the environmental groups, particularly in the West, Ronald Reagan underestimated the elevation of environmental values among the public at large. The hard-edged rhetoric used by the President and certain of his key officials, such as James Watt and Anne Gorsuch, during much of Reagan's first term, had the immediate effect of reinvigorating environmental organizations, many of which had been ready to proclaim the end of the Environmental Decade. Most of the administration's attempts to halt expenditures, roll back legislation, or delay implementation of regulations had only limited success. In certain instances, such as passage of the Safe Drinking Water Act Amendments in 1986, Congress, responding to the strong public concerns that had evolved around the issue of groundwater contamination, restructured this legislation initiative to forestall Reagan administration regulatory backbiting, specifically referring to the efforts of the Office of Management and Budget to undermine EPA standard-setting.

Environmental Standstill.   For the most part, however, environmentally sen-   11
sitive legislators were too busy fighting the Reagan administration's attempts to march backward to push forward with new laws or approaches. Reauthorizations of existing laws became pitched battles, with changes mostly a matter of detail. Much of the significant policymaking of the Reagan years took place within the bureaucracy, far from public, and often from Congressional, scrutiny. It is not surprising that the development interests tended to fare best in restricted forums where legal and technical expertise, which can be purchased, are at a premium.

Rather than insisting upon opening agency forums and broadening con-   12
flict, some environmental groups actually cooperated in restricting public access. A great deal was made of new opportunities for negotiation and environmental mediation. Emphasis was put upon finding common ground for agreement, not upon distinguishing environmental and development viewpoints. Leaders of environmental groups were congratulated for their growing maturity, reasonableness, and sound management of what had become large-scale organizations. Instead of publicly regretting the lack of substantial accomplishment in cleaning up the environment, environmental leaders satisfied themselves that the network of regulatory laws put in place in the 1970s was not dismantled.

The apparent failure at full-blown deregulation and dismantling of legis-   13
lation, however, did not prevent the emergence of a number of new or revised approaches, some of which were embraced by both Reaganites and environmental groups. These placed the environmental issue on the level of competing technologies and reallocation of resources and minimized the role of both the government and public action. Reaganites emphasized the move toward privatization and private markets in place of government intervention, a position which attracted those environmentalists who had come to focus on government subsidies as a major source of environmental abuse. In the area of solid waste management, for example, growing environmental concerns over landfills, which in turn contributed to the price escalation of the fees per pound of waste, helped stimulate the reappearance of the incineration industry. Privatization-oriented measures, such as tax breaks and the reduction of federal grants, aided that shift, which the environmental movement was slow to address. During the late 1970s, in fact, several environmental groups even welcomed the development of this "waste-to-energy" technology, only to modify their positions later as community and neighborhood groups, worried about air contaminants, hazardous ash residue, and local neighborhood impacts, took the lead in opposing this newly touted technical solution.

The Private Sector.   The focus began to shift to the private sector as the prob-   14
lems of regulation, expensive and inefficient subsidies, and the costs of cleanup
multiplied. Water markets, for one, were identified by some in the water industry—that unique collection of public agencies and private interests—as the
best way to salvage long-standing water policies designed to stimulate irrigated agricultural production and urban development. A number of environmental groups identified with this approach, calling it a "win-win" alternative to the construction of new and potentially environmentally destructive
facilities. Yet markets also allowed pricing inequities to continue, even providing an additional benefit for those landowners wishing to either bail out
of the system or maneuver to obtain an additional profit from arrangements
that had amounted to billions of dollars in federal transfer payments to western agriculture. The buyers, meanwhile—the rapidly expanding urban com-
plexes in places like San Diego, Denver, and Phoenix—saw markets as the
way to sustain development plans in the face of newly emerging "slow growth"
movements. These movements were different from the environmental constituencies, more distinctly neighborhood- and community-oriented, focused
on the urban and industrial environment, though not unsympathetic to fears
about abuse of the natural environment.

These new social movements have compounded the complexity of the en-   15
vironmental agenda. They have raised concerns about toxics and hazardous
wastes. They worry about residential groundwater contamination and car-
cinogenic water disinfection byproducts more than protecting in-stream flows.
They have placed questions of housing, transportation, air quality, and even
economic development on the agenda, which the traditional environmental
agenda either had failed to address or addressed inadequately. These questions, however, are fundamental environmental issues. They reflect patterns
of industrialization and urbanization, the primary sources of environmental
degradation.

Environmental issues are social issues; the natural environment and the   16
human environment are intricately linked in this industrial age. Some groups
have begun to connect apparently disparate concerns such as environmentalism and feminism into a new discourse that places the abuses of industrialization in the context of daily life. Furthermore, unlike the traditional agen-
das of the nationally-oriented environmental organizations, the focus of many
of these community, neighborhood, and various "single issue" groups is local. Their issues are as much about community and democratic control as
about "natural" environmental degradation, where the focus tends to be on
national and bureaucratic solutions.

These divergent forms of environmental politics help to develop larger   17
perspectives on the environment and future political approaches. Traditional
environmentalism, aside from its long-standing interest in scenic protection,
has developed as a crisis-oriented, reactive form of politics, seeking to address
questions of "clean-up" and more effective regulation of the extraordinary
brew of new products and production processes that have heightened the po-

tential of large-scale environmental deterioration. Though this environmentalism also seeks to promote concepts of conservation and "source reduction," these are often articulated in the form of programs to make urban and industrial interests more efficient in their operations, rationalizing rather than restructuring the production process.

The Grassroots Movement. In contrast, the more populist grassroots environmentalism promotes the concept that the needs of the community, and, in its more radical form, the workplace, take precedence. Traditional environmentalism has focused primarily on protecting nature and rationalizing the system while reducing its more obvious environmental abuses. Grassroots environmentalism, dealing with everyday problems from toxics to growth, has questioned how the system functions, at least on a local and single-issue level. . . .

What is most striking about these grassroots movements is their democratic thrust, similar in some ways to the emergence of the student, civil rights, and women's movements a generation earlier. Instead of embracing expertise, they have become examples of how to develop "self-taught experts." Instead of seeking to lobby or litigate more effectively, they have become advocates of popular action and citizen lawsuits, influencing legislative debate by their mobilizing efforts rather than lobbying skills. They have become organizations of members, in neighborhoods and communities, rather than groups with organized mailing lists and membership dues which are situated in offices that take the place of communities. Most important, they have begun to demand an accounting of how actions by industries and developers, the government as well as the private sector, affect people in their day-to-day lives and impact both the environments around us and the larger natural—and social—environment.

There is a rich historical tradition related to what can be called a democratic and populist environmentalism. These were the movements that emerged in the late 19th century to address the extraordinary abuses of early industrialization and urbanization, when issues of foul air, dirty water (which killed thousands of people in countless epidemics of infectious diseases), the horrendous noises and din of the new industrial and urban order, the suffocating and overcrowded cities, and the problems of rotting and infected foods dominated the urban and industrial landscape. Rivers, streams, mountains, and wilderness were, to be sure, casualties of this new order, part of the same package of development. The movements that emerged—public sanitarians, municipal housekeepers, social feminists, both "sewer socialists" and radical syndicalists, and a range of other reformist and revolutionary movements of the moment—represented an environmental tradition much as John Muir and Gifford Pinchot did with their romantic and utilitarian impulses.

Today, the issues of the industrial and urban order are more complex and yet more extensive in their impact on peoples' lives and environments. The new grassroots movements of the 1980s are part of a range of efforts that

18

19

20

21

seek to address the consequences of this order, whether in terms of nuclear politics, economic dislocation, or the problems of the environment writ large or small. In this sense, environmentalism can be seen not as an "interest group" seeking better regulation or protection of scenic resources, but as an essential component of a new democratic politics. It is a politics where "risk" is no longer just a question of what contaminant we are prepared or not prepared to live with, but a question of dealing with the hazards of an undemocratic society where the decisions that affect our lives are made elsewhere.

✹

ANALYZING THE ARGUMENT

1. Gottlieb and Ingram's essay is divided into five points: protective laws, governmental acts, environmental standstill, the private sector, and the grassroots movement. Explain how each of these sections is related to the point they make.
2. Where do you first discover Gottlieb and Ingram's thesis? State it in as few words as you can. [*Harbrace* 28d; *Hodges'* 32d]
3. What opposing arguments, if any, do Gottlieb and Ingram acknowledge? How do they deal with them? [*Harbrace* 32c and 32e; *Hodges'* 36c and 36e]
4. In "Government Intervention Can Protect the Environment" do Gottlieb and Ingram rely primarily on the appeal to credibility, the appeal to reason, or the appeal to the emotions and values of their readers? Are all three appeals present? Supply evidence to support your answer. [*Harbrace* 32d; *Hodges'* 36d]
5. How effective is Gottlieb and Ingram's introduction to this argument? Does their use of the crossroads image at the beginning of paragraph 1 support the thesis? If so, how? If not, why not? [*Harbrace* 28f(1); *Hodges'* 32f(1)]
6. Comment upon the meaning and rhetorical effect of each of the following phrases: *backfired* (paragraph 1), *tradeoffs* (paragraph 2), *high tech* (paragraph 3), *clout* (paragraph 10), *privatization* (paragraph 13), *bail out* (paragraph 14), *brew* (paragraph 17), *impact* (paragraph 19). [*Harbrace* 13a and 14a; *Hodges'* 19a, 20a, and 23e(2)]
7. Do Gottlieb and Ingram rely primarily upon inductive or deductive reasoning, or do they make use of another model? Explain. [*Harbrace* 31e, f, and g; *Hodges'* 35e, f, and g]

The Environmental Mindset
Rush Limbaugh III

In 1983, long-time radio broadcaster Rush Hudson Limbaugh III (1951–) launched his talk show, *The Rush Limbaugh Show*. Limbaugh's on-air persona as an outspoken critic of liberals, feminists, and social activists immediately made him a controversial media figure, but it also brought him nationwide attention. His talk show soon emerged as a nationally syndicated radio and television program, reaching millions of listeners and viewers. Recently, Limbaugh introduced a new nationally syndicated radio program, the *Rush Limbaugh Morning Update*. Limbaugh also visits 45 cities across the nation in his Rush to Excellence Tour each year. The following selection is from Limbaugh's book of social commentary, *The Way Things Ought to Be*.

I used to think environmentalists were a bunch of political liberals who 1
were just using a different angle to advance their cause. Some of that goes on. But it goes beyond merely advancing liberalism. There are two groups of people that have made environmentalism their new home: socialists and enviro-religious fanatics. And they have chosen two new constituencies which cannot speak or disagree and therefore cannot refuse their "help and assistance": animals and trees.

With the collapse of Marxism, environmentalism has become the new 2
refuge of socialist thinking. The environment is a great way to advance a political agenda that favors central planning and an intrusive government. What better way to control someone's property than to subordinate one's private property rights to environmental concerns.

The second group that has latched on to the environmental movement are 3
people who believe it is a religion; that God is the earth and that God is nothing more than the earth. Actually, it is a modern form of pantheism, where nature is divine. This group wants to preserve the earth at all costs, even if it means that much of the Third World will be forever condemned to poverty. Rather than elevate the Third World, they want to move us closer to Third World conditions. That's somehow cleaner, and purer. It's the way things were before Western white people came along and terrorized the earth by inventing things. They want to roll us back, maybe not to the Stone Age, but at least to the horse-and-buggy era.

Both of these groups are consumed with egocentricity. They behave as 4
though they believe the world began the day they were born and that it's going to end the day they die.

Now, I've spoken about the leaders of the radical environmental move- 5
ment. The followers are also interesting. They are the people who just want
to feel good; the people who want to receive accolades for their perceived care
and concern for the environment. Then we have the media who willingly serve
as conduits for all of these predictions, studies, prophecies, and tall tales that
the environmentalist wackos disseminate.

But there are also many average Americans who consider themselves en- 6
vironmentalists. It is quite natural to want a clean planet, with clean water
and air for ourselves and our children. It is quite commendable to not want
to destroy that which enables us to live. So, if some scientist comes along and
is given credibility by the media, it is not surprising that a lot of people believe him. That is how hundreds of thousands of people are mobilized for the
cause and end up on the Mall in Washington and in Central Park in New York.

What these decent people have to realize is that regardless of what per- 7
spective they have—socialist, religious, or whatever—a common characteristic of those in the radical environmental movement is the belief that private
property rights will have to be severely curbed in this country. That's what is
behind the move to take private land out of circulation to preserve wetlands,
and the efforts to save the spotted owl. If it rains in your backyard one day
and you have an inch of water there, all of a sudden your yard becomes a
wetland and you can't build anything there.

This hostility to private property, my friends, is based on the belief that 8
human beings can't be trusted to own very much of the land; that we are selfish and cursed with the desire to change nature. We are 4 percent of the world's
population here in America and we use 25 percent of the world's resources.
How dare we be so selfish. Never mind the fact that our country feeds the
world. Never mind the fact that our technology has improved life everywhere
on this planet.

I believe that many environmental leaders are quite sincere, but that they 9
all operate from a fundamentally different viewpoint than most other people.
You and I and the vast majority of other people work for a living. We hold
jobs in which we produce something or perform a service. We create commerce.

Most of the people running environmental groups don't work. What they
do is persuade other people to donate to their cause. They live well, with a 10
fair amount being siphoned off for expenses, conferences, and high salaries.
They've become dependent on the income from donations. These people want
to improve their standard of living and so they have to build up their donations. There are only so many people who will give to create bird sanctuar-
ies in this country. That's why some environmentalists have gone into crisis
mongering to increase the level of their donations. Their appeals and their
scare tactics are designed to transform people into foot soldiers in the army
of doomsday environmentalism.

It's interesting to note which environmental hazards these people really 11
worry about. It is those that are caused by business or man-made things.
Consider the danger of radon gas. If there is one environmental problem that

is real, it is radon. Some Easterners have homes where radon seeps in from under the ground and reaches levels many times beyond what is considered safe. But there is no hysteria over radon. Why? Because it's natural, man didn't put it there. There are no dramatic calls for radon studies, nor any calls for evacuations. Everything that happens in their deified nature is somehow acceptable. Things will work themselves out. Well, man-made disasters can also work themselves out. Take the *Exxon Valdez* spill. We were told that the cleanup would take hundreds of years. Now we see that through natural processes and the incredibly resilient powers of the planet, the tide has taken care of much of the damage that man didn't clean up. And, would you believe that more fish were caught last year than ever before in Prince William Sound?

My friends, the earth is a remarkable creation and is capable of great rejuvenation. We can't destroy it. It can fix itself. We shouldn't go out of our way to do damage, but neither should we buy into the hysteria and monomania which preaches, in essence, that we don't belong here. We have a right to use the earth to make our lives better.

12

✳

ANALYZING THE ARGUMENT

1. What can a reader infer from the first paragraph about the argument that will follow? Point to specifics in the paragraph that suggest the nature of the argument.

2. Limbaugh focuses on two types of environmentalists. What are they? How does he characterize them? Does he view environmentally minded "average Americans" in the same way? Why or why not?

3. Are there any underlying assumptions upon which the argument is based? If so, what are they? If not, how can you tell?

4. Comment upon the kind of appeal that Limbaugh makes in "The Environmental Mindset." Is the primary appeal to logic? to the attitudes and values of the reader? to Limbaugh's credibility? to more than one of these? Point to evidence in the essay to support your answer. [*Harbrace* 32d; *Hodges'* 36d]

5. What is Limbaugh's thesis and why does it occur where it does? What would be the effect if it came in the middle of the essay? at the end? [*Harbrace* 28d; *Hodges'* 32d]

6. How would you describe Limbaugh's tone in this essay? Does he address the topic from an objective viewpoint or from his own strong beliefs about it? Does he address his readers in a formal voice? a conversational voice? or something in between? [*Harbrace* 29a; *Hodges'* 33a]

7. Does the argument contain any concessions to those who would be likely to disagree? If so, where and what are the concessions? If not, why? [*Harbrace* 32c and 32e; *Hodges'* 36c and 36e]

8. What does Limbaugh's use of *my friends, we,* and *you and I* suggest about his intended audience? Does Limbaugh reveal other assumptions about his audience? If so, what are they? How can you tell? [*Harbrace* 28a; *Hodges'* 32a]

SUGGESTIONS FOR DISCUSSION AND WRITING: A LIFE-AND-DEATH ISSUE DEBATED

1. With your classmates—in discussion groups or, if your instructor prefers, as a whole class—list (1) all the specific arguments leveled against private involvement in environmental action in the six essays just presented, and (2) all the specific arguments presented in favor of it in the essays. (You might also want to list points for and against government involvement.) After each point, write in parentheses the names of the essayists who advance it. This analysis will help you to see the essays in relation to one another and should also help you carry out the other suggestions that follow here.

2. With your classmates, list as many possible arguments as you can think of—both for and against private/government involvement in environmental action—that are not advanced by any of the writers in this section.

3. In his essay, "Toward a Land Ethic," Aldo Leopold asserts that conservationists can be classified according to their view of nature as either a commodity or a biotic system. Analyze the essays in this section to discover which of these views informs the arguments set forth by each essayist. Which of these views of nature would you say predominates in the arguments in this chapter? Which of these views do the essayists find most objectionable?

4. Whatever positions they may take on who should control environmental action, a number of the authors focus either mainly or partly on ways that policies and regulations have been evaded. Summarize these objections and then argue either that such objections can or that they cannot be conclusive as arguments concerning who should control environmental action.

5. Choose any practice you encounter frequently that you consider potentially harmful to the environment (for instance, packaging fast food in styrofoam containers, dumping old engine oil in the garbage) and argue as convincingly as you can for the discontinuation of that practice. (You may need to do a little research.)

6. Several of the essays in this chapter discuss the reasons why people become active in environmentalism. Working in small groups, or if your instructor prefers, as a whole class, identify and discuss what motives for environmental action are revealed in the essays written by Leopold, Limbaugh, Pell, and Ingram and Gottlieb. Which motives, if any, appear to be based solely on assumptions made by the authors? How can you tell? How would you characterize environmental activists?

7. The majority of essays in this section discuss environmental protection in terms of economic issues; however, as Leopold has shown, economic concerns are not the only reason (or even the primary reason) for protecting the environment. Danger to all of life as we know it from pollution and unsound use of the environment is a far more urgent issue. Write an essay for an audience of your classmates arguing for or against a government tax on air conditioners (which uses large amounts of environmentally damaging freon). As with the essays you have read, you will need to consider such questions as whether the benefits to the society balance the effects on the environment, whether the preservation of the environment overrides any perceived benefit to society, who would be most damaged by such a tax, whether such a tax would actually reduce use of freon (an analogous situation is the gasoline tax)—and there are undoubtedly other considerations. You may use any evidence you draw from these essays, and you may wish to consult other sources.

Chapter 11

The Essay Examination: A Student Writer across the Disciplines

Essay examinations impose a variety of constraints on the writer. Pressure of time is the most obvious, but others are important as well. In the time allowed (usually fifty minutes, rarely more than two or three hours), you must produce answers that are:

Exactly responsive to the question asked,

Complete and factually accurate,

Convincingly supported by specific details,

Coherent and well organized,

Clearly and concisely written, and

Free of grammatical and mechanical errors.

Faced with these requirements, obviously you should do everything you can in advance to make the task go smoothly. And there is much that you can do. From the first day of the course, discipline yourself to *think critically* about the material presented in class and in your reading rather than merely trying to absorb it all. As you take notes in class, jot down reminders ("TEST?") to yourself about points that could become the basis for essay-examination questions. If you listen (and watch) closely, you will usually be able to discern what information your instructor considers especially important. Unlike instructors, written texts cannot raise their voices or punctuate the air with gestures, but they have their own ways of providing emphasis. Which topics are given the most space? Which topics are explicitly mentioned in chapter titles or in headings within the chapters? What terms are italicized for emphasis or defined at length, or both? In your textbooks look at the beginnings of chapters for lists of "learning objectives," the concepts or subjects you should have mastered when you read the chapter. Also pay particular attention to material at the ends of chapters that may summarize key points. Thinking critically also means looking for relationships among the facts or concepts you encounter; essay questions very often focus on such relationships, as all three of

401

Anne Nishijima's essays in this section illustrate. If you do all of these things, you will find there is a benefit besides being prepared for examinations: you will learn a great deal more from the course than you would have otherwise.

Your notebook can be an important resource. Use it not only as a place to deposit information gained from lectures and class discussions but also as a journal in which you anticipate questions and try out answers. A few days before the examination, review your notes to sort out again what is most important, searching for relationships you might have missed earlier in the semester. See if you can develop new questions, and plan answers to them.

When the examination begins, take a few minutes before starting to write to budget your time. Some experts advise about twenty percent of the time you allocate to a question should be spent in planning, about seventy percent in writing, and about ten percent in reviewing and revising what you have written. Glance through the entire examination before you begin to do anything else. If the examination requires that you answer several questions, budget the most time for the questions that are worth the most points. It is usually a good idea to answer those questions first. However, if you draw a blank about them at that moment, working on another question may stimulate your thinking and help you recall the information you need.

Essay-examination questions are usually carefully worded and often specify the method you should use in your answer: compare, define, analyze, explain, argue, and so on. However the question is phrased, make sure your answer responds to it exactly. Even if you feel insecure about your ability to answer well, resist the temptation to wander from the question asked to discuss a topic you think you can handle better; such digressions will almost always cost you more than you could hope to gain. As you plan your answer, try jotting down (inconspicuously in the margin or a corner of the page) a few key words or phrases that stand for the main ideas you intend to cover; such a list—a small working plan—will help to ensure that you don't skip anything important, an easy thing to do when you are writing under pressure.

When you begin writing, get right to the point in your first paragraph. Your reader should be able to see immediately that you have grasped the question and are on your way to answering it. For example, a common type of essay question quotes an assertion from one of the assigned readings and asks you to agree or disagree, defending your position with evidence drawn from the course. In such a situation, begin your essay with a clear statement of the position you are taking. Not only will such a statement up-front demonstrate to your reader that you are on the right track; it will also help you *stay* on the track as you write the essay.

Be sure to support any generalizations with specifics: details, examples, illustrations, quotations. It is these particulars, not your general statements, that will convince your instructor that you really know what you are talking about. Be direct and confident in your tone; an answer written with assurance is more likely to convince a reader than one that is larded with unnecessary qualifications or that seems apologetic.

In the time you have set aside for revision, reread your essay and make corrections and any other changes you think will improve it. Don't hesitate to cross out or insert material, but make the changes as neatly as possible. Check to make sure your sentences are clear and grammatical and that spelling and punctuation are correct.

The following pages present Anne Nishijima's answers to essay-examination questions in three courses: American Intellectual History, Introduction to Shakespeare, and Vertebrate Zoology. The answers for the history and Shakespeare tests show Nishijima's revisions, visible as crossed-out and inserted material.

Examination 1:
American Intellectual History
Anne Nishijima

The question in this examination is unusually broad, offering little guidance, but Anne Nishijima quickly finds a topic she wishes to pursue and writes directly to that point. Nishijima sets herself a difficult task: to argue the importance of environment in the determination of an individual's worldview, an exploration of the nature-nurture theme. In fact, the choice is probably too ambitious—forcing her to sacrifice the kind of specific detail that a more restricted, and therefore more manageable, topic would have permitted; however, she carries it off remarkably well. Notice that her primary method of development is that of cause and effect; for further discussion of this development strategy, see chapter 5.

QUESTION: This examination is in two parts. The first, consisting of a series of short-answer questions, is to be completed and handed in before going on to the second part, and in any event after thirty minutes of the exam have lapsed. *The second part is to be answered in the form of an essay, drawing upon the readings, lectures, discussions, and your own considered reflections on American intellectual life during the Age of Henry Adams and William James.*

ESSAY:

What determines a person's point of view? Why does one thinker see fit to agree with his colleagues' philosophy, or his society's philosophy, when another feels called upon to choose a different, possibly new, direction? ~~While Henry Adams was prophesying the doom of mankind and others of his social and intellectual ilk were Specifically, why how did William James happen of Pragmatism his philosophy of Pragmatism when all about him, men of equal intelligence were bogged down still caught up in still bogged down with Social Darwinism?~~ If biography is ~~construed to mean~~ defined as one's temperament and heritage, then biography alone cannot explain innovation. The influence of people, ideas, and experience must be brought to bear on temperament ~~and the mind~~ before it can be inspired to originate anything of its own. Genetic makeup, which is the only part of

404

heritage that is not ~~brought~~ shown to the individual by people, ideas, and experience, is not sufficient. ~~Twins~~ Many people of vastly different genetic background can hold the same opinions, and identical twins often think very differently from one another. Clearly, other factors must be involved.

William James's life and development as a philosopher illustrate the way in which outside influences shape the individual's thought. Although he grew up in and was, by virtue of his role as an intellectual, exposed to a high degree to Social Darwinism, ~~the prevalent philosop~~ he was not content to believe ~~what so many others~~ in it, for several reasons.

James's first influence was his father, who taught him to think and to reason. Henry James, Sr., stayed home during the day, having no trade that would keep him away, and amused himself by inventing *games* ~~things~~ to keep his children busy. On Sundays, they would be sent to the different churches in town to listen to the sermons so they could report *to their father* what had been said. Already, then, when most children are jealously ~~being brought up to in the "best" creed by their parents and are~~ being protected from subversive *creeds* ~~ideas~~ while their minds are still in the formative stage, the James children were being exposed to different interpretations of religion and philosophy.

~~As James grew older, he was educated in the proper and orthodox ways~~

~~When James came face to face with~~

~~When the time came for James to choose his avocation, he was undecided. He seemed only to know that he did not want to be a Social Darwinist.~~

~~Yet more than anything, James, when he began writing, was reacting against the ideas of his time.~~

~~This~~ Such exposure allowed William James to realize that options exist; the solution to a problem is not necessarily a given. ~~And~~ This concept was to become the foundation for his philosophy of Pragmatism.

We see, then, that the philosopher's upbringing is important. (Had Adams, for instance, been raised to think freely rather than to listen to the conversations of his elders and betters, he might have had a shot at leading a more optimistic life.) But James also shows us that the prevailing intellectual climate is at least as important.

Pragmatism was, to a large extent, a direct reaction against Social Darwinism. James held that, given a set of data, it is often possible to reach several conclusions and, therefore, choose one of several different directions. The Darwinist believed, however, that given the same set of data, only one conclusion could possibly result. Furthermore, that result would come about by itself. The Grand Pooh-Bah of Natural Selection would see to it that each course was continued to its end. To some, like Adams, the end was cold, lethargic doom. To others, it was the creation of a single perfect species. ~~But to James, even if events *were* controlled by unavoidable fate, the end might be either perfection or doom. Or it might be something entirely different.~~

Social Darwinism, then, had ~~run its course.~~ *OK* "Whatever is to happen," said the Darwinist, "there is nothing you or I can do about it. In fact, there's really no point in thinking about it." What philosophy could be more stultifying to an active, intelligent mind such as James's? Furthermore, the separation between rich and poor was getting rapidly wider, and social injustices were getting more and more horrifying. *OK* ~~Society~~ was ripe for conversion. Society embraced Progressivism, and philosophers were prepared to consider Pragmatism.

Social and intellectual climate, personal experience, all are part of the process by which a thinker like William James devises his philosophy. The influence of individuals also plays a part. The writings of Charles S. Peirce and Clifford both helped James refine his philosophic method, though in very different ways. Even the writers who criticized or objected outright to James's ideas aided him in straightening out any logical errors he may have made.

Although the nature-nurture question will never be answered satisfactorily, it is evident that outside influences are necessary to development. In the case of William James, I have endeavored to show some of these influences and their effects. Undoubtedly, temperament played a large role in determining these effects, ~~but temperament must in part~~ but equally, influences must determine the actions of the temperament. Biography, i.e., heritage and temperament, cannot act alone.

> INSTRUCTOR'S COMMENT: On balance, an attractive, even persuasive, answer, though one a bit short of the kind of illustrative detail that goes far to tie down any argument on behalf of a, at the least, disputable view. Still, an interesting response.

✳

Examination 2:
Introduction to Shakespeare
Anne Nishijima

Nishijima's task in her Shakespeare test is considerably more clearly defined than in the history test. Having considered the question carefully, she states her approach to it in her first sentence, then devotes most of the rest of the essay to supporting her case with specific details, illustrations, and examples. Her method of development—specified in the examination question—is that of comparison and contrast; for further discussion of this development strategy, see chapter 6.

QUESTION: Choose two important characters from different plays you have read so far in the term, and explore their essential similarities and differences. (40 points)

ESSAY:

Shakespeare's Richard III and Brutus are, in a sense, ~~mirror images~~ *opposites* of each other. Where the former is entirely self-directed, doing all he can to further his own cause, the latter puts aside his own desires and natural judgment to further what he believes is the cause of Rome and her citizens. Richard is savage and twisted, physically as well as mentally; Brutus is, above all, an honorable man. Yet two so different characters wind up in similar plights, fighting to maintain hold on a crown illegally seized.

One is tempted, to cite a closer parallel. Richard's mock refusal of the crown is inescapably similar to Caesar's refusal. Shakespeare himself asks us to make the comparison when he has Richard discuss how Julius Caesar built the Tower of London, a place of which Richard himself makes great use.

Yet there are similarities between Richard and Brutus. Both, it is true, are ambitious, though for different causes. Both are willing to kill those in power to get power for themselves. Both fight bravely and desperately in the end (assuming that the horse King Richard calls for is to be used to join the fray, not flee from it, and granting that Brutus' suicide is a brave act).

There the similarities end. The differences, which are more widespread, can be seen clearly in, for example, their relationships with their allies and co-conspirators. Richard uses Hastings and Buckingham (and anyone else he can) for his own ends, fully intending to get rid of them permanently when their usefulness is ended. Brutus, on the other hand, remains faithful to his co-conspirators and even treats his enemy, Marc Antony, with fairness and consideration. And whereas Richard kills everyone ~~who might get~~ who stands in his way, Brutus, at some risk to himself, persuades the conspirators not to kill Antony, whose presence on the scene is certainly dangerous to Brutus.

A very clear difference is seen in their treatment of their women. Brutus loves his wife, and mourns her death with despair and convincing restraint. Richard woos and marries Anne with scorn, for political reasons only, does her in, and then proposes to go after young Elizabeth. One can easily imagine him reacting to Anne's death with a show of crocodile tears in contrast to Brutus' reluctance to show and succumbs to his more plausible grief.

Richard, of course, is capable of acting as though he were every bit as honorable as Brutus. Before others he is always the injured party, longing to be friends with Elizabeth's brothers who refuse, unjustly, to trust him. He is the noble lord protector who must explain, ever so sadly, to the young princes that they must not trust their uncles. But Shakespeare is careful to provide us with frequent monologues from Richard in which he states his true aims, lest we too may be taken in by him.

One could try to read Brutus' character in the same way, and see him as a clever, ambitious man eager to take advantage of his fellow citizens' ~~discontent~~ disenchantment ~~of~~ with Caesar. One could believe Antony that Caesar put aside the crown deliberately and sincerely, not disingenuously. But such a reading is hard to maintain in the absence of Richard-like monologues, and overt glimpses of Brutus' dissembling.

Finally, there is the argument between Brutus and Cassius towards the end of *Julius Caesar*. It is rare in drama, where time and space are limited by the confines of the stage and the audience's attention span, to have two characters have ~~an arg~~ a dispute that is amicably settled, unless that is the main subject of a comedy. But the argument, and its subsequent in *Julius Caesar*, peaceful conclusion, prove beyond all doubt the essential differences between Brutus and Richard. It is very characteristic of Brutus to keep his temper and make friends again ~~to~~ with Cassius, even though Cassius (unbeknownst to Brutus) has deceived him. On the other hand, it would be greatly out of character for Richard to back down in an argument, or to wish to make peace, even with so loyal an ally as Buckingham.

Richard and Brutus are, therefore, like parallel arrows that point in opposite directions. The similarity in their circumstances is brought about by opposite goals and intentions.

> **INSTRUCTOR'S COMMENT:** You write well and knowingly about the two characters, and on balance one certainly agrees with you about the essential differences between the two. Yet there is a good deal of similarity, too, and I think you could go further in acknowledging and exploring the parallels. It is not just a forced reading of *Caesar* that sees Brutus as somewhat self-congratulatory and self-deceived in believing that murder is good. He is human and appealing, in contrast to Richard, but his actions don't seem all that different, whatever his intentions.

✳

Examination 3:
Vertebrate Zoology
Anne Nishijima

Nishijima's zoology test provides the most specific directions, though she must still choose the particular groups of animals she will write about. Note, incidentally, that this essay contains no obvious revisions. It was, however, revised. The examination was of a special kind you may sometimes be given: the "take home" examination. In such a test, you are allowed to write at home, referring to notes and books as necessary. Obviously, more time—typically a day or two—is available, and a clean copy can be handed in. In developing her answer, Nishijima combines several methods, especially description, comparison and contrast, and classification and division—all of which she handles extremely well. (For discussions of these strategies, see chapters 3, 6, and 7.)

QUESTION: Describe the adaptations of a group of predators that allow them to hunt effectively, and the adaptations of prey that help them elude carnivores. Discuss the relationships between these adaptations of adversary animals.

ESSAY:

The big cats of Africa, the lion and cheetah in particular, have like all cats developed a set of adaptations which allow them to chase down their prey. Aside from the forward-oriented eyes and sharp tearing and shearing teeth that are universal in mammalian carnivores, felines have exceedingly flexible backbones and strong shoulder musculature. With this kind of physique, a running cat can reach forward with its fore paws, pull itself rapidly over the ground, bend its back to reach forward with the hind paws, and then straighten the back to begin another stride with its fore paws. In this way, the feline is permitted a long stride for fast sprinting. However, such a strategy is a compromise. What a cat gains in speed it loses in endurance. The animal tires quickly and cannot run long distances because much of the forward force created by the hind limbs against the ground is lost to the flexibility of the vertebral column.

It is here that the ungulates have "found" their advantage. They are provided with stiff backbones that transmit the force of the hind legs against the ground into forward motion. Thus, although the animal cannot run as fast as its feline predator, and does not have as long a stride, it can run farther. If it becomes aware that it is being stalked, it can outrun a would-be killer fairly handily. To aid in perceiving prey, ungulates have laterally oriented eyes, large ears, and a tendency to form herds in which some animals are keeping watch at any given time.

Perhaps in response to these defensive mechanisms, various cats have developed ways of quite literally catching their prey by surprise. Lions are colored like the sun-dried grass in which they hunt. The males, with their impressive and conspicuous manes, do not hunt. It is the more inconspicuous females who do the hunting, and though they are less speedy than some felines, they make up for it with strategy, hunting in groups.

The cheetah, hunting in the same environment as the lion, also has concealing coloration, being dappled with small black spots on a dun background. Such dappling helps to mask the outline of an animal. Its claws are not fully retractable so that it has good traction, and it has particularly large scapulae and strong pectoral musculature on a long and supple body. With such assets, it does not need to hunt in groups, and so it is a solitary creature by and large, though its cubs spend an unusually long time with their mother learning hunting techniques.

Thus, predators and prey have developed skills and strengths that complement each other. Which developed in response to what is a chicken-and-egg question; probably they evolved in leap-frog fashion, each kind of animal responding to the other simultaneously. In the end, they reached a balance that allows predators to catch enough prey for their species to survive, and the prey sufficient means of escaping to perpetuate their species. Both, in the long run, are successful.

INSTRUCTOR'S COMMENT: Nicely done. Excellent choice of subject. Your command of species is impressive, and the whole is *very* well written.

✳

✳

Chapter 12

Writing from Research

Preparing a research paper can be a highly rewarding experience that you will remember with a sense of achievement long after college. The key is, first of all, to choose a subject that genuinely interests you and that you would like to learn more about; next, to limit and focus the subject so that you can do a thorough job with it in the time and space you have; and, finally, to work systematically, following time-tested procedures that will help you avoid becoming disorganized or overwhelmed.

The two research chapters of *Harbrace* (33 and 34) and *Hodges'* (37 and 38) guide you through the process in detail. This chapter of *The Resourceful Reader* is intended to help you by supplementing handbook chapters with additional examples, particularly a "case study" of one student's progress from a rough idea to a finished paper.

Between *Harbrace* (and *Hodges'*) and *The Resourceful Reader* you have nine researched papers available to you as examples, seven by students and two by professional scholars. The student papers are Katie Frushour's and Adrienne Harton's in *Harbrace* 34 and *Hodges'* 38, the three student essays in *Harbrace* 35 and *Hodges'* 39*, and Bill Wallace's and Barbara Kiger's in this chapter. The professionally written examples are both in this text: "The Harlem Renaissance: One Facet of an Unturned Kaleidoscope" by Darwin Turner in chapter 2 and "'We can't dance together'" by María Rosa Menocal in chapter 9. As you examine these essays, however, bear in mind that they do not all employ the same documentation style or even the same level of documentation. Five of the student essays and the essay by Menocal use the documentation style of the Modern Language Association of America (MLA), the style you are most likely to be asked to use in a college composition course. Turner's essay follows an older documentation style that uses *ibid.* and traditional footnotes for citations. Kiger's and Harton's essays follow the style of the American Psychological Association (APA), the most widely used style in the social sciences.

One of the most important challenges in writing a research paper is finding an appropriate subject. The advice in *Harbrace* 28b and *Hodges'* 32b

---

*These three essays do not appear in the *Harbrace Handbook, Brief Thirteenth Edition*.

and the questioning methods discussed in *Harbrace* 28c(1) and *Hodges'* 32c(1) can help you. Whatever subject you choose, it should be something that genuinely interests you. If a subject is assigned to you, of course, you may have a problem unless you are lucky; however, even a subject that seems to leave you cold can often be given an interesting focus if you consider it from different angles. Try some of the procedures described in *Harbrace* 28c(1), and *Hodges'* 32c(1).

Finding a general subject was fairly difficult for Bill Wallace, whose research paper appears in this chapter. His assignment was vague—write a research paper on a literary topic using at least five different sources. Wallace conferred with the instructor and with other students to try to pin down something he would be interested in doing. Noting a possible connection between his interest in fantasy fiction, information from a mythology course he was taking, and an assignment in the previous semester's English literature course, he decided to write about J. R. R. Tolkien's use of northern European mythology to create his mythic world.

Wallace began his research by consulting the library's online computer catalog. He found several books by Tolkien that seemed to be suitable and that his library had. He printed out the bibliographic information for each source—author, title (and subtitle, if any), and quite a bit of publishing information including whatever he would need if he later decided to use that source. He then switched to the MLA and *Reader's Guide* online databases to see what he could find on Tolkien's mythology in journals and magazines.

As he discovered possible sources, Wallace built his working bibliography, cutting and pasting from the database to his word processing program. (Instead of using a computer, he could have gone to the library and written the information on index cards or in a notebook, as researchers have done for years.) When he looked at the books and articles themselves, he added to each entry a one-sentence statement of what the book or article was about. This would come in handy when he decided to limit his topic to the mythological associations as revealed in a comparison of *Beowulf* and *The Hobbit*.

A sample entry that he printed for his working bibliography from a database follows.

AUTHOR: Provost, William.
TITLE: Language and myth in the fantasy writings of J. R. R. Tolkien.
SOURCE: Modern Age v. 33 (Spring '90) p. 42–52.

In creating his "works cited" list, Wallace carefully followed MLA style, which was the style specified by his instructor. [*Harbrace* 33b, 33g and h, and 34; *Hodges'* 37b, 37g and h, and 38] To do so, he cut and pasted from his working bibliography, making whatever adjustments were required to conform to MLA style. If Wallace had been using cards, he would have entered information for each source, carefully following MLA, which would later have enabled him to type the information from his cards directly into his final list of "works cited." When Wallace completed his working bibliography, he had 17 entries representing material that seemed promising.

Wallace had found a number of sources but still lacked a clear direction for his research project. Wisely, he decided to consult a biographical dictionary of literary topics, which included a substantial essay on Tolkien. He found a reference to Tolkien's efforts to make his fantasy world seem real. This reference suggested the direction Wallace's essay finally took—the role played by the mythology of northern Europe in the creation of Tolkien's world. Wallace was lucky to find a way to focus his project so quickly. A good rule of thumb is that if you find dozens of sources on your topic, your subject is too broad; if you find fewer than a dozen, it may be too narrow.

With this focus, Wallace was on his way. He also found—a pleasant surprise after his initial frustration—that he was more excited about this topic than he had expected. In fact, this is not surprising; it is almost always easier to be interested in specifics than in generalities. He began to read the source materials and take notes. The key to successful note taking is to find and evaluate useful passages quickly and efficiently, checking tables of contents and indexes and then skimming the pertinent pages for information related to the chosen topic. Wallace created computer files to hold bits of information or comments that he thought he would be able to use in his paper, a new file for each source. In each case, he had to decide how he would write down what he found—whether to summarize, paraphrase, or quote. [*Harbrace* 33f; *Hodges'* 37f] Each note file contained the author's name flush left on the first line and the page number from which the note came on the right margin. Additionally, Wallace entered a descriptive heading, such as "weapon" or "dragon," to help him classify and arrange his information.

Bill Wallace

Professor McLeod

English 102.A9

November 10, 1996

J. R. R. Tolkien's Mythology

If history were to be forgotten and our concept of God along with it, people would still require something to believe in. The stories of J. R. R. Tolkien could record myths as readily believed in as were those the ancients found in the stories of Homer and Vergil. As Augustus M. Kolich notes in the <u>Concise Dictionary of British Literary Biography,</u>

> [t]he driving passion of John Ronald Ruel Tolkien's literary life was to make his "fairy stories" so complete in description and detail, so varied in character and action, so expansive in philosophy and religion, as to be "real." (369)

This strong sense of reality derives in large part from familiarity. Tolkien used familiar childhood tales and traditional legends as a core around which he solidified a mythology for western civilization that in its conception is truly northern European, a coalescence of Teutonic and Celtic myth:

> A number of the beings in Tolkien's works are completely supernatural. These include the Valar, Wizards, Elves, Dwarves, Bombadil and Goldberry, Ents, and such evil creatures as Sauron, the Orcs, and the Balrog. They belong to the classes of beings which, at one time or another and in one form or another, were worshipped as gods by Celts, Teutons, and indeed most European peoples. Beings analogous to them were revered in most parts of the world. (Noel 98)

The creation of this mythic world grounded in the northern European mythos, that rich lode of legend, fable, and "fairy stories," was a task for which Tolkien was uniquely prepared, for Anglo-Saxon language and literature and its sources in myth and legend were his area of scholarly expertise.

A comparison of the Anglo-Saxon poem <u>Beowulf</u> with <u>The Hobbit</u> clearly reveals the origins of Tolkien's fables. Beginning with the monsters in both works, one easily finds similarities between Grendel and Gollum. For instance, each has his own underground lake habitat. Tolkien describes Gollum's in <u>The Hobbit:</u>

416

There were strange things living in the pools and lakes in

the hearts of mountains. . . . Deep down here by the dark

water lived old Gollum, a small, slimy creature. (78-79)

Although we are not shown Grendel's lair immediately when we meet

him, we soon find that he, too, like Gollum and like everything

else dark and slimy, has his home in an underground lake:

He went before with a few wise-men to spy out the country,

until suddenly he found mountain trees leaning out over

hoary stone, a joyless wood: water lay beneath, bloody and

troubled. (Tuso 25)

We see the true nature of Grendel's habitat only when Beowulf

fights Grendel's mother:

Then the earl saw that he was in some hostile hall where no

water harmed him at all, and the floods' onrush might not

touch him because of the hall roof. (27)

But Grendel and Gollum share other similarities besides the un-

derground habitat. Both use stealth to attack, though each employed

his own style. In The Hobbit Gollum had the One Ring, which made

him invisible. This, coupled with his natural stealth, made him a

dangerous opponent indeed. But the Gollum that we are most familiar

with, the Gollum from Lord of the Rings, no longer has the ring

and must rely on his natural instinct, much like Grendel. Grendel

used the cloak of night to hide his actions, being thereby both

visible and invisible. "There came gliding in the black night the

walker of darkness" (Tuso 13). Clearly, if size were to be over-

looked, the descriptions of the two monsters are virtually inter-

changeable.

A comparison of The Hobbit and Beowulf can also clearly show

that Tolkien probably based much of his characterization of Smaug

on the dragon from the final episode of Beowulf. To be specific,

the generic worm of Beowulf inhabits a barrow—a burial mound (39).

Early Germanic peoples often buried their kings and mighty heroes

in barrows with all their treasure. The well-characterized (and

well-heeled) dragon of The Hobbit, Smaug, lived in the same kind

of place, the kind of place the Beowulf Poet called the "lonely

mountain" (35).

Furthermore, the word "barrow" is derived from the Old English

word "beorg" which is related to the German word "berg" meaning

"mountain" (Noel 168). This language connection supports the assertion that a close relationship can be drawn between Beowulf and
"The King Under the Mountain," the chapter from The Hobbit describing Smaug. If we substitute the word "barrow" for "mountain," the
connection is obvious: "The King Under the Barrow."

A study of the weapons that helped both Bilbo and Beowulf defeat their monsters supports the idea that Tolkien derived many of
his ideas for The Hobbit from Anglo-Saxon sources. Sting, Bilbo's
blade, is instrumental in allowing its owner to defeat Gollum at
playing the game of riddles and so save his life (80). Sting is
thus comparable to the victory-blessed blade that allows Beowulf to
finally put an end to the Grendel family (27). Both tales make much
of named, magical, ancestral weapons, and Tolkien emphasizes the
theme by endowing Bard with a similar weapon named "Black Arrow."
Furthermore, "Black Arrow" gives Bard the edge he needs to finally
slay Smaug (237), just as the magical giant sword aids Beowulf
(although luck also plays an important part in the deaths of both
Smaug and Grendel's mother).

A further symmetry can be seen in the characterizations of the
heroes themselves. In both tales, there are actually two key heroes, the young hero and the old hero. In Beowulf, the old hero
and the young hero are the same person revealed to us at different
times of life, whereas in The Hobbit, the young hero and the old
hero are separate characters, Bilbo and Thorin, respectively. Both
stories show how the young hero triumphs and how the old hero dies.
Bilbo, the young hero of The Hobbit, lies in wait invisibly to
triumph over Gollum, just as Beowulf lies in wait for Grendel to
attack Heorot once more. The young Beowulf triumphs over Grendel
and the water hag, but the old Beowulf is killed fighting the
barrow dragon and with his death buys the dragon's treasure for his
people. Although the old hero of The Hobbit, Thorin, does not die
fighting the dragon, he is killed in the battle of the five armies
defending his people's claim to Smaug's halls of gold.

In Beowulf the young warrior Wiglaf provides the lucky assistance that allows Beowulf to finally kill the dragon and win its
treasure for his people, though Beowulf dies in the attempt. In
The Hobbit it is the young warrior, Bard, who actually kills the
dragon, allowing Thorin's friends and fellow dwarves to claim the
enormous treasure of Smaug's huge barrow-mound. These echoes of

<u>Beowulf</u> that are found in <u>The Hobbit</u> clearly show the strong influence of Anglo-Saxon/Teutonic myth and legend in Tolkien's first work, an influence that can be continuously seen throughout his later works.

Tolkien also draws upon northern European roots for the poetry which gives vigor to his world and his characters. Primarily through kennings, Tolkien's poetry shows influence not only of Teutonic sources, but also of medieval Celtic sources (Rogers 33). Including these recreations of early Germanic and Celtic forms allowed Tolkien to make his fiction seem more real, a technique only now being used by a few end-of-the-century writers. Perhaps it was Tolkien's view of himself as a philologist first that inspired him to do so (Kolich 372).

Tolkien captures and molds the amorphous legends and tales of ancient Europe into a solid mythology that captures the modern spirit (Provost 42). But, alas, mythologies must be built over time. It took Tolkien his whole life to concentrate the scattered myths of Europe into an all-encompassing work, <u>The Silmarillion</u> (Kroeber 522). Undoubtedly the culmination of his life's work, the development of a modern Western mythology that began with <u>The Hobbit</u> reached its culmination in this last and final book which allows us a glimpse of the reservoir from which flowed <u>The Hobbit</u> and <u>The Lord of the Rings.</u>

Works Cited

Kolich, Augustus M. "J. R. R. Tolkien." <u>Concise Dictionary of British Literary Biography: Modern Writers.</u> Vol. 6. Detroit: Gale, 1991.

Kroeber, Karl, "J. R. R. Tolkien." <u>British Writers.</u> Sup. II. New York: Scribner's, 1992.

Noel, Ruth S. <u>The Mythology of Middle Earth.</u> Boston: Houghton, 1977.

Provost, William. "Language and Myth in the Fantasy Writings of J. R. R. Tolkien." <u>Modern Age</u> 33 (1990): 42–52.

Rogers, Deborah W. "Literary Backgrounds." <u>J. R. R. Tolkien.</u> Boston: Twayne, 1980.

Tolkien, J. R. R. <u>The Hobbit.</u> New York: Ballantine, 1937.

Tuso, Joseph F., ed. <u>Beowulf: A Norton Critical Edition.</u> New York: Norton, 1975.

America's Forgotten People

Barbara Kiger

Sociology 243

Professor Ortega

March 3, 1993

Running Head: Forgotten People

America's Forgotten People

Living in the inner city, I witnessed a great number of homeless people struggling to survive the winter months. Each time I
passed one of their cardboard homes or noticed them sleeping in
the doorways of abandoned shops, I became more and more interested
in the impact of homelessness; but it was really not until I
learned that the younger sister of one of my high school friends
had become homeless that I was motivated to look into the problem
carefully.

"Widespread homelessness in the U.S. may be dated back from
the period immediately following the Civil War" when men whose
platoons had been disbanded were on the move (Hopper, 1990, p. 13).
At this time, the homeless men were referred to as "hoboes, tramps,
gandy dancers, and knights of the road; only later were 'bums' and
'derelicts' common epithets" (p. 13). Today, homelessness affects
all types of people, cutting across race, gender, and age barriers.
Frequently homeless people have been "stripped of traditional social
roles and brutalized in a variety of ways" (D'Ercole & Struening,
1990, p. 141). On the street, these people lack adequate shelter,
clothing, and food. They are often robbed and victimized physically
and sexually. Struening and Padgett (1990) assert that "many homeless persons are afflicted by both mental and physical comorbidi-
ties, imposing a tremendous burden on their lives" (p. 66). In
fact, many homeless people suffer from alcoholism, drug abuse,
and such chronic diseases as AIDS as well.

These days, men are not the only homeless people. Women, too,
who live on the streets endure this victimization and disease,
yet most of them have fled to the streets to avoid the same experiences in the home. For instance, most women become homeless due
to domestic violence and eviction. And because of the victimization
regularly directed at homeless women, they experience higher levels
of fear than do homeless men (D'Ercole & Struening, 1990, p. 141).
And not only does this social problem impact women; many women are
forced to bring their children to the streets with them and to try
to nurture these children in this dangerous environment. That a
woman is responsible for caring for children no doubt also raises
her level of fear, often leading to depression or other mental
illnesses. D'Ercole and Struening's study confirms that sixty-three

percent of a shelter sample of homeless women were mothers, of
whom twenty-seven percent had some college education or were college graduates (p. 145). The education and marital status of these
women varied greatly, yet most had children, and several had their
children with them on the street. Although D'Ercole and Struening
focus on homeless women in their study, their findings imply a
significant problem regarding homeless children, concerning whom
there are few studies.

One study, however, was completed by Janice Molnar, William R.
Rath, and Tovah Klein (1990). In their article, "Constantly
Compromised: The Impact of Homelessness on Children," Molnar et al.
claim that "one in four preschoolers lives in poverty" and that
within the rising number of homeless, the number of homeless
children is increasing the fastest (p. 109). In fact, the 1989
U.S. Conference of Mayors reported that children and families
account for thirty-eight percent of homeless people. In addition
to safety hazards, homeless children encounter many health hazards
while living on the streets. For instance, a large number of homeless children have high lead levels in their blood and suffer from
vitamin and mineral deficiencies, leading to anemia and slow wound-
healing (Molnar et al., 1990, p. 111). These children are extremely
susceptible to disease and receive little health care and few
immunizations because the parents do not know where to take the
children for medical help (p. 113).

However, physical distress is only one facet of children's life
on the street. Most of these children are exposed to this harmful
environment during the stages of cognitive and social development.
In a New York City shelter sample of preschool children, Phillips
and Hartigan observed "language delays, problems in conceptualizing
cause-and-effect relationships and time sequencing, difficulty in
organizing behavior (especially in transitions), and a lack of em-
pathy and the difficulty in the ability to share" (Molnar et al.,
1990, p. 115). The effects of homelessness on children are many,
especially during the preschool years; yet homelessness affects
adolescents in much the same way.

Homeless adolescents consist of both throwaways and runaways.
Throwaways are socially rejected teens who have generally experienced prolonged abuse and neglect and are finally forced to leave

home. In a study of homeless adolescents, Thomas Gullota (1978) discovered that the average age that a youngster is expelled from the home is about fifteen (p. 545). Because these adolescents are rejected by their parents and usually have few friends, they often choose to commit delinquent acts in an attempt to be accepted by their peer group on the streets (Heir, Korboot, & Schweitzer, 1990, p. 763). Heir et al. assert that although "both runaways and throw-aways [in an Australian sample] were found to have high scores on hostility, antisocial tendency, depression, and social isolation," throwaways were generally less aggressive than runaways, and female throwaways were more socially isolated than female runaways (pp. 769-770). Runaways, teens between the ages of eleven and seventeen who decide to leave home without parental consent (Brennan, Huizinga, & Elliott, 1978, p. 2), generally run away from home to escape family conflicts or to get the attention of their alienated parents. Most of these teens leave home with "no specific destina-tion" in mind, and, therefore, end up on the streets (Orten & Soll, 1980, p. 252). Often these girls and boys become delinquent, espe-cially those with low self-esteem, powerlessness, normlessness and high societal estrangement (Brennan et al. 1978, p. 242). However, Henggeler, Edwards, and Borduin (1987) contend that "families of female delinquents are more dysfunctional than those of male delin-quents" (p. 200), and the study completed by D'Ercole and Struening (1990) shows that most homeless women were once runaways or lived in a foster home (p. 143).

In any case, none can deny that the quality of life the home-lessness experience deteriorates. Not only those who have left home to find a better situation but also those who are forced to move to the streets are often disappointed to find life on the streets so difficult. The physical and emotional hardships quickly take their toll leaving these people destitute, trying to cope with mental illness, alcoholism, drug abuse, and poor health. Because of the large number of homeless, solutions to the problem are far in the future. Although many health and housing programs have been instated, most of these people end up in prisons or stay on the streets. Perhaps early intervention or better communication could decrease the number of runaways, now at 1.2 million a year (Hersch, 1988, p. 31), but the problems of those who are mentally ill or who have been evicted from their homes are entirely different from those of runaways. Breakley and Fischer (1990) suggest that "service planners must consider the diversity of the people affected and the variety of problems that compound their difficulties" (p. 43).

Perhaps the answer does lie in the hands of policy makers, but that certainly looks like just another instance of buck-passing. No one seems to be considering how the problem of homelessness will proliferate; homelessness appears to beget homelessness. Unless everybody takes some responsibility to do something practical about the problem now, in the long run, homelessness may be everybody's problem.

References

Breakley, W., & Fischer, P. (1990). Homelessness: the extent of the problem. Journal of Social Issues, 46(4), 31-47.

Brennan, T., Huizinga, D., & Elliott, D. (1978). The social psychology of runaways. Lexington, MA: Lexington Books.

D'Ercole, A., & Struening, E. (1990). Victimization among homeless women: implications for service delivery. Journal of Community Psychology, 18, 141-152.

Gullota, T. (1978). Runaway: reality or myth. Adolescence, 13(52), 15-20.

Heir, S. J., Korboot, P. J., & Schweitzer, R. D. (1990). Social adjustment and symptomology in two types of homeless adolescents: runaways and throwaways. Adolescence, 25(100), 761-771.

Henggeler, S., Edwards, J., & Borduin, C. (1987). The family relations of female delinquents. Journal of Abnormal Child Psychology, 15(2), 199-209.

Hersch, P. (1988, January). Coming of age on city streets. Psychology Today, 28-37.

Hopper, K. (1990). Public shelter as "a hybrid institution": homeless men in historical perspective. Journal of Social Issues, 46(4), 13-29.

Molnar, J. M., Rath, W. R., & Klein, T. P. (1990). Constantly compromised: the impact of homelessness on children. Journal of Social Issues, 46(4), 109-124.

Orten, J. D., & Soll, S. K. (1980). Runaway children and their
    families. <u>Journal of Family Issues, 1</u>(2), 249-261.

Struening, E., & Padgett, D. (1990). Physical health status,
    substance use and abuse, and mental disorders among homeless
    adults. <u>Journal of Social Issues, 46</u>(4), 65-81.

Chapter 13

For Further Reading:
Some Classic Essays

The Allegory of the Cave
Plato

SOCRATES,
GLAUCON. The
den, the prisoners:
the light at a
distance;

And now, I said, let me show in a figure how far our 1
nature is enlightened or unenlightened:—Behold! human beings living in an underground den, which has a mouth open
towards the light and reaching all along the den; here they
have been from their childhood, and have their legs and necks
chained so that they cannot move, and can only see before
them, being prevented by the chains from turning round their
heads. Above and behind them a fire is blazing at a distance,
and between the fire and the prisoners there is a raised way;
and you will see, if you look, a low wall built along the way,
like the screen which marionette players have in front of
them, over which they show the puppets.

I see. 2

the low wall, and
the moving figures
of which the
shadows are seen
on the opposite
wall of the den.

And do you see, I said, men passing along the wall car- 3
rying all sorts of vessels, and statues and figures of animals
made of wood and stone and various materials, which appear over the wall? Some of them are talking, others silent.

You have shown me a strange image, and they are 4
strange prisoners.

Like ourselves, I replied; and they see only their own 5
shadows, or the shadows of one another, which the fire
throws on the opposite wall of the cave?

True, he said; how could they see anything but the shad- 6
ows if they were never allowed to move their heads?

And of the objects which are being carried in like man- 7
ner they would only see the shadows?

Yes, he said. 8

And if they were able to converse with one another, 9
would they not suppose that they were naming what was
actually before them?

Very true. 10

And suppose further that the prison had an echo which 11
came from the other side, would they not be sure to fancy
when one of the passers-by spoke that the voice which they
heard came from the passing shadow?

No question, he replied. 12

To them, I said, the truth would be literally nothing but 13
the shadows of the images.

That is certain. 14

And now look again, and see what will naturally fol- 15
low if the prisoners are released and disabused of their error. At first, when any of them is liberated and compelled
suddenly to stand up and turn his neck round and walk and
look towards the light, he will suffer sharp pains; the glare
will distress him, and he will be unable to see the realities
of which in his former state he had seen the shadows; and
then conceive some one saying to him, that what he saw before was an illusion, but that now, when he is approaching
nearer to being and his eye is turned towards more real existence, he has a clearer vision—what will be his reply? And
you may further imagine that his instructor is pointing to
the objects as they pass and requiring him to name them,—
will he not be perplexed? Will he not fancy that the shadows which he formerly saw are truer than the objects which
are now shown to him?

Far truer. 16

And if he is compelled to look straight at the light, will 17
he not have a pain in his eyes which will make him turn
away to take refuge in the objects of vision which he can
see, and which he will conceive to be in reality clearer than
the things which are now being shown to him?

True, he said. 18

And suppose once more, that he is reluctantly dragged 19
up a steep and rugged ascent, and held fast until he is forced
into the presence of the sun himself, is he not likely to be
pained and irritated? When he approaches the light his eyes
will be dazzled, and he will not be able to see anything at
all of what are now called realities.

*The prisoners
would mistake
the shadows for
realities.*

*And when
released, they
would still persist
in maintaining
the superior truth
of the shadows.*

*When dragged
upwards, they
would be dazzled
by excess of light.*

Not all in a moment, he said.   20

He will require to grow accustomed to the sight of the   21
upper world. And first he will see the shadows best, next
the reflections of men and other objects in the water, and
then the objects themselves; then he will gaze upon the light
of the moon and the stars and the spangled heaven; and he
will see the sky and the stars by night better than the sun
or the light of the sun by day?

Certainly.   22

At length they will   Last of all he will be able to see the sun, and not mere   23
see the sun and   reflections of him in the water, but he will see him in his
understand his   own proper place, and not in another, and he will contem-
nature.   plate him as he is.

Certainly.   24

He will then proceed to argue that this is he who gives   25
the season and the years, and is the guardian of all that is in
the visible world, and in a certain way the cause of all things
which he and his fellows have been accustomed to behold?

Clearly, he said, he would first see the sun and then rea-   26
son about him.

They would then   And when he remembered his old habitation, and the   27
pity their old   wisdom of the den and his fellow prisoners, do you not sup-
companions of   pose that he would felicitate himself on the change, and pity
the den.   them?

Certainly, he would.   28

And if they were in the habit of conferring honors   29
among themselves on those who were quickest to observe
the passing shadows and to remark which of them went before, and which followed after, and which were together;
and who were therefore best able to draw conclusions as to
the future, do you think that he would care for such honors and glories, or envy the possessors of them? Would he
not say with Homer,

Better to be the poor servant of a poor master,

and to endure anything, rather than think as they do and
live after their manner?

Yes, he said, I think that he would rather suffer any-   30
thing than entertain these false notions and live in this miserable manner.

Imagine once more, I said, such a one coming suddenly   31
out of the sun to be replaced in his old situation; would he
not be certain to have his eyes full of darkness?

To be sure, he said.   32

And if there were a contest, and he had to compete in   33
measuring the shadows with the prisoners who had never
moved out of the den, while his sight was still weak, and before his eyes had become steady (and the time which would
be needed to acquire this new habit of sight might be very
considerable), would he not be ridiculous? Men would say of
him that up he went and down he came without his eyes; and
that it was better not even to think of ascending; and if any
one tried to loose another and lead him up to the light, let
them only catch the offender, and they would put him to death.

No question, he said.   34

This entire allegory, I said, you may now append, dear   35
Glaucon, to the previous argument; the prison house is the
world of sight, the light of the fire is the sun, and you will
not misapprehend me if you interpret the journey upwards
to be the ascent of the soul into the intellectual world according to my poor belief, which, at your desire, I have expressed—whether rightly or wrongly God knows. But,
whether true or false, my opinion is that in the world of
knowledge the idea of good appears last of all, and is seen
only with an effort; and, when seen, is also inferred to be
the universal author of all things beautiful and right, parent of light and of the lord of light in this visible world, and
the immediate source of reason and truth in the intellectual;
and that this is the power upon which he who would act
rationally either in public or private life must have his eye
fixed.   36

I agree, he said, as far as I am able to understand you.   37

Moreover, I said, you must not wonder that those who
attain to this beatific vision are unwilling to descend to human affairs; for their souls are ever hastening into the upper world where they desire to dwell; which desire of theirs
is very natural, if our allegory may be trusted.   38

Yes, very natural.   39

And is there anything surprising in one who passes from
divine contemplations to the evil state of man, misbehaving
himself in a ridiculous manner; if, while his eyes are blinking and before he has become accustomed to the surrounding darkness, he is compelled to fight in courts of law, or in
other places, about the images or the shadows of images of
justice, and is endeavoring to meet the conceptions of those
who have never yet seen absolute justice?

Margin notes:

But when they returned to the den they would see much worse than those who had never left it.

The prison is the world of sight, the light of the fire is the sun.

Nothing extraordinary in the philosopher being unable to see in the dark.

Anything but surprising, he replied. 40

Anyone who has common sense will remember that the 41
bewilderments of the eyes are of two kinds, and arise from
two causes, either from coming out of the light or from going into the light, which is true of the mind's eye, quite as
much as of the bodily eye; and he who remembers this when
he sees anyone whose vision is perplexed and weak, will not
be too ready to laugh; he will first ask whether that soul of
man has come out of the brighter life, and is unable to see
because unaccustomed to the dark, or having turned from
darkness to the day is dazzled by excess of light. And he will
count the one happy in his condition and state of being, and
he will pity the other; or, if he have a mind to laugh at the
soul which comes from below into the light, there will be
more reason in this than in the laugh which greets him who
returns from above out of the light into the den.

That, he said, is a very just distinction. 42

But then, if I am right, certain professors of education 43
must be wrong when they say that they can put a knowledge into the soul which was not there before, like sight into
blind eyes.

They undoubtedly say this, he replied. 44

Whereas, our argument shows that the power and ca- 45
pacity of learning exists in the soul already; and that just as
the eye was unable to turn from darkness to light without
the whole body, so too the instrument of knowledge can
only by the movement of the whole soul be turned from the
world of becoming into that of being, and learn by degrees
to endure the sight of being, and of the brightest and best
of being, or in other words, of the good.

Very true. 46

And must there not be some art which will effect con- 47
version in the easiest and quickest manner; not implanting
the faculty of sight, for that exists already, but has been
turned in the wrong direction, and is looking away from the
truth?

Yes, he said, such an art may be presumed. 48

And whereas the other so-called virtues of the soul 49
seem to be akin to bodily qualities, for even when they are
not originally innate they can be implanted later by habit
and exercise, the virtue of wisdom more than anything else
contains a divine element which always remains, and by
this conversion is rendered useful and profitable; or, on the

---

Margin notes:

The eyes may be blinded in two ways, by excess or by defect of light.

The conversion of the soul is the turning round the eye from darkness to light.

The virtue of wisdom has a divine power which may be turned either towards good or towards evil.

other hand, hurtful and useless. Did you never observe the narrow intelligence flashing from the keen eye of a clever rogue—how eager he is, how clearly his paltry soul sees the way to his end; he is the reverse of blind, but his keen eyesight is forced into the service of evil, and he is mischievous in proportion to his cleverness?

Very true, he said.   50

But what if there had been a circumcision of such na-   51
tures in the days of their youth; and they had been severed from those sensual pleasures, such as eating and drinking, which, like leaden weights, were attached to them at their birth, and which drag them down and turn the vision of their souls upon the things that are below—if, I say, they had been released from these impediments and turned in the opposite direction, the very same faculty in them would have seen the truth as keenly as they see what their eyes are turned to now.

Very likely.   52

Yes, I said; and there is another thing which is likely,   53
or rather a necessary inference from what has preceded, that neither the uneducated and uninformed of the truth, nor yet those who never make an end of their education, will be able ministers of State; not the former, because they have no single aim of duty which is the rule of all their actions, private as well as public; nor the latter, because they will not act at all except upon compulsion, fancying that they are already dwelling apart in the islands of the blessed.

Very true, he replied.   54

Then, I said, the business of us who are the founders of   55
the State will be to compel the best minds to attain that knowledge which we have already shown to be the greatest of all—they must continue to ascend until they arrive at the good; but when they have ascended and seen enough we must not allow them to do as they do now.

What do you mean?   56

I mean that they remain in the upper world: but this   57
must not be allowed; they must be made to descend again among the prisoners in the den, to partake of their labors and honors, whether they are worth having or not.

But is not this unjust? he said; ought we to give them a   58
worse life, when they might have a better?

You have again forgotten, my friend, I said, the inten-   59
tion of the legislator, who did not aim at making any one

Neither the uneducated nor the overeducated will be good servants of the State.

Men should ascend to the upper world, but they should also return to the lower.

class in the State happy above the rest; the happiness was to be in the whole State, and he held the citizens together by persuasion and necessity, making them benefactors of the State, and therefore benefactors of one another; to this end he created them, not to please themselves, but to be his instruments in binding up the State.

True, he said, I had forgotten.   60

The duties of philosophers

Observe, Glaucon, that there will be no injustice in compelling our philosophers to have a care and providence of others; we shall explain to them that in other States, men of their class are not obliged to share in the toils of politics: and this is reasonable, for they grow up at their own sweet will, and the government would rather not have them. Being self-taught, they cannot be expected to show any gratitude for a culture which they have never received. But we have brought you into the world to be rulers of the hive, kings of yourselves and of the other citizens, and have educated you far better and more perfectly than they have been educated, and you are better able to share in the double duty. Wherefore each of you, when his turn comes, must go down to the general underground abode, and get the habit of seeing in the dark. When you have acquired the habit, you will see ten thousand times better than the inhabitants of the den, and you will know what the several images are, and what they represent, because you have seen the beautiful and just and good in their truth. And thus our State, which is also yours, will be a reality, and not a dream only, and will be administered in a spirit unlike that of other States, in which men fight with one another about shadows only and are distracted in the struggle for power, which in their eyes is a great good. Whereas the truth is that the State in which the rulers are most reluctant to govern is always the best and most quietly governed, and the State in which they are most eager, the worst.   61

Their obligations to their country will induce them to take part in her government.

Quite true, he replied.   62

And will our pupils, when they hear this, refuse to take their turn at the toils of State, when they are allowed to spend the greater part of their time with one another in the heavenly light?   63

They will be willing but not anxious to rule.

Impossible, he answered; for they are just men, and the commands which we impose upon them are just; there can be no doubt that every one of them will take office as a stern necessity, and not after the fashion of our present rulers of State.   64

The statesman must be provided with a better life than that of a ruler; and then he will not covet office.

Yes, my friend, I said; and there lies the point. You must contrive for your future rulers another and a better life than that of a ruler, and then you may have a well-ordered State; for only in the State which offers this, will they rule who are truly rich, not in silver and gold, but in virtue and wisdom, which are the true blessings of life. Whereas if they go to the administration of public affairs, poor and hungering after their own private advantage, thinking that hence they are to snatch the chief good, order there can never be; for they will be fighting about office, and the civil and domestic broils which thus arise will be the ruin of the rulers themselves and of the whole State.   65

Most true, he replied.   66

And the only life which looks down upon the life of political ambition is that of true philosophy. Do you know of any other?   67

Indeed, I do not, he said.   68

A Modest Proposal
Jonathan Swift

Clergyman, Irish patriot, critic, poet, Jonathan Swift (1667–1745) is considered by many to be the greatest satirist in the English language. Born in Ireland to English parents who had settled there, Swift spent much of his early career in London, where he wrote his first important satires, *A Tale of a Tub* and *The Battle of the Books* (both published in 1704). He became a leading writer for the Tory party and as a reward for his services was appointed Dean of St. Patrick's Cathedral in Dublin. He spent the rest of his life in that post, involving himself deeply in Irish politics. His masterpiece, *Gulliver's Travels* (1726), embodies Swift's increasing disgust with his fellow human beings. "A Modest Proposal," written in 1729, reflects his mordant view of callous British administrators and absentee landowners whose indifference to the sufferings of the Irish poor during a time of famine filled him with indignation.

FOR PREVENTING THE CHILDREN OF POOR PEOPLE IN IRELAND FROM BEING A BURDEN TO THEIR PARENTS OR COUNTRY, AND FOR MAKING THEM BENEFICIAL TO THE PUBLIC

It is a melancholy object to those who walk through this great town or travel in the country, when they see the streets, the roads, and cabin doors, crowded with beggars of the female-sex, followed by three, four, or six children, all in rags and importuning every passenger for an alms. These mothers, instead of being able to work for their honest livelihood, are forced to employ all their time in strolling to beg sustenance for their helpless infants, who, as they grow up, either turn thieves for want of work, or leave their dear native country to fight for the Pretender in Spain, or sell themselves to the Barbadoes. 1

I think it is agreed by all parties that this prodigious number of children in the arms, or on the backs, or at the heels of their mothers, and frequently of their fathers, is in the present deplorable state of the kingdom a very great additional grievance; and therefore whoever could find out a fair, cheap, and easy method of making these children sound, useful members of the commonwealth would deserve so well of the public as to have his statue set up for a preserver of the nation. 2

But my intention is very far from being confined to provide only for the children of professed beggars; it is of a much greater extent, and shall take in 3 the whole number of infants at a certain age who are born of parents in effect as little able to support them as those who demand our charity in the streets.

As to my own part, having turned my thoughts for many years upon this   4
important subject, and maturely weighed the several schemes of other projectors, I have always found them grossly mistaken in their computation. It is true, a child just dropped from its dam may be supported by her milk for a solar year, with little other nourishment; at most not above the value of two shillings, which the mother may certainly get, or the value in scraps, by her lawful occupation of begging; and it is exactly at one year old that I propose to provide for them in such a manner as instead of being a charge upon their parents or the parish, or wanting food and raiment for the rest of their lives, they shall on the contrary contribute to the feeding, and partly to the clothing, of many thousands.

There is likewise another great advantage in my scheme, that it will pre-   5
vent those voluntary abortions, and that horrid practice of women murdering their bastard children, alas, too frequent among us, sacrificing the poor innocent babes, I doubt, more to avoid the expense than the shame, which would move tears and pity in the most savage and inhuman breast.

The number of souls in this kingdom being usually reckoned one million   6
and a half, of these I calculate there may be about two hundred thousand couple whose wives are breeders; from which number I subtract thirty thousand couple who are able to maintain their own children, although I apprehend there cannot be so many under the present distresses of the kingdom; but this being granted, there will remain an hundred and seventy thousand breeders. I again subtract fifty thousand for those women who miscarry, or whose children die by accident or disease within the year. There only remain an hundred and twenty thousand children of poor parents annually born. The question therefore is, how this number shall be reared and provided for, which, as I have already said, under the present situation of affairs, is utterly impossible by all the methods hitherto proposed. For we can neither employ them in handicraft or agriculture; we neither build houses (I mean in the country) nor cultivate land. They can very seldom pick up a livelihood by stealing till they arrive at six years old, except where they are of towardly parts; although I confess they learn the rudiments much earlier, during which time they can however be looked upon only as probationers, as I have been informed by a principal gentleman in the county of Cavan, who protested to me that he never knew above one or two instances under the age of six, even in a part of the kingdom so renowned for the quickest proficiency in that art.

I am assured by our merchants that a boy or a girl before twelve years   7
old is no salable commodity; and even when they come to this age they will not yield above three pounds, or three pounds and half a crown at most on the Exchange; which cannot turn to account either to the parents or the kingdom, the charge of nutriment and rags having been at least four times that value.

I shall now therefore humbly propose my own thoughts, which I hope   8
will not be liable to the least objection.

I have been assured by a very knowing American of my acquaintance in   9
London, that a young healthy child well nursed is at a year old a most delicious, nourishing, and wholesome food, whether stewed, roasted, baked, or
boiled; and I make no doubt that it will equally serve in a fricasse or a ragout.

I do therefore humbly offer it to public consideration that of the hundred   10
and twenty thousand children, already computed, twenty thousand may be
reserved for breed, whereof only one fourth part to be males, which is more
than we allow to sheep, black cattle, or swine; and my reason is that these
children are seldom the fruits of marriage, a circumstance not much regarded
by our savages, therefore one male will be sufficient to serve four females.
That the remaining hundred thousand may at a year old be offered in sale to
the persons of quality and fortune through the kingdom, always advising the
mother to let them suck plentifully in the last month, so as to render them
plump and fat for a good table. A child will make two dishes at an entertainment for friends; and when the family dines alone, the fore or hind quarter will make a reasonable dish, and seasoned with a little pepper or salt will
be very good boiled on the fourth day, especially in winter.

I have reckoned upon a medium that a child just born will weigh twelve   11
pounds, and in a solar year if tolerably nursed increased to twenty-eight
pounds.

I grant this food will be somewhat dear, and therefore very proper for   12
landlords, who, as they have already devoured most of the parents, seem to
have the best title to the children.

Infant's flesh will be in season throughout the year, but more plentiful in   13
March, and a little before and after. For we are told by a grave author, an
eminent French physician, that fish being a prolific diet, there are more children born in Roman Catholic countries about nine months after Lent than at
any other season; therefore, reckoning a year after Lent, the markets will be
more glutted than usual, because the number of popish infants is at least three
to one in this kingdom; and therefore it will have one other collateral advantage, by lessening the number of Papists among us.

I have already computed the charge of nursing a beggar's child (in which   14
list I reckon all cottagers, laborers, and four fifths of the farmers) to be about
two shillings per annum, rags included; and I believe no gentleman would re-
pine to give ten shillings for the carcass of a good fat child, which, as I have
said, will make four dishes of excellent nutritive meat, when he hath only
some particular friend or his own family to dine with him. Thus the squire
will learn to be a good landlord, and grow popular among the tenants; the
mother will have eight shillings net profit, and be fit for work till she produces another child.

Those who are more thrifty (as I must confess the times require) may flay   15
the carcass; the skin of which artificially dressed will make admirable gloves
for ladies, and summer boots for fine gentlemen.

As to our city of Dublin, shambles may be appointed for this purpose in   16
the most convenient parts of it, and butchers we may be assured will not be
wanting; although I rather recommend buying the children alive, and dressing them hot from the knife as we do roasting pigs.

A very worthy person, a true lover of his country, and whose virtues I   17
highly esteem, was lately pleased in discoursing on this matter to offer a refinement upon my scheme. He said that many gentlemen of this kingdom,
having of late destroyed their deer, he conceived that the want of venison
might be well supplied by the bodies of young lads and maidens, not exceeding
fourteen years of age nor under twelve, so great a number of both sexes in
every county being now ready to starve for want of work and service; and
these to be disposed of by their parents, if alive, or otherwise by their nearest relations. But with due deference to so excellent a friend and so deserving
a patriot, I cannot be altogether in his sentiments; for as to the males, my
American acquaintance assured me from frequent experience that their flesh
was generally tough and lean, like that of our schoolboys, by continual exercise, and their taste disagreeable; and to fatten them would not answer the
charge. Then as to the females, it would, I think with humble submission, be
a loss to the public, because they soon would become breeders themselves:
and besides, it is not improbable that some scrupulous people might be apt
to censure such a practice (although indeed very unjustly) as a little border-
ing upon cruelty; which, I confess, hath always been with me the strongest
objection against any project, how well soever intended.

But in order to justify my friend, he confessed that this expedient was put   18
into his head by the famous Psalmanazar, a native of the island Formosa, who
came from thence to London above twenty years ago, and in conversation
told my friend that in his country when any young person happened to be
put to death, the executioner sold the carcass to persons of quality as a prime
dainty; and that in his time the body of a plump girl of fifteen, who was crucified for an attempt to poison the emperor, was sold to his Imperial Majesty's
prime minister of state, and other great mandarins of the court, in joints from
the gibbet, at four hundred crowns. Neither indeed can I deny that if the same
use were made of several plump young girls in this town, who without one
single groat to their fortunes cannot stir abroad without a chair, and appear
at the playhouse and assemblies in foreign fineries which they never will pay
for, the kingdom would not be the worse.

Some persons of a desponding spirit are in great concern about that vast   19
number of poor people who are aged, diseased, or maimed, and I have been
desired to employ my thoughts what course may be taken to ease the nation
of so grievous an encumbrance. But I am not in the least pain upon that matter, because it is very well known that they are every day dying and rotting
by cold and famine, and filth and vermin, as fast as can be reasonably expected. And as to the younger laborers, they are now in almost as hopeful a
condition. They cannot get work, and consequently pine away for want of
nourishment to a degree that if at any time they are accidentally hired to

common labor, they have not strength to perform it; and thus the country and themselves are happily delivered from the evils to come.

I have too long digressed, and therefore shall return to my subject. I think 20 the advantages by the proposal which I have made are obvious and many, as well as of the highest importance.

For first, as I have already observed, it would greatly lessen the number 21 of Papists, with whom we are yearly overrun, being the principal breeders of the nation as well as our most dangerous enemies; and who stay at home on purpose to deliver the kingdom to the Pretender, hoping to take their advantage by the absence of so many good Protestants, who have chosen rather to leave their country than to stay at home and pay tithes against their conscience to an Episcopal curate.

Secondly, the poorer tenants will have something valuable of their own, 22 which by law may be made liable to distress, and help to pay their landlord's rent, their corn and cattle being already seized and money a thing unknown.

Thirdly, whereas the maintenance of an hundred thousand children, from 23 two years old and upwards, cannot be computed at less than ten shillings a piece per annum, the nation's stock will be thereby increased fifty thousand pounds per annum, besides the profit of a new dish introduced to the tables of all gentlemen of fortune in the kingdom who have any refinement in taste. And the money will circulate among ourselves, the goods being entirely of our own growth and manufacture.

Fourthly, the constant breeders, besides the gain of eight shillings sterling 24 per annum by the sale of their children, will be rid of the charge of maintaining them after the first year.

Fifthly, this food would likewise bring great custom to taverns, where the 25 vintners will certainly be so prudent as to procure the best receipts for dressing it to perfection, and consequently have their houses frequented by all the fine gentlemen, who justly value themselves upon their knowledge in good eating; and a skillful cook, who understands how to oblige his guests, will contrive to make it as expensive as they please.

Sixthly, this would be a great inducement to marriage, which all wise na- 26 tions have either encouraged by rewards or enforced by laws and penalties. It would increase the care and tenderness of mothers toward their children, when they were sure of a settlement for life to the poor babes, provided in some sort by the public, to their annual profit instead of expense. We should see an honest emulation among the married women, which of them could bring the fattest child to the market. Men would become as fond of their wives during the time of their pregnancy as they are now of their mares in foal, their cows in calf, or sows when they are ready to farrow; nor offer to beat or kick them (as is too frequent a practice) for fear of a miscarriage.

Many other advantages might be enumerated. For instance, the addition 27 of some thousand carcasses in our exportation of barreled beef, the propagation of swine's flesh, and improvement in the art of making good bacon, so much wanted among us by the great destruction of pigs, too frequent at our tables, which are no way comparable in taste or magnificence to a well-grown, fat, yearling child, which roasted whole will make a considerable figure at a lord mayor's feast or any other public entertainment. But this and many others I omit, being studious of brevity.

Supposing that one thousand families in this city would be constant customers for infants' flesh, besides others who might have it at merry meetings, particularly weddings and christenings, I compute that Dublin would take off annually about twenty thousand carcasses, and the rest of the kingdom (where probably they will be sold somewhat cheaper) the remaining eighty thousand.   28

I can think of no one objection that will possibly be raised against this proposal, unless it should be urged that the number of people will be thereby much lessened in the kingdom. This I freely own, and it was indeed one principal design in offering it to the world. I desire the reader will observe, that I calculate my remedy for this one individual kingdom of Ireland and for no other that ever was, is, or I think ever can be upon earth. Therefore let no man talk to me of other expedients: of taxing our absentees at five shillings a pound: of using neither clothes nor household furniture except what is of our own growth and manufacture: of utterly rejecting the materials and instruments that promote foreign luxury: of curing the expensiveness of pride, vanity, idleness, and gaming in our women: of introducing a vein of parsimony, prudence, and temperance: of learning to love our country, in the want of which we differ even from Laplanders and the inhabitants of Topinamboo: of quitting our animosities and factions, nor acting any longer like the Jews, who were murdering one another at the very moment their city was taken: of being a little cautious not to sell our country and conscience for nothing: of teaching landlords to have at least one degree of mercy toward their tenants: lastly, of putting a spirit of honesty, industry, and skill into our shopkeepers; who, if a resolution could now be taken to buy only our native goods, would immediately unite to cheat and exact upon us in the price, the measure, and the goodness, nor could ever yet be brought to make one fair proposal of just dealing, though often and earnestly invited to it.   29

Therefore I repeat, let no man talk to me of these and the like expedients, till he hath at least some glimpse of hope that there will ever be some hearty and sincere attempt to put them in practice.   30

But as to myself, having been wearied out for many years with offering vain, idle, visionary thoughts, and at length utterly despairing of success, I fortunately fell upon this proposal, which, as it is wholly new, so it hath something solid and real, of no expense and little trouble, full in our own power, and whereby we can incur no danger in disobliging England. For this kind of commodity will not bear exportation, the flesh being of too tender a consistence to admit a long continuance in salt, although perhaps I could name a country which would be glad to eat up our whole nation without it.   31

After all, I am not so violently bent upon my own opinion as to reject any offer proposed by wise men, which shall be found equally innocent, cheap, easy, and effectual. But before something of that kind shall be advanced in   32 contradiction to my scheme, and offering a better, I desire the author or authors will be pleased maturely to consider two points. First, as things now stand, how they will be able to find food and raiment for an hundred thousand useless mouths and backs. And secondly, there being a round million of creatures in human figure throughout this kingdom, whose sole subsistence put into a common stock would leave them in debt two millions of pounds sterling, adding those who are beggars by profession to the bulk of farmers, cottagers, and laborers, with their wives and children who are beggars in effect; I desire those politicians who dislike my overture, and may perhaps be so bold to attempt an answer, that they will first ask the parents of these mortals whether they would not at this day think it a great happiness to have been sold for food at a year old in the manner I prescribe, and thereby have avoided such a perpetual scene of misfortunes as they have since gone through by the oppression of landlords, the impossibility of paying rent without money or trade, the want of common sustenance, with neither house nor clothes to cover them from the inclemencies of the weather, and the most inevitable prospect of entailing the like or greater miseries upon their breed forever.

I profess, in the sincerity of my heart, that I have not the least personal 33 interest in endeavoring to promote this necessary work, having no other motive than the public good of my country, by advancing our trade, providing for infants, relieving the poor, and giving some pleasure to the rich. I have no children by which I can propose to get a single penny; the youngest being nine years old, and my wife past childbearing.

Liberty or Death
Patrick Henry

Patrick Henry (1736–1799) was a shopkeeper who educated himself to become one of Virginia's leading trial lawyers. Having starting his law practice in 1760 at the age of twenty-four, Henry—always sharp-tongued—became a public figure three years later when, in arguing "The Parson's Cause" case, he denounced King George III as a tyrant for reversing a law passed by the Virginia House of Burgesses. Two more years found him in the House of Burgesses himself and at the center of the Stamp Act crisis; it was Henry who presented the seven "Virginia resolutions" against the act, reportedly closing his speech with a statement that George III should profit from the example of Julius Caesar (who was assassinated by members of his senate). When this raised cries of "Treason!" from the assembly, Henry is supposed to have answered, "If this be treason, make the most of it." His most famous statement, however, is the one with which the following selection concludes. The speech, calling for an armed militia, was delivered on March 23, 1775, in St. John's Church, Richmond, to the second Virginia Convention.

Mr. President: No man thinks more highly than I do of the patriotism, as 1 well as abilities, of the very worthy gentlemen who have just addressed the House. But different men often see the same subject in different lights; and, therefore, I hope it will not be thought disrespectful to those gentlemen if, entertaining as I do opinions of a character very opposite to theirs, I shall speak forth my sentiments freely and without reserve. This is no time for ceremony. The question before the House is one of awful moment to this country. For my own part, I consider it as nothing less than a question of freedom or slavery; and in proportion to the magnitude of the subject ought to be the freedom of the debate. It is only in this way that we can hope to arrive at truth, and fulfill the great responsibility which we hold to God and our country. Should I keep back my opinions at such a time, through fear of giving offense, I should consider myself as guilty of treason towards my country, and of an act of disloyalty toward the Majesty of Heaven, which I revere above all earthly kings.

Mr. President, it is natural to man to indulge in the illusions of hope. 2 We are apt to shut our eyes against a painful truth, and listen to the song of that siren till she transforms us into beasts. Is this the part of wise men, engaged in a great and arduous struggle for liberty? Are we disposed to be of the number of those who, having eyes, see not, and, having ears, hear not, the things which so nearly concern their temporal salvation? For my part, whatever anguish of spirit it may cost, I am willing to know the whole truth to know the worst, and to provide for it.

I have but one lamp by which my feet are guided, and that is the lamp of experience. I know of no way of judging of the future but by the past. And judging by the past, I wish to know what there has been in the conduct of the British ministry for the last ten years to justify those hopes with which gentlemen have been pleased to solace themselves and the House. Is it that insidious smile with which our petition has been lately received? Trust it not, sir; it will prove a snare to your feet. Suffer not yourselves to be betrayed with a kiss. Ask yourselves how this gracious reception of our petition comports with those warlike preparations which cover our waters and darken our land. Are fleets and armies necessary to a work of love and reconciliation? Have we shown ourselves so unwilling to be reconciled that force must be called in to win back our love? Let us not deceive ourselves, sir. These are the implements of war and subjugation; the last arguments to which kings resort. I ask gentlemen, sir, what means this martial array, if its purpose be not to force us to submission? Can gentlemen assign any other possible motive for it? Has Great Britain any enemy, in this quarter of the world, to call for all this accumulation of navies and armies? No, sir, she has none. They are meant for us: they can be meant for no other. They are sent over to bind and rivet upon us those chains which the British ministry have been so long forging. And what have we to oppose to them? Shall we try argument? Sir, we have been trying that for the last ten years. Have we anything new to offer upon the subject? Nothing. We have held the subject up in every light of which it is capable; but it has been all in vain. Shall we resort to entreaty and humble supplication? What terms shall we find which have not been already exhausted? Let us not, I beseech you, sir, deceive ourselves longer. Sir, we have done everything that could be done to avert the storm which is now coming on. We have petitioned; we have remonstrated; we have supplicated; we have prostrated ourselves before the throne, and have implored its interposition to arrest the tyrannical hands of the ministry and Parliament. Our petitions have been slighted; our remonstrances have produced additional violence and insult; our supplications have been disregarded; and we have been spurned, with contempt, from the foot of the throne! In vain, after these things, may we indulge the fond hope of peace and reconciliation. There is no longer any room for hope. If we wish to be free—if we mean to preserve inviolate those inestimable privileges for which we have been so long contending—if we mean not basely to abandon the noble struggle in which we have been so long engaged, and which we have pledged ourselves never to abandon until the glorious object of our contest shall be obtained—we must fight! I repeat it, sir, we must fight! An appeal to arms and to the God of Hosts is all that is left us!

They tell us, sir, that we are weak; unable to cope with so formidable an adversary. But when shall we be stronger? Will it be the next week, or the next year? Will it be when we are totally disarmed, and when a British guard shall be stationed in every house? Shall we gather strength by irresolution and inaction? Shall we acquire the means of effectual resistance by lying supinely on our backs and hugging the delusive phantom of hope, until our enemies shall have bound us hand and foot? Sir, we are not weak if we make a proper use of those means which the God of nature hath placed in our power. Three millions of people, armed in the holy cause of liberty, and in such a country as that which we possess, are invincible by any force which our enemy can send against us. Besides, sir, we shall not fight our battles alone. There is a just God who presides over the destinies of nations, and who will raise up friends to fight our battles for us. The battle, sir, is not to the strong alone; it is to the vigilant, the active, the brave. Besides, sir, we have no election. If we were base enough to desire it, it is now too late to retire from the contest. There is no retreat but in submission and slavery! Our chains are forged! Their clanking may be heard on the plains of Boston! The war is inevitable—and let it come! I repeat it, sir, let it come.

It is in vain, sir, to extenuate the matter. Gentlemen may cry, Peace, Peace— but there is no peace. The war is actually begun! The next gale that sweeps from the north will bring to our ears the clash of resounding arms! Our brethren are already in the field! Why stand we here idle? What is it that gentlemen wish? What would they have? Is life so dear, or peace so sweet, as to be purchased at the price of chains and slavery? Forbid it, Almighty God! I know not what course others may take, but as for me, give me liberty or give me death!

The Declaration of Independence
Thomas Jefferson

A man with an astonishing range of talents, Thomas Jefferson (1743–1826) served as a member of the Virginia House of Burgesses, as a delegate to the Continental Congress (where he drafted the Declaration of Independence), as governor of Virginia, as ambassador to France, and then as our first secretary of state (under George Washington), our second vice-president (under John Adams), and, from 1801 to 1809, our third president. He was also a scientist, an inventor, an architect, a farmer, a historian, and one of the most original political and social philosophers of his day, becoming president of the American Philosophical Society in 1979. Retiring to his beloved Monticello in 1809, he went on to found the University of Virginia, whose campus and buildings he designed. It was only logical that Jefferson's colleagues in the Second Continental Congress of 1775–76 should choose him to draft the Declaration of Independence, for he was already one of the most articulate men of his—or any—time. Jefferson's complete draft is reproduced here as Garry Wills has reconstructed it from Jefferson's published papers. Brackets and underlining indicate the parts of Jefferson's original draft that were struck out by the Congress (one member of which was Benjamin Franklin). Revisions that were inserted appear either in the margin or in a parallel column.

A Declaration by the representatives of the United states 1
of America, in [General] Congress assembled.

When in the course of human events it becomes nec- 2
essary for one people to dissolve the political bands which
have connected them with another, and to assume among
the powers of the earth the separate & equal station to
which the laws of nature and of nature's god entitle them,
a decent respect to the opinions of mankind requires that
they should declare the causes which impel them to the
separation.

We hold these truths to be self evident: that all men are 3
created equal; that they are endowed by their creator with

certain

∧ [inherent and] inalienable rights; that among these are life,
liberty & the pursuit of happiness: that to secure these
rights, governments are instituted among men, deriving their
just powers from the consent of the governed; that whenever any form of government becomes destructive of these
ends, it is the right of the people to alter or to abolish it,

445

& to institute new government, laying it's foundation on such principles, & organising it's power in such form, as to them shall seem most likely to effect their safety & happiness. Prudence indeed will dictate that governments long established should not be changed for light & transient causes; and accordingly all experience hath shewn that mankind are more disposed to suffer while evils are sufferable than to right themselves by abolishing the forms to which they are accustomed. But when a long train of abuses & usurpations [begun at a distinguished period and] pursuing invariably by the same object, evinces a design to reduce them under absolute despotism it is their right, it is their duty to throw off such government, & to provide new guards for their future security. Such has been the patient sufferance of these colonies; & such is now the necessity which constrains them to ∧ [expunge] their former systems of government. The history of the present king of Great Britain is a history of ∧ [unremitting] injuries & usurpations, [among which appears no solitary fact to contradict the uniform tenor of the rest but all have] ∧ in direct object the establishment of an absolute tyranny over these states. To prove this let facts be submitted to a candid world [for the truth of which we pledge a faith yet unsullied by falsehood].

alter

repeated

all having

He has refused his assent to laws the most wholesome 4
& necessary for the public good.

He has forbidden his governors to pass laws of im- 5
mediate & pressing importance, unless suspended in their operation till his assent should be obtained; & when so suspended, he has utterly neglected to attend to them.

He has refused to pass other laws for the accommo- 6
dation of large districts of people, unless those people would relinquish the right of representation in the legislature, a right inestimable to them, & formidable to tyrants only.

He has called together legislative bodies at places un- 7
usual, uncomfortable, and distant from the depository of their public records, for the sole purpose of fatiguing them into compliance with his measures.

He has dissolved representative houses repeatedly [& 8
continually] for opposing with manly firmness his invasions on the rights of the people.

He has refused for a long time after such dissolutions 9
to cause others to be elected, whereby the legislative powers, incapable of annihilation, have returned to the people

at large for their exercise, the state remaining in the mean time exposed to all the dangers of invasion from without & convulsions within.

He has endeavored to prevent the population of these 10 states; for that purpose obstructing the laws for naturalization of foreigners, refusing to pass others to encourage their migrations hither, & raising the conditions of new appropriations of lands.

He has ∧ [suffered] the administration of justice [totally 11 to cease in some of these states] ∧ refusing his assent to laws for establishing judiciary powers.

obstructed
by

He has made [our] judges dependant on his will alone, 12 for the tenure of their offices, & the amount & payment of their salaries.

He has erected a multitude of new offices [by a self as- 13 sumed power] and sent hither swarms of new officers to harrass our people and eat out their substance.

He has kept among us in times of peace standing armies 14 [and ships of war] without the consent of our legislatures.

He has affected to render the military independent of, 15 & superior to the civil power.

He has combined with others to subject us to a juris- 16 diction foreign to our constitutions & unacknoledged by our laws, giving his assent to their acts of pretended legislation for quartering large bodies of armed troops among us; for protecting them by a mock-trial from punishment for any murders which they should commit on the inhabitants of these states; for cutting off our trade with all parts of the world; for imposing taxes on us without our consent; for depriving us ∧ of the benefits of trial by jury; for transporting us beyond seas to be tried for pretended offences; for abolishing the free system of English laws in a neighboring province, establishing therein an arbitrary government, and enlarging it's boundaries, so as to render it at once an example and fit instrument for introducing the same absolute rule and these ∧ [states]; for taking away our charters, abolishing our most valuable laws, and altering fundamentally the forms of our governments; for suspending our own legislatures, & declaring themselves invested with power to legislate for us in all cases whatsoever.

in many cases

colonies

He has abdicated government here ∧ [withdrawing his 17 governors, and declaring us out of his allegiance & protection].

by declaring us out
of his protection
& waging war
against us

He has plundered our seas, ravaged our coasts, burnt   18
our towns, & destroyed the lives of our people.

He is at this time transporting large armies of foreign,   19
mercenaries to compleat the works of death, desolation &
tyranny already begun with circumstances of cruelty and
perfidy ∧ unworthy the head of a civilized nation.

scarcely paralleled
in the most
barbarous ages,
& totally

He has constrained our fellow citizens taken captive on   20
the high seas to bear arms against their country, to become
the executioners of their friends & brethren, or to fall themselves by their hands.

excited domestic
insurrections
amongst us, &
has

He has ∧ endeavored to bring on the inhabitants of our   21
frontiers the merciless Indian savages, whose known rule of
warfare is an undistinguished destruction of all ages, sexes,
& conditions [of existence].

[He has incited treasonable insurrections of our fellow   22
citizens, with the allurements of forfeiture & confiscation
of our property.

He has waged cruel war against human nature itself, vi-   23
olating it's most sacred rights of life and liberty in the persons of a distant people who never offended him, captivat-
ing & carrying them into slavery in another hemisphere or
to incur miserable death in their transportation thither. This
piratical warfare, the opprobrium of *infidel* powers, is the
warfare of the *Christian* king of Great Britain. Determined
to keep open a market where *Men* should be bought & sold,
he has prostituted his negative for suppressing every legislative attempt to prohibit or to restrain this execrable commerce. And that this assemblage of horrors might want no
fact of distinguished die, he is now exciting those very people to rise in arms among us, and to purchase that liberty
of which he has deprived them, by murdering the people on
whom he also obtruded them: thus paying off former crimes
committed against the *Liberties* of one people, with crimes
which he urges them to commit against the *lives* of another].

In every stage of these oppressions we have petitioned   24
for redress in the most humble terms: our repeated petitions
have been answered only by repeated injuries. A prince
whose character is thus marked by every act which may de-

free

fine a tyrant is unfit to be the ruler of a ∧ people [who mean
to be free. Future ages will scarcely believe that the hardi-
ness of one man adventured, within the short compass of
twelve years only, to lay a foundation so broad & so undis-
guised for tyranny over a people fostered & fixed in principles of freedom].

Nor have we been wanting in attentions to our British 25 brethren. We have warned them from time to time of attempts by their legislature to extend ∧ [a] jurisdiction over ∧ [these our states]. We have reminded them of the circumstances of our emigration & settlement here, [no one of which could warrant so strange a pretension: that these were effected at the expense of our own blood & treasure, unassisted by the wealth or the strength of Great Britain: that in constituting indeed our several forms of government, we had adopted one common king, thereby laying a foundation for perpetual league & amity with them: but that submission to their parliament was no part of our constitution, nor ever in idea, if history may be credited: and,] we ∧ appealed to their native justice and magnanimity ∧ [as well as to] the ties of our common kindred to disavow these usurpations which ∧ [were likely to] interrupt our connection and correspondence. They too have been deaf to the voice of justice & of consanguinity, [and when occasions have been given them, by the regular course of their laws, of removing from their councils the disturbers of our harmony, they have, by their free election, re-established them in power. At this very time too they are permitting their chief magistrate to send over not only souldiers of our common blood, but Scotch & foreign mercenaries to invade & destroy us. These facts have given the last stab to agonizing affection, and manly spirit bids us to renounce for ever these unfeeling brethren. We must endeavor to forget our former love for them, and to hold them as we hold the rest of mankind enemies in war, in peace friends. We might have been a free and a great people together; but a communication of grandeur & of freedom it seems is below their dignity. Be it so, since they will have it. The road to happiness & to glory is open to us too. We will tread it apart from them, and] ∧ acquiesce in the necessity which denounces our [eternal] separation ∧ ! 26

We therefore the representatives of the United States of America in General Congress assembled do in the name, & by the authority of the good people of these [states reject & renounce all allegiance & subjection to the kings of Great Britain & all others who

We therefore the representatives of the United States of America in General Congress assembled, appealing to the supreme judge of the world for the rectitude of our intentions, do in the name, & by the authority of the good people of these colonies, solemnly publish &

Margin notes (left column):

an unwarrantetable
us

have and we have
conjured them by
would inevitably

we must therefore
and hold them as
we hold the rest
of mankind,
enemies in war, in
peace friends.

may hereafter claim by, through or under them: we utterly dissolve all political connection which may theretofore have subsisted between us & the people or parliament of Great Britian: & finally we do assert & declare these colonies to be free & independant states,] & that as free & independant states, they have full power to levy war, conclude peace, contract alliances, establish commerce, & to do all other acts & things which independant states may of right do. And for the support of this declaration we mutually pledge to each other our lives, our fortunes & our sacred honour.

declare that these United colonies are & of right ought to be free & independant states; that they are absolved from all allegiance to the British crown, and that all political connection between them & the state of Great Britain is, & ought to be, totally dissolved; & that as free & independant states they have full power to levy war, conclude peace, contract alliances, establish commerce & to do all other acts & things which independant states may of right do.

And for the support of this declaration, with a firm reliance on the protection of divine providence we mutually pledge to each other our lives, our fortunes & our sacred honour.

The Prevailing Opinion of a Sexual Character Discussed

Mary Wollstonecraft

Mary Wollstonecraft (1759–1797), a major figure in the history of the struggle for women's rights, was well known in her own time not only as an advocate of women's rights but as a political thinker on a more comprehensive scale. In an age when it was notoriously difficult for a woman to support herself financially, Wollstonecraft (whose father's drinking had ruined the family) supported herself first as a governess, the traditional occupation for single women, and then by working for a London publisher, James Johnson. After spending several years in France observing the French Revolution at first hand, she returned to London and again worked for Johnson, becoming part of the group of influential radicals he gathered about himself, of which William Blake, William Wordsworth, and William Godwin were also members. Eventually she married Godwin, and not long afterward she died giving birth to a daughter, Mary (who later became the wife of the poet Percy Bysshe Shelley and wrote the novel *Frankenstein*). *A Vindication of the Rights of Women,* from which the following section is taken, argues mainly for intellectual rather than social or political rights for women.

To account for, and excuse the tyranny of man, many ingenious arguments have been brought forward to prove, that the two sexes, in the acquirement of virtue, ought to aim at attaining a very different character: or, to speak explicitly, women are not allowed to have sufficient strength of mind to acquire what really deserves the name of virtue. Yet it should seem, allowing them to have souls, that there is but one way appointed by Providence to lead *mankind* to either virtue or happiness. 1

If then women are not a swarm of ephemeron triflers, why should they be kept in ignorance under the specious name of innocence? Men complain, and with reason, of the follies and caprices of our sex, when they do not keenly satirize our headstrong passions and groveling vices.—Behold, I should answer, the natural effect of ignorance? The mind will ever be unstable that has only prejudices to rest on, and the current will run with destructive fury when there are no barriers to break its force. Women are told from their infancy, and taught by the example of their mothers, that a little knowledge of human weakness, justly termed cunning, softness of temper, *outward* obedience, and a scrupulous attention to a puerile kind of propriety, will obtain for them protection of man; and should they be beautiful, every thing else is needless, for, at least, twenty years of their lives. 2

Thus Milton describes our first frail mother; though when he tells us that   3
women are formed for softness and sweet attractive grace, I cannot compre-
hend his meaning, unless, in the true Mahometan strain, he meant to deprive
us of souls, and insinuate that we were beings only designed by sweet attractive grace, and docile blind obedience, to gratify the senses of man when he
can no longer soar on the wing of contemplation.

How grossly do they insult us who thus advise us only to render ourselves   4
gentle, domestic brutes? For instance, the winning softness so warmly, and
frequently, recommended, that governs by obeying. What childish expressions,
and how insignificant is the being—can it be an immortal one? who will con-
descend to govern by such sinister methods! "Certainly," says Lord Bacon,
"man is of kin to the beasts by his body; and if he be not of kin to God by
his spirit, he is a base and ignoble creature!" Men, indeed, appear to me to
act in a very unphilosophical manner when they try to secure the good conduct of women by attempting to keep them always in a state of childhood.
Rousseau [whom Wollstonecraft argues against earlier, in a passage omitted
here] was more consistent when he wished to stop the progress of reason in
both sexes, for if men eat of the tree of knowledge, women will come in for
a taste; but, from the imperfect cultivation which their understandings now
receive, they only attain a knowledge of evil.

Children, I grant, should be innocent; but when the epithet is applied to   5
men or women, it is but a civil term for weakness. For if it be allowed that
women were destined by Providence to acquire human virtues, and by the exercise of their understandings, that stability of character which is the firmest
ground to rest our future hopes upon, they must be permitted to turn to the
fountain of light, and not forced to shape their course by the twinkling of a
mere satellite. Milton, I grant, was of very different opinion; for he only bends
to the indefeasible right of beauty, though it would be difficult to render two
passages which I now mean to contrast, consistent. But into similar inconsis-
tencies are great men often led by their senses.

"To whom thus Eve with *perfect beauty* adorn'd
"My Author and Disposer, what thou bidst
"*Unargued* I obey; So God ordains;
"God is *thy law, thou mine:* to know no more
"Is Woman's *happiest* knowledge and her *praise.*"

These are exactly the arguments that I have used to children; but I have   6
added, your reason is now gaining strength, and, till it arrives at some degree
of maturity, you must look up to me for advice—then you ought to *think,*
and only rely on God.

Yet in the following lines Milton seems to coincide with me; when he   7
makes Adam thus expostulate with his Maker.

"Hast thou not made me here thy substitute,
"And these inferior far beneath me set?
"Among *unequals* what society

"Can sort, what harmony or true delight?
"Which must be mutual, in proportion due
"Giv'n and receiv'd; but in *disparity*
"The one intense, the other still remiss
"Cannot well suit with either, but soon prove
"Tedious alike: of *fellowship* I speak
"Such as I seek, fit to participate
"All rational delight—

In treating, therefore, of the manners of women, let us, disregarding sensual arguments, trace what we should endeavour to make them in order to cooperate, if the expression be not too bold, with the supreme Being.   8

By individual education, I mean, for the sense of the word is not precisely defined, such an attention to a child as will slowly sharpen the senses, form the temper, regulate the passions as they begin to ferment, and set the understanding to work before the body arrives at maturity; so that the man may only have to proceed, not to begin, the important task of learning to think and reason.   9

To prevent any misconstruction, I must add, that I do not believe that a private education can work the wonders which some sanguine writers have attributed to it. Men and women must be educated, in a great degree, by the opinions and manners of the society they live in. In every age there has been a stream of popular opinion that has carried all before it, and given a family character, as it were, to the century. It may then fairly be inferred, that, till society be differently constituted, much cannot be expected from education. It is, however, sufficient for my present purpose to assert, that, whatever effect circumstances have on the abilities, every being may become virtuous by the exercise of its own reason; for if but one being was created with vicious inclinations, that is positively bad, what can save us from atheism? or if we worship a God, is not that God a devil?   10

Consequently, the most perfect education, in my opinion, is such an exercise of the understanding as is best calculated to strengthen the body and form the heart. Or, in other words, to enable the individual to attain such habits of virtue as will render it independent. In fact, it is a farce to call any being virtuous whose virtues do not result from the exercise of its own reason. This was Rousseau's opinion respecting men: I extend it to women, and confidently assert that they have been drawn out of their sphere by false refinement, and not by an endeavour to acquire masculine qualities. Still the regal homage which they receive is so intoxicating, that till the manners of the times are changed, and formed on more reasonable principles, it may be impossible to convince them that the illegitimate power, which they obtain, by degrading themselves, is a curse, and that they must return to nature and equality, if they wish to secure the placid satisfaction that unsophisticated affections impart. But for this epoch we must wait—wait, perhaps, till kings and nobles, enlightened by reason, and, preferring the real dignity of man to childish state, throw off their gaudy hereditary trappings: and if then women do not resign the arbitrary power of beauty—they will prove that they have *less* mind than man.   11

Where I Lived, and What I Lived For
Henry David Thoreau

Henry David Thoreau (1817–1862) remains for many Americans the most appealing of those nineteenth-century writers and thinkers known as the Transcendentalists (of whom Thoreau's friend Ralph Waldo Emerson was the most eminent). Well educated in the Greek and Latin classics and also in the modern languages, Thoreau briefly taught school and then worked as a tutor in his hometown of Concord, Massachusetts. In 1845 he built his now-famous cabin on some property belonging to the Emerson family near Walden Pond and began his experiment in simplifying his life to understand its real values. *Walden*, from which the following selection is taken, records and reflects upon that experience. Begun in 1846, *Walden* was not published until 1854, seven years after Thoreau had left the cabin. During those years he had published his first book, *A Week on the Concord and Merrimack Rivers*, based on his journal of a trip with his brother John, and his famous essay "Civil Disobedience," whose doctrine of nonviolent resistance was later to influence both Mahatma Gandhi in his struggle for an independent India and the Reverend Martin Luther King, Jr., in his struggle for civil rights for black Americans.

1 I went to the woods because I wished to live deliberately, to front only the essential facts of life, and see if I could not learn what it had to teach, and not, when I came to die, discover that I had not lived. I did not wish to live what was not life, living is so dear, nor did I wish to practice resignation, unless it was quite necessary. I wanted to live deep and suck out all the marrow of life, to live so sturdily and Spartan-like as to put to rout all that was not life, to cut a broad swath and shave close, to drive life into a corner, and reduce it to its lowest terms, and, if it proved to be mean, why then to get the whole and genuine meanness of it, and publish its meanness to the world; or if it were sublime, to know it by experience, and be able to give a true account of it in my next excursion. For most men, it appears to me, are in a strange uncertainty about it, whether it is of the devil or of God and have *somewhat hastily* concluded that it is the chief end of man here to "glorify God and enjoy him forever."

2 Still we live meanly, like ants; though the fable tells us that we were long ago changed into men; like pygmies we fight with cranes; it is error upon error, and clout upon clout, and our best virtue has for its occasion a superfluous and inevitable wretchedness. Our life is frittered away by detail. An honest man has hardly need to count more than his ten fingers, or in extreme cases he may add his ten toes, and lump the rest. Simplicity, simplicity, simplicity! I

say, let your affairs be as two or three, and not a hundred or a thousand; instead of a million count half a dozen, and keep your accounts on your thumbnail. In the midst of this chopping sea of civilized life, such are the clouds and storms and quicksands and thousand-and-one items to be allowed for, that a man has to live, if he would not founder and go to the bottom and not make his port at all, by dead reckoning, and he must be a great calculator indeed who succeeds. Simplify, simplify. Instead of three meals a day, if it be necessary eat but one; instead of a hundred dishes, five; and reduce other things in proportion. Our life is like a German Confederacy, made up of petty states, with its boundary forever fluctuating, so that even a German cannot tell you how it is bounded at any moment. The nation itself, with all its so-called internal improvements, which, by the way, are all external and superficial, is just such an unwieldy and overgrown establishment, cluttered with furniture and tripped up by its own traps, ruined by luxury and heedless expense, by want of calculation and a worthy aim, as the million households in the land; and the only cure for it, as for them, is in a rigid economy, a stern and more than Spartan simplicity of life and elevation of purpose. It lives too fast. Men think that it is essential that the *Nation* have commerce, and export ice, and talk through a telegraph, and ride thirty miles an hour, without a doubt, whether *they* do or not; but whether we should live like baboons or like men, is a little uncertain. If we do not get out sleepers, and forge rails, and devote days and nights to the work, but go to tinkering upon our *lives* to improve *them,* who will build railroads? And if railroads are not built, how shall we get to Heaven in season? But if we stay at home and mind our business, who will want railroads? We do not ride on the railroad; it rides upon us. Did you ever think what those sleepers are that underlie the railraod? Each one is a man, an Irishman, or a Yankee man. The rails are laid on them, and they are covered with sand, and the cars run smoothly over them. They are sound sleepers, I assure you. And every few years a new lot is laid down and run over; so that, if some have the pleasure of riding on a rail, others have the misfortune to be ridden upon. And when they run over a man that is walking in his sleep, a supernumerary sleeper in the wrong position, and wake him up, they suddenly stop the cars, and make a hue and cry about it, as if this were an exception. I am glad to know that it takes a gang of men for every five miles to keep the sleepers down and level in their beds as it is, for this is a sign that they may sometime get up again.

Why should we live with such hurry and waste of life? We are determined to be starved before we are hungry. Men say that a stitch in time saves nine, and so they take a thousand stitches to-day to save nine tomorrow. As for *work,* we haven't any of any consequence. We have the Saint Vitus' dance, and cannot possibly keep our heads still. If I should only give a few pulls at the parish bell-rope, as for a fire, that is, without setting the bell, there is hardly a man on his farm in the outskirts of Concord, notwithstanding that press of engagements which was his excuse so many times this morning, nor a boy, nor a woman, I might almost say, but would forsake all and follow that sound, not mainly to save property from the flames, but, if we will confess the truth, much more to see it burn, since burn it must, and we, be it known, did not set it on fire,—or to see it put out, and have a hand in it, if that is done as handsomely; yes, even if it were the parish church itself. Hardly a man takes a half-hour's nap after dinner, but when he wakes he holds up his head and asks, "What's the news?" as if the rest of mankind had stood his sentinels. Some give directions to be waked every half-hour, doubtless for no other purpose; and then, to pay for it, they tell what they have dreamed. After a night's sleep the news is as indispensable as the breakfast. "Pray tell me anything new that has happened to a man anywhere on this globe,"—and he reads it over his coffee and rolls, that a man has had his eyes gouged out this morning on the Wachito River, never dreaming the while that he lives in the dark unfathomed mammoth cave of this world, and has but the rudiment of an eye himself.

For my part, I could easily do without the post-office. I think that there   4
are very few important communications made through it. To speak critically, I never received more than one or two letters in my life—I wrote this some years ago—that were worth the postage. The penny-post is, commonly, an institution through which you seriously offer a man that penny for his thoughts which is so often safely offered in jest. And I am sure that I never read any memorable news in a newspaper. If we read of one man robbed, or murdered, or killed by accident, or one house burned, or one vessel wrecked, or one steamboat blown up, or one cow run over on the Western Railroad, or one mad dog killed, or one lot of grasshoppers in the winter,—we never need read of another. One is enough. If you are acquainted with the principle, what do you care for a myriad instances and applications? To a philosopher all *news,* as it is called, is gossip and they who edit and read it are old women over their tea. Yet not a few are greedy after this gossip. There was such a rush, as I heard the other day at one of the offices to learn the foreign news by the last arrival, that several large squares of plate glass belonging to the establishment were broken by the pressure,—news which I seriously think a ready wit might write a twelvemonth, or twelve years, beforehand with sufficient accuracy. As for Spain, for instance, if you know how to throw in Don Carlos and the Infanta, and Don Pedro and Seville and Granada, from time to time in the right proportions,—they may have changed the names a little since I saw the papers,—and serve up a bull-fight when other entertainments fail, it will be true to the letter, and give us as good an idea of the exact state or ruin of things in Spain as the most succinct and lucid reports under this head in the newspapers: and as for England, almost the last significant scrap of news from that quarter was the revolution of 1649, and if you have learned the history of her crops for an average year, you never need attend to that thing again, unless your speculations are of a merely pecuniary character. If one may judge who rarely looks into the newspapers, nothing new does ever happen in foreign parts, a French revolution not excepted.

What news! how much more important to know what that is which was   5
never old! "Kieou-he-yu (great dignitary of the state of Wei) sent a man to

Khoung-tseu to know his news. Khoung-tseu caused the messenger to be seated near him, and questioned him in these terms: What is your master doing? The messenger answered with respect: My master desires to diminish the number of his faults, but he cannot come to the end of them. The messenger being gone, the philosopher remarked: What a worthy messenger! What a worthy messenger!" The preacher, instead of vexing the ears of drowsy farmers on their day of rest at the end of the week,—for Sunday is the fit conclusion of an ill-spent week, and not the fresh and brave beginning of a new one,—with this one other draggle-tail of a sermon, should shout with thundering voice, "Pause! Avast! Why so seeming fast, but deadly slow?"

Shams and delusions are esteemed for soundest truths, while reality is fabulous. If men would steadily observe realities only, and not allow themselves to be deluded, life, to compare it with such things as we know, would be like a fairy tale and the Arabian Nights' Entertainments. If we respected only what is inevitable and has a right to be, music and poetry would resound along the streets. When we are unhurried and wise, we perceive that only great and worthy things have any permanent and absolute existence, that petty fears and petty pleasures are but the shadow of the reality. This is always exhilarating and sublime. By closing the eyes and slumbering, and consenting to be deceived by shows, men establish and confirm their daily life of routine and habit everywhere, which still is built on purely illusory foundations. Children, who play life, discern its true law and relations more clearly than men, who fail to live it worthily, but who think that they are wiser by experience, that is, by failure. I have read in a Hindoo book, that "there was a king's son, who, being expelled in infancy from his native city, was brought up by a forester, and growing up to maturity in that state, imagined himself to belong to the barbarous race with which he lived. One of his father's ministers having discovered him, revealed to him what he was, and the misconception of his character was removed, and he knew himself to be a prince. So soul," continues the Hindoo philosopher, "from the circumstances in which it is placed, mistakes its own character, until the truth is revealed to it by some holy teacher, and then it knows itself to be *Brahma*." I perceive that we inhabitants of New England live this mean life that we do because our vision does not penetrate the surface of things. We think that this *is* which *appears* to be. If a man should walk through this town and see only the reality, where, think you, would the "Mill-dam" go to? If he should give us an account of the realities he beheld there, we should not recognize the place in his description. Look at a meeting-house, or a court-house, or a jail, or a shop, or a dwelling-house, and say what that thing really is before a true gaze, and they would all go to pieces in your account of them. Men esteem truth remote, in the outskirts of the system, behind the farthest star, before Adam and after the last man. In eternity there is indeed something true and sublime. But all these times and places and occasions are now and here. God himself culminates in the present moment, and will never be more divine in the lapse of all the ages. And we are enabled to apprehend at all what is sublime and noble only by the perpetual instilling and drenching of the reality that surrounds us. The universe constantly and obediently answers to our conceptions; whether we travel fast or slow, the track is laid for us. Let us spend our lives in conceiving then. The poet or the artist never yet had so fair and noble a design but some of his posterity at least could accomplish it.

Let us spend one day as deliberately as Nature, and not be thrown off the track by every nutshell and mosquito's wing that falls on the rails. Let us rise early and fast, or break fast, gently and without perturbation; let company come and let company go, let the bells ring and the children cry,—determined to make a day of it. Why should we knock under and go with the stream? Let us not be upset and overwhelmed in that terrible rapid and whirlpool called a dinner, situated in the meridian shallows. Weather this danger and you are safe, for the rest of the way is down hill. With unrelaxed nerves, with morning vigor, sail by it, looking another way, tied to the mast like Ulysses. If the engine whistles, let it whistle till it is hoarse for its pains. If the bell rings, why should we run? We will consider what kind of music they are like. Let us settle ourselves, and work and wedge our feet downward through the mud and slush of opinion, and prejudice, and tradition, and delusion, and appearance, that alluvion which covers the globe, through Paris and London, through New York and Boston and Concord, through Church and State, through poetry and philosophy and religion, till we come to a hard bottom and rocks in place, which we can call *reality*, and say, This is, and no mistake; and then begin, having a *point d'appui*, below freshet and frost and fire, a place where you might found a wall or a state, or set a lamppost safely, or perhaps a gauge, not a Nilometer, but a Realometer, that future ages might know how deep a freshet of shams and appearances had gathered from time to time. If you stand right fronting and face to face to a fact, you will see the sun glimmer on both its surfaces, as if it were a cimeter, and feel its sweet edge dividing you through the heart and marrow, and so you will happily conclude your mortal career. Be it life or death, we crave only reality. If we are really dying, let us hear the rattle in our throats and feel cold in the extremities; if we are alive, let us go about our business.

Time is but the stream I go a-fishing in. I drink at it; but while I drink I see the sandy bottom and detect how shallow it is. Its thin current slides away, but eternity remains. I would drink deeper; fish in the sky, whose bottom is pebbly with stars. I cannot count one. I know not the first letter of the alphabet. I have always been regretting that I was not as wise as the day I was born. The intellect is a cleaver; it discerns and rifts its way into the secret of things. I do not wish to be any more busy with my hands than is necessary. My head is hands and feet. I feel all my best faculties concentrated in it. My instinct tells me that my head is an organ for burrowing, as some creatures use their snout and fore paws, and with it I would mine and burrow my way through these hills. I think that the richest vein is somewhere hereabouts; so by the divining-rod and thin rising vapors I judge; and here I will begin to mine.

The Death of the Moth
Virginia Woolf

Virginia Woolf (1882–1941) is best known for experimental novels such as *Mrs. Dalloway, The Waves,* and *To the Lighthouse,* but she was also influential as a critic and essayist. Born in London, the daughter of the eminent scholar Sir Leslie Stephen, Woolf was educated at home and read voraciously in her father's large library. She married journalist Leonard Woolf in 1912 and with him founded the Hogarth Press, which published works by several prominent artists, intellectuals, and writers known as the Bloomsbury group. Introspective and prone to depression, Woolf drowned herself in 1941. "The Death of the Moth," published posthumously, reveals her powers of observation and echoes a recurrent theme in her fiction, the interaction of time and consciousness.

Moths that fly by day are not properly to be called moths; they do not 1 excite that pleasant sense of dark autumn nights and ivy-blossom which the commonest yellow-underwing asleep in the shadow of the curtain never fails to rouse in us. They are hybrid creatures, neither gay like butterflies nor sombre like their own species. Nevertheless the present specimen, with his narrow hay-coloured wings, fringed with a tassel of the same colour, seemed to be content with life. It was a pleasant morning, mid-September, mild, benignant, yet with a keener breath than that of the summer months. The plough was already scoring the field opposite the window, and where the share had been, the earth was pressed flat and gleamed with moisture. Such vigour came rolling in from the fields and then down beyond that it was difficult to keep the eyes strictly turned upon the book. The rooks too were keeping one of their annual festivities; soaring round the tree tops until it looked as if a vast net with thousands of black knots in it had been cast up into the air; which, after a few moments sank slowly down upon the trees until every twig seemed to have a knot at the end of it. Then, suddenly, the net would be thrown into the air again in a wider circle this time, with the utmost clamour and vociferation, as though to be thrown into the air and settle slowly down upon the tree tops were a tremendously exciting experience.

The same energy which inspired the rooks, the ploughmen, the horses, 2 and even, it seemed, the lean bare-backed downs, sent the moth fluttering from side to side of his square of the window pane. One could not help watching him. One was, indeed, conscious of a queer feeling of pity for him. The possibilities of pleasure seemed that morning so enormous and so various that to have only a moth's part in life, and a day moth's at that, appeared a hard fate, and his zest in enjoying his meagre opportunities to the full, pathetic. He flew vigorously to one corner of his compartment, and, after waiting there a second, flew across to the other. What remained for him but to fly to a third corner and then to a fourth? That was all he could do, in spite of the size of the downs, the width of the sky, the far-off smoke houses, and the romantic voice, now and then, of a steamer out at sea. What he could do he did. Watching him, it seemed as if a fibre, very thin but pure, of the enormous energy of the world had been thrust into his frail and diminutive body. As often as he crossed the pane, I could fancy that a thread of vital light became visible. He was little or nothing but life.

Yet, because he was so small, and so simple a form of the energy that was   3 rolling in at the open window and driving its way through so many narrow and intricate corridors in my own brain and in those of other human beings, there was something marvelous as well as pathetic about him. It was as if someone had taken a tiny bead of pure life and decking it as lightly as possible with down and feathers, had set it dancing and zigzagging to show us the true nature of life. Thus displayed one could not get over the strangeness of it. One is apt to forget all about life, seeing it humped and bossed and garnished and cumbered so that it has to move with the greatest circumspection and dignity. Again, the thought of all that life might have been had he been born in any other shape caused one to view his simple activities with a kind of pity.

After a time, tired by his dancing apparently, he settled on the window   4 ledge in the sun, and, the queer spectacle being at an end, I forgot about him. Then, looking up, my eye was caught by him. He was trying to resume his dancing, but seemed either so stiff or so awkward that he could only flutter to the bottom of the windowpane; and when he tried to fly across it he failed. Being intent on other matters I watched these futile attempts for a time without thinking, unconsciously waiting for him to resume his flight, as one waits for a machine, that has stopped momentarily, to start again without considering the reason of its failure. After perhaps a seventh attempt he slipped from the wooden ledge and fell, fluttering his wings, on to his back on the window sill. The helplessness of his attitude roused me. It flashed upon me that he was in difficulties; he could no longer raise himself; his legs struggled vainly. But, as I stretched out a pencil, meaning to help him to right himself, it came over me that the failure and awkwardness were the approach of death. I laid the pencil down again.

The legs agitated themselves once more. I looked as if for the enemy against   5 which he struggled. I looked out of doors. What had happened there? Presumably it was midday, and work in the fields had stopped. Stillness and quiet had replaced the previous animation. The birds had taken themselves off to feed in the brooks. The horses stood still. Yet the power was there all the same, massed outside indifferent, impersonal, not attending to anything in particular. Somehow it was opposed to the little hay-coloured moth. It was useless to try to do anything. One could only watch the extraordinary efforts

made by those tiny legs against an oncoming doom which could, had it chosen, have submerged an entire city, not merely a city, but masses of human
beings; nothing, I knew, had any chance against death. Nevertheless after a
pause of exhaustion the legs fluttered again. It was superb this last protest,
and so frantic that he succeeded at last in righting himself. One's sympathies,
of course, were all on the side of life. Also, when there was nobody to care
or to know, this gigantic effort on the part of an insignificant little moth,
against a power of such magnitude, to retain what no one else valued or desired to keep, moved one strangely. Again, somehow, one saw life, a pure bead.
I lifted the pencil again, useless though I knew it to be. But even as I did so,
the unmistakable tokens of death showed themselves. The body relaxed, and
instantly grew stiff. The struggle was over. The insignificant little creature now
knew death. As I looked at the dead moth, this minute wayside triumph of
so great a force over so mean an antagonist filled me with wonder. Just as life
had been strange a few minutes before, so death was now as strange. The
moth having righted himself now lay most decently and uncomplainingly composed. O yes, he seemed to say, death is stronger than I am.

Copyrights and Acknowledgments

Index of Authors and Titles